Cambridge Studies in Chinese History, Literature and Institutions
General Editors
Patrick Hanan and Denis Twitchett

STATESMEN AND GENTLEMEN

Statesmen and Gentlemen is an important study of a crucial subject in
Chinese social history: the way in which, during the twelfth and
thirteenth centuries, China's ruling meritocracy was transformed into
a locally-rooted elite whose principal aim was the consolidation of their
power, wealth and influence on a local rather than a national and
dynastic basis. Professor Hymes offers a remarkable picture of the institutional and social changes this process entailed, but he also examines
in detail the subtle ways in which the elite's perception of itself and its
social role changed and it came to offer powerful support to local self-
defense, social welfare, religious cults and temple-building. The result is
the first work in English to impart a real feeling of the texture of life in
the provinces under the Sung.

GLEN DUDBRIDGE. The *Hsi-yu Chi*: A Study of Antecedents to the Sixteenth-Century Chinese Novel

STEPHEN FITZGERALD: China and the Overseas Chinese: A Study of Peking's Changing Policy 1949–70

CHRISTOPHER HOWE: Wage Patterns and Wage Policy in Modern China, 1919–1972

RAY HUANG: Taxation and Government Finance in Sixteenth-Century Ming China

DIANA LARY: Region and Nation: The Kwangsi Clique in Chinese Politics, 1925–37

CHI-YUN CHEN: Hsün Yüeh (A.D. 148–209): The Life and Reflections of an Early Medieval Confucian

DAVID R. KNECHTGES: The Han Rhapsody: A Study of the *Fu* of Yang Hsiung (53 B.C.–A.D. 18)

J. Y. WONG: Yeh Ming-ch'en: Viceroy of Liang Kuang (1852–8)

LI-LI CH'EN: Master Tung's Western Chamber Romance (*Tung hsi-hsiang chu-kung-tiao*): a Chinese *Chantefable*

DONALD HOLZMAN: Poetry and Politics: The Life and Works of Juan Chi (A.D. 210–63)

C. A. CURWEN: Taiping Rebel: The Deposition of Li Hsiu-cheng

P. B. EBREY: The Aristocratic Families of Early Imperial China: A Case Study of the Po-Ling Ts'ui Family

HILARY J. BEATTIE: Land and Lineage in China: A Study of T'ung-Ch'eng County, Anhwei, in the Ming and Ch'ing Dynasties

WILLIAM T. GRAHAM: The Lament for the South: Yü-Hsin's 'Ai Chiang-nan Fu'

HANS BIELENSTEIN: The Bureaucracy of Han Times

MICHAEL R. GODLEY: The Mandarin-Capitalists from Nanyang: Overseas Chinese Enterprise in the Modernization of China 1893–1911

CHARLES BACKUS: The Nan-chao Kingdom and T'ang China's Southwestern Frontier

VICTOR H. MAIR: Tun-huang Popular Narratives

IRA E. KASOFF: The Thought of Chang Tsai

A. R. DAVIS: T'ao Yüan-ming (A.D. 365–427): His Works and Their Meanings

Statesmen and Gentlemen

THE ELITE OF FU-CHOU, CHIANG-HSI, IN NORTHERN AND SOUTHERN SUNG

ROBERT P. HYMES

Department of East Asian Languages and Cultures,
Columbia University, New York

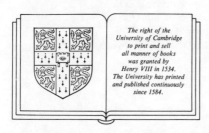

The right of the
University of Cambridge
to print and sell
all manner of books
was granted by
Henry VIII in 1534.
The University has printed
and published continuously
since 1584.

CAMBRIDGE UNIVERSITY PRESS

CAMBRIDGE

LONDON NEW YORK NEW ROCHELLE

MELBOURNE SYDNEY

Published by the Press Syndicate of the University of Cambridge
The Pitt Building, Trumpington Street, Cambridge CB2 1RP
32 East 57th Street, New York, NY 10022, USA
10 Stamford Road, Oakleigh, Melbourne 3166, Australia

© Cambridge University Press 1986

First published 1986

Printed in Great Britain at the University Press, Cambridge

British Library Cataloguing in Publication Data

Hymes, Robert P.
Statesmen and gentlemen: the elite of Fu-chou,
Chiang-hsi, in Northern and Southern Sung. –
(Cambridge studies in Chinese history, literature and institutions)
1. China – Social conditions – 960-1644
I. Title
951'.02   HN733

Library of Congress Cataloguing-in-Publication Data

Hymes, Robert P.
Statesmen and gentlemen.
(Cambridge studies in Chinese history, literature, and institutions)
1. Elite (Social sciences) – China – Fu-chou shih
(Fukien Province) – History. 2. Fu-chou shih (Fukien
Province, China) – History. I. Title. II. Series.
HN740.F8H95 1986   305.5'2'0951245   85-26949

ISBN 0 521 30631 0

AL

To DEBORA *and* SAUL

CONTENTS

MAPS

ACKNOWLEDGEMENTS

In the years (too many) of research, writing, and rewriting that have led to this book, I have accumulated debts, scholarly and personal, to many people. My greatest debt is to my graduate advisor, Robert Hartwell: the book bears the imprint of his teaching, and of his work, on almost every page. Some of the directions he has pointed me in are directions I expect to travel for as long as I do research in Sung social history. I am proud to call myself his student.

Other teachers must be thanked for leading me into the study of Chinese history and showing me what might be learned there. First among these were Hans Bielenstein, Wm. Theodore de Bary, and David Johnson. In graduate school and after I have been privileged to learn from Susan Naquin, Nathan Sivin, and Denis Twitchett. All have continued to teach me as my colleagues and my friends. All have made their mark in one way or another upon this book.

Work is shaped, and thinking molded, by fellow students and academic peers as well as by teachers. For reading and criticizing my work, for sharing their own work with me, for seeing things before I saw them, for hours and days of talk and argument, I have to thank Karen Alvarez, Peter Bol, John Chaffee, Hugh Clark, Patricia Ebrey, Benjamin Elman, Constance Johnson, Joseph McDermott, Paul Smith, John Stuermer, Richard von Glahn, Ann Waltner, and Linda Walton. All have helped me, perhaps more than they know.

My wife, Debora M. Worth, has traveled farther with me and put up with more from me than could reasonably have been expected. I owe her, truly, more than I know how to say.

EXPLANATORY NOTES:
TERMS AND UNITS

(1) Circuit, prefecture, county, etc.

In this book I follow E.A. Kracke and others in translating the term *lu*, used in Sung to identify an administrative unit roughly comparable to the modern province, as 'circuit,' and in using 'prefecture' as a comprehensive term for the next highest level of administration, equivalent to the Ming and Ch'ing *fu*, but in Sung comprising four distinct types, called *fu* ('superior prefecture'), *chou* ('regular prefecture'), *chün*[a] ('military prefecture'), and *chien* ('industrial prefecture'). (See E.A. Kracke, *Civil Service in Early Sung China*, p. 48.) When in Sung a general term was needed to express the general administrative category to which all these four belonged, recourse was often had to the word *chün*[b], which in earlier dynasties had identified a similar but formally distinct unit most often translated as 'commandery.' Where the word appears in Sung texts with the more general meaning, I translate it too as 'prefecture.'

Below the prefecture I depart from Kracke in rendering *hsien*, the lowest unit for whose administration regular officials were employed, as 'county' rather than as 'subprefecture.' This accords with common practice in studies of the Ming and Ch'ing dynasties and avoids confusion with the Ch'ing unit usually called 'subprefecture,' which was quite a different thing. Below the county, in Sung, was the *hsiang*, which I translate as 'canton,' following Brian McKnight (*Village and Bureaucracy in Southern Sung China, passim*). There remains the lowest administrative unit appearing in the sources for Sung Fu-chou: the *tu*. The word is an abbreviation of *tu-pao*, 'superior guard,' a unit in the *pao-chia* police and mutual surveillance system of middle and late Northern Sung. Originally an organizational unit comprising a fixed number of households (500 in Fu-chou), by middle Southern Sung – when the term first appears in Fu-chou sources – it had transformed itself into a unit of administrative geography. (For this process see McKnight, pp. 75–8.) A reasonable English equivalent is hard to find. 'Superior guard' itself seems too cumbersome and obscures the unit's geographic character. As the *tu* originated in a local police and defense organization, the word 'precinct' has a certain attraction; but this is associated in English with cities, while the *tu* was fundamentally rural. I have evaded the issue here by using *tu* itself.

(2) Family

The entities that I here call 'families' are not all simply households, nor even extended kin groups existing at single moments in time, but in many cases groupings enduring over a considerable period. I use the term to mean a set of men and women, whether contemporaries or separated by time and generations, who share a surname and whom the sources identify firmly as (patrilineal) kin. A source may do this by placing two people in a more or less exact relation (father to son, elder to younger first cousin, etc.) or by naming them as members of some more general grouping of kinsmen: 'the Wang *shih*' or 'the Tseng *tsu*' or 'the Lo *chia*,' for example. Thus a 'family' may be a household that does not survive the death of its founder, or a lineage-sized set of kin spanning three centuries. The ambiguity is unfortunate but unavoidable; there is no better term; and in fact the Chinese word *chia* (literally 'household' or 'family') appears in the sources with exactly the same range of meanings. Some of the wider, long-lived 'families' I deal with were certainly descent groups of some fair degree of corporation by the late Sung or the Yüan, judging by their possession of written genealogies and/or common property, but I avoid the term 'lineage' except in a few cases in order not to imply more than the sources can certainly show. The issue of corporateness is not, in any case, crucial for the arguments that I will frame here. On this issue in Fu-chou, however, see my article 'Marriage, Descent Groups, and the Localist Strategy in Sung and Yuan Fu-chou,' in *Kinship Organization in Late Imperial China, 1000–1940*, ed. Patricia B. Ebrey and James L. Watson, forthcoming from University of California Press.

(3) Fu-chou

On the physical and administrative geography of the prefecture of Fu-chou during the Sung, see the Introduction. As is made clear there, the prefecture's boundaries changed several times during the course of the dynasty. 'Fu-chou' meant different things at different times. For the sake of continuity, I treat as part of Fu-chou for the purposes of this study all territory that lay within it at any time during the Sung. Thus I have traced the elite of Nan-feng County throughout Sung, although the county was ceded from Fu-chou in 991. For this larger unit, comprising all the territory ever part of the prefecture in Sung, I use the term 'greater Fu-chou.' Certain questions, however, can only be answered for the prefecture as officially constituted at some particular time; in these cases I refer to 'Fu-chou proper.'

The choice of a prefecture as my unit of study needs some comment. The work of G.W. Skinner has argued forcefully and convincingly that in many respects the 'natural' units of Chinese society were not counties, prefectures, and provinces (circuits in Sung), but *marketing* areas based on physiographic, not political, divisions. Why not take as one's field of inquiry the city trading area of which Fu-chou city was the center — an area that very probably comprised the entire drainage area of the Ju river and thus, with some exceptions, the two prefectures of Fu-chou and Chien-ch'ang Chün in their entirety? The answer has to do with sources. On the one hand the data on markets in Sung are simply inadequate to reconstruct the marketing area of Fu-chou city in any but the most speculative way. One might then simply take the physiographic region itself, the Ju River's drainage area, as proxy for the marketing area; but here again one would be stymied by the sources. Local gazetteer materials in Sung, crucial sources for a study of the kind attempted here, are excellent for all of Fu-chou's five counties, but inadequate for all but one of the four counties of the region's other prefecture, Chien-ch'ang Chün[a]. What might make sense as a unit in social and economic terms would thus be a very poor unit in historiographic terms: the sources for its various component parts would vary so drastically in quality and quantity that any generalization about differences or similarities among those parts would be suspect, if not wholly groundless. The choice of an administrative unit — Fu-chou itself — as one's field thus seems dictated by the sources. I take some care further on to place Fu-chou within a physiographic framework, and attempt throughout to be sensitive to the influences of physiography. See for instance the discussion of local militia organization on pp. 149—50.

A NOTE ON THE MAPS

The maps of Fu-chou and its region supplied here derive from two chief
sources. The first is a set of forty-six topographic maps scaled at 50,000:1,
surveyed between 1921 and 1934 and engraved between 1938 and 1943,
presently held at Osaka University and listed in Nunome Chōfu, *Chūgoku
hondo chizu mokuroku: Tōkyō Daigaku Sōgō Kenkyū Shiryōkan shozō
shiryō* (Osaka: Osaka Daigaku Ajiashi Kenkyūkai, 1976), pp. 148–50, as
nos. 12 through 59, 63 through 79, 86 through 89, and 96 in the series for
Chien-ch'ang. These maps bear no markings of latitude and longitude. The
same maps are also to be found in the collections of the National Diet Library
and the Tōyō Bunko in Tokyo and are listed, under the same numbering, in
Nishimura Kanoe, *Chūgoku hondo chizu mokuroku: Kokuritsu Kokkai
Toshokan oyobi Tōyō Bunko shozō shiryō* (Tokyo: Kyokutō Shoten,
1967), pp. 15–17. The second source is a set of thirteen maps scaled at
200,000:1, engraved in 1925 and printed in 1931, presently among the
holdings of the Map Division of the Library of Congress, bearing the following
titles: Yü-kan, Tung-hsiang, Lin-ch'uan, Nan-feng, Chien-ning, Lo-p'ing, Kuei-
ch'i, Kuang-tse, Shao-wu, Kao-an, Ch'ing-chiang, Chi-an, Piao-hu. Each of
these maps covers one degree of longitude, thirty minutes of latitude; the set
forms most of a square running from 115° to 118° east longitude and from
26°30' to 29° north latitude: only the northwest and southwest corners are
missing.

   Of these two sets the first, judging by internal evidence and comparison
with noncartographic sources, is much the more accurate; unfortunately, it
is incomplete for the Fu-chou region. Thus in constructing my own maps I
have been forced to rely on the second set for the basic geographic framework
(administrative boundaries, river courses, etc.) while using the first set, where
possible, as a corrective reference for the location of smaller features such as
mountains, towns, and villages. Though reliance on the second set has involved
some sacrifice of geographic precision, for the questions I treat in this study
the loss appears negligible. As supplementary sources I have made considerable
use of the lists of place names (generally at the town and village level) found

in Ch'ing dynasty local gazetteers. These usually arrange the place names in order by *tu* unit and generally give more comprehensive coverage than even the first set of maps: low-level place names mentioned in Sung sources can often be found in a gazetteer list — which indicates the *tu* to which they belong — even when they do not appear on the corresponding maps. By locating on the maps as many places as possible from the gazetteer lists it has been possible to reconstruct the location and approximate extent of each *tu*. In this way the Sung places found in the lists but not in the source maps have been assigned locations which are, on the prefectural scale, fairly precise.

INTRODUCTION

Purpose and background

This book is about change. Its setting in time, the Chinese dynasty known as Sung (960–1278), was together with its predecessor the T'ang (618–907) a time of massive transformations in society, economy, politics, and culture. Its subject, the Sung social and political elite, was (it has been argued) a fundamentally new class, different in character and far more fluid in personnel than the elites of T'ang and before. Its setting in space, Fu-chou, a single prefecture in South China, was itself insignificant in T'ang and first became politically and culturally important under the Sung. The changes of late T'ang and Sung, then, are background and context to all that will be discussed here. More specifically and more centrally, I will focus on a new and further transformation of the elite, a shift that finds its pivot not in the T'ang/Sung transition but at the midpoint of Sung. But the book is also about stability. As I will try to show, despite general social and economic change, despite a system of civil-service examinations that some have argued promoted rapid social movement up and down, and despite the transformation of its way of life in the course of the dynasty, the Fu-chou elite was a remarkably continuous body.

Some background is in order here. In the transformation of China that begins in middle T'ang and continues deep into Sung, much is still little understood; but much else is already clear. Most striking of all perhaps is sheer demography. Between the eighth and eleventh centuries China's population balance shifted dramatically from the north — traditionally the heartland of Chinese civilization — to the south. The total population, level or growing only very slightly for centuries before, more than doubled; apart from the capital region, virtually all growth was in the south.[1] This growth fed on migration from the north, torn by repeated war and disorder between the middle eighth and late tenth centuries; but it fed too on a growing southern production of rice. Denis Twitchett has shown the growing dependence of the T'ang court and northern population centers on rice shipped from the Huai-nan and lower Yangtse regions well to the south; northern demand, and the vast canal system that connected it to southern supplies, partly

1

fuelled the emergence of rice in this period as the most important food crop in China.[2] The same relation persisted, if anything even more acutely, in Sung, which in fact followed the short-lived governments of the intervening Five Dynasties (908—959) in placing its capital well to the east of those of T'ang, at K'ai-feng, nearer and more accessible to the canals from the south. The imperial sponsorship of new early-ripening strains from Southeast Asia forty years into the dynasty gave the process further impetus.[3] In a sense the rise of rice, and the demographic upsurge of the south that was its accompaniment, laid the basis for the whole series of economic and social changes that shaped Chinese society in T'ang, in Sung, and after.

What were these changes? In the economic sphere, first of all an enormously expanded commerce. Katō Shigeshi and Denis Twitchett have demonstrated, in middle and late T'ang, the breakdown of an older system of government markets and state-regulated trade in the capitals and larger population centers, the growing importance of commercial taxes for state revenues, and the emergence, even in the public pronouncements of the scholar-official class, of a new and relatively tolerant attitude toward trade and merchants.[4] Commercial expansion was reflected in the growing importance of money. Katō has shown the rise of gold and silver as private media of exchange beginning in T'ang; Robert Hartwell, Ch'üan Han-sheng, and Sogabe Shizuo have dealt with the emergence and expansion of paper money under Sung.[5] Expanding trade and the sheer increase of population are reflected again, as Shiba Yoshinobu among others has shown, in an unprecedented growth of cities and a multiplication of smaller market-centers in the countryside.[6] G.W. Skinner has argued that the levels of urbanization reached in Sung were probably never exceeded in later Chinese history.[7] Secondary industries sprang up or, where already in existence, grew enormously to serve urban and rural markets. Hartwell's work has revealed the extraordinary scale and technical sophistication of the iron industry in Northern Sung, apparently unequalled in Europe before the seventeenth century, and has shown its direct dependence on the capital market.[8] Margaret Medley has described the emergence of mass-production techniques and other evidences of incipient industrialization in the manufacture of porcelain, both for the state and for popular consumption, under the Sung and its successor the Yüan.[9] Porcelain, among other goods, flowed into the rapidly expanding Sung sea trade, which served markets in Southeast Asia, Japan, the Philippines, and as far away as the East African coast.[10]

Sea commerce depended crucially on the mariner's compass, one of three inventions of world-historical note that emerged in China in this period. The others were gunpowder, which by late Sung was being applied extensively in warfare, and book printing, first by the woodblock method and later, though never as importantly, by movable type.[11] One may debate the relative economic and political importance of these three; but in the cultural sphere printing must surely take pride of place. A true book industry emerged for the first time. Classical texts, long available only by laborious copying from manuscript to manuscript, could now be reproduced in far greater quantities and at far lower (though still by no means negligible) cost. The collected prose and poetry of respected authors, volumes of sample examination answers, collections of edicts and memorials, histories — the whole foundation of a scholar's or an official's education — were now to be had, if not always quite legally, as objects of commerce. Manuals of agriculture and domestic economy, texts on medicine, divination, astronomy, and geography, elite and semi-popular religious texts, were written or reproduced on a scale entirely unprecedented. In the cities, handbills, notices, and virtual daily newspapers sprang up, often quite outside the law, leaking in advance court decisions and appointments to the educated elite.[12] In city and countryside alike, religious propagandists distributed pamphlets or posted broadsheets and so brought their message to readers who might then spread it among their acquaintances.[13] Literacy and its uses were available more cheaply and so more widely than ever before.

All of these changes, again, are not the focus of this study, but its context. It would seem on the face of it, however, that they cannot have left the structure of society and politics, in particular the distribution of wealth, power, and prestige, unaltered. And indeed, since the work of Naitō Torajirō early in this century, historians of China have come to agree that between middle T'ang and early Sung the social and political elite was fundamentally transformed.[14] An ancient oligarchy or, in some formulations, an aristocracy of 'great clans', virtual monopolists of office and informal power throughout the period of disunion from the third to the seventh centuries, and still powerful through much or all of T'ang, gave way, it is argued, to a much broader, more fluid class: in the terminology of Japanese scholars, the 'newly-risen bureaucrats' of Sung, whose status rested not on heredity but on current presence in office.[15] Their rise has been traced variously to the new civil service examination system, a T'ang creation continued and elaborated under Sung; to the new political careers afforded by the powerful military governors of the latter half of T'ang, with their extensive personal followings and political staffs; to the unprecedented economic opportunities that followed from T'ang and Sung commercial expansion; or to all of these together. But the greatest attention, surely, has gone to the examinations. For Ch'en Yin-k'o and E.G. Pulleyblank, the exams were the ground on which, in middle T'ang and after, a new *'literati* gentry' challenged and finally defeated the aristocracy.[16] For Sudō Yoshiyuki they were the means by which the early

Sung state drew into office, and so tamed, 'powerful families' newly arisen from the chaos of late T'ang and Five Dynasties.[17] For E.A. Kracke, Sudō, and others, the exams were throughout Sung a source of new blood in the bureaucracy, a guarantee of rapid and constant movement of families up and down, in and out of office, which by itself defined social status.[18]

To the broadest outlines of this picture of elite transformation the present study offers no dissent. One may argue about timing, about the completeness of the T'ang aristocracy's dissolution, and about causes; but that there was a discontinuity – that the elite of Sung was in some way fundamentally new – seems to me beyond dispute. Its heavily southern origins, at least by a century into the dynasty, are by themselves difference enough from the elite of T'ang. It is just as clear that the examinations, in Sung even more than in T'ang, crucially influenced the elite's way of life. It is beyond this point that questions arise. As will become clear, I would especially dispute the notion that the exams were a constant and powerful conduit of 'new blood' into the elite. But more generally, for all the importance granted to the Sung elite – to its newness, its fluidity, its involvement with the exams, its cultural persona as *literati* – in defining the character of Chinese society in Sung and after, still *as elite, as social group*, it has until recently remained remarkably little studied. In particular it is only recently that students of Sung, following the lead of historians of the Ming and Ch'ing dynasties, have begun to investigate the elite in a specific setting – to do local history.[19] The present study is one essay in that direction. The Sung elite, I would argue, cannot be properly understood unless it is considered in a local, as well as a national, frame.

This of course is not a theoretically neutral statement, nor even merely a heuristic prescription. To argue that the Sung elite cannot be understood apart from locality is to suggest that its social position is not reducible to its role in the overarching national state. In my first chapter I seek partly to demonstrate this by examining critically in local terms two aspects of the elite–state relation: the role of the exam system, as presented particularly in the work of Kracke; and the social importance of office. These are particularly apt subjects for local study. The exam process, though it culminated in the capital, reached down into the localities and drew on a local pool far broader than the group that (at any stage) succeeded. In a local context one can look at men who never held office alongside those who did; without this it is hard to gauge the significance of what distinguished them, office itself. My concluding section too takes up in part the same theme of elite–state relations by considering the elite's role in several crucial fields of local action, especially in the latter half of Sung, in relation to the regulating, restraining, and controlling power of the state. The notion of the elite's real independence of the state is half the message of my book.

The other half has to do, again, with change. To say that the Sung elite was always, from one angle, a local entity is not to say that its relation to its locality never altered. In large part this study is intended as a contribution to an emerging body of work that sees fundamental discontinuity, in some ways as important as the earlier transformations of the T'ang–Sung transition, between the two halves of Sung. For the first 150 years after the Sung founder's unification of China, in the period afterward known as Northern Sung, China proper – apart from a relatively small territory on the northern border – was a single empire under Chinese rule. After 1127, North China – the area north of the Huai River – was ruled by a 'barbarian' non-Chinese people, the Jurchen (ancestors of the Manchus), whose Chin dynasty confronted and periodically warred with a reduced, though still numerically and geographically superior, Sung state: as we now know it, the Southern Sung. This division lasted until another Northern people, the Mongols, conquered first the Chin and then the Sung, reuniting China in 1278. But the earlier conquest, that of Chin, along with internal processes that preceded it, may have produced in Southern Sung a society radically different from what had been before. The difference seems in many ways to connect Southern Sung much more closely than Northern Sung to the dynasties that followed. This is the burden, in particular, of recent work by Robert Hartwell.

Much of Hartwell's position, as it touches specifically on Sung, is restated in the central chapters of this book and so need not be dwelt on at too great length here. In brief, Hartwell argues that the Northern Sung elite was divided between a nationally oriented, nationally marrying, bureaucratically striving 'professional elite' of long-lived high officeholding families, and a locally oriented 'gentry' pursuing a diversified strategy of local success in which office (and not necessarily high office) was only one component; but that in Southern Sung these two merged into a single locally rooted stratum essentially similar to the earlier gentry. In Southern Sung and henceforward the Chinese elite pursued a far more strongly localist strategy, marrying, interacting, and striving within a quite limited geographical frame. For Hartwell the Northern Sung 'professional elite' is in fact more like the aristocracy of T'ang than like the elites of later dynasties.[20]

Hartwell's work, then, argues for a Northern/Southern Sung split in a particularly stark form. His is by no means the only work, however, in which the division has emerged as important. Within his own field of concern, Hartwell's work on changing marriage patterns has been duplicated independently by that of Ihara Hiroshi, work too little known in this country. But the same split has appeared in work with radically different concerns. It is perhaps first to be seen in the classic 1950 article of Wm. Theodore de Bary, 'A Reappraisal of Neo-Confucianism.' Here de Bary pointed out the centrality

of politics, and specifically a politics focused on the state and its reforming
and transforming capacities, in the thought of the Confucian revival of
Northern Sung, and commented suggestively on the shift away from political
concerns (at least in this state-centered form), and toward the cultivation of
self, in the form of Neo-Confucianism that gradually became dominant in
Southern Sung, the form associated with Chu Hsi.[21] In a third quite different
area of concern, Shuen-fu Lin calls attention, in his study of the poet Chiang
K'uei, to a new focus in the lyric poetry of Southern Sung, specifically to the
rise in the thirteenth century of the *yung-wu* song, in which 'the poet shrinks
from the vast world of his lived experience and concentrates his creative
vision on one tangible object.' Lin explicitly attempts to relate this development to new Southern Sung social circumstances, particularly a tendency
toward 'voluntary withdrawal from public life into a private life devoted to
self-cultivation or to artistic and scholarly pursuits.' Parallel changes may be
seen as well, Lin suggests, in other arts, particularly painting.[22]

The central chapters of my study are in considerable part a confirmation
(with some differences of focus) and an elaboration *at the local level* of
Hartwell's findings on changes in the elite; and the concluding chapters seek
to locate one motive for the changes in the relative weakness of the Southern
Sung state. I touch there only in passing on the possible relation of all this
to de Bary's, not all on its relation to Lin's work. In my fourth chapter,
however, I present what seems to me clear evidence that, in the ideal sphere,
the elite's view of itself and of its own role changed fundamentally between
Northern and Southern Sung in a way that parallels the changes in practise
documented both here and in Hartwell's work. The world of ideas and
ideals, then, is by no means irrelevant to the problems treated here. If indeed
a shift between Northern and Southern Sung expressed itself in many different
areas of life and thought, a major task of future work, surely, is to relate
these diverse transformations to one another, to discover and explain their
connections. This book cannot go beyond proposing this as a project — it is
work for many hands — and suggesting that the connections are there.

In sum, this study attempts to explore these questions: what was the
character of the social elite of Sung China? What role did it play in its home
localities? What was the relation of its status, its power, its scope of action,
to the authority of the state? How did this relation, and the elite's role,
change in the course of the Sung?

Method

This, then, is a work of local history; it deals with the Sung elite as it is
found in one South Chinese prefecture, Fu-chou in Chiang-hsi circuit. What,
at the outset, do I mean by 'elite'? As one of my primary questions is the

social importance of office, it has seemed important to define 'elite' fairly broadly at the start: not, for instance, to limit its scope to the degreeholding or officeholding group and so decide the question by terminological sleight of hand. I have taken my theoretical lead, in a rough-and-ready way to be sure, from students of social stratification in other societies and periods, who have commonly distinguished, though in widely varying terms, three 'dimensions' along which a society may be stratified; three 'resources' to which its members may have unequal access: wealth, power, and prestige. In looking for a Fu-chou elite I have looked for men and women whose access to wealth, power, or prestige was, in the local scheme of things, especially privileged: whose control of material resources, hold over men's actions and decisions, or special place in the regard of their contemporaries, set them apart from Fu-chou society as a whole and made them people to be reckoned with.

This way of setting out may not be wholly uncontroversial. Wealth, power, and prestige, it may be argued, are — however commonsensical they may seem — the categories of Western social scientists, derived from the study of stratified *European* societies. For at least one of the three, prestige, there is probably no adequate single equivalent in the language of the Sung Chinese. In taking them as a starting point, does one distort the social reality of Sung China? Clearly I think not. There is certainly no overarching theory of stratification available that one may simply apply to any society one chooses to study. Yet there is surely value, if one hopes to understand the differences as well as the likenesses between societies, in approaching them with at least partly similar questions. What is impermissible is to assume that the sources and cultural components of prestige, of power, or — though this is perhaps less problematic — of wealth, are the same in Sung China as elsewhere. This, as I think will become clear below, I do not assume. That Sung men at least implicitly recognized each of the three categories, distinguished them from one another, saw them as desirable, strove for them, and used them in comparing and evaluating one another, seems to me to emerge clearly from the sources. I will suggest further on that one of the fundamental social categories of the Sung Chinese themselves, the notion of the *shih* ('gentleman', 'literatus'), corresponds rather well to the elite as defined here.

It is one thing to look for wealth, power, and prestige; it is another to know when one has found them. Given the character of the sources — the lack of adequate testimony on property or income, for example — one needs to consider the problem of criteria. These should be fairly specific, if one is to know just whom one is talking about. A source may tell us that X is 'very rich' or that 'all his neighbors looked on him with awe'; but it is hard to know just what this means, how this places X in a social universe. For my study of Fu-chou I define seven (by no means mutually exclusive) categories of men and women as members of the elite. The seven, with brief explanations, follow.

(1)   Officeholders. The importance of office as a source of prestige, power, and indeed wealth in 'traditional' China is a commonplace among historians. While at his post, an officeholder exercised formal authority within some officially defined field of action, and often considerable informal authority as well. Out of office, at home in his own district or elsewhere, a man with a background of office was often in a privileged (though not necessarily uniquely privileged) position in dealing with local officials and so influencing decisions that might affect local interests. Office brought with it as well a number of fiscal and legal privileges for the holder's household *vis-à-vis* the state: I discuss these in later chapters. I will argue further on that office was not, as has sometimes been suggested, an ultimate and all-determining mark of high status; but to deny that office was important would be folly.

(2)   Graduates of the prefectural examination, or other men certified locally or regionally as academically eligible to compete for office in the exams at the capital. A passing grade in the prefectural exam seems to have been, in the local sphere at least, in some respects a more crucial step than success in the capital exam, to which it gave access. In Southern Sung Fu-chou the right to use an agent as legal proxy — one of the most important privileges of the 'official household' — was in fact shared by all households that had produced even a single pre-fectural graduate. By passing at the prefecture a man showed his ability to compete on at least even terms with the sons of Fu-chou's most illustrious officeholding and scholarly families.

(3)   Major contributors of funds or lands to Fu-chou Buddhist or Taoist temples. Building a temple, as we shall see, was an expensive proposition. For Sung the commemorative stelae on which the names of temple builders and donors have survived are not, as in some later examples, long lists that include the contributor of a few paving-stones along with the project's leading figures: here only the most important contributors are mentioned. Thus even when the record does not tell how much was contributed, the presence of a man's name is evidence of considerable wealth. It is clear too, indeed the act of carving a stela implies, that for many a very considerable prestige attached to the act of donation, which marked a man as charitable and community-minded. It seems likely as well that by his gift a donor might exert real influence over a temple's affairs: this was in itself a kind of social power.

(4)   Organizers of and major contributors to the founding or building of schools, academies, libraries, bridges, waterworks, or gardens. Once

again the mention of a man as contributor, or especially as sole builder, in records of the building or repair of dams, bridges, schools, etc. is evidence of considerable wealth. Beyond this, a leading role in such projects brought with it or even presupposed influence or power in local affairs. The decision to build a bridge, or the decision to site it at a certain spot, for example, could be highly controversial, since different local groups might be affected in different ways. Thus the construction of Fu-chou city's major bridge in 1225 was opposed by boat owners who knew they would lose the income they currently earned by ferrying.[23] The Ch'ien-chin Dam project in 1251 drew opposition from some who feared it would disrupt established irrigation patterns downstream from the dam.[24] The capacity to achieve a goal over the opposition of others is virtually a definition of power. Other projects might be significant in other ways. The man or woman who built an academy or library could attract famous scholars and teachers to his neighborhood, thus at once establishing important social connections, achieving a reputation for beneficence, providing tutors for sons, and reorienting local academic networks around his (or her) family and posterity. The builder of a spectacular or tasteful garden could similarly make his own property a focus of local elite social life, strengthening his own prestige and his potentially useful connections.

(5)   Organizers or leaders of local defense activities or of (formal or informal) local programs of charity or famine relief. That a military organization, if effective, exerts power goes without saying; the capacity to create or to take the leadership of such an organization implies a fair degree of power or influence to begin with. As we shall see, leadership in local defense seems often to have required considerable wealth as well. Wealth, or the power and influence needed to affect the disposition of wealth by others, is implied too by leadership of famine relief programs or the founding of local welfare institutions.

(6)   Men connected by friendship, master—student ties, or common membership in academic or poetic societies or cliques, to members of categories (1) through (5). The social importance of master—student ties was given formal recognition as a basis for recommendation or protection in the recruitment and educational systems of the Sung state. Friendship and academic or poetic collegiality were not so formally recognized; but it cannot be doubted that close acquaintance with the wealthy or powerful gave opportunities to exert one's own influence over local or even national affairs or to enlarge one's reputation.

(7)   Affinal kin of members of categories (1) through (5). In the third chapter I will argue, on the basis of several cases, that wealth and

reputation were criteria for a proper match both in sons-in-law and in daughters-in-law, and thus that marriage will usually have joined families of generally similar social position. If this is true, it is reasonable to treat marriage with a local elite member as in itself evidence of family wealth and/or prestige and hence of local elite membership even before the marriage. Once the marriage has taken place, the case is even stronger: affinal relations were universally recognized in Sung, as in other periods of Chinese history, as channels for the communication of social or political advantage and the exertion of power and influence. Compare the discussion in Chapter 1 of the range of kin an official was formally allowed to sponsor or protect.[25]

The diversity of these criteria obviously reflects the state of the sources rather than theoretical predilection: this is a *working* definition. Each criterion is reasonably specific, and each is in some way evidence of special access, within the local scheme of things, to wealth, power, or prestige. Vague references to wealth, to an academic vocation, or to charitable practices are disregarded.

This elite, then, though viewed as local, includes officeholders, no matter how high they may climb. Philip Kuhn, in his pathbreaking study of militarization in the Ch'ing, carefully distinguishes the 'local elite' from a 'national elite' and 'provincial elite', whose members had influence and connections beyond a single locality.[26] The distinction is essential for the wider field Kuhn treats. For my purposes the central question is whether a man maintained some presence in Fu-chou, some commitment to local affairs. So long as this is so, so long as he continues to play a role in Fu-chou society, I include him in the 'Fu-chou elite', though his commitments and connections may reach to the court and beyond.

Why study Fu-chou? At the outset the choice of setting was partly accident: I deliberately looked for a prefecture that lay outside the lower Yangtse region, the source of so much of our picture of Sung and post-Sung China; Fu-chou proved to be especially well provided with source material. Throughout Sung, Fu-chou was large enough and populous enough, and produced *chin-shih* and officials consistently enough, to be thought significant in national terms; yet not so large or so politically central as to be wholly untypical of its time. But Fu-chou is interesting for another reason: it was home to two Sung men especially well remembered by later generations of Chinese. Wang An-shih, prime minister and 'reformer,' the man around whose policies the great political struggles of late Northern Sung took shape, came from Lin-ch'uan, Fu-chou's metropolitan county. Slightly more than a century later Lin-ch'uan's eastern neighbor, Chin-ch'i County, was the home of Lu Chiu-yüan, Southern Sung Neo-Confucian philosopher and leading rival

to the central intellectual figure of his time, Chu Hsi. Thus in the two halves
of the dynasty a major political movement and an influential philosophical
school found their leaders in Fu-chou men. Though biography is far from my
purpose here, the prospect of reconstructing something of the social milieu
from which these two men emerged has been from the outset an attractive
one.

A sketch of the setting

A gentleman who planned a journey to Fu-chou in late Southern Sung
could consult two contemporary handbooks to the sights, landmarks, and
historic spots of South China: *The Scenery of the World Recorded* of Wang
Hsiang-chih and Chu Mu's *Scenic Views of the World.*[27] In each, under
'Customs and Manners,' he would find brief passages from descriptions of
Fu-chou by three prominent men of Sung. If his library housed the works
of all three he could, if curious, refer to these for a fuller account.

From Tseng Kung (1019–83), writing in 1050, he would learn:

> Fu [. . .] abounds in good fields; thus disasters of flood or drought,
> caterpillars or locusts, are few. Its people delight in agriculture and so
> provide enough for themselves; thus the horses and oxen pasturing in
> its mountains and valleys are not gathered in, and the five grains piled
> in the countryside are not walled up. At peace, they know nothing of
> the alarm of drumbeats or of the service of conscription.[28]

From Hsieh I (1069–1113), in 1110:

> Though Lin-ch'uan is but a small county for Chiang-hsi, its city is
> placed on the banks of the Ju River, and the Ling-ku, T'ung-ling, and
> other ridges ring it about like screens. [. . .] Of old it had Wang Hsi-
> chih, Hsieh Ling-yün, and Yen Chen-ch'ing as its prefects; thus its
> customs and manners are imbued with scholarship and refinement,
> with a love of affairs and an esteem for spiritual force. It has had Yen
> Shu and Wang An-shih as its natives; thus its communities delight in
> reading books and excel in literary expression.[29]

And from Chou Pi-ta (1126–1204), who alone among these three was not
a Fu-chou man himself, writing in 1202:

> The land south of the great river is divided into two circuits, east and
> west. Going from the eastern to the western the first place one comes
> to is Fu-chou. Though as a prefecture it was established and disestablished
> irregularly from Three Kingdoms to Sui and T'ang, yet today's Chien-
> ch'ang Prefecture, with its seat at Nan-ch'eng and overseeing Nan-feng,
> and what has been taken into Fu-chien as Shao-wu Prefecture, were all

originally subordinate counties of Fu. Not only the extent of its land
but the abundance of its people surpasses the entire circuit. In the
flourishing abundance of its great men too it excels other prefectures.
This dynasty gives greatest weight to the scholarly degrees. The *Lin-
ch'uan Gazetteer* devotes a whole chapter to a name-list [of degree-
holders], beginning with Yüeh Shih and continuing down through
1180, giving name and surname. [. . .] During two hundred years,
worthies and great talents have come in close succession. If one should
try to tell of the most illustrious, Yen Shu's promotion of worthies and
love of the good, Wang An-shih's literary scholarship and righteous
action, Tseng Kung's service as covenantor for our culture – these are
what a man should exert himself toward. The Yüehs, the Tsengs, the
Wangs, whose fathers and sons, elder and younger brothers have followed
one upon the other in the exam lists – these are what a family should
exert itself toward.[30]

When the traveller reached his goal, he would see that not all said here
was strictly true. Neither 'flood and drought' nor 'the alarm of drumbeats'
were, in his own time, unknown in Fu-chou; and it was only by historical
sleight of hand that Chou Pi-ta could elevate it to Chiang-hsi's largest and
most populous prefecture. But the words of Tseng, Hsieh, and Chou contain
much that contemporaries remarked on again and again when they spoke of
Fu-chou: its ridge-and-valley landscape, especially in the southern counties;
the nestling of its city in a bend of the Ju River; the productiveness of its
fields; and the scholarship and exam successes of its sons – in particular the
remarkable achievements of its most prominent families.

Hsieh I commented on the placement of the city on the banks of the
Ju; this siting was a clear expression of the river's crucial role in Fu-chou's
geography and economy. For the city itself, however, this role was by Sung
times not unproblematic. The local military leader who in 885 shifted the
seat of prefectural government to this site from one less well watered had
adjusted political arrangements to natural realities. By middle Sung the
relation ran in the opposite direction: the river's course was a human artifact,
maintained with difficulty. The northern part of Fu-chou, in which the city
lay, was relatively flat, and the Ju here had the character of an aging stream,
meandering irregularly across a barely sloping floodplain. Over time its natural
tendency had been to shift, or to spawn branches flowing, northeast of the
city and so to remove or reduce the supply of water and the transport route
on which urban residents and the prefecture's traders depended. To combat
this trend Fu-chou officials and locals in Southern Sung built and repeatedly
rebuilt a dam just south of the city, diverting part of the fugitive river back
into its older course past and around the city's eastern and northern bounds.[31]

In 885 the seat, and the settlement around it, could simply be moved; by middle Sung the growth of urban population had made the river more easily shiftable than the city. The difference epitomizes the transformation of Fu-chou, with its city, from demographic backwater to major population center.

Rivers and streams in large measure defined Fu-chou, and articulated its relation to its surroundings. The Ju not only fed and watered the city; with its tributaries it drained almost the whole prefecture and, further off, virtually all of southeastern Chiang-hsi circuit. (See Maps 1–4.) From its source in the far south of Nan-feng County[32] (part of Fu-chou until 991), it flowed north and northeast through Nan-feng and Nan-ch'eng County (under Sung no longer a Fu-chou county), then turned northwest and re-entered Fu-chou, flowing through Lin-ch'uan County, past the city, on northwest and out of the prefecture into neighbouring Hung-chou, and eventually north into the P'eng-li, now called P'o-yang, Lake.[33] The river and the territories it drained were thus components of the larger P'o-yang basin; the major river supplying the lake, the Kan, flowed through the prefectures bordering Fu-chou on the west; a third major river, the Hsin, drained those to Fu-chou's north (see Map 1). On a smaller scale, the Ju defined Fu-chou itself: after 991 the prefecture comprised (with some exceptions, to be dealt with below) the drainage area of all the Ju tributaries that joined the river within the boundaries of Lin-ch'uan County. Within Lin-ch'uan and most of its eastern neighbor Chin-ch'i County, again, flat lowlying lands predominated; but the rest of the prefecture was largely composed of a vast number of low but often quite steep hills and mountain ridges, from which hundreds of streams flowed rapidly down into numerous rather clearly defined and narrow river valleys. Men of the time remarked often both on the hills and on the abundance of streams. Water transport was so convenient and so crucial to Fu-chou's economic life that a special class of diviners found their sole livelihood in predicting, from details of shape and construction, the future of boats and ships.[34]

The Ju had always been Fu-chou's backbone; but Fu-chou had not always been the same prefecture. Its earliest administrative ancestor, Lin-ch'uan commandery, had been founded by the Wu Kingdom in 257; the name Fu-chou ('Pacified Prefecture') was first given in the late sixth century by the conquering Sui dynasty. At the end of the T'ang the prefecture governed four counties: Lin-ch'uan and Nan-ch'eng in the north, Ch'ung-jen and Nan-feng in the south. This was the composition of Fu-chou when it fell under the control of the Southern T'ang, one of the so-called Ten Kingdoms that divided South China between the fall of T'ang and the Sung reunification in 976. In the last years of Southern T'ang and the first years of Sung a series

Map 1. Sung China (c.1050) and Fu-chou.

of administrative changes transformed Fu-chou's position. On the one hand
two new counties were created: I-huang County in 968, from three cantons
of Ch'ung-jen; and Chin-ch'i County in 994–1005, out of territory of Lin-
ch'uan and the neighboring prefecture of Jao-chou. On the other hand
Nan-ch'eng County (in 969) and then Nan-feng County (in 991) were ceded
from Fu-chou to create a new prefecture in its old eastern territories: this was
Chien-ch'ang Chün.[35] (See Maps 2 and 3.) The resulting boundaries remained
unchanged for almost a century and a half. In 1149, because of the threat of

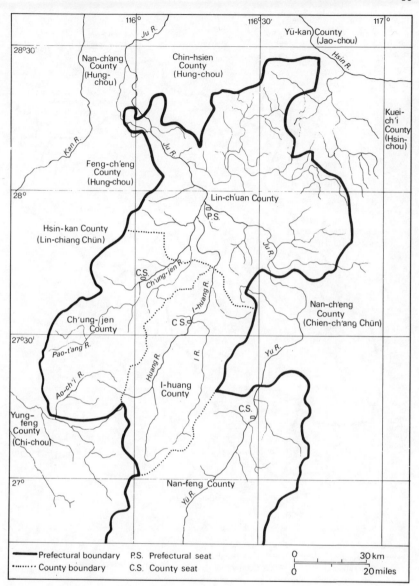

Map 2. Fu-chou in 975.

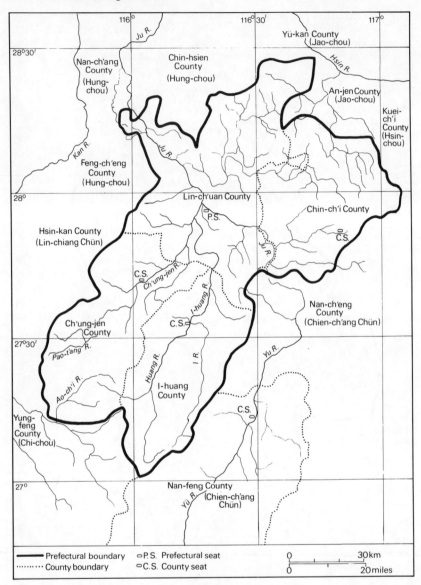

Map 3. Fu-chou and Nan-feng County, 1005–1148.

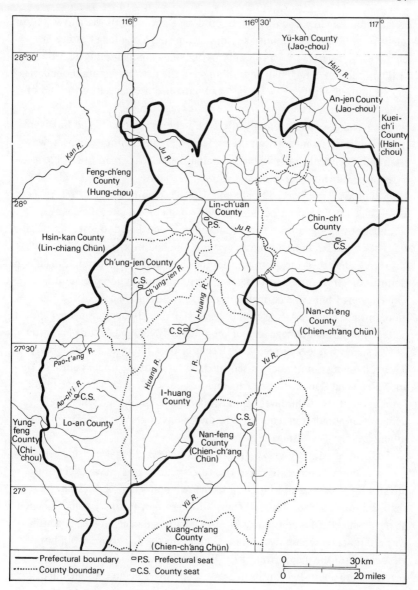

Map 4. Fu-chou and Nan-feng County, 1149–1512.

banditry on Fu-chou's southwestern borders, a new county was carved out of territory of Ch'ung-jen County and of neighboring Yung-feng County in Chi-chou: this became Lo-an County. After some compensating adjustment of the borders of Lin-ch'uan and Ch'ung-jen, the new prefectural boundaries were stabilized within a few years[36] and remained unchanged to the end of Sung, through the Yüan, and into the Ming (see Map 4).

These changes fundamentally altered Fu-chou's relation to the Ju River. In its middle T'ang incarnation the prefecture, spanning four counties, was essentially identical to the whole Ju drainage area. The creation of Chien-ch'ang Chün divided the same area into two separate prefectures, which by 1005 comprised six, by 1149 eight counties. This multiplication itself reflects, as we shall see, enormous population growth. Yet even after the changes, administrative geography – for the most part – continued to rest in intelligible ways upon the structure of the Ju system. Fu-chou proper after 991, as we have seen, embraced the Ju tributaries that joined the river within Lin-ch'uan County, the prefecture's seat of government; its companion prefecture, Chien-ch'ang Chün, was definable in turn as the drainage area of the Ju's more upward course. At the county level, similarly, I-huang coincided almost perfectly with the drainage area of the I-huang River, and Ch'ung-jen (after 1149), somewhat less perfectly, with that of the Ch'ung-jen (or Pao-t'ang) River. Nan-feng County comprised the tributaries of the upper course of the Ju, Nan-ch'eng County those of its middle course. Of such cases one might form a rule: that at this level administrative geography, even when the demands of population required it to divide physiographic systems, did not otherwise seriously disregard them.

To divide a territory into political units, however, was even for a central-ized state more complicated than this rule would suggest. Two exceptions are striking, and may give insight into the real political processes that shaped units of administration. The addition of new territory from Chi-chou at the creation of Lo-an County in 1149 greatly enlarged an area in south-western Fu-chou whose rivers drained, not into the Ju system at all, but, westward into the major river of the P'o-yang basin, the Kan. This area in fact made up about two-thirds of Lo-an's territory. Lo-an thus included, in effect, fragments of two quite separate river systems, flowing (at least locally) in opposite directions and separated by quite a steep watershed. The only parallel elsewhere in Fu-chou lay in the far northeast, where signifi-cant parts of Chin-ch'i County were watered by streams flowing north into the third major P'o-yang basin river, the Hsin.

These arrangements were, from the administrative point of view, distinctly strange. For the state the seats of counties and prefectures were in the first place stations for the collection of revenue. Tax goods and money were to be delivered first to the county, forwarded by counties to the prefecture, then shipped on to the capital or elsewhere as (in theory) the center might direct. In South China abundant waterways made these processes easier and less expensive than in the drier north, where taxes (and trade as well) might often have to move by land. Yet the inclusion of territory from outside the Ju system in Lo-an and Chin-ch'i placed the demands of the fiscal system — that taxes should move from these areas to their county seats and thence to Fu-chou city — in direct conflict with the transport capacities of the region's river systems.

The sources on the creation of Chin-ch'i and Lo-an supply no reasons for the odd composition of their territory. As to consequences, however, there is more evidence. In later chapters I will argue that in Chin-ch'i the distinctness of the northeastern region found social expression in the interaction of local elite families (see Chapter 2, pp. 75–81) and that in Fu-chou as a whole the poor correspondence of administration and physiography in the southwest and northeast had major impact on the organization of local militias (see Chapter 5, pp. 139–50). In Lo-an it is known that the transfer of territory from the seemingly 'natural' parent county of Yung-feng in Chi-chou was the occasion of lawsuits that led temporarily to its return.[37] In Lo-an, however, the old Chi-chou territory was not the only anomaly: the entire county was inaccessible by water transport from the rest of the prefecture. Its isolation prompted the county's exemption from forced sales of rice to the state, known as Harmonious Purchase;[38] Lo-an was also allowed to ship its regular rice taxes in the form of cash. These were significant fiscal advantages: contemporaries saw Harmonious Purchase as an especially onerous exaction. One might expect that Lo-an's favored status would make it attractive to land buyers from outside Fu-chou; and indeed it is recorded that in 1271 half of all the arable land in the canton transferred from Chi-chou belonged to a family surnamed Lo that lived across the western border, in Yung-feng County.[39] The Los will thus have avoided levies which they would have had to pay if their lands had lain within their own prefecture. There seems little question that, for the state, fiscal rationality would have been better served by attaching much or all of Lo-an County (and so having its tax goods shipped) to Chi-chou. It is just as clear, however, that once fiscal privileges were granted — and their granting, given Lo-an's peculiarities, was probably inevitable — the preservation of Lo-an's connection to Fu-chou must have been crucially important both for local landowners and for absentees like the Los. In the event, then, it would seem to be the interests of locals, not of the state, that were ultimately served by the disposition of Lo-an's territory. The evidence is indirect, and the test of '*cui bono?*' can of course never be decisive; but the example suggests that local interests and pressures could be as important as central needs in deciding the structure of local administration.[40]

The splitting of the Ju River system between two prefectures, again, rested on an almost explosive growth of population.[41] This, as we have seen, was characteristic of all of South China from late T'ang into Sung; the P'o-yang basin was a particular beneficiary. In middle T'ang the region was home to just over one quarter of a million households; by the 1070s these had grown to more than 1.7 million.[42] This was nearly sevenfold growth while the population of Chinas as a whole, though expanding steadily, had at most doubled. In 1223 the circuit of Chiang-hsi, which included much but not all of the P'o-yang basin, was the most populous in the reduced empire of Southern Sung, its ten prefectures housing 2,267,798 households: some ten or eleven million people.[43]

Fu-chou's population followed much the same course. (Here and below, see Appendix II: Population.) At the T'ang founding Fu-chou's registered population had numbered just over seven thousand households. By 742 the total had more than quadrupled.[44] After 742 it doubled again by the 980s or so, tripled by 1016. More of this increase than is apparent surely took place in late T'ang and Five Dynasties, since the first Sung figures are probably depressed by incomplete control of the new territory of South China. But in any case Fu-chou's population had grown roughly tenfold, though in the meantime, as we have seen, the prefecture had lost almost half of its territory. The relation of people to space, clearly, was transformed.

Under Sung, Fu-chou's population increased — in absolute terms at least — as dramatically as in T'ang. By 1176 the prefecture housed slightly more than a million people; between 1176 and 1262 there was, at least apparently, very little further growth. By the midpoint of Sung, Fu-chou's growth had moved it into a position of fair prominence in the empire. In 1102, when Chiang-hsi's population was second among all circuits, Fu-chou ranked third among Chiang-hsi prefectures.[45] In the empire only fourteen of about three hundred prefectures, including the capital, were more populous.[46] Fu-chou at this period, with about 200 persons per square mile, was about as densely peopled as the state of Illinois in 1970.[47] The population, of course, was not evenly distributed, but concentrated more heavily in the flatter northern territories of Lin-ch'uan and Chin-ch'i County than in the mountainous counties to the south. Even the southern counties, however, had population densities higher than the average for Chiang-hsi circuit: this was, in contemporary terms, a well-settled prefecture.

Perhaps one of every eight Fu-chou residents in Sung lived in a town or city.[48] The proportion is not unimpressive, as Fu-chou was by no means the main trading center of the P'o-yang region; and it may even have been higher.

There is good evidence that, as in the larger Sung cities studied by Shiba Yoshinobu,[49] in Fu-chou too urban settlement had pushed well past the old city walls or official urban bounds, for the most part established in late T'ang or Five Dynasties. In the prefectural seat in Lin-ch'uan County there were three extramural 'boroughs' recognized by the state: one, lying across the river from the city's eastern gate, stretched for at least 1.5 kilometers from the riverbank.[50] In Ch'ung-jen and Lo-an County similar secondary market districts or urban wards faced the county seat from the opposite bank of each county's main river.[51] Here there is no evidence that the urban character of the extramural population was officially recognized; if it was not, then Fu-chou's urban population was considerably larger than the official figures show. In any case such extramural settlement is evidence that the growth of Sung population, here as elsewhere, was urbanizing growth: evidence again that Fu-chou was transformed between T'ang and Sung.

The population expansion and influx of T'ang, Five Dynasties, and Sung — accompanied, one assumes, by the opening of extensive new lands to cultivation — presumably played a part in creating the economic base from which the local elite families of Sung would enter into the highest levels of national political life. Unfortunately the sources are far less informative on economic changes, indeed on economic life in general, than on the cultural and political achievements that presumably in part rested on them. On the local economy in T'ang no information at all survives,[52] and for the Sung itself only the most static picture is possible. Like the P'o-yang basin in general, which throughout Sung was of great importance as a producer and exporter of rice,[53] Fu-chou was known largely as an agricultural prefecture[54] where rice culture took pride of place. I have already touched on the importance of early-ripening strains of rice; these were well established in Fu-chou by the 1090s, when the prefecture each year produced two separate rice crops: 'early' and 'late.'[55] Fu-chou rice culture was heavily dependent on artificial irrigation works such as dams and storage-ponds, and by the 1250s the use of bamboo-pipe waterwheels (*t'ung-ch'e*) to bring water from streams up onto high banks was commonplace in at least some counties.[56] By these methods Fu-chou's farmers in Southern Sung produced, it seems, around 3,000,000 *shih*, or about 147,000 tons, of rice each year.[57]

Where did this rice go? First of all to local consumption. In 1271 a prefect took the people of Fu-chou to task for their dislike of any grain but rice for a daily staple;[58] Hsieh K'o two hundred years before had described his prefecture as a wealthy one, whose people 'eat their fill of rice and fish.'[59] Second, to the state, either as autumn tax sent to the capital or, in Southern Sung, as 'Harmonious Purchase' rice shipped to the vast armies stationed along and above the Yangtse. Finally, a good proportion of the local crop was sold to merchants who took it out of Fu-chou to sell it elsewhere.[60] Even in years of local drought and famine, when Fu-chou prices were at their highest, demand elsewhere was so great that local rice growers could expect a still higher price from travelling merchants.[61] Rice processed locally, under the direction of a number of 'wealthy households,' into red yeastcake was similarly exported to distant parts of the empire, where it would be used in the production of wine.[62] Fu-chou, it seems, was by a considerable margin a net exporter of rice;[63] and the gains to be had by selling rice stores to out-going traders were an economic mainstay of a good many wealthy families.[64]

Of other grains and of non-agricultural products we know much less. Wheat and barley were perhaps considerably less important than rice; the 1271 prefect commented at length on Fu-chou farmers' wastefulness in not, as a rule, planting their rice lands in wheat or barley between the rice harvest and the next sowing.[65] In every county, still, dry lands made up at least half the cultivated area, and in the hilly, less populated counties to the south the proportion seems to have been much higher. The major products of these lands, apart from wheat, were perhaps tea and textile crops, including kudzu and ramie.[66] Among local secondary industries, textile production was again probably one of the most important;[67] others were mining (of gold, silver, iron, and copper),[68] porcelain manufacture,[69] printing,[70] papermaking,[71] shipbuilding,[72] and – illegal as often as not, but still a thriving industry – bronze casting.[73] Most of these again fed into a thriving national commerce; for bronze vessels, paper, and printing at least, Fu-chou had some reputation across the empire.

This all too sketchy description of the Fu-chou economy has so far not touched on the social relations on which economic life was founded. Hard information is barely to be had. Throughout the Sung, some thirty to forty percent of Fu-chou's households were formally registered as owning no land within the prefecture; only a fifth or so of these were urban.[74] Some considerable number, one would think, must have supported themselves as tenants or hired workers on other people's land. Contemporary testimony, though vague, does give evidence of high rates of tenancy and, in some parts of the prefecture, of extensive and continuous tenanted holdings by single wealthy families.[75] One of the most restrictive forms of Sung land tenure – the so-called *ti-k'o* status, whose holder was legally obligated to remain attached to a certain piece of land and was regarded as standing in the relation of servant to master with the land's owner – is attested in a Fu-chou lawcase. This very case, however, demonstrates that a *ti-k'o* might own land of his own, might have *ti-k'o* of his own working that land, and could be *ti-k'o* with respect to one piece of land while taking part in very different sorts of tenancy arrangements on other land or with other owners.[76] Here, certainly, the picture of a 'manorial' economy that we find in the work of Sudō Yoshiyuki, Mark Elvin, and others seems too simply and broadly drawn.[77] Sung tenancy relationships in general took a number of different forms, with widely varying consequences for the legal and actual status of the tenant.[78] Relations of control and obligation were not simple. In Fu-chou, for example, we learn from the prefectural administrator Huang Chen in 1272 that landlords were preventing tenants from planting wheat on their rented lands (as a second crop between the rice harvest and the next planting) because a wheat crop would yield no rent.[79] If landlords could not force the paying of rent for wheat planted on their lands, rental arrangements must have been governed either by long-term contractual arrangements or by well-established custom that owners could not defy. That they were able nonetheless to prevent the planting of wheat suggests considerable informal control over their tenants' actions – but control that did not extend to terms of rental. We are dealing with complex sets of relationships here: relationships on which the Fu-chou sources shed only intermittent light.

We should not in any case conceive rural Fu-chou society as epitomized in the relation of landlord to landless tenant or farm worker. Not all tenants – not even all *ti-k'o*, as we have seen – were landless; and more important, not all the landless, or all rural dwellers of little wealth, lived by farming. Anecdotal sources reveal a broad and varied array of non-elite occupations in the countryside: weaver, carpenter, kiln worker, barber, dyer, lacquerer, painter, snail-boiler, musician, diviner, spirit medium, to name a random few.[80]

Our picture, again, is not only a vague but a static one. Yet change, we can be sure, did take place. Much of Fu-chou's economic life in Sung, given the sheer facts of demography, must have been essentially new, perhaps dating from late T'ang at the earliest. But apart from this, and much later, two important and recurrent new developments in Southern Sung will have had a disruptive effect on economic life, as on life in general. The first was drought and consequent loss of crops. The Fu-chou sources record drought and/or dearth under Northern Sung in only two years, more than a century apart: 1004 and 1109. Contemporary descriptions stress the rarity of drought in the period.[81] For Southern Sung, in contrast, the sources show drought or dearth in 1136, 1140, 1171 to 1173, 1180, 1182, 1186, 1187, 1204, 1221, and 1271.[82] The effects of these crop failures, it seems, were selective: in the worst droughts there were families with much grain to sell, and the disparities were the focus of controversy and even disorder.[83] A second disrupting influence was increasing disorder itself: war and 'banditry.' In Southern Sung the countryside and cities of most Fu-chou counties repeatedly suffered considerable destruction by invading soldiers from the Chin empire to the north or by bandits, usually from other prefectures.[84] The effects of dearth on the one hand and of disorder on the other cannot be measured; yet one may speculate at least that the livelihood of those less able to defend themselves, or to afford a year or two of bad crops, became considerably less secure in Southern than in Northern Sung. We will see in Chapters 5 and 6 something of the response of the local elite to these new social facts of Southern Sung.

For all of this, Fu-chou remained, in regional terms, a significant economic center; indeed it was in Southern Sung that it first received official recognition of its economic and political importance, with the siting in its prefectural city of the circuit office of the Intendant for Ever-Normal Granaries.[85] This agency, which supervised the state's charitable and price-stabilizing granaries, famine-relief programs, and water-control measures for all of Chiang-hsi circuit, was one of four circuit-level organs that formed the highest level of Sung administration below the central agencies in the capital. In Chiang-hsi the two most important of these, the financial and military intendancies, were sited in Hung-chou, bordering Fu-chou to the northwest; in effect this was the circuit capital. The third, the judicial intendancy, sat in Chi-chou, adjoining Fu-chou on the west. This scattering of circuit organs among three adjacent prefectures reflects consistent Sung central policy, intended partly to prevent the emergence of power centers rivalling the capital at the regional level.[86] But the choice of Fu-chou as one of the three sites signals the state's judgement of its position. Even in relation to its own P'o-yang region, as we shall see further on, this position was new in Sung.

New, too, was Fu-chou's political and cultural prominence within the empire. During T'ang Fu-chou had been of little political importance. No local men, apparently, achieved any prominence on the national scene; no 'great families' from Fu-chou found place on the national lists of aristocratic clans.[87] In Sung, as Chou Pi-ta's account above suggests, the situation was transformed. The change may have begun under the interim kingdoms of Wu and Southern T'ang: at least two Fu-chou men held office in this period, and a third was recommended as Fu-chou's leading candidate for the *chin-shih* degree, but refused to go.[88] All three came from families that were to achieve national prominence under Sung. Only four years after the reunification, in 980, Fu-chou produced its first Sung *chin-shih*.[89] Twenty-one others followed in the dynasty's first thirty years; by the end of Northern Sung 216 men of greater Fu-chou had achieved degrees. By the end of Sung the total was 628 for Fu-chou proper, 745 for greater Fu-chou.[90] In Chiang-hsi circuit only the 925 *chin-shih* from Chi-chou and the 647 from Chien-ch'ang Chün exceeded the number for Fu-chou proper.[91] These were Fu-chou's southwestern and eastern neighbors; the territory of the three formed a broad, continuous swath across the center of Chiang-hsi circuit. Under Southern Sung only thirteen prefectures (of about 150 in the empire) produced more *chin-shih* than Fu-chou.[92] Fu-chou's position as a producer of degreeholders in Sung seems to reflect fairly closely its new demographic rank in the empire.[93]

Within Fu-chou, however, the distribution of degrees changed significantly over time, and its relation to population was never a simple one. Under Northern Sung the metropolitan county, Lin-ch'uan, most populous of the four counties of Fu-chou proper but still housing no more than 45 per cent of its total population, produced nearly two-thirds of its *chin-shih*. The other third or so were divided among Ch'ung-jen, Chin-ch'i, and I-huang in proportions that bore no relation whatever to their respective population or population density. Under Southern Sung, Lin-ch'uan's share of Fu-chou's *chin-shih*, though still by far the largest among the four districts surviving from Northern Sung, had fallen to just below half; even lower if one takes into account the new county of Lo-an. Unless the distribution of population had in the meanwhile shifted drastically in Lin-ch'uan's favor, this was still a disproportionate share. There had been only a partial move toward adjusting *chin-shih* to population. Yet the sheer fact was that more than half of Fu-chou's *chin-shih* now came from the four less densely populated, more nearly 'peripheral' counties: this represented a sharp change. Men from the outlying counties may have brought different backgrounds and perspectives with them into the national bureaucracy. The shift represents, then, a significant difference between Northern and Southern Sung; of such differences we shall see much more further on.

It is not only by sheer numbers of *chin-shih*, however, that one can see Fu-chou's new importance as a source of national talent. At the higher levels of the Sung political structure, eight men from greater Fu-chou reached the rank of chief or assisting councillor of state: among these, of course, was Wang An-shih.[94] In literature, Wang and the earlier chief councillor Yen Shu were famous poets in their own time and ever after; and in late Northern and early Southern Sung four Fu-chou men were prominent members of the so-called 'Chiang-hsi school' of poetry.[95] In philosophy, again, the Chin-ch'i County man Lu Chiu-yüan became, in the twelfth century, the leader of one of the two or three most influential schools of Sung Neo-Confucianism. Yüeh Shih, Fu-chou's first *chin-shih* in Sung, was the author of the first national gazetteer of the reunited empire, the *T'ai-p'ing huan-yü chi*. At the fall of Sung, Fu-chou men were to be prominent in the last-ditch resistance to the invading Yüan led by the Chi-chou man Wen T'ien-hsiang; others were to collaborate with the invaders and gain national fame under the new dynasty.[96]

In sum, Fu-chou had become in Sung a prefecture of some political and cultural importance in national elite circles. Indeed it is largely to this that we owe the wealth of documents that make a study of the elite possible. In this respect Fu-chou is clearly not 'typical'; one must treat it instead as one of about thirty prefectures, across the empire, whose natives played a considerable part in the political, social, and cultural leadership of Sung.

Before closing this background sketch of Fu-chou it is worth considering again its position within its region. As we have seen, Fu-chou was in effect a 'new' prefecture on the national scene. In this respect, however, it was typical of prefectures in the P'o-yang basin: the region as a whole seems first to have risen to national importance in Sung. Fu-chou's emergence may thus be seen, on the one hand, as a reflection of the growth of its region; but on the other hand, not all parts of the region developed in the same way or to the same degree.

Skinner, in his richly suggestive and already vastly influential work on regional systems, has proposed that large areas of Chinese social and economic history are explicable as a process of the 'filling up' of a number of relatively separate physiographic regions by Chinese settlement, accompanied and followed by the internal articulation and integration of the subregions of each larger region into a largely distinct socioeconomic system. Each region, once integrated, was marked by the coexistence and interdependence of a highly developed 'core', where economic resources (including population) were concentrated, and a relatively undeveloped 'periphery'.

There seems good reason to see the emergence of the P'o-yang basin between middle T'ang and Sung as an example of the first filling up and internal differentiation of a macroregion along Skinner's lines.[97] I have already remarked on the enormous expansion of the region's population between the eighth and late eleventh centuries. This brought an increase in average population density from about nine to nearly fifty persons per square kilometer.[98] But the increase was not evenly distributed. In middle T'ang, densities varied from about six in Ch'ien-chou, southernmost prefecture of the region, to between eleven and twelve in Hung-chou, later the circuit capital, and about sixteen in Chiang-chou to the north, where the lake waters drained into the Yangtse. Fu-chou, at somewhat more than nine, fell almost precisely on the mean. By the 1070s, population density had almost tripled in Ch'ien-chou,[99] but had increased more than four times in Chiang-chou, nearly five times in Hung-chou, and between seven and eight times in Fu-chou. The distribution of population, already uneven in T'ang, had become far more uneven by middle Sung.

Population density by itself is a crude measure; but the increasing demographic disparities of the P'o-yang basin prefectures between T'ang and Sung surely reflect greater integration and internal differentiation within the region. It is doubtful whether economic integration had advanced far enough in

T'ang to justify speaking of a core or periphery at that period; but there were already relatively core-like areas — what one might call a 'proto-core' — in the lowlands centered around the lake and its outlet into the Yangtse, and a 'proto-periphery' in the mountainous south. By Sung the population data themselves would suggest that a real core and periphery had emerged, as areas already core-like differentiated themselves further and further from the incipient peripheries around them. The trend calls to mind Skinner's view of periphery formation as a process partly induced by the cores themselves: 'the very process of urbanization in the regional cores proceeded at the expense of urbanization potential in the surrounding peripheries. [. . .] Urban development in the core areas caused urban underdevelopment in the peripheries.'[100]

Where, in all this, does Fu-chou fit? In T'ang, once again, Fu-chou's population density was almost exactly the average for its region. The case in Sung was sharply different: Fu-chou's average density, about 75 persons per square kilometer, was in the 1070s close to the highest in the P'o-yang basin.[101] As we have seen, even its least populated counties had densities higher than the regional average. Ranking somewhere between proto-core and proto-periphery in T'ang, the prefecture, or much of its territory, seems clearly to have belonged to the regional core in Sung. Viewed from the other side, the T'ang proto-core, in the process of developing into the core of Sung, had expanded. The Sung core, then, included an 'old core' territory inherited from the proto-core of T'ang and 'new core' in the areas around it. Judging by population density, Fu-chou was not the only 'new core' prefecture: Yüan-chou and Lin-chiang Chün too had densities far above the average for the region, and the same is true of the more populous counties of Chi-chou (particularly Lu-ling, the metropolitan county), of Hsin-chou, and of Chien-ch'ang Chün.[102] The demographic equilibrium-point of the P'o-yang basin had moved outward from the lands immediately surrounding the lake to a second ring of territory lying west, south, and east of the older core.

The expansion of the proto-core of T'ang, the 'old core' of Sung, to include the new Sung core prefectures is perhaps reflected in the political sphere as well. No P'o-yang basin prefecture seems to have been important as a producer of national political figures in T'ang. But the T'ang great-clan lists did record the surnames of prominent families in just three prefectures of the region: these were precisely the three proto-core prefectures, Hung-chou, Jao-chou, and Chiang-chou.[103] In Sung, by contrast, Chi-chou, Lin-chiang Chün, Fu-chou, and Chien-ch'ang Chün all joined Hung-chou and Jao-chou as major producers of officials through the *chin-shih* examination: indeed the new core prefectures were on the whole even more successful in the exams than those of the old core.[104]

Fu-chou's sudden emergence onto the national scene in Sung, then, reflects two partly distinct processes: on the one hand the demographic rise of the P'o-yang basin as a whole; on the other hand the absorption of a number of new prefectures, or their more populous counties, into the developing regional core. Fu-chou is 'new' in two senses: as part of a 'new' macroregion and, within the macroregion, as 'new' core. If one is to draw broader conclusions about Sung from the findings of research on Fu-chou, or simply to compare Fu-chou to other prefectures, one must bear in mind these special aspects of its place within the Sung empire.

1

EXAMINATIONS, OFFICE, AND SOCIAL MOBILITY

The Fu-chou elite and the examinations

A visitor to Fu-chou in any third year during Sung would have found the government offices in the county and prefectural seats rather busier than usual. In the spring the customary decree had come down ordering the authorities in the prefectures and the capital to prepare to examine a new group of candidates for civil office. By this time each would-be candidate had deposited with the authorities in his county the 'family-guarantee certificate' that was in effect his application for admission to the exams. The county officials in turn had forwarded the certificates to the prefecture, where the truth of the statements in them was checked and a list of candidates compiled.[1] Now, with the arrival of the decree, it was the task of the prefectural officials and their superiors at the circuit capital to choose, from among their subordinates, several men who would oversee the exam, pose the questions, and grade the answers. By the autumn the candidates would begin to arrive in the prefectural city, and on the fifteenth day of the eighth month they would take their places in the examination hall for three days of tests.[2] The grading officials would have perhaps six weeks to sift through hundreds of papers (three for each candidate) and produce a ranked list of thirty-nine men[3] qualified to move on to the next stage. These prefectural graduates (chü-jen), after much feasting and celebration in their honor, were expected to present themselves in the capital by the end of the tenth month; the following spring they would repeat the three-day examination process in the capital, this time in competition with the favorite sons of the two or three hundred other prefectures of the Sung empire. In a typical year most of the thirty-nine would fail here; but several would survive this and the final, less competitive re-examination in the presence of the emperor and so attain the degree of chin-shih, qualifying them for appointment to office. This was the prize at which thousands at home had aimed; these were the cream — by official standards at least — of Fu-chou's intellectual crop. There were other routes to office, and these may in fact have come to account for more officeholders than the chin-shih process;[4] but in prestige, and in

29

chances for advancement once in office, the *chin-shih* offered much that the others did not.

Fu-chou men seem to have taken some pride in their prefecture's record in exam competition. In 1202 the preceptor of the prefectural school joined with local men to celebrate Fu-chou's achievements by carving on stone the names of all those who had achieved the *chin-shih* up to that time. Chou Pi-ta, a high official from neighboring Chi-chou, contributed a laudatory essay to be inscribed along with the names, singling out some of the most famous men and the most successful families as models for posterity. But beneath the pride at times it is not hard to detect a certain anxiety, even fear, that the successes of the past would not continue into the future. Another list of successful candidates, all of them from I-huang County, was carved into the outer walls of a newly rebuilt pagoda in I-huang's seat in 1223. The county's failures in the last four exams, it was thought, were the result of the pagoda's collapse in 1210; the new pagoda with its inscribed list would win super-natural favor for I-huang and reverse the frightening trend.[5]

The uncertainty of degree competition shows up most clearly in the strivings of individual candidates. It expressed itself in a search for strategies that could assure success for one man against hundreds or thousands. Some of these were simple and obvious. Lu Chiu-yüan, before applying to take the exams, read through the other candidates' certificates posted on public gates to learn which classic each had picked as his specialty; then he went home and made himself an expert on the one nobody had chosen, the *Rites of Chou*.[6] Another strategy, stranger to modern eyes perhaps, but apparently common in Sung, was to search for signs or omens, either in one's dreams or in everyday life, that could guide one's course of study. Of Wang I (courtesy-name Mao-sheng), a man of Ch'ung-jen County in early Southern Sung, we are told:

> [. . .] Mao-sheng's father had dreamed that in his house a large notice-board had been hung up, and from beside it someone spoke: 'This is the theme for the assigned poem when your sons and grandsons attain their degrees.' It was obscure and disordered and not fully legible; he recognized only the last word, 'beauty.' So he instructed his sons that all possible themes with the word 'beauty' in them should be brought together . . . Mao-sheng struggled on [without passing] until 1156, when he found in the road a coin from [the T'ang year-period] K'ai-yüan. He thought to himself: 'This year I am to be sent up to the capital by exemption from the prefectural exam, and now on New Year's Day I find money. Can it be that the policy question in the capital exam will touch on this?' On this account he inquired into money, its generalities and its fine points, preparing himself extensively.

> In 1157 he went to the capital: the assigned poem was 'Listen every-
> where and exhaust the world's beauty.' [. . .] The first page of policy
> questions asked about money. Thus he passed.[7]

Sometimes the signs told of other means to success. Lo Tien, also of
Ch'ung-jen, was to achieve the *chin-shih* in 1175 and ultimately reach high
office.

> Originally his given name had been Wei-yüan. [. . .] He studied at a
> country estate southwest of the city, and there dreamed that the
> reporter of exam standings had come, and that his own given name
> [appeared on the list as] Tien. Thus he changed it, and in 1168 passed
> the prefectural examination.[8]

Several other Fu-chou men passed the exams only after changing their names
as suggested in a dream;[9] there is no way of knowing how many others did
the same yet failed. But the examinations, along with office, marriage, and
death, do seem to have been a recurrent theme, if not an obsession, in Fu-
chou men's dreams. A common practice, apparently, was to pray at the
shrine of some local deity and ask for a dream in reply.[10] Not all dreams
were read as practical instructions: the uncertainties of lifelong study and
competition made some men hope to learn, not *how*, but simply *whether*
they might pass, and to search their dreams for answers. Sometimes the
answers they found seemed to decide the prospects of whole families:

> T'u Cheng-sheng, whose courtesy-name was Shih-piao, attained a
> degree and became administrator of Hsiang-t'an. He dreamed that
> there was a yellow dragon at his ancestral residence, Upon-the-Plain.
> It flew up and passed over places, separated by a stream, called Deer
> Pond and White Tea; then it stopped. The T'u family was an office-
> holding lineage. When Shih-piao awoke he was not pleased. He told
> people about the dream, and said: 'The official standing of Upon-the-
> Plain is to be interrupted by the rise of White Tea.' The next year
> T'u Ssu-yu passed the exam: he was precisely of the White Tea branch
> [of the family.] Ultimately a series of court officials and prefects, and
> ten county administrators, succeeded him, while Upon-the-Plain, all
> lonely and silent, has not had [another] official to this day, in forty-
> two years.[11]

But if men looked to dreams for sure answers to the uncertainty that
plagued them, they looked in vain, since dreams could be read in various
ways. Wang I, whose father's dream had provided a poetry-theme for study,
had once had a dream of his own:

In 1140 he and his elder brother Mao-ch'ien had prayed for dreams.
[. . .] He dreamed of a man who said to him: 'Your name will not be
below that of Chang Chin-ch'eng.' [Chang had passed first on the list
in 1132.] He awoke and rejoiced, saying that he would someday
achieve a degree as lofty as Mr Chang's. He had already passed at the
prefecture, and went to the capital exam in the spring of 1142 [. . .]
When he entered the exam, at the spot where he was to have his desk
there happened to be the signature of a predecessor: 'Chang Chin-
ch'eng,' in three large characters to the right of his seat. He thought
that this surely confirmed his earlier dream and was delighted all the
more. But that year he was not successful. Probably what the god
had told him referred only to the order of seating.[12]

I have dwelt on these stories — which were told as true by contemporaries
of the men who appear in them — because they show clearly the hold that
the competition for degrees exerted over the day-to-day concerns of those
involved in it. The examinations invaded men's dreams — indeed, they were
invited in — and shaped the way a man saw such an everyday happening as
finding an old coin in the road. This is not surprising, since some men spent
decades trying again and again to achieve a degree. The pervasiveness of the
concern with the exams is reflected even in the attitudes of those who rejected
it. The men who founded academies devoted to study for its own sake — such
as the Lin-ju Academy, founded in Fu-chou's prefectural city in 1248 —   .
deliberately and quite explicitly distinguished their enterprise from that of
the common run of scholar, who (so they said) studied only for the sake of
a degree.[13] Similarly, we may gather something of common attitudes towards
success in the exams from the admiring reports of the rather ostentatious
response of Lu Chiu-yüan. On the day the news of his success was brought,

> [. . .] he chanced to be visiting [his brother] Suo-shan. While he was
> playing the lute, the messenger arrived. Not until his piece was finished
> did he question him; he played one more piece, then returned home.[14]

Thus did Lu draw a line between himself and those for whom a degree was
a lifetime's dominating goal.

What made the goal so dominating? What drew hundreds of men into the
examination halls every three years, most of them not for the first time? In
part the question seems to answer itself: what drew them was the hope for
office. Office meant income, privileges, prestige; and office was the role in
society toward which much of traditional ethical thought directed the true
gentleman. But the question recurs when one considers the odds: these men
who devoted twenty or thirty years to study in hopes of reaching the *chin-shih*
were laying a wager they were very likely to lose. Most cannot have failed to

know this. What kept so many in the game for so long? Part of the answer may be the facilitated degree: this was earned by passing a special, lenient exam granted to men who, having passed several times at the prefecture, had repeatedly failed the normal exam in the capital, and had reached an advanced age. The degree was sharply distinguished from the regular *chin-shih*, and gave access to only very low-ranking offices. But another part of the answer may be that the career that exam candidates were pursuing was actually a fairly flexible one, with more than one acceptable goal. Office was the ultimate prize, but a life of study offered other possibilities. This seems to be the message of Yüan Ts'ai, author of an influential household manual of Southern Sung date:

> The son of a gentleman, if he has no hereditary stipend to maintain him, and no real estate to rely on, but wants to make a plan for serving his parents and supporting his dependents, can do no better than be a scholar [*ju*]. One whose talent is so fine that he is able to study the *chin-shih* curriculum may, if of the highest quality, take a degree and reach wealth and office, or, if of lesser quality, open his gates and give instruction to receive a teacher's stipend. One unable to study the *chin-shih* may, if of higher quality, work with brush and paper at writing letters for others, or, if of lesser quality, punctuate texts and act as a tutor to children.[15]

Thus scholarship gave a man opportunities for other respectable sorts of work, even if he never achieved a degree or reached office. Yüan's testimony suggests that it was in part the availability of these fallbacks that drew so many men into the scholarly vocation and degree competition despite the odds. In effect the system fed on itself, since the exams continually created a pool of would-be candidates on whom a teacher could draw, while the possibility of turning to teaching (as well as writing letters, punctuating texts, etc.) in turn encouraged men to persist and so kept the pool large. Men need not be totally discouraged by repeated failure, if their studies were capable of supporting them respectably in the meantime.

Certainly teaching was an important part of elite social life in Fu-chou, particularly important for those who had yet to succeed, or who were re-signed to failure, in the exams. Again and again in funerary inscriptions or biographies we read of men who failed, then returned home to gather students around them and live out their lives as teachers of classics or poetry. For the young man just beginning his career, on the other hand, teaching held special advantages: family tutors came to be included among the dependents an official could nominate for entry into a special, less demanding qualifying exam for the *chin-shih*, held not at the prefecture but at the circuit capital.[16]

Even without this privilege, the teacher who was admitted to the household of a wealthy or influential man, spent hours each day with his sons and grandsons, and earned his respect and trust, had formed a tie that might serve him well in later years. Among other things, a promising young scholar was an attractive choice for a son-in-law –

> Fu-chai [Lu Chiu-yüan's brother] entered the prefectural school and attended his elder brothers in their reciting and discussing. [Lu Chiu-yüan] waited on him in his studies. His culture and refinement, his mild and harmonious manner, amazed everyone. There was an old scholar who said to Wu Mou-jung: 'You have a beloved daughter and would like a fine son-in-law; none could excel this young gentleman.' Thus [Wu] formed a marriage connection with him. [. . .][17]

– and none had a better chance to show his scholarly worth close at hand than a family teacher. Connections of this kind were easily formed only because of the constant demand for teachers; and this demand – even despite the growing influence in Southern Sung of models of study and teaching that took scholarship as a prime value in itself, apart from questions of ambition – grew originally out of, and ultimately rested upon, the examination system.[18]

It is clear, then, that the examinations were enormously influential in Fu-chou elite society, shaping the directions in which a great many men steered their lives. But a larger claim has been made for the exams in Sung and after: that they brought into the government a broad and continuous stream of 'new' men, men without any family background in office; that they served as a major route of social mobility. I turn to this question in the next section.

The examinations and social mobility: I

The systematic study of social mobility in China in relation to the official system of civil service examinations begins with E.A. Kracke's 1947 article, 'Family versus Merit in Chinese Civil Service Examinations under the Empire.'[19] Investigating the two nationwide examination lists surviving from Sung, Kracke found that both in 1149 and in 1256 well over half the men attaining the *chin-shih* degree had had no officeholder in the paternal line in three preceding generations; he concluded that the examinations were a significant channel of new talent into office and thus a factor promoting a more fluid society. Soon afterward, in one section of a wide-ranging study of Sung officialdom, the Japanese scholar Sudō Yoshiyuki largely duplicated Kracke's research on the exam lists.[20] Kracke's method was later adopted by Ping-ti Ho, who applied it to the far more numerous surviving exam lists from the Ming and Ch'ing dynasties and found again that the percentages of new men were quite high, though rather lower than in Sung.[21]

Kracke's work has been a major pillar of support for the view of Sung society as highly fluid, with a social elite whose openness to newcomers was unusual among 'traditional' societies.[22] This view derives from the examination research if one accepts two premises: first, that the percentages of 'new men' derived by Kracke represent fairly accurately the rate of movement into office by men with no previous family history of office or degrees; second, that entry into office or the acquisition of a degree was a leap from one social stratum into another: that the line dividing official from non-official distinguished the ruling stratum of society from the ruled, and that social equality with those holding offices or degrees depended crucially on acquiring the same qualification for oneself. Without this second premise the significance of the rate of movement from nonofficial families into office is, at best, much reduced.[23]

The truth of the second premise – that officialdom and 'elite' (or 'ruling class') were one – is an empirical question; it may well have varied from period to period, or even from place to place. Recent research on Ming and Ch'ing has tended to diverge from it a good deal;[24] I will deal with its adequacy in Sung Fu-chou further on in this chapter. The first premise – that 'new men' are correctly counted by Kracke's method – has hardly gone unattacked;[25] but Kracke's work still awaits a full re-examination. Ideally this would require an exhaustive check of the men in Kracke's lists for further biographical data; I cannot attempt this here. My intentions are more limited: to explore more fully the statistical implications of a flaw in Kracke's method that others have already pointed out; and to draw on material from Fu-chou as a partial empirical check on my conclusions.

The main potential weakness of Kracke's method was noted by Kracke himself:[26] the exam lists give information only on the three immediate paternal ascendants of the candidates. Possible offices of members of collateral lines (uncles, great-uncles, cousins of a higher generation) are left unrecorded. How crucial a weakness is this? Kracke finds rates of 'new men' of roughly 56 and 58 per cent respectively in 1148 and 1256: by how much might these percentages plausibly be reduced if all male paternal relatives were recorded? (Here I leave aside for the moment the question of affinal relations.)

By way of an answer, one must consider what Kracke's statistic represents. In effect, the ancestors on whom Kracke has information may be considered as a *sample* (though a highly nonrandom one) taken from the population of all the male paternal relatives of the successful candidates. Of the sample a certain proportion have held office. One way of proceeding then might be to draw from the sample conclusions about the population as a whole: the percentage of officeholding ancestors in the sample might be assumed to reflect the percentage of officials among all male paternal relatives in the three generations preceding the candidates. That is, if 44 per cent of all fathers, grandfathers, and great-grandfathers held office — one might argue — then about 44 per cent of all uncles, great-uncles, and (say) third cousins once removed, taken as a group, must also have held office, though of course just which candidates had which officeholding relatives would be absolutely unknowable. Had Kracke adopted this approach he would certainly have been open to attack for the nonrandomness of his sample; but such an attack, and any defense against it, would have to deal with the question, just *how* the particular nonrandomness of this sample affected the result: how the choice of these particular three kinship positions skewed the proportion of officeholders in the sample with respect to that in the entire population of relatives. On this issue a variety of assumptions could be adopted which would affect one's conclusions in correspondingly various ways. By the procedure he pursues, Kracke in fact adopts one of the most radical possible assumptions: that the choice of these three relatives for the sample has the effect of *exhausting* (completely or nearly) the officeholders in the population, at least for those candidates without office among the sampled three. Only on this assumption can the proportion without recorded official ancestry equal, perfectly or nearly, the proportion without any officeholding kinsmen.

To show the significance of this assumption for the interpretation of Kracke's percentages, let us assume a situation in which upward movement by new men simply did not occur. What might one then expect to find in Kracke's lists? For instance: assume that the candidates in the lists came from an absolutely homogeneous set of kin groups; that each kin group regularly produced officials; that each male kinsman stood an equal chance of gaining office, no matter which of his relatives also held office; and (for the sake of argument) that this chance was one in six. As each kinsman thus would also have five chances in six (0.833) of *not* gaining office, the chance that any particular man's father, grandfather, and great-grandfather all had held no office would be 0.833 cubed, or 0.578: nearly 58 per cent. About this proportion of Kracke's candidates, on these assumptions, should have no recorded official ancestry. This is virtually the same as Kracke's own percentages of new men, but it is founded on the assumption of no real mobility. That is: even where office is the monopoly of a limited number of families, if the likelihood that any single member will gain office is relatively small, then the operations of chance alone may assure a relatively large number of men whose three lineal ascendants (as opposed to other relatives) have held no office. Thus, *Kracke's percentages are perfectly consistent with even the total absence of mobility in his sense.*[27] At the same time, they are consistent also with Kracke's own view, which treats the actual rate of mobility as identical to the apparent proportion of new men. But of course a statistic that fits equally well into two such divergent pictures of 'reality' is simply useless. Kracke's figures by themselves cannot be interpreted, and give no definite answer to the question whether rates of movement of new men into office were high or low. These conclusions apply a fortiori to the further attempts of Kracke and Sudō to divide the candidates with recorded official ancestry into those with more officeholding relatives and those with fewer.[28]

In all of this I have avoided the issue of what kin unit one should treat as significant in mobility studies for Sung China. Kracke's conclusions might be rescued if one argued that in fact only direct lineal ties determined social status or were politically effective. But this assumption would fly in the face of much of what we know about kinship ties in Sung and in other periods. In the first place, some Sung men lived in joint households, whose members shared descent from a deceased ancestor several generations before them. (Lu Chiu-yüan's family is one example.) A *chin-shih* candidate who came from such a family might thus be a member of the same property-owning and (formally) residential unit as a host of cousins, uncles, and great-uncles, any of whom might hold office. But apart from these cases, which seem to have been rare when the common ancestor was *not* an official, it is clear that effective kin ties normally extended well beyond the household as such. Some of the best evidence for this comes from official rules which specified the relatives a bureaucrat of a certain rank might aid in various career-related ways. The state designed these rules partly in order to obviate corruption and informal nepotism, and so attempted to include within their scope the relatives a man of position might want to help — or those who might expect his help — if legal provision were absent. One such set of rules governed the privilege of 'protection' (*yin*), by which court officials could name relatives who would be awarded official standing without having to pass the exams. For higher officials the range of kin that might be protected extended to the limits of the five mourning grades (*wu-fu*), including, for instance, cousins descended from a common patrilineal great-great-grandfather, and a narrower range of affinal kin. The privilege of gaining access for a relative to the special qualifying exam at the circuit capital — available to officials of considerably lower rank — covered, at its greatest extent, about the same range of kinsmen. The government, then, expected that patrilineal kin of a rather considerable distance, and affines within a narrower range, would be in contact and would seek aid from one another. It should be remembered as well that Sung saw the rise of the new-style corporate lineage, which at least in theory sought to extend ties of mutual aid and ritual cooperation even beyond the mourning grades. In fact, of course, the effectiveness of relatively distant ties will have varied considerably from family to family or from person to person; but one cannot justly claim that only lineal connections could transmit status or mediate joint action.

The discussion so far has been largely a priori. What empirical support can be drawn from the case of Fu-chou? The 1148 list includes four greater Fu-chou men,[29] the 1256 list another fourteen.[30] Leaving aside three members of the imperial lineage,[31] out of the remaining fifteen, seven have at least one officeholder recorded among their three ascendants.[32] Thus eight of the fifteen, or 53.3 per cent, are Kracke's 'new men'; this proportion compares well with his nationwide percentages. Below I list the eight and discuss what is known of them from other sources on Fu-chou.

1. Chang Chün-chung of Lo-an County, *chin-shih* 1256.[33] The 1256 list records only his great-grandfather's name, with no indication of office. According to the Lo-an gazetteers, however, Chün-chung was a member of the Chang[a] family of Nan-ts'un[34] (see Appendix I, no. 3), which by this time had produced twenty prefectural graduates since 1150, including *chin-shih* in 1172,[35] 1223,[36] and 1229.[37]

2. Chao Pang of Nan-feng County, *chin-shih* 1148.[38] No information survives on him save what the 1148 list records.

3. Ch'en Chen-yen of Ch'ung-jen County, *chin-shih* 1256.[39] Although no office is recorded for his three ancestors in the 1256 list, the Fu-chou and Ch'ung-jen gazetteers identify him as the nephew (*chih*) of Ch'en Yüan-chin, *chin-shih* in 1211 and a high official thereafter.[40] Further, the 1256 list records Chen-yen's great-grandfather's name as Ch'en Ming-shih, who is also recorded in the funerary inscription of Yüan-chin's father Ch'en K'ai as K'ai's father, thus Yüan-chin's grandfather.[41] This confirms Ch'en Chen-yen's connection to Ch'en Yüan-chin.

4. Ch'en Ju of Lin-ch'uan County, *chin-shih* 1149.[42] The list records no office for his three ancestors; but his agnate Ch'en K'ang-ch'eng had achieved a *chin-shih* degree ten years before him. The exact relation between K'ang-ch'eng and Ju is not recorded; K'ang-ch'eng had been the first to move to the current family residence at Ku-yüan.[43] In any case Ch'en Ju, when he achieved his own degree, was already serving in office as assistant instructor of the prefectural school in Ho-chou, Huai-nan-hsi circuit. Thus even if there had been no previous history of office in his family, it would be wrong to count him as an instance of movement into office *through the examinations.*

5. Ho Shih of Lo-an County, *chin-shih* 1256.[44] According to the Lo-an gazetteers, whose testimony is confirmed by contemporary sources (see Appendix I, no. 18), Shih was a member of the Ho family of

Hsi-fang,[45] which by 1256 had produced eleven prefectural graduates since 1121, with *chin-shih* in 1151[46] and 1223.[47]

6. Liao Tzu-shih of Lo-an County, *chin-shih* 1256.[48] While the list records no office among his three ancestors, it gives his mother's maiden name as Tseng, and locates his place of residence in Chung-i canton. Elsewhere I shall show the strong tendency of prominent Fu-chou men in Southern Sung to marry women from prominent families close to home; in this case the Tseng surname matches that of an important family of Chung-i canton, the Lo-shan Tsengs, who had been producing prefectural graduates since 1195, including a *chin-shih* in 1250;[49] a related family of Tsengs, at Pan-ch'iao in a different canton, had produced *chin-shih* in 1169,[50] 1175,[51] and 1181.[52] It is very probable in view of Liao Tzu-shih's residence that his mother was a member of the Lo-shan Tseng family. The probability is strengthened by the fact that the Lo-shan Tsengs are known to have intermarried before this with people surnamed Liao: a construction record for a temple hall built in 1183 names among the participants a woman named Liao Chüeh-chen, and identifies her as the wife of the older brother of one Tseng Yung,[53] whose nephews Tseng Hui and Tseng Hsieh[54] are identified by the gazetteers as Lo-shan men.[55]

7. Tseng Hui-ti of Lo-an County, *chin-shih* 1256.[56] The list records this man's place of registration as Wang-hsien township in Yün-kai canton. A Yüan funerary inscription for one Tseng Yeh identifies the Wang-hsien Tsengs as a 'leading lineage' in Southern Sung, mentioning in passing both Tseng Hui-ti (not by name) and an earlier lineage man who 'used his wealth to achieve office' and served as supervisor of a market town.[57] In 1230 a Tseng Hsin, also a Wang-hsien Tseng, had made major contributions of grain for provisions when the local government was attempting to pacify and resettle bandits:[58] since office was often given in exchange for this sort of service, Hsin may in fact be the lineage's earlier officeholder.

8. Chang Yu-hsin of Lin-ch'uan County, *chin-shih* 1256.[59] The absence of office among his three lineal ancestors is confirmed by the funerary inscription of his father Chang Wen-huan.[60] There had, however, been previous *chin-shih* of this Chang[b] surname from Lin-ch'uan, in 1211,[61] 1214,[62] 1217,[63] and 1247.[64] Of these, Chang Tzu-hsien, *chin-shih* in 1217, was the son of Chang Chieh-fu, who had studied with Lu Chiu-yüan.[65] Chieh-fu is in turn named in the funerary inscription of a Jao Ying-tzu as Jao's teacher.[66] Jao Ying-tzu is a member of a family whose home was in Ch'ung-jen but whose members appear by late Southern Sung to have been living in Lin-ch'uan.[67] According to Chang

Wen-huan's funerary inscription, Wen-huan's wife (thus Yu-hsin's mother) was of the Jao surname.[68] This double occurrence of connections between Changs and Jaos suggests that Yu-hsin may have been a member of the same family as Tzu-hsien and so have had a background of officeholding.

To summarize these eight cases, all of whom Kracke must count as 'new': five (Chang Chün-chung, Ch'en Chen-yen, Ch'en Ju, Ho Shih, Tseng Hui-ti) clearly had patrilineal kinsmen who had held office before they achieved their own degrees; for one (Chang Yu-hsin) there is inconclusive evidence suggesting that he too may not have been the first of his family to hold office; one was very possibly connected to an officeholding family through his mother; and one has left no record apart from the exam list. Kracke's percentage of 'new men' is reduced here from 53.3 percent to between 6.7 and 20 percent, depending on how one counts uncertain cases and how one views maternal kin. This second point is especially important: is a man 'new' if his only connection to previous officeholders runs through his mother? His contemporaries probably would have seen him as representing a new family, since patrilineal kin were kin *par excellence.* Yet clearly his case is more complicated than simple upward movement by a man without official ties.

Despite the small numbers, the evidence is highly suggestive. It is clear that a man could have a family background of office and yet show no officeholder among the three lineal ancestors in Kracke's lists. Fu-chou evidence from other examination years suggests that this may have happened fairly often. Thus a T'u family of I-huang County produced its first *chin-shih*, the brothers T'u Ta-lin and T'u Ta-k'uei, in 1091. These were followed by brothers and first cousins in 1094, 1100, 1118, and 1154. All six of these men fit Kracke's criterion, as none had a lineal ancestor with office; if there were lists like Kracke's for the years in which these men passed, all would appear to be new men. Yet four of the six had been preceded in office by at least two brothers or first cousins at the time of their degree. The other two, passing in the same year, might both be called 'new men' yet represent only one new family.[69]

A similar case is the Lu family of Chin-ch'i County. After Lu Yün achieved the *chin-shih* in 1145, his cousins Lu Chiu-ling and Lu Chiu-yüan passed in 1169 and 1172 respectively, followed by their grand-nephew Lu Chün in 1211. None of these four men had officeholders among their three lineal ancestors, yet only Lu Yün came from a family then new to office.[70] The family of Ho Shih (no. 5 above) provides a third example: Shih passed in 1256, and his brother Ho T'ien-sheng followed him in 1271. In the meantime their agnate Ho Lin had passed in 1262, followed by his own brothers: Ho

Yao in 1265 and Ho Hsi-chih and Ho Meng-niu in 1274. An uncle of these four, Ho Ku, had passed in 1223. Of these seven men, only Ho Ku had an officeholder among his three lineal ancestors: this was Ho Ssu, great-great-grandfather of Ho Lin and his brothers.[71] The other six, then, would appear on an exam list as new men. Yet all seven came from a kin group that had produced officials before their own degrees; five, at the time of their degrees, had relatives as close as an uncle or a brother currently in office. Among the T'us, Lus, and Hos Kracke's method would discover sixteen new men where there are at best four, representing only three different families or lineages.

On both methodological and empirical grounds, then, Kracke's figures cannot be accepted as they stand: everything suggests that they greatly overestimate the speed at which men unrelated to officials moved into office. At the same time there can be little hope of determining 'correct' rates for Fu-chou or, I suspect, for any other region during Sung. The difficulties are both empirical and theoretical. First, the data are not there: Kracke's exam lists — or any other list of degreeholders, for one year or for many, that one might compile — simply contain too many men of whom no other record survives. This is a consistent problem for *chin-shih* from Fu-chou, and makes the calculation of apparent rates of movement an exercise of doubtful value.[72] Second, as we have seen, some *chin-shih* were related to earlier officeholders only distantly or through their mothers. I have argued that Kracke's method, which leaves these relationships (and indeed much closer ones) out of account entirely, simply cannot capture the real situation. But on the other side, is it reasonable — assuming that one's prime interest is movement in and out of *office*, as opposed to some wider sense of social mobility — to group a man whose third cousin twice removed once held office together with one whose three uncles are currently serving? The whole enterprise of dividing *chin-shih* into two neatly distinct groups and measuring their relative proportions may be simply misfounded. There were not 'new' families on the one hand and 'old' families on the other: men were connected to officials through a whole range of relationships, near and distant, and of different kinds. In exploring the relation between family background and recruitment to office it may be more useful to study *how* men made use of whatever connections they had, or how they created new connections — to study means and strategies — than to try, in the face of inadequate sources, to calculate 'rates of movement.' In the section that follows I will approach the question of social mobility and its relation to the examinations once more, from a somewhat different angle.

The examinations and social mobility: II

If we are interested in the examinations and the relation they may or may not have borne to processes of social mobility, then a particularly strategic figure is the man who is first in his family to reach the *chin-shih.* From what backgrounds did such men come? It is possible to answer this question, at least in part, for thirty-four first *chin-shih* from greater Fu-chou during Sung.[73] These thirty-four are listed and discussed at the end of this chapter. Here I deal with them as a group.

For all but two of the thirty-four,[74] at least one (and for most, two or more) of the following statements is true:

1. Previous members of the same family had held office, whether through facilitated degree, as reward for contributions to the control of bandits or to famine relief, by hereditary privilege, or by other routes not specified. (Eleven cases.)

2. At least one previous family member, often a considerable number, had passed the prefectural exam but failed at the capital. In no case does the first prefectural graduate precede the first *chin-shih* by less than twenty-two years; usually the gap is much longer. (Seventeen cases.)

3. Members of the family had earlier distinguished themselves as men of wealth and local influence through local militia activity, by organizing or contributing to famine relief or other local welfare activities, by founding or building temples, libraries, or academies, or by providing lands for official building projects. (Eleven cases.)

4. Members of the family were connected by marriage to other families with an earlier record of success in the exams and in office. (Thirteen cases.)

5. Members of the family had associated as friends, members of poetic or academic cliques, partners in local defense organizations, or as students or teachers, with other families with an earlier record of office and degrees. (Fifteen cases.)

Evidently we are dealing here overwhelmingly with men of the local elite, as defined earlier (pp. 8–9). Especially striking is the evidence of association, as rough social equals, with families and men, within Fu-chou and without, whose records of office and degreeholding were long and outstanding: I will return to this point further on. For some, elite membership can only be shown for a fairly recent period; but for others it extends back for decades and generations. Though the numbers are not large, and while evidence for a good number of other men in the same position is simply lacking, it would seem from what positive evidence there is that even *chin-shih* who were the first from their families were drawn largely from families already, in other respects, traveling in elite circles and playing elite roles.

Why should this be so? Certain reasons seem obvious. Examination success depended on education. The advantages that wealth conferred on any man who wanted an education of the right sort are obvious and have often been remarked on.[75] In the process of seeking an education, young men will also have sought contact with prominent intellectual figures within the local elite, since this sort of contact may have been essential for gaining familiarity with the most important current academic and literary trends. Moreover the odds against passing the capital exam may have made it unlikely that the man who succeeded should be the first of his family to sit for it. But beyond these obvious considerations there may also have been institutional constraints that, in effect, imposed social restrictions on access to the *chin-shih* degree.

In Lu Chiu-yüan's funerary inscription for the Chin-ch'i County man Ko Keng, we read:

> There was a practitioner of the arts of the Five Phases named Huang Shih, who had long traveled the neighborhood and whose comings and goings often brought him to our house. Each time the decree for the examinations came down, [people] would ask him whose name would be sent up. Shih would always say 'Ko Ts'ai-mei,' and that was all. When this did not come true, people would all laugh, but Shih would say: 'This is because they only pick those whose talents are well known.'[76]

Here Huang Shih seems to be complaining that the prefectural examination is somehow biased in favor of men of established reputation. A similar comment, dealing with the neighboring prefecture of Chi-chou, appears in the works of the late Southern Sung man Wen T'ien-hsiang:

> Chi is a very great prefecture, its examination candidates number ten thousand or more; yet it is generally those whose reputations are prominent that ultimately pass.[77]

Complaints like these were not uncommon: perhaps they should be taken seriously. If so, one must explain how an examination process that made a virtual fetish of preserving the anonymity of the candidate from the grading officials – first pasting over the candidate's name on his paper, then rewriting all the answers in a uniform hand – could favor better-known scholars over others.

The process leading up to competition in the prefectural exam is still not wholly clear, but there is good reason to believe that personal guarantee by local men of note was, formally or informally, a prerequisite. I have already mentioned the 'family-guarantee certificate' (*chia-pao chuang*) that men were required to submit in order to be admitted as candidates in the prefectural exam. Only one official source refers to the document by this name:[78] others

refer simply to a 'family certificate' (*chia-chuang*), which was presumably
the same thing.[79] At least two other sources use the full term: these are two
prefaces by Wen T'ien-hsiang of Chi-chou. One I have already quoted a part
of: it deserves fuller quotation here.

> Sun Yu-pin of my neighborhood likes to socialize widely. When he
> receives someone's trust he is always true to it. Most of the gentlemen
> in my area are his acquaintances. At the triennial examinations, those
> who wish to be given guarantee in order to take the exam will often
> turn their certificates over to him so that he will send them up to the
> authorities. Yu-pin grudges no effort: at every exam he contracts as
> many as several hundred guarantees. On the day the results are posted,
> many from his list will pass; and always there are some who go on from
> there to pass at the Ministry of Rites [i.e. to achieve the *chin-shih*]. He
> has been active in several exams. Today once again the decree of the
> [examination] year is about to come down, and men are contending
> with one another [for his guarantee], in the view that Yu-pin is effective.
> Even Yu-pin cannot manage it by himself. One day he brought his list
> and appealed to me: 'You, sir, were once someone on my list. Will you
> preface it for me?' I could not refuse this.
>
> We find in the *Rites of Chou*, under the Grand Instructor [*ta ssu-t'u*]:
> 'He taught the myriad people in the Three Matters and made them his
> guests, to promote them.' This was the spirit of the Neighborhood
> Recommendation and Local Selection system [*hsiang-chü li-hsüan*].
> Checking under the Century Master [*tsu-shih*], we find that five and
> ten families, five and ten men, were further made to protect and care
> for one another: criminal punishments and rewards were shared;
> the entire guarantee-unit was implicated as a group. [. . .] The *chin-
> shih* began under Sui and T'ang; this dynasty inherited it without
> change. As time went on, abuses and problems gradually emerged.
> These the emperors have used every device to prevent and prohibit: the
> family-guarantee certificate is one such [device]. To be sure, the
> examinations are different from the Neighborhood Recommendation
> and Local Selection system, but in their legislative purpose they are
> more or less the same. [. . .]
>
> Chi is a very great prefecture, its examination candidates ten thousand
> or more; yet it is generally those whose reputations are prominent that
> ultimately pass. Yu-pin henceforth will spread his net widely to miss
> no one, so that the names of a thousand Buddhas may all be gathered
> on one list. [. . .][80]

Wen hardly tells us all that we might like to know about the family-
guarantee certificate; but it does seem clear that a genuine local guarantee

was involved. It is especially telling that Wen seems to see the certificate as a point of similarity between the T'ang–Sung examination system and the Neighborhood Recommendation/Local Selection system described in the *Rites of Chou*, since this stressed local responsibility – and liability – for the men who were selected. What was being guaranteed here? The 'family certificate' referred to in other sources supplied information on the prospective candidate's family background and residence. Candidates were required to have lived in the prefecture for a certain period and to have no one among their ancestors who had engaged in certain occupations – merchant, clerk, priest – or committed certain crimes. Presumably a man like Sun Yu-pin, in supplying his guarantee, provided his personal assurance that all the information in the certificate was correct.

Reliance on local guarantee would have had certain advantages for local officials. Candidates for the prefectural exam were to be vouched for by officials of their county, who were at least in theory punishable for guaranteeing men later found wanting in character.[81] At the prefecture, the staff of the prefectural school was expected to check the information in the family certificates and report to the school's preceptor, who was then to guarantee the men admitted as candidates.[82] Now, district and prefectural officials were not natives,[83] and remained at their posts for a few years at most. They cannot often have had personal knowledge of the men it was their responsibility to vouch for. How were they to judge the truth of the material on residency or ancestry in a family certificate, much less speak for a candidate's personal character? One likely resort was to judge the certificate by its guarantor: if he was a man of some prominence, someone known personally or by report, then his guarantee, perhaps, could be taken on faith. But this will have made certain local men – renowned scholars or teachers, officials in retirement, men known to local government – the most attractive guarantors. It becomes understandable then that some men may, like Sun Yu-pin, have provided guarantees for hundreds of candidates for the same exam. But a local guarantor too is likely to have contracted guarantees only for men known to him personally or by reputation: this is why Wen T'ien-hsiang remarks on Sun's particularly wide circle of acquaintances. In this way the need for guarantee both from officials and from a prominent local man will have served as a filter that excluded, or at least hindered, men without established connections, hence reputation, within the local elite.[84]

All of this, however, does not fully explain the remarks of Huang Shih and Wen T'ien-hsiang, who seem to suggest that reputation was an advantage that favored some men *even among the candidates admitted to the exam*. It is very possible that the candidate's anonymity was not in fact absolute, despite the rules. In the factional conflict over so-called 'false learning' in the capital during the 1190s, the opponents of Chao Ju-yü's faction put about charges to this effect. Here is Yeh Chu, writing in 1197:

> At the triennial examinations when school entry is decided, they recognize each other by using strange words and phoneticizations, and immediately place a paper [by one of their own] in the first ranks, thereby causing truly talented and capable men to be rejected.[85]

This suggests a deliberate, sinister plot against the principle of anonymity. Perhaps there were such plots, but very often conscious effort may not even have been necessary. Scholars – officials and commoners – traveled together, exchanged letters and poems, debated questions of politics and philosophy, and so came to know one another's personal mode of argument, style of composition, or special approaches to political and intellectual issues. A paper by a man one knew well might advertise its author no matter what its calligraphy. Lü Tsu-ch'ien served as grading official at the capital in the year Lu Chiu-yüan was sent up. On reading Lu's paper, we are told, he said: 'This is surely the essay of Lu Tzu-ching [Chiu-yüan's courtesy-name] of Chiang-hsi.'[86] But further, as Yeh Chu suggested, whole circles of scholars might come, through long association, to share certain points of style, issues of recurrent concern, or key technical terms: a paper might then be recognizable not as a particular man's work but as the product of a certain group or school.[87] If a grading official, knowing the school and approving of it, chose to pass the papers he recognized, there need not be anything sinister or corrupt about it. The principle of anonymity was far from universally accepted in Sung: a common, and very respectable, view held that anonymity made it impossible to judge the candidate's character, and so substituted mere technical competence for personal worth as a standard of judgement. A grading official may well have felt that a due consideration for the welfare of his ruler and his people required that he find ways around the candidate's anonymity. What makes this relevant to the issue at hand is that these tendencies may once more have served incidentally as a social filter through which some men would pass more easily than others. The chance of having one's personal style recognized, or of being a member of a group with a recognizable common style, was small for a man whose family was not yet well established in the local elite. One had a 'reputation' only if one was known to the sort of people whose business it was to determine reputations.

In all of this, of course, there is much that is speculative. What is certain is that *no direct evidence* shows any significant access to degrees in Fu-chou by men from families without wealth or influence, without previous success in the exams, and without social connections to already influential families or to officialdom.

Any proper assessment of the role of the examinations and the *chin-shih* degree in local society must take account of two further points. The first, which emerges from the list of thirty-four first *chin-shih*, has already been touched upon: families had no difficulty maintaining local prominence, as evidenced by continuous production of prefectural graduates, despite a long period without a *chin-shih*. The Chan family of Lo-an County, it seems, had produced sixteen prefectural graduates over 194 years before a member finally reached the *chin-shih* in 1242 (six, in eighty years, are beyond question);[88] the Ku-t'ang Ch'en family went through ninety-four years and six prefectural graduates before the seventh and eighth achieved the *chin-shih* in 1268; Li Liu's first relative to pass at the prefecture preceded his *chin-shih* by eighty-eight years. The Tai family of I-huang County (Appendix I, no. 45), which had sent up *chin-shih* in 1049, 1135, and 1151, went on to produce eight prefectural graduates before the next member passed the *chin-shih* exam ninety-nine years later in 1250.[89] These cases are far from untypical.

It is impossible to tell whether any Chans, Ch'ens, Lis, or Tais gained minor office through facilitated degrees during their long years of *chin-shih* drought. This raises the second issue: the *chin-shih* proper was not the only important way for a family to place its sons in office. Even leaving aside recruitment by protection, which was available only to the kinsmen of fairly high-ranking officials, two other routes loom large in the sources. One was reward-office, granted for local action useful to the state: bandit control, famine relief, etc. This was clearly important for several Fu-chou elite families,[90] and the fragmentary sources may conceal a good many others. The second route was the facilitated degree. Despite the very low rank of the offices to which this gave access, it was quite important from a local point of view. Judging by the few years for which the number of facilitated degrees nationwide is known, and by those included on the prefectural exam lists of the I-huang County gazetteers, facilitated degreeholders often out-numbered regular *chin-shih*.[91] What gave the institution its special importance was that, like reward-office, it granted special consideration on the basis of purely local distinction. A man need only show his ability to compete success-fully with others from his own prefecture, and attain a certain longevity, to gain access to a route in which competition was slight, at times nonexistent.[92] In a prefecture with little tradition of scholarship or education, whose men had poor chances in a demanding examination against nationwide com-petition, the facilitated degree must have had enormous importance as a virtual guarantee to the local elite that it would not be denied occasional participation in the national bureaucracy. In Fu-chou, where *chin-shih* abounded, it still provided a sort of backup assurance that a family capable

of competing convincingly in local academic circles probably would not be
shut out of opportunities for low office simply by the vagaries of chance (or
talent).

The view of the examinations that emerges from all this is rather different
from the picture that Kracke's work would suggest. What of the ultimate
goal of the exams, office itself? How is one to view the position of officeholders and the importance of office in local society? This is the problem of
the section that follows.

Office and the elite

I have treated the 'local elite' in effect as a single social stratum, encompassing men and families both with and without office and degrees, and
serving as a pool from which, for the most part, officeholders and degreeholders were drawn. Is this an adequate view? Or did officeholders in fact
constitute a separate stratum of their own, set above the rest of society? It
may seem that in defining the local elite so as to include various sorts of
men who did not hold office, I have begged the question. But in fact one
might treat 'elite' as an appropriate rubric for a wide range of wealthy,
influential, or famous people and still hold that officeholders formed a
separate and special group – the uppermost stratum within the elite, perhaps.
In what follows I will argue that in Sung Fu-chou, at the local level, this was
not the case.

It is no part of my purpose to claim that office was not an important
goal for the Fu-chou elite. I will argue further on that in Northern Sung
the goal of office – or more specifically high office – was in fact central to
elite strategies. Even focusing only on local aims, and apart from obvious
questions of prestige and self-respect, office could support the local position
of elite families in a number of ways: the income that an official brought in
need not have been the most important of these. A household headed by an
official held the special status of 'official household' (*kuan-hu*) *vis-à-vis* the
state. This entailed a number of fiscal privileges – chiefly exemption from
various local service duties – which varied with time, with level of office,
and with route of entry. For wealthy families the privileges must often have
meant relief from a considerable financial burden, or from the trouble of
evasion. Probably just as important, however, was another privilege: the right
to use an agent (*kan-jen*) as one's proxy in court cases. Agents were forbidden,
like other 'servants', from testifying against their employers, even when they
had been ordered to act illegally; and in cases of tax arrears local officials
were to treat the agent, not his master, as responsible.[93] This amounted, then,
to a virtual immunity from normal legal procedures. In a prefecture known
for its litigiousness, where recourse to the law seems to have been a usual

means of extending one's own property or resisting the encroachments of others, such an immunity was crucially important.[94]

The state granted privileges of this kind at least partly in order to set off officials and their households from society at large: the state's intention, evidently, was precisely to establish officialdom as a higher stratum, not only in their bureaucratic capacities, but in everyday life in their home districts. The social hierarchy was to be made to correspond as perfectly as possible to the bureaucratic hierarchy. How faithfully were the wishes of the state, in this respect, reflected in social reality? The question is complex, since social standing is a phenomenon of many dimensions; but one approach to an answer is through the evidence of interaction and association. Ruling strata, ruling classes, elites, are — in theory — *social* entities: they have to do with the ties and associations that join people, or exclude them. If officialdom, *at the local level*, made up a separate, higher social stratum, then one would expect officeholders, *at the local level*, to associate mainly with each other, or to associate with non-officials only in limited, clearly hierarchical ways — as patron to client, for example. This is not at all what the sources show.

Hsieh I (1069–1113) and Hsieh K'o (1073–1116) were brothers from Lin-ch'uan County. Both are remembered today, when they are remembered at all, chiefly as members of the so-called 'Chiang-hsi school' of poetry, a circle of poets of late Northern and early Southern Sung who modeled their work on that of the great Northern Sung poet Huang T'ing-chien. The collected works of both Hsieh brothers have survived. Hsieh I's works preserve what amounts to a piece of everyday, yet special, social interaction, frozen in writing. This is a sacrificial essay (*chi-wen*) for the deceased Wang Po-keng (given name Wang Ko), a *chin-shih* in 1097 and sometime preceptor of the government school in Ch'u-chou, Huai-nan-tung circuit.[95] A sacrificial essay was written for reciting at a sacrifice, then to be burned; the essay we have is Hsieh I's draft version. Ten men have come together, partly to mourn their lost friend and partly, in the way of mourners then as now, to accuse him:

> Oh woe! Why would you not stay a little for us? Why, all at once, did you cast us aside and leave? Did you not think of the wind at the lattice window, the lamplight, the cold of the night, reading and sighing with hunger? Did you not think of wandering east of the river, of bathing your feet in South Lake, of burning incense and meditating in deserted temples? Did you not think of chatting and arguing about past times and present, criticizing faults and merits, getting excited, [. . .] of drinking at night and continuing till dawn, gesticulating, laughing and singing? [. . .] Did you not think of helping your ruler to benefit the people, of cleansing away the muddy and raising up the pure?

[. . .] Did you not think of buying fields, building a house, digging a pond, planting bamboo, and forming a compact for a life in retirement? If things as trivial as this are not for Po-keng to think about, then did you not think of your younger brothers' and sisters' marriages, and of how their ceremonies were to be brought about? Did you not think of your parents' approaching old age, and of how they were to be provided with delicacies? Though your friends, we grant, are not worth talking about, how could you bear to discard your mother and younger brothers without a backward glance?[96]

I have quoted this at length because its tone is important: it is literary, yet intimate. These, it seems, are men who have shared Wang Ko's travels, have sat up drinking, arguing, and singing with him, have looked forward to sharing retirement with him, and now can pose affectionate but accusing questions to his spirit. The essay's opening tells us their names:

In the first year of Cheng-ho [1111], in the second month, on the eighteenth day, the friends, Wu Ch'en with his younger brother Ho and nephew Yü, Hsieh I with his younger brother K'o, Ch'en Chih-ch'i with his younger brother Yen-kuo, Huang Shu, Chi Tuan-ch'ing, and Chiang Yeh, have respectfully, with an offering of pure libations, made a declaration to the spirit of their friend who is gone, the Professor, Po-keng.[97]

Further on we read that Wu Ho is to manage Wang's burial; that Hsieh I has written a record of conduct and asked a Mr Lü to compose the tomb inscription; that Wu Ch'en and others are to handle the marriage arrangements for Wang's younger siblings; and that one 'Chü-jen' has written proposing that an official posthumous name be requested for Wang.

Who are the cast of characters here? They are worth considering one by one.

1. Hsieh I was, once again, a prominent poet. He had twice passed the prefectural exam but failed at the capital; after this he gave up trying for office. He had traveled with Wang Ko before Wang's *chin-shih*; when Wang left for office in Ch'ang-sha he asked Hsieh to write him a farewell essay.[98] Later Hsieh, through Wang's introduction, was to present his writings to the prominent official and scholar Lü Hsi-che, member of an illustrious North Chinese official family. In this way he came to know Lü's son Hao-wen, also an official, and Hao-wen's son Pen-chung. Hsieh and Lü Pen-chung became close friends.[99] It was Pen-chung who first identified the 'Chiang-hsi school'.

2. Hsieh K'o, like his brother, failed in the *chin-shih* exam, never held

office, and associated with Lü Hsi-che and his descendants: Lü Pen-chung wrote a colophon to his collected works.[100] Hsieh K'o's wife, a woman surnamed Tung from neighboring Chin-ch'i County, was the daughter of a *chin-shih* and the sister of two others.[101] It appears that no Hsieh had held office by the time Hsieh I and Hsieh K'o died.

3. Ch'en Chih-ch'i took the prefectural exam but never passed.[102] His father's sister had married a *chin-shih* of the Chiang surname;[103] his mother too was surnamed Chiang and may have been a *chin-shih*'s niece; his own sister married Chiang Yeh below.[104] Presumably all these Chiangs were of one family. Ch'en had no patrilineal kin in office. He and his three brothers were all friends of Hsieh I.

4. Ch'en Yen-kuo, actually not Chih-ch'i's brother, but his cousin,[105] also took and failed the prefectural exam.[106] A student of Hsieh I, he was married to a woman surnamed Wang (no relation to Wang Ko: the characters are different), whose father held office and whose grandfather had been a *chin-shih* in 1057.[107]

5. Huang Shu, another failed candidate in the prefectural exam, was a son of one of the oldest wealthy families in Lin-ch'uan.[108] His mother's brother Wu Ti-chi studied with Hsieh I, who came to know Huang Shu through Wu. Huang's sister married Wang Fu (again unrelated to Wang Ko), a *chin-shih*; two of his female first cousins married prefectural graduates. There is no evidence that any Huang had held office.

6. Chi Tuan-ch'ing was the son of Chi Fu, a *chin-shih* in 1085. His brother Ch'ing-ch'ing received office through protection by his father, but a disabling eye disease prevented Tuan-ch'ing from making use of the same privilege. A granddaughter of his father's — his own daughter or niece — married the brother of Ch'en Chih-ch'i above; another married Hsieh Mai, either a brother or a first cousin of Hsieh I and Hsieh K'o. Hsieh I himself 'followed Chi Fu for a very long time.'[109]

7. Chiang Yeh, a prefectural graduate, was as we have seen the husband of Ch'en Chih-ch'i's sister, and may have been related to at least two, perhaps more, *chin-shih* of the Chiang surname from Lin-ch'uan.

8. Wu Ch'en, Wu Ho, and Wu Yü are not recorded elsewhere.[110]

9. 'Mr Lu,' whom Hsieh I asked to write Wang Ko's tomb inscription, and 'Chü-jen', who wrote proposing that a posthumous name be created for Wang, are surely one and the same man: Lü Pen-chung, whose courtesy-name was Chü-jen. Lü, the only man mentioned in the essay who was not from Fu-chou, was at this time holding one of a series of local offices in North China.[111]

Thus, of the ten friends who sacrificed to the officeholder Wang Ko, and took it upon themselves to arrange his burial and put his affairs in order, not one was himself an officeholder. Only two (Chi Tuan-ch'ing, Chiang Yeh perhaps) seem to have had patrilineal kin in office. Of the others, some were connected to officials through their mothers, some through their wives or sisters, some chiefly as friends or students: the lack of office in their own families did not exclude them. It was not death's equalizing power that brought the ten together: a web of long-established ties bound most of them before Wang Ko died. Two men undertook to write the commemorative texts associated with the mourning and burial: one, Lü Pen-chung, called in from outside, was an official; the other, his close friend Hsieh I, was not. Would Hsieh's local network of ties have been very different if he had passed, not failed, at the capital? It is hard to see how. The line that divided official from 'commoner' seems to have meant little in this circle.

I have examined this case so closely because it is a virtual paradigm of local elite social life in Fu-chou throughout Sung. Everywhere one finds dense networks of connections – agnatic, affinal, scholarly, and personal – joining official and commoner. The distinction was certainly recognized: later I will argue that in Northern (not in Southern) Sung, at the national and even the prefectural (cross-county) level, certain wider-ranging forms of marriage were open only to families with some history of office. But the same families, within their own counties, were tied closely to families without office in all the ways we have seen here. In Southern Sung the case is if anything even clearer: consider the family backgrounds of Ch'en Yüan-chin (no. 5 in the list of first *chin-shih*), Hsieh Kung-tan (no. 8), Jao Tzu-yung (no. 14), Li Liu (no. 16), or Liang Ch'eng-chang (no. 17). The local scholarly circle that focused on Lu Chiu-yüan in the late twelfth century – including both his students and the broader group of associates who did not formally accept him as their teacher – encompassed men with high office, low office, and no office at all, with no evident distinction drawn between them.[112] Official and commoner, or men from officeholding and commoner families, came together, as we shall see, in any number of local projects: militia organizing, famine relief, the building of bridges and temples. In short, the sources simply will not support the notion that office was the badge of a distinct local social class or stratum. In local society, office was only one of a number of resources that affected a man's social position and determined the relationships into which he could enter.

The argument of this chapter can be retraced as follows. First, the rates of movement of 'new' men into office that emerge from a count of the three lineal ancestors recorded on exam lists are without clear significance and probably, if taken at face value, severe overestimates. Yet there seems little basis for substituting some other, 'correct' rate: the whole notion of 'new' men becomes rather unclear when one considers a wider range of kin. Judging from the evidence we have, *chin-shih* emerged chiefly from families already in one way or another involved in 'elite' pursuits – pursuits likely to be available mainly to those with wealth, informal power, or strategic social ties. I have argued that institutional, as well as social, constraints worked to limit access to the *chin-shih* in just this way. In any case, the *chin-shih* was neither the only major route to office, nor essential for maintaining elite position. Finally, office itself did not, at the local level, define a separate stratum, but was simply one important factor influencing local position: one important prize for which elite families competed. If one seeks to define an upper social stratum at the local level in a way that accords with social reality but takes into account the importance of office, then it seems best to focus, not on officialdom itself, but on the much broader group whose members were likely to try for office and sometimes to reach it, likely to compete for degrees and sometimes achieve them, and likely to interact and intermarry with officeholders. This group seems to overlap more or less completely with the 'local elite' as so far defined.

This approach will find strong resonances, too, in the conceptions of Sung men themselves. The term most used in Sung to talk of an uppermost social group and its members – the group, in fact, to which virtually all Sung authors clearly felt they belonged – was *shih*. Now one cannot read Sung texts in any depth and suppose that all *shih*, or even most of them, are officeholders. All the kinds of men that in my working definition fall within the 'elite', whether or not they hold office, turn up as *shih* in the sources. The term, it seems, points to men of a common general style of life. Literacy; a certain leisure; the capacity realistically to consider seeking office; the circles in which a man traveled – all these went to mark him as a *shih*.[113] Again, in my reading of the sources, the *shih* group and my 'elite' – in fact though not by definition – appear more or less coterminous.

What, then, was the role of the examinations in Sung Fu-chou? It was dual: on the one hand, through the *chin-shih* degree proper, to recruit from among the elite a group of officials qualified and competent (by contemporary standards) to advance into the higher levels of the bureaucracy; on the other hand, through the facilitated degree, to increase the occasional availability of minor office (and of the legal status of 'official household') to elite families. In both roles the examinations acted to confirm, and to validate officially, high social status that was already well established locally.

List of First Chin-shih

1. Chan Yüan-chi of Lo-an County, *chin-shih* 1242, was a member of the Ya-pei Chan family[114] (see Appendix I, no. 1), which had produced six prefectural graduates since 1162 and probably an earlier ten between

1048 and 1123, when the territory to become Lo-an was still part of
neighboring Ch'ung-jen. In 1149 at the creation of Lo-an, a member of
the family had donated the periodic marketplace he owned as the site
of the new county capital, for which he also built streets and offices.[115]
Another member was a friend of the 1169 *chin-shih* Tseng Feng, who
wrote a construction record for him mentioning that he had studied
with Tung Te-hsiu, a member of a family that had been producing
chin-shih since 1015.[116] (For the Tung family see Appendix I, no. 59.)
Another man apparently of the same family (judging by his surname
and by the location close to the family residence) was a major contributor to the construction of a temple in the county seat in 1183.[117]

2. Chang O of Lo-an County, *chin-shih* 1172, was the first *chin-shih* from
    the Nan-ts'un Chang family[118] (see Appendix I, no. 3); this family had
    previously produced prefectural graduates in 1150,[119] 1153,[120] and
    1171.[121]

3. Ch'en Ting-te of Lo-an County, *chin-shih* 1268, was with Ch'en Tzu-
    sheng (below) the first *chin-shih* from the Ku-t'ang Ch'en family,[122]
    which had produced six other prefectural graduates since 1174 (see
    Appendix I, no. 8).

4. Ch'en Tzu-sheng of Lo-an County, *chin-shih* 1268, passed in the same
    year as his relative Ch'en Ting-te above.[123]

5. Ch'en Yüan-chin of Ch'ung-jen County, *chin-shih* 1211.[124] The funerary
    inscription of his father Ch'en K'ai gives an account of the family's
    past: during the later reign periods of Northern Sung, in the first two
    decades of the twelfth century, the Ch'ens were reputed to be one of
    the wealthiest families of the county. K'ai's father Ming-shih studied
    poetry with Wang Tsao, Han Chü, and Sun Ti, all prominent officials
    from other prefectures who during their lives spent time as visitors or
    held office in Fu-chou.[125] Locally, Ch'en Ming-shih formed a poetry
    society with his fellow Ch'ung-jen men Wu Tseng, Wu I, and Ho I.[126]
    The last was an 1154 *chin-shih* who eventually reached the post of
    Minister of Works;[127] the former two were both members of a family
    that between 1052 and 1163 produced at least eight prefectural
    graduates, four of whom went on to become *chin-shih* (see Appendix I,
    no. 67). Wu Tseng, author of the *Neng-kai-chai man-lu*, a famous
    collection of jottings and remarks on various topics, obtained office
    by presenting his works to the throne,[128] while Wu I was *chin-shih* in
    1163 and held a number of circuit-level posts.[129] Thus by the early or
    middle twelfth century, Ch'en Yüan-chin's ancestors, already established
    as a wealthy family, were associating, apparently as equals, with promi-
    nent officeholders and literary figures from their own county and other

prefectures. Yüan-chin's younger brother, Ch'en Meng-chien, passed the prefectural exam together with him in 1210.[130]

6. Chi Fu of Lin-ch'uan County, *chin-shih* 1079.[131] According to his funerary inscription, the Chi family had for several generations been first in its township (*li*) in wealth, and Fu's father had earned local repute by canceling the debts of people to whom he had lent money.[132]

7. Chu Ching of Nan-feng County, *chin-shih* 1073,[133] was the first of three *chin-shih* among the sons of Chu Shih, who was known in his county for generations afterward as the epitome of humble virtue brilliantly rewarded. Shih had, so the story ran, given up most of his meager salary as a teacher to save two debt-prisoners he encountered on the road; his sons' academic and bureaucratic successes were heaven's recompense (see Appendix I, no. 14). Unlike most 'poor teachers' at the time, Chu Shih was, however, the son of a woman surnamed Tseng, whose grandfather Tseng Chih-yao had been *chin-shih* in 983 and financial intendant of Liang-che circuit under T'ai-tsung, and whose first cousins Kung, Chao, and Pu had reached high central offices under Wang An-shih after 1068.[134] Thus the examination successes of Chu Shih's sons followed closely upon his affinal kin's accession to central power in the capital.

8. Hsieh Kung-tan of Ch'ung-jen County, *chin-shih* 1214,[135] was the first of three *chin-shih* from a family that was to continue producing prefectural graduates down to the end of Sung (see Appendix I, no. 20). All that is recorded of his ancestry is that his grandfather Hsieh Ta-jen had been a prefectural graduate in 1153,[136] and that his father Hsieh Chiu-ch'eng had visited the high official Hsieh O of nearby Lin-chiang Chün, had been received by him with ceremony as his 'clansman' (in this context simply meaning man of the same surname), and had received from him a set of family instructions.[137] However, at least five years before his *chin-shih* Kung-tan had married the daughter of the high official Ho I[138] (on whom see no. 5, above, under Ch'en Yüan-chin).

9. Hsieh Yüan of Lin-ch'uan County, *chin-shih* 1160,[139] was the grandson of Hsieh K'o and grandnephew of Hsieh I:[140] see above, pp. 49–52. Two generations before Hsieh Yüan his ancestors were associating and intermarrying with officeholders and prominent literary figures of their own prefecture and elsewhere (for fuller sources on the family, see Appendix I, no. 21).

10. Hsü Meng-ling of I-huang County, *chin-shih* 1223,[141] was the first *chin-shih* from the Cha-p'u Hsü family, which had produced at least three previous prefectural graduates since 1137, of whom two had

received facilitated degrees, in 1165[142] and 1172[143] (see Appendix I, no. 24). The first of these facilitated degreeholders, a man named Shih-wei, had married the daughter of his fellow I-huang man Tsou T'ao,[144] the son of Tsou Yü, who had passed the *chin-shih* exam in 1082.[145]

11. Hsü T'ang of I-huang County, *chin-shih* 1166,[146] was the first *chin-shih* from the Hsia-shih Hsü family (see Appendix I, no. 25), which had produced four prefectural graduates since 1123, of whom one had attained a facilitated degree in 1150.[147]

12. Huang Chieh of Lo-an County, *chin-shih* 1253,[148] was a member of the Pa-t'ang Huang family, which had produced five previous prefectural graduates since 1204 (see Appendix I, no. 28). According to the preface to the family's early Yüan genealogy, its founder had come to the present home in 1014; within two generations the family had grown wealthy from its agricultural holdings; after the beginning of Southern Sung (1127) the family took up education for the first time.[149] A member named Huang Ch'ung-i studied with Chu Hsi's prominent disciple Huang Kan (1152–1121)(probably while the latter was administrator of Lin-ch'uan between 1208 and 1210[150]) and later became the head of the Lin-ju Academy in the prefectural seat.[151]

13. Huang Fu of Nan-feng County, *chin-shih* 1112,[152] according to the funerary inscription of his grandson Huang Wen-sheng, was the son of a man named Huang Lü-chung, who had held office as police inspector (*ssu-li ts'an-chün*) of K'ang-chou in Kuang-tung circuit;[153] Lü-chung was not a *chin-shih* and it is not recorded how he entered office.

14. Jao Tzu-yung of Ch'ung-jen County, *chin-shih* 1214:[154] his relative Jao Yen-nien had been friends with his fellow Ch'ung-jen man the 1154 *chin-shih* and Minister of Works, Ho I (who had died in 1209),[155] had studied with Lu Chiu-yüan (1139–92),[156] and in 1210 during a severe famine had made large-scale sales of grain at 30 per cent below current market prices, earning the prefect's recommendation for appointment to office but refusing to accept it. Earlier, in 1195, another relative had taken the prefectural exam but failed and soon afterward built a library at his home[157] (see Appendix I, no. 31).

15. Ko Feng-Shih of Chin-ch'i County, *chin-shih* 1169,[158] was the son of a man named Ko Keng. According to Keng's funerary inscription his ancestors had not held office but generation by generation had enriched their family through agriculture. In 1127, with the loss of the North, Ko Keng was one of the organizers and officers of the Chin-ch'i militia, which played a major role in defending the prefecture against Chin invaders and a variety of 'bandits.' Keng's leading role would

presumably have brought him into contact with the family of Lu
Chiu-yüan (see below under no. 20), and indeed Keng is recorded as
having been a guest in the Lu household in Chiu-yüan's childhood
(i.e., in the 1140s and 1150s). In 1135 Keng was a chief seller of grain
at reduced prices for relief of a famine caused by a drought the previous
year[159] (see Appendix I, no. 34).

16. Li Liu of Ch'ung-jen County, *chin-shih* 1208,[160] was the first *chin-shih*
surnamed Li from his county and eventually reached the fairly exalted
post of Minister of Personnel (*li-pu shang-shu*). His father, grandfather,
and great-grandfather had held no office, but his great-grandfather
Li Ch'ih had entered the *Pi-yung*, the upper level of the Imperial
Academy, sometime before 1121, but had died in his early twenties;[161]
a collateral relative of Liu's grandfather's generation, named Li Hao,
had also been sent up by the prefecture to the capital exam in 1118.[162]
Liu's grandfather, Li Yen-hua, was a friend of the 1163 *chin-shih* Wu
Hsieh and of his elder brother Wu Hang, a prominent local scholar and
founder of the Huan-ch'i Academy in the county seat. Both Wus were
members of a Ch'ung-jen family that had been producing *chin-shih*
at least since 1053 (see Appendix I, no. 67), as was Wu Tseng, who
sought Li Yen-hua's advice on textual points in writing his *Neng-kai-chai man-lu*.[163] Yen-hua's elder brother reached office as the sheriff
of an unspecified county;[164] his name and route of entry to office
are not recorded, but he may have been any one of a number of prefectural graduates, surnamed Li but not further identifiable, who passed
in the middle and late twelfth century.[165]

17. Liang Ch'eng-chang of Lin-ch'uan County, *chin-shih* 1190, was the only
Fu-chou man of his surname to receive the *chin-shih* in Sung. He was
the son of a woman surnamed Huang of the same county.[166] His
mother's sister was the wife of a man named Wu Chien and the mother
of the wife of Lu Chiu-yüan.[167] Wu Chien was the son of a low-
ranking official, was himself three times a prefectural graduate (in
1153, 1156, and 1162) but refused to try for a facilitated degree;[168]
his nephew Wu Ping-jo first passed at the prefecture in 1156 and
eventually reached the *chin-shih* in 1185.[169] (For this Wu family see
Appendix I, no. 71.) Lu Chiu-yüan's family in the meantime had
produced three *chin-shih* between 1145 and 1172.[170] (For the Lus see
Appendix I, no. 42.) Thus by the time of his own degree Liang Ch'eng-
chang was connected through his maternal aunt to four previous
chin-shih.

18. Liu Yao-fu of Chin-ch'i County, *chin-shih* 1175, the first *chin-shih* of
his surname from this county, had been preceded in the prefectural

exam by at least one relative, a man named Liu Chang, who had passed
during the Shao-hsing reign period (1131 to 1162).[171] Two generations
before Liu Yao-fu a relative named Liu Tao-cheng had built a Taoist
temple near the family residence, with a sacrificial altar beside it for
the worship of the family's ancestors.[172] Yao-fu himself studied with
Lu Chiu-yüan from the age of seventeen (around 1163) until his entry
into the Imperial Academy at twenty-four[173] (see Appendix I, no. 39).

19.   Lo Tien of Ch'ung-jen County, *chin-shih* 1175,[174] at the time of his
death in 1194 serving as Signatory Official of the Bureau of Military
Affairs, a post conferring the status of Assisting Councillor on its
holder,[175] was the first *chin-shih* of his surname from Fu-chou and had
no officeholders among his three paternal ascendants. It would appear,
however, that by the first decades of Southern Sung some members of
his lineage were holding office as well as building temples in the vicinity
of his family residence; and Lo Tien's mother, a woman of the Miu
surname, was apparently the daughter (but perhaps a niece) of a woman
from a family in I-huang County that had earlier produced a number
of *chin-shih* and prefectural graduates.[176]

20.   Lu Yün of Chin-ch'i County, *chin-shih* 1145, was the first member of
Lu Chiu-yüan's family to reach the *chin-shih*.[177] In 1127 his lineage-
mate Lu O had been the overall commander of the Chin-ch'i local
militia that was instrumental in keeping Chin troops and neighboring
bandits away from the prefecture[178] (see above under Ko Feng-shih,
no. 15). Lu Chiu-yüan's own account of his family presents it as 'poor,'
but the context makes it appear that this refers only to the family's
lack of extensive holdings in land: for generations the family had
depended chiefly on its drug-retailing business, which by Lu Yün's
generation was supporting over a hundred people within a single enormous household and providing funds for a family school as well.[179]
This suggests anything but poverty. An outsider's account of the Lus'
role in the 1127 local militia describes them at that time as extremely
hao,[180] a term used for wealthy and powerful families who practiced
a kind of de facto rule within their localities (see Appendix I, no. 42).

21.   Mo Jo of Lin-ch'uan County, *chin-shih* 1271,[181] and his brother Mo
Lei-hsien (see below) were the only two *chin-shih* of this surname from
Fu-chou during Sung. Their family, however, was intermarried with a
Kung family of the same county, and a third brother, Meng-k'uei, had
left the Mo family to become the adopted heir of a childless Kung and
in 1268 had passed the *chin-shih* exam under his adoptive surname.[182]
Meng-k'uei was not the first Kung to achieve office: his adoptive elder
cousin Kung Huan had been *chin-shih* in 1217.[183]

22. Mo Lei-hsien of Lin-ch'uan County, *chin-shih* 1271,[184] was the brother of Mo Jo above[185] and *chin-shih* in the same year.

23. Sun Yu-ch'ing of Lin-ch'uan County, *chin-shih* 1166,[186] and the first of four *chin-shih* produced by his family between 1166 and 1260 (see Appendix I, no. 44), was the grandson of a man named Sun Yen, who had been a clerk in the prefectural seat, responsible for the administration of the Fu-chou jail.[187] Yu-ch'ing had possibly been preceded in the prefectural exams by his father Sun Hsün, who reached the *chin-shih* after him, in 1175.

24. Teng Kang of Chin-ch'i County, *chin-shih* 1220,[188] was the first *chin-shih* from a family whose private self-defense organization had since 1127 been the main supplier of troops and officers for the multi-family Chin-ch'i militia, the mainstay of Fu-chou local defense throughout Southern Sung[189] (see above under Ko Feng-shih, no. 15, and Lu Yün, no. 20; for the Tengs see Appendix I, no. 47). At the beginning the Tengs (and other families involved in the militia) were under the general leadership of a member of Lu Chiu-yüan's family, as noted above; but after about 1175 the Lus appear to have dropped out, and the Tengs came to fill the post of overall commander from their own ranks. Throughout Southern Sung few if any funds for the supply of the militia came from official sources; expenses for training and supplies for a considerable number of soldiers (several thousand as of 1175) had to be borne by the Tengs themselves. By the mid-twelfth century two family members are known to have passed the prefectural exam. Lu Yün, prefacing the Tengs' genealogy in 1146, remarked that the Lus and the Tengs had been intermarrying for generations; it is thus virtually certain that the second wife of Lu Chiu-yüan's father, a woman surnamed Teng, came from this family.[190]

25. Teng Yüeh-li of Lin-ch'uan County, *chin-shih* 1178,[191] was by origin a man of neighboring Nan-ch'eng County in Chien-ch'ang Chün. He had moved to Fu-chou on his marriage to the daughter of the 1142 Lin-ch'uan *chin-shih* Li Hao, who was also originally a Nan-ch'eng man. (On Li Hao's family see Appendix I, no. 37.) After moving to Fu-chou Teng Yüeh-li studied with Lu Chiu-yüan and then passed the *chin-shih* exam, two years after his father-in-law's death.[192]

26. Ts'ao Shih-hsiu of I-huang County, *chin-shih* 1106.[193] Shih-hsiu was the first *chin-shih* from a family that was to produce two more, as well as ten other prefectural graduates by the end of Sung (see Appendix I, no. 50). The family had been founded by a supervisor of Huang-t'ien Chen (the garrison town which was soon afterward promoted to I-huang County) under the Southern T'ang kingdom in 971, before Sung's

absorption of Chiang-hsi. A relative four generations before Shih-hsiu had been a prefectural graduate sometime in the first half of the eleventh century and received a facilitated degree in 1070.[194] Shih-hsiu's grandfather had distinguished himself in a minor military post on the northern border; another man of his grandfather's generation, along with two sons, had received military titles for successful anti-bandit activities locally.[195]

27. Tseng Ying-lung of Lo-an County, *chin-shih* 1250,[196] was the first *chin-shih* from the Lo-shan Tseng family (see above, p. 39), which had produced ten other prefectural graduates since 1195 (see Appendix I, no. 53) and had been locally active in temple construction during the 1180s.[197] A twelfth-century member of the family, Tseng Hui, is known to have married the granddaughter of a Ch'ung-jen man named Miu Chao, whose grandsons passed the prefectural exam in 1183, 1189, and 1195;[198] Miu's wife (Hui's wife's grandmother) was the daughter of a Wang family of I-huang County that had been producing *chin-shih* and facilitated degreeholders since 1112.[199] (For the Mius, see Appendix I, no. 43; for the Wangs, no. 60.)

28. Tu Yü-te of I-huang County, *chin-shih* 1135,[200] was the only *chin-shih* of his surname from Fu-chou in Sung but was also a grandson of Tu Tzu-yeh,[201] who had been a prefectural graduate in 1056, had reached a facilitated degree in 1073, and had founded the Lu-kang Academy near his home and taught Wang An-shih there in Wang's youth.[202] Another relative, Tu Ch'ien, had been a prefectural graduate in 1075 and 1087.[203]

29. T'u Ta-lin of I-huang County, *chin-shih* 1091,[204] was the son of a man named T'u Chi, who had built a library near his family's residence and invited local scholars to come there to study, and to teach his sons into the bargain.[205] Elsewhere the family is recorded as having been 'a wealthy surname of the county' for three generations before that of T'u Ta-lin.[206] Five of T'u Chi's sons and nephews went on to pass the *chin-shih* exam; Ta-lin was the first (see Appendix I, no. 58).

30. Wang Tsai of I-huang County, *chin-shih* 1112,[207] was the first of two *chin-shih* from the I-nan Wang family, which was also to produce four facilitated degreeholders and in all nine prefectural graduates by 1249 (see Appendix I, no. 60). An earlier family member named Ch'en had passed the prefectural exam in 1056.[208]

31. Wu Chü-hou of Lin-ch'uan County, *chin-shih* 1063,[209] was the first *chin-shih* of this surname from his county. Neither his great-grandfather nor his grandfather had held office; his grandfather, however, had married the daughter of Yen Shu (famous in later dynasties and today

chiefly as a lyric poet), who had been *chin-shih* in 1005 and reached the office of Chief Councillor in the late 1030s.[210] Wu Chü-hou's father, who was thus the maternal grandson of a Chief Councillor, held office as Executive Inspector (*lu-shih ts'an-chün*) of Ch'ih-chou in Chiang-tung circuit – a low post which he probably reached by hereditary privilege through his affines; and in the next generation Chü-hou passed the *chin-shih*.

32. Wu Ming-yang of Chin-ch'i County, *chin-shih* 1271,[211] was a member of the Hsin-t'ien branch of the Wu-t'ang Wu family; although the first member of any branch to receive the *chin-shih* degree, he had been preceded in office by a large number of relatives from his own and other branches, who had reached office through routes unrecorded, perhaps by facilitated degree, perhaps as a reward for local defense or famine relief activities (see Appendix I, no. 66). Ming-yang's great-great-grandfather, for example, had served as sheriff of Han-kuang County in Ying-chou, Kuang-tung circuit; his intervening ancestors had held similar low-level posts.[212] The Wus had clearly been involved in local defense: see the discussion of the cluster of Chin-ch'i families in Chapter 2, pp. 75–77. A member named Wu Hsün studied with Lu Chiu-yüan.[213] By about 1240 a man of the family had married a woman related to Ko Feng-shih (see no. 15 above).[214]

33. Wu Ping-jo of Lin-ch'uan County, *chin-shih* 1185,[215] and the first in his family to receive a degree, was the nephew of Wu Chien, who had been a prefectural graduate in 1153, 1156, and 1162, but refused to try for the facilitated degree. Wu Chien's father Wu Wan had held the low rank of *ti-kung-lang*, and Chien's son Wu Wen-sheng served as the registrar of Wu-ning County in Hung-chou, Chiang-hsi circuit.[216] Chien's daughter married Lu Chiu-yüan in 1167; they had been betrothed since 1148. Wu Chien had been a fellow-student of Lu's elder brothers at the prefectural school.[217] (See Appendix I, no. 71.)

34. Wu Jung of I-huang County, *chin-shih* 1169,[218] was the earliest *chin-shih* from the I-tung Wu family, which was to produce three others and at least six prefectural graduates in all by the end of Sung (see Appendix I, no. 70). Jung was preceded on the prefectural exam by his grandfather Wu Yü, who passed in 1144 and received a facilitated degree in the same year as Jung's *chin-shih*.[219]

2

THE ELITE AND ITS ORIGINS

We do not know, and probably cannot know, how often new families moved into the Fu-chou local elite and thence, perhaps, into office. But a great many elite families succeeded remarkably well in holding their position once they had achieved it. Table I shows the known period of elite membership for seventy-three such families[1] during Sung.[2] All of these, at the time of their first Sung office or examination success, lived in Fu-chou.[3]

In several respects the evidence that underlies this table and decisions made in its construction minimize, for most families, the apparent period of elite membership. First, as to evidence: of the six counties of greater Fu-chou, surviving gazetteers provide lists of prefectural graduates for only three. In the other three counties (Lin-ch'uan, Chin-ch'i, and Nan-feng) many families whose earliest record is a *chin-shih* listing may in fact have had a long previous history of success in the prefectural exam.[4] As to the table's construction: families who claimed to be (or whom others represented to be) branches of older lineages living in other counties appear in the table only from the earliest provable date of elite membership at their ultimate place of residence.[5]

In view of these biases in the table it is all the more striking that for these seventy-three families the average period separating the earliest and latest Sung evidences of local elite membership exceeds 140 years. This figure, moreover, considerably underestimates the families' real durability, since more than half can be traced well into the succeeding Yüan dynasty (1279–1368) or even beyond.[6] Sixty-five were still prominent at the end of Sung; the other eight disappear from the Fu-chou sources after membership in the local elite for an average of 118 years. All of these eight originated in Northern Sung, and prominent members of three are known to have emigrated from Fu-chou to other prefectures; it is very possible that such emigration (which I will discuss in detail in Chapter 3), rather than downward mobility, accounts for the disappearance of the other five as well.

Ten families in Table I produced no *chin-shih* degreeholders in Sung. For these ten the average period of elite membership during the dynasty is only about seventy-two years. While this might seem evidence that families

Table I. *Timespans of Fu-chou elite families in Sung*

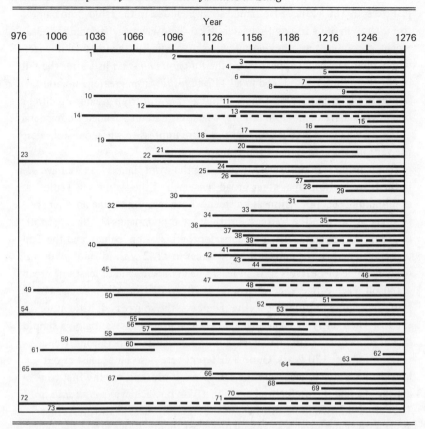

Number indicates family's location in Appendix I. Broken bar represents gap in sources concerning family during indicated years.

required success in the *chin-shih* examination in order to maintain their local position (a notion I have disputed in the previous chapter, p. 47), in fact it is more nearly evidence for the opposite view. All these families first appear in Southern Sung and continue to the last years of the dynasty: their relatively short span is the combined result of their late emergence in the records and the limiting of the table's scope to Sung. For six of the ten there is evidence of continued prominence under the Yüan.[7] It would seem that the failure to produce *chin-shih* here reflects the short period of elite membership, rather than vice versa. There are no similar families known to have originated in Northern Sung: this again suggests that local elite status, maintained over a long enough time, tended almost inevitably to culminate in the achievement of a *chin-shih* degree.

The remaining sixty-three families in the table produced in Sung a total

of 286 *chin-shih.* (For these families the average period of elite membership
just exceeds 160 years.) Five families not included in the table, who came
to Fu-chou in Sung having first established themselves as officeholders elsewhere, account for another eleven *chin-shih.*[8] Finally, the imperial lineage,
whose members begin appearing on the Fu-chou *chin-shih* lists after the fall
of Northern Sung,[9] produced in all 112 *chin-shih* from greater Fu-chou in
Southern Sung. Thus 409 of the 745 Sung *chin-shih* from greater Fu-chou can
be shown to have come from families whose elite status spanned a considerable
period.[10] That this is so is again all the more impressive when one considers
the very incomplete state of the available sources.

Yet caution is in order here. I am using the word 'family', as we have seen
in the Introduction, in a rather broad sense. All of the families in Table 1 are,
at minimum, sets of patrilineal kinsmen whose relation to one another is
securely attested in the sources; but they are by no means all the same sort
of group. As opposite extremes, consider the Lis of Lin-ch'uan and the Tungs
of Lo-an. The Lis first appear in the sources in 1142 with Li Hao's *chin-shih*
degree. Three of Li Hao's sons, at least one grandson, and at least one great-
grandson reach office, the last around 1270. Aside from the marriages of
Hao's daughters to other local elite members, the sources tell little more of
the Lis. Their entry in Table I (no. 37) thus represents, essentially, a simple
line of descent with officeholders in four consecutive generations over a
period of about 130 years. Quite a different case — so far at least as our
knowledge is concerned — are the Tungs. Four brothers are the first to
appear, passing the prefectural exam in 1014; one achieves a *chin-shih* in
1015. In 1033 two more brothers of the first four pass at the prefecture,
along with two sons and a nephew of one of them; all five attain the *chin-
shih* in 1034. This begins a history of success in the examinations unparalleled
by any other Fu-chou family. But the twenty-four *chin-shih* and hundred or
so prefectural graduates that emerge by 1271 belong, it seems, to several
separate lines of descent: by middle and late Sung the Tungs have the look
of an extensively ramified kin group. By Yüan at latest they are a 'lineage'
(*tsu*) with a printed genealogy (no. 59 in Table I).

Now for the Lis it is clear that, in one descent line at least, elite status
simply reproduced itself from one generation to the next. But among the
Tungs it is perfectly possible — the sources do not tell the precise relationships of most of the men they record — that individual households or lines
moved up or down, even dropped out of the elite or re-emerged into it, while
the group taken as a whole continued consistently to produce prefectural
graduates, *chin-shih*, and other officeholders. Between the Lis and the Tungs,
among the Fu-chou families reconstructed here, lies a broad range of possible
degrees of complexity. None of these families, we can be sure, was as vast and

internally differentiated as the elite lineages familiar from nineteenth-century Kwangtung, which might number in the thousands or tens of thousands. The sources seem to find it extraordinary when one 'family' (*chia*) or 'surname' (*hsing*) or, occasionally, 'lineage' (*tsu*) can boast even a few hundred members. But even a group of this size or smaller has room for internal stratification and internal movement up or down. It makes sense to speak of continuity here – indeed the common identity and continuous success of many of these families were recognized and remarked on by contemporaries – but this continuity should not be taken to exclude smaller-scale movement and change.

The table itself hardly suggests changelessness. Though only eight families vanish from the sources during Sung, still, 'new' families (families of whom there is no earlier record) continue to appear throughout the dynasty. Particularly remarkable is the number that emerges in the first decades of Southern Sung: eighteen families, or roughly a quarter of the whole group, in the thirty years immediately following the fall of the north (1127–56), and another seven by 1176, amounting to a third of all the families in only a sixth of the dynasty. This is not, I think, a chance phenomenon; I will return to it in the next chapter.

By the end of Sung, still, the Fu-chou elite – or a significant part of it – was genealogically a rather old stratum. In early Sung it had been entirely new: hardly any of its families can be traced back as elite members through the Southern T'ang kingdom and into T'ang. Where then did it come from? How did the families that made it up find their places there? What were their origins, in place and in social character? It is the aim of this chapter to pursue these questions: to pursue rather than wholly to answer, since as we shall see there is much that is obscure in the Fu-chou elite's background. In the pursuit, however, certain striking patterns do emerge. I begin with the question of geographical origins.

Migration

Fu-chou, as we have seen, was in many ways an upstart prefecture: its position of relative prominence – social, political, academic – did not precede Sung, and must have rested ultimately upon the tremendous expansion of its population between middle T'ang and early Sung. There is every reason to suppose that this expansion depended largely on migration into Fu-chou from other parts of China; yet for the great mass of Fu-chou's population there is simply no direct evidence. For the ancestors of the elite, however, the case is different: the evidence of immigration is abundant. Indeed, one can go further: no Sung elite family claims unambiguously, in the sources that survive, to have lived in Fu-chou before about the middle of T'ang. As far as one can tell, there were no old indigenous families among the Fu-chou elite.[11] Based upon elite claims of origin one can reconstruct a rather striking pattern of migration: this was conditioned rather strongly, it seems, by political changes over time. It is crucial, however, to distinguish carefully two sorts of claims: those which refer to places of origin associated with the great aristocratic families of the Six Dynasties, the Sui, and the T'ang; and those which do not. The first sort of claim I disregard in the discussion that follows; this deserves some comment here.

It is generally accepted that, during the centuries separating the fall of the Han dynasty from the rise of the T'ang, Chinese society and government were dominated by an aristocracy or oligarchy of great clans, who maintained high social status and access to office for generation after generation.[12] The role of these clans in T'ang, and how far into the dynasty their dominance continued, have been the focus of considerable dispute; but recent work appears to justify the view that their power and prestige were still considerable until late in T'ang.[13] Each clan was associated with a specific place-name – a 'choronym', to use the term coined by David Johnson[14] – which identified its traditional family home. Thus, for example, calling a man a 'Chao-chün Li' or a 'Ch'ing-ho Ts'ui' identified him as a member of an old and powerful clan. By T'ang, if not before, it did not necessarily identify the actual place of residence of the man himself, of his immediate family, or even of any living members of the clan.[15]

Most students of the great clans have held that they had largely or entirely disappeared by early Sung.[16] The claims of some Sung men to great clan descent have been dismissed as unserious or as attempts by individual families to magnify their own status – attempts which were successful, if at all, only in the eyes of those who made them. The point is not wholly uncontroversial; but it cannot be denied that the validity of Sung claims is presently, at best, moot.[17] Further, since already in T'ang choronyms were not claims of resi-dence, a Sung Fu-chou man's claim to association with a medieval choronym may have little relevance to the question of his geographical origins. Most Fu-chou families that claim great clan descent, in fact, also name one or more other places, not identifiable as great clan choronyms, as their residence after their departure from the traditional clan home and before their migration to Fu-chou. Thus it seems wisest, in treating elite migration, to disregard all claimed places of origin that seem clearly to be references to great clan choronyms.[18] Among Sung men from Fu-chou, such claims are recorded for ten families.[19]

There remain fifty-five elite families for whom one can discover a time of migration to Fu-chou, a place of origin, or both. The time is known for forty-seven: seven of these claim a founding ancestor who came to Fu-chou during the T'ang. But of these seven, three arrived at or near the end of the dynasty; only three are known to have migrated earlier, during the first half of the eighth century.[20] Seventeen founding ancestors arrived during the Five Dynasties period,[21] another seven just after the founding of Sung.[22] The remaining sixteen migrated during Sung proper, in the course of the eleventh, twelfth, or thirteenth centuries.[23] Clearly, then, the most concentrated wave of migration fell in and about the tenth century, spanning the end of T'ang, the Five Dynasties, and the first decades of Sung. This is far from surprising: first, these years lie within the period when most of Fu-chou's explosive early population growth must have occurred; second, the century witnessed enormous social and political upheavals, especially in North China, and migration seems to have been a common response everywhere.[24]

What is more surprising is where the migrants came from. It would be natural to picture the filling up of the former backwaters of South China in and around the tenth century as a pouring of refugees down from the north. The picture that emerges for the Fu-chou elite is strikingly different. Places of origin are recorded for 41 of the 47 dated immigrants. Thirty-six of these appear on Maps 5 and 5a: the first groups together the ancestors who arrived at the end of T'ang, during Five Dynasties, or in early Sung;[25] the second shows those who arrived during the rest of the Sung. In one respect the maps are similar: in both periods a noticeable proportion of the newcomers were people from the Kan River–P'o-yang Lake basin, Fu-chou's own region. The proportion, however, was far higher in the earlier period: fifteen of twenty-two, as opposed to four of fifteen. Otherwise the difference is striking: while during most of Sung the migrants came from widely scattered areas of China (with a strong concentration in the southeast, to be sure), in the earlier period virtually all migration had originated in an area which under Sung was to become the two circuits of Chiang-nan-tung and Chiang-nan-hsi.[26] For most of the tenth century this had been the territory of the Wu kingdom (902–37) and its powerful successor the Southern T'ang (937–75).[27] In this earlier period the most distant migrant point of origin, shared by four elite ancestors, was Chin-ling (under Sung, Chiang-ning Fu; later Nanking): this was the capital of Southern T'ang. Six ancestors, these four among them, came during the tenth century from the northeastern regions of later Chiang-tung circuit. This lay well outside the P'o-yang basin, and no eleventh-, twelfth-, or thirteenth-century migrants came from the same area.

The pattern revealed here is remarkable. Again, during the Five Dynasties, when the south offered a fairly peaceful prospect as against the almost continuous wars of the north, one might have expected evidence of large-scale migration to Fu-chou from North China. Instead, most migrants came from other parts of Fu-chou's own physiographic region. But even this, it

Map 5. Places of origin claimed by elite families migrant in late T'ang, Five Dynasties, and early Sung (excluding T'ang great clan choronyms).

1. Ai of Lin-ch'uan County: Mu-chou, Liang-che circuit (Ch'eng Chü-fu, *Hsüeh-lou chi* 22/16a–17a)
2. Chang[a] of Chin-ch'i County: Jao-chou, Chiang-tung circuit (Wei Su, *T'ai-p'u yün-lin chi* 6/15b–16a)
3. Chang[b] of Lin-ch'uan County: Jui-chou, Chiang-hsi circuit (Huang Chen, *Huang-shih jih-ch'ao* 97/10b-12b)
4. Ch'en of Tung-ch'uan in Lo-an County: Kan-chou, Chiang-hsi circuit (Ho Chung, *Chih-fei-t'ang kao* 4/9a–10b)

seems, mistakes the real pattern. Chin-ling was neither part of the same region as Fu-chou nor even especially close by; in fact, even after the founding of Sung, only four of fifteen later migrants came from places farther away. The special connection of Chin-ling to Fu-chou in the tenth century was purely political: Fu-chou lay within a state whose capital was Chin-ling. In both the earlier period and the later, migrants came from widely scattered parts of the 'nation'; but during seven decades of the tenth century the nation was Wu or Southern T'ang, only a small part of the area later unified under Sung. The real political status of the southern 'Ten Kingdoms' in this period is still in some respects an open question; but it seems from the evidence of migration offered here that the political boundaries of Wu and Southern T'ang exerted rather more influence − at least on this one aspect of social behaviour − than one might have expected.[28] While the state remained small, so did the area that fed migrants to Fu-chou; when the state grew, Fu-chou's field of attraction grew as well.

Office and wealth

The elite families of Fu-chou, it seems, were in large part the descendants of immigrants. But what were these families like − migrant or not − in

---

5. Ch'eng of Ch'ung-jen County: Hui-chou, Chiang-tung circuit (*WWC* 73/6a−7a)
6. Hsieh of Lin-ch'uan County: Chiang-ning Fu, Chiang-tung circuit (Hsieh I, *Ch'i-t'ang chi* 9/18b−20b)
7. Jao of Lin-ch'uan County: Chiang-ning Fu, Chiang-tung circuit (Lü Nan-kung, *Kuan-yüan chi* 19/5b−8a)
8. Ko of Chin-ch'i County: Jao-chou, Chiang-tung circuit (Lu Chiu-yüan, *Hsiang-shan hsien-sheng ch'üan chi* 28/7a−11a; *WWC* 80/12a−13a)
9. Li of Ch'ung-jen County: Hung-chou, Chiang-hsi circuit (Wei Liao-weng, *Ho-shan hsien-sheng ta-ch'üan chi* 79/4a−6a)
10. Liu of Chin-ch'i County: Chien-ch'ang Chün, Chiang-hsi circuit (Wei Su, op. cit., *hsü-chi* 1/12b−13a)
11. Ou-yang of Ch'ung-jen County: Chi-chou, Chiang-hsi circuit (Ou-yang Ch'e, *Ou-yang hsiu-chuan chi,* front matter)
12. Teng of Chin-ch'i County: Jao-chou, Chiang-tung circuit (*WWC* 79/10a−11b; Wei Su, op. cit. 3/14b−16b)
13. Ts'ai of Lin-ch'uan County: Chiang-ning Fu, Chiang-tung circuit (Su Sung, *Su Wei-kung wen-chi* 57/9b−14a)
14. Tseng of Nan-feng County: Chien-ch'ang Chün, Chiang-hsi circuit (*MKNF* 14/2a−b)
15. Wei of Chin-ch'i County: Chien-ch'ang Chün, Chiang-hsi circuit (Wei Su, op. cit. 6/1a−2a; Huang Chin, *Chin-hua Huang hsien-sheng wen-chi* 32/18b−20b)
16. Wu[a] of Hsin-t'ien in Chin-ch'i County: Hsin-chou, Chiang-tung circuit (Ch'eng Chü-fu, op. cit. 16/12a−13b; Li Ts'un, *Ssu-an chi* 23/18a−21b, 23/4a−7a, 6b−11b)
17. Wu[a] of Lin-ch'uan County: Chiang-ning Fu, Chiang-tung circuit (Yü Chi, *Tao-yüan hsüeh-ku lu* 43/2b−4b)
18. Yen of Lin-ch'uan County: Jui-chou, Chiang-hsi circuit (Ou-yang Hsiu, *Ou-yang Wen-chung kung chi* 22/7b−12b)
19. Yü[a] of Chin-ch'i County: Shao-wu Chün, Fu-chien circuit (Li Ts'un, op.cit. 24/16a−17a)
20. Yü[b] of Lin-ch'uan County: Hui-chou, Chiang-tung circuit (Ch'eng Chü-fu, op. cit. 18/5a−6b)
21. Yüan of Lin-ch'uan County: Chien-ch'ang Chün, Chiang-hsi circuit (Yü Chi, op. cit. 43/12b−13b)

Map 5a. Places of origin of elite families migrant in eleventh, twelfth, and thirteenth centuries.

1. Ch'ao of Lin-ch'uan County: K'ai-feng Fu (Tseng Kung, *Yüan-feng lei-kao* 46/11a–b)
2. Chou of Ch'ung-jen County: Lu-chou, Huai-nan-hsi circuit (*WWC* 79/5a–b)
3. Huang of Pa-t'ang in Lo-an County: Yüeh-chou, Ching-hu-pei circuit (Ho Chung, *Chih-fei t'ang kao* 4/18a–20a)
4. Huang of Chin-ch'i County: Jao-chou, Chiang-tung circuit (Wei Su, *T'ai-p'u yün-lin chi* 9/2a–3a)
5. Huang of Lin-ch'uan County (family of Huang Jen-chieh): Lin-an Fu, Liang-che circuit (see note 34, no. 2)

the time before they joined the Fu-chou elite? What sort of people were their ancestors? Less can be said by way of answer than one might wish; but the question deserves at least some discussion.

The pattern of tenth-century migration to Fu-chou might easily be explained if officeholders under Wu or Southern T'ang, appointed to posts in Fu-chou, made up a considerable proportion of the immigrants. The hypothesis is attractive, and may even be true, but cannot be confirmed on the evidence available: only four of the migrants in this period are reported to have been officials or relatives of officials, and only one held a post in Fu-chou.[29] In fact it is easier to show an officeholding background for migrants in other periods. Five of the seven ancestors who arrived in T'ang were officials, and four held office in Fu-chou.[30] Another family, whose ancestor had migrated in middle T'ang, produced officials under Southern T'ang.[31] A man from a family with no record of migration served as the superintendent during Southern T'ang of the garrison town that would later become I-huang County.[32] In all, then, only eleven Sung elite families are known to have claimed officeholders among their ancestors before Sung.[33] All of these ancestors held very low posts; this makes the claims entirely plausible, since descendants framing false claims could surely have done better for themselves. But the numbers are small: the best one can say is that a significant minority of Sung elite families in Fu-chou were descended from officials of earlier dynasties.

It is in Sung that officeholding immigrants come to the fore. Eleven of the sixteen families who arrived in the eleventh, twelfth, and thirteenth centuries had held office before coming to Fu-chou.[34] Five stand above the rest in prominence: these are the Ch'ao, Meng, and Huang families, immigrants to Lin-ch'uan County in late Northern or early Southern Sung, all of particularly illustrious pedigree; and the Lin and Lou families, Southern Sung migrants of

6. Huang of Lin-ch'uan County (families of Huang Piao and Huang Tz'u-shan): Hung-chou, Chiang-hsi circuit (see note 35, no. 3)
7. Kuan of Lin-ch'uan County: Ch'u-chou, Liang-che circuit (*KHFC* 47/34b and *CPT*, p. 3618)
8. Li of Lin-ch'uan County: Chien-ch'ang Chün, Chiang-hsi circuit (*YLTT* 10422/2b–9a)
9. Lin of Lin-ch'uan County: Fu-chou, Fu-chien circuit (*KHFC* 47/39a)
10. Liu of Chin-ch'i County: Lin-chiang Chün, Chiang-hsi circuit (Wei Su, 5/24a–25b)
11. Lou of Lin-ch'uan County: Hsiu-chou, Liang-che circuit (Yü Chi, *Tao-yüan hsüeh-ku lu* 43/13b–15b)
12. Meng of Lin-ch'uan County: K'ai-feng Fu (Han Yüan-chi, *Nan-chien chia-i kao* 21/11a–14a)
13. Shih of Ch'ung-jen County: Mei-chou, Ch'eng-tu-fu circuit (*WWC* 72/4a–6b)
14. Teng of Lin-ch'uan County: Chien-ch'ang Chün, Chiang-hsi circuit (*KHFC* 57/2b; Lu Chiu-yüan, *Hsiang-shan hsien-sheng ch'üan chi* 16/8b–10b)
15. Yü[c] of Ch'ung-jen County: Lung-chou, Ch'eng-tu-fu circuit (Yü Chi, 43/4b–7b)

somewhat less notable background.[35] No other Fu-chou families founded by
Sung officeholder immigrants were as successful in their new home as these.
Yet though all five continued to achieve office for at least a time after their
arrival, as a group their record is not outstanding among Fu-chou families,
many of whom, at the time of the migrants' arrival, were of far less long and
lofty pedigree. Only two of the five, the Mengs and the Lous, clearly maintained themselves in the local elite down to the end of Sung; and for the
Lous this was not an astonishing achievement, since they had only arrived
in the late twelfth or early thirteenth century. Evidently immigration with
a previous family history of office was not, in Sung, an especially advantageous route into the Fu-chou elite.[36]

Why should this have been so? There are, in fact, good reasons to believe
that, during Sung, immigrant families would have found it hard to establish
themselves firmly and surely in their new surroundings. Transplanted families,
it seems, were neither quickly nor automatically accepted into the existing
networks of elite social relationships. One evidence is their marriage pattern,
which ranged far afield of Fu-chou: this was quite the opposite, as we shall
see, of the typical Southern Sung local elite marriage pattern, which had a
strong local focus. During a major drought in 1271 the new Fu-chou prefect
Huang Chen, working against considerable local elite resistance to establish
an effective program of relief grain sales, recruited men of rank living in, but
not native to, Fu-chou — and only such men — as the informal local administrators and propagandists for the program. He seems to have expected these
men to identify with his own, outsider's, view of the problem and not to be
hopelessly compromised by relationships to the resisting local families.[37]
Other evidence suggests that local officials, when hearing lawsuits, commonly
gave special consideration to suits brought or offenses suffered by 'sojourning'
families, apparently in the view that these were otherwise at a disadvantage
in confrontations with natives.[38]

For an immigrant family's prospects, slow integration into local social
networks might be fatal. If local guarantee was a prerequisite for the prefectural examination, newcomers might be at some disadvantage in sending
sons to the exams with any regularity. But more important: to maintain
itself over the long term a family would need a firm property base, probably
in land. As we shall see further on, contemporaries regarded Fu-chou, especially in Southern Sung, as a highly contentious and litigious prefecture.
A major focus of litigation was landed property; and lawsuits seem as often
as not to have been simply extensions of extralegal, and sometimes violent,
struggles between families. During Southern Sung, in a local milieu where
some families maintained permanent private armed forces of considerable
size,[39] while others were capable of gathering them in emergencies,[40] and

where local officials admitted their inability to control the rural forces under their nominal jurisdiction,[41] a family might be unable to rely on the law alone to protect its lands. Instead it might need to exert either physical force or personal and social influence in its own defense. For a family not yet integrated into local social networks, influence was perhaps hard to come by; and physical force would require large numbers of kinsmen or dependents. Is this why the Mengs, who seem to have immigrated *en masse*,[42] are one of two migrant families that maintained elite position down into the Yüan, while other, rather less successful immigrants like the Ch'aos and Huangs, seem to have arrived as single nuclear families?[43]

From the eleventh century on, then, Fu-chou seems to have been rather rocky soil for migrant elite families. If this is so, much had changed since a century or so before, when many of the families later to be Fu-chou's most illustrious had first arrived. Perhaps the earlier families found hardly any established social networks ready to resist or deny their entry. But it is also likely that by the eleventh century Fu-chou's best lands were beginning to fill up, and that elite competition for property was growing more intense. By 1175 the rapid population growth of earlier years was nearly ended. This may reflect an overall pressure of population on the land that made Fu-chou less attractive than before to ordinary landseeking migrants and at the same time limited natural growth. But presumably the best lands had been taken by the first to come: it is plausible then that the pressure on these lands — the lands the elite was most likely to compete for — was intense as much as a century before population growth as a whole slowed down.

Many families, again, have left no record of any officeholding ancestry before their entry into the Fu-chou elite; and for many that have — especially those who immigrated before Sung — there is a considerable lapse of time between their earlier office and their first appearance in the elite in Fu-chou. What else can be said of their backgrounds? Here the sources grow sparse: funerary inscriptions and biographies hardly exist for people who were not, on the criteria used here, members of the elite, and the sources on elite members only occasionally touch on their families' earlier period of obscurity. Those that do, however, usually refer to a time of accumulation of wealth. Thus the Huang family of Pa-t'ang in Lo-an County, we learn, after their immigration in 1014 'in the beginning devoted themselves to agriculture and attended to what was fundamental; one or two generations later the family property had grown abundant.'[44] The ancestors of the Ko family of Chin-ch'i County 'for generations devoted themselves to their fields and made their family wealthy.'[45] The founders of the Lu family, also of Chin-ch'i, on their first arrival in the district 'bought fields and made their living; their wealth became prominent in their neighborhood.'[46] Sometimes it is simply a history of wealth, rather than the process of its accumulation, that draws comment: the Ch'en family of Ch'ung-jen County 'between Cheng-ho [1111–18] and Hsüan-ho [1119–25] were known as leaders in wealth;'[47] the Chi family of Lin-ch'uan County 'in the beginning [...] led their area in wealth and property.'[48] The ancestors of Cheng Sung of Lo-an County 'were for generations leaders of their canton in wealth;'[49] those of T'u Ta-hsiang of I-huang County 'were for three generations a rich surname of the district;'[50] and the family of Yüeh Ta-chang 'during Ch'ung-ning [1102–06] and Ta-kuan [1107–10] were leaders in wealth.'[51]

It is hardly surprising to find an elite family proclaiming a tradition of wealth or celebrating the efforts of founders in acquiring it.[52] What one does *not* learn, however, is crucial: how rich were the ancestors? How rich is the family now?[53] How did it accumulate its wealth? As to the last, the examples already cited are typical: they stress 'what was fundamental,' that is, agriculture. That agriculture, particularly the cultivation of rice, was the mainstay of Fu-chou's economy is, of course, beyond doubt. Still one may justly wonder whether other sources of wealth – commerce in particular – were not important in the early career of many an ambitious family. In wondering this one departs a good distance from the sources, which preserve clear mention of commercial activity – apart from the sale of grain – for only five local elite families.[54] Only one, the Lu family of Chin-ch'i, is said to have gained most of its wealth in trade – in this case a family drug business.[55] Yet there are some hints that commerce was indeed important for others as well. The founder of the Chan family, for example, came in 1034 to settle at a place whose name at the time – Yen-ch'eng Shih – indicates that it was then already a market town. With time the town acquired the name of the family, coming to be called Chan Hsü: 'Chan Market.' The change apparently reflected the family's acquisition of the market as its own, since in 1149 Chan Ta-t'ung contributed the marketplace to the government as the location for the seat of the newly founded county, Lo-an.[56] Whether the Chans themselves engaged in trade or not, their ownership of the marketplace would assure them an income in fees or rents paid by merchants and so make their wealth at least partly dependent on commerce.[57]

Few other sources are so suggestive, in part because the loss of the original Sung gazetteers of Fu-chou makes it impossible to identify beyond doubt more than two or three Sung market towns.[58] We would have no inkling of the Chans' ownership of a market if they had not decided to donate it to the state. Their example, then, suggests that commercial involvements lurk undetected in the pasts of other families (or indeed in their presents). The same may be true of other forms of enterprise. Who were the 'wealthy households' who specialized in the manufacture of rice yeastcake for export? Who managed the local porcelain industry? Who made Fu-chou an important center of bronze production? Answers to such questions are simply not to be had; but the fact that we find no record of local elite participation in any of these may betray the conventional bias of funerary inscriptions and biographies more than it reflects reality.

In this section and the one preceding I have explored virtually all that the Fu-chou sources have to say about the character of local elite families before they joined the local elite. Apart from an intriguing pattern of geographical origins, and evidence that Sung office did not guarantee successful entry into the Fu-chou elite from outside, this has proved to be remarkably little. But if we expand the notion of 'origins' to focus on elite families *as they are when we first see them in the elite*, rather more of interest emerges. I turn to this in the next section.

Regional clusters and the move into the elite

Chin-ch'i County, the northeasternmost county of Fu-chou and the least productive of degreeholders, was the home, during Southern Sung, of thirty-one *chin-shih*. Of these, thirteen were members of families that had already produced *chin-shih* in Northern Sung.[59] The remaining eighteen, all apparently from families whose official success did not precede Southern Sung, include four whose places of residence are unknown,[60] and fourteen, representing seven different families, whose residences are identifiable: these were the Ko, Liu, Lu, Teng, Wei, Wu, and Yang families.[61] Their residences are shown on Map 6. It will be seen that five of the families (Ko, Lu, Teng, Wei, and Wu) lived in the north-eastern corner of their county. Unlike the rest of Chin-ch'i this area is watered by a river system draining, not west into the Ju River, but rather north into the Hsin River system of neighboring Hsin-chou and Jao-chou.[62] As these five families account for twelve of the fourteen *chin-shih*,[63] and as this part of the county appears to have been represented by only one elite family in Northern Sung,[64] the region seems to emerge rather strikingly in Southern Sung as a breeding ground for the elite.

The dates of the five families' first *chin-shih* (Lu Yün in 1142; Ko Feng-shih in 1169; Teng Kang in 1220; Wei Kuo-ts'ai in 1235; Wu Ming-yang in 1271) would make it appear that the region emerged only gradually. Actually, however, for all but the Wei family the rise to importance in the Fu-chou elite can be shown to have come in the first decades of Southern Sung. More importantly, these four families make their first appearance engaged in a common enterprise: the defense of the prefecture and circuit against Chin invaders, renegade Sung troops, and bandits immediately after the fall of the north in 1127. The Chin-ch'i militia that came into existence at this time will be dealt with in detail in Chapter 5;[65] here it is enough to note that

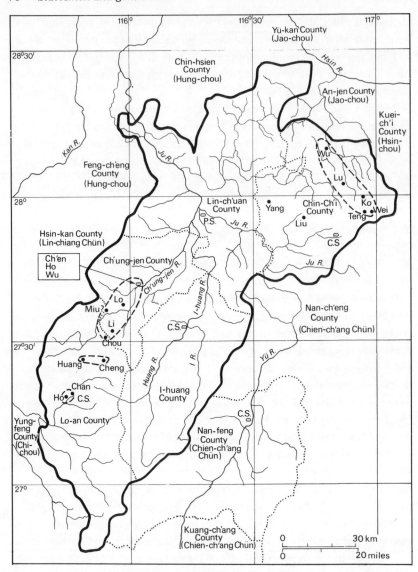

Map 6. Regional groupings of elite families.

the Lus provided overall leadership in the early years, and again when defense preparations were being made in 1175;[66] that the Tengs were perhaps the chief supplier of troops and officers and contributed funds as well;[67] and that Ko Keng (the father of Ko Feng-shih above) also played a leadership role.[68] As for the Wus, a gazetteer biography reports that a member of the family named Wu Ch'e made financial contributions to defense measures during Chien-yen (1127–30);[69] and a Yüan funerary inscription tells us that at the beginning of Southern Sung the family had provided refuge and protection to official families from all over the prefecture.[70]

After the four families' emergence in local defense activities, the Lus produced a *chin-shih* in 1142, the Kos in 1169; a member of the Teng family had been awarded a military office by 1135,[71] and two sons had passed the prefectural exam by 1175;[72] Wu Ch'e had been awarded a military rank and then the lowest civil rank by the 1130s,[73] while a relative named Wu Pang-chi reached the office of sheriff of Han-kuang County in Ying-chou by the middle 1100s. Thus within two or three decades all four families had obtained some form of official standing. All were to continue as prominent local elite families at least down to the end of Sung.

It is virtually inconceivable that with their common involvement in defense preparations around 1127 these families would not have come into contact; and there is evidence of connections among them from early on. Thus Lu Chiu-yüan recalled Ko Keng's visiting his home in his childhood, and Ko Keng's sons were among his students.[74] In 1146 a Lu noted that his family and the Tengs had been intermarrying for generations.[75] The earliest explicitly recorded contact between the Wu family and one of the other three is the tutelage of one Wu Hsün under Lu Chiu-yüan,[76] but still one's impression is strong that these four families, all living in one fairly small, physiographically integral region of Chin-ch'i County, rose into the local elite as a group.

A rather similar cluster of families comes from Ch'ung-jen County. Fuchou as a whole produced fewer, and in large part less illustrious, high court officials in Southern Sung than in Northern Sung; but a number of its highest Southern Sung officials came from Ch'ung-jen. The 1154 *chin-shih* Ho I reached the post of Minister of Works in 1209.[77] Earlier, the 1175 *chin-shih* Lo Tien had risen quickly to be Signatory Official of the Bureau of Military Affairs, a post of assistant-ministerial rank, by his death in 1194 at the age of forty-five.[78] The 1208 *chin-shih* Li Liu eventually reached the post of Executive of the Ministry of Personnel;[79] and the 1211 *chin-shih* Ch'en Yüan-chin rose to be Military Intendant in Kuang-hsi circuit[80] – a post lower than the others, yet still fairly successful for a Southern Sung Fu-chou man. Each of these was the first *chin-shih* from his family. The residences

of the four are shown in Map 6 (along with those of certain other families of
the same region who will be dealt with below). It may be seen that all four
lived in an area watered by the upper (western) course of the Ch'ung-jen
River and its tributaries. Two lived in or just outside the county seat, through
which the river passed as it flowed east and north toward an eventual confluence with the Ju River in Lin-ch'uan County; the other two lived further
upstream in mountainous areas drained by the river and tributary streams.
As the still higher course of the Ch'ung-jen in Lo-an County was apparently
not navigable in Sung,[81] the families as a group were living at the uppermost
navigable end of the Ch'ung-jen River system, a rather well-defined physiographic region from the perspective of Fu-chou as a whole.

While the *chin-shih* dates given for the four men above would once again
suggest that their families emerged at widely differing times, in fact all four
can be placed with complete or fair certainty in the local elite by the last
decades of Northern or the first decades of Southern Sung. Thus Li Liu's
great-grandfather Li Ch'ih was sent up to the Imperial University sometime
between 1103 and 1121,[82] and his collateral relative Li Hao was likewise
sent up in 1118;[83] a son of Li Ch'ih held office as a county sheriff;[84] and
from early in Southern Sung the family had social connections to other
prominent officials and scholars of their county. (On this, more below.)
On Ho I's family there is no information before he passes the prefectural
exam in 1153, although a man of the same surname (the first on the exam
lists) had passed in 1137 and may have been a relative.[85] Ch'en Yüan-chin's
family had been, we are told, the wealthiest in the county at the end of
Northern Sung; his grandfather Ch'en Ming-shih had studied poetry in the
1130s with three different officials from other prefectures who sojourned
for several years or retired in Fu-chou, and had formed a poetry society
together with Ho I and two officeholding members of the neighboring Wu
family.[86] As for Lo Tien, although his record of conduct informs us only that
'his family had for generations cultivated scholarly works, but their house
had not yet flourished'[87] — a sentence whose vagueness is if anything greater
in the original Chinese[88] — there is convincing evidence that men of his
family had been active in local construction, married with other local elite
families, and even held office by the first ten or twenty years of Southern
Sung.[89]

Thus all four of these families seem to make their appearance within a
period of forty years or less. Further, there is evidence of their association
with each other, directly and through common connections to a fifth family.
I have mentioned Ch'en Ming-shih's membership in a poetic society together
with men of an officeholding family surnamed Wu. This family, living in or
just outside the county seat[90] (see Map 6), had produced one *chin-shih* in

1053[91] (and perhaps an earlier one in 1002);[92] another member had passed
the prefectural examination in 1126 and attained the *chin-shih* in 1132.[93]
In the early years of Southern Sung a number of other men of the family
became prominent, either reaching office or making a scholarly name for
themselves locally. During the Shao-hsing period (1131–62) Wu Hang,[94] his
brother Wu Hsieh,[95] and their lineage-mate Wu Tseng[96] all presented their
writings to the throne with an eye to being appointed to office in return.
Tseng, known to later generations as the author of the *Neng-kai-chai man-lu,*
received office and rose to be Office Chief of the Ministry of Personnel;
Hsieh eventually (in 1163) passed the *chin-shih* exam and reached the post
of Professor to the Imperial Family in the Western Capital; Hang never
reached office, but in 1156 founded the Huan-ch'i Academy near his residence. Tseng's younger cousin Wu I also passed the *chin-shih* in 1163 and
rose to be Fiscal Supervisory Official of Hu-nan circuit.[97] Thus this family,
already successful in the exams in Northern Sung, achieved especial prominence in the first decades of Southern Sung. Members were to continue
passing the prefectural and *chin-shih* exams to the end of the dynasty. By
official standards, then, the Wus were the most successful family of this
highly successful region of Ch'ung-jen County.

Ch'en Ming-shih's connection to the Wus is already established. It is recorded elsewhere that Li Liu's grandfather Li Yen-hua was a friend of Wu
Hsieh and Wu Hang, and that Wu Tseng consulted him in the compilation
of the *Neng-kai-chai man-lu.*[98] Ho I was a member of the same poetic society
as the Wus and Ch'en Ming-shih, apparently before his departure for office
in 1154.[99] Lo Tien appears to have worked as a family teacher for the Wus
before his *chin-shih,*[100] and his family was also indirectly connected, through
marriage, to the Lis.[101] Thus we find once again a group of families living in
the same region, emerging at roughly the same time, and already connected
to each other in the period of their emergence. There is no evidence here, as
there is in Chin-ch'i, of their involvement in some common enterprise; but I
would suggest that their rise as a group may have been the result of their
associations (direct or indirect) with their already prominent neighbors, the
Wu family.

Two other families may belong to the same regional grouping: these produce no high officials, but emerge near the same time and live (either certainly
or probably) in the same region. One is the Chou family of Huai-jen, a place
which after 1149 belonged legally to Lo-an County but which lay just on the
border between that county and Ch'ung-jen,[102] very near the Li family (see
Map 6): a first prefectural graduate in 1140[103] was followed by two more in
1174[104] and 1189.[105] Li Yen-hua (see above) is recorded as marrying a
daughter of a 'Lo-an *chin-shih*' named Chou Kuang (as the name does not

appear in the exam lists for Lo-an or Ch'ung-jen, the man may well have been a military degreeholder), and one of his granddaughters married a Chou Shan-fu:[106] it seems very likely that these are of the Huai-jen family. The second example is a Miu family, apparently intermarried with both the Los and the Lis by early Southern Sung (see nn. 89 and 101 above). An elite family by around 1130 on the evidence of a member's marriage to a woman related to *chin-shih*, the Mius in the next generation acquired three office-holding sons-in-law (two of them from the Lo family), and in the next pro-duced three prefectural graduates, in 1183, 1189, and 1195.[107] The family's residence in the same region is less certain: it appears in Map 6 with a question mark.[108]

The surviving sources on these two groups of families, one in Chin-ch'i and one in Ch'ung-jen, are exceptionally rich; it is difficult, given the sort of material that more commonly comes to hand, to find other, equally clear examples of groups united in time, space, and personal association when they first emerge. One may point to the Cheng family of Lo-an and the Huang family of T'ung-fu in the same county: both appear on the prefectural exam lists for the first time in 1249;[109] their residences lie close together in the northern part of the county (see Map 6); and they were already intermarried in 1230, when the Chengs first achieved office for their role in local defense.[110] No earlier local elite families from just this area of Lo-an, lying between the county's two river systems, are known. One other possible example is worth mentioning: in the large area of Ch'ung-jen County that was later to become Lo-an, only two families can be placed in the local elite as early as Northern Sung. One, the Chan family, came from the market town that would eventually be the Lo-an county seat;[111] the other, the Ho family, was its virtual neighbor, living just outside the town, to the west (see Map 6).[112]

All these examples, but especially the Chin-ch'i and Ch'ung-jen groups that I have dwelt on at some length, suggest that families often 'rose' into the elite not singly, but in groups, tied together by scholarly, marital, or organizational connections. In Southern Sung, at least (for Northern Sung the evidence does not admit of a judgement), these groups were based in physiographic regions of some integrity: viewed from the outside the rise of a group amounts to the absorption of a region, with its leading families, into the elite networks of the prefecture and the nation.

Again, the evidence is good only for Southern Sung. Of our four examples, only the Chan/Ho pair belongs to Northern Sung, and here there is no direct evidence of their association at this early date.[113] It may well be, for instance, that the tight network of elite families centered (so far as the sources are concerned) on Hsieh I and Hsieh K'o (Chapter 1, pp. 49–52) formed a regional as well as a social unity: but no source records the exact place of residence of any of these families. This is in fact typical for Northern Sung: with some exceptions, it is generally only the most illustrious elite families of Northern Sung that can be placed at a definite residence. For Southern Sung the sources become much more informative. Even where they do not directly identify a man's residence, they generally give enough auxiliary geographic information to make locating a residence an easy matter. This historiographic shift is very probably no accident. There is good reason to believe that a specific place of residence within its county or prefecture became a more central part of an elite family's identity in Southern Sung: that its exact placement in a local framework was now crucial. This development would parallel a whole cluster of changes in elite behavior, and in notions of elite roles, that divide Northern from Southern Sung. These form the subject of the two chapters that follow.

3

ELITE TRANSFORMATION:
FROM NORTHERN TO SOUTHERN SUNG

Marriage

In 1057 Wang An-shih wrote to his fellow Fu-chou man Wu Fen, then Executive Inspector of Chiang-ning Fu, recommending that Wu choose Wang Ling (no relation to An-shih), a man of Yang-chou in Huai-nan-tung circuit, to be his daughter's husband.[1] Receiving no reply, Wang wrote again:[2]

> I do not know whether or not the petition that I previously addressed to you reached your presence. Wang Ling has presently gathered a following of students in Chiang-yin. In his knowledge of letters and in his actions he is truly an outstanding gentleman. Some may have conveyed to you that he acts improperly; none of this is worthy of your belief. Here I have thoroughly examined his conduct, and at bottom he only maintains restraint and is content in his poverty. Recently those studying with him have greatly increased: he is by no means absolutely poor, all the more as his dependents are few and quite easily supported. Though he has not taken the examinations, on my reckoning those who do take the examinations today do not necessarily reach a degree; nor do they always avoid falling into extreme poverty. I ask again your consideration [. . .]

Soon afterward Wu Fen did give his daughter to Wang Ling. His consent was surely owing to Ling's sponsorship by Wang An-shih, who was not only a successful young official but also the son of Wu Fen's own sister.[3] What is striking in the letter is Wang An-shih's evident belief — without having heard from Wu — that Wu's objections to Wang Ling might center on his 'poverty'[4] and on his failure to take the exams, thus on his lack of prospects for an official career. Clearly Wang An-shih assumed that wealth and prospects were common concerns of fathers seeking husbands for their daughters.

Wang's letter is one of a very few documents in which Sung witnesses of the Fu-chou scene remarked on the standards that elite families used (or ought to use) in choosing marriage partners. Yet through these few sources runs a common theme. In a collection of miscellaneous jottings on topics contemporary and ancient, the Northern Sung man Wei T'ai (fl. ca. 1105) recorded a brief anecdote about the Fu-chou man Yen Shu:

> When Yen was superintendent of the Southern Capital, Fan Chung-yen, having gone into mourning, was serving as acting director of the capital school. One day Yen said to Fan: 'One of my daughters has reached marrying-age. I will rely on you, sir, to choose a son-in-law for me.' Fan said: 'In the school there are the candidates Fu Kao and Chang Wei-shan. Both are cultivated in their conduct; both will someday be high ministers. Either would be a suitable son-in-law.' Yen said: 'That being so, which would be the better?' Fan said: 'Fu is careful and diligent; Chang is rougher-hewn but of more eminent talent.' Yen said: 'Then I will take Fu Kao as my son-in-law.' Fu Kao later changed his name; he is the same man as the Assisting Councillor Fu Pi.[5]

Like Wang An-shih with Wu Fen, Fan assumed that prospects for high office — along with considerations of personal character, to be sure — would be a prime concern for Yen as a prospective father-in-law.

Other sources suggest — sometimes only by implication — the importance of sheer wealth. In the funerary inscription of Huang Ssu-yung (ca. 1169–1208) we find: 'In choosing wives for his sons he did not go by wealth, but always went by generations of great scholarship and by local reputation.'[6] Here wealth is denied as a standard for marriage-making; but the very denial of it for this man appears to take it for granted for most; and the standard proposed in its place — a long family history of success in scholarly pursuits and prominence in one's locality — not only does not exclude wealth but would seem to imply it as a precondition. The meaning surely is simply that, given a choice between two families, Huang would not always choose the wealthier, if local fame and the length of the family's history of scholarship tipped the balance the other way. The funerary inscription of the late Sung – early Yüan man of Lo-an County, Yu Te-hung, informs us that 'The custom of the world counsels that, in taking a wife, one choose one whose family's resources are greater than one's own, in hopes of a generous dowry.'[7] Here again wealth appears as a standard for the wife-seeker. Finally there is a postscript to the funerary inscription of Cheng Sung's mother (see Chapter 2, n. 110), a late Southern Sung woman of the Huang surname, who found herself an early widow:

> At that time my sister [the subject] was just thirty-one years old, with only one daughter, who was still at home. She took up what her husband's family had left after the draining expenses of bandit defense. [Her husband and his brother had earned honors for using their wealth to fund a local self-defense force against bandits in 1230] [. . .] Before

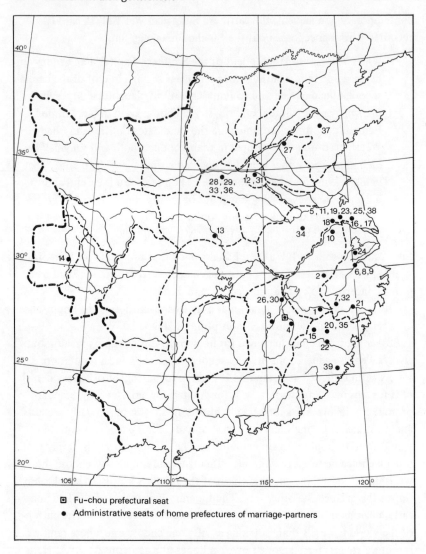

Map. 7. Northern Sung local elite marriages outside the prefecture

1. Woman surnamed Kuei, of Kuei-ch'i County in Hsin-chou, wife of Chu Shih-heng of
    Chin-ch'i County: cf. Appendix I, no. 12. Married 1073. (Hsieh I, *Ch'i-t'ang chi*
    9/15b–17a)
2. Hsieh Pi, of Hsi County in Hui-chou, husband of woman surnamed Hou of Nan-feng
    County. Married before 1012. (*SS* 460/6b–7a)
3. Woman surnamed Ho, of Lin-chiang Chün, wife of Ts'ai Ch'eng-hsi of Lin-ch'uan
    County: cf. Appendix I, no. 49. Married probably by 1065. (Su Sung, *Su Wei-kung
    wen-chi* 57/9b–14a)

4. Wang Wu-chiu, of Nan-ch'eng County in Chien-ch'ang Chün, husband of daughter of Tseng I-chan of Nan-feng County: cf. Appendix I, no. 54. Married 1059. (Tsou Hao, *Tao-hsiang hsien-sheng wen-chi* 37/7a–b)

5. Wang Chi, of Chiang-tu County in Yang-chou, husband of daughter of Tseng I-chan of Nan-feng County. Married by 1072. (Tseng Kung, *Yüan-feng lei-kao* 46/13a)

6. Kuan Ching-hui, of Ch'ien-t'ang County in Hang-chou, husband of daughter of Tseng I-chan of Nan-feng County. Married by 1053. (Ibid., 46/3b–4b)

7. Chiang Pao of K'ai-hua County in Ch'ü-chou, husband of daughter of Tseng Pu of Nan-feng County: cf. Appendix I, no. 54. Married 1094. (Ch'eng Chü, *Pei-shan chi* 31/16a–18b)

8. Woman surnamed Ch'iang, of Ch'ien-t'ang County in Hang-chou, wife of Tseng Chao of Nan-feng County: cf. Appendix I, no. 54. Married by 1081. (Yang Shih, *Kuei-shan chi* 29/2a–20b)

9. Woman surnamed Ch'iang, of Ch'ien-t'ang County in Hang-chou, wife of Tseng Hsün of Nan-feng County: cf. Appendix I, no. 54. Married by 1118. (Wang Tsao, *Fu-ch'i chi* 27/17b–20a)

10. Woman surnamed Huang, of Chiang-ning Fu, wife of Tseng Chih-yao of Nan-feng County: cf. Appendix I, no. 54. Married 975. (Wang An-shih, *Lin-ch'uan chi* 99/3a–4a)

11. Woman surnamed Chu, of T'ien-ch'ang County in Yang-chou, wife of Tseng I-chan of Nan-feng County. Married between 1014 and 1047. (Ibid., 93/1a–3b and Tseng Kung, op. cit. 46/9a–10a)

12. Woman surnamed Ch'ao of K'ai-feng Fu, wife of Tseng Kung of Nan-feng County: cf. Appendix I, no. 54. Married probably by 1060. (Tseng Kung, op. cit. 46/11a–b)

13. Woman surnamed Wei, of Hsiang-yang County in Hsiang-chou, wife of Tseng Pu of Nan-feng County. Married by 1070. (Li O, *Sung-shih chi-shih* 87/5a)

14. Woman surnamed Su, of Mei-shan County in Mei-chou, wife of Tseng Tsung of Nan-feng County: cf. Appendix I, no. 54. Married 1100. (Tseng Hsieh, *Yün-chuang chi* 5/28b–30b)

15. Woman surnamed Wu, of Shao-wu Chün, wife of Tsou T'ao of I-huang County: cf. Appendix I, no. 57. Married by 1107. (Sun Ti, *Nan-lan-ling Sun shang-shu ta-ch'üan chi* 63/14a–16b)

16. Chou Yen-hsien, of Hai-ling County in T'ai-chou, husband of daughter of Wang Kuan-chih of Lin-ch'uan County: cf. Appendix I, no. 60. Married c. 1035 (Wang An-shih, op. cit. 96/8b–9b)

17. Woman surnamed Chou, of Hai-ling County in T'ai-chou, wife of elder brother of Wang An-shih of Lin-ch'uan County: cf. Appendix I, no. 60. Married probably by 1059. (Ibid.)

18. Shen Chi-ch'ang of Yang-tzu County in Chen-chou, husband of daughter of Wang I of Lin-ch'uan County: cf. Appendix I, no. 60. Married probably by 1066. (Tseng Kung, op. cit. 45/4b–6a)

19. Chu Ming-chih of T'ien-ch'ang County in Yang-chou, husband of daughter of Wang I of Lin-ch'uan County. Married probably by 1066. (Ibid.)

20. Wu An-ch'ih of P'u-ch'eng County in Chien-chou, husband of daughter of Wang I of Lin-ch'uan County. Married probably by 1066. (Ibid.)

21. Yeh T'ao of Lung-ch'üan County in Ch'u-chou, husband of daughter of Wang An-kuo of Lin Ch'uan County: cf. Appendix I, no. 60. Married probably by 1080. (Wang An-shih, op. cit. 91/8a–9a)

22. Chang K'uei of Sha County in Nan-chien-chou, husband of daughter of Wang I of Lin-ch'uan County. Married c. 1038. (Ibid., 99/5b–6a)

23. Man surnamed Yang of Chiang-tu County in Yang-chou, husband of daughter of Wang Kuan-chih of Lin-ch'uan County. Married probably by 1030. (Ibid., 97/9b–10b)

24. Chang Wen-kang of Wu-ch'eng County in Hu-chou, husband of sister of uncle of Wang An-shih of Lin-ch'uan County. Married by 1072. (Ibid., 97/11b–12a)

25. Wang Ling, of Yang-chou, husband of daughter of Wu Fen of Chin-ch'i County: cf. Appendix I, no. 65. Married c. 1058. (Wang Ling, *Kuang-ling chi, fu-lu* 13b)

26. Li Chieh-fu, of Hsin-chien County in Hung-chou, husband of daughter of Wu Meng of Chin-ch'i County: cf. Appendix I, no. 65. Married 1057. (K'ung Wu-chung, *Tsung-po chi* 17/14a–15a)

27. Kuo Shen-hsi of Ta-ming Fu, husband of daughter of Wu Yu-lin of Ch'ung-jen County. Married probably c. 1030. (Liu Chih, *Chung-su chi* 11/18a–23a)
28. Ch'en Chien-su, of Ho-nan Fu, husband of daughter of Yüen Huang-shang of I-huang County: cf. Appendix I, no. 72. (Wang An-shih, op. cit. 99/9b–10b)
29. Woman surnamed Huang, of Ho-nan Fu, wife of Yüeh Hsü-kuo of I-huang County: cf. Appendix I, no. 72. Married c. 1018 (Yin Chu, *Ho-nan hsien-sheng wen-chi* 15/6b–7b)
30. Li Hsiu-yung, of Feng-ch'eng County in Huang-chou, husband of sister of Yen Shu of Lin-ch'uan County: cf. Appendix I, no. 73. Married before 1025. (Lü Nan-kung, *Kuan-yüan chi* 19/10a–11b)
31. Woman surnamed Wang, of Hsien-p'ing County, K'ai-feng Fu, wife of son of Yen Shu of Lin-ch'uan County. Married c. 1045. (Chang Lei, *Chang Yu-shih wen-chi* 60/4a–5a)
32. Woman surnamed Wu, of Hsi-an County in Ch'ü-chou, wife of Yen Chao-su of Lin-ch'uan County: cf. Appendix I, no. 73. Married probably by 1065 (Hsieh, I, op. cit. 9/11a–12a)
33. Fu Pi, of Lo-yang County in Ho-nan Fu, husband of daughter of Yen Shu of Lin-ch'uan County. Married probably by 1040. (Ou-yang Hsiu, *Ou-yang Wen-chung kung chi* 22/7b–12b)
34. Yang Ch'a, of Ho-fei County in Lu-chou, husband of daughter of Yen Shu of Lin-ch'uan County. Married probably by 1040. (Ibid.)
35. Woman surnamed Li, of Chien-an County in Chien-chou, wife of Yen Shu of Lin-ch'uan County. Married probably by 1021. (Ibid.)
36. Woman surnamed Chang, of Ho-nan Fu, wife of Yen Ch'eng-yü of Lin-ch'uan County: cf. Appendix I, no. 73. Married by c. 1055. (Liu Pin, *P'eng-ch'eng chi* 39/517–518)
37. Fan Shih-chi, of Ch'ing-chou, husband of daughter of Ts'ai Ch'eng-hsi of Lin-ch'uan County. (Su Sung, loc. cit.)
38. Woman surnamed P'ang, of Yang-chou, wife of Wang Chien of Lin-ch'uan County. Married by c. 1080. (Hsieh I, *Ch'i-t'ang chi* 8/13b–15a)
39. Ts'ai Pien, of Hsien-yu County in Hsing-hua Chün, husband of daughter of Wang An-shih of Lin-ch'uan County. Married by 1076. (*SS* 472/5a)

---

long the family's finances were growing more prosperous daily. Consequently she was able to marry her daughter to a son of [a property or income of] two thousand *shih*.[8]

Here both the importance of wealth in a son-in-law and the importance of one's own wealth in getting one are clear.

These examples – which make up the entire direct testimony of the available sources – suggest that elite families used such standards as official standing or wealth, prospects for office, length of pedigree, scholarly renown, and local reputation in choosing both sons-in-law and daughters-in-law.[9] Whatever may usually or ideally have been the relative position of the two families involved in a marriage, the importance of the same criteria for both parties would lead one to expect elite families to find their marriage partners in families of roughly the same social standing as their own; and the evidence on the actual marriages of the Fu-chou elite, in both Northern and Southern Sung, overwhelmingly confirms this expectation. 'One takes a wife to match oneself,' remarked the Southern Sung prefect Huang Kan.[10]

None of this is at all surprising. Yet the marriage standards of Fu-chou men were by no means stable during the Sung. A glance back at the examples will show that, of the five, only the two from Northern Sung specifically mention officeholding as a criterion; in the Southern Sung examples we find only wealth, pedigree, scholarship, and local standing. It would be absurd to deduce from so little evidence a change in elite aims in marriagemaking. But in fact, as we shall see, the difference may be no accident. Fu-chou elite marriage patterns changed dramatically between Northern and Southern Sung. The most striking difference, and a fair place to start in considering the broader changes in the elite between Northern and Southern Sung, is the geographical range of marriages. About five hundred marriages of Fu-chou elite members are recorded; of these, the residence of each partner is identifiable for about one hundred. These are the chief basis for the discussion that follows.

Map 7 displays the places of registration of Northern Sung Fu-chou elite marriage partners who were not themselves from Fu-chou. It will be seen that these are spread over the more populous south-eastern and northern regions of Northern Sung (with one exceptional case in Szechwan). Aside from five cases in prefectures that directly bordered Fu-chou, there are four regions of particular concentration. One is the northwestern section of Fu-chien circuit, comprising Chien-chou, Nan-chien-chou, and Shao-wu Chün, which accounts for four cases (15, 20, 22, 35). Lying further north is a cluster of six cases (2, 6, 7, 8, 9, 32) in the Che River valley. Continuing north, we find the largest cluster, ten cases, in the group of prefectures that surrounded the junction of the lower Yangtse River with the southern limb of the canal system leading north to the capital (5, 10, 11, 16, 17, 18, 19, 23, 25, 38). Finally, there are seven cases (12, 27, 28, 29, 31, 33, 36) in the capital prefectures in the north: Ho-nan Fu (modern Lo-yang), Ta-ming Fu, and the capital proper, K'ai-feng Fu. Only six cases do not fall clearly into one of these four rather well-defined regions.[11] Simple proximity probably accounts for the concentration in northwestern Fu-chien; but the other three were areas of especial political or economic importance during Northern Sung. I will return to this further on.

Who were these Fu-chou families who married outside the prefecture? Leaving aside one woman of whose family nothing is known,[12] the thirty-eight remaining marriages involve only nine local families. Six of these account for thirty-four marriages: they are the Ts'ai, Wang, and Yen families of Lin-ch'uan, the Tseng family of Nan-feng, a Wu family of Chin-ch'i, and the Yüeh family of I-huang. These six had a great deal in common. All produced their first *chin-shih* during Fu-chou's first thirty years under Sung rule (four of them before 992). All went on to have impressive, even spectacular success in the examinations during the early to middle eleventh

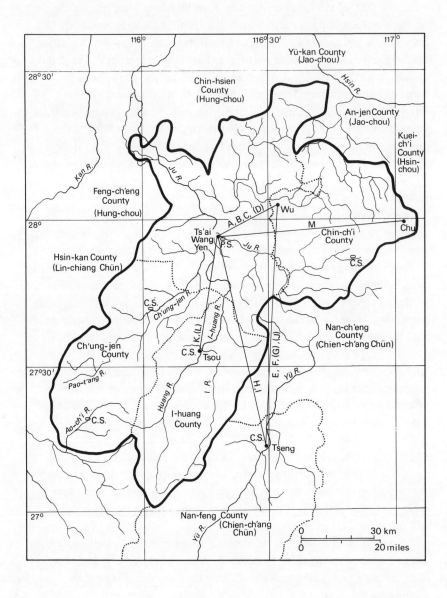

Map 8. Northern Sung marriages within greater Fu-chou.

(Note: Letters in parentheses indicate speculative identification of one partner)

A. Marriage of Wang I to daughter of Wu Min. Married before 1021. See her funerary inscription in Tseng Kung, *Yüan-feng lei-kao* 45/4b–6a.
B. Marriage of Wang An-shih to daughter of Wu Fan. See funerary inscription of her nephew Wu Ch'üeh in Sun Ti, *Nan-lan-ling Sun shang-shu ta-ch'üan chi.*
C. Marriage of Yen Chao-su to daughter of Wu Fan. Married probably before 1040. See funerary inscription of Yen's second wife in Hsieh I, *Ch'i-t'ang chi* 9/11a–12a.
(D.) Marriage of daughter of Wu Fen to Yen Hsiu-mu, judging by surname and other marriage connection between the families probably a member of the Lin-ch'uan Yens. See Wu Fen's funerary inscription in Wang An-shih, *Lin-ch'uan chi* 98/10a–b.
E. Marriage of Wu Min to daughter of Tseng Chih-yao. Married by 1014. See her funerary inscription in ibid., 100/3a–b.
(F.) Marriage of Tseng I-chan to woman surnamed Wu, of unidentified family but possibly of Chin-ch'i Wus. Married around 1014. See her funerary inscription in ibid., 100/3b–4b.
(G.) Marriage of Tseng I-ts'ung to woman surnamed Wu, of unidentified family but possibly of Chin-ch'i Wus. Married by 1025. See her son's funerary inscription in Tseng Kung, op. cit. 46/10a–b.
H. Marriage of Tseng Yü to daughter of Wang An-kuo. Married by 1115. See Tseng Yü's funerary inscription in Wang Tsao, *Fu-ch'i chi* 28/1a–5b.
I. Marriage of Wang An-kuo to daughter of Tseng I-chan. Married probably by 1060. See Wang's funerary inscription in Wang An-shih, op. cit. 91/8a–9a, and long note on Tseng I-chan's wives and children in *MKNF* 12/7b–8a.
(J.) Marriage of Tseng Chia to woman surnamed Wu from Chin-ch'i County, not specifically identified but surely member of Wu family above. See note on Tseng in *MKNF* 12/17a–b, which cites Wu Tseng, *Neng-kai chai man-lu.*
K. Marriage of Yen Fang to daughter of Tsou Chi of I-huang County. Married probably by 1080. See Yen's funerary inscription in Hsieh I, op. cit. 9/4a–8b.
(L.) Marriage of daughter Ts'ai Ch'eng-hsi to man named Tsou Fan, not identified but possibly of family of Tsou Chi above. See Ts'ai's funerary inscription in Su Sung, *Su Wei-kung wen-chi* 57/9b–14a.
M. Marriage of Yen Fang's daughter to Chu Liang of Chin-ch'i County. Married probably by 1100. See Yen's funerary inscription in Hsieh I, loc. cit.

---

century.[13] All but the Wu family are known to have achieved offices of considerable influence in the capital by the 1070s at the latest.[14] Thus marriage outside the prefecture in Northern Sung was especially characteristic of families very much of a single type: successful early and often in the competition for *chin-shih* degrees, and nationally renowned by middle Northern Sung. It must be stressed, however, that while several of the families produced men who reached the highest offices in the Sung state, their marriages outside the prefecture began before they had risen so high. Ministerial rank was by no means a prerequisite for making a long-distance marriage. Many supporting examples can be found among the marriages in Map 7. The Tsengs had made at least four marriages at great distances from Fu-chou (see 6, 10, 11, 12) well before Tseng Pu and his brothers reached high capital posts. The Wangs were tied to a number of families in the lower Yangtse region before Wang An-shih achieved power at court (see 16, 17, 23, and probably 18–20). But the clearest evidence comes from other families, who never approached the achievements of the Tsengs, Wangs, et al. Neither Wu Yu-lin (27) nor Wang Chien (38), nor any member of their families before them, held office in the capital; yet Wu's daughter married a man from the northern auxiliary capital, Ta-ming Fu, while Wang's wife came from Yang-chou, on the lower Yangtse. This is not to disregard the importance of office as a qualification for long-distance marriage — I will argue that it was a virtual prerequisite — but simply to emphasize that the office need not be among the highest.

What of the spouses? What sorts of families were at the other end of the transaction? Very often they seem to have been of very much the same type as their Fu-chou partners: officeholders at least; often families that had reached office, through the *chin-shih* or other means, early in Sung, repeated the achievement a number of times thereafter, and (in many but not in all cases) placed men in influential posts in the capital by the middle or later eleventh century.[15] Thus for example the wife of Tseng I-chan, a woman surnamed Chu from T'ien-ch'ang County, Yang-chou (11), was the grand-niece of a man who had reached a salary-rank of the third grade under Chen-tsung, having held several prefectships; his son (her first cousin once removed) reached the prefectship of Lang-chou; and the woman's father and brothers held low offices.[16] Chou Yen-hsien, husband of Wang Kuan-chih's daughter (16), was the grandson of a man who had been prefect of T'ai-chou at the beginning of Sung and the son of a man who had served in several prefect-ships, as Judical Intendant of Fu-chien, and as Supervisory Official for Salt and Iron of the Finance Commission.[17] These examples are typical. While some of the families extend in office back before the beginning of Sung (of the six Fu-chou families this is demonstrable only for the Tsengs and Yüehs),[18] and a few others emerge somewhat later than their Fu-chou counterparts, families without significant background in office do not appear.

A marriage sometimes began a relationship between two families that would endure in later generations. Most notable are the three generations of Tsengs (in direct paternal line beginning with Tseng Chao) who married women of the Ch'iang family of Ch'ien-t'ang County. (Two of these are nos. 8 and 9 on Map 7; the third is Tseng Hsieh, Chao's grandson.)[19] Similarly Chou Yen-hsien (no. 16) married Wang Kuan-chih's daughter, while his own younger sister married the elder brother of Kuan-chih's grandnephew Wang An-shih (no. 17). Although cases of this kind were clearly not uncommon, from the Fu-chou evidence there is no basis for seeing them as typical or as representing preferred marriage strategies; rather the evidence suggests that families most frequently attempted to spread their marriage network rather widely.

A second aspect of Northern Sung marriage patterns emerges when one maps the marriages made *within* greater Fu-chou by families who also married outside. These are shown in Map 8. (Each numbered line represents a connection of two families by at least one marriage —see the legend for Map 8 — and the endpoints of each line are the residences of the families of the partners.) The map is very incomplete, involving only a small number of marriages, as for most Northern Sung marriages within Fu-chou one cannot identify the residence of both partners. Still, the skeletal outline of a pattern seems clear: a network of marriages connected the most prominent families of four different counties. Some of these marriages spanned a considerable distance in relation to the counties' sizes. Of particular interest is the triangle joining the Tseng, Wang, and Wu families, with at least one marriage and perhaps four connecting the Tsengs and Wus, two connecting the Wus and Wangs, and two connecting the Wangs and Tsengs.

In Northern Sung, then, a certain kind of family spread its marriage net across the empire and, within Fu-chou, across county boundaries. What of Southern Sung? Map 9 shows the Southern Sung marriages within Fu-chou for which the residences of both partners are known. The difference from Map 8 is striking. Here marriages are made largely within a single county; where they connect two counties, one partner lived just across the boundary (thus 4, 9, 10, 17, 18, 21, and 28). One exception meets the eye: the marriage of Lu Chiu-yüan of Chin-ch'i to the daughter of Wu Chien of Lin-ch'uan (20) covers a distance comparable to the Northern Sung marriages and connects families in separate counties, neither of whom lives close to the intervening border. In a sense, though, this exception proves the rule. The Wu family, though living in the prefectural city, is known to have owned land in Chin-ch'i County: in fact this was probably for some time the family's only land.[20] The Wus thus may have been close neighbors of the Lus in respect to their property if not their residence. For the rest, the longest distances covered by Southern Sung marriages here are similar to the shortest in Map 8.

Once again, however, this map of Southern Sung patterns is fragmentary, representing only about thirty marriages. The picture it presents may be augmented by examining other marriages, for which only one partner's residence is known. Often in Southern Sung funerary inscriptions one finds wives, mothers, or sons-in-law listed only by surname, or by surname and given name, with no indication of their family or place of residence. As a rule these are not included in Map 9.[21] Yet in many cases the surname is that of a prominent family known to have lived not far away. Taken individually such cases would be inconclusive, but taken as groups they are highly significant. In Map 10 I have plotted three examples: these are groupings of otherwise unidentifiable spouses sharing a single surname, plotted at the residences

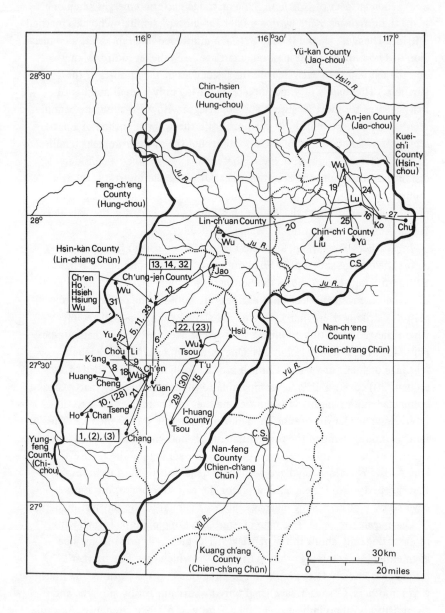

Map 9. Southern Sung marriages within Fu-chou.

(Note: Numbers in parentheses indicate speculative identification of one partner)

1. Marriage of woman of lineage of Ho Yao to father of Chan Ch'ung-p'u. Before 1246. (*WWC* 74/10b–13b)
(2.) Marriage of Ho Chan to woman surnamed Chan. Before 1207. (Ch'eng Chü-fu, *Hsüeh-lou chi* 16/16b–17a)
(3.) Marriage of Ho Meng-lung to woman surnamed Chan. Before 1229. (Ibid., 16/13b–14b)
4. Marriage of daughter of Ch'en P'eng-fei to Chang Mu. Before 1237. (Ch'en Yüan-chin, *Yü-shu lei-kao* 6/6b–9a; *TCLA* 7/20b)
5. Marriage of granddaughter of Ch'en Yüan-chin to Li Chün. Probably by 1275. (*WWC* 75/10b–11b)
6. Marriage of sister of Ch'en Yüan-chin to grandfather of Yüan Hung-tao. Probably between 1200 and 1230. (Ibid., 86/6a–7b)
7. Marriage of woman of Huang family of T'ung-kang to adoptive father of Cheng Sung. Before 1230. (Ho Hsi-chih, *Chi-lei chi* 5b–7b)
8. Marriage of Cheng Sung to woman of K'ang family of Lung-i. By 1271. (*WWC* 74/3a–5a and Huang Chen, *Huang-shih jih-ch'ao* 78/24a–b)
9. Marriage of brother of Chou Ch'i-wu, sister of Wu Ch'eng. Probably by 1275. (*WWC* 72/14a–15a)
10. Marriage of great-aunt of Ho Chung to grandfather of Wu Ch'eng. Probably between 1200 and 1220. (Ibid., 34/1a–3b)
11. Marriage of granddaughter of Ho I to Li Hsiu. Before 1253. (Ibid., 75/10b–11b)
12. Marriage of great-granddaughter of Ho I to Jao Ying-tzu. Probably after 1230; before 1244. (Liu K'o-chuang, *Ho-ts'un hsien-sheng ta-ch'üan chi* 63/6bff.)
13. Marriage of daughter of Ho I to Hsieh Kung-tan. Before 1209. (*TCCJ* 8b/5b–6a)
14. Marriage of granddaughter of Hsiung P'u to Wu Ch'ih. Probably by 1183. (Ch'en Yüan-chin, op. cit. 6/18b–20b)
15. Marriage of Hsü Shih-wei to daughter of Tsou T'ao. (Sun Ti, *Nan-lan-ling Sun shang-shu ta-ch'üan chi* 63/14a–16b; *TCIH* 25/21b)
16. Marriage of Ko Chi-tsu to great granddaughter of Lu Chiu-yüan. Probably by 1275. (*WWC* 80/12a–13a)
17. Marriage of woman of lineage of Li Liu, two generations later, to Yu Te-hung. Probably by 1254. (Ibid., 74/17a–18b)
18. Marriage of Li Chü-ch'uan to woman of Tsou family of Shih-pei. Probably c. 1190. (Ibid., 57/8a–b)
19. Marriage of Liu Kuo-chen to woman of Wu family of Hsin-t'ien. Probably by 1275. (Ibid., 82/2b–3b)
20. Marriage of Lu Chiu-yüan to daughter of Wu Chien. Probably by 1169. (Lu Chiu-yüan, *Hsiang-shan hsien-sheng ch'üan chi* 27/8a–10a)
21. Marriage of Tseng I-yüan to woman of Yüan family. Around 1262. (*WWC* 78/8a–9a)
(22.) Marriage of woman surnamed Tsou to Wu K'un-sun. By 1275. (*WWC* 83/4a–5a)
(23.) Marriage of woman surnamed Tsou to Wu I. Probably before 1262. (*WWC* 79/6a–7a)
24. Marriage of woman of Ko family to man of Wu family of Hsin-t'ien. (Ibid., 79/8b–10a)
25. Marriage of Wu Te-p'u to woman of Yü family of Li-yüan. Probably by 1266. (Ibid., 82/5b–7a)
26. Marriage of Wu Ch'eng to woman of Yü family of Chu-ch'i. Probably by 1275. (Ibid., 32/10a–11a)
27. Marriage of woman of Ko family to man surnamed Chu (of 'a prominent lineage'). Probably by 1260. (Ibid., 79/8b–10a)
(28.) Marriage of Ho Yao to woman surnamed Wu. Probably by 1270. (*WWC* 74/10b–13b)
29. Marriage of Tsou Tsung-kao to daughter of T'u Ta-hsiang. Probably soon after 1127. (*TCIH* 45g/93a–95a)

of the families with whom they marry. In each case these residences are clustered around or near the residence of a prominent elite family of the same surname. These clusterings strongly confirm the short-distance Southern Sung marriage pattern suggested by Map 9. The three examples, it will be seen, are concentrated in the same counties (Chin-ch'i, Ch'ung-jen, and Lo-an) that are best represented in Map 9: these are the examples for which the records of marriage are most frequent; but similar support can be brought to bear from other counties.[22]

One must not press too far the contrast drawn here between Northern and Southern Sung. Even the Northern Sung families most successful in office maintained marriage contacts within their own counties. The Chu family in Map 8, for example, made three recorded marriages within Chin-ch'i.[23] The Tsengs, as we have already seen (p. 55), married a daugther to another Chu family, from their own Nan-feng County, who had yet to produce an office-holder. The granddaughters of Chi Fu (p. 55) had married commoners from their own county, Lin-ch'uan. And among elite families with little or no official pedigree a more localized pattern may have been close to the norm throughout Northern Sung: this emerges from a check of the marriages within Hsieh I's circle of friends and associates.[24] Still the difference in Southern Sung is clear: there is no evidence at all of the kind of intercounty marriage network that Map 8 reveals for Northern Sung. Thus families highly successful in the exams or office, such as the Lus of Chin-ch'i, the Hos, Lis, or Los of Ch'ung-jen, and the Tungs of Lo-an, *do not* marry with each other across county lines. Instead each seems, in its Fu-chou marriages, to be deeply involved in a marriage circle within its own county, connecting it to families far less successful by official standards as well as to some whose success matches its own.[25] The marriages that do cross county lines in Southern Sung seem to do so incidentally, and are not in any clear way different from those that do not. If a marriage network encompassing the entire prefecture existed, it did so only as the summation of a large number of much smaller and more closely focused local and county networks.

What of the other side of Northern Sung marriage? Was Fu-chou, in Southern Sung, still part of a national marriage network? Map 11 shows all

---

(30). Marriage of daughter of Tsou T'ao to T'u Chung-sheng. Between 1127 and 1153. (Sun Ti, op. cit. 63/14a—16b)

31. Marriage of Li Hu to daughter of Wu Hung of Ch'ing-yün canton. Before 1188. (Wei Liao-weng, *Ho-shan hsien-sheng ta-ch'üan chi* 79/6a—8a)

32. Marriage of Huang Ping-yen to woman of Ch'en family. Probably by 1260. (Yü Chi, *Tao-yüan hsüeh-ku lu* 40/9a—10b)

33. Marriage of grand-niece of Ch'en Yüan-chin to granddaughter of Li Liu. By 1275. (Yü Chi, *Tao-yüan hsüeh-ku lu* 40/9a—10b)

the Southern Sung marriages of Fu-chou elite families that crossed prefectural boundaries. A first glance suggests that the network had thinned out markedly at the edges: only seven cases of nineteen lie outside the P'o-yang basin. A closer look at the families involved here shows the change to be even more drastic. Nine of the nineteen marriages were made by just five Fu-chou families, surnamed Ch'ao, Huang, Li, Meng, and Tung. All of these had connections to Fu-chou that were in some way tenuous or anomalous. The Ch'aos, Huangs, and Mengs (A, B, J, and K on the map), all ostensibly of Lin-ch'uan County, have been touched on before: all had first reached office elsewhere, then migrated to Fu-chou in later Northern or early Southern Sung. Similarly, Li Hao was by origin a man of Nan-ch'eng County in Chien-ch'ang Chün, whose grandfather had immigrated to Lin-ch'uan. His sons-in-law (D and E) came from his prefecture of origin. Finally, the Tungs of Lo-an County (L, M, N) lived in Yün-kai canton, originally territory of Yung-feng County in Chi-chou. Their residence did not become part of Fu-chou until the creation of Lo-an in 1149. Throughout the twelfth century the most prominent members of the family, including those whose marriages appear here, maintained their old identity as Chi-chou men, living, teaching, and siting their graves in that prefecture's seat in Lu-ling County, far from the family's ancestral residence.[26] The family seems to have reoriented itself in the direction of Fu-chou by around 1200.[27] We have here, then, four families of recent immigrants and one whose place of residence had been shifted into Fu-chou by bureaucratic fiat – 'administrative immigrants,' in effect. These account for nearly half the known Southern Sung marriages outside the prefecture.[28]

Taking away these marriages – eliminating families whose attachment to Fu-chou was recent – transforms the picture in Map 11: this is illustrated in Map 12. All but two of the remaining marriages (F and G) were made with partners who lived in prefectures sited, like Fu-chou, in the northern area of the P'o-yang drainage basin. Of these, all but one partner (S)[29] came from prefectures that directly bordered Fu-chou. For two of these (I and R) the county of origin is not recorded; but the others lived in counties that shared a border with the Fu-chou counties of their marriage partners. These liaisons, then, may have covered as short a distance as any made within a single county. In short, true long-distance marriages in Southern Sung Fu-chou were, with a pair of exceptions, a peculiarity of families new to the prefecture. The exceptions, the marriages of Lo Tien and his daughter to people from coastal prefectures in Fu-chien circuit, do indeed cover a fair distance, but do not essentially alter a pattern that is clear: indigenous families, in Southern Sung, even when they married outside the prefecture, as a rule stayed well within Fu-chou's immediate region. Of the widely ramified national marriage network of Northern Sung there is no trace.

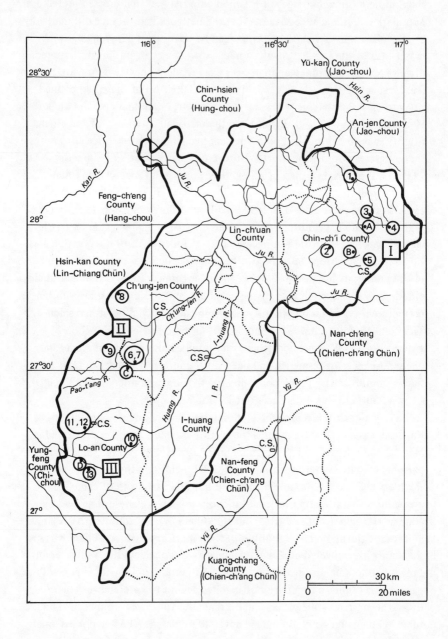

Map 10. Groupings of spouses sharing surnames of nearby families (Southern Sung).

I. A grouping of families with marriage-partners surnamed Yü in Chin-ch'i County.
   A. Huo-yüan, residence of Yü lineage. (Wei Su, *T'ai-p'u yün-lin chi* 6/2b—4a; Li Ts'un, *Ssu-an chi* 14/2a—3b and 24/16a—17a)
   B. Li-yüan, residence of Yü 'line,' family of wife of Wu Te-p'u (*WWC* 82/5b—7a)
   1. Residence of Wu T'ien-kuei (died c. 1273), whose wife is surnamed Yü. (Ibid., 81/8a—9a)
   2. Residence of Liu T'ien-ch'i (fl. c. 1270), whose first wife is surnamed Yü. (Ibid., 86/17b—18b)
   3. Residence of Lu Chiu-hsü (1123—87), whose wife is surnamed Yü. (Lu Chiu-yüan, *Hsiang-shan hsien-sheng ch'üan-chi* 28/3a—4a)
   4. Residence of Ko Keng (1107—90), whose second wife is surnamed Yü; and of his daughter, whose husband is named Yü Pang-kuang. (Ibid., 28/7a—11a)
   5. Residence of Chou Kuei-fang (1253—1313), whose wife is surnamed Yü. (Ch'eng Chü-fu, *Hsüeh-lou chi* 20/14b—16a)
   Compare also marriage no. 25 on Map 9.
II. A grouping of families with marriage-partners surnamed Chou in the Ch'ung-jen County-Lo-an County border area.
   C. Huai-jen, residence of Chou family. (Hung Mai, *I-chien chih, chih-i* 2/6a—b; Huang Chen, *Huang-shih jih-ch'ao* 78/16b—19b, 24a—b)
   6, 7. Residence of Li Yen-hua (1112—92), whose wife is daughter of a 'Chou Kuang of Lo-an County', and of his granddaughter, whose husband is named Chou Shan-fu. (Wei Liao-weng, *Ho-shan hsien-sheng ta-ch'üan chi* 79/4a—6a)
   8. Residence of man surnamed Wu (fl. c. 1160), whose daughter marries a 'Chou T'an of Lo-an.' (Ch'en Tsao, *Chiang-hu ch'ang-weng chi* 35/16b—18b)
   9. Residence of Wu Lung-ch'i, whose wife (1253—1324) is surnamed Chou. (*WWC* 83/9b—11b)
III. A grouping of families with marriage-partners surnamed Tung in Lo-an County.
   D. Liu-fang, residence of Tung family.
   10. Residence of Chang Yüan-ting (1259—1319), whose mother is surnamed Tung. (*WWC* 79/2a—3b)
   11, 12. Residence of Ho Hung-chung (1207—76), whose wife is surnamed Tung; and of Ho Lin, whose wife is also surnamed Tung. (Ch'eng Chü-fu, *Hsüeh-lou chi* 16/16b—17a; Ho Hsi-chih, *Chi-lei chi* 17b—20a)
   13. Residence of Tseng Feng (1140—c. 1208), whose mother is surnamed Tung. (Huang Kan, *Mien-chai chi* 32/8b—9a)

The migrant families, with their wider-ranging pattern, present a fascinating problem. Some of their marriages can be explained by the survival of ties to their old prefectures: thus Tung I marries a woman of Chi-chou (L), and Li Hao gives his daughters to men from Chien-ch'ang Chün (D, E). But some are not so easily explained: Huang Ch'ing-ch'en (B), Meng Huan (K), and Tung Ch'ang-i and his daughter (M, N) all found their spouses as far from their old prefectures as from Fu-chou. Were these families in fact preserving the Northern Sung pattern? The cases are simply too few to answer this question; but it suggests an interesting corollary. Had the Fu-chou elite merely dropped out — perhaps because of reduced opportunities to make connections at long distance — of a national network that then continued without it? To this, at least, the answer seems clearly to be no. A dramatic decline in long-distance marriage in Southern Sung has been shown previously by Robert Hartwell

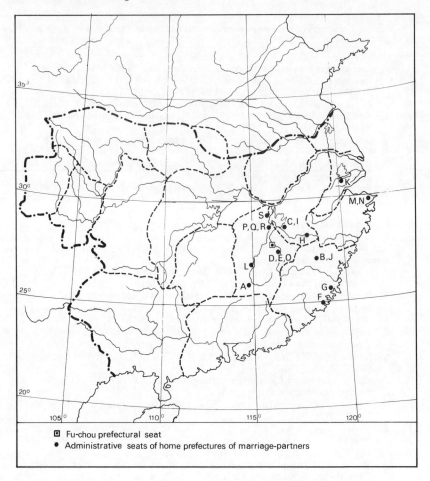

☐ Fu-chou prefectural seat
● Administrative seats of home prefectures of marriage-partners

Map. 11. Southern Sung local elite marriages outside the prefecture.

A. Woman surnamed Ch'en, of Kan-chou, wife of Ch'ao Tzu-yü of Lin-ch'uan County. Probably c. 1150. (Chou Pi-ta, *Wen-chung chi* 75/1a–3a)
B. Woman surnamed Chu, daughter of Chu Yeh and granddaughter of Chu Hsi, of Chien-chou, wife of Huang Ch'ing-ch'en, son of Huang Ssu-yung of Lin-ch'uan County. By 1208. (Huang Kan, *Mien-chai chi* 38/11a–13a)
C. Feng Wen-tsai, of An-jen Hsien in Jao-chou, husband of daughter of Keng of Chin-ch'i County. By 1190. (Lu Chiu-yüan, *Hsiang-shan hsien-sheng ch'üan-chi* 28/7a–11a)
D. Tseng Tsun, of Nan-feng County in Chien-ch'ang Chün, husband of daughter of Li Hao of Lin-ch'uan County. Probably by 1165. (*YLTT* 10422/4b–8a)
E. Teng Yüeh-li, of Nan-ch'eng County in Chien-ch'ang Chün, husband of daughter of Li Hao. Between 1176 and 1178. (Lu Chiu-yüan, op. cit. 16/5a–6a)
F. Liu Yüan-kang, of Chin-chiang County in Ch'üan-chou, husband of daughter of Lo Tien of Ch'ung-jen County. By 1194. (Yüan Hsieh, *Chieh-chai chi* 12/1a–35a)
G. Woman surnamed Ch'en, daughter of Ch'en Chün-ch'ing of P'u-t'ien County in Hsing-hua Chün, second wife of Lo Tien of Ch'ung-jen County. (Chu Hsi, *Chu Wen-kung*

and Ihara Hiroshi: Fu-chou was not unique.[30] The notion that opportunities for broader contacts had declined, however, deserves further comment. The Northern Sung sources show very clearly that the first contact with a potential spouse from outside Fu-chou, the contact that led ultimately to marriage, was very often made in office. Yen Shu may serve as one example:

> When he was dismissed from the Bureau of Military Affairs, he became prefect of Ch'en-chou. [Chang Shih-kao] at just this time was the prefectural judge there. Yen Shu was selecting a wife for his son, and thought only the Chang family a proper choice.[31]

Was this sort of opportunity for contact less available in Southern Sung? Again the answer, for Fu-chou at least, seems to be no. Fu-chou men, indeed men from all parts of the P'o-yang region, had less chance in Southern Sung of reaching the very highest offices.[32] Yet at least forty-six Southern Sung Fu-chou men (excluding immigrants) held some office in the capital and so had the opportunity to meet successful officials from all over the empire. Nor was the capital the only likely setting for such contacts, as Yen Shu's example shows. In Maps 13a–13f I have plotted the major posts held by Fu-chou men at the county, prefectural, and circuit level for Northern and Southern Sung.

---

wen-chi 96/36a)
H. Man surnamed Chang, of Kuei-ch'i County in Hsin-chou, husband of daughter of Lu Chiu-kao of Chin-ch'i County. By 1191. (Lu Chiu-yüan, op. cit. 28/12a–16b)
I. Woman surnamed Ch'en, of Jao-chou, wife of Lu Huan-chih of Chin-ch'i County. Probably by 1170. (Lu Yu, *Wei-nan wen-chi* 38/9b–11b)
J. Woman surnamed Chou, daughter of Chou Wu-chung, of P'u-ch'eng County in Chien-chou, wife of Meng Tse of Lin-ch'uan County. Probably by 1148. (Han Yüan-chi, *Nan-chien chia-i kao* 21/11a–14a)
K. Woman surnamed Jui, daughter of Jui Hui, of Wu-ch'eng County in Hu-chou, wife of Meng Huan of Lin-ch'uan County. (*KHFC* 47/42a–b; *SYHA* 77/12b)
L. Woman surnamed Chou, granddaughter of cousin of Chou Pi-ta, of Lu-ling County in Chi-chou, wife of Tung I of Lo-an County. Probably by 1200. (Chou Pi-ta, op. cit. 75/11b–12a)
M. Woman surnamed Lin, daughter of Lin Pao, of Yin County in Ming-chou, wife of Tung Ch'ang-i of Lo-an County. (Ibid., 72/7a–9a)
N. Lin Tsu-hsia, grandson of Lin Pao, of Yin County in Ming-chou, husband of daughter of Tung Ch'ang-i of Lo-an County. Before 1177. (Ibid.)
O. Cheng Kuo-hua, of Nan-ch'eng County in Chien-ch'ang Chün, husband of woman surnamed Wang of Lin-ch'uan County. Probably by 1235. (Pao Hui, *Pi-chou kao-lüeh* 6/24a–25a)
P. Woman surnamed Lo, daughter of Lo Pi-yüan, of Chin-hsien County in Hung-chou, wife of Wei Ho of Lin-ch'uan County. Probably around 1240. (Liu K'o-chuang, *Hou-ts'un hsien-sheng ta-ch'üan chi* 162/15b–22a)
Q. Woman surnamed Ch'en, of Feng-ch'eng County in Hung-chou, wife of Wu Hao of Ch'ung-jen County. Probably by 1180. (Ch'en Yüan-chin, *Yü-shu lei-kao* 6/17a–18b)
R. Woman surnamed Chao, of Hung-chou, wife of Yen Ta-cheng of Lin-ch'uan County. Probably by 1208. (Ts'ao Yen-yüeh, *Ch'ang-ku chi* 20/19a–23b)
S. Ts'ao Kun, son of Ts'ao Yen-yüeh, of Tu-ch'ang County in Nan-k'ang Chün, husband of daughter of Yen Ta-cheng. Probably by 1227. (Ts'ao Yen-yüeh, loc. cit.)

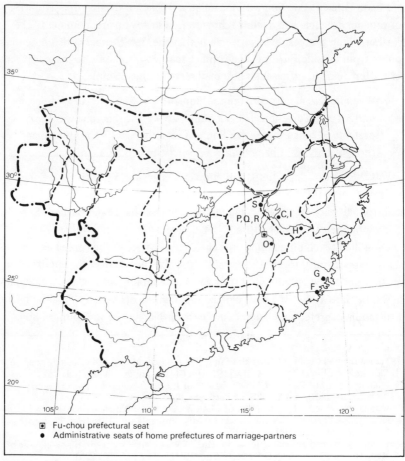

☒ Fu-chou prefectural seat
● Administrative seats of home prefectures of marriage-partners

Map 12. Southern Sung local elite marriages outside the prefecture (excluding recent migrants). See legend for Map 11.

Three points emerge: first, in both periods there was a significant concentration of posts within Fu-chou's own circuit and region; second, this concentration was undeniably more marked in Southern than in Northern Sung; but third, in both periods posts were scattered over much of the empire of the time – in Southern Sung over a much wider area than the Fu-chou elite's marriage network. The men who held these offices had every opportunity to make contacts far from Fu-chou. Ho I, for instance, served as prefect of Ch'üan-chou in Fu-chien circuit, as circuit intendant or assistant intendant in Ching-hu-nan, Che-hsi, and K'uei-chou circuits, and in academic, censoral, and ministerial posts in the capital. Yet his daughter, granddaughter, and great-granddaughter all married into families living in his home county, Ch'ung-jen (11, 12, and 13 in Map 9). His neighbor Li Liu held staff posts in the circuit intendancies of Szechwan and Liang-che circuit, and served as Executive of

Map 13a. County administrators and vice-administrators from Fu-chou during Northern Sung.

the Ministry of Personnel in the capital; but again all the recorded marriages of his sons and descendants lie close to home within Fu-chou (5, 11, and 17 in Map 9, and others not listed). Lu Chiu-yüan held academic posts in the capital, and his son Lu Ch'ih-chih served on the staff of the military inten-dancy of Che-hsi circuit; yet one will search the sources in vain for any Lu who married outside Fu-chou's immediate region.

Southern Sung men not only had opportunities to form ties far from Fu-

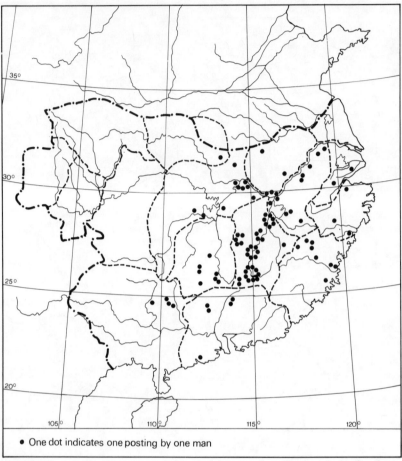

Map 13b. County administrators and vice-administrators from Fu-chou during Southern Sung.

chou: they formed them. This is clearest in the academic sphere: in Southern as in Northern Sung, Fu-chou scholars often found teachers (and Fu-chou teachers their students) far from home. As one example, I have plotted in Map 14 the men who, though not Fu-chou residents, took instruction from Lu Chiu-yüan and called themselves his students. The student–teacher tie was a serious and often a lasting one: men did not form it carelessly. Lu's network of strong personal ties, in this sphere, reached across four circuits, with particular strength (as will hardly surprise historians of thought) in Che-tung circuit.[33] It was not a lack of contacts that kept him, his brothers, his sons, and their daughters from marrying far abroad.

In sum, then, marriage networks contracted doubly between Northern and Southern Sung. On the one hand a clear intercounty network that had

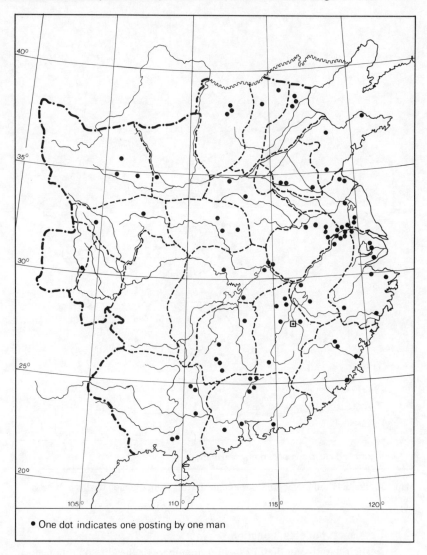

Map 13c. Prefects and prefectural vice-administrators from Fu-chou during Northern Sung.

joined some of Fu-chou's most illustrious families broke down; on the other hand the Fu-chou elite no longer, as a rule, extended its marriage ties to other regions of the empire. Marriage had become localized and, where not localized, regionalized, even while other sorts of connections joining Fu-chou to the rest of the empire — friendship, academic ties, contacts in office — continued undisturbed.

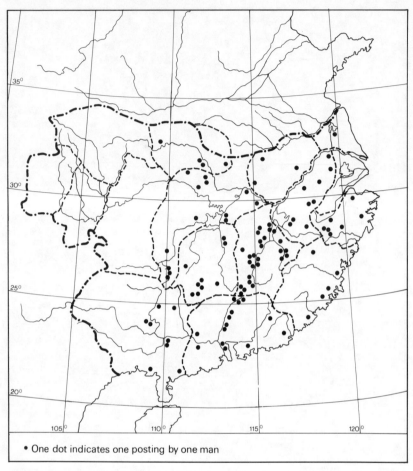

• One dot indicates one posting by one man

Map 13d. Prefects and prefectural vice-administrators from Fu-chou during Southern Sung.

Residence, building, donation

In their day-to-day life in Fu-chou, members of the elite maintained, on the one hand, various private residences and estates; on the other hand, they involved themselves from time to time in the founding, building, or material support of various local institutions, monuments, and architectural landmarks. These might be private studies, libraries, or landscaped gardens, intended mainly for personal use or the entertainment of friends and colleagues; or they might be such 'public' institutions as temples, forts, granaries, bridges, and schools or academies. For some men — much more often in Southern than in Northern Sung — one can map fairly precisely both their residences and the sites where they built or made donations. The evidence, especially for

Map 13e. Officeholders from Fu-chou in circuit administrations during Northern Sung.

Northern Sung, is not all that one might wish; but the outlines of a pattern do emerge.

Map 15 shows the local residences, estates, and sites of construction or donation of two Northern Sung families, the Tsengs of Nan-feng and the Yüehs of I-huang. (The sites are indicated by numbers; the lines join all the sites of one family and are only for convenience of reference, with no significance in themselves.) Both these families, as we have seen, are representatives of a single type, both in their success in exams and office and in their marriage patterns. The map reveals that each ranged rather broadly across counties.

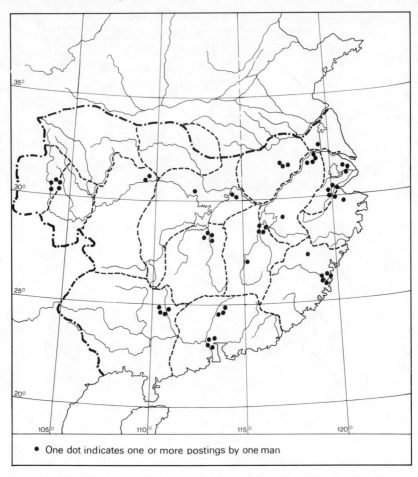

• One dot indicates one or more postings by one man

Map 13f. Officeholders from Fu-chou in circuit administrations during Southern Sung.

The Tsengs, apparently from the beginning, maintained a family residence in Nan-feng's county seat (no. 1), and established or acquired gardens, studios, and a river-viewing tower (2–6) within the city walls. Tseng Chih-yao had already established a large, separate residential estate for his retirement: this was in the neighboring county of Nan-ch'eng, at Ma-ku Mountain, some forty kilometers from Nan-feng city (11). Later, when Tseng Kung's father Tseng I-chan was cashiered and sent home, he came back to establish a new long-term residence in the Fu-chou prefectural city in Lin-ch'uan County, where he had earlier held office and where Kung's grandmother was already living.[34] Tseng Kung and his brothers (Pu and Chao) lived and studied in Lin-ch'uan, and Kung, when he reached office, founded a charitable estate for his family just outside the city (12), about ninety kilometers from the family residence in

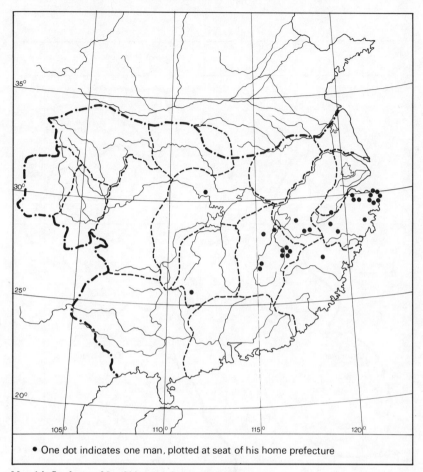

• One dot indicates one man, plotted at seat of his home prefecture

Map 14. Students of Lu Chiu-yüan from outside Fu-chou.

Nan-feng. He also founded a second estate in Chin-ch'i County, but its exact
site is unrecorded.[35] All this cannot be seen simply as a move away from Nan-
feng: connections to the original family home endured. Tseng Kung was
buried at the Buddhist temple Tseng Chih-yao had founded, and his brother
Pu, then at court, obtained a decree granting the temple to the family of a
'Merit Cloister' (*kung-te yüan*)[36] in Kung's honor (10). Still later, Pu built a
temple for a local deity on the border dividing Nan-feng from I-huang County
(8). The family seems to have maintained real connections to two widely
separate places of residence within greater Fu-chou.

For the Yüehs one finds a cluster of five temples, both Buddhist and
Taoist, in the northwestern part of Ch'ung-jen County (including the county
seat), all of which were built by Yüeh Shih or received lands from him

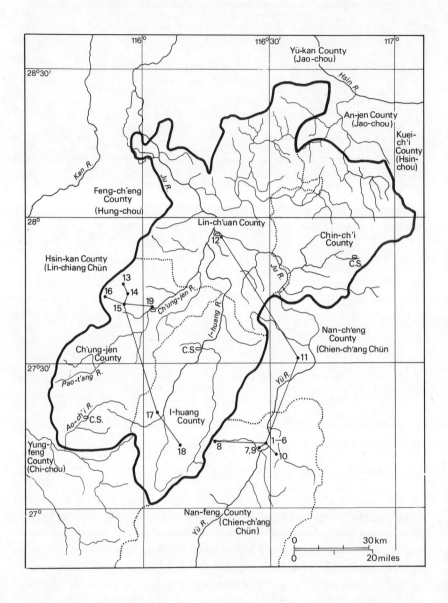

Map 15. Donation, building and residence: the Nan-feng Tseng family and the I-huang Yüeh family.

A. *Tseng family:*

1. Feng-ch'in Quarter, established in honor of Tseng Chih-yao when his sons and grandsons achieved fame: marked the place that had been the family's residence for generations. (*MKNF* 3/5b)
2. Chung-ho Tower, built by Tseng Chih-yao. (Ibid., 3/30a)
3. Study maintained by Tseng Kung. (Ibid., 3/6a; Tseng Kung, *Yüan-feng lei-kao* 17/10a–11a)
4. Chiang Tower, bought and renovated by Tseng Chü. (*MKNF* 3/27b–29a)
5. Nan Hsüan, a study built by Tseng Kung as a place of retirement. (Ibid., 3/25a–b)
6. Jung-ch'in Garden, established by Tseng Chih-yao for his mother on his return from office. (Ibid., 3/18a)
7. Ch'ing-yün Pavilion, built by Tseng Kung. (Ibid., 3/11b)
8. Chün Mountain Shrine, built by Tseng Pu, who also requested and received state recognition for the god in whose honor it was built. (Ibid., 3/8b–9b; Tseng Chao, *Ch'ü-fu chi* 4/4a–6a)
9. Ch'i-shan Ching-she, a retreat and place of study built by Tseng Wu and his brothers for their teacher, a man surnamed Yen. (*MKNF* 3/8b–9b)
10. Hall of Buddhas of Ch'an-tse Temple, built by Tseng Chih-yao; in 1095 officially obtained by Tseng Pu as Merit Cloister for the family, and given new name Ch'ung-chüeh Pao-tz'u Ch'an Temple. (Liu Hsün, *Shui-yün-ts'un kao* 3/4a–6a)
11. Yün Chuang, estate founded by Tseng Chih-yao on his retirement. (*MKNF* 3/30a–b)
12. Charitable estate established by Tseng Kung. (Yü Chi, *Tao-yüan hsüeh-ku lu* 35/2a–3a; Wei Su, *T'ai-pu yün-lin chi* 5/10b–11b)

B. *Yüeh family*

13. An-yüan (Buddhist) Temple: lands donated by Yüeh Shih. (*TCCJ* 2d/34b–35a)
14. Shang-ch'eng (Buddhist) Temple: lands donated by Yüeh Shih. (Ibid., 2d/30b)
15. Chung-shan (Buddhist) Temple: lands donated by Yüeh Shih. (Ibid., 2d/31a)
16. Ch'i-chen (Taoist) Temple: lands donated by Yüeh Shih. (Ibid., 2d/51a)
17. Residence at Huo-yüan. (*TCIH* 13/6a, 25/1b; *KHIH* 5/1a; *CCFC* 11/3b; *WWC* 49/13a)
18. Charitable estate established by family. (*TCIH* 7/4b, 14/23a–b; *KHIH* 3/1b–2b, 18b)
19. Tung-lin (Buddhist) Temple, built by Yüeh Shih, who also donated lands. (*TCCJ* 2d/1b)

(13–16 and 19). Further, a construction record for another temple in the county seat, written by Yüeh Shih himself, records that in his youth he lived north of this temple – no distance is specified, but the same general area is clearly meant.[37] At the same time Yüeh Shih was associated with another place of residence, at Huo-yüan in I-huang County, some fifty kilometers to the south of the Ch'ung-jen seat (17). There is evidence that his family had been associated with, if not resident in, Huo-yüan already by the end of T'ang.[38] In any case, members of his family went on to establish a charitable estate in I-huang, about twenty kilometers farther to the southeast (18). Yüeh Shih himself was buried in Ch'ung-jen, near one of his temples (6):[39] apparently connections with that area had been to some degree maintained.

Thus for both families one finds a binuclear pattern involving two areas of

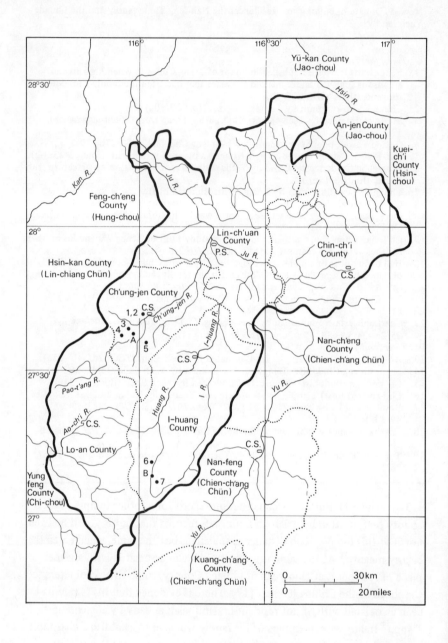

residence, estate-founding, and/or construction activity, with evidence in both cases that simple abandonment of one in favor of the other had not (yet) occurred. In both cases the two areas are in separate counties and, on the prefectural scale, a good distance apart.

Southern Sung men simply did not act this way.[40] Instead, they concentrated their building and donation, and their residences, within relatively small areas of a single county. Examples are legion; there is no space here to map them all. Map 16 shows two more or less typical cases: the Lo family of Ch'ung-jen and the Hou family of I-huang.

There probably was still a tendency in Southern Sung for the men most successful in office to establish new residences; but the moves covered a shorter distance, always within a single county. Thus Li Liu's immediate family moved from the ancestral home (see Map 6) to the county seat, about twenty kilometers away, when Liu reached high office;[41] he himself built in both places,[42] and with the fall of Sung his family returned to the ancestral home.[43] His neighbor, Ho I, at first active around his family's original home in the southern part of the county seat,[44] also opened up a large new residential mountain estate somewhat farther from the seat, ostensibly to escape the city noises.[45] But such moves in Southern Sung never appear to have taken a man or his family out of the general vicinity of their place of origin. The tendency for the range of residence and construction in this period to coincide with the field of marriages is striking.[46] Caution is appropriate, since the evidence from Northern Sung touches only two families. Still, the evidence there is suggests that the change in marriage patterns within Fu-chou was in some degree paralleled by a change in other spheres of local action.

Map 16. Donation, building and residence: the Ch'ung-jen Los and I-huang Hous.

I. A group of sites associated with the Lo family of Ch'ung-jen County (for references see Appendix I, no. 41).
A. Lo residence.
1. The Ta-hua-tsang (Buddhist) Temple, built by Lo Min-te and sons in 1140–52.
2. The P'u-an (Buddhist) Temple, rebuilt by Lo Yen after 1127.
3. The Lung-yen (Buddhist) Temple, rebuilt in 1131–62 and endowed with new properties by Lo Min-te.
4. The Hua-yen (Buddhist) Temple, rebuilt in 1176 with donations from Lo Wei and others.
5. A stone bridge, built between 1165 and 1173 by Lo Pang-yen.
II. A pair of sites associated with the Hou family of I-huang County (for references see Appendix I, no. 19).
B. Hou residence.
6. Lung-chi Fort, built by Hou Ting in 1230.
7. Hall of Buddhas of the Mi-lo Temple, rebuilt by Hou Ting in 1234.

Emigration

In a short piece entitled 'Poems on Thinking of Ying'[47] in his collection
of miscellaneous notes and comments, the *Jung-chai sui-pi,* the Southern
Sung man Hung Mai remarked:

> When officials rise from the fields, and are ennobled as dukes and high
> officers, there are many who call their father's and grandfather's old
> house not fit to live in, and change and renovate their dwellings. Many
> as well are those who, from medicine's being unavailable, or food and
> drink hard to get, move from their villages to the county seat, or from
> the county seat to the prefectural city.

The reference to local moves strikes a familiar note in view of the findings of
the preceding section. But Hung Mai goes on to remark that a longing for
new surroundings often led officials to abandon their home regions entirely:
he offers Ou-yang Hsiu and Su Shih as examples.[48] This peculiar trait of Sung
officialdom was later pointed out, with further examples, by the Ch'ing
scholar Chao I,[49] and has recently been discussed by Japanese researchers.[50]
In Fu-chou, emigration seems once more to differentiate a certain type of
Northern Sung family from the elite families of Southern Sung.

The funerary inscription of Ts'ai Ch'eng-hsi (1035–84; see below, p. 305,
n. 14) tells us that, in the course of his fairly successful career,

> [...] he had travelled to Ching-k'ou, seen its mountains and rivers,
> and delighted in them. He said: 'When I am old, I must return here.'
> [When he died], Chü-hou [his son], in accordance with the instruc-
> tions he had left, chose a spot in Tan-t'u County [...] [and buried
> him there]. He therefore made his residence in Jun-chou; and so they
> became Jun-chou people.[51]

Here 'Ching-k'ou' is an unofficial name for Jun-chou, in Liang-che circuit;
Tan-t'u was one of its counties. The earliest surviving gazetteer of Jun-
chou lists Ts'ai Chü-hou among its *chin-shih,*[52] confirming the move the
inscription reports. Chü-hou and a son, Ts'ai Tse-chi, are included in the Fu-
chou gazetteers' *chin-shih* lists as well,[53] but these lists by themselves are not
sufficient evidence as to whether a family had already abandoned Fu-chou.[54]
Later, the 1124 and 1172 *chin-shih* degrees of a cousin of Ts'ai Ch'eng-hsi
and the cousin's great-grandson also appear in the Fu-chou lists.[55] Here it is
impossible to know whether these too are holdovers on the lists, who had
actually emigrated, or whether this branch of the family had remained in
Fu-chou. In any case, no local record of the family exists for after 1172.

The Ts'ais are in most respects typical of the Northern Sung emigrant
families of Fu-chou. Part of the Tseng family of Nan-feng (the branches of

Tseng Chao and Tseng Pu) similarly removed to Jun-chou, and from there
to other prefectures, breaking contact with the ancestral home by about 1127
(though other branches of the family remained in Nan-feng and Lin-ch'uan).[56]
The Wang family of Lin-ch'uan (see below, p. 305, n. 14) seems to have
begun moving away almost from its first access to office: one branch migrated
to Chen-chou in Huai-nan-hsi circuit,[57] a later branch (the immediate family
of Wang An-shih) to Chiang-ning Fu (modern Nanking) in Chiang-tung
circuit.[58] The Wangs' in-laws, the Wus of Chin-ch'i (see below, p. 305, n. 14),
also diverged, one branch moving to T'ang-chou in Ching-hsi-nan circuit,
another to Ch'ang-chou in Liang-che circuit.[59] The Yüehs of I-huang (see
below, p. 306, n. 14) moved to Ho-nan Fu (Loyang) before the mid eleventh
century, though they returned to Fu-chou at the fall of Northern Sung.[60]

These emigrant families are five of the six I have dealt with already in my
discussion of marriage patterns, who achieved *chin-shih* early in Sung and
went on to produce middling-to-high officeholders by the 1070s. The sixth of
these, the Yen family of Lin-ch'uan, seems to have established a firm presence
in Hsü-chou in Ching-hsi-pei circuit in the first half of the eleventh century,
but evidently never wholly severed its connections to Fu-chou.[61] Thus all six
families of this type tended to establish themselves in other prefectures.

Where did they go? Three, the Ts'ais, Tsengs, and Wangs, moved to a
cluster of three prefectures lying adjacent to one another on either side of the
lower Yangtse, around its junction with the major canal system that connected
the southeast, and ultimately all of the south, with the capital in the north.
These are Jun-chou, destination of the Ts'ais and Tsengs, and Chen-chou and
Chiang-ning Fu, destinations of the two branches of the Wangs. This region
was, in Northern Sung, the major economic nexus of the empire: through
its cities and waterways passed (apart from a private trade of enormous
volume) the six million *shih* of tax rice that the southern circuits shipped
each year to the capital. During much of Northern Sung an official apparatus
of considerable size, centered in this region, was devoted to the administration
and control of these shipments. Both economically and politically, then, this
was a critical region. Two other families, the Yüehs and the Yens, established
themselves, somewhat earlier, in the vicinity of the capital prefectures in the
north. These moves too took the families who made them closer to the
political and economic 'action' of the empire as a whole. One branch of the
Wu family seems anomalous in having moved to T'ang-chou, which was
allied geographically (though not administratively) with the still quite undeveloped Ching-hu circuits of central China; but the other branch, in moving
to Ch'ang-chou, joined the Ts'ais, Tsengs, and Wangs in the critical lower
Yangtse region. The overall tendency is clear: the Fu-chou families of Northern
Sung most successful in exams and office moved, temporarily or permanently,
to the major economic and political centers of Sung China.

In Southern Sung this simply did not happen. Men who reached high office might shift their residences locally; but after 1127 not a single important official or prominent family is known to have left Fu-chou. The change is particularly striking because within the empire as a whole elite migration had by no means ended: we have seen that a number of official families migrated into Fu-chou.

One point needs comment: the two regions that received most of the Fu-chou emigrants are the very two that account for more than half of the long-distance elite marriages in Fu-chou. Does emigration in itself account for the marriage pattern? Is the apparently far-flung network a mirage, and did Fu-chou men and women in fact simply find their spouses, reasonably enough, in their new homes? It might appear so at least in the case of the Wangs: most or all of their marriages in the lower Yangtse region were made after Wang Kuan-chih was buried in Chen-chou, and after Wang I established a residence in Chiang-ning Fu.[62] It is far from clear just when the Wangs cut their ties to Fu-chou, or when the last Wang lived there. Certain of Wang An-shih's brothers seem to have had sons who remained in Fu-chou into early Southern Sung;[63] but perhaps these were exceptions. Perhaps, then, by the 1060s or so the Wangs conceived of themselves as Chiang-ning people and married accordingly. Yet it is hard, on this assumption, to account for the marriage of Wang I's daughter in 1055 to Wu An-ch'ih of P'u-ch'eng County in Fu-chien circuit.[64]

It is even harder to account for the marriages of other families in the same way. Wu Fen moved to T'ang-chou, far from the lower Yangtse, but took a Yang-chou man as his son-in-law.[65] The families of Tseng Pu and Tseng Chao did not establish themselves in Jun-chou before the late eleventh century; yet their father and grandfather had formed marriage ties in the region, and in the adjoining Che valley, several decades earlier;[66] and their similar ties to families in the capital, in the Ching-hu region and in Szechwan seem to have no connection whatever to their migration.[67] The Yens established themselves in Hsü-chou, near the capital, but one of their marriage partners lived in the Huai-nan region just north of the Yangtse, another in the southern reaches of the Che River valley.[68] And how is one to explain the marriages of Wu Yu-lin's daughter (to a man of Ta-ming Fu in the far north) or Wang Chien (to a woman of Yang-chou on the lower Yangtse), when neither Wu nor Wang moved away from Fu-chou? Clearly emigration cannot by itself explain the Northern Sung marriage pattern. Yet just as clearly it cannot be sheer coincidence that the families who emigrated, or who at least established a secondary residence elsewhere (e.g. the Yens), are those who had practiced long-distance marriage most extensively. In the next section I will propose an explanation of the whole complex of changes that has emerged so far.

Family strategies in Northern and Southern Sung

From the evidence presented so far it appears that there was between Northern and Southern Sung a sort of general retrenchment of Fu-chou elite families within their localities. There is good reason to see this retrenchment as the result of a transformation of family strategies for self-advancement and maintenance of status.

Suppose that the head[69] of an imaginary Sung family aimed, first, to place as many of his sons (grandsons, nephews, grandnephews, younger brothers) as possible in office; second, evenutally to see them achieve offices of the highest possible rank. What strategy might best serve these aims? Consider first the number of family offices. In Sung only two routes to office would have been important to a man planning his sons' advancement: the *chin-shih* degree and the privilege of protection (*yin*). (The facilitated degree required too long a waiting period and was too dependent on chance longevity to be relied on by family strategists.) The *chin-shih* degree was clearly the route to be preferred, but it was conditioned strongly by the vagaries of luck and talent: a *chin-shih* can never have been thought a sure thing. Protection, on the other hand, was a nearly automatic route to office for men related to officials of sufficient rank. But to guarantee this privilege to large numbers of dependents it was necessary − if one did not hold fairly high office oneself − to provide oneself somehow with high official kin.

Next consider the second aim: the achievement of high rank − something clearly possible only for a very small proportion of officials. Men who finished near the top of the list in the *chin-shih* exam seem to have moved immediately into career paths that led often to the higher central offices;[70] but for others the rise to high rank, if it occurred, depended chiefly on recommendations from other officials for strategic posts that brought good prospects to their bearers. In particular the so-called academic assignments (*kuan-chih*), overwhelmingly influential for the careers of the men who filled them, depended either (again) on outstanding performance in the exam or on recommendation by high officials.[71] Contemporaries testified that these posts were frequently to be had through private agreements and deals.[72] A family that hoped to advance its members to higher office through recommendations had first to increase and strengthen its connections to other men of rank within the bureaucracy.

For both these aims, then, marriage was a critical resource. Protection was available, within a certain distance, to affines: families that managed to acquire a number of men of sufficient rank as inlaws could count on placing their sons periodically in low-ranking offices. And although recommendation could not legally be obtained from relatives by blood or marriage, a family that formed a large number of marriage ties within the

circle of middle-to-higher officials would naturally increase its chances for
indirect connections (through shared affinal ties to some third family, or
through marriage to a family with useful non-kin connections) to men whose
recommendations would be valuable.[73] Both aims, in sum, could be advanced
by spreading one's marriage net widely among families of established official
background. Limiting one's marriages geographically would serve little
purpose and might be counterproductive. Within one's home locality one
might maintain ties to (in official terms) less illustrious families as a prop
to one's local position and to reinforce one's economic base; but one would
also seek out spouses from officially prominent families both within the
prefecture, regardless of district, and in other regions entirely if that was
where they were to be found.

Why should a family pursue these aims? So far I have treated the two as
separate, but they would more probably be aspects of a single strategy: one
might in fact require the other. First, the chances of any one man's reaching
high office were shaky enough (even assuming the best of prospects, early
death often intervened) that families who made it their central goal will have
been merely reasonable if they tried to maximize the number of their entries.
Despite the disadvantaged status of protection as a route to office, still, in
absolute numbers, a good many high officials began their careers in this
way.[74] Second, placing as many sons and grandsons as possible in office
would increase the number of at least reasonably attractive sons-in-law that
one could offer other families. Thus where the ultimate aim was to reach
high office, maximizing the *number* of offices would follow logically. It is
not difficult to understand in theory why a father might pursue high office
for his sons: high office meant presence at court, access to the emperor; it
meant a part in the ruling of the empire, influence over decisions that might
affect the lives of all the elite. The family that sought these things, then, was
well advised to find marriage partners in families with office.

Now imagine a second Sung family. Unlike the first, this one aimed
neither to gain office for as many of its members as possible nor (at least
as a matter of family strategy) to advance its members to the highest possible
rank. Rather it sought only to guarantee that some members would from time
to time reach office, both in order that at least some members of the family
might maintain the various legal privileges associated with *kuan-hu* (official
household) status, and for the sake of the social prestige that officeholding
members reflected on their families. A family with these goals would be
adequately served by concentration on the exam system (both for the
occasional *chin-shih* and for the slightly more frequent facilitated degree)
and, especially in the early stages of its rise, on other routes to minor ranks,
such as reduced-price sales of grain in time of famine or bandit defense in

periods of local disorder. For these latter routes, and for regular access to the exams, the best foundation would be to maintain an abundant family property and to establish close social relationships with other wealthy, powerful or influential families in one's own locality. A solid property base and firm involvement in local elite social networks would serve, in periods when one's family might be out of office, to preserve the family's local position and maintain a foundation from which later generations could again reach office. Since officeholding, while still important, need not be required of *every* son, and since there were many other, and some better, sources of wealth, it would make sense to diversify the family's commitments, sending some sons into the exams, some into trade, some perhaps into military service or militia leadership, and training some as managers of the family property. It would be highly advantageous too to use marriage to bind local connections, and there would be no special value in marriage with more prominent families farther off, since their support might be of little use in a local context. Thus from families who did not aim chiefly to reach high office one would expect a marriage pattern concentrated in their own locality and region, with the official rank (if any) of their partners not necessarily determining their choice.

The changes in marriage patterns that have been traced from Northern to Southern Sung reflect, I would argue, a shift from the first to the second strategy. Northern Sung families, following the first, married out; Southern Sung families, following the second, married close to home. What is crucial here is that the Northern Sung strategy would be available chiefly, perhaps only, to those already established in office: a family would not, until at least one man held office, be a desirable match for families elsewhere who pursued the same strategy. Thus the marriages in Map 7, as we have seen, were almost all made *after* the Fu-chou families had reached office through the *chin-shih* exam. As evidence from the other side we have the case of Hsieh I and Hsieh K'o (see Chapter I, pp. 49–52): as we have seen, neither they nor any member of their family before them held office. They were prominent as poets both locally and nationally in their own lifetimes; they were joined by marriage connections (in Hsieh K'o's case) to officeholders within the Fu-chou elite. Yet even despite friendships and disciple–master relationships with one of the most prominent officeholding families of North China, the Lüs, their own family, it seems, never married outside the prefecture. At the national level – though not at home – office was the key to marriage.

Other changes from the Northern to Southern Sung followed the same shift in strategies. A family that sought marriage partners from the important officeholding families of its own prefecture would be well served by extending its presence in other respects – residence, donation, etc. – over a wide area of the prefecture. A family that aimed instead to strengthen its local base and position, and to make marriages close to home, need not spread its resources so thin. Eventually, a family that hoped to perpetuate itself in high office and to maintain its position in a national marriage network might think it advantageous to move to an area where day-to-day life would bring it more often into contact with officials and men from officeholding families. The areas which received the Northern Sung emigrants from Fu-chou, because of their economic and political centrality, were not only among the most successful in the empire in producing officials – this, after all, was true of Fu-chou's own region – but also, *unlike* Fu-chou's region, had heavy concentrations of official posts through which higher-ranking officials were likely to pass: court posts in the case of the capital and its region; key regional financial positions in the case of the lower Yangtse. Thus to emigrate to these regions meant to increase one's chances of coming to know men from the most successful families from all parts of China. On the other hand, for a Southern Sung family concerned to keep its strong local base, emigration would not be attractive unless firm and rapid integration into the existing local social networks of the destination were assured; I have argued that this was unlikely.

Yet even a family whose chief concern was its local base – a family with no fundamental interest in emigration – might be compelled to emigrate, if the local base became difficult or impossible to maintain. The Ch'aos and Mengs, for instance, apparently took up permanent residence in Fu-chou only after their homes in the north were lost to the conquering Chin at the fall of Northern Sung. Other immigrants, in Southern Sung, generally came from parts of China closer than Fu-chou to regional or national centers:[75] in this respect these moves were just the opposite of those made by Northern Sung Fu-chou men. It is tempting to see here an almost forced movement from more to somewhat less densely populated (and so less land-poor) areas, as elite families tried to plant firm roots in a local soil – if not in their own original home, then somewhere else.

In the light of all this, we may recognize in a passage from the household manual of Yuan Ts'ai, quoted in part earlier, perhaps a peculiarly Southern Sung view of a son's proper ambitions.

> The son of a gentleman, if he has no hereditary stipend to maintain him, and no real estate to rely on, but wants to make a plan for serving his parents and supporting his dependents, can do no better than be a scholar (*ju*). One whose talent is so fine that he is able to study the *chin-shih* curriculum may, if of the highest quality, take a degree and reach wealth and office, or, if of lesser quality, open his gates and offer instruction, thus receiving a teacher's stipend. One unable to study the

chin-shih may, if of higher quality, work with brush and paper at writing letters for others, or, if of lesser quality, punctuate texts and work as a tutor to children. If one is incapable of being a scholar, then medicine, the Buddhist or Taoist clergy, agriculture, commerce, and the miscellaneous arts may all support life without disgracing one's forebears. Any of them may properly be done.

What is most striking here is not only the range of occupations open to a 'gentleman's' (*shih-ta-fu*) son, but the premise that lies behind the whole: that office, scholarship, and the rest are necessary only for the man with neither 'hereditary stipend' nor 'real estate' to rely on. Where local position is the standard, evidently, wealth comes crucially to the fore.

The explanation offered here for the changes in elite behavior between Northern and Southern Sung — a shift from a national strategy centered on high office to a basically localist one, seeking occasional office as one element of status but not concentrating on bureaucratic position above all else — essentially parallels, with some elaboration and with certain differences of focus, the analysis proposed by Robert Hartwell in his provocative and profoundly important recent study of China's transformation between middle T'ang and middle Ming.[76] The Northern Sung families of Fu-chou who married nationally and emigrated correspond roughly to Hartwell's 'professional elite'; the Southern Sung elite that married locally and stayed at home, and those Northern Sung families, less successful in office, who were unable to pursue the national marriage strategy, are, more or less, Hartwell's 'gentry.' The data offered here on marriage distance with the prefecture and on patterns of residence, donation, and construction, not available to Hartwell in his nationally-focussed research, strengthen the case for a fundamental shift toward localism. My evidence on the behavior of Northern Sung non-officeholders with connections outside Fu-chou (such as the Hsiehs) confirms the essentially bureaucratic orientation of the 'national' strategy.

Some caution, however, is in order. Hartwell treats the professional elite and gentry, in Northern Sung, as distinct groups deliberately pursuing different strategies. This may in part reflect the empire-wide perspective of his research. A division between two sorts of families, distinguished most crucially perhaps by their relative success in producing high officeholders in consecutive generations, may appear particularly salient at the national bureaucratic level; for here a history of success may make all the difference in a family's marriage prospects and factional influence. But from a local perspective, and judging once again by the standard of social interaction and association, the distinction seems overdrawn. It is hard, in Fu-chou at least, to see two clearly separate groups. Some families married extensively far from home; but the same families, as we have seen, made other marriages within their own counties, sometimes forming connections to families without any history of office of their own. Men clearly outside Hartwell's professional elite, men excluded from the national marriage network by their families' lack of office, formed strong connections of other kinds to families of distant origins and of the highest bureaucratic pedigree: the Hsiehs, with their ties to the Lüs, are an example. The collected works of Wang An-shih and Tseng Kung, high office-holders from Fu-chou's most illustrious 'professional elite' families, are filled with evidence of their interaction, as friends and rough social equals, with men who belong, in Hartwell's terms, to Fu-chou's 'gentry.' In moving away from Fu-chou, families like the Wangs and Tsengs did in the end set themselves apart — literally and physically — from those who stayed behind. But to show that this step marked their departure from one social group and entry into another, one would have to show that after the move they drastically altered their patterns of contact and association, and not only in geographic terms: that they interacted more exclusively than before with other members of the 'professional elite.' This, I suspect, one could not show. I would argue then that there were in Northern Sung not two distinct social groups, but one broad group whose members varied widely (and probably continuously rather than dichotomously) in opportunity and success.

If this is so — if no clear boundary of social interaction distinguishes two groups within the Northern Sung elite — it would be somewhat surprising to find two (and only two) distinct strategies of advancement — one a 'national' or 'bureaucratic' strategy, the other an anticipation of the 'localist' strategy of Southern Sung — pursued as deliberate alternatives to one another. The evidence as it stands is consistent, I think, with quite a different view: that the elite as a whole shared the ultimate goal of high office, but that the surest means to that goal were available (in the case of long-distance marriage) or even useful (in the case of emigration) only to families who had already achieved office. For their fellows without this qualification, the first step to high office — office itself — remained to be achieved; and for this a concentration on wealth, education, and connections at home was surely the most appropriate, if not the only, strategy available. Thus even where these less successful families of Northern Sung seem to anticipate most clearly the behavior of the Southern Sung elite — in their marriages in particular — they may simply be pursuing the first stage of a strategy with quite different final aims, a strategy (if it succeeded) whose later stages will take them in sharply different directions. If so, closer inquiry should perhaps reveal differences between the two — the Northern Sung 'first stage' and the strategy of Southern Sung — that would reflect their differing ultimate goals. In Northern Sung, for example, the prefectural examination at the capital in K'ai-feng drew thousands of candidates from across the empire, who chose to try to qualify for the succeeding *chin-shih* exam there rather than in their home prefectures. Many of these were men from families without previous office. In Southern Sung the capital prefectural exam at Hang-chou never attained equivalent importance. Were the candidates of Northern Sung seeking, already at this stage, to establish a presence and form connections in the capital that would serve them afterward? Were such connections of less interest to the candidate of Southern Sung? Other, similar examples, once the question is raised, may not be hard to find; the issue demands further study. For the present, however, I would suggest that where Hartwell sees in the Northern Sung/Southern Sung shift one group, previously distinct, being absorbed into another group and so adopting its-strategy, we see instead simply the replacement, for the elite as a whole, of one broadly shared strategy by another.[77]

Why should strategies have shifted in this way? There is much work to be done before this question can be answered confidently; but any likely answer, or part of an answer, will surely take one of two forms. First, the Northern Sung goals may have become undesirable. Second, they may have become, no matter how desirable, unfeasible. What might have made high office less desirable? In the first place – to anticipate in part the issues of latter chapters – there is reason to think that the center exerted less power over the prefectures and counties in Southern than in Northern Sung, and hence, on the one hand, that central office yielded fewer direct benefits, and, on the other hand, that influence over central decisions was less relevant to an elite family's day-to-day life, wherever it might choose to live. At the same time, one of the most prominent intellectual tendencies of Southern Sung, represented by Chu Hsi among others and deriving from Ch'eng I in Northern Sung, took a rather pessimistic view of central politics and questioned whether a man of high moral character could, in the near term at least, achieve much there. This tendency may have reinforced the effects of any practical decline in the significance of central office; its own origins, as Wm. Theodore de Bary and Michael Freeman have argued, lay at least in part in the factional conflict surrounding the reform program of Wang An-shih in the 1070s.[78] The factional struggles of middle and later Northern Sung may also have played a more direct role in making high office less and less desirable, by making it more and more dangerous. The man caught out on the wrong side might face – apart from his own exclusion from office – the ostracism of his sons from the examinations, like Tseng Chao[79] among others, or banishment to the malarial south, like Su Shih. At the beginning of Southern Sung the murder of the hawkish general Yüeh Fei by the 'peace party' of Ch'in Kuei – however much later regimes might condemn the deed – could only be read as upping the factional ante still further.

If the Northern Sung aims became less desirable in Southern Sung, did they also become less feasible? Again the factionalism of late Northern Sung may be crucial: it is to this that Hartwell, for instance, gives especial explanatory weight. A man could not now avoid choosing sides, once he rose to a certain level; but choosing sides in turn almost guaranteed that later on, when the other side was in, his family would be out. It may have seemed less and less rational to plan one's marriages, and much else, in order to gain continuous access to court, when the new, fiercer style of court politics would periodically make access difficult or impossible. Still, it was not only at the top that the older strategy could be made unfeasible. The increasing local disorders of Southern Sung, not only in Fu-chou but almost everywhere in China, may have made it far more difficult to maintain wealth and property — particularly at a distance — and so have forced families to plan for the preservation of their local position and property base above all else.

In what proportion each of these factors contributed to a change in family strategies must remain for now uncertain. What is certain is that a number of tendencies of his time could have converged to impel a Southern Sung man to direct his attention and ambitions less toward matters central and bureaucratic and more toward his own locality and community. If the change was partly conditioned by developments in central politics, it may well have exerted its own influence on those politics in turn. This is not the place to explore this issue at length. Still it should at least be noted that one prime means of factional recruitment and expansion was, after the change, no longer available. A faction leader in Northern Sung who hoped to expand his political base to include bureaucrats from regions other than his own had the network of interprefectural and interregional marriages to work with. Here were pre-existing ties, with a certain inherent content of moral duty and reciprocal obligation, which might be exploited, at second and third removes, to recruit followers whom otherwise the leader might never have come to know. In Southern Sung these ties were no longer available. What other ties between elites whose origins lay in different regions could stand in their place? Perhaps mainly *academic* ties: master—student connections, or the relation of student to fellow student. One would expect academic connections, then, to become in Southern much more than Northern Sung a major means of factional recruitment and political alliance.[80] (This is not to say that men chose their teachers with politics in mind, but simply that once established, the tie might sometimes be used for political ends.) It cannot be wholly coincidence that one of the most bitter factional conflicts of Southern Sung — the struggle over 'false learning' in the late 1190s — focused precisely on issues of scholarship and of master—student connections?[81] The effects of the change may indeed have been permanent. The recurring political role of private local academies and of academic or literary societies from the Southern Sung through the Ch'ing, and the attempts of courts and emperors to abolish, control, or coopt them have their origins, perhaps, in a partial substitution of academic for affinal connections in faction-building that first takes place in Southern Sung.[82]

Before concluding the argument of this chapter, this seems the place to return to an issue raised in the last one. We have seen that a very significant number of Fu-chou elite families first emerge into the view of the sources during the early decades of Southern Sung. In part this too may be the consequence of the changes then taking place in elite strategies. If elite families, including those already in office, gave new attention to maintaining a firm local position through marriage and other social ties, and so withdrew from — or more precisely dissolved — the former national marriage network, they must have increased the number and strength of the ties, whether of marriage, friendship, or collegiality, that connected them to other families in their own locality. In effect, established elite families of Northern Sung pedigree will have had to reach further 'down' into the society of their own localities for partners in marriage and other joint social enterprises. The 'new' families, now with greater access to guarantee for the exams (thus a greater chance of producing degreeholders), and with newly multiplying connections to other families likely to have left records, thus achieved a degree of local note that made them likely to be mentioned in the sources still available. Seen from one angle, what went on here may be 'social mobility'; seen from another, it was a local expansion and internal ramification of the elite social network. In any case the emergence of regional groupings of 'new' families such as the Wus, Ch'ens, Lis, Los, and Hos of Ch'ung-jen County, or the militia families of Chin-ch'i County, which we have seen in Chapter 2, must in part find its explanation here.

In this chapter I have traced a pattern of changes in the behavior of the Fu-chou elite between Northern and Southern Sung, changes that suggest a broad redirection of elite strategies toward local position and local concerns. The strategies themselves must chiefly be inferred from actions: with few exceptions, Sung men do not, in their writings that have come down to us, tell us their thoughts and plans in the areas of life in question here. In the chapter that follows I will turn to forms of evidence that seem to speak more directly of the Sung elite's thoughts, in order to argue that the change in strategies proposed here was paralleled by a transformation in ideal notions and public models of the proper role of the gentleman in society.

4

ELITE IDEALS AND THE 'LOCAL GENTLEMAN'

In 1182 Lu Chiu-yüan wrote to one Ch'en Shou, then vice-administrator of Fu-chou. Recently, as he told Ch'en, he had spoken with several friends who had some reputation as administrators of counties; the conversation had focused on 'matters of the relationship between a prefecture or county, its clerks, and the people:'

> On the whole, their view was that the prefecture or county should not be concerned with accumulated arrears [in tax payments]. What people call 'accumulated arrears' are all merely nominal obligations with no correspondence to reality [*yu-ming wu-shih*]; they are simply an excuse for provocations and disturbances by clerks. Someone who knows how to administer a county will, without fail, ask the prefecture to [allow him to] hand in each month only the money for that month and, if there are old arrears, to shelve them and wait until later on. If one hands them in at a relaxed pace and according to the current situation at the time, then the county will be well managed. Someone who is good at administering a prefecture must likewise reach an agreement with the counties to make full payment each month of that month's money, without asking about arrears. In this way one may have real gains [*shih-te*]. If one is only concerned with adjusting accumulated arrears, in the end he will have to levy new monies, taking without recompense. This will only create an occasion for bribe-taking by crafty clerks. [. . .] If it should happen that the Minister of Finance or the Director-General urges one to adjust accumulated arrears, one absolutely does not respond. No matter how they scold in their official communications, one absolutely disregards it [. . .] These too are the established views of those who know how to administer a prefecture or a county. I have presumed to report them to you: perhaps there is something in them worthy of adoption.[1]

Here, Lu – a serving official himself – coolly advised a local administrator in his own home prefecture to disregard the instructions of his superiors on questions of taxation and revenue. In a follow-up letter Lu pressed the point home again. The advocates of various political views at the present day, he suggested, could be divided into those for whom the people were chief and those who saw themselves as chief.

> Those whose proposals treat the people as chief will not fail to restrict the depravities of the clerks and relieve the strength of the people. If, as may be, one cannot then avoid falling short in finances and revenues, and so does not gain the confidence of his superiors, it is best that the blame should fall on oneself. As for those whose proposals treat themselves as chief, they will invariably start by regarding the management of finances and revenues as their major task, and will invariably use the excuse of arrears and deficits to weaken and diminish the people.[2]

The local official, then, should act as a buffer, seeking — even at his own peril — to shield the local people from a revenue-seeking state that might try to insist on extracting its past-due taxes.

There can be no doubt that Lu is talking of Fu-chou: he is not dealing in the abstract. The passage from the first letter leads directly into a recommendation of a man who Lu feels may be of some help:

> My kinsman has a relative by marriage, one Wang X, who is the new administrator of Lo-an county. This man is an extremely capable official; he handles matters carefully and confidentially; he knows how to run a family. If he were made responsible for some matter, there would surely be [results] well worth seeing.

In a similar way Lu follows his discussion of those who 'make themselves chief' with this advice:

> I hear that recently the steps taken by county administrator Su are highly questionable. His only thought is to get things done quickly; he has not the slightest concern for the people. His measures are often laughable. It would be my good fortune if you might find a way to reprove him.

In these two letters to Ch'en, then, Lu does three things: he urges, in rather strong terms, a basically localist, anti-fiscalist view of a local official's responsibilities; he recommends an in-law, already holding office in another of Fu-chou's counties, for special responsibilities at the prefectural level; and he urges the disciplining of the administrator of his own home county, Chin-ch'i. In short, Lu Chiu-yüan here confronts a Fu-chou local official in the role of *advocate* — for his prefecture and county, or for a particular view of their interests — and in the role of personal *intermediary* — in this case for his in-law, Mr Wang.

These were accustomed roles for Lu. His collected works preserve a rare wealth of letters to officials serving in Fu-chou or at the circuit capital, written mainly during the 1180s and 1190s: in most of these he draws attention to some local problem and urges — sometimes implicitly, but more often explicitly — some corresponding action. Through all the letters run two consistent themes: warnings of the ill intentions and untrustworthiness of government clerks and their powerful local patrons or allies; and attacks on the negligence or downright malfeasance of local officials, past and present. His specific concerns are chiefly economic: he writes to urge the elimination of various special levies;[3] to solicit official funds and sanction for a charitable 'normal-purchase' granary to be managed by his brother;[4] to protest plans to sell off various local estates, nominally under state ownership but long since the *de facto* property of their 'tenants,' to private holders;[5] and — again and again — to notify officials of impending problems with the Fu-chou rice crop.[6] In a unique example he writes to support an unnamed felon's confession and plea for leniency.[7] Throughout, he uses the self-humbling formulas appropriate to letters of this kind; yet it is clear that Lu sees himself as a full and legitimate participant in the affairs of his home district. To Ch'en Shou he writes:

> I deeply regret that I cannot be at your side to assist you in some small way [. . .] When in any matter there is something you would deign to ask me, let me know in a scrap of paper giving a rough account, and I will bend my inadequate efforts to it.

Lu Chiu-yüan's activity as local advocate to officialdom is exceptionally well documented; but the role was hardly his alone. A number of the clearest other examples are worth listing here:

1. In 1100 the assisting councillor Tseng Pu intervened at court to achieve official recognition and 'enfeoffment' of a local popular deity in his home county, Nan-feng. This resolved a longstanding issue that had been a source of some dissatisfaction at home.[8]
2. Teng Chou, a Ch'ung-jen County man and a prefectural graduate in 1134, proposed to the vice-administrator of his county that the banditry and disorder in its southwestern region could be controlled, and the local population assured of peace, if a new county were established on part of Ch'ung-jen's territory. This was in the 1140s; in 1149 the petitions sent up by local and circuit officials in response to Teng's proposal were granted, and Lo-an County was created.[9]
3. In 1175 the Chin-ch'i man Liu Yao-fu, then in the capital, approached the high official Chou Pi-ta with a proposal for a reorganization of his county's militia that he thought would induce one important but reluctant family to participate.[10]

4. In 1175 Lu Chiu-ling, brother of Lu Chiu-yüan, wrote to the administrator of Chin-ch'i County outlining his own view on the proper organization of local defense.[11]

5. Wu K'o-ch'eng of Lo-an County, a local gentleman and scholar active in the late twelfth and early thirteenth centuries, is said to have been sought out by each new county administrator for his advice both on scholarly matters and on 'the essentials of caring for the people.'[12]

6. In 1268 the Nan-feng gentleman Liu Hsün joined with several office-holding natives of his prefecture (Chien-ch'ang Chün) to make a special appeal to the court, taking note of the grain riots and general banditry that had followed recent flooding in Nan-feng, and asking that the district be exempted both from the state's Harmonious Purchase program and from normal land taxes: this was granted.[13]

7. In 1271, during a famine, the Lo-an county man Yu Te-hung, hearing that the county administrator was planning a program of relief sales in which grain would be sold every third day, persuaded him to enlist the aid of local wealthy families for a shift to daily sales.[14]

8. During the same 1271 famine, the Lo-an prefectural graduate and historiographer Cheng Sung, son of a militia leader, intervened with the prefect to excuse from punishment a neighboring family that was refusing to sell its grain.[15]

9. At around the same time the Lin-ch'uan gentleman Yen Fu-hsin advised the prefect of the very high rates of interest — often reaching 100 percent — charged by the wealthy households of Fu-chou, and urged the prefect to prohibit such practises. The prefect issued a public notice urging the rich to bear in mind the ties of mutual dependence that bound them to the poor.[16]

10. Yüan Li-Ch'u (b. 1250) of Ch'ung-jen County, son of an officeholder and himself a failed candidate in the prefectural exam, before the fall of Sung had 'stayed as a guest in the offices of the prefecture and the county, taking part in the planning and discussions as if he were a subordinate official.'[17]

In calling all these men 'local advocates' I am not implying that they represented some single network of local interests, or that the local elite spoke with a united voice. Quite the contrary: some of those listed here may have had entirely different views of the local interest (or conflicting personal interests of their own), may even have worked at cross purposes. Yu Te-hung and Cheng Sung seem good examples. What unites all these cases is that in each of them a Fu-chou man, in order to influence the course of local events and the actions of government, intervenes directly and openly with local or central officials — not in his formal capacity as an official himself (though several clearly use their official status to good advantage), but simply as a native, with a native's interest in and knowledge of the affairs of his own district. Each seems to take for granted that to influence the governing of his home is a part of his proper role.

Nine of the ten cases date, like Lu Chiu-yüan's letters, from Southern Sung. The one Northern Sung example, Tseng Pu's intervention on behalf of a local deity, seems somehow on a different plane from the rest, which largely involve fundamental fiscal, economic, and military questions – issues in which local and state interests were most likely to conflict. In asking the court to honor a deity, Tseng asked it to make no particular concession, to take no particular risk. In asking officials to abolish certain levies, exempt certain counties from basic taxes, organize local defense in certain ways, or strike at certain financial practises of wealthy families, men like Lu Chiu-yüan, Liu Yao-fu, or Yen Fu-hsin asked for real sacrifices, demanded real risks. In drawing distinctions – as Lu Chiu-yüan did – between local interests, or even political morality, and the demands of the state, or in resisting – as Cheng Sung did – the efforts of officials to make their will effective, they took, perhaps, real risks themselves. These men of Southern Sung, in short, were injecting themselves into local government in the most fundamental ways.

There is simply no sign of this in the Northern Sung sources. The collected works, funerary inscriptions, and biographies of high Northern Sung officials like Wang An-shih, Yen Shu, Tseng Kung, and Tseng Chao preserve no record of their open intervention with local or central officialdom on behalf of their prefecture, their county, or any clear local interest whatever. Some of these men, of course, spent much of their lives away from Fu-chou, first accompanying fathers at their posts, then holding offices of their own; and many, as we have seen, eventually established new permanent residences in other parts of China. But absence cannot explain everything: Lu Chiu-yüan, after all, wrote his letters to Ch'en Shou from a capital post; Liu Yao-fu acted in the capital to influence (so he hoped) local government policy at home. Wang An-shih, Tseng Kung, and the rest were active in Fu-chou affairs in other ways – building temples and composing inscriptions for them; attending local academies; corresponding, when away, with friends and relatives at home; even writing to Fu-chou officials. What we do not see them doing is intervening in local government, seeking benefits for their counties, their neighborhoods, or their families.

This omission seems even more striking when one detects it in the works and life stories of men like Hsieh I and Hsieh K'o: Northern Sung men who held no office and lived virtually their entire lives in Fu-chou. It is from this sort of man – the 'resident gentleman' or 'gentleman in retirement', as funerary inscriptions often call him – that one might expect the deepest involvement in the affairs of his own county and his own prefecture. In some respects, as we shall see, the expectation is confirmed: the biography of a man of this kind, even in Northern Sung, often dwells at some length on his charities to his lineage, to his neighborhood, and to the local people at large. A man (and sometimes a woman) may be shown dispensing grain to the hungry, supplying coffins to the bereaved poor, providing medicine and doctors to the sick; but again, he will not – in Northern Sung, and in Fu-chou sources – be shown counselling local officials how best to manage his county.

What does this mean? Did Southern Sung elite men play a wholly new local role, a role unknown in Northern Sung? Had Northern Sung men left local government to local officials, and concentrated (if they held office) on governing other places and influencing larger policy decisions, or (if they did not) on aiding their neighborhood in strictly private and personal ways? This seems extremely unlikely. To believe it, one would have to suppose either that Northern Sung men did not use the resources they had – prestige, connections, personal eloquence – to influence matters that were important to them; or else that they thought local government, the practical fulfillment (or annulment) of central decisions, unimportant. One can believe that Fu-chou came to seem less and less important to men like Wang An-shih or Yen Shu as they rose in the official hierarchy and shifted their residences elsewhere; but what of men like the Hsiehs and their circle, and the many others – officeholders or not – who never moved away? As family strategies, in Southern Sung, shifted from a focus on central office back to the locality, it may be that men spent more of their time than before trying to influence the conduct of local government; but it is not plausible that until this time they had hardly tried at all. It seems to me that the change was probably more historiographic than historical, and reflects a broader change in the way local action was *viewed*. It was now more widely accepted than before that the local elite would, and even should, intervene in local government; the intervention was celebrated where once it would have been passed over in silence. Compilers of collected works and authors of biographies now transcribed papers or reported anecdotes that once they would have omitted as unfitting or, at best, as of no importance for an understanding of the character and position of their subject. Though a man's official responsibilities, if any, gave him no formal authority in his own county or prefecture, it was now thought proper that, as a gentleman, he should speak and act openly on their behalf.

Perhaps one may go further and say that in Southern Sung the role of 'local gentleman' in general commanded new respect; that local commitments and involvements were now thought as deserving of praise as, for instance, performance in office. There is other evidence that suggests precisely this. Among the institutions of official religion in Fu-chou (as elsewhere) in the

Sung were certain shrines or altars (*tz'u*) at which sacrifices were offered to figures of the recent or distant past who in life had been connected in some way to Fu-chou and who, for various reasons, were thought worthy of local reverence. Often (though not always) placed at or near the official prefectural or county school, these shrines are presumably the institutional ancestors of the sacrificial tablets for former worthies and scholars found (often in far larger numbers) in the official school-temples of the Ch'ing dynasty;[18] they were in fact sometimes referred to as 'shrines to former worthies.' As an institution they were perhaps not wholly new in the Sung; but they do, in Fu-chou and elsewhere, multiply considerably and seem to assume new importance in the course of the dynasty. The men they honored were not, it appears, treated precisely as gods[19] – not prayed to for aid, for example – but were offered homage through sacrifices to their spirit. To call these shrines institutions of 'official religion' is perhaps to pigeonhole them more neatly than is appropriate: they were established, not (as a rule) at the bidding of the central government, but more or less *ad hoc* by officials serving in Fu-chou. In a few cases their official builders were evidently responding to appeals or agitation from the local elite; in other cases the balance of initiative is unclear. Similar shrines were founded in private local academies to honor their founders or the teachers whose doctrines they promoted. Leading figures in the Neo-Confucian movement came to take a strong interest in such shrines in both official and private settings, and sometimes acted to promote them and perhaps to turn them in specifically Neo-Confucian directions. (On this more in a later chapter.) The spread of shrines of this kind is thus hard to class as a phenomenon purely of official religion. Those I deal with here, however, were without exception formally established by Fu-chou local administrators. In these officials' eyes their purpose, presumably, was on one hand to express gratitude to men whose benefits to the community and the world were still felt; and on the other to provide moral exemplars for the living – probably chiefly the local elite, who it seems were expected to join the officials in attendance at the sacrifices – to emulate.[20]

The shrines, then, provided models; but models of what kind? It is revealing to compare the set of shrines established before the fall of the North with those built or rebuilt during Southern Sung. Northern Sung shrines were dedicated to four men: Yen Chen-ch'ing (after 1055), a prominent official of the middle T'ang dynasty who had once been prefect of Fu-chou;[21] Su Chien (after about 1100), who had administered Ch'ung-jen County in the 1050s;[22] Ti Ming-yüan (after the early 1100s), who had served as Fu-chou prefect a few years before;[23] and Wang An-shih (after 1106), the Fu-chou man whose tenure as chief councillor had set the course of factional politics at court for the rest of Northern Sung.[24] Of the four, only one was a Fu-chou man; the others were outsiders and local officials, representatives of the state in Fu-chou. The shrine to the one native, Wang An-shih, is known to have been established at local request.

The picture shifts drastically in Southern Sung. Yen, Su, Ti, and Wang still received their sacrifices; but seven new shrines appeared, honoring nineteen new men, seven from Northern and twelve from Southern Sung.[25] Only one was a local official: Huang Kan, prefect of Fu-chou in the early 1200s.[26] All the rest were Fu-chou natives. Some, like Yen Shu, Tseng Kung, Tseng Chao, or Lo Tien, had reached high central office. But six of the new men had never held office of any kind: these included poets (Hsieh I, Hsieh K'o, Tseng Chi-li), scholars (Wu Hang), a teacher famous chiefly for his system of household economy (Lu Chiu-shao), and a political martyr — Ou-yang Ch'e, executed in 1127 for sending up, as a commoner, a memorial denouncing current policies and political actors at court. Most owed their reputations largely to what they had done at home; some — the Hsiehs, Ou-yang Ch'e, Tseng Chi-li — probably had, by the time they began to receive sacrifices, little real renown outside Fu-chou. Still others, like Lu Chiu-yüan and Lu Chiu-ling, had held office but never risen very high: the Lus achieved national renown, but this grew out of the teaching they had done and the students they had gathered in Fu-chou and (in Chiu-yüan's case) just across the border in neighboring Hsin-chou. Only two of the Southern Sung men who came to receive sacrifices were remembered chiefly for their service in office, thus for what they had done outside Fu-chou: these were the assisting councillor Lo Tien and the Executive of the Ministry of Rites, Li Hao.

It would seem, then, that in Northern Sung Fu-chou the shrines to local worthies were used above all to glorify the state and its agents, on the one hand by celebrating the contributions that governing officials had made to Fu-chou, on the other by honoring the one Fu-chou man who had risen highest and achieved most in the state. In Southern Sung, though this purpose was not wholly abandoned, a new one came to the fore: to celebrate the achievements of Fu-chou men themselves, including those with no connection to the state. More: the state had at some time rejected some of those most celebrated here. Wu Hang had submitted his writings to court but had been rebuffed for a violation of a taboo character. Hsieh I, Hsieh K'o, and Lu Chiu-shao had failed in the exams. Some had themselves rejected the state's overtures: Hsieh I (later in life) and Tseng Chi-li had both refused opportunities for office. One, Ou-yang Ch'e, was the state's victim. It is not officeholding and service to the nation (in the conventional sense) that are being celebrated here. This is all the more striking as the shrines were the work, at least in some consider-able part, not of local men but of prefects and county administrators — men with no permanent stake in Fu-chou but with considerable stake, one would presume, in the bureaucracy.

These two phenomena – the transformation of the role of shrines to local worthies, and the new evidence of local elite intervention in local government (evidence which, I have argued, need not express a new reality) – reflect, I would suggest, the spread in Southern Sung of a new, or a newly dominant, ideal of the gentleman's role: an ideal which valued local commitments and contributions at least as highly as action in official capacities and on the national scale. The elite of Fu-chou, in effect, was now legitimized as a *local* elite.

Where else may we turn for evidence of this new ideal? To a surprising source, perhaps, and one with no special connection to Fu-chou. The Neo-Confucian philosopher Chu Hsi, founder of a system of thought that was to become, in highly simplified and thus distorted form, the state orthodoxy of all succeeding dynasties, has long been known chiefly as a teacher of moral self-cultivation. Wm. Theodore de Bary, in a seminal essay on the origins of Neo-Confucianism, suggested thirty-five years ago that the moral and personal emphasis in Chu's thought might be seen as a conscious move away from the state-centered political and institutional reformism of Neo-Confucian forerunners in Northern Sung, a move with roots in the memory of the disastrous factional struggles surrounding Wang An-shih's reforms.[27] I have already suggested the congruence of this philosophical shift with the changes in practical strategies traced in the preceding chapter. But there is more in Chu Hsi than this. In moving, like his Northern Sung predecessors the Ch'eng brothers, away from the state and a state-centered politics, Chu Hsi, for one, did not abandon institutional reform. Rather, as de Bary has more recently proposed and as I have argued elsewhere, one may extract from Chu's writings elements of an innovative and comprehensive institutional program for social reformation, a program, however, whose milieu is not central but local.[28] Three institutions, none of them Chu's invention, are fundamental to the program: the private local academy (*shu-yüan*), the community granary (*she-ts'ang*), and the community compact (*hsiang-yüeh*). Each has been extensively studied elsewhere; I will describe them only briefly here.

The local academy, essentially a school with an associated ritual center, might be private, semi-private, or state-sponsored, but was most commonly conceived – even when founded by local administrators – as an institution largely independent of the state apparatus and of the normal state-run prefectural and county schools. Though there had been private academies in Northern Sung, some of them quite important, in its capacity as alternative to the official school the academy was largely a phenomenon of Southern Sung and after. The academy 'movement,' as it is sometimes called, was hardly the creation of Chu Hsi; as John Chaffee has pointed out, the wave of academy foundings that is so striking in Southern Sung was well under way when Chu came on the scene.[29] Yet as Chaffee also argues, the influence of Chu's activity in this sphere, in particular of his rules for the White Deer Grotto Academy in Nan-k'ang and of his reaffirmation of the academy's function as a place of disinterested study in a world where education was aimed largely at success in the examinations, was enormous. Chu Hsi's followers and disciples were among the most active founders of new academies in the period that followed.

The community granary was the scheme originally of Chu Hsi's friend Wei Shan-chih, who had put it into practise in Chien-yang County in Chu Hsi's own prefecture Chien-chou in the 1160s. Chu borrowed the idea with some modifications and was able to see it promulgated by the throne during the 1180s as an officially approved institution available for adoption by interested local administrators and private gentlemen. The scheme was put into effect, by Chu's followers and others, in many parts of China. I will trace in a later chapter its spread in Fu-chou. In its general principle of operation the plan resembled Wang An-shih's national 'Green Sprouts' program of Northern Sung. A granary, endowed with an initial stock of rice, was to make loans from the stock to farmers in planting season for repayment after the harvest. In other respects, however, the plan diverged sharply from Wang An-shih's: no interest (after an initial period in which the founding investment was recouped) was to be charged, but only a three per cent wastage fee; and the granary was to serve a specific and generally small locality and to be managed (and some-times founded and endowed) by local gentlemen rather than by agents of the state. The object was, through voluntary and locally-based action, to help the farmer by meeting his need for credit without imposing oppressive interest charges.[30]

The community compact, adopted by Chu Hsi with considerable modifi-cations from the Northern Sung thinker and official Lü Ta-chün (1031–82), differed from the other two institutions dealt with here in not being put widely into practise in Chu's own time. It is clear nonetheless that Chu him-self meant the plan as a serious contribution to the reformation of local communities, and intended it to be put into effect. The 'compact' (*yüeh*) was a voluntary association or agreement among the members of a community, aiming at the promotion of moral and social order through mutual exhorta-tion and admonition, common ritual, and organized mutual aid. Members were to be enrolled on registers and their good and bad conduct recorded, brought to the attention of other members at regular meetings, and publicly praised or blamed. Membership was voluntary, but members were to be expelled in case of repeated offenses against the rules or spirit of the compact. A finely worked program of community ritual was to bind members to one another and promote a proper recognition of distinctions of age, virtue, and social position.[31]

What is most striking about this cluster of institutions is that each was in some respect a substitute, or an alternative, for a specific state institution of Chu Hsi's own time or of Northern Sung. Thus one may see in the community compact a voluntarily based, non-coercive version, founded in natural com- munities, of the *pao-chia* units of mutual surveillance instituted from the center by Wang An-shih and others and still surviving, in modified or degenerate forms, in Chu Hsi's day. The community granary clearly represented a transfer of the method of Wang An-shih's long-rescinded Green Sprouts law to a voluntary and locally based welfare institution. The academy was a direct alternative to the contemporary official school, an institution that once again had its origins in the centralizing national reformist efforts of the Northern Sung statesmen Fan Chung-yen and Wang An-shih. In a sense Chu Hsi, and those who joined him in promoting these institutions, were proposing to accomplish on the foundation of the local community, and voluntarily, what Wang An-shih had tried to do through the state and from the center. A shift from a central to a local focus in elite conceptions is perhaps nowhere clearer than here.

What purposes led Chu Hsi and some among his followers to promote institutions of this character? Most simply, of course, the material and moral repair of local society. Farmers were to be given the means to plant without mortgaging their independence; students and scholars were to be taught and edified; malfeasance and impropriety were to be detected and condemned, virtue praised, charity and cooperation encouraged and organized. Yet at one remove from these direct purposes, surely, was another, rather more abstract: to give institutional expression and structure to the local community as some- thing apart from the state and its local organs. Chu Hsi sought to define a level of society, and a sphere for social action, not (as he saw it) well defined before: a level lying between the family and the lowest reaches of the state apparatus; the level of the 'community' (*hsiang* or *she*). We may see this as well in Chu's ritual compilation, the *I-li ching-chuan t'ung chieh*. Here he divided the seventeen sections of the classical ritual text the *I-li* into hierarchical social levels, of which one — lying between 'family ritual' (*chia li*) and 'ritual of countries and kingdoms' (*pang-kuo li*) — was 'community ritual' (*hsiang li*). The categories were an innovation, and Chu's own. In de Bary's words, Chu Hsi 'sought to incorporate the principle of voluntarism into community structures which might mediate between state power and family interest.'[32]

It would be foolish to claim that Chu Hsi and his followers, or Southern Sung Neo-Confucians more broadly, were in any meaningful sense 'localist.' There is little question that, as compared to Confucian activists of the Northern Sung, they de-emphasized service in office. Yet if one route to the reformation of society lay, for Chu, in local institutional innovation, another, at least as important, lay in the moral reform of the highest central authority, the emperor himself, through teaching and admonition and through his own self-cultivation. Chu, and the Neo-Confucians of his time more generally, hoped to bind together again a polity and moral order that seemed to them to have come apart; their ideas for local reform should be seen as one element in what would ultimately have been a larger integration of society.

The point, then, is not to find 'localism' in Neo-Confucian philosophy but to point out — and here I return to the line of argument of the chapter as a whole — that through his plans for the three reforming institutions Chu offered the gentleman a set of channels for virtuous social action that could be pursued in a purely local sphere; thus he gave stress to the gentleman's local role in a way quite uncharacteristic of Northern Sung thinkers.[33] In this respect Chu and his followers were in resonance with the other commentators on elite life whose evidence we have seen here: the authors of biographies and compilers of collected works, and the sponsors of shrines to local worthies. The three groups of commentators overlapped partly — Neo-Confucian philosophers did sponsor shrines, did compile biographies and collected works — but by no means completely. There is strong foundation for the conclusion that, for many in the elite, Southern Sung ideal images of the gentleman were informed by a new stress on locality. Virtue could be displayed, obligations to society fulfilled, as laudably in local action as in office.

All this was the ideal. But the ideal was not without foundation in the realities of the time. New channels of local action did emerge among the Fu-chou elite in Southern Sung, quite apart from (though surely not unrelated to) the changes in strategies treated in the preceding chapter. In part these new channels must have been influenced by the reworking of ideal images we have seen here, and must have influenced it in their turn. But a separate phenomenon may independently have influenced both the ideal and the practise: this was the real weakness of the Southern Sung state, which opened whole new fields of action to the local elite in the countryside. This problem is taken up in the chapters that follow.

5

LOCAL DEFENSE

The men of the Fu-chou elite in Southern Sung, as we have seen, withdrew from the ties of marriage that in Northern Sung had bound them to the elites of other parts of China; they built and made donations only in the immediate vicinity of their residences; they gave up the habit of emigration that had drawn those most successful in office out of Fu-chou; in sum, they undertook what appears a general retreat from relatively distant involvements in favor of their home counties and localities. With roughly parallel timing, such more articulate witnesses and judges of elite life as found occasion to author biographies, compile collected works, promote particular men for honor at shrines to local worthies, or offer (in Chu Hsi's case) plans for social reform, came to give new attention and attribute new value to local involvements and local benefactions as elements of the good character of a gentleman. We see then on the one hand a change in practical family strategies, never spoken of directly in the testimony of the elite itself; and on the other hand a change in articulated ideal images and standards of valuation, a change which in itself offers little evidence as to the course of actual behavior. I have argued that the two, though directions of influence or even order in time cannot as yet be sorted out, are clearly related. In all of this, however, little has been said, apart from questions of marriage, residence, and the like, about the real, broader role of the Fu-chou elite. What, in fact, did the elite *do*? What was its role in local society? How, and for what, did it act? In the present chapter and the two that follow I will take up three fields of action that won the attention, particularly in Southern Sung, of the Fu-chou elite. The first is local defense, an especially acute issue after the Chin conquest of North China. The second is social welfare, rather broadly conceived so as to include, along with relief of famine and the provision of cheap rural credit, such economically beneficial and sometimes 'charitable' acts as irrigation maintenance and bridgebuilding. The third is religious life; and here for once we may gain a glimpse, though only a glimpse, of parts of society that stood below, or at least outside, the elite. The purpose of these chapters, then, is at least partly descriptive: the character of the elite cannot be understood without attention to certain things it did. But a deeper question runs throughout. In each of these fields of action, what were the relative shares, and the relative power, of the elite and the state? How, if at all — and if the evidence will show it — did this relation change, as so much else changed, between Northern and Southern Sung? This last problem I will take up in more general form in Chapter 8.

During his tenure as prefect of Fu-chou between 1271 and 1273 the late Sung Neo-Confucian scholar Huang Chen addressed a memorial to the Department of Ministries, asking permission to eliminate a fort in Lo-an County. In support of his request he offered a discussion of the problem of 'fort troops' (*chai-ping*):

> Of all the things that harm the people of this prefecture, none does so more profoundly than fort troops. Whenever they receive a dispatch, thirty to fifty men set their weapons in order and go out to plunder the villages. With long continuance this has become established custom; despite severe restraints it has not been corrected. Since I came to this post, though I have labored to curb false suits, I have not dared to hand over to this crew the authority to injure the people; but those in the outer counties I have never managed entirely to restrain. Worst of all is Lo-an County, which is extremely far from the prefectural seat and [so] is the most inaccessible to my intervention. No matter how great or small the trouble, the fort troops invariably persuade the county clerks to dispatch them into the countryside. The spoils from each round of pillage and plunder are divided three ways, with one share each for fort troops, county clerks, and fort officers. There are fixed rules [for the division] ; it is so in every case. Now while on the one hand I have deputed officials to travel the counties, inquire into the people's distress, and plan how to suppress [the problem] , still to suppress it is not as good as to cut it off at the root. I have investigated: Lo-an is one county but has three forts. One of them, located in the county seat, is called the County Fort. One, located on the border with Yung-feng County of Chi-chou, is called Chao-hsi Fort. One, located only fifteen *li* from the county seat, is called Tseng-t'ien Fort. I am humbly aware that Yung-feng abounds with bandits, and that earlier people set up Chao-hsi Fort in order to resist them; it has both dis-advantages and benefits and may not lightly be set aside. As for the county seat, it has both the sheriff's office and the County Fort, which of course is quite unnecessary; but as the latter has no fort officer and is headed by the county administrator, it is still controllable. Only Tseng-t'ien Fort is established in an area of peaceful communities and causes disorder in a countryside into which the eyes and ears of the

prefecture and county do not reach; it is wholly harmful and has never
rendered the slightest particle of benefit. That it should be eliminated
is clear.[1]

Two points here are especially worth noting: first, that Huang found himself entirely unable to control fort troops once they went out into the
countryside and so, despite his efforts to reduce local disorders associated
with lawsuits, had made it his policy to keep the troops in their forts; second,
that he was unable to enforce even this policy in the 'outer counties,' that is
outside of Lin-ch'uan. Huang further makes it clear that county administrators
of Lo-an too had failed to maintain control over a fort that lay only fifteen *li*
(roughly five miles) from the county seat. All this is important chiefly because these fort troops, by middle Southern Sung, constituted the main
official military forces available to the prefect and county administrators for
the control of the countryside and for defense against banditry or local
rebellions.

This had not always been true. In Northern Sung, after 1041, the prefect
had at his disposal a full command of troops – four or five hundred men – of
the regular imperial army; by early Southern Sung the force had doubled. All
troops were stationed in the prefectural city, under the prefect's immediate
supervision. During Southern Sung these regular forces ceased to exist. Very
probably they had lost considerable strength early on through transfer to the
hard-pressed border armies: the state was in desperate need of soldiers to
fight the Chin. The rest of their forces may have been used to stock the forts
that local officials created in response to increasing banditry: three of these
were placed in or near the prefectural city, but the rest stood far off on the
borders or in outlying counties like Lo-an.[2] In all, the forces theoretically
under official control seem to have been rather larger in Southern than in
Northern Sung, but they were now dispersed throughout the countryside, not
concentrated at the center. That they should now become less amenable to
central control was only natural. The dispersal was deliberate strategy, it
seems: a measure of direct control was surrendered to gain an outward screen
against bandit incursions and general disorder. But the strategy seems to have
failed: little real protection was gained.

In Southern Sung, apart from the fort troops, each county was provided
with between seventy and a hundred 'bowmen,'[3] subject to the command of
the county sheriff and serving a variety of policing functions. There is nothing
to suggest, however, that these forces played a significant role in the defense
of the countryside or the suppression of uprisings.[4] Similarly, while state-run
militia units, called *pao-wu*, seem to have existed in Fu-chou at various times
during Southern Sung, there is no evidence that these could or ever did
play any part in defense against organized banditry, as opposed to simple

surveillance and reporting of crimes or disturbances at the village level.[5] The fort troops were the officials' major weapon, and it would seem that they were an ineffective one. Military weakness in the countryside was a constant worry for Fu-chou officials in Southern Sung.[6]

Against this background it is hardly surprising that private local defense organizations emerged as an important force in the same period. In what follows I will deal with what the surviving evidence reveals of their history.

The Chin-ch'i militia

The fall of the capital in the north to the Jurchen Chin invaders in 1126 and the Sung's subsequent retreat to the south began a period of constant war and internal disorder that was to last some years into Southern Sung. From the beginning of this period the Sung government, hard pressed by the weakness of official armies and faced with local rebellions and renegade government troops as well as repeated incursions by Chin troops, encouraged the formation of local self-defense forces, whether organized by officials or by private locals, and gave official recognition to such forces where they already existed.[7] In the seventh month of 1127 it was decreed that these organizations in all circuits be granted the name 'Loyal and Dutiful Patrolling Societies' (*Chung-i hsün-she*).[8] One such force was a militia, or an association of militia units, in Chin-ch'i county.[9]

Contemporaries called the Chin-ch'i militia the 'Two Societies of the Tengs and the Fus' (*Teng-Fu erh she*): this reflected the role of a Teng family (see above, p. 75) and a Fu family (Appendix I, no. 74) in its organizing and leadership. A fragmentary gazetteer of the Ching-ting period (1260–4) preserves an account of the court's edict that local militia be formed, and of the local reaction:

> In Chin-ch'i there were the Two Societies of the Tengs and the Fus, who responded to the order. The head of the Teng society was named [Teng] P'ang. The head of the Fu society was named [Fu] An-ch'ien. Both were courageous and loved duty. They disbursed their families' wealth to support militiamen [. . .] The two families' sons and grandsons inherited their posts.[10]

Again, in an account entitled 'About the Militiamen of Chin-ch'i,' dated 1175, and included in the collected works of the Southern Sung official Chou Pi-ta, we learn:

> The great surnames of Chin-ch'i in Fu-chou, the Teng family and the Fu family, each have several thousand militiamen. They cover their heads with hoods of red lacquer bark and are called the Red Heads. They are feared far and near, and are known as the Two Societies of the Tengs and the Fus.[11]

Similarly in the Chin-ch'i gazetteers' biographies of the militia leaders Teng P'ang and Fu An-ch'ien the defense activities of the 1127–30 period are described as a cooperative enterprise of the two families, the Tengs operating in the north and east of the county and the Fus in the south and west.[12] It is clear from these various sources that the Tengs and Fus were families of especial importance in the militia at its inception; and as will be seen, the Tengs were to remain throughout Sung and into Yüan the local family most closely associated with defense activities. Yet from the beginning other families were prominently involved. According to Chou Pi-ta:

> Previously there was also in that county a Lu family that was the most dominating in the countryside. In past years the Financial Intendancy had named them to act as Overall Commander of the Societies (*tu-she*), with the Tengs and the Fus both subordinate to them.[13]

These Lus are, of course, the family of the philosopher Lu Chiu-yüan, whose own record of conduct for his elder brother Lu Chiu-ling confirms the family's military role:

> In Chien-yen [1127–30], with the coming of the caitiff bandits [i.e. Chin invaders], the Master's lineage man [Lu] O rose righteously in answer to [the court's] recruitment. Thereafter bandits flourished and, one after another, violated the territory of the prefecture: O was summoned each time to assemble a following and provide defense. Frequently he was able to drive the enemy away; the prefecture and the villages relied upon him.[14]

Thus, from the first official recognition of the militia, the Tengs and Fus had in fact been subordinate to a member of the Lu family. Nor were these three the only important participants of whom record survives. Two others, as we have already seen, were the Kos[15] and the Wus,[16] neighbors of the Tengs and the Lus (see above, p. 75). A third family, the Lans, at least once provided a commander for operations against bandits from nearby Kuei-ch'i county in Hsin-chou.[17]

If the Tengs and Fus each commanded one society, while the Lus provided overall leadership for the two together, how did the Kos, Wus, and Lans fit in? The structure of the militia is far from clear, but geography yields a strong clue. As we have seen, the Tengs, Kos, and Wus all lived, along with the Lus, fairly close together in the northeastern part of Chin-ch'i. The Lans came from precisely the same region. The Fus, on the other hand, lived in the far south of the county, on a westward-flowing tributary of the Ju River. The Teng society, once again, is said to have patrolled the north and east of Chin-ch'i, while the Fu society held down the south and west. Each society built and manned a private fort: the Teng society at a place called Pai-ma, the Fus at Han-p'o Ridge.[18] As Map 17 makes clear, each fort lay deep within the

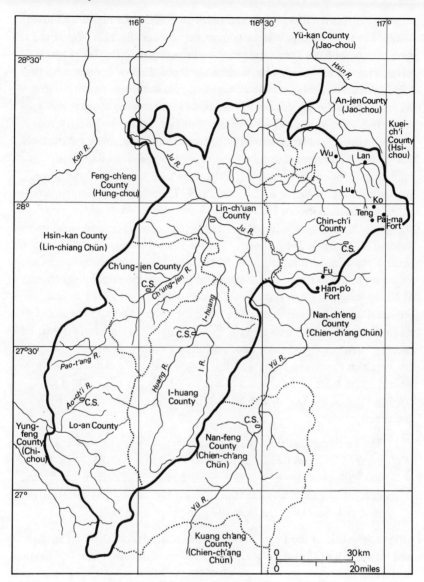

Map 17. Chin-ch'i militia. Family residences and forts.

territory patrolled by its society and near the residence of the commanding family. Given all of this it seems almost certain that the Kos, Wus, and Lans were members of the Teng society and so subordinate to the Tengs themselves. This would explain why, despite the other families' involvement, the militia's name mentions only the Tengs and Fus. But if this reconstruction is correct, then the sources tell a great deal about the Teng society, but — apart from its commanders — very little about its Fu counterpart.

The Chin-ch'i militia was an enduring institution, but hardly a static one. The picture I have drawn so far applies chiefly to the time immediately following its founding. In later years the Teng family seems to have moved gradually to a position of overall authority. The process was not, apparently, entirely smooth. Between 1127 and 1135 the militia had fought successful engagements against Chin incursions and at least eleven separate uprisings by 'bandits' or renegade Sung soldiers.[19] After 1136 there appears to have been relative peace in the prefecture until 1175, when tea bandits rose in the Ching-hu region (modern Hupei and Hunan) and spread to the neighboring circuits of Kuang-tung and Chiang-hsi.[20] As the disturbance drew near Fu-chou, preparations for defense began. At around this time, one Liu Yao-fu, a student at the Imperial University in the capital who in the previous year had passed as number one in the school's qualifying exam for the *chin-shih*, paid a visit to Chou Pi-ta, then holding an influential post in the capital. I have already cited, from Chou's record of the visit, Liu's account of the Two Societies and of the Lus' overall leadership. Liu went on to discuss the current situation:

> The Fu family has already taken its leave; but a son of the Teng family, named P'ang, has two sons. The elder is thirty or so, the younger something over twenty; both are martial figures of extraordinary reputation [. . .] On hearing that tea bandits had arisen, they trained strong men and recommended themselves to the prefecture.[21]

As to the role of the Lus, Liu traced the circumstances that had arisen since the death of the man (Lu O, whom he does not name) who had held the leadership post:

> Local people have advised making the office hereditary [i.e., passing it on to another Lu] ; the county [administration] too, on checking into the old archives,[22] has found it appropriate. From this the thoughts of the sons of the Teng family have tended toward indolence, for they fear that if they receive orders from the Lus, then the credit will not be their own.[23]

In order that the approaching local defense efforts might once more benefit from the Tengs' participation, Liu suggested to Chou that the Fu-chou prefect should seek them out and, with ceremony, ask them to take up the position of leaders of an independent society, not subordinate to Lu leadership. Chou thought the idea a reasonable one and had it conveyed to the emperor, who considered it but rejected it out of the fear that it would 'too much disturb people' — probably a euphemism for provoking local disorder. What is important here is the evidence that the Tengs, fifty years after the founding of the Chin-ch'i militia, were reluctant to accept a second-ranking position any longer, and that their importance to the defense preparations was such that high officials were prepared to entertain compromises that would bring them back in.

In the record of conduct of Lu Chiu-ling cited above one may read of some of the same events from the Lus' point of view:

> By this time [Lu] O had died. His old troops wanted the Master [i.e., Lu Chiu-ling] to lead them and made requests to that effect of the prefecture [administration]. At the time the Master happened to be in Ch'ien-shan county of Hsin-chou. On hearing of the alarms he returned in haste. When he reached his home the appellants filled his gates. He declined; they did not leave, but grew daily more numerous. The Master and his brothers and followers discussed how duty was to be done. It happened that the prefecture's commission had already come down; the Master was inclined to accept it. Some were displeased [. . .] [24]

This confirms Liu Yao-fu's reference to the desire of locals and officials to continue Lu O's post within the same family. There follows an account of the objections raised by unnamed followers or Lu family members against Lu Chiu-ling's acceptance of the position. Significantly, one view expressed was that leadership of the militia was a role that a self-respecting man would not accept (the Lus had by now produced two *chin-shih*: Chiu-ling was one) and should be taken instead by a 'bold and forceful man of military might.'[25] Chiu-ling rejected this alternative partly on the grounds that the power associated with the post, if it fell into the wrong hands, could wreak havoc in the countryside even if the bandits themselves never arrived. Presumably both sides in the argument were speaking, not abstractly, but with the real alternative leadership represented by the Tengs in mind. The two families, allies of old and in-laws for generations, now faced each other as competitors for the supreme position in the militia. The competition was perhaps part of a more general contest for dominance in the region of Chin-ch'i that was home to both. Judging from official recognition alone — which may not be a reliable standard — the Lus seem to have maintained their position this time around. The issue, however, became academic when the tea bandits failed to reach Fu-chou.[26]

Liu Yao-fu's approach to Chou Pi-ta may in itself be evidence of other conflict or tension among local families. Liu was, though he apparently made no mention of it to Chou, a student of Lu Chiu-yüan.[27] Yet in his recommendation that the Tengs be freed from the Lus' authority, he seems to have been working in the Tengs' favor and against the interests of his teacher's own family. His proposal was in fact an odd one: since the Lus would presumably have retained their authority over other militia families, two separate organizations with no unifying command would have been established around families virtually next door to each other in the northeast of the county. The potential for conflict between the two seems obvious, and probably prompted the emperor's rejection of the proposal. It is possible that Liu was motivated by a sincere and perfectly disinterested desire to see the fullest possible participation by the Tengs in the impending anti-bandit campaigns; but another explanation is conceivable. Liu's family lived in the west-central part of the county, well outside the mountainous northeastern region with its northward-flowing rivers that was the home of the Tengs and Lus. Among a fair amount of surviving information on Liu and his family[28] there is no evidence of involvement in the local militia, or of any other military activity. I would suggest that Liu or his family feared that a unified northeastern militia organization would give the Lus *de facto* authority over all or most of the county, including the area of his own residence. If instead the militia leadership were divided among two northeastern families, their competition might prevent either from extending its power to other parts of Chin-ch'i. This, of course, is speculation. Yet it is interesting too that soon after this Liu broke with Lu Chiu-yüan's teachings, condemning them in such harsh terms that Chu Hsi, himself Lu's philosophical rival, was moved to rebuke Liu for his too extreme attacks.[29] The temptation is strong to see here a penetration of local family rivalries into the field of philosophical discourse.

There is no record of direct Lu participation in Chin-ch'i militia activity after 1175;[30] it would seem that after the passing of the bandits in that year the family's ties to the militia were allowed to dissolve. The Tengs' position in the meantime seems to have risen. Chou Pi-ta reports that as of 1175 the Fu family, in 1127 leaders of a society and coequal with the Tengs, had 'taken their leave.' It is not clear from this whether they had withdrawn from militia activity or merely asserted their own independence of Lu supervision. In any case, when in 1230 the other districts of Fu-chou were overrun by bandits from T'ing-chou in Fu-chien circuit, a descendant of Fu An-ch'ien, named Fu T'i, was again to be found as an officer at the family's old stronghold, Han-p'o Fort, in the far south of the county. This time, however, overall leadership at the fort was in the hands of a member of the Teng family; indeed the Tengs' activity in this period covered all of the county and even the prefectural city itself in Lin-ch'uan.[31] Apparently their attempts to assert their own authority, dating back at least to 1175, had succeeded.

What was the relation of the Chin-ch'i militia to the state? Certain clues emerge from what little the sources tell us of the militia's structure. In decreeing the creation of Loyal and Dutiful Patrolling Societies in 1127, the court had issued detailed instructions as to their internal organization. The sizes of various hierarchical units were clearly specified, along with the titles of their respective officers.[32] The titles of several of the Chin-ch'i militia leaders are recorded: one, that of Lu O, corresponds roughly to the form required by the state.[33] The others seem to bear no relation whatever to the regulations.[34] Lu O, as overall leader, was the man most likely to deal directly with local officials; it made strategic sense, perhaps, for him to bear the title the rules prescribed. For his subordinates, it seems, there was no such need. The point is telling. It would have cost little for the militia to adopt the state's *terms* even if its actual organization was largely self-determined: that it did not suggests that even the pretense of conformity was unnecessary. Elsewhere we learn that the registers (of membership, payment, etc.) of the Teng-Fu societies were always privately held, never in the possession of the government. This too was a departure from the official regulations, and meant that the bureaucratic wherewithal for direct official control of the body of the militia did not exist.

Perhaps, then, the state controlled the militia, not directly, but through its leaders? Formally, of course, an imperial decree had created it and authorized its commanders to take the field on the state's behalf. The fragmentary Sung gazetteer — a work compiled under official auspices — shows the Two Societies mobilizing in 1127 in 'response' to the court's decree.[35] Yet even this leaves unclear whether the Societies in fact had existed before and 'responded' by declaring their readiness, or whether they came into existence after and through the decree. Teng P'ang's biography, however, tells us that P'ang had raised troops in 1126, before any formal moves by the government, and that it was his success against bandits in that year that brought him and his following to the state's attention.[36] Similarly, Chou Pi-ta implies that Lu O was 'chosen' as overall leader because his family was already in fact ' the most dominating in the countryside.'[37] Whatever the exact balance of private and official initiative that brought the militia into being, in certain respects the state simply gave official sanction to a set of circumstances that was independent of its will.

This was no less true in later years. The events of 1175 show that for the Lus the acceptance or rejection of Lu Chiu-ling's 'appointment' as militia leader was a matter to be weighed in private within the circle of family and students, and not a command that demanded obedience. The discussion recounted by Lu Chiu-yüan centered around issues of propriety, prestige, the security of Lu's family and neighborhood, and the danger of the post's falling

into the wrong hands — all essentially personal or local concerns. It seems
clear too that the initiative for the transfer of the post to Lu Chiu-ling came
from militia troops and other locals. Likewise the Tengs were prepared to
back out of the militia out of the conviction that there would be no credit in
it for them; and Liu Yao-fu and Chou Pi-ta clearly accepted that the Tengs
had the power to withdraw. Here the state was in the position of waiting on
the pleasure of powerful locals, some of them officeholders and some not.

The same problem confronted the state once again near the end of Sung.
In 1259 or 1260 the Hsin-chou man and 1256 *chin-shih* Hsieh Fang-te, later
famous for his heroic refusal to serve the Yüan, received orders to organize a
militia defense of Jao-chou, Hsin-chou, and Fu-chou against Mongol troops,
who at about this time had sacked the cities of Jao-chou and Lin-chiang
Chün.[38]

According to his biography in the *Sung shih*, Hsieh 'persuaded the Two
Societies of the Tengs and Fus and various great families [to join him],
obtained over ten thousand militia troops, and protected Hsin-chou.'[39] The
use of the word 'persuaded' (*shui*) is significant in itself; and a Chin-ch'i
gazetteer preserves a letter from Hsieh to a member of the Teng family which
reveals that persuasion — rather than direction or compulsion — is precisely
what was involved.[40] The letter was written in 1260[41] to Teng Yüan-kuan, a
man who had studied at the Imperial University during the 1250s and was to
achieve a *chin-shih* in 1265,[42] but at this time had yet to hold office. Much in
the letter that appears obscure or rambling becomes clear if one assumes a
previous correspondence between the two: an official dispatch from Hsieh to
the Tengs and a response from Teng Yüan-kuan expressing a variety of reasons
for reluctance to join Hsieh. In response Hsieh attempted to soothe feelings
injured by the peremptory character of his earlier communication, and to
answer Teng's arguments. Thus:

> In troubling you, I am not saying that I can bend [to my will] a great
> worthy [such as yourself]. Loyalty to the ruler and concern for the
> state have been your constant thought. Having made suggestions and
> proposals you will surely [also] manifest practical achievement [. . .]
> In using an official dispatch and not a personal letter I know that I have
> been at fault. But a gentleman will not hold others responsible for strict
> details: he takes their intentions as sufficient [. . .]

Evidently Teng Yüan-kuan had again raised the issue of credit and who would
receive it, for Hsieh noted:

> Whether the merit is manifested by oneself or others there is not
> time to calculate. [. . .] Today one who would preserve those who are
> perishing and aid those who are in danger becomes a contender against

Heaven; one who would stand apart and act alone becomes an enemy of men [. . .] With Heaven and men joined in malice [towards one], how will one's merit be established?[43]

Apparently Teng was proposing (again) to maintain independence of any external leadership and to act as the family saw fit. While in the end the Tengs did join Hsieh (who after the fighting was over reported the name of the leading Teng officer to the court and so procured him a low military office as a reward),[44] the letter shows that they had felt free to decide otherwise, and that a man of official standing found it necessary to cajole them into joining. It seems that once again the Tengs were chiefly concerned with what benefits their participation might bring their family. Though the government sanctioned the Chin-ch'i militia, rewarded it, and in theory commanded it, it did not in fact control it.

Other local defense activity

The Chin-ch'i militia was apparently the most long-lived organization of its kind in Fu-chou, and certainly the most important. Yet others appeared from time to time, and in general private action against bandits was quite common. The evidence dates chiefly (though not exclusively)[45] from Southern Sung — this surely reflects a real increase in local social disorder — and divides naturally into three periods of intense defense activities: the years from 1127 to 1135, immediately after the fall of Northern Sung; 1229—30, when bandits from T'ing-chou and elsewhere threatened every county of Fu-chou; and the end of Southern Sung, with invasions by Mongol troops on the one hand and an upsurge of internal disorder on the other. These are the same periods, of course, that were critical in the history of the Chin-ch'i militia.

No purpose would be served by discussing one by one and in detail the Fu-chou men from outside Chin-ch'i County who are known to have involved themselves in local defense.[46] From an examination of the men as a group, however, certain points emerge. In the first place, each man's activities appear strongly localized within his own county or the area around his residence (this cannot be determined for every man, but holds true where the area of activity is recorded) and occur as a response to disorder in his own area rather than in the prefecture as a whole. Not one is known to have taken part in defense outside his county. This contrasts with the case of the Chin-ch'i militia, which was active in several counties of Fu-chou and occasionally outside the prefecture.[47] Second, while no Chin-ch'i militia family had any apparent history of office at the militia's inception (rather all achieved office within a few decades of their participation), from the cases outside Chin-ch'i it is clear that men from families with a long previous history of office, or men with office of their own, often figured significantly in local defense. For

example, Hsü Tso-lin of I-huang, who led resistance to bandit invasions of
that county in 1133, was a member of a family that had produced its first
chin-shih in 985 and five others since that date.[48] Hou Ting of the same
county, who resolved after the widespread destruction of 1230 not to allow
a repetition, and so built a private fort in the mountains near his home and
manned it with a thousand privately hired militiamen, came from the same
family as Hou Shu-hsien, a 1046 *chin-shih* who had played a prominent part
in Wang An-shih's program of river control and hydraulic construction in the
1070s.[49] Tung Chü-i of Lin-ch'uan, who organized the 1230 resistance in his
county, had achieved the *chin-shih* in 1181 and served as Military Control
Commissioner in Szechwan after reaching fairly high office in the capital;
his elder brother Chü-hou had preceded him as a *chin-shih* in 1178.[50] Chao
Pu-tz'u of Ch'ung-jen, who led three hundred men in defense of his county
in 1230, was a member of the imperial lineage.[51] Though in 1175 some of
Lu Chiu-ling's students and family had argued that local militia leadership
was an inappropriate role for a man of scholarship and rank,[52] in fact the role
was played by officeholders, scholars, and men from scholarly and officeholding families, as well as by men from families of wealth or informal
power who had yet to achieve official or scholarly renown.

What is most striking about local defense activity outside Chin-ch'i is that
it seems to have been chiefly provisional, and limited largely to the short
term. Though there are certain periods for which one knows nothing of the
Chin-ch'i militia, the fact that several of the same families turn up more than
once (the Lus in 1127 and 1175, the Kos in 1127 and 1230, the Tengs and
Fus in 1127, 1175, 1230, and after 1261), and that the name 'Two Societies
of the Tengs and Fus' survives from 1127 at least to 1261, suggests considerable continuity. It seems almost certain that the organization, or at least
parts of it, existed in the interim periods as well. Outside Chin-ch'i, however,
only one family is known to have involved itself in private local defense in
more than one generation.[53] This was the Cheng family of Lo-an County. In
1230 Cheng Feng-hsiang was awarded one of the lowest civil offices for his
merit in defense against bandits, and in 1275 the government allotted fields
producing an annual rent of 800,000 *shih* to his son Cheng Sung as a financial
base for the organizing and training of militia troops for use against the
invading Mongols.[54] Elsewhere elite involvement was sporadic, and militia
organizations *ad hoc*, springing up only in response to a crisis.

This difference in the organization of local defense in Chin-ch'i and other
Fu-chou counties seems to be reflected in each county's security. Aside from
the sections of gazetteers dealing with military activity, which briefly note
the years in which bandits, rebels, or Northern invaders crossed the borders
of each county,[55] a wide variety of sources on Fu-chou very often yields

incidental references to cases of property destruction, looting, or killing by bandits. When one brings together all these scattered references (which come exclusively from Southern Sung), a rough but reasonably clear picture emerges of the degree to which the various districts were affected. It appears that Chin-ch'i was much the most secure, at least up until the Sung-Yüan transition. Before 1276, of the six county seats in greater Fu-chou only Chin-ch'i had never been occupied or sacked by bandits. Lin-ch'uan city, the seat of the prefecture, was held at least briefly by bandits in 1133, after being besieged several times in the previous few years; each time, the Chin-ch'i militia played a crucial part in driving away or defeating the occupying or besieging troops.[56] Ch'ung-jen city was burned almost entirely around 1130, and in 1230 the county school as well as several rural Buddhist temples were destroyed.[57] In I-huang the county seat's official buildings and at least two urban temples were burned in 1130; in 1230 the city was almost wholly reduced to ashes.[58] The Lo-an county seat suffered the same fate in 1230, when too its county administrator was captured and only released through a subterfuge by two prominent locals, who convinced the bandits that they had carried off the wrong man.[59] In the same year bandits are reported to have destroyed the genealogy (thus presumably the home or library) of a Huang family of Pa-t'ang, north of the Lo-an city.[60] Nan-feng city was burned in 1230, again in 1258, yet again in 1268, and finally once more in 1275 – all of this before the Mongols' arrival, itself particularly bloody in Nan-feng.[61] There is not the slightest record of destruction of this kind in Chin-ch'i.[62] Evidently the Chin-ch'i militia was a rather effective force. Evidently too, it was not for lack of need that similar forces did not emerge elsewhere.

What made Chin-ch'i different? Why were there not in every county families like the Tengs or Fus, who would take on the task of local defense and make it their own for generation after generation? Part of the answer, again, may lie in geography. The Tengs and Fus were military specialists; so also – insofar as they were involved in militia activity for more than a single generation – were the Lus, the Kos, and, in Lo-an, the Chengs. G.W. Skinner has suggested that, on the national scale, military service was likely to be the specialty of families from the periphery – from areas on the less developed, usually mountainous edges of physiographic macroregions; he proposes that the same principle may apply at lower levels as well.[63] The residences of the Tengs, Fus, Lus, and Kos have been shown on Map 15; the Cheng residence appears in Map 16, further on. Leaving aside the Fus, all these families lived in what may reasonably be called 'peripheral' areas of the physiographic microregion that partly coincided with Fu-chou: in or near mountainous regions that defined watersheds between the major river systems of the P'o-yang region, the Ju and Hsin Rivers in Chin-ch'i, the Ju and Kan rivers in

Lo-an. But this is not the whole picture. The watershed between the Ju and the Kan systems, after all, defined much of Fu-chou's western border; and part of the northern border closely followed the watershed between the Ju and the Hsin. Yet here we find no militia families. Rather, we find the Tengs, Lus, Kos, Wus, and Chengs precisely where major regional watersheds did *not* coincide with prefectural boundaries — where physiography and administration, so to speak, were out of phase. The Lus, Kos, Wus, and Tengs lived on the Hsin River side of the Hsin—Ju watershed, where it lay well *within* Chin-ch'i county; elsewhere the territories of the two systems were administratively separate. The Ju—Kan watershed split Lo-an County in two, physiographically but not administratively; and here, on the Kan side, the Chengs made their home.

What, if anything, made these anomalous areas likely breeding-grounds for militia specialists? In a sense these were the most 'peripheral' areas of all. In northeastern Chin-ch'i, for instance, access from the prefectural city — and so, one would expect, control by the prefectural government — was hindered by the hills, which made water traffic impossible and land travel more difficult than elsewhere. From the other side, the authorities in Hsin-chou to the north had no jurisdiction whatever over the southernmost reaches of 'their' river system, since these lay within a different prefecture. Here, in theory, was an ideal haven for bandits, who could strike in either direction and flee — across the watershed from Fu-chou or across the border from Hsin-chou. But here, too, was the greatest need for an indigenous elite defense force to fend bandits off; and here were the conditions that might allow one to recruit and train private troops on a permanent basis with relatively little fear of official hindrance: indeed a force that began as 'bandits' might find it convenient, if circumstances changed, to transform itself into a 'militia.' At the same time the area was — assuming protection could be provided — a likely conduit for trade between the Hsin and Ju systems. A family that could guarantee interregional traders clear passage through the hills could assure itself a regular income in service fees. Here, then, were motive and opportunity to make private militia action a family specialty.

In any case, the facts are clear: in much of Fu-chou, no indigenous, effective, permanent, private force emerged to fill the vacuum left by the state. here the elite turned to militia activity only when the need was immediate and the danger close to home. The Chin-ch'i militia surely would not have thrived as it did if the state had been able to project an effective, controllable armed presence into the countryside; but its rise evidently depended on local peculiarities as well. Where the state, in effect, had withdrawn, the local elite did not everywhere, or automatically, rush in.

6

SOCIAL WELFARE

The Chin-ch'i County man Chu Te-yu, who died in 1107, was the nephew
of an officeholder, a member of a family that was to continue producing
officials down into Yüan,[1] and a friend of the poet Hsieh I. In his funerary
inscription for Chu, who himself had held no office, Hsieh undertook to give
an idea of his friend's character:

> All his life he delighted in charitable practices and would give aid to men
> in emergencies; though they knocked at his gate in the middle of the
> night, he never failed to answer. When people in his neighborhood were
> hungry and lacked food, were cold and lacked clothing, were sick and
> lacked medicine, or had died and had no coffin; when their sons and
> daughters grew to adulthood but [through poverty] did not marry; or
> when people were students of Buddhism or Taoism but had not taken
> the cloth — they relied on Te-yu to fulfill their desires. The petitioners
> were uncountable.[2]

The picture drawn here of a man of wealth and renown who acts as patron
to his neighborhood, dispensing charity to all who cannot afford the
necessities of life or the amenities of social intercourse, is far from an uncommon one in the funerary inscriptions and biographies of Fu-chou men
throughout Sung. Thus one may read very similar accounts of Tseng Chieh of
Nan-feng county (fl. c. 1100), who indeed is supposed to have impoverished
his family through his largesse;[3] of the wife of Miu Chao of Ch'ung-jen county
(1110–91) after her husband's death;[4] and of Yüeh Ta-chang (1160–1241)
of Ch'ung-jen,[5] among many others. In fact an account like this one — down
to the very words used — is so much characteristic of a certain kind of Sung
funerary inscription (one whose subject had no official career, or only a very
brief one) that one simply cannot accept it at face value as a description of
a specific person. Still one may read it as evidence, if not of the character or
acts of its subject, then of the currency of a certain ideal of cultivated
behavior. This was how, on one view, a proper man of means, living at home,
was supposed to act.

Further on I will argue that, even as ideal, not all aspects of this view necessarily won the unanimous assent of the local elite of Fu-chou. As a description of typical behavior it simply cannot be evaluated, though there seems ample room for skepticism. Still there is considerable evidence of Fu-chou elite participation in certain more specific charitable institutions or activities. I will deal below, first with a welfare institution, already briefly treated earlier, that became rather popular among the Fu-chou elite in Southern Sung: the community granary; second with the role of the elite in famine relief in times of agricultural crisis; and third with its involvement, and that of the state, in water control and bridgebuilding.

Community granaries

The administrative cities of Sung China were the sites of a variety of institutions that one may loosely regard as serving social welfare functions. The operation of these institutions in Northern Sung cannot be recovered in any detail from the Fu-chou sources, but for most of Southern Sung the prefecture was the administrative seat of the Chiang-hsi circuit Intendancy for Ever-Normal Granaries. Whether these granaries retained, during Southern Sung, their original role of price-stabilization through strategically timed purchases and sales of rice is unclear (though the fragmentary Sung gazetteer suggests that they did).[6] They do, however, appear to have played the role of 'charitable granaries' (*i-ts'ang*), issuing relief grain, during famines, out of stores founded on rents from government-owned local lands. A separate 'Normal Sale Granary' (*p'ing-t'iao ts'ang*), established in 1252 and maintained jointly by the Intendancy and the prefectual administration, had taken over at least part of the Ever-Normal Granaries' price-stabilizing function.[7] From Fu-chou sources, however, there is not the slightest evidence that during Southern Sung these government-founded and government-run granaries extended their benefits beyond the prefectural city,[8] and there is some direct evidence that they did not.[9] Rather, in the countryside charity and relief were very often officially seen (even when the state played an instigating role) as the province of the men of wealth and reputation who lived there. One institution that gained some currency in this context was the community granary, by origin, as we have seen, the scheme of Chu Hsi.

The Lu family of Chin-ch'i County were, it seems, the first to apply Chu's plan in Fu-chou. Lu Chiu-yüan held office from 1184 to 1186 as Revising Official in the capital's Bureau of Edicts and Statutes[10] and in that capacity had been involved in the compilation of existing statutes and edicts on relief and welfare. He had thus become familiar and, despite his philosophical differences with Chu, had been impressed with the community granary proposal, which had been promulgated in 1181.[11] Thus when in 1188 (Lu Chiu-yüan having since returned home) the Chiang-hsi Intendant of Ever-Normal Granaries, Chao Ju-ch'ien, tried to recruit Fu-chou locals to found community granaries, Lu Chiu-yüan's elder brother Lu Chiu-shao responded, and a granary was established near the Lu residence under Chiu-shao's administration. It served an area of only two *tu* units (out of a total of forty-nine in the county), but according to Lu Chiu-yüan these were the only part of the county without resident wealthy families who might provide rice loans in the granary's absence. Here the farming people were largely tenants either on official estates or on land of absentee officeholding households: in spring and summer, when they needed rice, they had until now been forced to travel to purchase grain from wealthy families in other cantons. In the year after its founding, in a time of drought, the areas served by the granary, almost alone in the county, were well supplied with rice.[12] Nothing is known of the history of this granary in later years.

Lu Chiu-yüan implies that his brother had been the only one to respond to Chao Ju-ch'ien's call for local men to found community granaries.[13] The establishment of the Lu granary, however, may have been one of two events that disseminated knowledge of Chu Hsi's scheme among the Fu-chou local elite: the other was the founding of a community granary in 1194 by two brothers from a Wu family in Nan-ch'eng, the metropolitan county of the neighboring prefecture of Chien-ch'ang Chün.[14] Whereas earlier community granaries seem mainly to have been established some distance away, in Fu-chien and Liang-che circuits, Nan-ch'eng directly bordered Fu-chou's Lin-ch'uan, Chin-ch'i, and I-huang counties; furthermore the founding Wu brothers were students of Pao Yang,[15] who along with two of his own brothers had studied with Lu Chiu-yüan until Lu's death in 1192, afterward leading his students elsewhere to become followers of Chu Hsi.[16] The Paos and Wus must still have had personal connections in Fu-chou only two years after Lu's death, and the founding of this granary six years after the Lus established their own may have done much to reinforce interest in the plan in Fu-chou. Thus, Ts'ao Yao-tzu of I-huang (member of a family that had produced three prefectural graduates since 1070, and father of a 1208 *chin-shih*)[17] is known to have made plans in the mid-1190s to establish a granary on Chu's model, but died without fulfilling his ambition.[18] Jao Shih-heng, also of I-huang and an 1185 *chin-shih*, founded a community granary on his retirement from office, probably early in the thirteenth century.[19] A community granary managed by the Jao family of Ch'ung-jen[20] seems to have been founded at around the same time.[21] Thus the last decade of the twelfth and first decades of the thirteenth century seem to have been the time of the first flowering of the community granary in Fu-chou.

Two later community granaries were both associated with militia activity.

At the time of bandit trouble in 1230 the leaders of the Teng Society of Chin-ch'i, because official supplies were forthcoming only for one of their forts, made contributions of their own grain and solicited similar contributions from other local 'great families' as provision for their troops during the fighting. After order had been restored, they used the remaining provisions to stock two granaries in the general vicinity of their residence and 'copied the method of Chu Hsi's community granary, distributing in the spring and collecting in the fall' in order to provide grain to members of the Society who lacked it.[22] Similarly, when Hou Ting of I-huang built a fort and organized a militia after the 1230 disorders, he gave 3,000 *shih* of his own rice and accepted contributions from other wealthy men among his kin for a granary in the fort. This store was intended for the use of his troops in case of renewed banditry, but in the meantime it 'followed the law of Ch'un-hsi' (1174–89) – that is, Chu Hsi's community granary plan – and made spring loans to farmers at 20 per cent interest 'in hopes of increasing its stores.'[23] Clearly a community granary could be made to serve functions more specific than the general welfare of local farmers. It is striking as well that a granary by this time could be described as following Chu Hsi's plan despite (in Hou's case) the clear absence of any intention to eliminate interest, and despite an equally clear concern for increasing stores beyond the original investment. The tendency for community granaries to continue indefinitely the taking of interest, frequently at rates higher than 20 per cent, seems to have become endemic: by 1271 the prefect Huang Chen was ready to comment approvingly on one Li I of Chin-ch'i, whose community granary 'took only 20 per cent interest,'[24] and noted that the granary of the Ch'ung-jen Jao family, probably about sixty years old by this time, regularly took in large amounts of interest in years of good harvest.[25] It would appear from Huang's testimony that there were by this time quite a large number of community granaries in Fu-chou, all privately established and administered.[26]

The essential characteristic of the community granary as first conceived, and undoubtedly an important reason for its repeated adoption by elite families, was that although it served a charitable function (the provision of rice loans at low interest or interest-free at a time of year when grain prices were invariably high), it was designed to pay for itself and so to require little long-term sacrifice from its founders, whether these were county administrators or local gentlemen. This was the object of an initial period in which interest was levied in order to pay back the original investment of grain. Thereafter losses of grain, whether through spoilage or through failure to repay, were to be covered by the 3 per cent handling charge. However, from early on it became evident that in fact a granary run on this model would not necessarily pay for itself, since the likelihood of borrower default in years of poor harvest was high. Thus Lu Chiu-yüan, soon after his brother had begun administering their community granary, sought further official funds for a normal-purchase granary to supplement it:

> The community granary of my humble county is, to be sure, presently of benefit to the farmer; but I have never been at ease about it. For while the years are continuously prosperous and the fields constantly fertile, its benefits may be lasting; [but] if the fields are not constantly fertile and there should be a year of dearth, then there will be distribution but no collection, and when in the following years there is a lack of seed and provisions there will be nothing with which to supply it. It would be best to establish concurrently a granary for normal purchase and, in times of prosperity, to make grain purchases to obviate the problem of a fall in grain prices that might harm the farmer, while in times of dearth making grain sales, so as to abort the schemes of rich people to shut up their granaries and drive up prices. Let one split what is purchased into two parts, always retaining one as provision to make up the deficits of the community granary in times of dearth. This will truly make for long-term accumulation.[27]

The normal-purchase granary proposed here is precisely the same institution as the normal-sale granary maintained by the state, but in this case privately run. Here what is crucial is that it is offered as a means to maintain the rice supplies of a community granary that cannot recover on all its loans. The proposal makes sense only if the normal-purchase granary itself was a profit-making institution, and in fact it could be: variations in rice prices were great enough that one could undersell the market when the price was high, overpay when the price was low, and still sell for more than one paid. With competent administration the problem of grain losses should not arise, as no grain changed hands without payment. At the same time, insofar as the granary helped to stabilize rice prices and spare rural families the worst effects of extreme price swings, it could justly be seen as performing a charitable function. Thus it was precisely the sort of self-funding charitable institution that the community granary had been intended to be. Lu Chiu-yüan elsewhere remarks that 'normal purchase can be instituted by itself; a community granary cannot necessarily be instituted by itself.'[28] In view of this it is not surprising that in Southern Sung Fu-chou normal-purchase (or normal-sale) granaries were established both as adjuncts to community granaries and in their stead.[29] I have mentioned above Ts'ao Yao-tzu's desire to establish a community granary: when in 1198 his sons undertook to carry out the spirit if not the letter of his wishes, the granary they founded was in fact (though not in name) a normal-sale granary.[30] The Ch'ung-jen men Jao Meng-k'uei and

Ch'en Yüan-chin, both officeholders of prominent family background,[31] founded a normal-sale granary in their own county at some time in the early or middle thirteenth century.

A second solution to the problem of the survival of a community granary was simply to charge interest at a rate high enough to offset losses from defaulters. The evident tendency, with time, to retain interest as a permanent feature, and to push the rate well above 20 per cent, may in fact reflect the widespread adoption of this solution by Fu-chou elite members; but these tendencies may be accounted for more simply by the wish to make the community granary a profitable venture. This would not necessarily have violated the spirit of the institution in the minds of its administrators, since normal private interest rates at the time were so high — sometimes reaching 100 per cent[32] — that rates well in excess of 20 per cent could still be seen as representing a real sacrifice. Once it was conventionally accepted that profit was a proper function of a granary based in theory on Chu Hsi's model — as it certainly must have been by the 1240s, when Hou Ting's use of the institution to increase the store of supplies for his troops was recorded without comment — one would expect the granaries to begin to act more and more as any lending institution whose function is profit might act. And indeed in 1271, at a time of drought, one finds the administrator of the community granary of the Jaos of Ch'ung-jen County refusing outright to make loans to poor families, in the expectation that they will be unable to repay.[33]

A third possible solution to the community granary problem was simply to abandon the notion of a self-replenishing charitable institution and to accept the need for continual input of new funds. This was the solution proposed by prefect Huang Chen: he suggested that a privately-run granary should collect rents from fields attached to it and in poor years simply distribute its stores as grants rather than as loans. This was essentially the system followed by the Charitable Granaries under the Intendancy in the prefectural city; but these, of course were governmental institutions. There is no evidence of widespread private adoption of such a system. Huang Chen's proposal seems to have been largely out of touch with the real trend of local elite practice.

We cannot know to what extent the community granary, or its complement the private normal-purchase granary, achieved their purposes of making credit more easily available to the farmer or of stabilizing grain prices in the countryside. Chu Hsi's own plan, certainly, cannot be called entirely successful, if only because later versions of the institution he promoted diverged significantly — in making interest charges a permanent feature — from Chu's scheme.[34] The divergence from Chu, however, can be looked at from still another side. Certain members of the Fu-chou elite, it seems, had learned that profit could be had by offering, on the foundation of a relatively large permanent store of grain and on a scale presumably broader than the activity of typical rural lenders of the time, credit at less than customary interest rates. Where Wang An-shih had undersold private creditors to swell the revenues of the state, the community granary, as modified, could be used — especially when the original stock, as was often the case, was provided by the state — to undersell competing lenders for private gain. In the notion behind the community granary (especially when it was used in tandem with a normal-purchase granary), we may also see a forerunner of the interest in cost-free charities that one finds in certain Ming dynasty morality books. But for the purposes of my central argument here, the community granary and private normal-purchase granary are important because through them, as through the private local militias that arose in the same period, men of the Fu-chou elite moved, on a private and local basis, into an institutional and social space left vacant by the withdrawal or failures of state power.

Famine relief

Although community and normal-purchase granaries were very often founded hard on the heels of famines and by men who had been recently involved in famine relief,[35] they were not specifically designed for years of poor harvest; they were to serve year in and year out as a cushion for poor and middling farmers in seasons when food was scarcest and prices were highest. In the drought-provoked agricultural crises that were a recurrent feature of Chiang-hsi rural life in Southern Sung, recourse was had to other, *ad hoc* measures, in which once again members of the local elite frequently played an important role. Thus in the funerary inscription of Ko Keng of Chin-ch'i County we learn that, in 1139:

> [...] the year was one of drought. The next year the people had difficulty buying rice, one *tou* of rice exceeding ten cash; the wealthy people were shutting up their granaries. At this time [Ko Keng] took the lead in lowering the price and distributing his rice. To those who came empty-handed he granted loans on the spot.[36]

Similarly of Ko Keng's neighbor Lu Chiu-kao we are told:

> In the *ting-wei* year of Ch'un-hsi [1187] in Chiang-hsi the year was one of drought. In Fu-chou it was severe; and of Fu-chou's five counties it was most severe in Chin-chi. The Granaries Office [i.e. the Intendancy of Ever-Normal Granaries] and prefect gave their attention to relief; they separately deputed Liao Shih to oversee it. Liao was acquainted with the theory that it is best to find one's men locally, and that nothing is worse than for clerks to take part. He came to the house and questioned [Lu] about plans and policies, then drafted him as canton officer

[. . .] In the next year relief sales were implemented: [Lu] issued grain
and received grain, all without the abuses of other times. The villages,
rejoicing, did not know it was a year of dearth.[37]

These examples are only two of about fifteen, gathered from funerary
inscriptions and other sources, of Fu-chou men involved in the sale of grain at
less than market prices as an extraordinary response to famine; most of these
fall in Southern Sung.[38] The two examples cited here illustrate two recurrent
themes in famine relief in Fu-chou. First, in Lu Chiu-kao's funerary inscription reference is made to the 'theory' (*shuo*) that famine relief should be run
or provided by local men, and that government clerks should be barred from
influencing the process. This was rather a commonplace of Southern Sung
thinking.[39] Second, in Ko Keng's inscription we find that Ko, when he lowered
his prices in 1139, was deviating from the current practice of wealthy local
families, who were refusing to sell.

The reluctance or refusal of most wealthy families to sell their rice, or to
sell below current prices, in times of dearth is mentioned repeatedly in Fu-
chou sources. Thus in the funerary inscription of Huang Ssu-yung of Lin-
ch'uan County we are told that Huang, during a shortage of the early 1200s,
was the only man in his area to sell his grain at reduced prices and so provide
relief to local communities.[40] One might dismiss such references in funerary
inscriptions as attempts to magnify the virtues of their subjects by setting
them against a background of their supposed moral inferiors, if it were not
that rather extensive documentation survives of the struggle during a 1271
famine between the Fu-chou administrator Huang Chen and large numbers of
wealthy local families, who had closed their granaries to purchasers and were
awaiting further price rises. These documents are an invaluable source for the
study of Sung famine relief. They cannot be dealt with fully here; but one
aspect of the case requires examination.

From his arrival in Fu-chou in the fourth month of 1271 Huang Chen
began issuing public notices urging the wealthy families of the prefecture to
cease hoarding rice and begin selling, despite the likelihood that higher prices
could be obtained later on.[41] On the tenth day of his service in the prefecture he issued a notice listing the names of hoarders in Lo-an County. As the
list uses what appear to be the men's courtesy names, almost none of them
is directly identifiable.[42] Their surnames, however, are as follows: Chan
(three men), Tseng (five men), K'ang (one man), Chou (one man), Huang
(eleven men), Ch'en (two men), Ch'iu (one man), Teng (one man), Chang
(two men), and Cheng (two men).[43] One may compare the surnames of the
reconstructed Lo-an local elite families listed in Appendix I who were
present in 1271: Chan, Tseng, Chou, Huang, Ch'en, Teng, Chang, Cheng, Chu,
Ch'üeh, Ho, Li, Tung.[44] The coincidence of eight surnames here suggests that

many of the wealthy hoarders may in fact have been members of the re-constructed elite families,[45] and that the hoarding problem (to describe it from Huang Chen's point of view) was endemic in Lo-an.

A month later Huang was directing his attention specifically at two of the Lo-an men on the earlier list, now identified more circumstantially: one sur-named Chou, from a place called Huai-jen; and one surnamed K'ang, from a place called Lung-i.[46] The earlier history of the Chous of Huai-jen has been discussed in the second chapter. Of the K'angs nothing is known before this date; but their place of residence, Lung-i, is identifiable from later gazetteers and lies in the same general northeastern part of the district as Huai-jen[47] (see below, Map 18). Huang first ordered the vice-administrator of Lo-an, a Mr Liang, to go into the countryside, force the opening of the Chou and K'ang granaries, and administer the selling of their hoarded rice.[48] A month later in another public notice Huang acknowledged that the problem of the Chou grain was still unresolved, since the vice-administrator had gone first to the K'ang household; the news of his mission had spread to the Chous, who had emptied their granaries, hidden their grain, and now claimed to have none left to sell. Thus Huang now ordered Liang's superior the Lo-an administrator, Mr Shih, to take Liang's place in the countryside and compel the sale of the Chou rice.[49] Shortly afterwards he issued a further notice repeating this order. Here he further commented that 'vice-administrator Liang, whom I had deputed, was not very vigorous in his assignment, but every day drank the Chou household's fine wine and napped in their cool beds.' In the meantime, as he had heard, the potential rice-purchasers in the area, in fear of later retaliation by the Chou family, were expressing considerable reluctance to show up for the promised sales of Chou grain.[50]

Huang's comments on the Chou case suggest the considerable influence that local elite families (of whom the Huai-jen Chous were hardly a particularly illustrious or powerful example) could wield both over officials — even those sent specifically to control them, like vice-administrator Liang — and over the less well-off households around them. As no later public notices about the cases have been preserved, there is no way of knowing whether in the end the Chous were compelled to sell. By dropping the subject of the K'angs, the notices seem to imply that they, at least, had given in. But other evidence indicates they had not.

In the funerary inscription of Cheng Sung of Lo-an, Cheng's friend Wu Ch'eng tells us:

> He was several times tested at the Board of Rites [i.e. in the *chin-shih* examination] but failed; but through his poems he came to the notice of the prefect, who was then carrying out famine relief. There was a local wealthy household that shut up its granary, and the prefect was

going to take punitive steps. [Cheng] came to the rescue and obtained remission [for them] ; the wealthy household in gratitude formed marriage ties with him [...] His wife, of the K'ang family, had all the wifely virtues [...] [51]

Cheng Sung was thirty-six in 1271;[52] as his wife's surname was K'ang, it is virtually certain that the case discussed here is that of the K'angs of Lung-i, who evidently took Cheng as their son-in-law when he intervened with the prefect (Huang Chen) on their behalf. The nature of his intervention is left entirely vague, but the K'angs would surely not have rewarded him with their daughter if his contribution had been to persuade them to give in. It would seem instead that Huang dropped the issue of the K'angs in his second and third notices because Cheng had persuaded him to drop it or had worked out some compromise satisfactory to the K'angs. The Cheng family's history of militia activity (see above, p. 148) may perhaps have strengthened Cheng's influence here. The first list of hoarders, it is worth recalling, had included two men surnamed Cheng. The residences of the K'angs, Chous, and Chengs are indicated in Map 18.

The cases of the K'angs and the Chous suggest the real difficulties a Southern Sung official might face in trying to impose his will on local elite families in the countryside. On the existing evidence the point should not be pressed too far. It does appear from Huang Chen's public notices and memorials as a whole that most wealthy locals began selling their grain during the first several months of his term. A prefect might, like Huang Chen, find punishment sometimes beyond his means;[53] but he could still resort to rewards. Thus Huang's success — if success it was — may have owed much to the schedule of compensation that he offered, at about this time, for voluntary rice sales. Men who sold 10,000 *shih* or more were to receive office; those already in office were to be promoted.[54] True to his word, at the close of the relief program Huang asked the court to grant appointments for five men whose sales together amounted to almost 110,000 *shih* — a quantity half again as great, for example, as the 'Harmonious Purchase' tax quota for the entire prefecture in 1271.[55] The promise of rewards gave Huang an entering wedge into the circle of reluctant wealthy families. Once several of them had broken ranks and sold large quantities of rice in hopes of office, the sellers' boycott would be weakened, the price would begin to fall, and others might follow suit rather than watch it fall further. If reward-offices were, for the local elite, an important first route into officialdom, they were also, from the other side, one of the very few reliable means an activist local official had for gaining the cooperation he needed.

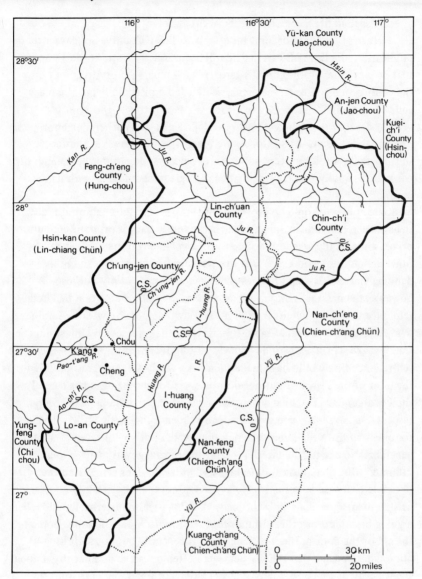

Map 18. Residences of K'ang, Chou, and Cheng families of Lo-an County.

A speculative digression on social thought

Huang Chen did not limit his efforts to Lo-an County. Six days after his publication of a list of Lo-an rice hoarders, he issued a notice proclaiming that he was ordering the administrator of Lin-ch'uan County to go out into the countryside and open the granaries of a Jao household living at a place called Nan-t'ang.[56] According to Huang the Jaos, living in the county's seventy-seventh *tu*, owned extensive properties in three other, neighboring *tu*; most of the residents of all three were tenants of the Jaos. Yet the Jaos not only would not sell but went so far as to 'delude and confuse the feelings of the people, falsely proclaiming that each single *tu* should deal with its own affairs.'[57]

Some context should be provided for this passage: the assumption seems to have been common in Sung China that in times of crisis or in the agricultural off-season a family was responsible for the well-being of its own tenants or other agricultural workers.[58] It is this responsibility that the Jao family was denying and that Huang Chen was trying to enforce. For my purpose, however, the passage is important as perhaps the only source that makes any reference to the arguments framed in their own defense by wealthy families who refused to make relief sales. Even this hostile reference is almost impenetrably vague. If Huang is to be believed, the Jaos argued for a sort of local self-reliance that would have made them, as a wealthy family, responsible for the poor of their own *tu* but not of others. As Joanna Handlin has recently shown, arguments for what seems the same principle could be made on quite respectable grounds – and were made, by Ch'en Lung-cheng (1585–1645) for one – in the Ming dynasty, when they were clearly connected to a more general resistance to 'the interference of the central government in local affairs.'[59] But there is no way to know whether the Jaos articulated the principle nearly so systematically. In the sources there is certainly no dearth of statements (particularly by officials planning or administering famine relief) arguing on ethical or other grounds that wealthy rural families must come to the aid of the poor in times of famine.[60] In contrast (but not surprisingly), although it appears that relief-sellers were often only a small minority among the wealthy of Fu-chou, there is hardly any record of arguments from the other side.

Many of the arguments that officials and others used in exhorting local men to charity seem to imply an absence of ethical consensus on the issue. Huang Chen, in his repeated public notices urging the sale of stored rice, argues often from morality,[61] but almost as often from utility or from self-interest: the wealthy should sell now to secure high profits lest the price fall suddenly before they have sold,[62] virtuous action now will bring rewards in the future.[63] Utilitarian justifications for charity were commonplace. Thus

Lu Chiu-yüan's younger brother Chiu-shao argued that, so long as funds were sufficient, one should give assistance to others, because if one did not one would risk conflict with those who expected aid.[64] One reads Aesopian tales of families spared by bandits because of their record of relief sales or other charities,[65] and the Southern Sung man Yüan Ts'ai, in his manual of household management, makes the implied moral explicit: one should be charitable precisely in order that bandits will pass one by.[66] The use of such arguments from self-interest may reflect underlying disagreement or uncertainty as to the ethical basis — or more broadly, the basis in general rules of social behavior — of charity in general and of relief grain sales in particular. In fact, although no explicit ideological defense of abstention from charity or refusal to sell grain has survived, the elements that might go to make up such a defense were widely available from intellectual sources that commanded considerable social approval.

Lu Chiu-shao, whose justification of charity I have already cited, was the author of a set of family rules that spelled out in great detail the proper organization and management of a household and the role of each member. Contemporaries regarded the Lu family organization as something of a model,[67] and Chiu-shao's program of household management won particular praise.[68] Something of his approach to the problem may be gathered from several passages of his 'Daily Notes' (*Jih-chi*) that have been preserved in the Ch'ing compilation of Sung and Yüan philosophical schools, the *Sung-Yüan hsüeh-an*. It is evident that Lu Chiu-shao stressed economy, frugality, and careful budgeting with an eye to preserving the family property and, ultimately, preventing the breakup of the household. In a characteristic passage, Lu urges that one divide one's after-tax income into ten parts, putting aside three as provision against natural disasters and one for expenditures on sacrifices. The remaining six tenths one should split into twelve, one for each month; each of these should then be divided into thirty parts for the thirty days of the month. This final fraction is the highest expenditure allowed for each day. Lu stresses that one need not spend all of each day's share, but recommends 70 percent as a proportion to aim at. This will leave a further surplus. Then:

> For what is left over, establish separate books, and apply it to summer and winter clothing, repairs to walls and houses, doctors and medicines, entertaining, condolence calls, visits to the sick, and seasonal gifts. *If there is still some left over*, distribute it among the poor of the neighborhood and the lineage, worthy gentlemen in difficult straits, *tenants who are hungry or cold*, or passersby without means of support.[69]
> (Emphasis mine)

Here is a budgeting method in which (aside from provision for disasters and sacrifices) income is allotted first to the expenses of daily living; what is left goes first to periodic expenses (clothing, repairs, etc.), then to the amenities of social life — everything comprehended by the narrower sense of the word *li* — and only then to categories that one might call charity. Further on Lu advises those whose resources are limited:

> One who has few fields and ample expenses can only take the road of purifying his heart, being frugal and simple, and managing things so as to assure sufficiency of food. As to entertaining visitors, condolence calls, visits to the sick, seasonal gifts, or getting together for eating and drinking: these are not to be considered.[70]

Here *li* seems to be virtually excluded for a family whose income is stretched tight by its other expenses. In continuing, however, Lu softens this implication: 'I mean only that [in such circumstances] *one cannot use one's wealth* for *li*.'[71] (Emphasis mine.) He goes on to indicate ways in which the spirit of *li* can be fulfilled without the expenditure of wealth. For my argument, however, what is important is that if *li* — which took priority over charity in Lu's general statement — may not absorb wealth, then surely charity must be similarly excluded where resources are limited.

As I have already noted, Lu argues in favor of charity; but he does so on pragmatic grounds — stinginess makes enemies — that are extrinsic to his fundamental approach. (A contemporary might after all have argued that failure to give gifts at weddings and funerals — which Lu is willing to countenance — would likewise make enemies.) At bottom Lu is proposing a sort of ethic of economy that treats the continuance of the family, hence the maintenance of property, as primary and subordinates considerations of *li* (as customarily practiced at least), or of altruism beyond the household, to this central goal. One must not mistake this for an abandonment of ethical concerns, since the maintenance of a household over the generations — the avoidance of *p'o-chia*, the destruction of the family — was itself an ethical value of considerable respectability for many in Lu's time.[72] At the same time it is clear that Lu's standards leave considerable leeway for the household head to determine when his resources are adequate for the luxuries of *li* and charity, and when they are not. He proposes no such absolute rule as, say, the responsibility of a family for its tenants in time of need.

A second relevant ideological strand may be found in a manual of famine relief, the *Chiu-huang huo-min shu*, written around 1202 by another man of the P'o-yang Lake region, Tung Wei of Jao-chou, Fu-chou's northern neighbor. The book achieved a certain influence in later dynasties;[73] its influence in its own time is hard to measure, but the author's own performance in administration of famine relief while a local official had been praised in a decree by the emperor Ning-tsung,[74] and the book was presented to and accepted by the throne. One may assume then that the work received a certain exposure at the time and that the views it expressed were shared by at least some contemporaries. Most significant here is Tung Wei's evaluation of two strategies of famine relief. On the forcible lowering of rice prices (*i-chia*) by officials to allow poor people to buy, he argued:

> [Those who advocate this strategy] do not realize that if officials force down the price, then *k'o-mi* [rice brought in for sale by travelling merchants who have bought it in other regions] will not come in. If the price mounts in other places, and is low only in this area, then who will be willing to bring it here for sale? If it is not brought for sale, then within our borders people will lack food. Still less will the upper households with accumulated stores venture to offer them for sale. The hungry people will hold their money in their hands all day long but will have nowhere to go to buy. But if one does not force down prices, then not only will the boats and carts [bringing rice] flock to the spot, but the upper households too, afraid of being too late in selling, will compete to be the first to open their granaries; and the price of rice will fall of itself.[75]

In other words, the price should be allowed naturally to rise to a level that will attract sellers, who will respond to the opportunity for profit and provide the grain needed in the famine; the consequent increase in supply will in turn automatically drive the price back down. Tung also deals with a policy adopted by some local officials during famine called 'barring grain purchase' (*o-ti*) — a practice aimed at preventing the loss of rice from a prefecture or district to exporting merchants, which might lead to shrinkage of local supply and rises in prices. Against this Tung argues, in sum, that trade between prefectures or circuits is in fact the means by which *all* places can be supplied and famine relieved.[76] The empire — one's own prefecture no less than others — lives by trade.

Tung's discussion of both practices expresses a belief in the self-regulating and socially ameliorating capacities of an unrestricted commerce in grain. On this view, official action to limit artificially the prices at which goods are traded, or to hinder the free movement of goods from place to place, can only disrupt the operation of the supply and demand forces that would otherwise assure the feeding of the empire with a minimum of social friction. In this conception profit plays a crucial role. Arguing that where prices are artificially depressed, rice brokers from other districts will establish secret purchase contracts with wealthy locals at slightly above the official price (but still below the price elsewhere), Tung remarks: 'Men's pursuit of profit is like water's tending downward.'[77]

Sung men could hardly have failed to recognize here a dual allusion. First, to the great Han historian Ssu-ma Ch'ien, arguing against state intervention in commerce:

> When each person works away at his own occupation and delights in his own business, then, like water flowing downward, goods will naturally flow forth ceaselessly day and night without having been summoned, and the people will produce commodities without having been asked.[78]

Second, to Mencius, in his debate with Kao Tzu on the goodness or evil of human nature:

> 'It certainly is the case', said Mencius, 'that water does not show any preference for either east or west, but does it show the same indifference to high and low? Human nature is good just as water seeks low ground. There is no man who is not good; there is no water that does not flow downwards.'[79]

Tung would not have used the water-tending-downward metaphor if he had meant profit to be seen as even a necessary evil. For him, it seems, the urge to profit is (*a*) part of human nature, and (*b*) beneficial, since it is owing to it that a rise in price can act as a stimulus to supply and so counteract itself.

In Tung's free-market approach to famine relief and Lu's ethic of household economy we find, it seems to me, the elements that Fu-chou elite families could use to justify their refusal to sell their grain. Both tend to validate the free disposition of property by wealthy private households in ways that redound to the benefit of their domestic economy. Lu anchors this in the widely accepted value of the perpetuation of the household; Tung undercuts the competing claims of altruism or social obligation by arguing that an un-regulated rice market will better serve the very goals to which altruism aspires. Fu-chou abstainers from official relief sales programs could argue confidently that their first obligation was to assure a foundation for their posterity, and that, in any case, in refusing to sell before the price reached its natural level they were playing their allotted role in a market whose beneficial operations official action only hindered. They will have felt themselves on particularly firm ideological ground when local officials forbade them to export rice from Fu-chou; both Huang Chen in 1271 and his predecessor Huang Kan in 1208 in fact made this prohibition their first order of business.[80] Huang Chen repeatedly proclaimed his intention not to force down prices[81] — demon-strating the currency that Tung's position possessed — but his efforts to compel the sale of grain before prices rose further will have been read as, in effect, an artificial price ceiling.

This discussion has been frankly speculative, as there is no direct evidence of the ideology of the Fu-chou elite as it concerned famine relief. Still the likelihood that the elements of the position I have sketched had diffused widely in Fu-chou by late Southern Sung seems to me rather strong. The intellectual history of Sung (indeed of Chinese) ideas on famine relief and social welfare deserves more systematic attention than it has yet received. In the meantime one may not assume that the ethical basis proposed by activist local officials, when they urged local elites to act in certain ways, was generally shared by local elites themselves. Huang's difficulties with the Fu-chou elite may reflect not only the limits of a local official's power, but fundamental disagreement as to what *should* be done.

Irrigation, water control, and dam building

In the early 1200s, during his term as administrator of Lin-ch'uan County, Huang Kan was entrusted by the prefect of Fu-chou with composing a memorial to the throne on his behalf, discussing several problems of local administration. The last of these was the problem of irrigation works. Huang wrote:

> The fields of Chiang-hsi are lean, and often dry; except by reliance on the benefits of dams, storage ponds, wells, and dikes, they would in most cases be waste. The recurrent famines and droughts of recent years have all been largely due to the disrepair of irrigation works. The best course would be to reinstitute enforcement of the old law, deputing the vice-administrator of the prefecture and of each county first to register for every canton the breadth and depth of irrigation works and then, when the streams and rivers are dry and low, during free periods in the agricultural year, to entrust the superior guard units to assemble the people and dredge and deepen the bottoms and build up the tops [...] Though there be toil in the beginning, yet in the end it will benefit the people. Then Heaven's disasters will do no harm, and abundant harvests may be permanently assured.[82]

Huang poses two related issues here: the importance of man-made irrigation works in the region that included Fu-chou, and the role of the state in their construction and maintenance. The Fu-chou sources yield less information than one would wish on these issues; but in what follows I will attempt to make use of what has survived, concentrating once again on the relative roles of the state and the local elite.

Though in his memorial Huang discussed Chiang-hsi circuit in general, one may assume that, as he wrote on behalf of the Fu-chou prefect, his remarks on the importance of irrigation works applied to Fu-chou in particular. Similarly, when in 1192 Lu Chiu-yüan, from his post as administrator of

Ching-men Chün in Ching-hu-pei circuit, addressed a letter to the circuit military intendant comparing agricultural conditions in Ching-men with those more familiar to him in Chiang-tung and Chiang-hsi circuits, he will have had his home prefecture in mind:

> In Chiang-tung and Chiang-hsi the water from dams often reaches even the high and level places; hereabouts it cannot, for the dams they make are neither as many nor as good as in Chiang-tung and Chiang-hsi.[83]

Here Huang and Lu echo earlier remarks by the Northern Sung man Hsieh K'o:[84] all confirm the abundance and importance of irrigation dams in Fu-chou, something one would in any case have expected in a place where rice culture was crucially important and where (at least in Southern Sung) long periods of little rainfall in the growing season were not uncommon. More direct evidence is to be found in a fragment of a Sung gazetteer from the Ching-ting period (1260–4), which preserves a set of lists of the names of dams for all five counties of Fu-chou proper in later Southern Sung.[85] The numbers are startling: 342 dams in Chin-ch'i, 303 in Lin-ch'uan, 135 in Ch'ung-jen, 114 in Lo-an, and 61 in I-huang: a total of 995 dams,[86] or one for every 227 rural households recorded in the population records for the same period.[87] It seems likely that only the more important irrigation works of the prefecture would have acquired names and earned mention in a gazetteer; many small and makeshift dams may not be recorded.

If dams were abundant in Fu-chou, they were apparently rather small compared to the irrigation works of other regions of China. Figures survive for the numbers of works repaired or constructed in each circuit on government initiative between 1070 and 1076 under Wang An-shih's national program to revitalize irrigation systems; also recorded are the total acreages of land thus brought under (or restored to) irrigation in each circuit. For Chiang-hsi the average area watered by a new or repaired installation was 4.89 *ch'ing* (489 mou); to this one may compare the averages for Liang-che circuits (52.95 *ch'ing*), for Huai-tung circuit (60.74 *ch'ing*), or for Chiang-hsi's neighbors. Chiang-tung (20.99 *ch'ing*) and Fu-chien (14.27 *ch'ing*) circuits.[88] Comparable figures for specific dams in Fu-chou are rare. The gazetteer lists give watering-area figures only for the Po Pei ('Far-reaching Dam') in the far south of Lin-ch'uan County, which irrigated 63 *ch'ing*.[89] In view of its name, its place of honor at the head of the list and well apart from other dams in its canton, and the unique notation of its watering-area, one must assume that this dam was regarded as extraordinarily large in Fu-chou; yet it would have been little better than average among the Northern Sung dams recorded for Huai-tung and Liang-che. Similarly, when in a mid-Southern Sung funerary inscription for a Fu-chou woman, in an account of her reconstruction of a dam near her home, one finds a very unusual reference to the area it irrigated (20 *ch'ing*),[90] it is surely because the dam was unusually large. It would appear that, in Fu-chou, irrigation water was supplied in part by a rather large number of (for the most part) relatively small local dams.

As to the role of the local elite in the building, maintenance, and management of dams, direct evidence is sparse. Like most of the everyday miscellany of economic life, the repair or construction of irrigation works came in for little attention in the kinds of private sources that have survived; if inscriptional records were made, they were not taken into the collected works of the men who wrote them. There is the funerary inscription mentioned above, for the wife of Miu Chao of Ch'ung-jen County, who died in 1191:

> East of her house was Lo Dam, which watered fields in excess of twenty *ch'ing*. Its banks were given to collapsing, and those who made their living by the fields were distressed. She took on the yearly task of rebuilding it. The families who owned the fields enjoyed the full benefits but did not share in the labor or expense.[91]

But this reference is virtually unparalleled in other Fu-chou funerary inscriptions. A gazetteer biography of Chou Hsin-fu of Ch'ung-jen, who lived from 1222 to 1304, records his building an irrigation dam in the neighborhood of his home.[92] During the Shao-hsing period (1131–62) a wealthy Lin-ch'uan County man named Wang Chi-weng — not an officeholder, and entirely unrecorded elsewhere[93] — spent his own resources to build a large and important dike, later called the Ch'ien-chin Dam, near the prefectural city.[94] This was not strictly speaking a dam for the irrigation of fields: its purpose was to block off the new, unwanted second channel of the Ju River and so restore the old course, which flowed past and around the prefectural city, to its former level. In 1275 circuit officials sought a local volunteer to fund and organize a new restoration of the old channel — the problem was recurrent — and Cheng Sung of Lo-an County responded and received an office as his reward.[95]

These four are the only references of their kind in the Fu-chou sources. They are certainly few enough, but do show that members of the local elite sometimes involved themselves in the building and maintenance of irrigation and water-control works. In the light of these examples certain less unambiguous evidence appears significant: this is provided by the names of dams. The late Sung dam list for Chin-ch'i County includes a 'Lu Family Dam': this can be identified as located in Chin-ch'i's thirty-sixth *tu*.[96] This *tu* was also the site of Ch'ing-t'ien, the residence of the family of Lu Chiu-yüan.[97] In the same list are a 'Ko Family Dam,' and a 'Huang Family Dam.' The former can be located in the forty-third *tu*;[98] the Ko family of Chin-ch'i lived at Ko-fang in the forty-fourth *tu*, just next door to the forty-third.[99] The Huang Family Dam can be placed in the nineteenth *tu*;[100] a prominent Huang family is recorded in sources for Northern Sung living in the eighteenth *tu*, again just next door.[101] Two similar cases appear in the list for I-huang County: a 'Tai Family Dam,' and a 'Little Yüeh Family Dam.' The first of these can be placed in the eleventh *tu* of Ch'ung-hsien canton:[102] the prominent Tai family of I-huang lived at Huang-pei in the same *tu*.[103] The Little Yüeh Family Dam can be located in the fourteenth *tu* of the same canton;[104] the Yüeh family of I-huang lived at Huo-yüan, once again in the same *tu*.[105]

These matches of dam names with the surnames of local elite families in the same or adjacent *tu* cannot be mere coincidence; in all likelihood the dams bore the names of the families that owned, managed, or had built them. A great many other dams in the lists bear the names of families who cannot as easily be identified or for whom more than one identification is plausible. These too, I think, may be taken as evidence of the involvement of rural elite (and possibly other) families in the building, repair, or ownership of irrigation works.

The role of the state too can only be approached impressionistically. In principle, local officials — the vice-administrators of prefectures and counties in particular — were responsible throughout Sung for the adequate maintenance of irrigation systems within their jurisdictions. How fully these responsibilities were met in Fu-chou during Northern Sung is a question that is rather hard to answer. It is known, however, that under Wang An-shih's irrigation program nearly a thousand installations were built or repaired in the ten prefectures of Chiang-hsi circuit between 1070 and 1076.[106] Fu-chou was far more densely populated than all but one or two other prefectures in the circuit, and it does not seem very unreasonable to suppose that it received a proportionately large share of the benefits of the program. If between one-tenth and one-fifth of the irrigation works built or restored were sited in Fu-chou (more, or much less, seems unlikely), these would account for about the same fraction of the dams known to have been in existence at the end of Sung: about ten or twenty per cent. This is a rather significant portion for the state to have contributed in only seven of Sung's three hundred years. A central government capable of a program of this magnitude may also have been able to meet, through its agents in the prefecture, the more ordinary year-to-year tasks of inspection and maintenance.

There were no such vast central projects in Southern Sung. More, despite recurrent central government attempts to reassert official responsibility for irrigation throughout the empire, in Fu-chou real official involvement was sporadic, limited, and largely ineffective. Huang Kan's memorial of the early 1200s, quoted at the beginning of this section, makes it clear that the responsibility of the vice-administrators for irrigation had long been merely theoretical — 'the best course would be to *reinstitute* enforcement of the *old law* [. . .]' (emphasis mine) — and that no usable register of dams existed any longer in the prefectural city. It seems likely that the registration of dams, with notation of their size, depth, state of repair, etc. — in theory a major part of the official role in irrigation — in fact generally followed the pattern of the registration of lands: this, in Southern Sung Fu-chou, seems to have occurred, if at all, only at intervals of eighty years or more, with massive or total losses of registers in between.[107]

In 1271 Huang Chen, having acquired concurrently with his prefectship of Fu-chou the post of Intendant of Ever-Normal Granaries for Chiang-hsi circuit — an office that in theory brought with it responsibility for local irrigation systems within the circuit — sent around an administrative order to the vice-administrators of the various prefectures of Chiang-hsi, asking them to take steps to encourage repair of dams in their respective prefectures, and touching on the measures taken thus far in Fu-chou:

> [. . .] Most recently I have selected and deputed prefectural finance inspector Wu to make inquiries into repair and construction, using polite encouragement and not trucking with official paperwork, following what is appropriate in each case and not setting up fixed policy; step by step, we have gradually made a start. But the several other prefectures are widely separated from this office; I can only clasp my hands and dare not exceed my limits, for fear that matters may fail of completion and merely create disturbances. I humbly desire that the vice-administrators use all means to make personal inquiries as to whether or not there are under their jurisdiction any places where irrigation works have deteriorated and should be repaired, or where they have been taken over by powerful families and should be restored [to their previous situation]. One might select a fellow-official to go out alone and make personal inspection, or one might order each county official to ask sojourning-resident upper-grade households to take part.[108]

Here the reference to the avoidance of official paperwork echoed Huang's general promise to local wealthy families that in his program of famine relief he would refrain from the use of written dispatches, lists, and registers that might later be manipulated by clerks, and would conduct as much of his business as possible in person or through private intermediaries.[109] In this way he hoped to win the cooperation of the Fu-chou elite. In general Huang's order projects a rather diffident view of what could be accomplished through official involvement in the field of irrigation maintenance. Again the need for personal inquiries would suggest, as in Huang Kan's memorial, that reliable registers of dams were not being maintained as a matter of administrative routine. Of particular interest, however, is his reference to irrigation works that had been taken over by powerful families in the localities: again this suggests a well-established withdrawal of the government from rural involvement – a withdrawal that Huang was trying at least partly to reverse.

By a stroke of luck a document that records the upshot of Huang's efforts has also survived: this is a 'General Record of Repair and Construction in Fu-chou,' listing and discussing official construction projects during Huang's term. Huang wrote this in the spring of 1273, just before leaving Fu-chou to serve as Judical Intendant of Chiang-hsi:

> As to water control works, we have repaired Lin-ch'uan County's South Lake and Shu Dam, restored I-huang County's Chia-lo Dam and Ch'ung-jen County's Yung-feng and Wan-chin Dams, and dredged that district city's two Chou-t'ung Dams, which had been clogged for forty years. Whenever a dam had been appropriated by the powerful and crafty, it has been returned to its former state.[110]

It is immediately evident that in sheer numbers Huang's program – having accomplished the repair of six dams and a man-made lake – had made only a fractional impression on Fu-chou irrigation systems overall. But its limitations were not only numerical. Apart from Shu Dam, which cannot be located, all the works that Huang had repaired were sited inside or immediately outside the prefectural city or respective county seat.[111] This is shown on Map 19 (which also includes two other installations that will be discussed below). The official repair program had left most of rural Fu-chou untouched. Huang's remark on the restoration of the status of dams that had been previously appropriated is more ambiguous: it is unclear whether he was referring only to all the repaired dams or to all dams in Fu-chou. The former is considerably more plausible; but even if Huang had in fact restored all or most of the prefecture's dams to official control and regulation, it would appear from his own testimony and from the earlier remarks of Huang Kan that in general such reassertions of state authority in Southern Sung can only have been sporadic and short-lived. Huang Chen proclaimed as a triumph achievements that are simply dwarfed by the Northern Sung program of the 1070s.

Two other Southern Sung water-control projects are recorded. The first is the Ch'ien-chin dam (see above, p. 169), built and rebuilt to block off a second course of the Ju River for the sake of the prefectural city's water supply. Fu-chou prefects undertook the rebuilding of the dam and/or the cutting of a new channel past the city in the late 1230s and, when this was unsuccessful, again in 1251.[112] The second is the Pao-t'ang Dike, built around 1208 by the Ch'ung-jen County administrator, apparently (the inscriptional record is incomplete) to control the flow of the Ch'ung-jen River as it passed

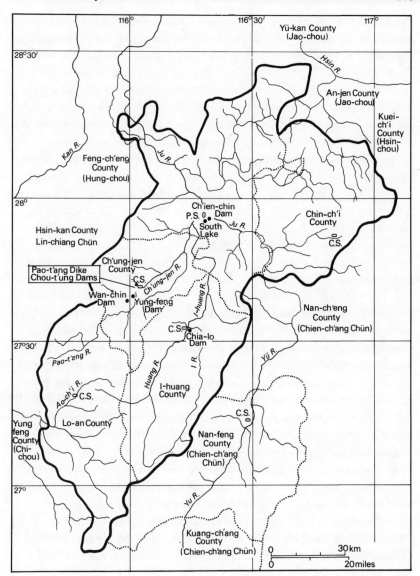

Map 19. Water-control works built by government.

through the middle of the county town.[113] Again, both these projects were sited at or just outside the prefectural or county seat (see Map 19), suggesting once more that official involvement in irrigation and water control in Southern Sung, when it occurred, clung to the cities and their immediate environs.

In view of this conclusion it is interesting to examine the roles of state and elite in a separate but similar area: bridgebuilding. Like irrigation maintenance, the repair and rebuilding of bridges was in Sung ideally regarded as one of the tasks of a local official.[114] Like dams, bridges performed important economic functions (by facilitating travel and commerce), and their construction or repair could absorb enormous quantities of provisions and money. It is impossible to say just how many bridges may have been built in Fu-chou during Sung; but records exist for twenty-two bridges in five of greater Fu-chou's six counties. Eighteen of these date from Southern Sung.[115] Of the eighteen, thirteen were private undertakings by local people (some officeholders, some not); one was the work of Buddhist monks; and four were built or rebuilt at least once by officials or with official participation. These last four were: the Wen-ch'ang Bridge, connecting the eastern gates of Lin-ch'uan's county seat (the prefectural city) with the east bank of the Ju River;[116] the Wen-ming Bridge, connecting the south gate of the Nan-feng County seat with the south bank of the Yü River;[117] the Huang-chou Bridge, crossing the Ch'ung-jen River to connect the northern and southern boroughs of the Ch'ung-jen County seat;[118] and the Ao-ch'i Bridge, connecting the Lo-an County seat with the market on the south bank of the Ao-ch'i River.[119] All of these, like the irrigation works already discussed, were located in or about the prefectural and county seats. Here again official initiative and enterprise seem not to have reached into the countryside.

In sharp contrast, bridges built privately were scattered throughout the Fu-chou countryside.[120] Even urban bridgebuilding was not an official monopoly: the Li-i Bridge, the equivalent in I-huang's county seat of the four listed above, was built in 1183 by the local gentleman T'u Hsiang-chung. Connecting the city with the east bank of the I-huang River, the bridge was over a thousand Sung feet in length, with lodgings for travelers at each end and a small temple in the middle housing a sculpted bodhisattva: all this was financed by T'u using only his own family's resources.[121] Even when officials involved themselves, they very frequently had recourse to the organizational and financial support of men of the local elite. For the 1225 reconstruction of the Wen-ch'ang Bridge the prefect solicited the aid of the Lin-ch'uan man, 1181 *chin-shih*, and high official Tung Chü-i in persuading other local men to participate. Yen Ta-cheng (see below, p. 000, n. 29) and Tung Chü-i's son Tung Hung-tao took on the task of managing funds and expenditures; Li Liu of Ch'ung-jen County contributed fields for the support of the Buddhist

temple that was to run the bridge and handle repairs.[122] Similar local elite
contributions are recorded, though in less detail, for the other three officially-
built bridges,[123] one of which (the Wen-ming Bridge in Nan-feng) had originally been the private project of the Northern Sung Nan-feng man
Chu Yen.[124] In short, the private bridge-building efforts of the local elite
spanned city and countryside; and if the surviving sources are any guide,
private projects far outnumbered those of local officials.

In bridgebuilding and in water control, then, the performance of the
Southern Sung state, or of its local representatives, was geographically restricted and on the whole rather ineffectual: its theoretical responsibilities (and,
in water control, its legal authority) were seldom fulfilled in practice. In
bridgebuilding the gap was abundantly filled by the local elite; in water
control, though the evidence is far more sketchy, Huang Chen's comments
suggest that the state's negligence again left the field open to local elite intervention. We know next to nothing of Northern Sung bridges,[125] but in water
control Northern Sung officialdom was capable, at least at times, of achievements far beyond what its Southern Sung successors could manage.

Here again, then, we see indications – perhaps less unambiguous in this
sphere than in others so far dealt with – of a retreat of the state from a kind
of power and activism in the countryside that it had at least laid claim to in
an earlier time; a retreat, whether voluntary or forced, that once again left a
space that men of the local elite could and did seek to fill. To be sure, not all
the processes we have seen in this and the preceding chapter that seem to fit
this pattern were in fact strictly parallel. In particular, the attitude of the
state and its agents to each of the elite involvements traced here, and the
degree to which, in each sphere, conflict rather than convergence of aims
informed the relationship of state to elite, surely varied greatly. A local
administrator might welcome the involvement of the local elite in bridgebuilding as relieving his own burdens; he might himself encourage or finance
the creation of privately-managed community granaries; and in times of
immediate military crisis he would surely be glad of the private local militia
that could come to the aid of his own limited forces. He, and his superiors
at court, would probably be more disturbed by the continuing presence of
the same militia in the countryside after the crisis had ended; by local elite
control of irrigation works; by the unforeseen uses to which, say, a community
granary, once in private hands, could be put, or the refusal of a granary
manager to fulfill the function for which the community granary was first
intended. The state in Southern Sung seems to have been as glad to invite the
local elite into some spheres of action as it was eager to exclude them from
others. (In one sphere, famine relief, as we have seen, the elite was not eager
to be invited; and the state found it hard to enforce the invitation.) Similarly,

elite men may have viewed some of the new involvements as golden opportunities, others as burdensome responsibilities to be accepted only because
the state's default made them inescapable. Nor should my constant use of the
words 'the Fu-chou elite' here give the impression of a united group with a
consensus as to its common interests. We have seen, for example, that one
elite man might set out to undermine the militia organization that another –
his neighbor and the brother of his teacher – was working to strengthen.
What is nonetheless common to everything dealt with in these chapters is a
movement of the elite – eagerly or willy-nilly, in convergence with state
interests or solely in the service of its own – into fields of action focused on
the locality, fields from which the state had withdrawn or where the state's
efforts had proven inadequate. The pattern as a whole is, once again, clearly
new in Southern Sung.

TEMPLE-BUILDING AND RELIGIOUS LIFE

Religion permeated life in Sung Fu-chou. Its forms were many and complex; to bring the various strands into orderly arrangement would be difficult and perhaps unfaithful to the facts. The changes from Northern to Southern Sung that I have been tracing so far are less obvious in this arena than elsewhere; but they do, I think, find some reflection here as well. I take as my point of attack three events in the history of Fu-chou religious life that, as I will argue, embody in different ways the themes — of center and locality, of state control and elite action — that have been central to much of what we have seen so far. The events bear little intrinsic relation to one another, though each was in some way new or out of the ordinary in its own time. Each can be recounted very briefly. First: at the beginning of the Hsüan-ho reign period (1119–25) of the emperor Hui-tsung, the T'ien-wang Buddhist temple in I-huang County was converted, by state decree, into a Taoist temple bearing the name Shen-hsiao. The change was brief: before long the temple had reverted to its original status and resumed its former name. Second: in the sixth month of 1190, during a drought in his home county, Lu Chiu-yüan offered private prayers for rain to the gods of Chin-ch'i's mountains and rivers. The texts of the prayers and of a prayer of thanks that Lu offered when rain did come were later gathered into Lu's collected works. Third: during his term as administrator of Fu-chou in the 1270s, Huang Chen — whom we have seen already in his struggle with wealthy ricehoarders — installed a portrait of the Neo-Confucian philosopher Chu Hsi in the ritual section of the official prefectural school, to encourage sacrifices to Chu by local scholars and gentlemen.

To show why these three events are of interest here, and something of what they meant in their own time, it is necessary to offer a broad background sketch of religion in Sung Fu-chou. The shrines to former worthies associated (more often than not) with official schools, which appear again here with Huang Chen's promotion of sacrifices to Chu Hsi, have already been touched on; they represent a tendency which, though important in itself, was perhaps largely tangential to the predominant forms of religious practice of the time. The other two of our three events, however, involve all of the three major spheres within which Fu-chou religious life (outside the household)[1] largely defined itself: Buddhism, Taoism, and the sphere of gods and spirits (*shen*).

At the end of Lu Chiu-shao's list of the uses that a householder might properly make of income budgeted to daily expenses but left unspent, he admonished his reader: 'Do not foolishly contribute to Buddhists or Taoists.'[2] Lu adds this so casually, and so briefly, that one could easily read it as a mere reiteration of conventional wisdom by a good Neo-Confucian, who assumes that his audience shares his assumptions and so does not dwell on the matter. In fact, however, in Sung Fu-chou the remark had enormous practical relevance and would have seemed deliberately controversial. It amounted to a repudiation of something commonplace among the local elite. In Fu-chou, to judge especially from the evidence of temple-building, Buddhism and Taoism both thrived.

Contemporaries were especially likely to comment on the strong position of Buddhism.[3] In this respect Fu-chou was typical of the P'o-yang basin as a whole. The abbot of the Pai-yün temple at Su Mountain in I-huang County, in an 1150 letter asking the visiting official Sun Ti to record the building of a sutra library at his temple, remarked: 'The great monasteries of Chiang-hsi are first in all the empire: eminent pagodas and fine halls are arrayed in hundreds.'[4] His figures were probably true even of Fu-chou alone. From gazetteer lists of temples and from inscriptional records preserved both in gazetteers and in collected works of local men, a list emerges of ninety-six Buddhist temples that were built or rebuilt, received donations of land, or were granted official names during the course of the Sung.[5] There is good evidence that this number represents only a fraction of the Buddhist temples that existed: in a variety of other sources, not directly concerned with temple-building or religion, one finds frequent passing references to the names of local temples, most of them missing from the list of ninety-six.[6] There can hardly have been less than several hundred Buddhist temples in Fu-chou through most of Sung.

For many of the known Buddhist temples no record survives but a date of construction or a name-grant. But among fifty-six temples of whose erection or renovation something more is known, the participation of local laymen in the project is attested for thirty-seven. Of these lay contributors or builders some are unknown from other sources and of unidentifiable pedigree; but the list includes men — both with office and without — from many of Fu-chou's most prominent elite families. The Wangs of Lin-ch'uan County — Wang An-shih's family;[7] the Tsengs of Nan-feng County — family of Tseng Kung;[8] the T'us[9] and Yüehs[10] of I-huang; the Los[11] of Ch'ung-jen; the Chous[12] of

Chin-ch'i: all are represented among the builders and donors of Fu-chou Buddhist temples. The projects often involved enormous expenditures: the sutra library of the Pai-yün Temple was built with lay donations of 20,000 strings of cash,[13] a sum that would have paid a year's summer tax money for all of Chin-ch'i County and left about 7,000 strings to spare.[14] The work could go on for years: the building of the Fu-ch'ing Temple in the Lo-an county seat comprised a series of projects that lasted from 1165 until 1191, spanning the terms of four abbots and drawing major contributions from at least six local elite families.[15]

Building a temple, or contributing to Buddhist establishments, need not always have implied a strong attachment to the tenets of Buddhism. The funerary inscription of the wife of Miu Chao (d. 1191) seems to show this for both Buddhism and Taoism:

> All her life she performed the spring and autumn sacrifices at the family's ancestral hall, and nothing else. The Buddhist and Taoist doctrines of prayer and reward she would not admit; [but] neither did she refuse to give when there were requests for donations.[16]

Similarly, when Tseng Kung was prevailed upon to record the building of a Hall of Buddhas for the Ts'ai-yüan Temple in Nan-feng County in 1048 – a project in which he he played no part himself – he devoted much of the essay to his regret at the skill of Buddhists in promoting their teaching and the lack of success, by contrast, of those like himself who followed 'the Way of the Sages.'[17] Clearly his personal commitment was to Confucianism and to a view of Buddhism as a competitor. Yet on his death Tseng Kung was buried at a Buddhist temple that had been partially constructed by his grandfather, and his brother Tseng Pu was able to have the court, in Kung's honor, declare the temple a private Merit Cloister for the family.[18] It would seem that contributions to Buddhists or to their temples were sometimes simply a conventional way for Fu-chou men to show their community-mindedness and spirit of charity. Thus in the passage already cited from the funerary inscription of Chu Te-yu (see above, p. 151), at the end of a typical list of charities we find: 'when people were students of Buddhism or Taoism but had not yet taken the cloth, they [too] relied on Te-yu to fulfill their ambitions.'[19]

But it would be a mistake to view all elite involvement with Buddhism in this way. It is obvious that genuine religious attachment to its scriptures and belief in its efficacy were common. Wang An-shih, in a letter to his friend Tseng Kung, tried to clear up a misunderstanding left over from an earlier exchange of letters:

> In my previous letter I suspected that you were not left much time for

reading *ching*, and made a remark to that effect. In your letter that
followed, you thought that what I had called *ching* must be Buddhist
sutras [*fo-ching*], and instructed me as to the Buddhist sutras' disruption of mores. When I say simply 'read *ching*,' how could I mean
anything but the Classics [*ching*] of the Chinese sages? [20]

Here is comfort for the scholar struggling with classical Chinese. The
confusion in this case, of course, stemmed from the two meanings of
the word *ching*: 'Classics' and 'sutras.' But Tseng Kung could not have
misinterpreted Wang's passing reference had he not taken it for granted that
perusing sutras was something a man of his station in his time and place might
well do, and that he could not assume his own views as to the social
destructiveness of Buddhist doctrine to be shared, even by his friends. To
the contrary, at times men of the Fu-chou elite expected direct social
benefits, supernaturally mediated, from the construction or repair of temples.
The following passage comes from an inscriptional record of the middle
1220s, commemorating the building of a pagoda for a Buddhist temple in the
I-huang county seat:

> In the southern part of the county seat there is a Buddhist temple. The
> temple had a pagoda, called T'ai-ho, which directly faced the county
> school. By tradition it had come to be called the Writing-Brush. It was
> built in 1142, but after only sixty-eight years it suddenly collapsed.
> In the four examinations after 1208 there was not one man [from this
> county] who reached the *chin-shih* degree. People were alarmed.[. . .]
> They all said: 'We must raise up the Writing-Brush!' And so they all
> made a joint petition asking me [the county administrator] to restore
> it to its former state. I thereupon deputed the prefectural graduate
> Hsü Te-hsin, a gentleman of the county named Liu Hsieh, and the
> monks Tsung-hsin, Tsung-an, and Miao-tuan to organize it. [. . .] On
> the top stone were recorded the names of all those who had passed the
> examinations since the beginning of the dynasty, and the thousand
> names of the Buddha. It was named the Thousand Buddha Pagoda.[. . .]
> Work was begun in the fall of 1222, and in the spring of 1223 it had
> just been completed, when the announcement of the *chin-shih* degrees
> for that year came down; it included the names of Hsü Meng-ling,
> T'u Hui, and Wan K'ai, all passing together. Then people said: 'How
> quickly the Writing-Brush has responded!' [21]

Here Buddhist ideas of the recompense to be had from good deeds clearly
have come together with 'wind and water' theory on the effects of the siting
of buildings; but in this mix the Buddhist elements have remained strong and
seem to be taken seriously, as evidenced by the engraving of the Buddha-names

together with the names of earlier degreeholders. The participant Hsü Te-hsin, who was eventually to achieve his own *chin-shih*, was the grandson of an 1166 degreeholder and a member of the Hsü family of Hsia-shih in I-huang, which had produced eleven prefectural graduates and two *chin-shih* since 1123. Liu Hsieh is not otherwise identifiable, but was not an officeholder or prefectural graduate at the time of his participation.

Other evidence of Buddhist belief comes from areas of life less public. The wealthy I-huang County gentleman Tsou Chih-ming got his kinsman, a Buddhist monk, to come to his home and recite a sutra to cure his painful sores.[22] The registrar of Chin-ch'i County, Wu Shih-liang, according to gossip circulating in his time, once paid monks of a temple he was staying in to recite sutras to end a mysterious rain of stones (they failed).[23] A military officer of Lin-ch'uan County contributed funds to a nearby temple after an *arhat* who had appeared to his daughter in a dream proved to be depicted in a painting, now in the family's possession, which had once belonged to the temple.[24] In the public sphere again, when prayers for rain to a T'ang dynasty monk associated with a temple in I-huang were answered after a long drought in 1163, the I-huang gentleman Huang Hsi recorded with approval the honors the county and court bestowed upon the monk.[25] In sum, elite involvement with Buddhism often reflected what seems real religious belief.

Much of what has been said here of Buddhism could be said equally of Taoism. It is hard to judge the relative appeal of the two among the Fu-chou elite. The sources available preserve firm record of fully 129 Taoist temples (*kuan*) built, named, or extant in Sung Fu-chou. Yet these sources are, there is little doubt, far more complete for Taoist than for Buddhist temples;[26] the real relative numbers of temples for the two are entirely uncertain. In any case it is hard to know what such numbers would mean if we had them. Direct record of elite involvement in the building of temples is in fact less abundant for Taoism than for Buddhism. Yet Taoist temple-building did attract a fair number of elite participants. Some details of construction or renovation are known for twenty temples; for twelve of these there is record of lay elite participation. Of especial interest is the evidence of the growing importance during Sung, particularly during Southern Sung, of certain local mountains reputed to be the earthly residences or places of sojourn of specific Taoist Immortals (*hsien*).[27] These cult centers and the Immortals associated with them clearly drew elite attention and belief. The family of Li Liu of Ch'ung-jen County (see Chapter 2, p. 78) in several successive generations built or renovated shrines on Mei Peak, northeasternmost part of Pa Mountain, cult center of a group of Four Immortals worshipped widely in the area, and very close to the Lis' own home.[28] Still more widely worshipped, it seems, were the Three Immortals or Three Perfected Lords of Hua-kai

Mountain, also in Ch'ung-jen but farther south. The local man Lo Pin, at some stage in his career an administrative official in a circuit military intendancy, prayed daily to the Hua-kai Immortals for a son (this was in 1151) and received a dream which foretold the birth of his three sons over the next few years.[29] An officeholder from neighboring Jao-chou in the middle twelfth century made yearly pilgrimages to Hua-kai Mountain, in fulfillment of a vow made in the hope (again) of obtaining a son.[30] The Ch'ung-jen man Hsiung P'u, at around the same time, regularly prayed and made frequent donations to the Hua-kai Immortals' shrine at the Chao-ch'ing Temple in the county seat.[31] The Nan-feng County gentleman and office-holder Huang Yüeh, somewhat later in the century, told the high official Chou Pi-ta, who was traveling through the county, of his yearly visits to his own local Three Immortals shrine at Chün Mountain near his home.[32] In sum, though donations to Taoist temples too may sometimes have been a mere gesture of community spirit, evidence of real belief is abundant.

At least as they are reflected in temple-building, active association with Buddhism and with Taoism were not mutually exclusive. The first Fu-chou *chin-shih* degreeholder, Yüeh Shih, built one Buddhist temple and donated fields to four others, but also gave land to one Taoist temple.[33] The Wu family of the Ch'ung-jen county seat can be definitely connected to at least one and probably two Taoist temples;[34] they very probably also built part of a Buddhist temple.[35] Yet most families for whom any record of temple construction has survived are only known to have been involved with one of the two teachings. This may be a function of imperfect sources; yet it is easy to believe that, where belief was strong and genuine, attachment to one of the two made involvement with the other unlikely.

The Fu-chou evidence suggests that Buddhism and Taoism occupied, particularly in relation to the broader activities of the elite and of local government, rather different social spaces. When men seek sons, health, relief from ill fortune, or most particularly a change in the weather, we are more likely to read of appeals to Immortals, to the residents of Taoist temples, or to wandering holy men of clearly Taoist affinities than to arhats, bodhisattvas, or Buddhist monks. Exceptions are not uncommon – some have already been cited – but on balance the evidence for activity of these kinds does seem to favor Taoism. In this respect Taoist belief seems to fulfill many of the same functions, as we shall see, as belief in gods and spirits (*shen*). The Buddhist clergy, on the other hand, seems far more directly involved, quite apart from supernatural functions, in the day-to-day social world. When in 1225 the Fu-chou administrator took the initiative in the rebuilding of Fu-chou's major bridge, which connected the prefectural city to the east bank of the Ju River, he deputed a Buddhist monk named

Miao-yen to keep the registers of laborers and funds that were required. After the bridge was completed, the prefect established a shrine to a local god to make sacrifices for the bridge's protection, but also had a new Buddhist temple built, supported by fields donated by the high official and Ch'ung-jen County man Li Liu. Miao-yen led his disciples in taking up residence at the temple; their duties were to make periodic prayers and sacrifices for the bridge, but also to manage it and to make repairs whenever needed.[36] Buddhist monks built two other local bridges independently of any official or lay instigation.[37] In about 1203, when the Intendant of Ever-Normal Granaries established the An-shou Hall, an institution designed for travelers and visitors to the prefecture who fell sick, he entrusted its management to the monks of the Cheng-chüeh (Buddhist) Temple in the prefectural city. Buddhist monks were also employed to run two paupers' graveyards and to carry out burials with proper Buddhist ceremonies.[38] In the 1271 famine Huang Chen used Buddhist temples as distribution sites in his program of free congee for the starving.[39] All of these were functions serving the public welfare; but the services of Buddhist monks were also often retained privately to provide care for the tombs of members of the local elite.[40] These temples might then become private family Merit Cloisters, as with the Nan-feng Tseng family and their Ch'ung-chüeh Temple (Map 15). Thus Buddhist monks and temples fulfilled a variety of social functions that were partly or wholly independent of their own religious activities. Apart from a considerable involvement in the practise of medicine, there is no evidence that the Taoist clergy too played such roles in Sung Fu-chou.[41]

It was not only by temple-building, donation, or prayer that the Fu-chou elite showed its attachment to Buddhism and Taoism: it also supplied recruits to the higher levels of both clergies. Jao Chieh, a poet of Lin-ch'uan County and friend to Hsieh I and Wang Ko (see above, pp. 49–52),[42] after a career of study with some of the most prominent scholar-officials of the empire, became a Buddhist monk and rose to be the abbot of the T'ien-ning Temple in Hsiang-yang County, Hsiang-chou (in Ching-hu-nan circuit).[43] The 1175 *chin-shih* Liu Yao-fu of Chin-ch'i County, on breaking with his teacher Lu Chiu-yüan, turned to Ch'an Buddhism and became a monk.[44] As it happened, a relative of Liu's had two generations earlier been a Taoist priest and built a Taoist temple.[45] Lo Yü of Ch'ung-jen County, son of the Assisting Councillor Lo Tien, entrusted the care of his parents' tomb to a man of his lineage who was a Buddhist monk;[46] another kinsman was head of the Shang-fang (Taoist) Temple at the end of Sung or beginning of Yüan.[47] At about the same time a member of the Lin-ch'uan Yen family and direct descendant of the chief councillor Yen Shu held the post of abbot of the Fu-sheng Temple in his native county.[48]

Most striking of all, however, (if a bit more speculative) is the case of the heads of the Chao-hsien (Taoist) Temple in the southern suburbs of the Lo-an county seat. According to a record of its reconstruction under the Yüan, since the Shao-hsing period (1131–62) it had been headed in succession by men surnamed Tu, T'an, Li, Tseng, Chan, Ch'en, Tung, and Hsü.[49] Now Li, Tseng, Chan, Ch'en, and Tung are all surnames of elite families prominent in Lo-an during Southern Sung.[50] As for Hsü (surname of the last head in Sung), the first examination graduate of this surname from Lo-an, Hsü Ying-ch'ang, had passed the *chin-shih* in 1242[51] and was cited as a wealthy rice-hoarder by Huang Chen in 1271;[52] he is reported to have lived in the south of the county seat, quite close to the temple. This neatly matches, in both time and place, the tenure of the temple head named Hsü. There remain the first two heads, a Tu and a T'an: neither bears the surname of any known Lo-an elite family. The list, however, begins with Shao-hsing, that is presumably with its first year, 1131. But the Chao-hsien Temple had not moved to its site in Lo-an until that county's creation in 1149; before this it had stood five *li* east of what was to be the Lo-an County boundary.[53] This clearly indicates a site in I-huang County. As it happens, Tu and T'an were the surnames of two families prominent in I-huang County precisely around the end of Northern and beginning of Southern Sung.[54] Thus it seems very probable that this Taoist temple had consistently drawn its head from among local elite families of its own county, and that when it moved from I-huang to Lo-an its recruiting pool changed accordingly.[55]

Buddhism and Taoism, it seems, were far and away the main objects of religious interest – at least public interest – for the Fu-chou elite. Somewhat apart from these lay the third of the three 'spheres' I have drawn at the outset: the sphere of *shen*, of gods and spirits. This is what is often, in discussions of Chinese society, called 'popular religion.' The term is not wholly apt, for reasons that will be seen; yet it is not wholly inappropriate either. In the Fu-chou material in Hung Mai's massive collection of twelfth-century occult gossip, the *I-chien chih*, the anecdotes that deal with *shen* are the most likely to involve characters drawn from outside the elite and officialdom. There can be little doubt that much of the world of gods, spirits, and demons is hidden from us by its especial association with levels of society that have left little record in the sources that survive. Yet both elite and state, in Sung, involved themselves in this world. For the elite, indeed, still more involvement may be concealed by a reluctance to admit to beliefs or practises that were not always seen as quite proper to a gentleman. One prominent actor in the world of *shen*, for instance, was a sort of practitioner known as a *wu*, a spirit medium, who could be called upon to communicate with a god or especially to detect, call out, and exorcize a demon. Though there is ample evidence of the role of *wu* in Fu-chou,[56] and though contemporaries commented on their importance in the Chiang-hsi region, particularly as alternatives to medical doctors,[57] no evidence survives of elite involvement with *wu* in Fu-chou. The silence, in this instance, is suspicious.

Some gentlemen saw nothing to be ashamed of, at least, in promoting the worship of a local *shen*. Not long after 1100 Tseng Chao of Nan-feng County, brother of the Assisting Councillor Tseng Pu, recorded the renovation and expansion of a shrine for a god associated with a mountain in his home county:

> Chün Mountain is the highest mountain of Nan-feng.[. . .] It is an old tradition that, during the Han, Wu Jui camped his army at the mountain. His general Mei Hsüan made sacrifices there. When the rite was complete, a shape like mounted soldiers waving weapons enveloped the mountaintop. Thus they called it Chün [Army] Mountain. The sacrifices made to it by people of this county had their origin in this. In the T'ang, during the K'ai-yüan period [713–41] it once again manifested spiritual evidences, and a great shrine building was built and ceremonies undertaken with still more devotion. Thereafter the shrine was moved several times. The present one, north of the Yü River and seven *li* from the district seat, is the remnant of one dating from 937 under Southern T'ang. In the prayers and sacrifices of the whole region, all requests have been promptly answered for over a thousand years, yet enfeoffment [of the god] had never been granted. The people were dissatisfied over this. The circuit intendant made requests of the court, but for a long time there was no response. In 1100 the present Assisting Councillor, Tseng Pu, memorialized: 'I am a man of Nan-feng, and know Chün Mountain. The words of the former circuit intendant were not false; I ask that his request be granted.' A decree then enfeoffed the god as Marquis of Excellent Benevolence; the shrine was called the Chün Mountain Temple of Numinous Response. When the decree came down, people of the county pooled their wealth and strength to expand the shrine and renovate it. When the shrine was completed the Assisting Councillor entrusted his younger brother [Tseng] Chao with making a record.[58]

This record does not show the full extent of Tseng Pu's own connection to the shrine: a later account by another of his kinsmen tells us that Pu himself had built it.[59] Thus we see here a local man using his considerable official influence to win state recognition – enfeoffment – of a popular deity associated with his own county. Such enfeoffment was common in Sung China for local gods and for the Immortals associated with Taoist cult

centers: the sections that have come down to us of the massive Sung compilation of edicts and regulations, the *Sung hui-yao*, record hundreds of acts
of enfeoffment scattered across the empire.[60] Several others are recorded in
Fu-chou; but in no other case do we find as clear record of local elite involvement as here with Tseng Pu.[61] More often the local initiative is represented
as being taken, at least formally, by local administrators: we shall see this
further on. Yet the administrators who ask state recognition of local gods
sometimes claim to be acting on behalf of local sentiment; it is not hard to
imagine, in the background, some elite initiative like Tseng Pu's. In such
cases, perhaps, we are not entitled to deduce belief from sponsorship: a spirit
of competition with the elites of other regions who had won recognition for
their own local gods, or a desire to improve one's name among the local
population, may have been motive enough. But as with Buddhism and Taoism
there is other evidence that elite men genuinely believed – or acted as if they
genuinely believed – in the powers of certain *shen*. We have already seen, in
the first chapter, the custom of praying to local deities for dreams that would
predict success or failure in the examinations. The Ch'ung-jen men Wang I
(in 1140) and Wu Tseng (around 1150) both prayed for dreams at the
Yang-shan Shrine in the prefectural city;[62] Wu is also reported, whenever he
was contemplating an action, to have consulted the Purple Lady, a deity then
and afterwards believed able to provide oracles through the planchette.[63]
Tsou Chi, a man of I-huang and a high official of the late eleventh century,
and Jao Tz'u-wei of Ch'ung-jen, who sought a degree about a century later,
prayed for their dreams at the prefectural shrine of the god of the earth, a
shrine whose spiritual power, we are told, was particularly famed.[64] The Jao
family, a 'great surname' of Lin-ch'uan County in Northern Sung, once built
a shrine to house, as a newly promoted god, what they believed to be a
demon that was possessing their daughter-in-law.[65] Elite men did not in
formal contexts tell these stories on themselves – did not, for instance, admit
to a father's or mother's worship of *shen* in funerary inscriptions – but
happily told them on one another, as gossip or tales worth hearing, to compilers like Hung Mai, whose work itself seems devoted to showing the reality
of divine and occult phenomena.

What, amid this plethora of forms and varieties of religion, was the role
of the state, or of its agents, the administrators of the counties and the
prefecture? As to *shen*, local officials, as we have seen, could find themselves,
like some members of the local elite, in the role of promoters and advocates.
In the summer of 1220 Fu-chou went five months without rain. As was
customary at such times, the prefectural administrator went out personally
to make sacrifices and pray for rain at various local religious institutions; the
drought continued. He then heard reports of one Ying-tse Shrine in Lo-an

County, where prayers for rain had often been answered. He had the god
(that is, its sculpted image) brought to the prefectural city and prayed to it
there: the rain came at last. At this he kept the god in the city and built a
fine new shrine there.[66] Similarly, when Huang Chen judged his prayers for
rain in 1271 to have been most effective at the Shrine of the Four Immortals
in Ch'ung-jen County, he granted the shrine's guardian Taoist priest the favor
of a special inscriptional record tracing its history and his own experiences
there.[67]

But local government could act to suppress, as well as to promote, the
practises, deities, and associations of local religion. Huang Chen during his
term issued the following notice:

> This official went out yesterday to receive the imperial decrees and
> saw, posted on the Wen-ch'ang Bridge, a printed placard entitled
> 'Commentaries of the Wu-yüan Shrine.' This must be the work of
> followers of the head of a *wu* shrine who have come here to swindle
> and coerce our people. I have ordered the three precinct officers [of
> the prefectural city] to remove and destroy these placards everywhere
> in and out of the city, and to seek out and expel these people.[. . .]
> I have posted notices before the prefectural office, requiring our people
> to respect themselves, fear Heaven and Earth, be filial to their fathers
> and mothers, honor the laws of the state and the Way of the world, and
> not to err in this way.[. . .] [68]

Huang does not explain what doctrine if any in the posted text has
offended him, but the reference to *wu* is significant. At about the same time
Huang oversaw the arrest, and transportation to a nearby prefecture, of a man
who had led another religious manifestation apparently forbidden: it is
referred to as 'poling boats to greet a god' (or perhaps 'greeting a god in
poling-boats'). Huang was sufficiently aroused to order the confiscation and
burning of all 'poling-boats' – it is unclear whether these were actual boats,
or vehicles of some ritual performance – belonging to shrines, Buddhist
temples, or private households. In 1273, after his transfer to the post of
Judicial Intendant of Chiang-hsi circuit in Chi-chou to the west, Huang issued
a notice prohibiting this same practise there, and remarked that in Fu-chou he
had 'burned over 1,300 poling-boats, torn down heterodox shrines, and
prohibited the Society of the God of Plagues and other societies.'[69] Finally,
in his continuing search for revenues with which to meet the prefecture's
Harmonious Purchase quotas, Huang appealed to the Military Intendant
of Chiang-hsi to turn over to him the fields the Intendant had recently
confiscated from a White Lotus temple in the course of a crackdown on
heterodox sects.[70]

These cases are spectacular and, it seems, unusual: sponsorship and patronage, or utter disregard, were for Fu-chou administrators clearly more likely approaches to the world of local *shen* than proscription and persecution. And there is no evidence at all of comparable official attacks on religious practises or institutions clearly supported by the elite. Still, particularly for *shen*, the problem of control, or at least of distinguishing what deserved promotion from what was tolerable on the one hand and what was pernicious on the other, was one with which at least some local administrators had to grapple. It remains unclear how they made their choices. At the center, systematic efforts to approach the problem had begun only late in Northern Sung. Under the emperor Che-tsung in 1095 it was for the first time decreed that each prefectural administration should survey and make a register of the shrines to deities in their jurisdiction, record the history of their establishment, and print the whole as a manual to be called *Sacrificial Statutes [ssu-tien] of X Prefecture.*[71] Under Hui-tsung in 1108 it was further proposed and decreed that an empire-wide *Sacrificial Statutes* be compiled as a check against the sometimes unreliable reports of prefectural authorities; this work was to distinguish deities and shrines worthy of enfeoffment from those of no benefit to the people, presumably with an eye to promoting the former and proscribing or discouraging the latter.[72] Che-tsung's and particularly Hui-tsung's reigns were periods of reformist legislation and a general urge toward centralization of power – under Hui-tsung more marked than ever again in Sung – and the impulse to control of *shen* embodied in the legislation of the *Sacrificial Statutes* was, it seems, one of many examples of overreaching in the period. Works of this name do indeed seem to have been compiled; but there is no evidence that they were ever, particularly in Southern Sung, vehicles of systematic and effective control of local *shen* worship. A discussion of the issue in a fragmentary late Sung gazetteer of Fu-chou displays a vagueness and looseness probably typical of the approach of local administrators in this period:

> Those [deities] that have rendered meritorious service to the common people should be included in the *Sacrificial Statutes*. But any who through abundance of substance and spirit have become gods and are accordingly worshipped by the common people, even though the *Statutes* do not record them, need not be opposed so long as they are not harmful to the state.[73]

As to what might harm the state, this, like much else, was in Southern Sung evidently left to local administrators to decide. Several decades before Huang Chen, Huang Kan, serving as administrator of Lin-ch'uan County, had judged a suit brought by a White Lotus temple and never hinted that he found this complainant less honorable than any other – indeed he decided in its favor.[74]

The religious role of the local administrator went well beyond the encouragement or occasional suppression of some few of the crowd of deities he encountered in local society. Through his office he was the supervisor of a religious domain of his (or of the state's) own. The boundaries of that domain are, and perhaps were at the time, entirely fuzzy: 'state religion' is in Sung as slippery a notion as 'popular religion.' The core of the domain comprised several religious institutions clearly the state's own: pre-eminently, the altars to the gods of land and grain (*she-chi*) and to the gods of wind and rain.[75] These replicated altars in the capital at which the emperor himself offered sacrifices; they had deep classical roots and had been a part of the state's ideological apparatus in dynasty after dynasty. To the same domain belonged the sacrifices local administrators were expected to offer to the gods of the prefecture's larger mountains and rivers. All these gods – of land and grain, of wind and rain, of mountains and rivers – were conceived classically, and usually in official ideology, as anonymous 'spiritual intelligences' governing their respective natural phenomena. They were not, in contrast to the vast majority of the gods worshipped by the populace at large, specific, historical, dead human beings. It is this that most clearly sets them apart. It is beyond this that boundaries grow fuzzy: we find apart from the classical gods of natural phenomena a number of more or less state-sponsored deities who had their origin in specific historical figures, and who had entered 'state religion,' in relatively recent times, from among the gods of the wider populace, which may still have actively worshipped many of them. The most prominent of these was surely the City God (literally God of the Walls and Moats) of the prefectural seat, a deity originating (in Fu-chou) in the apotheosis of a general of the Han dynasty.[76] What seems to justify placing this shrine and certain others within the boundaries of state religion is that, in Fu-chou at least, they were built by local administrators. Almost all of the gods involved originated outside Fu-chou: their local shrines are offshoots of some first shrine in another prefecture or in the capital.[77] We seem to deal here with gods whom the center or local officials have chosen as worthy for promotion throughout the empire or among the local populace at large, and to whom local administrators have accordingly built shrines. Two of especial interest are Kuan Chiang-chün ('General Kuan,' known in later dynasties as Kuan-ti, 'Emperor Kuan'), god of military loyalty and commercial honesty;[78] and Ma-tsu, goddess of seafaring:[79] these were to be among the most important gods of official and popular religion in the Ch'ing dynasty.[80] And finally, one must probably place within the domain of official religion – given always that the initiative in that domain may lie with local officials rather than with the center — the shrines to former worthies in or near the official schools; for these too, in Fu-chou, are recorded as the projects of local administrators.

What is striking in all of this is the shallowness of local elite involvement. The Fu-chou elite, as we have seen, was deeply and publicly involved in the building and the financial support of Buddhist and Taoist temples. Yet to this other complex of officially sponsored shrines, which were sited prominently in the prefectural city and whose active promotion by local administrators surely removed any question as to their social respectability, the elite offered, it seems, no similar support. Local men sometimes authored inscriptions when the various shrines and halls were built, and presumably took some part in the ceremonies they housed. But, to judge by the records we have, they did not build the shrines, contribute funds to their building, or otherwise offer financial or organizational support. This cannot simply reflect some peculiarity of records written for state-sponsored projects, since records of just the same kind of document quite fully the role of Fu-chou elite men in other official projects, such as the building of bridges, walls, or schools. There is reason to conclude that the local elite stood apart from this domain in a way that it did not from Buddhism or Taoism.

In a parallel way, the state and its agents seem rarely to have been associated with local Buddhist and Taoist establishments. To be sure, the court granted official temple names — almost on demand it seems, or on a scale that surely precluded serious selection or control — to Buddhist and Taoist temples in Fu-chou, as everywhere in the empire. But local officials, with rare exceptions, did not build or sponsor Buddhist or Taoist temples. For Taoism the exceptions are important; they include one of the three events I introduced at the outset, and will be dealt with further on. As to Buddhism, some official involvement is recorded in the building of only four temples or associated edifices. For one, the Writing-Brush Pagoda, an official acted only when asked to do so by local men, and at once delegated responsibility for the construction itself to members of the local elite. The project in any case was focused on the fortunes of the county in the examination system, a crucial institution of the Sung state. The Fu-ch'ing Temple in Lo-an County received official encouragement and funds from about 1161 because a temple was needed to make the customary local prayers and sacrifices on the emperor's birthday.[81] The Tung-shan Temple just outside the prefectural city was created in 1226 as part of an official bridgebuilding project so that its monks would take responsibility for the bridge's maintenance.[82] In both these cases officials involved themselves out of practical needs related to local government, having nothing to do with the practise of Buddhism for its own sake or the encouragement of particular tendencies in local religion. The circumstances surrounding the fourth example, which took place around

1060,[83] are unrecorded; but one suspects that similar pragmatic motives may have lain behind it. As the building of shrines to certain deities was the domain of the state, the building of Buddhist and Taoist temples was overwhelmingly the domain of the local elite. Whether through a consensus that divided responsibility for different religious spheres, or through disagreement over which tendencies deserved support and promotion, elite religion and state religion in Fu-chou were in certain respects clearly separate.

In this separateness of elite and official religious involvements, in the problem of official selection and control of *shen*, and in the sheer multiplicity of spheres, beliefs, gods, and practises, we see what for any observer familiar with Western religious history must be the most striking aspect of Sung religious life: the absence of any clear or systematic religious integration, whether in sheer fact or by law and regulation. Even to remark on this might seem to impose a standard based in Western experience, and ultimately perhaps in Judeo-Christian belief itself, on a Chinese reality that has no reason to conform to it. Deeper analysis, in any case, might even show that the apparent variety and disorder of religious life expressed, or was founded upon, consistent underlying cultural principles. But this solution would not have satisfied Sung observers themselves, for whom surface variety, difference, disintegration in religious belief and practise did often seem real problems. Lu Chiu-yuan, as we shall see, complained that in his day 'worship and prayer are scattered among the people and fill all the world,' rather than being organized in a clearly hierarchical system of levels of sacrifices on classical principles. The complaint was an utterly Neo-Confucian one and not uncommon in its time.

Too great a plenitude and variety of belief could be approached in various ways. One might try simply to talk them out of existence. Officials of Neo-Confucian bent, even in the act of honoring local Immortals for their abundant response to prayers for rain, could argue that rains were *really* brought, prayers really answered, by the nameless spirits of the mountains (as in the classics and on the primary altars of the state cult); or that Immortals were really simply virtuous men venerated as heroes by a grateful posterity (as in the shrines to former worthies in the schools).[84] But this was not an approach that could satisfy everyone. Hsiung P'u, as we have seen a lifelong devotee of the Three Perfected Lords of Hua-kai Mountain, one of whose special domains was the weather and who delighted in displays of thunder and lightning, was shocked, when he held office in Lei-chou in Kuang-nan, to discover there a god (*shen*) of thunder chief among those he was expected to pay his respects to; he resisted having anything to do with it.[85] Devotees of different Immortals clashed over the relative rank and power of their chosen favorites, and looked to divine intervention to settle the disagreement.[86] As we have seen, local administrators sometimes took strenuous action to eliminate religious tendencies of which they disapproved. Tseng Kung lectured Wang An-shih on the perniciousness of Buddhist scriptures and lamented the success of Buddhists in propagating their message. In sum, despite a considerable *de facto* toleration, the differences that divided Fu-chou men from one another in religion were not, to many at least, a small matter. The impulse to provide, by force or by the disguise of words, an integration that was otherwise lacking was, for some, real and strong.

In the variety and, at least to a considerable number of contemporaries, disorder of local religious belief there is no evidence of major change between Northern and Southern Sung. Yet in certain responses of elite and state to this situation – in certain attempts to provide at least partial integration of or through religion – one may see symptoms of the broader changes that I have traced in other chapters. Here I return to the three events with which I began, or to two of them in particular: the conversion of a Buddhist temple in I-huang County into a Taoist temple by state decree in late Northern Sung, and Huang Chen's promotion of sacrifices to Chu Hsi at the Fu-chou prefectural school near the end of the dynasty. We see here, I think, two efforts – contrasting radically in quality but above all in scale – to promote a translocal integration of society through a religious medium. It is the difference in the focus of integration that is most symptomatic of larger differences between Northern and Southern Sung.

The founding of the Shen-hsiao Taoist temple in I-huang was not an isolated event. Nor was this the first Taoist temple founded by imperial decree in Fu-chou. More than a century before, in 1008, the emperor Chen-tsung had ordered the establishment of Taoist temples bearing the name T'ien-ch'ing in every prefecture of the empire.[87] Fu-chou soon complied.[88] The decree was one element of a broader upsurge of innovating Taoist religious activity in the capital, with Chen-tsung himself at the center; the discovery of 'Heavenly Texts' purportedly sent by Heaven to the emperor, revelatory dreams by the emperor himself, and the performance of the time-honored *feng* and *shan* sacrifices to Heaven by Chen-tsung at Mt T'ai in Shantung all formed part of the same movement. A crucial element was the revelation that the first ancestor of the emperor's own Chao lineage was a powerful Taoist divinity who had previously been incarnated as the Yellow Emperor of highest antiquity and who was now to be recognized as the first founder of the Taoist religion, displacing Lao Tzu from his traditional position. Suzanne Cahill has shown the importance of this series of events and has suggested that by the adoption of a divine Taoist ancestor Chen-tsung 'sought [. . .] to borrow the charisma of a potent religious figure to lend legitimacy to his rule and his lineage,' while the Heavenly Texts 'confirmed

Sung's continued possession of the Mandate of Heaven.'[89] Within this enterprise, and viewed from the local level, the founding of the T'ien-ch'ing temples, and perhaps more the further creation by decree in 1012 of halls devoted to the emperor's revealed Incomparable Ancestor within each of the temples (this too is documented for Fu-chou),[90] put in place a national structure of Taoist religious institutions with a branch in each prefecture and its focus in the capital, centered on the highest imperial ancestor and thus, in this world, on the person of the emperor. An act, clearly, that aimed at an integration of (and through) religion, if an integration of a very specific sort.

The Shen-hsiao Temple of 1119 belongs to a second great phase of Taoist innovation at the Northern Sung court, similar in some ways to the first, but even more ambitious. Michel Strickmann has explored the developments of this period, which saw the short-lived establishment of Shen-hsiao Taoism, under the auspices of the Taoist Lin Ling-su and the emperor Hui-tsung, as the state religion of the Sung.[91] Deriving its authority from a newly conceived highest region of the heavens, the Divine Empyrean (*shen-hsiao*), and thus subordinating to itself all previous revelation and all earlier forms of Taoism, the new religion discovered the elder son of the supreme Jade Emperor, namely the Great Lord of Long Life, Sovereign of the Divine Empyrean, dwelling on earth in the person of emperor Hui-tsung.[92] The burst of activity that followed upon the installation of Shen-hsiao included the compiling and printing of an expanded and reorganized canon of Taoist scriptures, and – of more direct interest here – the creation by decree of Shen-hsiao temples in all prefectures of the empire. The focus of each of the temples was to be an image of Hui-tsung himself in his divine persona. The new temples were to be created from existing Taoist or, often, Buddhist temples.[93] The latter was the case in Fu-chou. The decree founding the Shen-hsiao temples was handed down in 1117; as we have seen, the Fu-chou temple was not, it seems, created until 1119.[94] In the same year an even more ambitious set of decrees set out, in essence, to abolish Buddhism entirely by absorbing all Buddhist temples, monks, and nuns, under new names and titles, into the new Taoist religious structure.

The effect of the Shen-hsiao innovations should not be overstated. By 1120 the major anti-Buddhist decrees had already been rescinded. In Fu-chou the effect may have been less than elsewhere. In some prefectures, neighboring Jao-chou for one, the Buddhist temples chosen for conversion to Shen-hsiao were among the most important local Buddhist establishments.[95] The T'ien-wang Buddhist temple, by contrast, was not only by all indications not an especially significant Fu-chou temple, but was sited in the subordinate county of I-huang rather than in the prefectural city. This, along with the relatively late date of the changeover (1119, responding to a decree of 1117), may reflect some resistance on the part of Fu-chou administrators or the local elite to the transformations dictated in the capital. (This despite the fact that one of Lin Ling-su's chief associates in his program, the Taoist Wang Wen-ch'ing, was by origin a man of greater Fu-chou.) I have found no evidence that the broader conversions of Buddhist establishments and personnel envisioned by the 1119 decrees were ever carried out in Fu-chou. But the ineffectiveness of the new measures at the local level (Chen-tsung's inno-vations seem in comparison far more real and effective in Fu-chou) should not obscure their meaning for those in the capital who undertook them. Here again, as under Chen-tsung, the court sought to establish a unified empire-wide hierarchical structure of Taoist institutions, based in the prefectures and centered in the capital. The new program went far beyond Chen-tsung's in its integrating aims by trying to absorb Buddhism into its framework and so remove at a blow one of the major strands of religious diversity in the empire. But again like Chen-tsung's, the new program focused reverence and worship above all on the emperor, to whom divinity now adhered not merely through his ancestors but through the previous incarnations of his own person. These two Northern Sung programs of religious integration of the empire placed at the center the man who more than any other personified the state.

There was in Southern Sung no state action from the center comparable to these Northern Sung programs of Taoist-style religious reconstruction. It may seem absurd to set alongside them Huang Chen's humble efforts, in the 1270s, to promote reverence and sacrifices for the philosopher Chu Hsi in Fu-chou. Certainly there is no similarity in scale, or seemingly in ambition. Yet Huang Chen's acts too may be seen as an effort, or part of an effort, to integrate society through religious means, and belong to an innovative tendency of some importance in Southern Sung, the upsurge of foundings of local shrines to former worthies. I have dealt with certain aspects of this phenomenon in an earlier chapter. Southern Sung Neo-Confucian thinkers, Chu Hsi among them, had from early on been among those prominent in the founding and promotion of the shrines. It seems clear that at the outset, for Neo-Confucians and others, the shrines had served to encourage reverence precisely for *local* 'worthies': men who came from the place where the shrine was established, who had spent a considerable time there, or who had served in office there; thus men who deserved the particular attention, gratitude, and reverence of the local populace and could be held up to them both as rallying-points of local pride and as models of how men of that place should act. In 1181 the administrator of Wu-yüan County in Hui-chou (Chiang-tung circuit) asked Chu Hsi himself to write a commemorative inscription for a shrine to the Neo-Confucian founders, Chou Tun-i and the

Ch'eng brothers, which the administrator had recently built in Wu-yüan. Chu at first refused, saying that, since Wu-yüan had been for these three men 'Neither their home, nor their place of sojourn, nor a district in which they held office,' and since the national *Sacrificial Statutes* gave them no place, the shrine in Wu-yüan was not appropriate.[96]

The Wu-yüan shrine, however, was representative of a major secondary strand in the development of the shrines to former worthies, a strand that seems to have gained in importance as Southern Sung wore on. This was the creation of shrines to certain men of national renown, most commonly to the founding figures of Neo-Confucian teaching and thought, even in places to which those figures had no special connection. Chu Hsi finally gave in to the Wu-yüan administrator, apparently persuaded by his argument that the shrine was made appropriate by the spontaneous reverence given Chou and the Ch'engs by scholars in all localities, including Wu-yüan. A random perusal of gazetteers will show that similar foundings took place in many parts of southeastern China in the course of Southern Sung, especially in the thirteenth century.[97] After the court instituted official sacrifices at the Confucian temple in the capital to Chou, the Ch'engs, and Chu Hsi himself in 1234 – a move probably conditioned chiefly by factional politics, the dynasty's worsening military situation, and the need to gather constituencies to the court's support – the tendency had the sanction of the central government.[98]

It is not clear when a shrine to Chu Hsi was first established at the Fu-chou prefectural school, or when sacrifices to him were first performed. Huang Chen tells us that when he arrived in office in Fu-chou, 'there remained only an empty room,' which suggests that a shrine had been established some time before but had fallen into disuse.[99] In any case, Huang copied from the nearby Lin-ju Academy, a semi-public academy devoted to Chu's teachings, an incription recording Chu's titles and offices; obtained from Chu's great-grandson in far-off Shao-hsing prefecture a copy of Chu's portrait; and put both on display 'in order that the Master's spirit may have something to cleave to and that the honoring and revering thoughts of the students may have something to attach to.'[100]

In the growth of this second, non-local, and strongly Neo-Confucian strand in the development of local shrines to former worthies, represented in Fu-chou by Huang Chen's efforts on behalf of Chu Hsi, what can we see? On the one hand, surely, simply a reflection of the growing following that Neo-Confucian scholarship, especially the brand represented by Chu Hsi, found among the elite and particularly the students of Southern Sung. Yet its expression in this particular setting – in shrines at first devoted explicitly to *local* exemplars – reflects, I think, something else as well: an effort, deliberate or spontaneous, by officials themselves of Neo-Confucian bent, to crown the local pantheon of worthies honored in and around the official schools — a pantheon which by its nature varied sharply from place to place — with a shared set of figures to be honored by all students and gentlemen throughout the empire. The shrines' founders set out, in other words, to provide a common focus for the reverence and worship of all the Sung elite.

It is here, then, that we may find a parallel to the Taoist integrating efforts of the Northern Sung. What is striking is the difference in the proposed common focus of reverence in the two cases: on the one hand, the emperor, personification of government and the state; on the other, Chu Hsi and his Neo-Confucian forebears, teachers and gentlemen first, officeholders (if at all) only second, and creators of a form of thought that elevated gentlemanly conduct, the ethics of everyday life, and scholarship above the pursuit of office or, indeed, above the conduct of politics as conventionally understood.

Where the court Taoists of Northern Sung, and their sponsoring would-be theocrats, erected their hierarchical structures from above, by governmental fiat, Neo-Confucian local administrators of Southern Sung pursued their own integrative vision piecemeal, at the local level — helped along, to be sure, by the eventual adoption of their moral exemplars by the court. When politics and office had retreated, for the elite, from the position they had once held in household strategies and in ideal self-conceptions, the founders of a nationally successful intellectual movement were perhaps most suited to be the focus of an empire-wide elite reverence that the Taoist innovators of an earlier time had tried to center on the emperor. There are reflections here, then, of the broader change I have been tracing elsewhere. In the third chapter I have proposed that as the nationwide ties of marriage and of common commitment to a court-focused enterprise that had bound at least a part of the Northern Sung elite dissolved, academic ties may have emerged in their place as a prime means of factional recruitment and of translocal elite connection in general. The enshrinement of the Neo-Confucian founders in prefectural schools across the empire may represent a parallel phenomenon in the religious sphere. There is support here too for what I have suggested in the fourth chapter: that the Neo-Confucian intellectual leaders of Southern Sung confronted the localizing tendencies of their time not as localists themselves, but as would-be integrators; but that in seeking ultimately to bring things together, they laid great emphasis on establishing a firm local foundation, and so devised or made use of institutions of a decidedly local cast.

Where in all of this can we fit the second of our three events, Lu Chiu-yüan's private prayers to the gods of the mountains and rivers to end a drought in 1190? Lu created no new institution of worship and sacrifice here, and sought no new integration of religion or of society through religion. His act was an isolated one and found, so far as I have discovered, no echo in the acts of men who came after him. It has the feeling rather of a *cri du coeur* and a rebuke of what Lu sees all around him. In praying for rain to the gods of the mountains and rivers, gods whose worship (as we have seen) was traditionally the province of the local administrator as the state's representative, Lu felt deeply that he trod upon ground not properly his. Yet the circumstances of his time, he thought, compelled him. The text of his prayer tells the story:

> Now I have heard that the Son of Heaven sacrificed to Heaven and Earth, and the feudal lords sacrificed to the famous mountains and great rivers within their territory; that the *yü-yung* altars were for sacrifices for rain or drought; that if a mountain or a forest, a river, a gorge, or a tomb could issue clouds and make rain, they sacrificed to it. The state has regular statutes; the responsibility lies with the authorities. Who, if it is not his appointed task, dare infringe upon this? But the chief councillors do not attend to [their proper task, which is] maintaining harmony, and instead take matters of practical administration for their task. The prefects and county administrators have no time for [their proper tasks, which are] cherishing and nourishing, and instead treat pressing for taxes as if it were governing. Discussing the Way, ordering the land, spreading transformative influences, all have become mere empty words. Registers, deadlines, lawsuits, budgeting – these are the real matters at hand. This has continued, day by day, for a long time. How much truer is it today, when our territory remains unrecovered; when, here in the southeast, our resources are limited, yet the weight of the massive expenses of the court, officialdom, walls, palaces, suburban sacrifices, and ancestral temples cannot easily be reduced; when from west to east we labor under a border of almost ten thousand *li*, and the costs of supporting troops take up eight to nine tenths of the whole. High officials and great ministers, whose compassion and generosity are real, who each day, with care and diligence, urge one another to duty and to reverence, turn instead to evil and confusion, or cling to the thought that one may go on as things have always been. Thus the people's strength sinks further by the day; the prefectures and counties fall each day deeper into distress; and the efforts of the prefects and county administrators to relieve the problems are not enough. This is the inevitable consequence of [our] circumstances. Though in sacrificing against drought or flood the administrators may want to exhaust their skill and sincere feeling, their basic duties and routine affairs take up most of [their time and

resources]. Thus worship and prayer are scattered among the common people and fill all the world. With long continuance this has become the norm. Though the law has its articles, the authorities never enforce them. This too is the inevitable consequence of circumstances.

Today it has not rained for a full month. The cracks in the soil are deep. The rivers and streams are shrunken; the dams and ponds are dried up. The sound of waterwheels fills the air, but the moisture does not soak through the fields. The color of worry is on men's faces, but their sighs do not find voice. The people's hearts are fearful.

As day led on to day, one of my visitors rebuked me: 'None who lives in this locality can fail to worry about the whole locality's affairs. When something is done by men as the norm and not prevented by law, for a man to hold alone to the tiniest details in the words of antiquity and to sit watching a disastrous drought, not once lending the resources of his heart to pray to the gods and so assist the prefecture and the county, comfort the neighbourhood, and share in the worries of his elders – surely this is just like notching one's boat in order to find a sword [that one has dropped in the water], or like failing to come to the aid of a drowning married woman [in order not to violate the taboo on male–female contact] !'

Thus I pondered: [. . .] I have served in office at court, and further have credentials in hand for a post in Ching; I wait my turn here at home. The prefecture and county [authorities], not disdaining my stupidity, treat me with the ceremonial one would offer an honored guest. My elders and my juniors often call to ask after me. If I truly cannot share in the worries of my elders and satisfy the hopes of my juniors, then my visitor's rebuke will not have been in error. Thus I undertake ritual abstentions and pray to you gods. [. . .][101]

Lu's visitor, we may presume, is urging him to pray to the gods worshipped by the populace at large – to do 'what is done by men as the norm.' In choosing a rather different course, though to the same end, Lu avoids taking part in the ills of contemporary custom, but at the same time steps, as he sees it, into a gap left by the state. The gap – the failure to perform, or to perform with adequate energy and attention, the traditional sacrifices to the gods of mountains and rivers, prescribed by the classics – grows partly out of moral failings that seem, for Lu, to antedate his own time. But it grows too out of problems Lu himself sees as special to Southern Sung. A long, hostile border, lined with troops who drain provisions and revenues northward; a state apparatus of imperial size and expense resting heavily upon a shrunken territory – these render the problems of central and local government so acute that religious duties fall by the wayside. As a consequence gods

multiply and are worshipped by those who ought not to worship: 'worship
and prayer are scattered among the common people and fill all the world.'

There is no general movement of the Fu-chou elite in the direction Lu has
laid out here; and the act of one man hardly constitutes social or religious
change. In blaming, even partly, the special conditions of Southern Sung for
what he saw as the religious disorder all about him, Lu was surely wrong: the
breakdown of the classical hierarchical system of worship, even insofar as it
ever existed quite so neatly, long preceded the Sung. Indeed, Lu must have
known this; his argument here may be conscious hyperbole. Yet in representing himself as drawn by the state's inaction, or ineffective action, into
doing reluctantly what the state ought to do itself, Lu speaks in terms that
do surely reflect the larger realities of his own time, and the Fu-chou elite's
view of those realities. In one sphere after another of local social life, as we
have seen, men of the Fu-chou elite in Southern Sung acted, reluctantly
or eagerly, to fill gaps left by the state's withdrawal, inaction, or ineffectiveness. That Lu framed the religious situation of his time as the consequence
of state inaction, pictured himself as drawn into reluctant action to fill the
gap for the sake of his community, and went on in fact to perform – as far
as I know, uniquely – sacrifices to gods that were traditionally the state's
own, suggests that he was applying habits of mind drawn from these other
spheres to the sphere of religion. That they did not, perhaps, quite fit the
facts of the case suggests all the more that they were rather strong habits.
In effect Lu draws for religion the picture I have drawn for local defense
and for social welfare. We need not wholly accept his picture to conclude
from it that the Fu-chou elite of Southern Sung – if Lu is its representative
– conceived itself, broadly, as playing the state's role in the absence of the
the state.

THE STATE IN FU-CHOU:
NORTHERN AND SOUTHERN SUNG

In preceding chapters we have seen a number of areas in which the power of the Southern Sung state was circumscribed or its field of action limited. In the military sphere, the inadequacy of official forces and the failure of local officials to control them, against a background of intensifying national and local war and disorder, allowed the rise of elite-run private militia organizations. The government's encouragement and sanctioning of these militias glossed over but could not fully disguise its inability to control them. In social welfare and famine relief the relevant organs of local government were sited exclusively in, and their efforts probably confined to, the prefectural and county seats. As famines and price squeezes became common in Southern Sung, again the apparent response to the state's absence was the rise of locally run (though sometimes officially initiated) rural welfare institutions such as community and normal-purchase granaries. Official views on the duty of wealthy locals to supply grain to poorer families in their vicinity did not command the agreement, in practice, of a good many local elite families; and their resistance in practice may have rested on respectable foundations in contemporary social thought. In at least one important case an official's direct efforts to force the sale of grain were thwarted or defused through the aid of a local man with a family background of militia action. In water management, official control and regulation were effective only sporadically if at all, while private appropriation of dams was a recurrent problem or perhaps an enduring condition. The state — despite its theoretical commitment to preserve and improve irrigation systems — built dams and dikes only in or near the administrative cities; and even there the works most crucial for government interests often went unrepaired for decades. In bridge-building the situation seems much the same, and here the very active role of the local elite is fully documented.

In all of this, had the state's power truly declined? The difficulty here is the scarcity of evidence for Northern Sung. Official troops were concentrated then in the prefectural city, and one may suppose with some confidence that they were therefore more easily controllable, a more effective instrument of official power; but there is no direct evidence of their use. One reason may be that their use was unnecessary. There seems to have been very little banditry or large-scale social disorder in Northern Sung Fu-chou, and certainly the threat of 'barbarian' invasion from the north, with the Liao lying half a continent away, was no threat at all. In effect the official forces of Northern Sung may simply have gone untested. The invasions and banditry of Southern Sung presented a new problem for local officials. The national scope of the crisis, and the need for soldiers on the border with Chin, virtually guaranteed that local officials in Fu-chou, well back from the front lines, would have to face the new problem alone: they could count on little material help from the center.

In social welfare and relief too, it may have been external circumstances, as much as the state itself, that had changed. As we have seen, famine struck Fu-chou in only two of Northern Sung's hundred and fifty years. In Southern Sung, serious dearth rarely skipped more than twenty years at a time. Contemporaries mentioned the problem of drought so rarely in Northern, so often in Southern Sung, that one must suspect a real climatic change. Beyond this, the steady growth of population up to middle Southern Sung must have put new pressure on land and so on supplies of grain: this may have made the offseason price rises more serious even in years of good crops. Thus it may be that fundamentally new, or newly severe, problems led to the rise of community granaries and normal-purchase granaries among the local elite. It was only in a time of dearth, too, that a local official had the *opportunity* to fail to force elite families to sell their grain, and thus to reveal the limits of his power. Perhaps, given recurrent shortages and elite resentment of past claims made on them, a Northern Sung official would not have done much better. Northern Sung officials in Fu-chou were not put to the test.

If we seem to see a decline in the effective power of local officials, then, it may reflect external conditions as much as any change in the state's own inherent capacities. But other evidence does suggest that, whether in response to these new conditions or for other reasons, the state itself had changed. In water control, for instance, we do not know directly that local officials in Northern Sung maintained registers of dams and kept up with routine repairs more consistently than they would do in Southern Sung. But the achievements of the program of the 1070s revealed a central government capable, through its local agents, of compensating massively for the accumulated neglects, if any, of previous years. Two centuries later Huang Chen tried to make up for what may have been a much longer period of neglect, and achieved relatively little. On the one hand, it seems, the difficulty of exerting coercive force in the countryside compelled him to keep his program voluntary and informal; on the other hand, he did not have the encouragement and resources of the central government behind him. This, perhaps, is the key: during Southern Sung, local officials were in many respects on their own. The days of far-reaching central legislation, directed uniformly at all localities − in Northern Sung generated nearly as enthusiastically by 'conservative' antireformers as by reformers like Fan Chung-yen or Wang An-shih − were past.

The shift is clear in the sphere of land registration. Formally, local officials in Northern and in Southern Sung were responsible for a complete revision of land and household registers − a full survey, with reassignment of households to the five fiscal grades according to the amount of their property − every three years. As we have seen, in Southern Sung this responsibility simply ceased to be met, and registers remained unchanged − or even rotted away − over periods of decades. Northern Sung Fu-chou provides little direct evidence; but the evidence for the empire as a whole suggests that Northern Sung registers, despite frequent abuses, were still revised regularly.[1] The process may often have been corrupted, as wealthy or powerful families used their influence over officials to avoid paying taxes or rendering service; but this is less important here than the window into the real situation in the countryside that the re-registration process itself will have provided for local officials. In Southern Sung this window was shut for eighty years at a time, or longer. Most important, the tendency for real tax burdens to become more and more inequitable with time led twice, in middle and late Northern Sung, to a centrally directed program of resurvey of lands, national or semi-national in scale. Each of these − one in 1072, one in 1112 − was in the end reversed by factional shifts in the capital; but the arguments raised against them − that they were being distorted so as to raise rather than redistribute local taxes; that farmers were destroying crops and property to avoid the tax increases − make it clear that the programs had reached down into the localities and affected them in fundamental ways.[2] In Fu-chou one of these programs increased local tax quotas considerably.[3] Here again we see the center taking control of its local agents so as to make its will effective at the prefectural and county level. The last nationwide land survey program in Sung came in 1142, fifteen years after the founding of Southern Sung.[4] For the rest of the dynasty, it was left to local officials to decide whether to undertake new registration; hardly any did.

In virtually all areas − apart from the forwarding of taxes to the center − the Southern Sung state systematically withdrew from uniform decision-making about real policy at the local level. Many decrees now merely offered possibilities to local officials, to accept or reject as they (or as the local population) chose. The original decree on local militias at the beginning of Southern Sung had ordered their formation wherever possible. Within a few years this was reversed: the imposition of new militias by local officials was prohibited, but localities that asked to keep their militias were to be allowed to do so. The decree on Chu Hsi's community granary plan in 1188 simply presented the program as an option for officials who wanted to adopt it and could find local men willing to run it. A circuit intendant, prefect, or county administrator who chose to survey lands, to revise the local service system,[5] to organize a *pao-wu* self-defense and police organization, to bring a new category of wealth into the tax structure,[6] or to revitalize – as Huang Chen attempted – official control of irrigation, could do so, as far as the center was concerned. The formality of an official request to the court might be required, but the center did not dictate policy on a broad scale. Yet in granting this freedom – perhaps willy-nilly – to local officials, the court could not also grant them the power it had exercised on its own behalf in Northern Sung. In the first place this freedom came to local officials precisely at the time when – in Fu-chou at least – their own coercive apparatus, the official military forces, had been dispersed through the countryside and so out of their control. In the second place, officials were surely in part weakened when they no longer had the authority of clear and uniform central policies backing their actions. A prefect might try a good many things, more or less on his own decision. But precisely because it was his own decision, if what he tried disrupted – even briefly – the flow of taxes, or provoked enough local resistance that the state could not help taking notice, the responsibility was all his own. Could he expect local people to cooperate, knowing this, if his policy was not to their liking? If some local man's connections to influential figures at court were better than his own, he might find himself reprimanded or transferred: the court, after all, had no special or permanent commitment to the policy he had chosen. What he gained in freedom of decision, then, he lost in security. It would be very surprising if most officials in this position had not chosen to play it safe and do little, even if registers rotted, dams fell into private hands, and fort troops divided booty with clerks.

In picturing the Southern Sung local official as a weakened figure, however, one must deal with two pieces of evidence that seem more refractory. First, as I have already remarked, Fu-chou's populace was extremely litigious: prefects and county administrators complained of endless processions of suitors filling their days with plaints and counter-plaints.[7] One might imagine that this tendency to take disputes before officials would yield to the state considerable real authority in a wide range of local affairs. Might not an ingenious official even use his role as judge as a lever to move strategic members of the elite toward goals of his own? Second, the state apparently managed, through its 'Harmonious Purchase' program, to extract ever-increasing quantities of rice from Fu-chou landowners, quantities that by the end of the dynasty equalled the regular autumn tax quotas.[8] In theory Harmonious Purchase was, as the name suggests, a program of government purchases of rice at market prices. But over time in Southern Sung it seems to have developed into a quasi-tax: depending on the period and the region of China, quotas for sale might be assigned to each household on the registers, regardless of willingness to sell; payment might be set far below the current market price; in some places the rice might simply be taken, with no payment at all.[9] If Harmonious Purchase quotas steadily rose in Fu-chou, is this a sign of effective state power in the countryside?

To this last question the answer, I think, is no. In the first place, the original aim of Harmonious Purchase under Southern Sung was to make up for vast quantities of regular taxes that no longer came in as reliably as they had in Northern Sung.[10] This was still one of its major functions in Fu-chou in the early 1200s, to judge by the testimony of Lin-ch'uan county administrator Huang Kan.[11] In Fu-chou, furthermore, the rice was paid for, right to the end of the dynasty.[12] By that time the price was indeed well below market rates: Huang Chen, addressing a local audience, argued that what was once a fair price had become unfair through remaining the same while market prices rose.[13] But so long as Harmonious Purchase served mainly to make up for regular taxes not paid, the payment of any price for rice formally owed the government amounted to a partial state subsidy of the taxpayer. This hardly seems to show the state's strength.

By the end of Sung, Fu-chou's Harmonious Purchase quotas were not an alternative, but a supplement to regular taxes, and Huang Chen suggests that their fulfillment involved real suffering for local people. But here the question becomes: who suffered? No data survive on the usual distribution of Harmonious Purchase allotments; but one can make educated guesses. Everything suggests that the Southern Sung local government found it much easier to extract revenues (no matter what the formal category) from some locals than from others. Lu Chiu-yüan tells us that while most Fu-chou commoners paid a surcharge on their land taxes, amounting to half again above their theoretical obligation, the families of officeholders and of clerks were charged — even as a matter of formal procedure — only the base amount.[14] Huang Kan, in the early thirteenth century, was unwilling to institute a formal program of relief grain sales during a famine, because he believed that wealthy families could shift the major selling burden to their middling and poor neighbors.[15] Huang Chen argued that 'the reason for the breakdown of finances and revenues [in local government] is the evasion of tax grain quotas by the great families,' and outlined the problem that would face any administrator who tried to repair the damage:

At the least, the clerks will have to suffer the consequence that the great families will see their pressing for taxes as the extortion of bribes, and go off to appeal to the circuit office. At the worst, the district administrator will have to suffer the consequence that the great families will view his pressing for taxes as tyrannical government, and fly to give word to the court. [. . .] If we press even one great family for its proper taxes, that great family's strength is enough to move and to shake, and disaster will come at once.[16]

Perhaps this is special pleading: Huang Chen was a local official himself. But his words gain in force when one recalls Lu Chiu-yüan's argument, framed nearly a century earlier and from the other end of the elite/local official relation, that an administrator ought not to concern himself with back taxes, ought in fact to protect his jurisdiction from the demands of the center. Huang Chen saw the 'great families' as obstacles to the restoration of 'finances and revenues'; Lu Chiu-yüan, who spoke for a great family if anyone did, had called the preoccupation with 'finances and revenues' (the very words are the same) a mark of moral bankruptcy, the logical consequence of 'treating oneself as chief.' Huang's references to 'appealing to the circuit office' or 'flying to give word to the court' recall Lu's letters to officials, impeaching the conduct of their subordinates. Lu several times intervened against specific taxes or revenue-raising devices in Fu-chou. Lu and Huang seem, at a distance of almost a hundred years, to be describing one another; and Lu's example makes Huang's complaint entirely believable.

None of this touches Harmonious Purchase directly. But if indeed local officials had to let officeholding families pay their taxes at a lower rate than others did; if they could not be sure of payment even at privileged rates; if they could not assume that the very enterprise of tax collection was ack-nowledged as legitimate; if they could not prevent wealthy households from shifting responsibility for relief sales to others; could they allot Harmonious Purchase quotas to the rich, the titled, or the powerful and expect them to be fulfilled? Huang Chen, after the court had repeatedly refused his petitions that it release Fu-chou from its Harmonious Purchase obligations until the famine was ended, still rejected the notion of Harmonious Purchase and instituted a program of 'purchase by invitation' — no quotas, he said, were to be assigned — directed solely at the rich. He seems to have assumed that Harmonious Purchase — despite the principle of allotment according to means, which in theory always underlay it — would in fact place an unfair burden on those with less to sell.[17]

If Harmonious Purchase was allotted inequitably, it becomes easier to account for the testimony of contemporaries, by late Southern Sung virtually unanimous, that it imposed — even in the best of years — an enormous burden in the countryside. Under Huang Chen, owing to a rapid increase in

Harmonious Purchase quotas, the total rice obligation of the prefecture
(counting Harmonious Purchase and regular rice taxes together) amounted to
180,625 *shih*, or nearly nine thousand tons, each year. A plausible estimate
of the total rice production of Fu-chou at around the same time, as we have
seen, is about three million *shih*: 147,000 tons. Even assuming that none of
the Harmonious Purchase rice was paid for — something we know was not the
case — this would amount to a total rice tax of only about six percent, not
an unbearable burden, one would think, for any but the poorest farmer.[18]

Huang Chen, of course, served in a year of famine, and one can understand
his concern; but in earlier years, when crops were good and Harmonious
Purchase quotas somewhat lower, it is hard to imagine that, as a sheer proportion of production, it represented a serious burden on the prefecture as a
whole. But if the burden was systematically shifted down the economic scale
— if middling and small farmers were in the end responsible for the defaults
of officeholders and the wealthy — it may very quickly have become in-
tolerable. The figures themselves, then, seem to suggest — if we are to accept
the word of contemporaries that Harmonious Purchase was a serious affliction
to the farmer — that purchase allotments had been shifted to those with less
to sell, because those with more were unwilling. In short there is no reason to
believe that, in Harmonious Purchase or in any other category of tax, the
Southern Sung local official managed to tap adequately the resources he most
needed to tap: those of the wealthy, the titled — the local elite.

What of the lawcourts? Here again it is not at all clear that the local
official formally responsible was in fact in charge. Huang Kan, in a judgement
on the case of one Professor Wei and his antagonist Hsiung Hsiang, expressed
a remarkably pessimistic view of what a judge could achieve. Wei, his eye on
Hsiung Hsiang's lands, had falsely charged Hsiung with harboring thieves; the
process of suits, countersuits, and jailings that followed had largely accomplished Hsiung's ruin. Huang Kan was helpless to do more than release several
men held under false charges and punish others who had administered
beatings at Wei's instigation. Against Wei himself he had no recourse. His
comment is almost pathetic:

> The customs of these times are such that anyone who lives in the
> countryside must, in various ways, employ the methods of a tyrant
> in order to control his locality; only then can he stand independent.
> Even an officeholder [like Wei] cannot avoid the influence of custom.
> But it would be grievous for a county office to *help* someone employ
> the methods of a tyrant. [...][19] (Emphasis mine)

Huang, who clearly holds Wei responsible for the death of one man, the
injury of several others, and the ruin of Hsiung Hsiang's family, here is

reduced to refusing to lend him positive aid. Clearly he does not believe that, as a judge, he can do much that is practical about the 'tyrannical' ways of a rural strongman.

Huang's other judgements seem all of a piece with this one. Convinced that one Prefect Tseng, a man of Lo-an County, has by false charges engineered the death in jail of two of his opponent's dependents, Huang asks that the circuit intendant investigate and, if his opinion is upheld, that the capital apply stern administrative discipline.[20] Evidently he is in no position to act himself. In a third similar case a certain Tseng K'ua, member of an officeholder's house-hold, has ruined one man and had two others thrown in jail through (as Huang maintains) false accusations. Huang recommends that the center discipline him if he brings any further false suits.[21] In these and other cases Huang responds in strikingly mild or hesitant ways to what he sees, or professes to see, as moral and legal outrages. There is no evidence here that his authority as judge gave him much real influence over affairs in the countryside. Instead the stronger of the two parties, through influence over the country sheriff's office, the prefectural bowmen, or jailers and clerks, has largely achieved the other's destruction by the time the case reaches Huang. He is left to pick up the pieces and, in effect, to refuse to sanction legally what has already been accomplished outside the law but with the help of its agents. All this is especially striking when one recalls that these judgements are presumably not a random sample of Huang's work, but were chosen for inclusion in his collected writings for their exemplary character, both as literary pieces and as records of action. These may be Huang's successes. There is coercive authority here, but it is exercised more often by coalitions of powerful locals with subordinate officials, clerks, and jailers than by the official in whose hands it formally rests.

Lu Chiu-yüan, in two of his letters to officials, had described, from a concerned local's point of view, the processes that seem to be at work in Huang Kan's legal cases. An especial problem in judging lawsuits, he believed, was the role played by clerks and jailers:

> Recently I saw Wang [the prefect of] Chi-chou, who said that a circuit intendant or a prefect should not too lightly put men in jail. For the official in charge of the jail is usually not the right sort of man; the clerks and soldiers are often in control. Once an ordinary commoner falls into jail he is at the mercy of the jailer-clerks. Under the whip, whatever one seeks one will find. [...] An official is a man of another place; a clerk is a man of this place. An official's term is up in two or three years; a clerk grew up and has had sons and grandsons here. When an official examines a matter, clerks are at his left and right, before and

behind him. Thus it is inevitable that an official will be deceived by
clerks and betrayed by clerks.[22]

But clerks do not always act alone or for themselves. Thus:

> Wily clerks and powerful families collaborate with one another, inter-
> twining to prey like grubs and maggots upon the people. [. . .] Powerful
> families amass great riches and close connections; together with those
> who adhere to them on either side they create some opening apart from
> the matter at hand to subvert our basic intention; they conspire in
> corroborative testimony within their coterie to substantiate falsehoods,
> skillfully crafting chapter and verse to jibe with the clerks and make
> their story stand up. I, a man of another place, hearing this all at once,
> am not well versed in the [local] customs; and within my office,
> secluded and exalted, the affairs of the villages do not reach my eye;
> the talk of the roads and lanes is not heard by my ear. [. . .] When
> hearing cases, one wants above all to get at the facts, and not to be
> tricked. This is something difficult even for the most brilliant. Even if I
> do get at the facts, these others may still be able to create hindrances
> and so limit the measures I take.[23]

All this will sound only too familiar to students of any dynasty after the
Sung, if not before. The machinations of clerks; the helplessness of the
official, an outsider, to understand what is happening around him; the ties
that join powerful and determined locals to the clerks: these are virtual
clichés in the historiography of China. Yet sometimes a cliché is a cliché
because it expresses a truth. Local officials in Sung Fu-chou *were* outsiders,
at their posts only for a few years, confronting a population whose interests
were by no means always the same as their own; clerks *were* natives,
employed for life, sometimes for generations within a single family. Huang
Kan's judgements document for single lawsuits the elite/clerk alliances that
Lu Chiu-yüan pictures as universal. Local men who brought suit to the
county or the prefecture did not, by that act, necessarily yield to local
officials — except formally — the power or the authority to resolve their
disputes; they might simply intend to use the coercive apparatus of the
courts and jails to gain ends which in mere private feuding they had not yet
achieved.

Litigiousness, then, need not automatically add to the power of the state
in local affairs. Nor, as I have argued, did rising Harmonious Purchase quotas
necessarily reflect a fiscal apparatus powerful enough to draw reliably on
the wealth of the local elite. Neither, in the present state of the evidence,
seriously threatens the conclusion that Southern Sung local government in

Fu-chou was on the whole weaker than it had been, at least during periodic bouts of intense activity, under Northern Sung. A part of the power lost, it seems — a part, in other terms, of the responsibilities abdicated — fell into the hands of the militia leaders, granary managers, and dam-builders of the local elite.

What has all this to do with the transformation of elite strategies? I have already suggested that as the power and activity of the state declined, central office seemed less crucial to elite families' interests, advancement, and survival; and that local disorder, aggravated by (and in turn aggravating) the state's military weakness, perhaps made property and position less secure and so redirected attention to the local base. But the retreat of the state also laid open, as we have seen, new fields of action at the local level, and with these a new or greatly expanded social role: the role of local magnate or, if one prefer, community leader. Various (and potentially conflicting) strands of Confucian and traditional ethics had long urged a gentleman to serve, support, and aid his family, and/or to serve and improve the larger social world. A state in firm control of its localities, perhaps, made unrestricted action in either direction difficult except through the medium of high central office. But a weakened state opened, at the local level, new ways of doing both. To be a big fish in a smallish pond was now not only safer than to leap the rapids in the capital, but more rewarding and less limiting than it would have been in the past. Whatever combination of factors first precipitated the shift toward a localist strategy, the weakening of the state in the localities surely helped to fill that strategy with a positive content of social action. This in turn, perhaps, made the strategy itself more thinkable and more respectable.

CONCLUSION

Through this essay in local history have run three themes of general significance, I think, for our understanding of Sung China. One is the elite's sheer
continuity. A second is the growing importance of locality in elite social life
and self-conceptions. A third, and perhaps the most important, is the separation — growing in Southern Sung, but in some respects already clear in
Northern Sung — of elite from state.

'Social mobility' in Sung — whether this means movement into the elite, or
simply (and questionably) movement in and out of office — probably can
never be measured. But in Fu-chou the persistence of a large number of elite
'families' (using the term broadly, to be sure) over many generations, even
centuries, is impressive. A few families, in Northern Sung, left; many new
ones emerged, especially in the early decades of Southern Sung; and beyond
the field of view that the sources afford, many others may have risen briefly
into the elite, only to fall out again; but there was never, from the beginning
of Sung to the end, a wholesale replacement of 'old' families by 'new.' Even
if we limit our attention to office-holding, the sort of constant turnover that
has sometimes been inferred from Kracke's examination statistics is, I think,
wholly imaginary. Most of the sixty or so elite families who were already
many generations old by the end of Sung were to persist well into Yüan or
even beyond.

The impression of continuity is even more striking where single families
involved themselves for generation after generation in some continuing
enterprise. A drug business supported the Lus as a single household for
ten generations. The Chin-ch'i militia drew the participation of the Tengs
and Fus for half the dynasty; the Tengs would continue their role right to
the end of the Yüan. The Cheng-chüeh Temple was closely connected to the
Tsengs of Nan-feng County for over two hundred years. A great deal happened,
a great deal changed, in Fu-chou under the Sung; but a significant part of the
local elite reproduced itself for generations despite wars, banditry, and the
transformation of its way of life.

That locality assumed new importance in Southern Sung, that the elite shifted its attention from national centers of power and from the pursuit of high office toward the consolidation of its home base, and that a sort of elite 'localism' emerged in the sphere of social ideals as well, form a second major argument of this study. The local retrenchment expresses itself in marriage, in patterns of residence and donation, and in a 'stay-at-home' policy that distinguishes Southern Sung families quite sharply from the emigrants of Northern Sung. Here my findings confirm and develop at the local level what Robert Hartwell had proposed on the basis of national data. I have argued that the changes must have expanded the network of purely local contacts and associations of the older elite families, and so may account in part for the large number of 'new' families that appear in early Southern Sung. An examination of two groups of the new families has shown that they emerged into the elite as clusters associated with definite and relatively small areas of the prefecture and joined by mutual connections from the start. Here again the social importance of locality is obvious.

In this picture, however, one element remains unclear: the position of recent immigrant families under the Southern Sung. In Fu-chou, at least, these maintained a marriage pattern rather like that of the officeholders of Northern Sung. Was this only a second resort, forced upon them by the difficulty of gaining acceptance into the elite networks of their new prefecture? Or did immigrants deliberately preserve an older, court-focused strategy, and does their migration itself – however different it may look from the centripetal emigration of Northern Sung – set them apart from the general local retrenchment of Southern Sung elites? I have already suggested quite a different interpretation of their moves: that they went from areas of greater to areas of lesser population-density and land-scarcity, precisely in order to find and maintain, in more congenial territory, a firm local base. But to settle the question would need a broader study of migrants in various regions of Southern Sung China. In either case, the existence of a special group that practised long-distance marriage – whether this was by choice or willy-nilly – may have had considerable significance for Southern Sung history. I have already suggested that the localizing of marriage had reduced the means available for the recruiting of factions at the capital. Did recent migrants now gain a special position in factional conflict through their broader connections? If changes in the ideal sphere were connected – as cause or as effect, or both – with the transformation of family strategies, did migrants, who maintained at least a part of the older strategy, hold to different ideals as well? These are questions worth pursuing. There seems little doubt, however, that Southern Sung migrants were a small and untypical group, and that the broader picture of emergent localism is not fundamentally altered by their presence.

This same emergent localism is closely connected to my third theme: the separation of elite from state. I use the word 'separation' precisely to suggest a process rather than a stable condition. It seems clear that the changes of Southern Sung — both the transformation of elite strategies and (what the transformation itself may partly reflect) the relative decline of state power — served to widen and to emphasize a gap between elite interests and state interests at the local level, and to confirm and strengthen the independence of elite status and social position from the efforts of the state to certify, to validate, and so to control it. Still, this independence was not wholly new. One may define the boundaries of the elite, as I have done at the outset, by standards that turn on the possession of wealth, power, or prestige; or one may allow the elite, as it were, to define its own boundaries, by the friendships, connections, and associations its members formed. On neither reckoning, even in Northern Sung, did elite and officialdom, or elite and degree-holding group, coincide. Yet it is in Southern Sung, once again, that the independence, the self-ratifying character of elite status becomes clearest. The elite strategy of Northern Sung had made participation in a prestigious network of empire-spanning marriages, at least, dependent on officeholding. Even the elite members joined by this network were involved too in webs of local connections that extended well beyond officialdom, and often acted as if status were not wholly dependent on office — as when Wang An-shih recommended Wang Ling, who had not even taken the exams, as a son-in-law for his officeholding affine Wu Fen. Yet in their pursuit of high office and court position as a central and life-defining goal these men did perhaps grant the state the role of status arbiter for at least the highest levels of the elite. In the Southern Sung the national marriage network and the strategy that had created it (leaving recent migrants aside) were gone, and with them had gone, surely, the last pretense that the state, now apparently weaker than ever at the local level, could decide and manage the distribution of high social status. Local administrators, Neo-Confucian or otherwise, perhaps recognized and even sanctioned this when they honored at their shrines — sometimes, perhaps, at the urging of the local elite itself — men without office, men whose claims to worth and renown were chiefly or wholly local.

In offering sacrifices to genuinely local heroes, the men who administered Fu-chou may in fact deliberately have attempted a *rapprochement* with an elite whose concerns diverged more and more openly, in Southern Sung, from those of the state. The crucial word here, perhaps, is 'openly': local interests and state interests had of course always been potentially, and often actually, distinct. Northern Sung men like Wang An-shih may have learned, as they rose in office, to identify their own interests almost wholly with those of the court or bureaucracy; but still they had relatives at home, surely, whose careers had not taken them as high, whose interests were thus more firmly rooted in local soil, and who might expect their well-placed kinsmen to serve these interests. Was it partly to cast off the burden of such expectations, to evade the potential conflict of state and local/familial interests—and not simply to gain the strategic advantages of the capital region and the Yangtse delta — that successful Northern Sung officeholders so often abandoned Fu-chou? Did they migrate not merely *to*, but also *away from*? The most famous genealogists of Northern Sung, the successful officials Su Hsün and Ou-yang Hsiu, limited the scope of their works to comparatively recent ancestors — not including the first migrant ancestor himself — and so circumscribed the range of living kinsmen who might fall within their 'lineage.' Even within this range, they focused chief attention on the direct lines that led to their own immediate kin. These limitations found justification in classical ritual principles; but were they also partly an attempt to restrict lineage solidarity, and so to escape the demands of more distant kin whose interests might be more purely local than the authors' own?[1] We may find here hints of conflicts of a sort that come further out into the open in Southern Sung.

We have seen that Southern Sung men frequently took the role of local advocate, of intercessor with local administrators on behalf of their kin, their neighbors, or a wider local community (however conceived); I have argued that the role was not so much new as newly honored, newly prized. But to honor a gentleman's local involvements and his activity as local advocate was at the same time implicitly to legitimate, sometimes openly to celebrate, local interests. These were now appropriate subjects for public discussion. (They may first have begun to be so, it is true, in the late Northern Sung, when 'conservative' statesmen like Su Shih argued that central policies — 'reforms' or not — must vary according to local peculiarities and special conditions.) What needs stressing once more is that local interests were sometimes conceived not simply as apart from, but as directly opposed to, the interests of the court and of the central and local bureaucracy. This is explicit in Lu Chiu-yüan's virtually seditious advice to local administrators on the question of tax arrears, and in his rejection of 'finances and revenues' as immoral concerns. It is implicit at least in the behavior of the Teng family when called upon for militia service in 1175 and 1261; in the discussions of the Lu family over the same issue in 1174; in the open defiance of Huang Chen's famine relief efforts and Cheng Sung's intervention on the K'angs' behalf in 1271; and in Huang Chen's discussions of the burden of Harmonious Purchase levies.

A new openness of conflict between state and local interests in Southern Sung may indeed reflect a change in historiographic attitudes more than in real conditions. But it still raises questions that need answers. I have speculated that Northern Sung officeholders evaded the issue by moving away; but this option was unattractive to Southern Sung men whose family strategies were focused on local position, on their identity as local gentlemen. So long as a man lived at home, he might resolve any conflict between state and locality by coming down on the side of his home and neighbors. But the same man might have to take part in like conflicts from the opposite side — not on his home ground, to be sure, but not always very far away — when he served in office. How did men resolve — indeed, did they recognize — the dissonance between the roles they played at home and those they were expected to play as administrators elsewhere? The question serves partly to show the limitations of the present study, in which for clarity of focus the official careers and administrative achievements of Fu-chou men have largely been left aside. Still it is worth asking. How did Lu Chiu-yüan reconcile his disdain for 'finances and revenues' with his taxgathering responsibilities when he administered Ching-men Chün in Ching-hu-pei circuit during the 1190s? On his own accounting as we have seen, a local administrator ought to shield his domain from the excessive or too urgent demands of regional or central authorities. Is this in fact how he, and other Southern Sung men of similar bent, acted or tried to act in office? Did they offer local elites elsewhere the protection they claimed to expect for themselves? Or must principled localism give way to bureaucratic pragmatism when the locality and the populace at issue were not one's own? Again, the issue can hardly have been new in Southern Sung, but it must have been informed with new tension when family strategies no longer pushed men out and up toward the highest offices and so, perhaps, toward identification of self with government, of social beneficence with state action. How, if at all, was this new tension expressed, and perhaps eased, in the intellectual currents of the time? This, I think, is a direction of inquiry into Southern Sung thought that no one has yet taken. Are there systematic differences, for example, between the portraits of local officials in biographical and eulogistic writings in Northern and in Southern Sung? Were there many competing formulations of the local administrator's proper role; or is Lu Chiu-yüan's view typical of the political thinking of his time? Such questions lead well beyond the bounds of this study, but they suggest directions of research that might be fruitful.

These questions bring us again into the realm of intellectual history. An old issue that may emerge with new force from what we have seen here is the social place and significance, in Southern Sung, of Neo-Confucianism. The Neo-Confucian movement — the strand of thought, or cluster of strands, that contemporaries called *tao-hsüeh*, 'the learning of the Way' — was, we must not forget, still new in Southern Sung, and had yet to win the status of official orthodoxy. Chu Hsi and other leaders of that movement, confronting a society and an elite in which locality and local action received new emphasis, took something of the same emphasis into their own plans for society's moral reconstruction. Yet at the same time, as I have argued, their own vision was in no real sense 'localist': the moral reconstruction they sought was, ultimately, the reconstruction and reintegration of an *empire*; hence their equal stress on the moral self-perfection of the emperor. Local communities were important because they were the building-blocks of which a new integration could be made. In practise, too, the Neo-Confucians built networks of scholarly and academic ties that were translocal, regional, even — in their summation at least — ultimately national. If the Neo-Confucian movement, then, in part reflected or absorbed the emergent localist tendencies that we find in elite strategies and broader self-conceptions in Southern Sung, in larger part, perhaps, it was in tension with them, even stood in opposition to them. If one looks at Southern Sung intellectual life for a direct reflection, or better, a direct translation into ideal terms, of the transformed condition of the elite that I have been tracing here, one will find it more easily in the privatist household ethic of Yüan Ts'ai[2] than in Neo-Confucianism taken as a whole.

It may be useful then to ask whether there was some particular social basis of the tendencies in Neo-Confucianism that seem in tension with much else in their own time. (The tension is not in the observer's eye only: the Neo-Confucian leaders saw *themselves* as standing in opposition to much that was current in their own society.) The answer might lie simply in the real social independence of the academic vocation — an independence whose social foundation was the elite's demand for and society's respect for the teacher, and which thus ultimately, and paradoxically, rested in part on the very examination system that Neo-Confucians, with their academies and their ideal of study for its own sake, reacted against. The notion of 'Confucianism' as a *profession* has recently been provocatively argued by John Dardess for the Yüan and early Ming dynasties.[3] But the question might be taken in other directions as well. Did the leading figures of the movement come from social backgrounds, or occupy social spaces, in any way special for the elite of their time? To ask such questions is to raise the specter of a materialist reductionism; but the point is rather to look for relationships, without prejudging directions and channels of influence. Social-background analyses of Chinese political or intellectual history have often been vitiated by categories so crude and so unverifiable as to be surely unreal — landlord versus merchant, aristocracy versus new gentry, and so on; but this need not make us reject the whole enterprise. Local study of the kind attempted here might provide categories more verifiable and, perhaps, more refined. To investigate the social backgrounds of the Neo-Confucian leadership would first of all require broader inquiry into the elites of the places they came from and lived in: we need a specific ground to view them against. From what we have seen here, patterns of marriage, residence, and migration are likely directions of inquiry.

Is it of any significance at all, for example, that Chu Hsi himself came from a family that had only recently migrated to the prefecture, Chien-chou in Fu-chien, in which it was registered? I raise these questions in only the most tentative spirit; but they may be worth asking.

Some of these issues are large ones; but they leave us within the bounds of the Sung. Hartwell, for one, has argued that the transformation of the elite between Northern and Southern Sung was permanent: that the Southern Sung 'gentry' (to use his term) was essentially the same social group, following the same strategy, as the 'local elite' (following Hilary Beattie) or the 'gentry' (using the term more broadly than is now usual) of Ming and Ch'ing. And in fact the Southern Sung elite reconstructed here does bear certain resemblances to later elites as discussed by Beattie, Jerry Dennerline, and others. Several aspects of elite life clearly continue or recur in Ming and Ch'ing: the centering of intellectual activity, especially when innovative or oppositional, on local, often private academies or literary associations rather than on the capital (something barely touched on here); the importance of private local militia, often formed of kin-based units; the role of private, local, yet formally organized institutions of social welfare – community granaries, charitable service estates, and the like; the importance of private initiative in water control; the frankness of local elite intervention in local government. Many of these are reminiscent of much earlier periods than the Sung – the Six Dynasties, for example – but their coexistence with a centralized recruitment system that penetrated the localities as deeply as the examination system did was certainly new in Southern Sung. Perhaps even more crucial is marriage: here work clearly remains to be done. I have elsewhere examined Fu-chou marriage patterns under the Yüan and concluded that, despite some tactical changes in response to new institutional realities, they essentially served the same locally focused strategy as those of Southern Sung.[4] For Ming and Ch'ing, both Beattie and Dennerline seem to find marriage networks focused locally or regionally.[5] Still it is far from certain that a national marriage network in the Northern Sung style never re-emerged, even temporarily, at higher levels or among special groups within the elite. Elite continuity between Southern Sung and Ch'ing – not necessarily in a genealogical sense, but in social and institutional terms – is a powerful organizing hypothesis that needs much further exploration.

To look in the other direction: how, in view of the fundamental transformation between Northern and Southern Sung, is one now to conceive the longer process of change that led from the aristocracy of T'ang to the post-Sung elite? Until recently historians have focused their answers on the T'ang–Sung transition itself. It may now be more adequate to think in terms of a 'dual transformation':[6] a first shift in personnel followed by a second shift of ways of life, of strategies. The first shift one might place at the T'ang–Sung transition with the disruption of the genealogical (and perhaps in a great many cases the biological) continuity of the great clans of the T'ang; or one might extend it into the Sung to encompass the rise of southerners, for the first time in any unified dynasty, to bureaucratic dominance. The Northern Sung elite that followed this first shift, as Hartwell has argued, still acted in many ways remarkably like the T'ang great clans: marrying nationally, living at national centers, pursuing high office and court influence above all else. The second shift, dividing Northern from Southern Sung, encompassed the change from national to local strategies. The elite that, in genealogical terms, persisted through this change not only had (as before) only vague connections to the T'ang clans, not only was largely southern in immediate origin, but now acted very differently.

If in fact the Northern Sung–Southern Sung shift was in significant ways permanent, the result must be, rather surprisingly perhaps, to give signal importance to the Chin conquest as a point of division in Chinese history: to make it appear more consequential than, for example, the conquest and reunification of the Yüan. The new Southern Sung conditions, of course, may partly have their roots in the factional conflicts of Northern Sung, with which the Chin had nothing at all to do. But if state weakness in Southern Sung also played a major part – by making influence at court seem less important; by making property and position in the localities less secure and so encouraging attention to them above all else; or by opening up new fields of action, in effect a new elite role, at the local level – then the Chin, which maintained constant pressure on the Sung state and drew its coercive means and material resources north to its borders, must also receive some credit. The Chinese subjects of the Ch'ing dynasty, thriving or chafing six centuries later under Manchu rule, lived perhaps in a society and polity shaped partly, and at a considerable remove, by the Manchus' own ethnic ancestors, the Jurchen.

In closing, I return to a note sounded briefly in my introduction. At the outset Fu-chou seemed an attractive focus for a local study partly, once again, because it was home to both Wang An-shih and Lu Chiu-yüan. What I had no reason to expect was that the two would prove to be, for Northern and Southern Sung respectively, virtual archetypes of the Fu-chou elite. This, in fact, they were. On one side of the divide stands Wang, the ambitious, successful career bureaucrat, who strove to reform society from the center, who was tied by marriage to leading officials of North and South China, and whose family established a second residence far off on the lower Yangtse, then left Fu-chou altogether. On the other side stands Lu, the occasional and irregular officeholder, who spent much of his life teaching at home or nearby, who worked tirelessly and openly to influence the governing of his home prefecture, who together with his brothers took an active role in local defense and in semi-public social welfare projects, whose marriage-kin came without exception from his own and neighboring counties, and whose lineal and collateral posterity still lived and thrived in Fu-chou at the moment of the Yüan conquest. The contrast epitomizes the gulf between the Northern and Southern Sung elites. Most of the broader processes of change I have discussed here appear, at the level of biography, as the transformation of Fu-chou from the springboard of Wang An-shih to the home of Lu Chiu-yüan.

LIST OF ABBREVIATIONS

(See List of Works Cited, below, p. 354, for full references on the sources listed here)

CCFC	Hsü Ta-ching et al., *Fu-chou Fu chih*
CPT	Ch'ang Pi-te et al., *Sung-jen* etc.
KHCC	Wang Yu-nien et al., *Chin-ch'i Hsien chih*
KHCJ	Ch'en Ch'ien et al., *Ch'ung-jen Hsien chih*
KHFC	Hsü Ying-jung et al., *Fu-chou Fu chih*
KHIH	Yu Chih-chang et al., *I-huang Hsien chih*
KHLA	Fang Chan et al., *Lo-an Hsien chih*
KHNF	Cheng Yüeh et al., *Nan-feng Hsien chih*
KHTH	Liang Ch'i et al., *Tung-hsiang Hsien chih*
KHYF	Lu Mei, *Yung-feng Hsien chih*
MKNF	Li Kuang-jun et al., *Nan-feng Hsien chih*
SCCA	Li Hsing-yüan et al., *Chi-an Fu chih*
SHY	*Sung hui-yao chi-pen*
SKCSCP	*Ssu-k'u ch'üan-shu chen-pen*
SPPY	*Ssu-pu pei-yao*
SPTK	*Ssu-pu ts'ung-k'an*
SS	T'o T'o et al., *Sung shih*
SYHA	Huang Tsung-hsi, *Sung-Yüan hsüeh-an*
SYHAPI	Wang Tzu-ts'ai, *Sung-Yüan hsüeh-an pu-i*
TCCC	Ch'eng Fang et al., *Chin-ch'i Hsien chih*
TCCJ	Sheng Ch'üan et al., *Ch'ung-jen Hsien chih*
TCChCh	Shao Tzu-i et al., *Chien-ch'ang Fu chih*
TCIH	Chang Hsing-yen, *I-huang Hsien chih*
TCLA	Chu K'uei-chang et al., *Lo-an Hsien chih*
TCLC	T'ung Fan-yen et al., *Lin-ch'uan Hsien chih*
TCTH	Li Shih-fen et al., *Tung-hsiang Hsien chih*
TCYF	Shuang Kuei et al., *Yung-feng Hsien chih*
TKIH	Cha Lung-a et al., *I-huang Hsien chih*
TSCC	*Ts'ung-shu chi-ch'eng*
WWC	Wu Ch'eng, *Wen-chung kung chi*
YLTT	*Yung-lo ta-tien*

APPENDIX I

RECONSTRUCTED ELITE FAMILIES

Below I list the sources used in reconstructing each of the seventy-three local elite families appearing in Table I in Chapter 2. The reconstruction of these seventy-three is reasonably secure; in a final section I list sources for nine uncertain or hypothetical cases: groups of men of one surname whose membership in a single family seems plausible but cannot be proven, or whose period of elite membership is unclear.

1. Chan of Lo-an County

a. Fourteen prefectural graduates, two of them *chin-shih*, listed as men of Ya-pei between 1162 and 1271 in *TCLA* 7/17bff. and *KHLA* 5/6 aff.

b. Ten prefectural graduates listed as men of Ch'ung-jen County between 1048 and 1123 (before the creation of Lo-an County; none thereafter) in *TCCJ* 7c/1b—4a and *KHCJ* 1/43b—47a.

c. Biographies of Chan Hao in *TCLA* 1/27a and *TCCJ* 6a/7a.

d. Biographies of Chan Ta-t'ung in *KHLA* 7/8b and *TCLA* 8/36a.

e. Preface to genealogy of Chan lineage in *WWC* 32/2b—3a.

f. Account of founding of Lo-an County in *SHY, fang-yü* 6, p. 27.

g. Account of founding of Lo-an County in record for construction of Fu-ch'ing Temple in Tseng Feng, 19/10a—13a.

h. Eight officeholders (not prefectural graduates) listed as men of Ya-pei in *TCLA* 7/4b—5b and *KHLA* 5/16b—18b.

i. Note on Ku-mei Academy in *KHFC* 33b/33a.

j. Record for construction of Shan-yüeh Hall in Tseng Feng, 19/20a—12a; cf. TCLA 1/27b—28a.

k. Biography of Chan Ch'ung-p'u in *KHLA* 6/6a—b.

l. Biographies of Chan Yüan-chi in *TCLA* 8/17b, *KHLA* 6/20b, and *KHFC* 59/11a.

m. Note on Chi-fang Garden in *TCLA* 2/47a.

n. List of temple heads in record for construction of Chao-hsien Temple in *WWC* 27/33a.

o. List of rice hoarders in Lo-an County in Huang Chen, 78/16b—19b.

N.B. m., n., and o. concern men whose membership in this family is likely but cannot be proven.

2. Chang[a] of I-huang County

a. Thirteen prefectural graduates, four of them *chin-shih*, listed as men of I-nan (the southern part of the county seat) between 1099 and 1260 in *TCIH* 25/4a–8b and 12bff.; *KHIH* 5/6bff.

b. Listing for 1256 *chin-shih* Chang Sheng-tzu in *Pao-yu ssu-nien teng-k'o lu* 41b.

3. Chang[a] of Lo-an County

a. Twenty-seven prefectural graduates, five of them *chin-shih*, listed as men of Nan-ts'un between 1150 and 1270 in *TCLA* 7/17aff. and *KHLA* 5/5bff.

b. Funerary inscription for Chang Yüan-ting in *WWC* 79/2a–3b.

c. Biographies of Chang Kuei-te in *TCLA* 8/5b and *KHLA* 6/17b.

d. Chang Mu mentioned as son-in-law in funerary inscription of Ch'en P'eng-fei in Ch'en Yüan-chin, 6/6b–9a.

e. List of rice hoarders in Lo-an County in Huang Chen, 78/16b–19b.

N.B. e. concerns men whose membership in this family cannot be proven.

4. Ch'en of Ch'ung-jen County

a. Funerary inscription of Ch'en K'ai and wife in Ch'en Yüan-chin, 6/4a–6b.

b. *Chin-shih* listing for Ch'en Chen-yen in *Pao-yu ssu-nien teng-k'o lu* 33a.

c. Funerary inscription of wife of Ch'en Yü-sun in Yü Chi, 20/1b–3a.

d. Examination listings and biography for Ch'en Yüan-chin in *TCCJ* 7b/3b, 7c/8b, and 8b/5a; *KHCJ* 1/52b and 53.

e. Examination listings for Ch'en Meng-chien in *TCCJ* 7c/8b and *KHCJ* 1/5ab.

f. Examination listings for Ch'en Shuo in *TCCJ* 7c/9b and *KHCJ* 1/54b.

g. Examination listings for Ch'en Chen-yen in *TCCJ* 7b/5b and 7c/10b–11a; *KHCJ* 1/57b–58a.

h. Record for reconstruction of Huang-chou Bridge in Huang Chen, 87/87/15b–16a (also in *TCCJ* 1f/3a).

i. Note on Yü-shu Academy in *TCCJ* 1g/2b.

j. Record for reconstruction of Ta-hua-ts'ang (Buddhist) Temple in *KHCJ* 3/8a–9a.

k. Note on Wen-lin Academy in *TCCJ* 1g/2b.

l. Funerary inscription of Ch'en Jung-tsu in *WWC* 75/9b–10b.

N.B. j., k., and l. concern men whose membership in this family cannot be proven.

5. Ch'en of Lin-ch'uan County: family of Ch'en I-chien

a. Biography of Ch'en I-chien in *KHFC* 47/29a.

b. Biographies of Ch'en Yüan-kuei in ibid., 61/4a–b; *SS* 450/1a–b; Wan Ssu-t'ung, 4/16b.

c. Listing for 1256 *chin-shih* degree of Ch'en Yüan-fa in *Pao-yu ssu-nien teng-k'o lu* 90b.

d. Examination listings for Ch'en I-chien, Ch'en Ch'eng-fu, Ch'en Yüan-kuei, Ch'en Yüan-chih, and Ch'en Yüan-fa in *TCLC* 36/6b, 7b, and 8a.

6. Ch'en of Lin-ch'uan County: family of Ch'en Ju

a. Listing for 1148 *chin-shih* degree of Ch'en Ju in *Shao-hsing shih-pa-nien t'ung-nien hsiao-lu* 12a.

b. Biographies of Ch'en Ju in *KHFC* 47/15b—16a and *TCTH* 13a/18b—19a.

c. Examination listings for Ch'en Ju in *TCLC* 36/4b and *TCTH* 11/5a.

d. Funerary inscription of Ch'en Yü in *WWC* 87/9b—11b.

7. Ch'en of Lo-an County: Tung-ch'uan

a. Two prefectural graduates listed as men of Tung-ch'uan in 1252 and 1270 in *TCLA* 7/23a and 25a; *KHLA* 5/12a and 15a.

b. Record for construction of West Garden in *TCLA* 2/47b.

c. Note on Tao-shan Academy in ibid., 4/68b.

d. Note on Tao-shan Bridge in ibid., 1/24b.

e. Note on West Tower in ibid., 1/29a.

f. Funerary inscription of Ch'en Shih-kuei in *WWC* 82/1a—3a.

g. Funerary inscription of Ch'en Shih-kuei in Ho Chung, 4/9a—10b.

h. Preface to genealogy of Tung-ch'uan Ch'en lineage in *WWC* 32/11a—b.

8. Ch'en of Lo-an County: Ku-t'ang

a. Eight prefectural graduates, including two *chin-shih*, listed as men of Ku-t'ang between 1174 and 1268 in *TCLA* 7/18aff. and *KHLA* 5/5a and 6bff.

b. Eight officeholders (not prefectural graduates) listed as Ku-t'ang men in *KHLA* 5/5a.

9. Cheng of Lo-an County

a. Four prefectural graduates listed as men of the county seat's southern quarter (or as men of Hsiao-pei who had moved to the southern quarter) in 1249, 1252, 1255 and 1270 in *TCLA* 7/22bff. and *KHLA* 5/12aff.

b. Biographies of Cheng Sung in *TCLA* 8/18a and *KHLA* 6/5b.

c. Biography of Cheng Sung in Wan Ssu-t'ung, 16/17a.

d. Funerary inscription of Cheng Sung in *WWC* 74/3a—65a.

e. Mention of Cheng Sung in record of conduct for Wu Ch'eng in Yü Chi, 44/2b—17a and *WWC*, end matter.

f. Postface to Huang Kao-yüan's colophon to funerary inscription of Cheng Sung's mother in Ho Hsi-chih, 5b/7b.

10. Chou of Chin-ch'i County

a. Funerary inscription of Chou Kuei-fang in Ch'eng Chü-fu, 20/14b—16a.

b. Funerary inscription of Chou Heng in Wang Chih, 11/131—133.

c. Biographies of Chou Kun in *TCCC* 23a/1a; *KHCC* 5/2a—b; *KHFC* 47/10b.

d. Biographies of Chou Heng in *TCCC* 25/1a; *KHCC* 5/4a—b; *KHFC* 69a/2b—3a.

e. Biographies of Chou Fu-hsien in *TCCC* 20/4b; *KHCC* 5/17b; *KHFC* 59/11a.

f. Record for construction of Yung-hsing (Buddhist) Temple in *TCCC* 33d/8b—10a.

g. Examination listings for Chou Ch'en, Chou Kun, Chou Mai, and Chou Kuo-hua in *TCCC* 17a/1a, 2a, 2b; *KHCC* 4/1b, 2b, 3b; *KHFC* 42/4b, 9b, 16a.

h. Biographies of Chou Ch'ing-sou in *KHFC* 57/9b; *SYHA* 77/10a; *SYHAPI* 77/15b.

N.B. h. concerns man whose membership in this family cannot be proven.

11. Chou of Lo-an County

a. Anecdote about Chou Hsiao-jo (mentioning his father Lung-chang and grandfather Chao and identifying all as men of Huai-jen) in Hung Mai, 2/6a—b.
b. Chou Hsiao-jo listed as prefectural graduate in 1189 in *TCLA* 7/18b and *KHLA* 5/7b.
c. Chou Chao listed as prefectural graduate in 1140 from Ch'ung-jen County (before creation of Lo-an County) in *TCCJ* 7c/4b and *KHCJ* 1/48a.
d. Chou Lung-chang listed as 1174 prefectural graduate in *TCLA* 7/18a and *KHLA* 5/6b.
e. Discussion of Chou family of Huai-jen as hoarders of rice in 1271 in Huang Chen, 78/16b—19b, 24a—b, 25b—27a, and 27a—28a.
f. Funerary inscription of Chou Ch'i-wu in *WWC* 72/14a—15a.

N.B. f. concerns man whose membership in this family cannot be proven.

12. Chu of Chin-ch'i County

a. Funerary inscription of woman surnamed Chu in Hsieh K'o, 10/3a—4b.
b. Funerary inscription of woman surnamed Chu in ibid., 10/4b—5b.
c. Funerary inscription of Chu Te-yu in Hsieh I, 8/18a—20a.
d. Listing for 1256 *chin-shih* degree of Chu Yu-chi in *Pao-yu ssu-nien teng-k'o lu* 96b.
e. Record for construction of Hsiao-yin Garden in Hsieh I, 7/12a—13b.
f. Funerary inscriptions of wife of Chu Shih-heng in ibid., 9/15b-17a and 10/3b—5a.
g. Biographies of Chu Fu in *KHFC* 57/8a—b; *SYHA* 77/7a.
h. Biography of Chu T'ai-ch'ing in ibid., 77/7b.
i. Record for reconstruction of Hsiao-yin Garden in *WWC* 54/8b—10b.
j. Funerary inscription of Chu Ssu-jung in Sung Lien, 49/7aff.
k. Biography of Chu Hsia in *KHCC* 5/23a—b.
l. Examination listings for Chu Hsien-ming, Chu Ch'i, Chu Yüan-ch'ing, Chu Ying-lung, and Chu Yu-chi in *TCCC* 17a/1b, 2b, and 3a; *KHCC* 4/1b, 2a, and 3b.
m. Biography of Chu K'o-chia in *KHFC* 57/9a.

N.B. m. concerns man whose membership in this family cannot be proven.

13. Chu of Lo-an County

a. Six prefectural graduates, including one *chin-shih*, listed as men of Chu-yüan between 1186 and 1265 in *TCLA* 7/12a and 18bff; *KHLA* 5/5a and 7bff.
b. Funerary inscription of Chu Kuei-fa in *WWC* 75/8a—9b.
c. Postface to poem granted by emperor to Chu Hsi-i in ibid., 57/7a—b.
d. Note on K'ua-ao Bridge in TCLA 1/25b.
e. Record for construction of Fu-ch'ing (Buddhist) Temple in Tseng Feng, 19/10a—13a.

14. Chu of Nan-feng County

a. Anecdote about Chu Shih in Hung Mai (*TSCC* edition), 20/154.
b. 'Record of the Hidden Virtue of the Chu Family' in *KHNF* 13/11a–12a.
c. Record for the founding of the Chi-ch'uan Estate and accompanying notes on construction of Wen-ming Bridge in *MKNF* 2/18a–19a.
d. Note on Chu Shih in *SYHAPI* 4/139.
e. Funerary inscription of Chu Shih's mother, surnamed Tseng, in Tseng Kung, 46/8b–9a.
f. Biographies of Chu Ching in *SS* 322/7b–8a; *SYHAPI* 4/155b.
g. Biography of Chu Hsiang in *MKNF* 19/5b–6a.
h. Biography of Chu Hsiu in ibid., 19/5a–b.
i. Biography of Chu Yen in ibid., 19/4b–5a.
j. Preface to genealogy of Chu lineage in Liu Hsün, 7/21b–22b.
k. Examination listings for Chu Ching, Chu Yen, Chu Hsiu, and Chu Huai in *KHNF* 5/2b–3a and 7a.

15. Ch'üeh of Lo-an County

a. Two prefectural graduates listed as men of Hsia-yüan in 1246 and 1273 in *TCLA* 7/22b and 25b; *KHLA* 5/11 and 15b.
b. Seven officeholders (not prefectural graduates) listed as Hsia-yüan men in *TCLA* 7/4b–5b and *KHLA* 5/16a–18b.

16. Fang of Ch'ung-jen County

a. Seven prefectural graduates listed as men of Chai-pien between 1206 and 1261 in *TCCJ* 7c/8bff. and *KHCJ* 1/52bff.
b. Woman surnamed Fang identified as mother of Ch'en Chen-yen in *Pao-yu ssu-nien teng-k'o lu* 33a.
c. Woman surnamed Fang named as mother of Yüan Hung-tao in *WWC* 86/6a–7b.
d. Woman surnamed Fang named as wife of Yü Yü in ibid., 70/13b–14b.
e. Fang Pi-chung named as husband of daughter of Wu Ch'ih in Ch'en Yüan-chin, 6/18b–20b.

N.B. b., c., d., and e. concern three women and one man whose membership in this family cannot be proven.

17. Ho of Ch'ung-jen County

a. Biographies of Ho I in *TCCJ* 8/a/1a; *KHCJ* 4/23b–24b; *KHFC* 47/23a–24a; *SS* 401/3b–4b.
b. Examination listings for Ho I in *TCCJ* 7b/2b and 7c/5a; *KHCJ* 1/48b.
c. Hung Mai's record for founding of estate in *TCCJ* 7/6a–8a.
d. Note on P'u-an (Buddhist) Temple in ibid.
e. Note on Moon Lake in ibid.
f. Colophon to poems by nephew of Ho I in *WWC* 57/10b–11a.
g. Examination listings for Ho Ch'ih in *TCCJ* 7b/3a and 7c/8a; *KHCJ* 1/51b.
h. Biography of Ho Chin in *TCCJ* 8b/9a.
i. Examination listings for Ho Chin in *TCCJ* 7b/6b and 7c/11b; *KHCJ* 1/59a–b.

j.   Examination listings for Ho Kuei-fa in *TCCJ* 7b/6a and 7c/11b; *KHCJ* 1/59a.
k.   Note on establishment of commemorative markers for Ho Chin and Ho Kuei-fa in *CCFC* 4/23a.
l.   Ho I's granddaughter named as mother of Li Chün in *WWC* 75/10b– 11b.
m.   Ho I's great-granddaughter named as wife of Jao Ying-tzu in Liu K'o-chuang, 63/6b.
n.   Ho I's grandniece named as wife of Yüan Li-li in WWC 76/1a–2b.

18. Ho of Lo-an County

a.   Twenty prefectural graduates, eight of them *chin-shih*, listed as men of Hsi-fang between 1150 and 1274 in *TCLA* 7/10a–12b and 17aff.; *KHLA* 5/2bff.
b.   Listing for Ho Jui as prefectural graduate from Ch'ung-jen County in 1119 (before the creation of Lo-an County) in *TCCJ* 7c/4a and *KHCJ* 1/47a. (See also *TCCJ* 7b/2b and 7c/5a.)
c.   Listing for Ho Ssu as prefectural graduate from Ch'ung-jen County in 1121 (before the creation of Lo-an County) in *TCCJ* 7c/4a and *KHCJ* 1/47a.
d.   Funerary inscriptions of Ho Hung-chung in Ch'eng Chü-fu, 16/16–17a and Ho Hsi-chih, 20b–21b.
e.   Funerary inscription of Ho Yao in *WWC* 74/10b–13b.
f.   Funerary inscription of Ho Lin in Ho Hsi-chih, 17b–20a.
g.   Funerary inscription of Ho T'ien-sheng in Ch'eng Chü-fu, 16/13b–14b.
h.   Funerary inscription of Ho Chung in Ho Chung, end matter 19a–21a.
i.   Biographies of Ho Shih in *TCLA* 8/22a; *KHLA* 6/12a–b; Wan Ssu-t'ung, 10/13a.
j.   Listing for 1256 *chin-shih* degree of Ho Shih in 14b.
k.   Preface to collected poems of Ho Yu-wen in *WWC* 15/13a–b.
l.   Mention of Ho T'ien-sheng and Ho Chung in letter from Ho Hsi-chih to Ch'eng Chü-fu in Ho Hsi-chih, 27b.
m.   Biographies of Ho Hsi-chih in *TCLA* 8/45a and *KHLA* 6/26b.
n.   Biographies of Ho Ku in *TCLA* 8/5a and *KHLA* 6/5b.

19. Hou of I-huang County

a.   Twelve prefectural graduates, three of them *chin-shih*, six of whom are listed as men of Hou-fang, between 1046 and 1261 in *TCIH* 25/2b–7b and 11aff.; *KHIH* 5/4bff.
b.   Note on 1054 construction and 1254 reconstruction of Mi-lo (Buddhist) Temple in *TCIH* 13/6b.
c.   Record for construction of Lung-chi Fort in Pao Hui, *Pi-chou kao-lüeh* 4/9b–11b.
d.   Biographies of Hou Shu-hsien in *TCIH* 29/2a–4a and *KHIH* 6/4a.

20. Hsieh of Ch'ung-jen County

a.   Preface to collection of writings of Hsieh family in *WWC* 24/5b–7b.
b.   Biographies of Hsieh Kung-tan in *TCCJ* 8b/5b–6a and *KHCJ* 4/40a– 41a.

c. Examination listings for Hsieh Ta-jen in *TCCJ* 7c/5a and *KHCJ* 1/48b.

d. Examination listings for Hsieh Kung-tan in *TCCJ* 7b/4a and 7c/9a; *KHCJ* 1/53a—b.

e. Examination listings for Hsieh Hung in *TCCJ* 7b/4b and 7c/8b; *KHCJ* 1/52a, 55a.

f. Examination listings for Hsieh Lin in *TCCJ* 7b/4a and 7c/9a—b; *KHCJ* 1/53b—54b.

g. Examination listings for Hsieh Tsung-tou in *TCCJ* 7c/11b and *KHCJ* 1/60a.

h. Farewell composition for Hsieh Yu-yüan in *WWC* 28/20b—21b.

i. Colophon to writings of Hsieh Kung-tan in *WWC* 55/17b—18a.

21. Hsieh of Lin-ch'uan County

a. Funerary inscription of Hsieh Yüan in Chu Hsi, 91/27b—29a.

b. Biography of Hsieh I in *KHFC* 59/2a—b.

c. Biography of Hsieh K'o in ibid., 59/2b—3a.

d. Discussion of Hsieh I and Hsieh K'o in *Chiang-hsi shih-she tsung-p'ai t'u-lu* 6b.

e. Discussion of Hsieh I and Hsieh K'o in Liu K'o-chuang, 95/10b.

f. Mention of Hsieh I in Lü Pen-chung, 2a.

g. Funerary inscription of Hsieh K'o's father-in-law Tung Ko in Hsieh K'o, 10/1a—2a.

h. Funerary inscription of Hsieh I's father-in-law Hsü Tzu-an in Hsieh I, 8/15b—16b.

i. Anecdote about Hsieh family in Hung Mai, *ting* 18/3a—b.

j. Note on Hsieh Min-hsing in *SYHAPI* 23/15a.

k. Mention of Hsieh Mai in funerary inscription of Chi Fu in Hsieh I, 10/5a—12a.

l. Examination listings for Hsieh Yüan, Hsieh Shu, and Hsieh Tzu-hsin in *TCLC* 36/4b, 6a, 6b.

22. Hsiung of Ch'ung-jen County

a. Preface to medical work in *WWC* 15/12b—13a.

b. Record for construction of Pai Hall in ibid., 42/6b—8b (also in *KHCJ* 4/86b—87b).

c. Examination listings for Hsiung Chih-ch'ang in *TCCJ* 7b/1b and 7c/2a; *KHCJ* 1/44b.

d. Anecdote about Hsiung P'u in Hung Mai, *chih-ching* 9/6a—b.

e. Examination listing for Hsiung P'u in *TCCJ* 7b/2a and *KHCJ* 1/46a.

f. Examination listings for Hsiung Chiang in *TCCJ* 7b/2a and 7c/3b; *KHCJ* 1/46b.

g. Examination listings for Hsiung Kuei in *TCCJ* 7b/3a and 7c/6a; *KHCJ* 1/49a—b.

h. Examination listings for Hsiung Chung-hsiung in *TCCJ* 7b/3b and 7c/6b; *KHCJ* 1/50a and 52a.

i. Examination listings for Hsiung Yu-tsung in *TCCJ* 7b/4a and *KHCJ* 1/53b.

j. Examination listings for Hsiung Yüan-lung in *TCCJ* 7b/5a and 7c/10a; *KHCJ* 1/55b—56a.

k. Examination listings for Hsiung Yu-hsüeh in *TCCJ* 7b/6b and 7c/11a; *KHCJ* 1/59b—60a.

23. Hsü[a] of I-huang County

a. Thirteen prefectural graduates, six of them *chin-shih*, listed between 985 and 1153 in *TCIH* 25/2a–b and 9b–21a; *KHIH* 5/1b–26b.
b. Seven of above identified through kinship notations as members of one family in *TCIH* loc. cit., and 36/1a–b; *KHIH* loc. cit., and 5/36b–37a.
c. Biography of Hsü Shih-lung in *KHIH* 5/36a–b; *KHFC* 66/2.
d. Account of founding of I-huang in *TCIH* 12/1b.
e. Biographies of Hsü Tso-lin in *TCIH* 36/1a–b and *KHIH* 5/36b–37a.
f. Preface to poems of Hsü Tso-lin in Sun Ti, *Nan-lan ling Sun shang-shu ta-ch'üan chi* 33/10b–11a.
g. Biographies of Hsü Cheng-luan in *TCIH* 29/1b and *KHIH* 6/15a.

24. Hsü[b] of I-huang County: Cha-p'u

a. Eight prefectural graduates, one of them a *chin-shih*, listed as men of Cha-p'u between 1137 and 1258 in *TCIH* 25/7a and 17bff.; *KHIH* 5/16aff.
b. Hsü Shih-wei identified as son-in-law of Tsou T'ao in the latter's funerary inscription in Sun Ti, 63/11b–14a (also in *TCIH* 45g/90a–92a).

25. Hsü[b] of I-huang County: Hsia-shih

a. Twenty-two prefectural graduates, four of them *chin-shih*, listed as men of Hsia-shih between 1123 and 1249 in *TCIH* 25/5b–7b and 16aff.; KHIH 5/10bff.
b. Record for reconstruction of T'ai-ho (Buddhist) Temple in *TCIH* 45b/39a–41a.
c. Note on construction of Hsin-hsing (Buddhist) Temple in *TCIH* 13/9b.
d. Funerary inscription of Hsü Wen-chien in *WWC* 72/12b–14b.

N.B. d. concerns man whose membership in this family cannot be proven.

26. Hsü[c] of I-huang County

a. Twenty-six prefectural graduates, five of them *chin-shih*, listed between 1053 and 1273 in *TCIH* 25/3a–8b and 10aff.; *KHIH* 5/3aff.
b. Nine of above identified through kinship notations as members of one family in *TCIH* 25/19a–27a and 29/8b; *KHIH* 5/13a–22a and 6/17b.
c. Anecdote about Hsü Shih-ying in Hung Mai (*TSCC* edition), 12/93.
d. Biographies of Hsü Yüan-lao in *TCIH* 29/8b and *KHIH* 6/17b.
e. Funerary inscription of Hsü Fu in Li Kou, 30/8b–9b.
f. Funerary inscription of woman surnamed Hsü in *WWC* 76/4b–6n.

N.B. e. and f. concern a man and woman whose membership in this family cannot be proven.

27. Hsü[c] of Lin-ch'uan County

a. Biographies of Hsü Tzu-shih in *KHFC* 47/4b–5a; *SYHA* 77/15b.
b. Note on Hsü Yüan-te in ibid.
c. Record for construction of Chao-chou (Taoist) Temple in *TCLC* 19/34a–35b.

   d. Examination listings for Hsü Tzu-shih, Hsü Yüan-te, Hsü Piao in *TCLC* 36/6a, 7a, 8a.

   e. Examination listings for Hsü Te-ch'üan and Hsü Hao in *TCLC* 36/5b.

N.B. e. concerns men whose membership in this family cannot be proven.

28. Huang of Lo-an County: Pa-t'ang

   a. Fourteen prefectural graduates, three of them *chin-shih*, listed as men of Pa-t'ang between 1204 and 1273 in *TCLA* 7/11b and 19bff.; *KHLA* 5/4b 8bff.

   b. Preface to genealogy of Huang lineage of Pa-t'ang in *WWC* 32/17a—18b.

   c. Biographies of Huang Ch'ung-i in *TCLA* 8/12b and *KHLA* 6/6a.

29. Huang of Lo-an County: T'ung-fu

   a. Nine prefectural graduates listed as men of T'ung-fu between 1249 and 1273 in *TCLA* 22bff. and *KHLA* 5/12aff.

   b. Two entrants into Imperial Academy listed as T'ung-fu men in *TCLA* 7/6a and *KHLA* 5/19a.

   c. Funerary inscription of woman of Huang surname from T'ung-kang in *WWC* 72/8b—9b.

   d. Officeholder Huang Po-ch'ing (not a prefectural graduate) listed as T'ung-kang man in *TCLA* 7/4b and *KHLA* 5/16b.

   e. Postface to Huang Kao-yüan's colophon to funerary inscription of woman surnamed Huang from T'ung-kang in Ho Hsi-chih, 5b—7b.

   f. Listing for T'ung-kang Pagoda, locating it at T'ung-fu, in *TCLA* 1/27b.

30. Huang of Nan-feng County

   a. Funerary inscription of Huang Wen-sheng in Lu Chiu-yüan, 24/4a—6a.

   b. Listing for 1148 *chin-shih* degree of Huang Wen-ch'ang in *Shao-hsing shih-pa nien t'ung-nien hsiao-lu* 32b.

   c. Biography of Huang Wen-ch'ang in *MKNF* 19/7b—8a.

   d. Note on Huang Fei in *SYHA* 77/16b.

   e. Note on Huang Nan in ibid.

   f. Biographies of Huang Shu in *MKNF* 22/3a—b; Lu Hsin-yüan, 31/8a.

   g. Examination listings for Huang Fu, Huang Yang, Huang Yüeh, Huang Wen-ch'ang, and Huang Shu in *KHNF* 5/3a—4b, 5b.

31. Jao of Ch'ung-jen County

   a. Funerary inscription of Jao Ying-tzu in Liu K'o-chuang, 63/6b.

   b. Biography of Jao Ying-lung in *TCCJ* 8/b7a; *KHFC* 49/31b.

   c. Biographies of Jao Yen-nien in *TCCJ* 8d/3b; *KHCJ* 4/26b—27a; *KHFC* 69a/3b; *SYHA* 77/11a; *SYHAPI* 77/16a.

   d. Mention of Jao Yen-nien in Huang Chen, 97/10b—12b.

   e. Anecdote about Jao Tz'u-wei in Hung Mai, *san-jen* 1/4b—5a.

   f. Examination listings for Jao Ying-tzu, Jao Ying-lung, Jao Tzu-yung, Jao Cho, Jao O, Jao Meng-lü, Jao Tsung-ying, and Jao Chih-sun in *TCCJ* 7b/4a—7a and 7c/9a—11a; *KHCJ* 1/53a—60b.

   g. Accounts of Jao Li role in community granary in Huang Chen, 75/9b—10b and 78/22b; *SS* 46/9b.

32. Jao of Lin-ch'uan County: family of Jao Kung

a. Examination listings (with extensive kinship information) for Jao Kung, Jao Ch'i, Jao Shih-ch'uan, Jao Meng, Jao Wen-tu, Jao Po-ta, Jao Hao-yü, and Jao Hui-ch'ing in *TCLC* 36/2a, 3a, 3b, and 4a.
b. Funerary inscription of Jao Huai-ying in Lü Nan-kung, 19/5b—8a.
c. Biographies of Jao Sung in *KHFC* 69a/2a; Li O, 29/15a.
d. Biography of Jao Tsu-yao in *KHFC* 47/43b—44a.
e. Biographies of Jao Tzu-i in ibid., 69a/1b—2a; Lu Hsin—yüan, 36/13b—14a; *SYHA* 2/29a.
f. Anecdote about Jao family in Hung Mai (*TSCC* edition), 12/92—93.

N.B. b., c., d., e., and f. concern men whose membership in this family cannot be proven.

33. Jao of Lin-ch'uan County: family of Jao Shih-heng

a. Biography of Jao Shih-heng in *KHFC* 66/1a; *TCLC* 46/1b.
b. Examination listings (with kinship information) for Jao Shih-heng, Jao Meng-lung, Jao Yüan, Jao Kuei-ling, and Jao Keng-lung in *TCLC* 36/5b, 7b, 8a.
c. Examination listings for Jao Shih-heng and Jao Meng-lung in *TCIH* 25/6a and 23a; *KHIH* 5/15b, 17b, and 18a.

N.B. All the above except Jao Meng-lung are listed by the Lin-ch'uan County gazetteer as men of Lin-ch'uan; Jao Shih-heng and Jao Meng-lung are listed by the I-huang County gazetteers as I-huang men. As the Lin-ch'uan gazetteer remarks, under Shih-heng's listing, that he was 'registered in I-huang,' the claim of the I-huang gazetteers seems to have some basis in fact. Whether dual residence or a change of registration is involved here cannot be determined.

34. Ko of Chin-ch'i County

a. Funerary inscription of Ko Keng in Lu Chiu-yüan, 28/7a—11a.
b. Funerary inscription of woman surnamed Ko in *WWC* 79/8b—10a.
c. Funerary inscription of Ko Chi-tsu in ibid., 80/12a—13a.
d. Mention of Ko Tsung-yün in biography of Teng P'ang in *TCCC* 22a/1a—5a.
e. Biography of Ko Yüan-che in *KHCC* 5/22a—22b.
f. Examination listings for Ko Feng-shih in *TCCC* 17a/2a and *KHCC* 4/3a.
g. Biography of Ko Keng in *TCCC* 22a/5b—6a.

35. Kung of Lin-ch'uan County

a. Funerary inscription of Kung Meng-k'uei in Ch'eng Chü-fu, 22/8a—9b.
b. Biographies of Kung Meng-k'uei in *KHFC* 49/33a; *SYHAPI* 58/48a.
c. Examination listings for Kung Huan and Kung Meng-k'uei in *TCLC* 36/6b and 8b,
d. Examination listings for Mo Jo and Mo Lei-hsien in *TCLC* 36/9a.

36. Li of Ch'ung-jen County

a. Funerary inscription of Li Yen-hua in Wei Liao-weng, 79/4a—6a.
b. Funerary inscription of Li Hu in ibid., 79/6a—8a.

c. Colophon to funerary inscriptions of Li Yen-hua and Li Hu in *WWC* 29/ *WWC* 29/12a—b.
d. Biographies of Li Liu in *KHCJ* ch. 4 and *KHFC* 47/48a—b.
e. Colophon to poems of Li Yen-hua and relatives in *WWC* 57/8a—b.
f. Funerary inscription of Li Ch'ou in *WWC* 75/15b—17a.
g. Funerary inscription of Li Chün in ibid., 75/10b—11b.
h. Record for construction of Mei-feng Shrine in ibid., 46/1a—3a.
i. Record for construction of Ch'eng-kang Library in ibid., 41/8b—9b.
j. Note on Nan-fu Pavilion in *TCCJ* 1g/1b and *KHCJ* ch. 3.
k. Record for Hsiang Spring in *WWC* 45/4b—5b.
l. Record for construction of Wen-ch'ang Bridge in *TCLC* 7/3a—5a.
m. Examination listings for Li Hao and Li Liu in *TCCJ* 7c/3b, 8b, and 7b/ 3b; *KHCJ* 1/46b and 52a—b.

37. Li of Lin-ch'uan County

a. Record of conduct and biographies of Li Hao in *YLTT* 10422/2b—9a.
b. Anecdotes about Li Hao in Hung Mai, *ping* 14/4a—5a.
c. Biography of Li Su in *KHFC* 57/4a; *SYHA* 77/15b.
d. Note on Li Fu in *SYHA* 77/15b.
e. Colophon to funerary inscription of Li Hao in Huang Chen, 91/38b— 29b.
f. Examination listings for Li Hao, Li Su, and Li Fu in *TCLC* 36/4b, 5b, and 6a.

38. Li of Lo-an County

a. Eight prefectural graduates listed as men of Ts'an-yüan between 1150 and 1249 in *TCLA* 7/17aff. and *KHLA* 5/5bff.
b. List of temple heads in record for reconstruction of Chao-hsien (Taoist) Temple in *WWC* 27/33a.
c. Taoist priest Li Kung-ch'en mentioned in record for construction of Yü-shan (Taoist) Temple in ibid., 47/4a—6a.

N.B. b., and c. concern men whose membership in this family cannot be proven.

39. Liu of Chin-ch'i County

a. Preface to genealogy of Liu lineage in Wei Su, 1/12b—13a.
b. Preface to genealogy of Liu lineage in Sung Lien, 12/449—450.
c. Biographies of Liu Yao-fu in *TCCC* 20/5a; *KHFC* 47/38a; *SYHA* 77/ 19a; *SYHAPI* 77/29a.
d. Preface to collected works of Liu Yao-fu in *WWC* 22/8a—b.
e. Anecdote about Liu Yao-fu in Hung Mai, *chih-i* 10/3a—4a.
f. Funerary inscription of wife of Liu T'ien-ch'i in *WWC* 86/17b—18b.
g. Funerary inscription of wife of Liu Kuo-chen in ibid., 82/2b—3b.
h. Biography of Liu Chieh in *KHCC* ch. 5.
i. Examination listings for Liu Yao-fu in *TCCC* 17a/2b and *KHFC* 42/ 12a.
j. Examination listings for Liu Chang in *TCCC* 17b/6b and *KHCC* 4/40a.

40. Liu of Nan-feng County

a. Funerary inscription of Liu Chao in Liu Hsün, 8/2b—4a.
b. Funerary inscription of Liu Hsi-t'i in ibid,, 8/1a—2b.
c. Funerary inscription of Liu Hsün in *WWC* 71/10a—12a.
d. Funerary inscription of Liu Hsün in Liu Hsün, 8/11a—12b.
e. Mention of residence of Liu Hsün in preface to genealogy of Tseng lineage in ibid., 7/37a—38a.
f. Funerary inscription of Liu Shan in ibid., 8/6a—9a.
g. Appointment decrees for Liu Chia and Liu K'uang preserved, with added colophons, by their descendant Liu Hsün in ibid., 7/13b—19a.
h. Biography of Liu Lin-shui in Wan Ssu-t'ung, 16/20a.
i. Biography of Liu Shan in *MKNF* 26/6b—7a.
j. Biography of Liu Yüan-tsai in ibid., 30/1b—2a.
k. Record for construction of Chiang Tower in ibid., 3/27b—29a.
l. Preface to genealogy of Liu lineage in Liu Hsün, *Yin-chü t'ung-i* 16/12a—14a.
m. Examination listings for Liu Chia, Liu Shih, Liu Yen, Liu K'uang, Liu Yin, and Liu To in *KHNF* 5/2a—b, 4b.

41. Lo of Ch'ung-jen County

a. Record of conduct of Lo Tien in Yüan Hsieh, 12/1a—35a.
b. Anecdote about Lo Tien in Hung Mai, *chih-i* 2/2b—3a.
c. Biography of Lo Yü in *KHFC* 47/44a.
d. Record of construction of Pai-yün Study in Liu Tsai, 23/19b—20a.
e. Biography of Lo Chien in *KHFC* 59/9a.
f. Biography of Lo Hsiang-tsu in *TCCJ* ch. 8.
g. Biography of Lo Hsien-k'o in ibid.
h. Biography of Lo Hsün in *KHFC* 57/11a—b.
i. Funerary inscription of woman surnamed Wang I in Ch'en Tsao, 35/13a—16a.
j. Record for construction of Ta-huang-ts'ang (Buddhist) Temple in *KHCJ* 3/8a—9a.
k. Note on Lung-yen (Buddhist) Temple in *KHCJ* ch. 3.
l. Notes on construction of P'u-an (Buddhist) Temple in *TCCJ* 2d/6b and *KHCJ* 3/11a.
m. Notes on Stone Bridge in *TCCJ* 1f/22b and *KHCJ* ch. 3.
n. Record for construction of Shang-fang (Taoist) Temple in *WWC* 47/14b—16a.
o. Anecdote about Lo Tien's mother in Hung Mai, *chih-ting* 4/5a.
p. Examination listings for Lo Pang-yen, Lo Yen, Lo Tien, Lo Sung-nien, Lo Hsün, Lo Mo, and Lo Chi-chung in *TCCJ* 7b/3a and 7c/8aff.; *KHCJ* 1/48bff.

42. Lu of Chin-ch'i County

a. Funerary inscription of Lu Chiu-ling in Lu Chiu-yüan, 27/1a—8a.
b. Funerary inscription of Lu Chiu-hsü in ibid., 28/3a—4a.
c. Funerary inscription of Lu Chiu-kao in ibid., 28/12a—16b.
d. Funerary inscription of Lu Ch'ih-chih in Wei Liao-weng, 73/11a—14a.

   e. Funerary inscription of Lu Huan-chih in Lu Yu, 38/8b—11b.

   f. Preface to collected works of Lu Huan-chih in ibid., 15/5b—7b.

   g. Discussion of Lu family in Lo Ta-ching, 5/9—10.

   h. Biography of Lu Chiu-shao in *KHFC* 56/1a—2a; *SS* 434/5b.

   i. Biography of Lu Chiu-ssu in *KHFC* 56/1a.

   j. Record of conduct of Lu Chiu-yüan in Lu Chiu-yüan, end matter.

   k. Biography of Lu Chung in *KHFC* 64/2a.

   l. Record for commemorative marking of residence of Lu family in *TCCC* 33d/20a—22a.

   m. Biography of Lu Yün in *KHFC* 47/33b—34a.

   n. Preface to work of Lu Yün in Chou Pi-ta, 53/1a—2b.

   o. Biography of Lu Chün in *KHFC* 47/45.

   p. Preface to funerary inscription of Lu Hung in *WWC* 47/4b—5a.

   q. Biography of Lu Hung in *KHFC* 64/2a.

   r. Note on awarding of office to Lu P'u in *SS* 46/9b.

   s. Examination listings for Lu Yün, Lu Chiu-ling, Lu Chiu-yüan, and Lu Chün in *TCCC* 17a/2a—b and *KHCC* 4/3a—b.

   t. Mention of Lu Chiu-yüan's great granddaughter in funerary inscription of Ko Chi-tsu in *WWC* 80/12a—13a.

43. Miu of Ch'ung-jen County

   a. Funerary inscription of wife of Miu Chao and Ch'en Tsao, 35/13a—16a.

   b. Funerary inscription of Miu Mu in *WWC* 72/7a—b.

   c. Preface to collected poems of Miu Mu in ibid., 15/7b—8a.

   d. Anecdote about woman surnamed Miu in Hung Mai, *chih-ting* 4/5a.

   e. Examination listings for Miu Ch'ien, Miu K'ang-chung, Miu K'uei, and Miu Jo-feng in *TCCJ* 7c/7aff. and *KHCJ* 1/50bff.

   f. Examination listings for Miu Pang-chih, Miu Ch'iu, Miu Meng-lung, Miu I-lieh, and Miu Shou-lao in *TCCJ* 7c/9aff. and *KHCJ* 1/53aff.

   g. Funerary inscription of woman surnamed Hsiung in Ch'en Tsao, 35/16b—18b.

N.B. f. and g. concern men whose membership in this family cannot be proven.

44. Sun of Lin-ch'uan County

   a. Funerary inscription of Sun Ch'e in Yü Chi, 43/1a—2b.

   b. Biography of Sun Ch'e in Wei Su, 7/23a—24b.

   c. Biography of Sun Hsün in *KHFC* 47/40a—41a.

   d. Examination listings for Sun Yu-ch'ing, Sun Hsün, Sun Meng-k'uei, and Sun Hsing-chih in *TCLC* 36/5a and 8a.

45. Tai of I-huang County

   a. Eighteen prefectural graduates, four of them *chin-shih*, listed as men of Huang-pei between 1048 and 1258 in *TCIH* 25/3aff. and *KHIH* 5/2bff.

   b. Note on founding of Ching-i Academy in *TCIH* 19/2b.

   c. Biography of Tai Ching-ch'en in ibid., 29/4a—b.

   d. Biographies of Tai Lin in *KHIH* 6/25a and *KHFC* 59/13a.

46. T'an of I-huang County

a. Seven prefectural graduates listed in 1130 and between 1243 and 1273, three of them identified as men of T'an-fang, in *TCIH* 25/17a and 29b–33b; *KHIH* 5/11a and 24b–28b.
b. Reference to T'an family in funerary inscription of Tsou Tz'u-ch'en in *WWC* 80/8b–10b.
c. Identification of place to which Tsou Tz'u-ch'en moved (according to the above, home of the T'an family) in record for construction of Hsien-yüan (Taoist) Temple in *WWC* 47/12b–14b.
d. Identification of place to which Tsou Tz'u-ch'en moved in his biographies in *TCIH* 31/5a and *KHIH* 6/10b.
e. Preface to genealogy of T'an lineage in *WWC* 32/12b–13a.
f. Funerary inscription of T'an Shih in ibid., 87/1a–2b.
g. Note on casting of bell for Pai-t'u (Buddhist) Temple in *TCIH* 7/7a.
h. Huang Chen's memorial asking rewards for sellers of relief grain in Huang Chen, 75/15a–16b.
i. Records of confiscation of fields from local strongman T'an Hu in *TCIH* 14/23a–b and *KHIH* 3/1b–2b, 18b.

N.B. h. and i. concern men whose membership in this family is probable but cannot be proven.

47. Teng of Chin-ch'i County

a. Preface to genealogy of Teng lineage in *WWC* 32/20b–21b.
b. Account of Chin-ch'i militia in Chou Pi-ta, 20/16b–17b.
c. Funerary inscription of Teng Hsi-yen in *WWC* 79/10a–11b.
d. Funerary inscription of woman surnamed Teng in ibid., 86/17b–18b.
e. Funerary inscription of Teng Ju-chen in Wei Su, *hsü-chi* 6/5a–7a.
f. Biographies of Teng P'ang in *TCCC* 22/1a–5a and *KHCC* 5/5b–7a.
g. Mention of Teng militia in *SS* 425/11a.
h. Record of painting of Yün-lin in Wei Su, 3/14b–16b.
i. Letter from Hsieh Fang-te to Teng Yüan-kuan in *TCCC* 33f/7b–9b.
j. Listing for 1256 *chin-shih* degree of Teng Fei-ying in *Pao-yu ssu-nien teng-k'o lu* 63b.
k. Examination listings for Teng Kang, Teng Fei-ying, and Teng Yüan-kuan in *TCCC* 17a/2b and 3a; *TCLC* 36/8b; *KHFC* ch. 42.

48. Teng of Lo-an County

a. Four prefectural graduates listed as men of Chao-hsi between 1159 and 1270 in *TCLA* 7/17bff. and *KHLA* 6/5aff.
b. List of rice hoarders in Lo-an County in Huang Chen, 78/16b–19b.

N.B. b. concerns men whose membership in this family cannot be proven.

49. Ts'ai of Lin-ch'uan County

a. Funerary inscription of Ts'ai Ch'eng-hsi in Su Sung, 57/9b–14a.
b. Biography of Ts'ai Chü-hou in *KHFC* 47/32b–33a.
c. Exam listing for Ts'ai Chü-hou in Yü Hsi-li, *Chen-chiang chih*.
d. Biography of Ts'ai Hsiao-kung in *TCLC* 47a/1b–2a.
e. Biography of Ts'ai Yüan-tao in *KHFC* 59/1b–2a.

f. Examination listings for Ts'ai Wei-shan, Ts'ai Tsung-yen, Ts'ai Tsung-ho, Ts'ai Yüan-chen, Ts'ai Yüan-tao, Ts'ai Ch'eng-hsi, Ts'ai Ch'ih, Ts'ai Chü-hou, Ts'ai Hsing-kuo, Ts'ai Hsing-tsu, Ts'ai Hsing-shih, Ts'ai Tse-chi, and Ts'ai Shen in *TCLC* 36/1b–2a, 3a–4a, 5a.

50. Ts'ao of I-huang County

a. Fourteen prefectural graduates, three of them *chin-shih*, listed between 1070 and 1273 in *TCIH* 25/5a–7b and 10bff.; *KHIH* 5/4aff.
b. Preface to genealogy of Ts'ao lineage in *WWC* 32/15a–16b.
c. Record for construction of charitable granary in *TCIH* 45b/28a–29a.
d. Postscript to record for construction of charitable granary in Chen Te-hsiu, 36/22a–23a.
e. Biographies of Ts'ao Hsi in *KHIH* 6/10a and *KHFC* 47/46a.
f. Record for construction of Ching-ssu Hall in Chen Te-hsiu, 25/3a–4a (also in *TCIH* 45b/42a).
g. Note on reconstruction of Lu-t'ou (Buddhist) Temple in *TCIH* 13/8a.

N.B. g. concerns man whose membership in this family cannot be proven.

51. Tseng of Chin-ch'i County

a. Funerary inscription of Tseng Chung-tzu in Ch'eng Chü-fu, 17/2b–4a.
b. Biographies of Tseng Yüan-tzu in *KHFC* 61/7b; *MKNF* 22/4a–5a; Li O, 66/21b.
c. Record for ancestral hall of Tseng lineage in Wei Su, 5/10b–11b.
d. Colophon to genealogy of Tseng lineage in Yü Chi, 40/4a–6a.
e. Memorial from Huang Chen to Tseng Yüan-tzu (then military intendant of Chiang-hsi circuit) in Huang Chen, 75/29a–30b.
f. Mention of Tseng Yü in record for reconstruction of Ch'ung-chüeh Pao-tzu Ch'an (Buddhist) Temple in Liu Hsün, 3/4a–6a.
g. Examination listings for Tseng Yü, Tseng Hung-tzu, and Tseng Yüan-tzu in *TCCC* 17a/2b and 3a; *KHCC* 4/3b.

52. Tseng of Lo-an County: Pan-ch'iao

a. Nine prefectural graduates, four of them *chin-shih*, listed as men of Pan-ch'iao between 1168 and 1264 in *TCLA* 7/10a–12a and 17bff.; *KHLA* 5/2b–5a and 6bff.
b. Preface to genealogy of Tseng lineage of Sung-chiang, Yung-feng Hsien, Chi-chou, in Tseng Feng, 17/1a–2b.
c. Different version of same preface preserved in modern genealogy of a Tseng lineage (or group of lineages) in Taiwan: *Tseng-shih tsu-p'u*, Taichung 1966, in collection of Columbia University.
d. Tseng Shih listed as 994 *chin-shih* from Sung-chiang in Yung-feng Hsien in *TCYF* 15/11a and 13a; *KHYF* 4/2a.
e. Tseng Chih listed as 1094 *chin-shih* in ibid.
f. Preface to Tseng Feng collected works in Yü Chi, 34/3a.
g. Preface to Tseng Feng collected works in Tseng Feng, front matter.
h. Preface to genealogy of Tseng lineage of Lo-shan in Lo-an County (see below) in *WWC* 32/5a–6b.
i. Biography of Tseng Feng in *TCYF* 22/8a–b.

j. Biographies of Tseng Feng in *TCLA* 8/10b; *KHLA* 6/1a–b; Lu Hsin-yüan, 28/20a–b.
k. Judgement by Huang Kan in law case of Prefect Tseng (identifiable as Tseng Feng) vs. Huang Kuo-ts'ai in Huang Kan, 32/8b–9a.
l. Funerary inscription of Tseng Yeh in *WWC* 39/15b–17a.
m. List of rice hoarders in Lo-an County in Huang Chen, 78/16b–19b.

N.B. l. and m. concern men whose membership in this family cannot be proven.

53. Tseng of Lo-an County: Lo-shan

a. Fifteen prefectural graduates, one a *chin-shih*, listed as men of Lo-shan in *TCLA* 7/11b and 19aff.; *KHLA* 5/8aff.
b. Preface to genealogy of Tseng lineage of Lo-shan in *WWC* 32/5a–6b.
c. Preface to Tseng Feng collected works in Yü Chi, 34/3a.
d. Preface to collected poems of Tseng Tou-lung in *WWC* 60/9a–b.
e. Biographies of Tseng Tou-lung in *TCLA* 8/17b and *KHLA* 6/6a.
f. Funerary inscription of Tseng I-yüan in *WWC* 84/10b–12a.
g. Funerary inscription of Tseng I-yüan's wife in ibid., 78/8a–9a.
h. Record for construction of Fu-ch'ing (Buddhist) Temple in Tseng Feng, 19/10a–13a.
i. List of temple heads of Chao-hsien (Taoist) Temple in *WWC* 27/33a.
j. List of rice-hoarders in Lo-an County in Huang Chen, loc. cit.

N.B. i. and j. concern men whose membership in this family cannot be proven.

54. Tseng of Nan-feng County

a. Colophon to genealogy of Tseng lineage in Yü Chi, 40/4a–6a.
b. Colophon to genealogy of Tseng lineage by Hsieh O in Tseng Kung (*SPPY* edition), front matter 17a–b.
c. Remarks on genealogy of Tseng lineage in Liu Hsün, *Shui-yün ts'un kao* 7/37a–38.
d. Record for construction of ancestral hall in Yü Chi, 35/2a–3a.
e. Record for construction of ancestral hall in Wei Su, 5/10b–11b.
f. Record for reconstruction of Ch'ung-chüeh Pao-tzu Ch'an (Buddhist) Temple in Liu Hsün, 3/4a–6a.
g. Account of Tseng surname in Teng Ming-shih, 17/6b–7b.
h. Letter from Ou-yang Hsiu to Tseng Kung in Ou-yang Hsiu, 47/10b–11b.
i. Mention of Nan-feng Tseng lineage in preface to genealogy of Tseng lineage of Lo-shan, Lo-an County, in *WWC* 32/5a–6b.
j. Mention of Nan-feng County Tseng lineage in preface to genealogy of Tseng lineage of Lo-shan, Lo-an County, in *WWC* 32/5a–6b.
k. Funerary inscription of Tseng Yeh in Tseng Kung, 46/1a–b.
l. Record of conduct of Tseng Chao in Yang Shih, 29/2a–20b.
m. Funerary inscription of Tseng Chih-yao in Wang An-shih, 92/1a–4b.
n. Funerary inscription of Tseng Chih-yao in Ou-yang Hsiu, 21/1a–4a. (See also the slightly different version in *KHNF* 16/51a–53b.)
o. Funerary inscription of Tseng Chüeh in Tseng Kung, 46/6b–7a.
p. Funerary inscription of Tseng Hsiang in ibid., 46/10a–b.

q.   Funerary inscription of Tseng Hsün in Wang Tsao, 27/17b.

r.   Funerary inscription of Tseng I-chan in Ch'en Shih-tao, 16/10b—11b.

s.   Funerary inscription of Tseng I-chan in Wang An-shih, 93/1a.

t.   Funerary inscription of Tseng Kung in Han Wei, 29/6b—11a.

u.   Record of conduct of Tseng Kung in Tseng Kung, *fu-lu*.

v.   Funerary inscription (*mu-chih*) of Tseng Kung in ibid.

w.   Transcription of recently excavated funerary inscription of Tseng Kung in Lo Yüan, 'Sung Tseng Kung mu-chih.'

x.   Funerary inscription of Tseng Tsai in Tseng Kung, 46/11b—12b.

y.   Funerary inscription of wife of Tseng Tung, surnamed Su, in Tseng Hsieh, 5/28b—30b.

z.   Funerary inscription of Tseng Yen in Lou Yüeh, 97/13b—22a.

aa.   Reference to descent of Nan-feng Tsengs in funerary inscription of Chin-ch'i Hsien man Tseng Yen-ch'ing in Huang Chin, 32/13a—14b.

bb.   Funerary inscription of Tseng Yu-lung in Liu Hsün, 8/4a—6a.

cc.   Funerary inscription of Tseng Yü in Wang Tsao, 28/1a—b.

dd.   Notes on Tseng Chao and Tseng Pu in *Ching-k'ou ch'i-chiu chuan* 2/4a.

ee.   Mention of place of burial of Tseng Chao in Chou Pi-ta, 165/15b—21a.

ff.   Biographies of Tseng Chi in *MKNF* 18/1b—2a; *TCLC* 43/4a—b; *SYHA* 57/11a; *SYHAPI* 57/10b.

gg.   Biographies of Tseng Chi-li in *TCLC* 43/5a—b; *KHNF* 7/19b; Lu Hsin-yüan, 36/17a.

hh.   Farewell composition for Tseng Chi-li in Chang Shih, *Chang Nan-hsüan hsien-sheng wen-chi* 3/53—54.

ii.   Colophon to collected letters of Tseng Chi-li in Chu Hsi, 83/17a.

jj.   Law case involving Tseng Chi-li's son Tseng Wei in Huang Kan, 32/13b—17a.

kk.   Biography of Tseng Chieh in *MKNF* 23/2b—3a.

ll.   Notes on Tseng Fa in *SYHA* 71/12a; *SYHAPI* 71/1a.

mm. Colophon to correspondence between Lü Pen-chung and Tseng Fa in Lü Tsu-ch'ien, *Lü Tung-lai wen-chi* 6/158—159.

nn.   Biography of Tseng Hung in *MKNF* 26/3b—4a.

oo.   Preface to poems of Tseng Hung in Yang Wan-li, 83/8b—10b.

pp.   Biography of Tseng Hung-li in *MKNF* 14/2a—b.

qq.   Reference to Tseng Hung-li (by title) in record for construction of Ch'i-shan Study in ibid., 3/8b—9b.

rr.   Biography of Tseng I-chien in ibid., 26/1a—b.

ss.   Letter from Tseng Kung to Chiang-hsi circuit intendant in Tseng Kung, 15/14a—15a.

tt.   Reference to Tseng Kung's Lin-ch'uan County residence in preface to work by Yen Shu in ibid., 13/5b—6b.

uu.   Biographies of Tseng Pu in Tu Ta-kuei, *hsia* 20/1a; *MKNF* 13/3a—4a.

vv.   Record for construction of Chün-shan Shrine in Tseng Chao, 4/4a—6a.

ww. Biography of Tseng Chih-yao in *MKNF* 23/1a.

xx.   Biographies of Tseng Shu-ch'ing in *SS* 459/10a; *MKNF* 23/2a.

yy.   Biographies of Tseng Ku in *SS* 448/1a; *MKNF* 22/1a—b; *TCLC* 44/3b.

zz.   Biographies of Tseng Tsao in *MKNF* 19/19a; *SYHAPI* 4/16ab.

aaa.   Notes on Tseng Tsun in *SYHA* 71/12b; *SYHAPI* 71/15b

bbb.   Record for construction of Tseng Tsun's study in Chang Shih, 4/82—83.

ccc. Biographies of Tseng Tui in *MKNF* 26/5a and *KHNF* 7/15a.
ddd. Note on Tseng T'ung in Yü Hsi-lu, 19/6a.
eee. Biographies of Tseng Wu in *MKNF* 22/1b–2a; *SS* 448/1b.
fff. Examination listings for thirty-three *chin-shih*, twenty-nine of them
before 1185 (compare the number given as of 1188 for the Tseng lineage
in Hsieh O's genealogy preface cited above) in *KHNF* ch. 5.

55. Tsou of I-huang County: I-nan

a. Nineteen prefectural graduates, five of them *chin-shih*, listed as men of
I-nan (the southern part of the county seat) between 1069 and 1265
in *TCIH* 25/3a–8b and 10bff.; *KHIH* 5/4aff.
b. Biographies of Tsou Fei-hsiung in *TCIH* 30/1b–3a; *KHIH* 6/8b; *YLTT*
7893/4a–b.
c. Note on statue of Buddha at Ta-lu Temple in *TCIH* 7/6a.
d. Record for sculpting of Buddha for Lung-ch'üan Temple in ibid., 45b/-
33a–34a.
e. Record for reconstruction of Dharma Hall of Lung-ch'üan Temple in
ibid.

56. Tsou of I-huang County: family of Tsou Tz'u-ch'en

a. Biographies of Tsou Chi in *TCIH* 29/4b–6a and *KHIH* 6/5b.
b. Anecdote about Tsou Chi in Hung Mai, *ping* 9/6b–7a.
c. Biography of Tsou Yung-nien in *TCIH* 29/6b–7a.
d. Listings for prefectural graduate Tsou Tang in ibid., 25/10b–13b.
e. Listings for *chin-shih* Tsou P'an in ibid., 25/7b and 29a; *KHIH* 5/23b.
f. Funerary inscription of Tsou Tz'u-ch'en in *WWC* 80/8b–10b.
g. Biographies of Tsou Tz'u-ch'en in *TCIH* 31/5a and *KHIH* 6/10b.
h. Postface to appointment certificates of Tsou Tz'u-ch'en's ancestors in
Ch'eng Chü-fu, 24/3a–b.
i. Record for construction of Hsien-yüan (Taoist) Temple in
WWC 47/12b–14b.
j. Listings for prefectural graduate Tsou Hsüeh-i in *TCIH* 25/29b–32b
and *KHIH* 5/24b–28a.
k. Listings for prefectural graduates Tsou Tz'u-ch'en and Tsou Tz'u-fu in
TCIH 25/33a and *KHIH* 5/28b.
l. Note on T'an-luan Study in *TCIH* 13/1a.
m. Note on I-weng Pavilion in ibid., 7/1a.
n. Record for construction of I-ch'üan (Buddhist) Temple in ibid., 45b/-
3b–4a.
o. Note on I-an Academy in ibid., 19/3a.

57. Tsou of I-huang County: family of Tsou Yü

a. Funerary inscription of Tsou T'ao in Sun Ti, *Nan-lan-ling Sun shang-
shu ta-ch'üan chi*, 63/14a–16b.
b. Funerary inscription of Tsou Tsung-mo in ibid., 63/11b–14a.
c. Inscription for Yün-yeh Study in ibid., 52/16b–17b.
d. Funerary inscription of Tsou Kai in ibid., 63/16b.
e. Farewell composition for Tsou Tsung-mo in ibid., 34/10a–11a.
f. Farewell composition for Tsou T'ao in ibid., 34/13a–14a.

g. Biographies of Tsou Yü in *KHIH* 6/6a and *KHFC* 47/11b—12a.
h. Examination listings for Tsou Yü in *TCIH* 25/3b and 11a; *KHIH* 5/4b—5a.
i. Examination listings for Tsou Yu-jen in *TCIH* 25/6b and 23a; *KHIH* 5/17b and 20a.
j. Examination listings for Tsou P'i-ch'eng and Tsou P'i-hsien in *TCIH* 25/13b and 16b; *KHIH* 5/10b.

58. T'u of I-huang County

a. Forty-six prefectural graduates, fourteen of them *chin-shih*, listed as men of Shih-lu between 1084 and 1270 in *TCIH* 25/3b—8b and 12aff.; *KHIH* 5/5bff.
b. Record for construction of I-ch'üan (Buddhist) Temple in *TCIH* 45b/3b—4a.
c. Biography of T'u Chi in *TCIH* 32/2a—b.
d. Anecdote about T'u family in Hung Mai, *san-jen* 1/3b—4a.
e. Anecdote about T'u Cheng-sheng in ibid., *san-jen* 4/3a—b.
f. Anecdote about T'u Ssu-yu in ibid., *chih-i* 2/5b.
g. Record for construction of T'ai-ho (Buddhist) Temple in *TCIH* 45b/35a—b.
h. Record for stele listing degreeholders from Fu-chou in Chou Pi-ta, 54/18a—19b.
i. Biographies of T'u Ta-ching in *TCIH* 30/1a—b and *KHIH* 47/32b.
j. Anecdote about T'u Ta-ching in Hung Mai, *san-jen* 4/3b—4a.
k. Funerary inscription of T'u Ta-hsiang in Sun Ti, also in *TCIH* 45g/-93a—95a.
l. Record for construction of Li-i Bridge in *TCIH* 45b/21a.

59. Tung of Lo-an County

a. Twenty-five prefectural graduates, including five *chin-shih* listed as men of Liu-fang between 1153 and 1274 in *TCLA* 7/10a—12a and 17aff.; *KHLA* 5/2b—5a and 6aff.
b. Eighty-two prefectural graduates, including twenty-two *chin-shih*, listed between 1015 and 1148 from Yung-feng County, Chi-chou (before the creation of Lo-an County); nine identified as men of Liu-fang: in *TCYF* 15/11b—14b and 16/1a—10a.
c. Farewell poem by Mei Yao-ch'en for Tung Ts'an of Yün-kai (canton) in Yung-feng County, in *SCCA* 36/7b.
d. Biographies for Tung Ts'an in *TCLA* 8/4b; *KHLA* 6/17b; *TCYF* 24/1a.
e. Listings for 1148 *chin-shih* degree of Tung Te-yüan in *Shao-hsing shih-pa nien t'ung-nien hsiao-lu* 12a.
f. Funerary inscription of Tung Kuan in Wang T'ing-kuei, 44/3a—5b.
g. Funerary inscription of Tung I in Chou Pi-ta, 75/11b—12a.
h. Funerary inscription of Tung Ch'ang-i in ibid., 72/7a—9a.
i. Preface to genealogy of Tung lineage of Yün-kai canton in *WWC* 32/20b—21b.
j. Farewell composition for Tung T'ien-chü in ibid., 24/12b—14b.
k. Farewell composition for Tung Ch'i-ch'ien in ibid., 26/18a—20a.
l. Biographies of Tung Te-hsiu in *TCLA* 8/13a; *KHLA* 6/21a; *SYHA* 77/14a.

m. Mention of Tung Te-hsiu (under courtesy-name Chung-hsiu) in record for construction of Shan-yüeh Hall in Tseng Feng, 19/20a–21a.
n. Biographies of Tung Liang-shih in *TCLA* 8/4a; *KHLC* 6/11b; *TCYF* 21/12a.
o. Biographies of Tung Te in *TCLA* 8/17b; *KHLA* 6/21a.
p. Mention of Tung Te in record for reconstruction of Lo-an County school in *WWC* 36/19b–22a.
q. Biographies of Tung Tun-i in *TCLA* 8/4a; *KHLA* 6/12a; *TCYF* 21/11b; *SS* 355/2b–3b.
r. Biographies of Tung Yü-ch'ien in *TCLA* 7/1b and *KHLA* 6/21a.

60. Wang of I-huang County

a. Nine prefectural graduates, two of them *chin-shih*, listed as men of I-nan between 1056 and 1249 in *TCIH* 25/4a, 7b, and 9bff.; *KHIH* 5/3aff.
b. Funerary inscription of woman surnamed Wang in Ch'en Tsao, 35/13a–16a.
c. Note on construction of Shan-hua (Buddhist) Temple in *TCIH* 13/7a.
d. Note on construction of Yu-hsin Hall in ibid., 7/5a.
e. Note on construction of Chi-ao Tower in ibid.
f. Note on construction of Ting-ao Academy in ibid., 19/2b.

61. Wang of Lin-ch'uan County

a. Funerary inscription of Wang Kuan-chih in Wang An-shih, 98/2b. 98/2b.
b. Funerary inscription of Wang I in Tseng Feng, 44/6b–8b.
c. Funerary inscription of Wang An-kuo in Wang An-shih, 91/8a–9a.
d. Funerary inscription of Wang An-jen in ibid., 96/1b–2b.
e. Funerary inscription of Wang Shih-hsi in ibid., 93/7a–b.
f. Funerary inscription of woman surnamed Wang in ibid., 96/8b.
g. Funerary inscription of woman surnamed Wang in ibid., 99/5b–6a.
h. Funerary inscription of Wang I's wife in Tseng Kung, 45/4b–6a.
i. Biographies of Wang An-li in *KHFC* 47/9a–12a; *SS* 327/8a–10a; Yü Hsi-lu, 20/10b.
j. Biographies of Wang An-shih in *SS* 327/1a–7a; Tu Ta-kuei, 14/1a; *KHFC* 47/3b–8a.
k. Anecdote about Wang Ch'un in Hung Mai, *chih-keng* 10/3a–b.
l. Discussions of Wang Hou-chih in Chang Kao, *K'uai-chi hsü-chih* 5/10b.
m. Preface to collected works of Wang An-li in Lou Yüeh, 51/12b–14b.
n. Anecdote about Wang Huan in Hung Mai, *chih-ching* 3/6a–b.
o. Remarks on Wang I and sons and grandsons in Chang Hsüan, 13b/46a–47a.
p. Biography of Wang P'ang in *SS* 327/6b–7a.
q. Biography of Wang Ti in Wang Ch'eng, 79/6a.
r. Record for construction of Chin-yao Pavilion in Ta-chung Hsiang-fu (Taoist) Temple in Wang An-shih, 83/10b–11a.
s. Record for construction of Ch'eng-pei (Buddhist) Temple in ibid., 83/3b.

t. Note on Ch'eng-pei Temple in *CCFC* 4/40a.

u. Note on naming of part of Fu-chou prefectural city in honor of Wang An-shih's having lived there in *YLTT* 10950/1b.

v. Record for renovation of sacrificial altar to Wang An-shih in *TCCC* 33b/18a—21b.

w. Preface to genealogy of Wang lineage in Wei Su, 10/2a—b.

x. Mention of Wangs in preface to genealogy of Tseng lineage in Yü Chi, 40/4a—6a.

y. Examination listings for Wang Kuan-chih, Wang I, Wang Chen-ch'ing, Wang I, Wang An-shih, Wang Hang, Wang An-jen, Wang An-li, and Wang P'ang in *TCLC* 36/1b—2n.

62. Wang of Lo-an County

a. Four prefectural graduates listed as men of Hu-p'ing in 1259 and 1265 in *TCLA* 7/23b—25a and *KHLA* 5/14a—b.

b. Biographies in *TCLA* 8/17b and *KHLA* 6/21b.

63. Wei of Chin-ch'i County

a. Record of conduct of Wei Lung-yu in Wei Su, 10/21b—23a.

b. Funerary inscription of Wei Yung-chi in Huang Chin, 32/18b—20b.

c. Preface to genealogy of Wei lineages of Lin-ch'uan County and Chin-ch'i County in Wei Su, 6/1a—2a.

d. Biography of Wei Su in *KHCC* 5/33a—5a.

e. Examination listings for Wei Kuo-ts'ai and Wei Yen-chen in *TCCC* 172/3a; *KHCC* 4/4a; *TCLC* 36/8a.

f. Memorial asking rewards for sellers of relief grain in Huang Chen, 75/15a—16b.

N.B. f. concerns men whose membership in this family cannot be proven.

64. Wei of Lin-ch'uan County

a. Funerary inscription of Wei Ho in Yüan Fu, 17/14a—16a.

b. Biographies of Wei Chen (or K'o) in *KHFC* 49/34b—35a; *SS* 415/7a—8a; *KHTH* 4/5b.

c. Note on founding of Chen-shuai Society in *TCLC* 16/31a.

d. Biographies of Wei Fu-chih in *KHTH* 4/26b; Wan Ssu-t'ung, 10/17b; Lu Hsin-yüan, 35/18a; *SYHA* 84/3b.

e. Mention of a Wei of Leng-shui in public notice on rice prices in Huang Chen, 78/22b—24a. Compare also *KHTH*, loc. cit.

f. Documents on law case of Professor Wei vs. Hsiung Hsiang in Huang Kan, 27/3b—9a, 29/8b—10a, 32/12—5a.

g. Examination listings for Wei Chen, Wei Ho, Wei Sung, and Wei Piao in *TCLC* 36/5b—6a, 7a, 9a.

h. Mention of Lin-ch'uan County Wei family in article on Wei surname in Teng Ming-shih, 3/42.

i. Preface to genealogy of Wei lineages of Lin-ch'uan County and Chin-ch'i County in Wei Su, 6/1a—2a.

N.B. h. and i. concern men whose membership in this family cannot be proven.

65. Wu[a] of Chin-ch'i County: family of Wu Min

a. Funerary inscription of Wu Fan in Wang An-shih, 98/8a—b.
b. Funerary inscription of Wu Fen in ibid., 98/10a—b.
c. Funerary inscription and biography of woman surnamed Wu in Wang Ling, 12b—14b.
d. Funerary inscription of woman surnamed Wu in Tseng Kung, 45/4b—6a.
e. Funerary inscription of woman surnamed Wu in K'ung Wu-chung, *Tsung-po chi* 7/11b.
f. Funerary inscription of Wu Ch'üeh in Sun Ti, 58/14b—18a.
g. Biographies of Wu Min in *KHCC* 5/1a—b and *KHFC* 64/1b.
h. Funerary inscription of Wu Min's wife and Wang An-shih, 100/3a—b.
i. Biography of Wu Fan in *TCCC* 24/1a.
j. Biography of Wu Hao in ibid., 26/1a—b.
k. Discussion of Wu residences mentioned in Wang An-shih's poems in Wu Tseng, 9/228.
l. Preface to poems of man surnamed Wu in Wang An-shih, 84/5a—b.
m. Examination listings for Wu Min, Wu Jui, Wu Meng, and Wu Su in *TCCC* 17a/1a and 2b; *KHCC* 4/1a and 2b.
n. Funerary inscription of Wu Hsing-tsung in Wang An-shih, 94/12a—13a.
o. Biography of Wu Hsing-tsung in *TCCC* 26/1b.
p. Biography of Wu Hsiao-tsung in *TCCC* 24/1b.
q. Examination listings for Wu Piao-wei and Wu Hsiao-tsung in *KHFC* 42/1b and *TCCC* 17a/1a.

N.B. n., o., p., and q. concern men whose membership in this family is uncertain.

66. Wu[a] of Chin-ch'i County: Hsin-t'ien and Wu-t'ang

a. Funerary inscription of woman surnamed Wu in *WWC* 82/2b—3b.
b. Funerary inscription of woman surnamed Wu in ibid., 84/3b—4b.
c. Funerary inscription of Wu Ch'en-tzu in Yü Chi, 18/28a—29b.
d. Funerary inscription of Wu Ch'en-tzu in Li Ts'un, 23/6b—11b.
e. Funerary inscription of Wu Ch'ing-hsi in ibid., ch. 24.
f. Funerary inscription of Wu En in *WWC* 81/8a—9a.
g. Funerary inscription of Wu Fei in ibid., 83/5a—6b.
h. Funerary inscription of Wu Fu-tzu in Li Ts'un, 23/4a—7a.
i. Funerary inscription of Wu Hou-tzu in Ch'eng Chü-fu, 20/13b—14b.
j. Funerary inscription of Wu I in Sung Lien, 22/805—806.
k. Funerary inscription of Wu K'o-sun in Ch'eng Chü-fu, 16/12a—13b.
l. Record of conduct of Wu T'ai-lien in Li Ts'un, 23/18a—21b.
m. Funerary inscription of Wu Te-hung in Ch'eng Chü-fu, 22/9b—10b.
n. Funerary inscription of Wu Te-p'u in ibid., 18/3a—4a.
o. Funerary inscription of Wu T'ing-lan in *WWC* 76/10a—11a.
p. Preface to genealogy of Wu lineage in ibid., 32/19a—20b.
q. Biography of Wu Ch'e in *TCTH* 13h/1a.
r. Biographies of Wu Ching-li in *KHFC* 57/10a; *SYHAPI* 51/4b.
s. Biography of Wu Chü in *TCTH* 13a/20b—21a.
t. Note on Wu Hsing-shih and Wu Hsün in *SYHAPI* 77/25b.

u. Biographies of Wu Jao in *TCTH* 13c/10b and *SYHAPI* 77/50b.

v. Biography of Wu K'o in *TCTH* 13c/11b—12a.

w. Biography of Wu Meng-ch'i in ibid., 13a/20a.

x. Biographies of Wu Ming-yang in *KHCC* 5/21a—b; *KHFC* 61/6b—7b; *KHTH* 4/7a—b; *SYHAPI* 88/37a.

y. Note on Wu Shih-heng in *SYHAPI* 51/46b.

z. Biographies of Wu Yü in *KHCC* 5/29b—30b; *TCTH* 13d/5b—6a.

aa. Examination listings for Wu Ming-yang and Wu K'o-sun in *TCCC* 17a/3b and *KHCC* 4/4a.

bb. Funerary inscription of Wu Po-wu in Hsieh I, 8/16b—18a.

N.B. bb. concerns man whose membership in this family cannot be proven.

67. Wu[a] of Ch'ung-jen County: family of Wu Tseng

a. Biographies of Wu Hang in *TCCJ* 8e/1b and *KHCJ* 4/22a—b.

b. Record for construction of sacrificial altar to Ou-yang Ch'e and Wu Hang in Ou-yang Ch'e, front matter.

c. Wu Hang's preface to Ou-yang Ch'e's collected works in ibid.

d. Biographies of Wu Hsieh in *KHFC* 59/4a—b and *SYHAPI* 45/167a.

e. Biographies of Wu I in *KHFC* 47/36b and *KHCJ* 4/39a—b.

f. Anecdote about Wu I in Hung Mai, *san-jen* 1/1b—2a.

g. Wu Hang's note on poetry of Wu Kuang in Li O, 40/3b.

h. Wu Hang's note on poetry of Wu T'ao in ibid.

i. Biographies of Wu Tseng in *TCCJ* 8b/3a—4a and *KHCJ* 4/22b—23b.

j. Preface to Wu Tseng's collected works in Lou Yüeh, 52/11b—13b.

k. Hung Mai, *chih-i* 2/4a—b.

l. Account of Ch'ung-jen County Wu lineage in funerary inscription of Huang-chou man Wu Yen in *WWC* 76/13b—15a.

m. Funerary inscription of Wu Ch'ih in Ch'en Yüan-chin, 6/18b—20b.

n. Funerary inscription of Wu Hao in ibid., 6/17a—18b.

o. Note on Huan-ch'i Academy in *TCCJ* 1g/3a.

p. Note on Chen-lo Garden in *KHCJ* ch. 3.

q. Examination listings for Wu Shan-fu, Wu Shang, Wu Tseng, Wu T'ao, Wu Pi, Wu I, Wu Hsieh, Wu Chang, Wu Tsung, Wu Kuan, Wu Ts'ung-lung, Wu Chien, Wu T'ai and Wu Chün-chao in *TCCJ* 7b/1b and ff. and 7c/1bff.; *KHCJ* 1/43bff.

r. Examination listings for Wu Yu-lin and Wu Shih in *TCCJ* 7b/1b and 5a, 7c/10a; *KHCJ* 1/43b and 56a.

s. Biographies of Wu Yu-lin in *KHCJ* 4/36a—b and *KHFC* 47/27b.

t. Funerary inscription of woman surnamed Wu in Liu Chih, 14/20b—21b.

u. Biographies of Wu Shih in *TCCJ* 8b/8a and 4/42a.

N.B. r., s., t., and u. concern two men and one woman whose membership in this family cannot be proven.

68. Wu[a] of Ch'ung-jen County: Ch'ing-yün canton

a. Preface to genealogy of Wu lineage of Ch'ing-yün canton in *WWC* 32/-8b—9a.

b. Funerary inscription of Wu Te-fu in ibid., 86/1a—2a.

c. Funerary inscription of woman surnamed Hsiung in Ch'en Tsao,

35/16b—18b.
d. Examination listings for Wu Ju-shan, Wu Ju-ling, Wu Li-i in *TCCJ* 8c/6b—7a and *KHCJ* 1/50a—b.
e. Examination listings for Wu Ju-ch'uan and Wu Ju-sung in *TCCJ* 7c/6a—7a and *KHCJ* 1/49b—50b.

N.B. e. concerns men whose membership in this family cannot be proven.

69. Wu[a] of Ch'ung-jen County: family of Wu Ch'eng

a. Record for conduct of Wu Ch'eng in *WWC*, end matter (also in Yü Chi, 44/2b).
b. Mention of Wu Meng-hsi in preface to collection of writings of Hsieh family in *WWC* 24/4b—7a.
c. Biographies of Wu Yung in *KHCJ* 4/68a and *KHFC* 61/5b.
d. Examination listings for Wu Meng-hsi, Wu Meng-wen, Wu Yung, and Wu Ch'eng in *TCCJ* 7c/11b and *KHCJ* 1/53a—60a.

70. Wu[a] of I-huang County

a. Six prefectural graduates, three of them *chin-shih,* listed as men of I-tung (the eastern part of the county seat) between 1144 and 1273 in *TCIH* 25/5b—7b and 18aff.; *KHIH* 5/12bff.
b. Funerary inscription of Wu Shun-tzu in *WWC* 83/4a—5a.
c. Funerary inscription of Wu I in ibid., 79/6a—7a.
d. Preface to genealogy of Wu lineage in ibid., 32/13b—15a.
e. Farewell composition of Wu I-feng in ibid., 30/19b—20a.
f. Biographies of Wu Jung in *TCIH* 29/7b—8a and *KHFC* 47/37b.

71. Wu[a] of Lin-ch'uan County

a. Funerary inscription of Wu Ting-weng in Yü Chi, 43/2b—4b.
b. Funerary inscription of Wu Chien in Lu Chiu-yüan, 27/8a—10a.
c. Colophon for calligraphy of Wu Ping-jo in *WWC* 61/15a—16b.
d. Funerary inscription of Wu Yung in Lu Chiu-yüan, 28/11a—12a.
e. Biography of Wu Yüan-tzu in *KHFC* 57/3b—4a.
f. Note on Wu Cheng-tzu in *SYHAPI* 58/34b, 40a.
g. Note on Wu Ch'eng-jo in ibid., 77/24b.
h. Note on Wu Hou-jo in ibid.
i. Note on Wu Hui-tzu in ibid., 58/34b.
j. Note on establishment of commemorative marker for Wu family in *YLTT* 10950/1b. (On the name of this marker cf. Yü Chi, loc. cit.)
k. Examination listings for Wu Ping-jo and Wu Yüan-tzu in *TCLC* 36/5b—6a.

72. Yüeh of I-huang County

a. Biographies of Yüeh Shih in *KHFC* 47/25b; *SS* 306/10b—12a; Tseng Kung, *Lung-p'ing chi* 14/1a—b; Wang Ch'eng, 115/3a—4a.
b. Examination listings for Yüeh Shih's sons and grandsons in *TCIH* 25/-2a—b and *KHIH* 5/1b—2a.
c. Funerary inscription of woman surnamed Yüeh in Wang An-shih, 99/9b—10b.

d. Funerary inscription of wife of Yüeh Hsü-kuo in Yin Chu, 15/6b—7b.
e. Examination listings for Yüeh Jen-chieh, Yüeh T'ing-chüeh, and Yüeh I in *TCIH* 25/18a—31a and *KHIH* 5/12b—25b.
f. Examination listings for Yüeh Fu and Yüeh Yüan in *TCIH* 25/7b and 32b; *KHIH* 5/23a—b.
g. Discussion of problem of Yüeh Shih's residence in *TCCJ* 8d/2a—3a.
h. Record for construction of Ch'ing-yün (Taoist) Temple in *TCCJ* 2d/- 1b—2a.
i. Record for reconstruction of Shang-fang (Taoist) Temple in *WWC* 47/14b—16a.
j. Listing for Yüeh Shih's *T'ai-p'ing huan-yü chi* in Ch'en Chen-sun, *Chih-chai shu-lu chieh-t'i* 8/15b.
k. Note on Yüeh Shih in Wang Hsiang-chih, 29/8a.
l. Record for sutra library of Yün-feng (Buddhist) Temple in *WWC* 49/13a.
m. Note on Yün-feng Temple in *TCIH* 13/16a.
n. Judgment on division of estate of Yüeh I in Huang Chen, 78/36a—40b.
o. Mention of Yüeh I in memorial asking dismissal of I-huang County Supervisor of Wine taxes in ibid., 75/20a—21a.
p. Colophon to genealogy of Yüeh lineage in *WWC* 55/10b—11a.
q. Note and construction record for Ch'i-chen Temple in *TCCJ* 2d/51a.
r. Note on Shang-ch'eng (Buddhist) Temple in ibid., 2d/30b.
s. Note on Chung-shan (Buddhist) Temple in ibid., 2d/31a.
t. Note on An-yüan (Buddhist) Temple in ibid., 2d/34b—35a.
u. Notes on Tung-lin (Buddhist) Temple in ibid., 2d/1b.
v. Notes on charitable estate in *TCIH* 7/4a and 14/23a—b; *KHIH* 3/1b— 2b, 18b.

73. Yen of Lin-ch'uan County

a. Funerary inscription of Yen Shu in Ou-yang Hsiu, 22/7b—12b.
b. Funerary inscription of Yen Fang in Hsieh I, 9/4a—8b.
c. Funerary inscription of Yen Ta-cheng in Ts'ao Yen-yüeh, 20/19a—23b.
d. Funerary inscription of Yen Shu's sister's son Li K'ang in Lü Nan-kung, 19/10a—11b.
e. Preface to genealogy of Yen lineage in Yü Chi, 32/8a—9a.
f. Biographies of Yen Chi-tao in *KHFC* 59/8b; Li O, 25/12b.
g. Funerary inscription of wife of Yüeh Hsü-kuo in Yin Chu, 15/6b—7b.
h. Biography of Yen Hsiao-kuang in *TCLC* 44/2a—b.
i. Biography of Yen P'u in Lu Hsin-yüan, 30/17b.
j. Biographies of Yen Tun-fu in *KHFC* 47/19b—21a; *SS* 381/5b/7a.
k. Colophon to work of Yen Tun-fu in Ou-yang Shou-tao, *Sun-chai wen-chi* 19/3b—4b.
l. Colophon to work of descendant of Yen Shu in Huang Chen, 91/23a—b.
m. Colophon to imperial calligraphy in possession of Yen Shu's descendants in ibid., 91/23b—24b.
n. Note on commemorative marking of part of prefectural city in *YLTT* 10950/1b.
o. Mention of Yen family's ancestor in funerary inscription of Chang Wen-huan in Huang Chen, 97/10b—12b.

p. Account of Yen family in *CCFC* 11/4a—9b.
q. Funerary inscription of Yen Shu's daughter-in-law in Chang Lei, *Chang Yu-shih wen-chi* 60/4a—5a.
r. Funerary inscription of Yen Shu's daughter-in-law in Liu Pin, 39/517.
s. Examination listings for Yen Shu, Yen Ch'ung-jang, Yen Sheng-ch'ing, Yen P'eng, Yen Chung, Yen Shao-hsiu, Yen Tun-fu, Yen Tun-lin, Yen Su, and Yen Ta-cheng in *TCLC* 36/1b—4a, 6a.
t. Memorial asking rewards for sellers of relief grain in Huang Chen, 75/15a—16b.
u. Mention of man surnamed Yen in public notice on problem of high-interest loans in Huang Chen, 78/33a—b.

N.B. t. and u. concern men whose membership in this family cannot be proven.

Uncertain Cases

74. Fu of Chin-ch'i County

a. Biography of Fu An-ch'ien in *KHFC* 61/5b—6a.
b. Biography of Fu T'i in ibid., 61/8a.
c. Mention of Fu An-ch'ien and Fu T'i in biography of Teng P'ang in *TCCC* 22/1a—5a.
d. Notes on Fu An-ch'ien in *TCCC* 18/8a and *KHCC* 5/7b.
e. Biographies of Fu Tzu-yün in *TCCC* 19/4b—5b; *KHCC* 5/16b—17a; *SYHA* 77/2b; *SYHAPI* 77/4a.
f. Preface to collected sayings of Fu Tzu-yün in *WWC* 18/15b—16b.
g. Record for construction of Ti-hua Hall in Li Ts'un, 15/6a—8a.
h. Note on burial place of Fu An-ch'ien in *TCCC* 7/10b.

75. Ho of Chin-ch'i County

a. Funerary inscription of woman surnamed Ho in Wei Su, 4/9b—11b.
b. Record for construction of Ch'ung-chen Pavilion in Li Ts'un, ch. 14.
c. Examination listings for Ho Shih, Ho Kuo-jui, and Ho Hsiu, in *TCCC* 17a/1b—2a; *KHCC* 4/2b, 40a.

76. Hsia of Lo-an County

a. Funerary inscription of Hsia Hsiung in *WWC* 75/6b—8a.
b. Funerary inscription of Hsia Yu-lan in ibid., 74/8b—10b.
c. Funerary inscription of woman surnamed Hsia in ibid., 75/15a—b.
d. Record for construction of Chao-hsien (Taoist) Temple in ibid., 47/7b—8b.
e. Notes on founding of Wu-chiang Ferry and Lan-yüan Bridge in *TCLA* 1/8a and 24b.
f. Mention of Hsieh Shun (probably same as Hsia Hsiung) in memorial asking abolition of Tseng-t'ien Fort in Huang Chen, 75/19a—20a.
g. Biography of Hsia K'o-ta in *KHLA* 5/9b.

77. T'an of Nan-feng County

a. Mention of T'an Meng-lin in 'Record of the Hidden Virtue of the Chu

Family' in *KHNF* 13/11a—12a.

b. Mention of T'an Meng-lin in record of the Chi-chuan Estate in *MKNF* 2/18a—19a.

c. Mention of the 'Three T'ans' and 'Two Chaos' in account of banditry in Nan-feng Hsien in Liu Hsün, 13/2b—7b (also in *KHNF* 14/77a—80b).

d. Biography of T'an Shih-yüan in *MKNF* 26/4b.

e. Notes on early generations of a Nan-feng Hsien T'an lineage in *Nan-feng T'an-shih hsü-hsiu tsu-p'u* 1a—4a.

78. Teng of Ch'ung-jen County

a. Biographies of Teng Chou in *KHCJ* 4/60a; *KHFC* 59/4b.

b. Biographies of Teng Ch'i in *KHCJ* 4/63a; *SYHAPI* 39/17b.

c. Biography of Teng Hu in *KHFC* 59/4b—5a.

d. Inscription on bell of Hou-shan Temple in *TCCJ* 9g/2b—3b.

e. Law case involving men surnamed Teng in *Ming-kung shu-p'an ch'ing-ming chi* pp. 168—71.

f. Examination listings for men surnamed Teng in *KHCJ* 1/46a, 46b, 47b, 48a, 50a, 51b, 52b, 57a, 58a, 59a, 60a; *TCCJ* 7b/2b, 5b, 6a.

79. Wu^b of Lo-an County

a. Funerary inscription of Wu Lung-hsiang in *WWC* 77/14a—15a.

b. Funerary inscription of wife of Wu Lung-ch'i in ibid., 83/9b/11b.

c. Biographies of Wu K'o-ch'eng in *TCLA* 8/17a; *KHLA* 6/5b; *KHFC* 59/-13b.

d. Mention of Wu K'o-ch'eng in record for construction of Yü-shan (Taoist) Temple in ibid., 47/4a—6a.

e. Mention of Wu Mao, Wu Chih-ch'üan, Wu Ching, and Wu Lung-chieh, in note in *KHLA* 5/15b—16a.

f. Examination listings for Wu Lung-chieh in ibid., and *TCLA* 7/26a.

g. Examination listings from Ch'ung-jen County for Wu Mao, Wu Chih-chüan, and Wu Ching in *KHCJ* 1/46a—47a; *TCCJ* 7b/2a.

h. Mention of Wu Mao, Wu Ching, and Wu Chih-ch'üan in list of men from territory of Lo-an County who passed exams before Lo-an's founding, in *KHLA* 5/1b—2a and *TCLA* 7/1b.

80. Yu of Lin-ch'uan County

a. Biography of Yu Yüan in *YLTT* 8843/12b.

b. Examination listings for Yu Luan and Yu Tsu-wu in *TCLC* 36/6a and 7a.

c. Anecdote about Yu Tsu-wu in Hung Mai, *san-jen* 4/2a.

81. Yü^a of Chin-ch'i County

a. Funerary inscription of Yü Jui in Li Ts'un, 24/16a—17a.

b. Funerary inscription of Yü Tou-hsiang in *WWC* 74/5b—7a.

c. Funerary inscription of woman surnamed Yü in Wei Su, 6/2b—4a.

d. Funerary inscription of woman surnamed Yü in *WWC* 82/5b—7a.

e. Mention of Yü lineage in record for construction of Ch'ing-ming Pavilion in Li Ts'un, 14/2a—3b.

f. Biography of Yü Shih-te in *KHFC* 49/36b.

g. Note on Yü Shih-te's residence in *TCCC* 18/1b.

82. Yü[b] of Lin-ch'uan County

a. Funerary inscription of Yü Ying-yüan in Ch'eng Chü-fu, 18/5a—6a.
b. Biographies of Yü T'ing-ch'un in *TCTH* 13b/1a—b; *KHTH* 3/9b; *SYHA* 77/16b; *SYHAPI* 77/20a.
c. Biography of Yü T'ing-hua in *TCTH* 13c/11a—b.
d. Biography of Yü Yüan-liang in ibid., 13d/4b.
e. Examination listings for Yü T'ing-ch'un and Yu Ping in *TCLC* 36/5a and 7a; *TCTH* 11/5b and 7a.

APPENDIX II

POPULATION

Fu-chou population trends before and during Sung are displayed in Table II and Figure I below.

The estimated Sung figures for individuals graphed here are derived by doubling those given in *KHFC* 22/3a—b and *TCLC* 21/3b—5a. This requires some explanation. Sung population figures have been the focus of considerable controversy, centering around the fact that, if taken at face value, the figures for individuals (*k'ou* or *ting*) yield an average household size that is implausibly low: in the area of two or two and a half. This quotient bears no resemblance to those of the dynasties preceding and following Sung, or indeed to that of any known premodern society; no student of Sung or of Chinese society in general has been willing to accept it. The issue won much attention from Japanese researchers in the 1930s and 1940s, with two general positions emerging: first, that the ratio of individuals was reduced by the omission of household members, fictitious division of households, and similar strategies aimed at reducing liability to various tax and service levies; second, that the existing figures for individuals include only males, who alone were subject to service duties, with perhaps some further reduction through tax-evasion strategies such as those above. The first position was defended, with differing

Table II. *Fu-chou population figures, to early Sung*

Period or Year	Households	Individuals	Source[*]
Chin[**] (265–419)	8,500	–	*Chin shu* 15/7b
Liu Sung[**] (420–478)	8,983	64,850	*Sung shu* 36/11a
Sui (585–618)	10,900	–	*Sui shu* 31/5a
T'ang: c. 625	7,354	40,685	*Chiu T'ang shu* 40/18b
T'ang: 713–41	24,988	–	*Yüan-ho chün-hsien chih* 28/753
T'ang: 742	30,600	176,394	*Chiu T'ang shu* 40/18b
Sung: 976–97	61,279	289,850[***]	*T'ai-p'ing huan-yü chi* 110/3a
Sung: 1008–16	90,333	427,962[***]	*KHFC* 22/3a

[*]All the figures listed here are also found together in *KHFC* 22/2b—3a.
[**]Chin and Liu Sung figures are for Lin-ch'uan commandery.
[***]On Sung figures for individuals, see below.

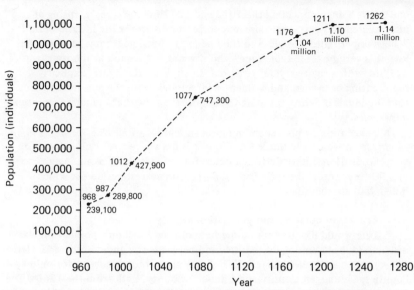

Figure I. Fu-chou's population during Sung (source: *KHFC* 22/3a–b.) All figures are rounded down to hundreds.

emphases, by Katō Shigeshi in articles appearing in 1930 and 1940 (Katō, *Shina keizaishi kōshō*, pp. 317–37 and 371–403) and by Hino Kaisaburō during the same decade (Hino, 'Sōdai no kiko o ronjite koko mondai ni oyobu'). The second was advocated by Miyazaki ('Tokushi sakki') and by Sogabe Shizuo. In a recent study of Sung and Chin population, Ping-ti Ho seems to regard the question as still unresolved (Ho, 'An Estimate of the Total Population of Sung-Chin China'); I find his hesitancy surprising, as to my mind the males-only view is convincing, especially as argued by Sogabe in three brilliant articles published during the war (Sogabe, 'Sōdai no koko tōkei ni tsuite no shin kenkyū'; 'Zoku Sōdai...'; and 'Zokuzoku Sōdai...'). Hence in interpreting the gazetteer totals for Fu-chou – themselves ranging between 2.26 and 2.42 per household, depending on the year – I have assumed the figures to represent only males and further assumed that males were roughly half the population, thus doubling the figures given to obtain my estimates. It will be seen that this yields an individual/household ratio of between 4.52 and 4.84, which is plausible though perhaps even a bit low. (For T'ang, as may be calculated from Table II, the ratios are 5.5 to 1 around 625 and 5.76 to 1 in 742; for Ming there are gazetteer figures for 1391 which yield a ratio of 5.25 to 1; see *CCFC* 7/1a.)

In Fu-chou there is good independent support for the males-only view. Wang An-shih, in an inscriptional record written in 1060 for the Chien-shan Pavilion in the prefectural city, comments that in Fu-chou 'the *men and women* of the population, counting them by ten-thousands, number some fifty or sixty' (Wang An-shih, 83/7b–9a; emphasis mine). Now the figures given for individuals in the gazetteers never reach 600,000: the highest, in fact, is 557,479, in the 1260s, separated from Wang's record by two centuries of further population growth. No figure survives for 1060 in the gazetteers, but figures do exist for 1012 and 1077. From Figure I it can be seen that if one draws a line connecting the 1012 and 1077 figures – representing an interpolated and very approximate course of growth for the interim period – Wang's upper figure lies close to the line in 1060; while it may be somewhat low, it is very possible that Wang, who was not in Fu-chou at the time, was working with a figure several years old. In any case the figure, explicitly representing both men and women, is far enough from the gazetteer figures for individuals in Northern Sung to support the view that the latter represent only males.

One exception to my general method should be noted: the *T'ai-p'ing huan-yü chi*, from which the figure for 976–88 is drawn, records only a total for households. Here I have derived a figure for individuals by assuming a ratio of 4.73 to 1: this is the ratio for 1008–16, the nearest period for which individuals are recorded.

County population and population density

One would like to know something of how Fu-chou's population was distributed, both among its counties and between city and countryside. Here the sources have rather less to tell. Full population totals survive for only two counties, Ch'ung-jen County and Chin-ch'i County, both from the 1260s. The figures are 68,244 households in Ch'ung-jen, 36,972 households in Chin-ch'i (*TCCJ* 3a/1a; *TCCC* 1/1a). The prefectural total in the same year was 247,320 households. Thus the two accounted for just over 40 percent of Fu-chou's households at the time: 27.5 percent and 14.9 percent respectively. There is no way to estimate the other county populations at the same time. For a period nearly two centuries earlier, however, one can calculate the approximate *rural* population, and rural population density, for each county of Fu-chou proper. The calculation is based on the numbers of *tu* units in each county.

The *tu* was originally the highest organizational level of the *pao-chia* system instituted on a national scale under Wang An-shih in 1073, and at the start was a unit of participating population, not territory. To calculate population from these units, however, is not as straightforward a matter as one might suppose: it would seem that the number of households per *tu* varied from region to region, despite national statutes that prescribed a uniform number. (See for instance Brian McKnight, *Village and Bureaucracy in Southern Sung China*, p. 79n.; and on local variations in general, pp. 74–9.) Officially the number of households for each *tu*, according to the final form of the system promulgated in 1073, was to be 250 (McKnight, p. 34). Now in Fu-chou it is clear that the *tu* units represented in Ch'ing dynasty gazetteers were already in existence before 1149. (The series of *tu* numbers for Lin-ch'uan County is missing about twenty numbers from the middle of the series; the gazetteers explain that these were the numbers of the *tu* transferred to Ch'ung-jen County after the creation of Lo-an County from Ch'ung-jen's territory in 1149.) It is reasonable then to suppose that they were created either during the system's first application in the 1070s or during its revival in the middle 1090s after a brief abolition in the conservative interregnum. Presumably a population estimate derived from a ratio of 250 households to one *tu* should correspond, at least roughly, to Fu-chou's rural population in the 1070s or 1090s. But when one multiplies by 250 the number of *tu* in the four counties of Fu-chou before 1149, the resulting figure (70,000 house-

Table III. *Rural population, ca. 1073, by county*

County	Households	Individuals (estimated)	Density*	% of total rural population
Lin-ch'uan	54,500	253,970	79.5	38.9
Ch'ung-jen	39,000	181,740	58.5	27.9
Chin-ch'i	24,500	114,170	68.9	17.5
I-huang	22,000	102,520	51.3	15.7
Total	140,000	652,400	65.5	100.00

*Density figures are in individuals per square kilometer.

holds) is considerably less than half the population for 1077 attested in other sources. To accept this figure for 1073 or for the 1090s one would have to believe that well over half of Fu-chou's population lived in cities: this is fantastic.

The number 250, then, seems clearly inapplicable in Fu-chou. Let us assume for a moment that the true ratio was instead 500 households for one *tu*. In this case the population estimate doubles to 140,000 households. Now this corresponds rather well to the 1077 figure of 160,480 found elsewhere. If contemporaneous, the two figures imply an urban share of 12.76 percent, which as we shall see corresponds closely to much later data on urban population supplied by gazetteers.

The 500-to-one ratio is not drawn from a hat. As first promulgated, the *pao-chia* law required precisely that each *tu* comprise 500 households; the number was halved to 250 several months later (McKnight, p. 34). It is more than plausible that the Fu-chou administration, having put the system into effect under the original regulations – having surveyed the rural households, organized the various units, and drawn up extensive and complicated registers in triplicate or quadruplicate – were simply unwilling, when the revised regulations came down, to redo the entire process and create 560 new *tu*. For another prefecture in the P'o-yang region, Fu-chou's neighbor Jao-chou, there is independent confirmation: the gazetteers for P'o-yang and Lo-p'ing Counties give 500 as the number of households in one Sung *tu* (*TCPY* 1/11- aff.; *TCLP* 1/4bff.). There can be little doubt, I think, that the numbers of *tu* in Fu-chou represent an original ratio of 500 households and date from the time of the system's first application in the 1070s. To convert households to individuals below I have used the multiplier 4.66, the same as for the 1077 figure in Figure I. In calculating population density here and elsewhere I use land area figures for Sung counties reconstructed on the basis of the Republican figures in Kuan Wei-lan, *Chung-hua min-kuo hsing-cheng ch'ü-hua chi t'u-ti jen-k'ou tsung-chi piao*, pp. 18–21.

Table III, then, shows rural population and density figures for each county of Fu-chou at the time of the application of the *pao-chia* system.

These figures show that Lin-ch'uan County, the seat of prefectural government and producer of more than half the prefecture's degreeholders, led other counties by a fair margin in rural population and population density. This is as one might expect. The figures also show that settlement was thicker in the northern counties (Lin-ch'uan and Chin-ch'i), where the terrain was on

Table IV

County	Households	Individuals (estim.)	% of total	Density
(Lin-ch'uan)	47,500	221,350	31.9	76.7
(Ch'ung-jen)	28,000	130,480	18.8	72.3
Chin-ch'i	24,500	114,170	16.4	68.9
I-huang	22,000	102,520	14.8	51.3
(Lo-an)	27,000	125,820	18.1	54.0
Total	149,000	694,340	100.0	63.1

the whole low and flat, and thinner in the much more mountainous southern counties (Ch'ung-jen and I-huang). The pattern shows up even more clearly if one examines the densities, not of the four counties as constituted in 1073, but of the pieces of territory that were to become the *five* counties of 1149 and after. These differed in that roughly the southern half of Ch'ung-jen County was incorporated into the new Lo-an County, while two southern cantons of Lin-ch'uan County were transferred to Ch'ung-jen. Since the numbers of *tu* in each transferred area are known (including those in the part of Lo-an transferred into the prefecture from what had formerly been part of Yung-feng County, Chi-chou), the rural populations and densities, as of 1073, of the five counties as they would appear in 1149 can be calculated. These appear in Table IV.

Here it becomes clear that the northern part of the pre-1149 Ch'ung-jen County — the part closest to Lin-ch'uan County, and which maps reveal to be far less mountainous than the region incorporated into Lo-an County — was similar in density to the northern counties, while the relative thinness of settlement in the southerly, more rugged areas of the prefecture — I-huang and what was to become Lo-an — is even clearer than in Table III.

The density figures given here, again, are for rural population only. For the prefecture as a whole, including urban population in the calculations raises overall population density to about 75 per square kilometer. And this figure, of course, did not remain static. By 1262 the overall density for the prefecture had risen to 103.6 per square kilometer; for Ch'ung-jen County, which had grown faster than the prefecture as a whole, overall density was at that time 176.2 per square kilometer.

Urban population

The Fu-chou sources supply two figures for urban population, spaced widely in time. The first is derived from the rural figures above. By comparing the rural household total in Table III with the gazetteer's overall figure of 160,480 households for 1077, one may conclude that urban households — or households officially counted as urban — made up about twelve or thirteen percent of Fu-chou's population during the 1070s. In the 1260s, according to the gazetteer, slightly more than 30,000 of 247,320 households lived in the prefectural and county seats: this is 12.4 percent (*TCLC* 21/3b–5a). If these numbers are roughly correct, the intervening hundred and ninety years had seen considerable absolute growth, but little relative change, in Fu-chou's urban population. On this, however, compare the discussion of extramural urban populations in the Introduction, p. 21.

APPENDIX III

ECONOMY

Rice production

In estimating figures for Fu-chou production of rice, my overriding assumption is that where gazetteer records for Lin-ch'uan and Chin-ch'i Counties (*KHFC* 33/13a—14a) divide county lands as of 1225—64 into *t'ien*, 'fields' (further divided into government and private *t'ien*), and *shan yüan lu-ti*, 'mountain, garden, and dry lands'), the first category refers exclusively to paddy fields. Now, for the other counties we find: for Lo-an County, a summary figure for *t'ien* and *yüan* ('garden') together; for I-huang County, figures for various ownership categories of *t'ien*; for Ch'ung-jen County, simple acreage figures categorized only by locality.

To deal with I-huang first: a possible assumption is that the figure given for *t'ien* refers once again only to paddy land, and that figures for other kinds of land are omitted. However, there exist separate land-tax records for I-huang which show that in the late eleventh or early twelfth century the total autumn tax in rice was 11,894 *shih*, while the average tax rate was roughly seven *sheng* per mou. As one hundred *sheng* equalled one *shih*, this would yield an acreage figure for private rice fields of about 169,924 mou. This is far less than the 1225—64 land figure of 476,315 mou of private *t'ien*. One must conclude either that there had been an enormous expansion of cultivated paddy land in the intervening century or so — an expansion seemingly bearing no relation to population trends in the same period — or that *t'ien* here does not refer to paddy alone, but in the absence of other categories is used in its most general sense to encompass all sorts of land. In the latter case one must adopt the earlier figure of 169,924 mou as the closest thing available to a figure for paddy fields in the later period. This, incidentally, represents just over 35 per cent of the gazetteer figure for *t'ien*. Next one must deal with Lo-an County. Here we know that the gazetteer figure (which derives uniquely not from 1225—64, but from 1174—89) includes both *t'ien* — paddy fields — and *yüan* — other, dry fields. The problem is to estimate what proportion is represented by the former. Now for Lin-ch'uan and Chin-ch'i the figures for *t'ien* roughly equal those for *shan yüan lu-ti*; for I-huang on the other hand, if the most conservative assumption is correct, only 35 per cent of the total is paddy. As I-huang and Lo-an resemble each other in having considerably less flat land and more hills than Lin-ch'uan and Chin-ch'i it seems reasonable to adopt this more conservative estimate for Lo-an as well. This would mean that 77,529 out of the 217,551 mou recorded in the gazetteer were paddy field. Finally there is Ch'ung-jen County: here the figures are completely uncategorized. Again a conservative estimate of the proportion of paddy may be adopted from I-huang: this yields 218,333 mou out of the 623,809 recorded. One may then total the figures for these three counties with those for Lin-ch'uan and Chin-ch'i (1,509, 166 mou and 633,141 mou respectively): the sum is 2,608,093 mou. On the other hand, if one seeks a maximum estimate, one may adopt quite opposite assumptions: that the I-huang *t'ien* figure includes only paddy lands, which had thus expanded enormously in the preceding century or so; that the Ch'ung-jen unlabeled figure likewise includes only paddy; and that in Lo-an the proportion of paddy resembled that in Lin-ch'uan and Chin-ch'i: about half of all lands. On these three assumptions, the total for paddy rises to 3,381,706 mou. The alternative figures vary, in opposite direction, by about 13 percent from my compromise estimate of three million mou.

To convert mou of paddy land into *shih* of rice I assume an average production of one *shih* per mou. This is a fairly conservative figure for Southern Sung: see for instance the average yields quoted for various prefectures in Sudō Yoshiyuki's study of Sung land-tax burdens in his *Chūgoku tochi seido kenkyū*, pp. 511–36. For the weight of a Sung *shih* of rice I follow Thomas Lee's recent study of the Sung merchant ship excavated at Ch'üan-chou in 1974: 'A Report on the Recently Excavated Sung Ship at Quanzhou and a Consideration of its True Capacity.'

Early- and late-ripening rice

In the collected works of the Sung Buddhist monk Hui-hung there is a poem entitled 'In Lin-ch'uan, Accompanying the Prefect Mr Hsü to Ching-shan to Pray for Rain: Written at the Shrine for Huang Hua-ku.' One couplet of the poem reads: 'The late rice is already on the ear/One rain will be enough to allow its harvesting' (Hui-hung, *Shih-men wen-tzu ch'an* 3/11a–b). Hui-hung lived from 1071 to 1128; the only Fu-chou administrator surnamed Hsü to serve in this period was Hsü Chung-fu, who took up the post in 1096 (*KHFC* 35/7a). The poem cannot thus have been written much after that date. Elsewhere in Hui-hung's works is a colophon to a painting of a lotus that had bloomed auspiciously in Ch'ung-jen County during the term of a county administrator surnamed P'eng; here we find: 'At the meeting of spring and summer it rained for several weeks in a row; the early rice reached the threshing floors' (Hui-hung, 23/23a–24a). Of the two men who might be county administrator P'eng, one served from about 1105, the other around 1117 (*KHFC* 35/18b–19a). Together the two references make clear the existence of two regular crops of rice in Fu-chou by the end of the eleventh century. This was not 'double-cropping': the two sorts of rice were grown on different lands. On this see Lu Chiu-yüan's discussion of 'early fields' and 'late fields' in Chiang-hsi in a letter to Chang Shen written from Lu's post in Ching-men Chün in the 1190s; this also specifies that the crop grown on early fields is Champa early-ripening rice (*Hsiang-shan hsien-sheng ch'üan chi* 16/2a–4a).

Waterwheels

In 1251 the Fu-chou prefectural administrator rebuilt the Ch'ien-chin Dam, which cut off an unwanted channel of the Ju River and redirected its water into the main stream flowing past the prefectural city. According to the inscriptional record of this project, objection to the rebuilding was raised on the grounds that 'from the breakaway stream east, through the years, people have often used *t'ung-ch'e* [bamboo-pipe waterwheels] to aid in irrigation. If we dam it and cut it off, people will lose this benefit.' This reference reinforces the impression one gathers from the names of certain dams in Sung Fu-chou: a Wheel-field Dam (*ch'e-t'ien pei*) in Chin-ch'i County (*YLTT* 2754/15a, column 1); a Water-wheel Dam (*shui-ch'e pei*) in the same county (*YLTT* 2754/12a, column 6); a Black river Two-channel-mouth Wheel Dam (*wu-chiang shuang-kang k'ou ch'e pei*) and a Two-channel-mouth Wheel Dam (*chuang-kang-k'ou ch'e pei*), both in Lo-an County (*YLTT* 2754/14a, columns 1 and 3); a Sour-wine Fields Middle Wheel Dam (*chiang-t'ien chung ch'e pei*), a Ch'ien Family Wheel Little-stream Dam (*Ch'ien-chia ch'e hsiao-kang pei*), and a Yang Family Wheel Dam (*Yang-chia ch'e pei*), all in Ch'ung-jen County (*YLTT* 2754/12b, column 8, and 13a, column 2); a Canal-back Wheel Dam (*keng-pei ch'e pei*) in I-huang County (*YLTT* 2754/13a, column 7); a Wheel-head Dam (*ch'e-t'ou pei*) in Lin-ch'uan County (*YLTT* 2754/10b, column 7). The translation of *ch'e* as 'wheel' in these names is in some degree speculative (except in the case of Water-wheel Dam), since 'cart' or 'wagon' is a possible alternative; but the association of the word with bodies of water or fields in many of the names suggests that these are irrigation-wheels of the kind referred to in the 1251 record.

In view of all this it is odd that Huang Chen, in his annual proclamation encouraging agriculture in 1272, expressed his puzzlement and dismay at what he thought was an absence of irrigation-wheels in Fu-chou, in contrast to his native Liang-che circuit (Huang Chen, 78/50a—52a). It would seem that Huang was not fully informed as to the agricultural practices of the prefecture. Sudō Yoshiyuki has used precisely this passage as evidence in a study of regional variations in the progress of agricultural technology and technique (*Sōdai keizaishi kenkyū*, pp. 73—138; the reference in question is on p. 113). The case suggests that one must be cautious in accepting such testimony from any single local official, particularly as to the absence of some practice. That water-wheels were less common in Fu-chou than in Liang-che does not seem unlikely. But as the technique was available and was used in at least some parts of the prefecture, its uncommonness may reflect different local conditions and needs, rather than technical backwardness. The progressiveness that Sudō perceives in Liang-che agriculture may simply reflect relative over-population and scarcity of land (in Fu-chou, by contrast, Huang Chen objected also to the large quantity of arable land that remained uncultivated), leading to the widespread and intensive adoption of techniques that elsewhere were as well known but simply would not pay where production could be increased by bringing unused lands under cultivation.

Wheat and barley

Between 1271 and 1273 in each of his yearly proclamations encouraging agriculture (*ch'üan-nung wen*), Huang Chen took Fu-chou farmers to task for not planting wheat or barley (*mai*: hereafter referred to simply as wheat), whether on rice lands between plantings of rice or on other, unused lands. He quoted arguments which Fu-chou farmers had used to him (or which he imagined they might use? it is unclear which) to justify not planting wheat, and set out to refute them one by one. From his testimony here, it would appear that hardly any wheat was planted in Fu-chou (Huang Chen, 78/47b–54a).

Other evidence, however, complicates the issue. Even in these proclamations, Huang acknowledges that in Fu-chou's 'outer counties,' that is outside Lin-ch'uan County, farmers did plant *hsiao-mai* (wheat in the strict sense). As Lin-ch'uan was the flattest and lowest-lying of Fu-chou's counties while the others were, in varying degrees, higher and hillier, it is precisely in Lin-ch'uan that one would expect the greatest concentration on paddy rice, and in other counties that one would expect wheat to assume some importance. Is Huang Chen's impression of wheat's unimportance conditioned by his own residence in the prefectural seat in Lin-ch'uan? Elsewhere, in his proclamations banning the use of rice to produce yeastcake (leaven) for export for use in winemaking. Huang notes that in Chin-ch'i County yeastcake is customarily manufactured from wheat (Huang Chen, 78/31a–32a). Wheat also formed a part (though a relatively small part) of the summer tax quota of Chin-ch'i between 1225 and 1264 (*TCCC* 9/1a–b; *KHCC* 2/1a–2a). There is reason, then, to think that Huang Chen in his proclamations encouraging agriculture overstated his case.

There are other reasons for supposing that Fu-chou's consumption of rice, in the absence of significant imports of rice or other grains, must have been supplemented by some quantity of locally produced grains other than rice, presumably wheat. As we have seen, a reasonable estimate of Fu-chou rice production in late Southern Sung is around three million *shih* per year. Now, at around the same time Fu-chou's population was somewhat in excess of one million. Sung men seem generally to have assumed that an average consumption of grain – rice was usually the grain they had in mind – would be one *sheng* per day; and that much less than this would be inadequate to support life. One *sheng* per day amounts in a year to something over three *shih*. Fu-chou's rice production, then, by contemporary standards was barely sufficient or indeed insufficient (three million divided by over one million yields less than three *shih* per person) to support its population. Given that we know that Fu-chou exported a significant proportion of its rice, the problem should become even more acute. It is true that drought-provoked famines recur with some frequency in Southern Sung; but these are at times of *reduced* rice production. No Southern Sung observer suggests that insufficiency of food was a chronic problem in Fu-chou; and both the seeming absence of significant rice imports and the fact, acknowledged by many contemporary witnesses, that a good deal of arable land went uncultivated in Fu-chou, would argue against a condition of permanent and severe pressure by population on food resources. One likely solution is to suppose, again, that local production of wheat, despite Huang Chen's claims, adequately supplied the difference. It is also possible, of course, that my estimate of rice production falls well below the reality, either because average yields exceeded one *shih* per mou or because figures for cultivated land are depressed by poor maintenance of registers and consequent underregistration. Yet even in the latter case, one would expect significant underregistration of population as well, which would restore the problem. In the present state of the evidence no certain solution is possible; but there is reason to think that Huang Chen is exaggerating; that rice production was greater than estimated; or both.

Tea

According to the *Sung hui-yao*, under the tea monopoly in the early years of Southern Sung Fu-chou's production quota was 21,726 catties per year: something over ten tons. The source for this figure is the *Chung-hsing hui-yao*, compiled in the 1130s (*SHY: shih-huo* 29/2). A much reduced quota — 3,600 catties — is cited from the *Ch'ien-tao hui-yao*, compiled around 1165 (*SHY: shih-huo* 29/4a); but this precipitous decline may reflect the vagaries of the monopoly system more than the real production in Fu-chou. Even the higher figure would make Fu-chou, from the point of view of the monopoly, only a minor producer of tea within its own circuit: Hung-chou to the northwest had a quota nearly a hundred times, Jao-chou to the north five times as high.

Without these official figures we would know virtually nothing of Fu-chou tea production. I have found only one reference in the wealth of private sources for Fu-chou. In Lu Chiu-yüan's funerary inscription for Ko Keng of Chin-ch'i County we read: 'There are many farming families who in their vegetable gardens plant tea and then use the extra to trade for what they lack. The cruel and crafty harass them with the monopoly prohibitions; as simple, ignorant people are not aware of the distinction [*pu chih so-pien*], one can obtain bribes in this way.' (Lu Chiu-yüan, 28/7a–11a.) To judge from this, small-scale production of tea outside the framework of the monopoly was common in Fu-chou.

Textiles

An anecdote in Hung Mai's *I-chien chih* tells of a merchant based in Lin-ch'uan County during Southern Sung who had organized something approaching a putting-out system for the production of some variety of hempen or linen cloth (*pu*). He loaned out capital (in money, not materials) each year to 'debtor households' in Ch'ung-jen, Lo-an, and Chin-ch'i Counties, as well as in Yung-feng County in Chi-chou to the west. In each place he had brokers who handled the lending of the money and the collecting of the product: every summer he went out personally from his base in the prefectural city to collect the cloth from each broker. One season's accumulation by a single broker amounted to several thousand rolls of cloth (Hung Mai, *chih-kuei* 5/1a–b).

Hung Mai does not tell us what fibre was used in the production of this cloth. Already in the T'ang dynasty, cloth produced from the kudzu vine (*ko-pu* or simply *ko*) had been established as a Fu-chou tribute good, to be sent up to the throne yearly. (See for example Tu Yu, 6/36.) This requirement was continued under the Sung (*SS* 88/10a; Yüeh Shih, 110/3b). The fragmentary surviving late Sung gazetteer of Fu-chou contains the story of a farmer who discovered a strange stone in his field and took it to a stream to wash it. A passing Taoist advised him not to wipe it off with his straw sandals, but to use 'kudzu cloth' instead (*YLTT* 10950/19a). The story itself cannot be taken at face value (the stone turns out to be transparent, with an image of the goddess Kuan-yin inside); but it does suggest that kudzu cloth was in common use in Fu-chou.

Another important textile crop, it seems, was ramie. Since James Polachek first made me aware of the importance of ramie culture in the Fu-chou region in the Ch'ing dynasty, I have looked for evidence of its cultivation or use locally during Sung. Evidence, though sparse, does survive. The existence of a Ramie Dam in Lin-ch'uan County and a White Ramie Dam in Chin-ch'i County as of about 1260 is suggestive (*YLTT* 2754/10b, column 6, and 14b, column 16). Ramie cloth was among the tribute goods of two of Fu-chou's immediate neighbors (Kan-chou to the south, Chi-chou to the west: see *SS* 88/9b—10a), but not of Fu-chou itself; but the Sung court seems to have been extremely conservative in its tribute requirements, often following T'ang precedent without change. (Compare the goods listed in *SS* 88/9b—10a with those in Tu Yu, 6/36.) Thus the absence of a crop from the tribute list in Sung is probably of little significance. More decisive evidence comes from the Yüan dynasty. An inscription made on a temple brick by Ch'ung-jen County construction workers in 1293 tells us that as of that date the autumn rice tax, for middle-grade households, was to be converted into and paid in equivalent quantities of ramie cloth. There is no evidence of a similar conversion practise in Sung; but it is inconceivable that ramie could have been so important fiscally only fourteen years after the Yüan conquest if it had not already been a well-established local product in late Southern Sung. (See Ch'ien Po-ch'üan, 'Ch'ung-jen Hsien T'ai-ho-ssu ta ch'uan-ming.') Also in Yüan, a gazetteer for Nan-feng County listed ramie cloth as one of three famous local products (quoted in Ch'ien Po-ch'üan). Again the crop's reputation in Yüan implies a long preceding period in which ti had become established locally.

Mining

Silver. The smelting of locally mined silver ore at Chin-ch'i County under Southern T'ang and in early Sung is mentioned in Yüeh Shih, 110/8a.

Gold. The official history of Sung lists Fu-chou as one of five prefectures in the empire with government offices for the mining of gold on its territory (*SS* 185/6b). No date is given; nor do we learn just where the gold is produced. Under Yüan it is recorded that around 1286 one hundred ounces of panned (not mined) gold were the annual production quota of Lo-an County.

Copper. The *T'ai-p'ing huan-yü chi* tells us that O-feng Mountain in Lin-ch'uan County was a source of mined copper (Yueh Shih, 110/3a).

Iron. According to the *Sung hui-yao*, the Tung-shan iron-mining station in Lin-ch'uan County was responsible each year for producing 117,000 catties of iron: this is something over fifty tons. As this was to be shipped to neighboring Hsin-chou for smelting, it is presumably ore that is referred to here (*SHY: shih-huo* 33/22a).

Porcelain

Recent excavations have shown that the Pai-hu Kiln in Lin-ch'uan County, a site of ceramic manufacture at least since the Sui dynasty, during Sung produced two types of greenish-glazed white porcelain bowls of moderate quality (Ch'en Po-ch'üan, 'Chiang-hsi Lin-ch'uan Nan-feng yao-chih tiao-ch'a'). The kiln is mentioned in contemporary sources (Huang Chen,

78/30a–32a). Apart from this, the names of a number of Fu-chou dams (as of about 1260) refer to kilns apparently located in the vicinity. Thus one finds a Tile-kiln Dam (*wa-yao pei*) in Chin-ch'i County; a Kiln-front Dam (*yao-ch'ien pei*) in the same county; and another Kiln-front Dam in Lin-ch'uan County (*YLTT* 2754/14a, column 4; 14b, column 8; and 11a, column 3 respectively). Nothing is recorded of the organization of any of these kilns; but Lu Chiu-yüan tells us that in Chin-ch'i most 'pottery households' were farming families who took the work in agricultural off-season (Lu Chiu-yüan 10/4a–5a). Elsewhere, Hung Mai tells the story of a murder committed at a kiln (probably in Lin-ch'uan County) by a man who 'made his living by the firing of porcelain' (Hung Mai, *san-jen* 1/3a–b). By the Yüan dynasty, officials responsible for porcelain production at the kilns in the major national porcelain production center, Ching-te Chen in Jao-chou, Fu-chou's northern neighbor, complained that the market for Ching-te Chen wares was being severely reduced by competition from kilns in Fu-chou. On this see Chiang Ch'i's 'Appendix on the Ceramic Industry' of 1322, in the translation by S.W. Bushell in *Oriental Ceramic Art*, pp. 178–83.

Shipbuilding

In early Southern Sung an official navy yard in Fu-chou, presumably located at or near the prefectural city, was charged with the construction of warships of twenty and twenty-six paddlewheels. The yard seems to have been abolished at the urging of the prefectural administrator Wang Tsao, from whose memorial we learn of its existence (Wang Tsao, 1/6b–7a). The importance of private ship- and boatbuilding in Fu-chou is reflected in the fact that, as we have seen, a large number of diviners in the prefecture supported themselves mainly by predicting the future of boats from the details of their construction (Hung Mai, *ting* 8/2a–b).

Papermaking

The *Fang-yü sheng-lan*, a national guide to sights and historic landmarks of the prefectures of the empire, lists as a famous local product of Fu-chou 'Ch'ing-chiang paper,' a sort of notepaper produced at Ch'ing-chiang Crossing in Chin-ch'i County (Chu Mu, *Fang-yü sheng-lan* 21/2a and 3b).

Bronzemaking

On official prohibitions of bronzemaking in Sung, motivated by the state's need for copper in its coinage and by concern over the size of the national currency, see the discussion in Jerome Ch'en, 'Sung Bronzes: An Economic Analysis.' In a memorial on just this subject in 1248, the Investigating Censor Ch'en Ch'iu-lu complained that 'bronze craftsmen especially abound in Lung-hsing, Lin-ch'uan, and Kuei-lin' (*SS* 180/14b). Here Lin-ch'uan is Fu-chou (known sometimes under its old commandery name of Lin-ch'uan) and Lung-hsing is Hung-chou, Fu-chou's northern neighbor.

NOTES

Introduction

1. See Mark Elvin, *The Pattern of the Chinese Past*, pp. 204–9; Robert Hartwell, 'Demographic, Political, and Social Transformations of China, 750–1550,' pp. 383–94; Hans Bielenstein, 'The Census of China during the Period AD 2–742'; Katō Shigeshi, *Shina keizaishi kōshō*, v. ii, pp. 330–7; Aoyama Sadao, 'Zui-Tō-Sō sandai ni okeru kosu no chiikiteki kōsatsu.'
2. Denis Twitchett, *Financial Administration under the T'ang Dynasty*, pp. 84–96.
3. See Ping-ti Ho, 'Early-Ripening Rice in Chinese History,' and Katō Shigeshi, *Shina keizaishi kōshō*, v. ii. pp. 659–75.
4. Katō Shigeshi, 'On the Hang or the Associations of Merchants in China'; Denis Twitchett, 'Merchant, Trade, and Government in Late T'ang.'
5. Katō Shigeshi, *Tō-Sō-jidai ni okeru kingin no kenkyū*; Robert Harwell, 'The Evolution of the Early Northern Sung Monetary System'; Ch'üan Han-sheng, 'Sung-mo ti t'ung-Huo p'eng-ch'ang chi ch'i tui-yü wu-chia ti ying-hsiang'; Sogabe Shizuo, 'Nan-Sō no shihei,' in *Sōdai zaisei shi*, pp. 268–332.
6. Shiba Yoshinobu, *Commerce and Society in Sung China*, pp. 126–64.
7. G.W. Skinner, *The City in Late Imperial China*, p. 28.
8. Robert Hartwell, 'A Cycle of Economic Change in Imperial China: Coal and Iron in Northeast China, 750–1350'; and 'Markets, Technology, and the Structure of Enterprise in the Development of the Eleventh-Century Chinese Iron and Steel Industry.'
9. Margaret Medley, *The Chinese Potter: A Practical History of Chinese Ceramics*, pp. 103–91.
10. Jung-pang Lo, 'Maritime Commerce and its Relation to the Sung Navy.' On the porcelain trade see also Gakuji Hasebe, *Sekai tōshi zenshū*, v. xii: *Sō*, pp. 266–96.
11. Joseph Needham, 'The Chinese Contribution to the Development of the Mariner's Compass'; L. Carrington Goodrich and Feng Chia-sheng, 'The Early Development of Firearms in China'; L.C. Goodrich, 'The Development of Printing in China and its Effects on the Renaissance under the Sung Dynasty.'
12. Chu Chuan-yu, 'A History of Chinese Journalism in the Sung Dynasty.'
13. See for instance Huang Chen's notice on a heterodox sect cited in Chapter 7, p.187.
14. For Naitō's views see for instance his 'Gaikakuteki Tō-Sō-jidai kan.'
15. On 'newly risen bureaucrats' see, among others, Sudō Yoshiyuki, 'Sōdai kanryōsei to daitochishoyū'; on the flourishing and the decline of the great clans see in particular Patricia Ebrey, *The Aristocratic Families of Early Imperial China*; David Johnson, *The Medieval Chinese Oligarchy* and 'The Last Years of a Great Clan: the Li Family of Chao Chün in Late T'ang and Early Sung'; Denis Twitchett, 'The Composition of the T'ang Ruling Class: New Evidence from Tunhuang'; Moriya Mitsuo, *Rikuchō monbatsu no ichi kenkyū*.
16. E.G. Pulleyblank, *The Background of the Rebellion of An Lu-shan*, pp. 47–60 and passim.; Ch'en Yin-k'o, *T'ang-tai cheng-chih shih shu-lun kao*, pp. 1–93.

17. Sudō, 'Sōdai kanryōsei,' p. 5 and pp. 33–76.
18. E.A. Kracke, 'Family versus Merit in Chinese Civil Service Examinations under the Empire'; Sudō, 'Sōdai kanryōsei,' pp. 56–64.
19. An important contribution is Harriet Zurndorfer's article, 'The Hsin-an Ta-tsu Chih and the Development of Chinese Gentry Society, 800–1600.' Two recent dissertations deal with the elite of T'ang and/or Sung in a local context: Hugh Clark, 'Consolidation on the South China Frontier: The Development of Ch'üan-chou, 699–1126,' Diss. University of Pennsylvania, 1981; and Richard Davis, 'The Shih Lineage at the Southern Sung Court,' Diss. Princeton University, 1980. Of these three scholars, Clark deals largely with different issues from those treated here; Zurndorfer approaches the Sung elite in ways that to a considerable degree parallel the approach I take here; and Davis, who treats status as in large part reducible to official standing, differs sharply in this respect from either Zurndorfer or myself. Four other recent dissertations do not center on the nature of the elite *per se* but are locally focused and contribute at least indirectly to our understanding of the elite: J.P. McDermott, 'Land Tenure and Rural Control in the Liang-che Region during the Southern Sung,' Diss. Cambridge University, 1978; John Stuermer, 'Polder Construction and the Pattern of Landownership in the T'ai-hu Basin during the Southern Sung Dynasty,' Diss. University of Pennsylvania, 1980; Mira Ann Mihelich, 'Polders and the Politics of Land Rec-lamation during the Northern Sung Dynasty 960–1126,' Diss. Cornell University, 1979; and Linda Ann Walton-Vargö, 'Education, Social Change, and Neo-Confucianism in Sung–Yüan China: Academies and the Local Elite in Ming Prefecture (Ningpo)', Diss. University of Pennsylvania, 1978. In Japan, important work on the elite in a local context has been done by Ihara Hiroshi, who has studied patterns of marriage and residence in two southeastern prefectures and in Szechwan (see Chapter 3, n. 30); Otagi Hajime has investigated a prominent Ma family of North China in his 'Godai Sōsho no shinkō kanryō – Rinshi no Bashi o chūshin to shite'; Morita Kenhi has studied a listing of 'famous lineages' of Sung dynasty Szechwan in '*Seido Shizokufu* shōkō.'
20. Hartwell, 'Demographic, Political, and Social Transformations,' pp. 405–25.
21. Wm. Theodore de Bary, 'A Reappraisal of Neo-Confucianism,' pp. 100–6.
22. Shuen-fu Lin, *The Transformation of the Chinese Lyrical Tradition: Chiang K'uei and Southern Sung Tz'u Poetry*, pp. 16–48.
23. *TCLC* 7/3a–5a.
24. *TCLC* 5/5a–7a.
25. I must stress here that while the rough similarity of the families entering into a marriage is a conclusion drawn from empirical cases, the inclusion of affines of local elite members within the local elite is, in this study, a matter of *definition*. Thus, for example, my research cannot be cited as having shown that 'local elite members were wholly endogamous'; rather this is the consequence of part of my working definition of the elite. That the definition itself is not without empirical grounding seems to me clear; but because it is a definition it can have no evidentiary value of its own.
26. Philip A. Kuhn, *Rebellion and its Enemies in Late Imperial China*, p. 4.
27. Wang Hsiang-chih, *Yü-ti chi-sheng* 29/3a–b; Chu Mu, *Fang-yü sheng-lan* 21/1b.
28. Tseng Kung, *Yüan-feng lei-kao* 18/4a–5b.
29. Hsieh I, *Ch'i-t'ang chi* 7/2b.
30. Chou Pi-ta, *Wen-chung chi*; *TCLC* 52/1a–b.
31. *KHFC* 66/1a; *TCLC* 5/5a–7a.
32. The river's source lay in a part of Nan-feng County that was split off to create Kuang-ch'ang County in 1138 (see below); thus sources from before that date locate it in Nan-feng, while those dating from Southern Sung or later place it in

Kuang-ch'ang. Up until the transfer of Nan-feng County in 991 (see below), the river's source and upper course lay in Fu-chou proper; after 991 they lay, along with the part of the middle course that passed through Nan-ch'eng County, in the neighboring prefecture of Chien-ch'ang Chün.

33. From its source until shortly after is re-entry into Fu-chou, the river was known as the Yü; north of its confluence with a smaller tributary stream at a place called Shih-men its name became Ju. See *TCLC* 5/5a–7a. Later sources give the name Ju to this tributary, also called the Ch'ing-chiang River, and thus explain the change of name of the larger river at this confluence; but no similar account appears in any discoverable Sung source. See *TCCC* 2/7a–b. Comparison of Sung sources describing the flow of Fu-chou rivers with the descriptions in late Ch'ing gazetteers and with modern topographic maps reveals no real disagreement. While the Sung accounts tend to be less detailed and exist for only a few of the prefecture's rivers, it would still appear that there was little major change in the larger streams between Sung and Ch'ing or Republican times. This is not entirely surprising, since except in the northernmost parts of the prefecture the terrain tended to be quite hilly: it is on flat floodplains that rivers are most likely to shift or vary their courses. Thus while using Sung sources where possible, I have made fairly confident use of more modern sources as well. For Sung the major sources are: Yüeh Shih, *T'ai-p'ing huan-yü chi* 110/4a–8a; Wang Hsiang-chih, *Yü-ti chi-sheng* 29/3b–6b; an account of the Lin and Ju Rivers in a 1251 inscriptional record for the reconstruction of the Ch'ien-chin Dam next to the prefectural city, in *TCLC* 5/5a–7a; an exhaustive description, exactly agreeing with modern topographic maps, of the Ch'ung-jen River in a *c*.1208 inscriptional record for the reconstruction of the Pao-t'ang Dike, in *TCCJ* 9f/22a–24b; a reference to the course of the Niu-t'ien River (also called the Ao-ch'i) in a 1271 public notice by the prefect of Fu-chou, in Huang Chen, *Huang-shih jih-ch'ao* 78/16b–19b.

34. Hung Mai, *I-chien chih*, *ting* 8/2a–b.

35. On the administrative geography of Fu-chou through 1005 see *TCLC* 1b/1b–2a; *TCCC* 1/1b–2a; *KHFC* 2a/4a; *TCIH* 3/3b; *KHTH* 1/16a; Yüeh Shih, *T'ai-p'ing huan-yü chi* 110/3a–8a; Wang Hsiang-chih, 29/1a–2b; *YLTT* 10949/9a–11a; Liu Hsü et al., *Chiu T'ang shu* 40/18b; Ou-yang Hsiu et al., *Hsin T'ang shu* 41/10a.

36. The sources on the creation of Lo-an County are a thicket of problems. The *Sung shih* tells us: 'Established in Shao-hsing 19 [1149]. They cut off four cantons from Ch'ung-jen and Chi-shui to attach to it. In the twenty-fourth year [1154] they returned Yün-kai Canton to Yung-feng' (*SS* 88/18a). The reference to Chi-chou's Chi-shui County here as a source of land for Lo-an is simply a mistake for Yung-feng County, as the concluding sentence would suggest; the mistake had earlier appeared in the most important chronicle of early Southern Sung (Li Hsin-ch'uan, *Chien-yen i-lai hsi-nien yao-lu* 159/1b, placed – apparently mistakenly – under the *first* month of 1149), and in the *Sung hui-yao*, which corrects itself midstream and gives a far more circumstantial account:

> In the twelfth month of Shao-hsing 19 [1149], a decree established Lo-an County at a place under Fu-chou's jurisdiction called Chan-hsü. They cut off three cantons, T'ien-shan, Lo-an, and Chung-i, from Ch'ung-jen County and one canton, Yün-kai, from Chi-shui County in Chi-chou, and attached them to it. They further cut off one canton, Ch'ien-ying, from Chi-shui County in Chi-chou and transferred it to Yung-feng County, and cut off two cantons, Hui-an and Ying-hsiu, from Lin-ch'uan County and transferred them to Ch'ung-jen County. This was in response to the request of the various offices of this circuit.

> In the eleventh month of Shao-hsing 24 [1154], it was decreed that Yün-kai canton in Lo-an County in Fu-chou revert to the jurisdiction of Yung-feng County in Chi-chou, and that Yung-feng County's Ch'ien-ying canton be once again under Chi-shui County in Chi-chou. *Before this, in 1149, they had established Lo-an Hsien and taken one canton, Yün-kai, from Yung-feng to be attached to Lo-an, and one canton, Ch'ien-ying, from Chi-chou to be attached to Yung-feng.* Coming to this time [i.e., 1154 as above], the taxpaying house-holders of Yün-kai canton, Chang Ta and others, had memorialized arguing that this canton was not served by water transport and that the carrying route was very long, so that it was hard to bring in [taxes]. Therefore, there was this decree.' (*SHY, fang-yü* 6, p. 27: emphasis mine.)

Here the second article, dealing with the 1154 decree, makes clear the error in the first, where the relevance and purpose of the transfer of Ch'ien-ying canton from Chi-shui to Yung-feng are completely obscure. Once again, however, we are told that Yün-kai reverted to Yung-feng County in 1154. Yet all other Sung and later sources agree in naming Yün-kai canton as one of four in Lo-an County. Thus for instance the late Sung and early Yüan Fu-chou man Wu Ch'eng, in a preface to the genealogy of a Tung family (see Appendix I, no. 59) resident in Yün-kai canton, remarked:

> In the middle years of Shao-hsing [1131–62] Fu-chou established the additional county Lo-an, and only then cut off Yün-kai canton from Chi-chou and attached it to Fu-chou. Since that time the Tung family have been people of Fu-chou. Today their connection to Fu-chou is long indeed [...]

(Wu Ch'eng, *Wen-kung chi* 18/10b–11b. Hereafter abbreviated as *WWC*.) Similarly the Yüan national gazetteer, the *Yüan i-t'ung chih*, lists Yün-kai as a canton of Lo-an; and the national *chin-shih* list for 1256 records the place of registration of on Tseng Hui-ti as Lo-an Country, Yün-kai canton (*Pao-yu ssu-nien teng-k'o lu* 11a). The solution is provided by two other sources. In 1160 the Lo-an sheriff Hsieh O recorded the erection of a stone tablet listing the names of Lo-an administrators up to that time. His account of the county's creation is as follows:

> In 1149 the Chiang-hsi circuit intendants [...] asked the court to cut off three cantons [of Ch'ung-jen County], Lo-an, Chung-i, and T'ien-shou, and further to cut off Yün-kai canton from Yung-feng [County] of Chi-chou, and separately establish a county called Lo-an [...] Before long, owing to suits by the people, they returned Yün-kai to Chi-chou. After its return, vigorous arguments went on for six years, and Lo-an obtained it once more (*TCLA* 10/21a–b).

Thus Yün-kai canton appears first to have been returned to Yung-feng, then to have been transferred again to Lo-an. This is supported by a late Ch'ing gazetteer for Yung-feng County, which records the return of the canton to Yung-feng in 1154 and its final cession to Lo-an in 1162 (*TCYF* ch. 2). Here the span of years is longer than in Hsieh O's record – indeed the record, done in 1160, could not have mentioned the retransfer of Yün-kai canton if the gazetteer were correct – but the basic outline is the same; it is even possible that the discrepancy over dates reflects a third return and retransfer of the canton. In any case its final incorporation into Lo-an County is clear.

37. *TCLA* 10/21a–b.
38. Huang Chen, 84/43b.
39. Huang Chen, 79/19a.
40. There is no direct evidence that the fiscal privileges of Lo-an County were shared by the areas of Chin-ch'i County that fed out of the Ju River system. It is

tantalizing, however, that the only other reference in the Fu-chou sources to ownership of land in one district by residents of another concerns a Wu family that lived in the prefectural seat in Lin-ch'uan County, but owned land in Chin-ch'i.

41. Population growth by itself, however, did not necessarily lead to a multiplication of administrative units. Skinner has argued that 'constraints of organizational scale' prevented the Chinese state, from Han through Ch'ing times, from increasing its administrative apparatus so as to match the expansion of population. The implication of Skinner's argument, as he himself points out, is that the smaller states of periods of disunion should have been more able than unified dynasties to extend their control into the countryside by increasing the number of administrative units at the local level. This is borne out by the administrative history of Fu-chou: the new prefecture of Chien-ch'ang Chün and the new county of I-huang were both created under the Southern T'ang kingdom that controlled only the P'o-yang basin and the region that is now southern Anhui province; and the establishment of Chin-ch'i as a county, nominally an act of the Sung state, in fact represented merely an administrative upgrading of a sub-county unit first cut off from Lin-ch'uan County under Southern T'ang. During Northern Sung, when China proper was more or less united, no truly new units were created in the Fu-chou region. Soon after the Chin conquest, however, the Southern Sung state, now in control only of the area south of the Huai River, established three new counties in or near Fu-chou: Lo-an County (see n. 36 above) and two new counties of Chien-ch'ang Chün, Kuang-ch'ang and Hsin-ch'eng. Cf. Skinner, *The City*, pp. 17–21.

42. Here I use figures from Tu Yu, *T'ung tien* 182/967–68; and from Wang Ts'un, *Yuan-feng chiu-yü chih* 6/9a–11a.

43. For Sung circuit totals for ca. 1077 and 1223 see Ma Tuan-lin, *Wen-hsien t'ung k'ao* 11/114–117. Complete or nearly complete figures for 1102 for most circuits can also be derived from the prefectual figures given in the *Sung shih* geographical monograph (*SS* ch. 85–90). These have been conveniently grouped by circuit by Fang Hao in his study of Sung population ('Sung-tai jen-k'ou k'ao-shih,' pp. 268–82).

44. This increase may well be slightly exaggerated through undercounting in the earlier years of T'ang, when state control was probably less than complete; but in view of the figures for Sui and earlier periods, when Fu-chou (or Lin-ch'uan commandery) was larger in area, the actual early T'ang figure cannot have been very much higher than the records show.

45. Fang Hao, pp. 268–82, tabulates the 1102 prefectural figures. These place Fu-chou in the correct relative position but appear to have shifted or exchanged figures for other prefectures: in particular, the figure given for Ch'ien-chou (placing it first in the circuit) almost surely belongs properly to Chi-chou, whose figure in turn seems to have been borrowed from the less populous Yüan-chou, next after it in the list. Compare the figures from two decades earlier given in Wang Ts'un, 6/9a–11a; these too place Fu-chou third among Chiang-hsi prefectures, fourth in the P'o-yang Lake basin. Note also that some of the 1102 figures, including the one for Fu-chou itself, seem to be carried over from earlier years: this emerges from comparisons with Wang Ts'un's numbers and with those in the Fu-chou gazetteers.

46. This is subject to some approximation owing to the considerations mentioned in note 45 above and to the fact that some prefectures are omitted from the 1102 list.

47. On population densities in Fu-chou see Appendix II: Population. For Illinois in 1970 see for example the *Information Please Almanac* for any year after 1970.

48. For urban population see Appendix II: Population.

49. Shiba, *Commerce and Society*, pp. 127–8.

50. On the extramural boroughs (*hsiang*) in Sung see for example *TCLC* 1b/4a. The borough lying east across the Ju River was called Kang-tung. In 1963 Chinese archaeologists excavated the tomb of a husband and wife who had lived from late Southern Sung through much of the Yüan dynasty. The couple's funerary inscriptions record their burial 'behind Hsin-chüeh Temple in Kang-tung Borough.' The tomb was discovered, according to the excavation report, '1.5 kilometers east of the Fu-chou city bridge.' See Ch'eng Ying-lin and P'eng Kua-fan, 'Chiang-hsi Fu-chou fa-hsien Yüan-tai ho-tsang-mu.'

51. The Ao-ch'i Bridge in Lo-an County, long built of wood and subject to repeated destruction by flood, was rebuilt in stone in 1235 and again in 1248. The bridge joined the district city, north of the Ao-ch'i River, to the river's south bank. Sung inscriptional records survive for both reconstructions: the first reports that the bridge connected the city with 'market precincts' south of the river; the second refers to the bridge as 'straddling the north and south markets.' In Ch'ung-jen County the Huang-chou Bridge, built of stone in the 1250s and again in 1270, played a similar role: an inscription for the second project refers to the 'north and south markets' that the bridge connected.

52. One vague indicator of growing local prosperity under T'ang may be the very large number of Buddhist temples that seems to have been built then. T'ang temples are known often to have functioned as the first clearers of new land for cultivation. For temples in T'ang see *TCIH* ch. 13; *TCLA* ch. 2; *TCCJ* ch. 2d; *TCLC* ch. 8; *TCCC* ch. 7. The Lo-an gazetteer, for instance, lists some twenty Buddhist temples built in T'ang, only three less than the number listed for Sung, though the attrition of sources must have been greater for the earlier period, and the population far lower. The other gazetteers draw similar pictures.

53. See for example the rather unsystematic treatment of rice production in Northern Sung by Sung Shee in *Sung-shih yen-chiu lun-ts'ung*, pp. 94–9; the much more satisfactory treatment by Ch'üan Han-sheng, 'Nan-Sung t'ao-mi ti sheng-ch'an yü yün-hsiao'; and Shiba Yoshinobu's recent discussion of official grain purchases in Northern and Southern Sung, which touches on the importance of Chiang-hsi circuit as a supplier of tax and Harmonious Purchase rice. (Shiba, 'Sōdai shiteki no enkaku.').

54. Thus the description by Hsieh K'o (1073–1116):

> Fu-chou is a wealthy prefecture in Chiang-hsi. Its fields are many and its soil is fertile, improved by the dams, ponds, and rivers that water it (Hsieh K'o, *Hsieh yu-p'an wen-chi* 8/6b–7b)

See also Tseng Kung's description quoted on p. 11 above. Both men were Fu-chou natives. Many other such passages could be cited, equally vague but confirming the contemporary image of the prefecture as one in which agriculture was highly successful.

55. On early and late-ripening rice in Fu-chou, see Appendix III: Economy.

56. On waterwheels in Fu-chou, see Appendix III: Economy.

57. On the quantity of rice produced in Fu-chou, see Appendix III: Economy.

58. Huang Chen, 78/47b–50a.

59. Hsieh K'o, 8/6b–7b.

60. See, among many references, Lu Chiu-yüan's letter to a Professor Ch'en arguing for the establishment of a privately run Normal Purchase granary in his neighborhood in Chin-ch'i County: '[. . .] the farming people are all poor; at the time of gathering of the grain many are no longer able to store it, but need urgently to sell it in order to provide for other expenses and liquidate debts. Should there be no one to purchase it, then the price must fall and the grain drain off into *the boats of rice-merchants* and the storehouses of the wealthy people' (Lu Chiu-yüan, *Hsiang-shan hsien-sheng ch'üan-chi*, 8/46–6a. Emphasis mine.)

61. See Chapter 6, pp. 157–61.
62. Huang Chen, 78/30a–32a.
63. There is not a single reference in any source to the import of rice into Fu-chou. The measures taken by local officials to shut the prefecture's borders to rice commerce during famine make sense only if Fu-chou's exports greatly exceed any imports.
64. See the materials on Huang Chen's efforts to persuade grain hoarders to sell during the famine of 1271 in Huang Chen, ch. 78; and cf. Chapter 6, pp. 157–61.
65. For wheat and barley in Fu-chou, see Appendix III: Economy.
66. For tea, kudzu, and ramie in Fu-chou, see Appendix III: Economy.
67. See Appendix III: Economy.
68. For mining in Fu-chou, see Appendix III: Economy.
69. For porcelain manufacture in Fu-chou, see Appendix III: Economy.
70. See for instance Su Pai, 'Nan-Sung ti tiao-pan yin-shua.'
71. For papermaking in Fu-chou, see Appendix III: Economy.
72. For shipbuilding, see Appendix III: Economy.
73. For bronzecasting, see Appendix III: Economy.
74. For population figures on *chu-hu* (property-holding households) and *k'o-hu* (households without any landed holdings in their place of registration) see *KHFC* 22/3a–b.
75. In exhorting the Fu-chou populace to cultivate wheat in 1271, Huang Chen evidently assumed that he was addressing himself mainly to tenants rather than to landlords or small independent farmers:

> In these times those who have fields do not cultivate; those who cultivate have no fields. You people toil and suffer all year, and the fields' owners sit and enjoy the benefits. But in cultivating wheat you need not pay rent: if you grow one *shih*, it is one *shih*; if you grow ten *shih*, it is ten *shih*. (Huang Chen, 78/48b.)

Elsewhere we are told that in the sixty-third, seventy-sixth, and seventy-eighth *tu* of Lin-ch'uan County at around the same time virtually all residents were tenants (*tien-hu*) of a Jao family that lived in the seventy-seventh *tu* (Huang, 78/19b–21b); and that in two *tu* served by a community granary in Chin-ch'i County in the 1190s 'the farming people rent either from "guest estates" [*k'o-chuang*] or from official estates; nor are more than a few of them lower-grade households with fields of their own' (Lu Chiu-yüan, 8/4b–6a). All these references seem to suggest high rates of tenancy in at least parts of Fu-chou.
76. *Ming-kung shu-p'an ch'ing-ming chi*, pp. 168–71. This case is neither dated nor explicitly identified as taking place in Fu-chou. However, the author of the judgement, Fan Ying-ling, is known to have been administrator of Ch'ung-jen County from 1219 to 1224, and to have attained some renown for the judgements he rendered there; other judgements of his in this collection can be dated or otherwise identified as coming from Ch'ung-jen. Further, this case involves as one party a member of a landowning family surnamed Teng and a piece of land (owned by the other party but presumably located in the vicinity) at a place called Nan-yüan. Now several Southern Sung Ch'ung-jen men of some scholarly reputation surnamed Teng are identified by gazetteers as resident in the county's twenty-fifth *tu* (e.g. Teng Chou, his son Teng Hu, and a Teng Ch'i: see *TCCJ* 7c/4b; *KHCJ* 1/47b, 4/60a, 63a; *KHFC* 59/4b–5a); and an inscriptional record for the casting of a bell in 1230 at a temple in the same *tu* lists three other men surnamed Teng as contributors (*TCCJ* 9g/2b–3b). The Ch'ung-jen gazetteer under the same twenty-fifth *tu* lists a place called Nan-yüan (*TCCJ* 1b/20a). Thus the occurrence of the surname Teng and the placename Nan-yüan in the

judgement by Fan Ying-ling strongly supports the case's location in Ch'ung-jen. In my remarks on the case I rely heavily on the discussion by Joseph McDermott in his recent dissertation on land tenure (Joseph McDermott, 'Land Tenure and Rural Control', pp. 153–61.

77. For Sudō's views on Sung tenancy, see especially the studies brought together in his *Chūgoku tochi seido kenkyū*; for Elvin's picture of Sung manorialism, which derives largely from Sudō, see *The Pattern of the Chinese Past*, pp. 69–83.

78. The stress McDermott places on the distinction between forms of tenancy which placed the parties in a 'master–servant' relationship (*chu-p'u chih fen*) and those which established only a 'landlord–tenant' relation (*chu-tien chih fen*) (McDermott, pp. 140–4 and ff.), is echoed independently in a recent article by Takahashi Yoshirō (Takahashi, 'Sōdai tenko no mibun mondai'). Yanagida Setsuko raised the study of Sung tenancy to a new level by accepting, and attempting to explain, its diversity. She thus attempted to unify a field of study split by the earlier work of Sudō Yoshiyuki and Miyazaki Ichisada, whose attempts to advance opposite single forms of tenancy as 'typical' or predominant were largely inspired by broader questions of periodization. See Yanagida Setsuko, 'Sōdai tochi shoyūsei ni mirareru futatsu no katachi.' The work of McDermott and Takahashi may be seen as further advancing the description and analysis of Sung tenancy as a phenomenon of systematic diversity.

79. Huang Chen, 78/52a–b. On the rent-free character of wheat crops see also n. 75 above. Peter Golas, in his recent survey of research on the Sung countryside, mentions landlords' failure to collect rent from a second crop on double-cropped land as a common Sung phenomenon. See Peter Golas, 'Rural China in the Sung.'

80. See, respectively, Hung Mai, *ting* 15/3b, *san-jen* 1/5a, *san-jen* 1/3a–b, *san-jen* 4/4b; Huang Chen, 78/36a–40b; Hung Mai, *chih-ching* 2/1a, *ting* 20/1a–b, *ting* 8/3a, *san-jen* 4/4a–b, *ting* 8/2a–b, *ting* 20/4a–5a.

81. See for instance Tseng Kung's remarks on p. 11.

82. *TCLC* 13/5b–7a; *TCCC* 35/1a–2a.

83. See Chapter 6, pp. 157–61.

84. See Chapter 5, pp. 139 ff.

85. In Southern Sung the full term was intendant of Ever-Normal (Granaries) and Tea and Salt Matters. The author of the national geographic manual the *Yü-ti chisheng*, writing in about 1221, reported that the intendant's office, located in Fu-chou's prefectural city, could not tell him in what year it had been established there (Wang Hsiang-chih, 29/3a). But a surviving fragment of a Sung gazetteer of the 1260s notes that the intendancy was first sited in Hung-chou, moved to Yüan-chou in 1127, then to Fu-chou in 1134 (*YLTT* 10950/6b). The Ch'ing gazetteer for Fu-chou, in its lists of men holding office there, records the names of intendants from 1135 on (*KHFC* 35/15a–16a).

86. See for instance Winston W. Lo, 'Circuits and Circuit Intendants in the Territorial Administration of Sung China.'

87. See for example Yüeh Shih, *T'ai-p'ing huan-yü chi* 110/3a. The sections on 'personages' (*jen-wu*) for each prefecture in this work are actually lists of surnames culled from a T'ang great clan list. For Fu-chou the annotation under this heading reads simply 'none'. On this list see David Johnson, *The Medieval Chinese Oligarchy*, pp. 67–8, 70, 73–88, 228–31.

88. This is Tseng Chih-yao of Nen-feng Hsien. See Wang An-shih, *Lin-ch'uan chi* 92/1a.

89. This was Yüeh Shih: see Chapter 3, n. 14.

90. These totals are calculated from the lists of degreeholders in the gazetteers; as these very occasionally contradict each other, omit men whose degrees are documented elsewhere, or include cases that other sources render more doubtful, a certain exercise of judgement has been required in arriving at a complete list: the

totals accepted could vary slightly – but only slightly – depending on one's criteria for the exclusion or inclusion of doubtful cases.

91. I am indebted to John Chaffee, who at an early stage of my research kindly shared with me his figures on the production of *chin-shih* by Chiang-hsi prefectures other than Fu-chou, the fruit of painstaking research of his own: these are the figures I use here. They have since appeared, along with corresponding figures for all other Sung prefectures, in his very important dissertation on Sung examinations and education. (John Chaffee, 'Education and Examinations in Sung Society', pp. 382–91.)

92. In Northern Sung it is harder to assess Fu-chou's performance, since the data are highly imperfect for many prefectures, especially in North China. See Chaffee, pp. 353–56. For Southern Sung see Chaffee, pp. 382–91.

93. This relation, however, needs a second look. I have remarked on the leading degreeholding position of the territory comprising Fu-chou, Chi-chou, and Chien-ch'ang Chün. These three produced well over half the *chin-shih* from the eleven prefectures of Chiang-hsi (56.5 per cent, to be precise; see Chaffee, p. 383). All three were among the circuit's most populous prefectures. But the circuit capital to the north, Hung-chou, although clearly the commercial as well as the political and military center of the circuit, and although far more populous than either Fu-chou or Chien-ch'ang Chün, produced considerably fewer *chin-shih*. A prefecture's success in the examinations, apparently, need not be a direct function either of its population or of its political and economic centrality. The patterns of regional or local success in the exams, and the factors that explain them, still await a full exploration. Chaffee, however, has made an important beginning by calling attention to the failure of national economic centers such as Ch'üan-chou and even Lin-an Fu to attain rates of examination success even nearly comparable to those of neighboring prefectures of somewhat lesser economic importance. Chaffee suggests that in the commercial centers of the empire specialized careers in trade may have drawn off far more of the potential degreeholding population than elsewhere. It is notable, on examining Chaffee's degreeholding totals for each prefecture, that in only two physiographic regions was the leading economic center also clearly the leader in degree production: in most regions it was clearly not.

94. The full list, in chronological order, is as follows:

1. Yen Shu of Lin-ch'uan County, chief councillor under Jen-tsung: cf. Ou-yang Hsiu, *Ou-yang wen-chung kung chi* 22/7b–12a.

2. Wang An-shih of Lin-ch'uan County, chief councillor under Shen-tsung cf. *SS* 327/1a–6b.

3. Wang An-li, An-shih's brother, assisting councillor under Shen-tsung: cf. *SS* 327/8a–10a.

4. Tseng Pu of Nan-feng County, chief councillor under Hui-tsung: cf. *SS* 471/10a–12a.

5. Wu Chü-hou of Lin-ch'uan County, assisting councillor under Hui-tsung: cf. Ko Sheng-chung, *Tan-yang chi* 12/4b–7b. Note: Wu is frequently identified as a man of Hung-chou, but (as the source above makes clear) was himself the first of his family to move to Hung-chou from Lin-ch'uan, which had been the family home for generations.

6. Tung Te-yüan of Lo-an County, assisting councillor under Kao-tsung: cf. *Shao-hsing shih-pa nien t'ung-nien hsiao-lu* 12a, and Chou Pi-ta, 75/11b–12. Tung was a resident of Yung-feng County, Chi-chou, at the time of his *chin-shih* degree in 1148; but the next year the canton that included his place of registration became part of the new district of Lo-an County in Fu-chou.

7. Lo Tien of Ch'ung-jen County, assisting councillor under Ning-tsung: cf. Yüan Hsieh, *Chieh-chai chi* 12/1a–35a.

8. Ch'en Tsung-li of Nan-feng County, assisting councillor under Tu-tsung: cf. *SS* 421/6a–8a.

95. These were Hsieh I, Hsieh K'o, Wang Ko (a *chin-shih* in 1097), and Jao Chieh (who became the Buddhist monk Ju-pi), all of Lin-ch'uan County. See for example Liu K'o-chuang, *Hou-ts'un hsien-sheng ta-ch'üan chi* 95/10b.

96. See for instance the cases of Ho Shih and his brother Ho T'ien-sheng of Lo-an County (Ho Chung, *Chih-fei-t'ang kao*, end matter, 19a–21a; Wan Ssu-t'ung. *Sung-chi chung-i lu* 10/13a.)

97. Skinner, *The City*, pp. 3–31, especially pp. 9–17. For Skinner, studying the Ch'ing dynasty, the P'o-yang basin is not in itself a separate macroregion, but rather part – indeed the less developed part – of a larger 'Middle Yangtse' macroregion that also encompasses the Tung-t'ing Lake and Han River basins to the west as well as the segment of the Yangtse valley that connects the three. But Skinner himself notes that this macroregion had evolved through a process of 'integration of the essentially autonomous economies that developed in the sharply defined subregions' and dates this integration to the Ch'ing. In Sung the Tung-t'ing Lake and Han River regions were, in comparison to the P'o-yang basin, on the whole undeveloped or newly developing areas. The circuit capitals and major population centers of Ching-hu-pei and Ching-hu-nan circuits (roughly equivalent to modern Hupei and Hunan provinces), for instance, had prefectural population densities in the 1070s of about 59 and 41 per square kilometer respectively. The former, the highest among prefectures of the Tung-t'ing and Han River regions in Sung, would have ranked only seventh, the latter only tenth, among the thirteen prefectures of the P'o-yang basin. Similarly E-chou, the ancestor of modern Wuhan, had a prefectural population density of about 58 – high enough to signal the beginnings of its emergence as a major population center lying between the two lake regions, but not impressive by the standards of the P'o-yang basin. On the basis of these and other population density figures it is clear that the more westerly areas of Skinner's Middle Yangtse macroregion were in Sung lagging well behind those to the east. One might then argue simply that the macroregion's core had shifted from east to west in later periods, and its periphery from west to east. In fact, however, there is little Sung evidence of strong integrative connections among the lake regions, the Han basin, and the middle Yangtse valley. I thus follow John Chaffee in treating the P'o-yang basin by itself as a single macroregion in Sung.

98. The estimated increase in density is less than the sevenfold increase in household numbers because the fairly conservative estimate used here for the ratio of individuals to households in Sung is far less than the recorded ratio in the T'ang. If the estimated ratio for Sung is too low, then the increase in density will have been correspondingly greater.

99. Ch'ien-chou proper had lost territory from T'ang to Sung with the founding of Nan-an Chün on part of its land. My Sung figure for 'Ch'ien-chou' thus includes the population and land area of Nan-an Chün.

100. Skinner, *The City*, p. 288. Unfortunately the rarity of *city* population data for Sung makes it impossible to investigate this process more closely.

101. In fact, it *was* the highest; but this was to some extent a function of Fu-chou's relatively small size and of the vagaries of prefectural boundary lines. Hung-chou, for example, where for a number of reasons one would expect to find the highest densities in the region, in fact had an average density in the 1070s of only about 57; but this seems chiefly to reflect the inclusion within its territory of a great deal of mountainous, sparsely populated land in the northwestern reaches of the P'o-yang region, particularly in the two counties of Wu-ning and Fen-ning. Figures for counties rather than for prefectures would yield a more precise picture and

probably move Fu-chou somewhat down from the top. The metropolitan country (Nan-ch'ang) of Hung-chou, for example, had a density of 113 per square kilometer in the mid-twelfth century, and this must have been higher in the 1070s, since the population of the prefecture as a whole is said to have dropped sharply during the wars of early Southern Sung. It is unlikely, in comparison, that the density of Fu-chou's metropolitan (and most densely populated) county, Lin-ch'uan, was much over 100 in the 1070s. This density would require a county population of about 68 500 households. The *rural* households of Lin-ch'uan at the time are known to have numbered about 54 500: see Table I. The difference of 14 000 households will then have been urban dwellers: but this is over two-thirds of the urban population of all four Fu-chou counties at the same time. A proportion much higher than this seems implausible.

102. Chi-chou in particular, in Southern Sung at least, may have contained the most densely populated areas of the entire circuit. As with Hung-chou, its average density is depressed by the sparsely populated, clearly peripheral counties of its mountainous southern and western reaches. When using prefectural averages for population density it is important to bear in mind the wide range of conditions that might exist within one prefecture. In Fu-chou itself, the southern counties, Ch'ung-jen and I-huang, to judge by their rural figures (see Table I), had overall densities not very much above the average for the circuit in the 1070s. It is only the lack of any figures for most counties in Sung that forces one to use prefectural totals in their place. Population densities for T'ang and Sung prefectures are calculated from Tu Yu, ch. 182, and Wang Ts'un, ch. 6, using land area figures reconstructed from the Republican figures in Kuan Wei-lan, *Chung-hua min-kuo hsing-cheng ch'ü-hua t'u-ti jen-k'ou tsung-chi piao*, pp. 18–21. I have also calculated county figures where possible, using Ch'ing gazetteers for the respective Chiang-hsi prefecture or county; but these are so few that I have only mentioned them occasionally.

103. See Johnson, *The Medieval Chinese Oligarchy*, p. 218, nos. 32 and 33; p. 220, no. Be-1; p. 227, nos. 82, 83, and 84; p. 231, nos. 64 and 65.

104. Chaffee, pp. 318 and 383.

Chapter 1

1. On this procedure (in considerably more detail) see *SHY*, *hsüan-chü* 16/8b–9a. For more on the family guarantee certificate, see below. On the Sung examination system in general see Chaffee; also Araki Toshikazu, *Sōdai kakyo seido kenkyū*.

2. In Fu-chou for the first half of Sung this was simply a large Buddhist temple in the prefectural city. In 1163 a prefect built a new hall to be used only for the examinations.

3. The quota for Fu-chou was fixed at thirty-nine in 1150; before that the number is not clear. See for example *KHIH* 5/29a.

4. See Chaffee, pp. 34–42.

5. *TCIH* 45b/39a. See the fuller discussion in Chapter 7.

6. Lu Chiu-yüan, 36/7b–8a.

7. Hung Mai, *chih-i* 2/5b–6a.

8. Hung Mai, *chih-i* 2/2b–3a.

9. See for instance the cases of Yüan Shih-ch'eng and Chou Hsiao-jo in Hung Mai, *chih-i* 2/6a–b; of Huang P'u in Hung Mai, *chih-i* 2/6b; and of Liu Yao-fu in Hung Mai, *chih-i* 10/3a–4a. The bare facts of all these cases – though not the dreams and changes of name themselves – are confirmed by gazetteers or other sources.

10. See for instance Hung Mai, *ping* 9/6b–7a; *chih-i* 2/4a–b; *chih-i* 2/5b–6a.

11. Hung Mai, *san-jen* 4/3a–b.

12. Hung Mai, *chih-i* 2/5b–6a. This and several of the other stories cited here from the

I-chien chih were taken by Hung Mai from a work called the *Record of Dreamed Omens*, compiled by a Mr Liu, himself a Fu-chou man.

13. This of course is a much commented-on aspect of the academy 'movement' in Southern Sung. On the Lin-ju Academy see *YLTT* 2265/8b–10a.
14. Lu Chiu-yüan, 36/8a.
15. Yüan Ts'ai, *Yüan-shih shih-fan* 2/40.
16. Chaffee, pp. 243–5.
17. Lu Chiu-yüan, 36/4b.
18. As evidence for this view one may cite the abundant testimony in sources of the Yüan dynasty that during the period of the abolition of the examinations the number of men studying the classics shrank dramatically. See for instance the funerary inscription of Wu Ch'en-tzu (1268–1339):

    > Before [Ch'en-tzu] was twelve years old, Lin-ch'uan was conquered. Many of those who had studied gave it up; but [Ch'en-tzu] still followed the scholarly masters Feng Te-i, Fu Yang-feng, and Hsieh Yüan-li (Yü Chi, *Tao-yüan hsüeh-ku lu* 18/28a–29b).

    The inscription of Tsou Tz'u-ch'en tells us that Tsou, who lived from late Sung through middle Yüan, 'never tired of teaching others,' but that when Yüan revived the examinations, 'the gentlemen studying under him grew even more numerous' (*WWC* 80/8b–10b). That the exams led men to study who otherwise would not was an assumption shared by most of those who discussed the issue of reviving the exams at the Yüan court. See for example John Dardess, *Conquerors and Confucians: Aspects of Political Change in Late Yüan China*, p. 64.
19. E.A. Kracke, 'Family vs. Merit in Chinese Civil Service Examinations Under the Empire.'
20. Sudō Yoshiyuki, 'Sōdai kanryōsei to daitochishoyū, pp. 48–77.
21. Ho, *The Ladder of Success in Imperial China: Aspects of Social Mobility, 1368–1911*, pp. 92–125.
22. Ho's work extended the same view through Ming and Ch'ing. This picture of China was largely dominant in historical work in English during the 1950s and 1960s and is not yet wholly superseded. Citations could be legion. According to one standard textbook: '[. . .] by Sung times hereditary status had become relatively unimportant. Social mobility had greatly increased in an economically more diversified society and had become justified by a greater acceptance of egalitarian principles.' (John K. Fairbank, Edwin O. Reischauer, and Albert M. Craig, *East Asia: Tradition and Transformation*, p. 140.) Another important introductory text is more circumspect but seems largely to accept Kracke's and Ho's conclusions:

    > It need hardly be said that having the means to pay for an education gave the wealthy class an enormous advantage. Yet the small amount of statistical evidence available suggests that a considerable number of successful candidates – at least thirty percent or more – may have come from households that had not produced officials in the immediately preceding generations. If such a large proportion of men could regularly achieve a new, higher status, the system must have kept privilege relatively fluid. (John Meskill, *An Introduction to Chinese Civilization*, p. 121.)

    In work on Ming and Ch'ing, two other contributors to the 'high mobility' view should be mentioned. Robert Marsh's study of prominent Ch'ing men suggests intriguingly that routes *other than* the exams were most important for the upward mobility of commoners into the bureaucracy, but supports the overall view that such mobility was quite frequent. (Robert Marsh, *The Mandarins: The Circulation of Elites in China, 1600–1900*, pp. 114–53.) Chang Chung-li's general study of

the gentry was an earlier attempt than Ping-ti Ho's to analyze the social background of officeholders, in this instance using biographies in local gazetteers
rather than examination lists. (Chang Chung-li, *The Chinese Gentry*, pp. 214–16.)
Ho, with appropriate examples, has pointed out the serious inadequacies of this
approach. (Ho, *Ladder of Success*, pp. 93–4.)

23. By way of (admittedly extreme) example: one certainly could not offer a rate of
movement into government positions by men without officeholding background
in the United States as an overall measure of social mobility, or even as something of particular importance for scholars interested in mobility. One would
want to know, of those without official background, what sort of background
they did have. If one sought some summary rate of movement into the upper
ranks of society, one would have to group government offices (and presumably
not all of them at that) together with various other occupations and social roles.
This is because, in the United States today, it simply will not do to see the government bureaucracy as a ruling class or stratum in itself.

It might be objected that, even if the Sung bureaucracy was not a ruling
stratum all to itself, still office brought its holder wealth, power, and prestige; a
man who gained office gained these. If social mobility, as many would argue, is
precisely movement along these three dimensions of social standing, is it wrong
then to see a man who moves into office as *ipso facto* upwardly mobile? The
difficulty here, once again, is that office, even in China, was undeniably not the
only source of wealth, power, or prestige; nor can one assume that it was always
their most effective source. It is conceivable for instance that some men who
entered the race for office did so only because their families had suffered economic setbacks and needed new sources of income. (This seems to be the implication of the opening lines of the passage cited earlier from Yüan Ts'ai's household
manual. Here the scholarly vocation, including the pursuit of degrees, is seen as
something of particular interest chiefly to men without inherited wealth, whether
from land or from official stipends.) Suppose that such a man did not make
enough in office to offset his family's other difficulties. His entry into office
might then represent only an ineffective attempt to interrupt a larger process of
downward mobility. Without a study of the personal and familial context within
which each 'new' man on an exam list reached office, one would be unable to
convert rates of movement into office into rates of social mobility. But these
considerations are wholly irrelevant if one grants that officeholders or degreeholders themselves (presumably together with their immediate families) constituted a separate social stratum resting above the larger society. This is the
explicit burden, for example, of Ping-ti Ho's restrictive definition of 'elite.'
(Ho, *Ladder of Success*, pp. 17–41.)

24. In fact the equation of the 'gentry' or the social elite with the degreeholding
and officeholding group (or with a part of it) was never accepted by all scholars
in the field. For contrary views in scholarship of the 1950s and 1960s see for
example Morton Fried, *The Fabric of Chinese Society*, pp. 180–217; Maurice
Freedman, *Lineage Organization in Southeastern China*, pp. 52–62, and the same
author's 1956 review of *The Chinese Gentry*, especially pp. 15–16; Wolfram
Eberhard, *Conquerors and Rulers: Social Forces in Medieval China*, pp. 42–47,
and *A History of China*, especially pp. 72–75. For the Ch'ing dynasty, Jonathan
Spence twenty years ago pointed out that the Ch'ing imperial bondsman and
official Ts'ao Yin included within his view of the elite of local society men whose
prominence derived from sources other than degree or office (Jonathan Spence,
Ts'ao Yin and the K'ang-hsi Emperor, pp. 79–81). Frederic Wakeman, at about
the same time, agreed, basing himself on Freedman's views (Frederic Wakeman,
Strangers at the Gate, p. 29n.). More recently Wakeman has argued at some length

for a conception of the gentry that would capture both its official character, as including the degreeholding group, and its social character, as local notables:

> [. . .] a degreeholder (i.e. specifically a *sheng-yüan*, the *lowest* degreeholder) stood lower in the social hierarchy than certain other kinds of local notables whose families were regarded as *shih-chia* or *wang-tsu* – eminent lineages of a high social pedigree. Indeed these households, even if devoid of degreeholders, apparently belonged to what would be regarded by contemporaries as the local gentry of a county. (Wakeman, *The Fall of Imperial China*, p. 25.)

In his introduction to an edited volume of studies of local social change in Ch'ing published in the same year, Wakeman appears to use the word 'gentry' itself in its more restrictive sense; but conceptually both his own introduction and most of the studies included discuss local society in terms which stress, not simply the division between degreeholder and nondegreeholder, but such other issues as specific personal, social, and political connections, wealth, and landholding (Frederic Wakeman and Carolyn Grant, eds., *Conflict and Control in Late Imperial China*. See especially Jerry Dennerline, 'Fiscal Reform and Local Control: The Gentry-Bureaucratic Alliance Survives the Conquest,' pp. 86–120; and James Polachek, 'Gentry Hegemony: Soochow in the T'ung-chih Restoration,' pp. 211–56). Two other important recent studies need mention here. R. Keith Schoppa, in his article on the social elite of late nineteenth-century Szechwan, finds more men without than with degrees among his functionally defined elite (R. Keith Schoppa, 'The Composition and Functions of the Local Elite in Szechwan, 1851–1874'). Hilary Beattie, in her enormously important study of T'ung-ch'eng in Ming and Ch'ing, reconstructs its landholding-based elite and shows that a large number of elite lineages persisted for hundreds of years. She notes that:

> [. . .] when one attempts to describe and define this elite in a strictly local context, rather than from the standpoint of the central government, it is extremely difficult to make clear-cut distinctions between persons with formal academic qualifications and those without. [. . .] Individuals with this kind of formal status were surprisingly few [. . .] and the vast majority had relations, friends, and in-laws who, despite their lack of qualifications, still lived in the same economic and social milieu as themselves. (Hilary Jane Beattie, *Land and Lineage in China: A Study of T'ung-ch'eng County, Anhwei, in the Ming and Ch'ing Dynasties*, p. 315.)

This passage, as we shall see, could apply with at least equal force to Sung dynasty Fu-chou.

It now seems generally accepted among students of Ming and Ch'ing that any proper understanding of the elite must deal both with office (or degrees) and with wealth and informal (or purely local) status and power. See for instance John K. Fairbank, 'Introduction: The Old Order,' in *The Cambridge History of China*, vol. 10, Part I: *Late Ch'ing, 1800–1911*, ed. John K. Fairbank, p. 13.

25. See Maurice Freedman, rev. of *The Chinese Gentry*, for the earliest strong objection to the neglect of relatives not in the direct paternal line. A more recent study draws on an entirely different kind of source to derive percentages of Ch'ing local officials (not only degreeholders) with official kin connections far higher than those Ho finds for degreeholders in the same period. The key here as well is the inclusion of a wider range of kin. See Odoric Wou, 'The Political Kin Unit and the Family Origin of Ch'ing Local Officials.'

26. Kracke, 'Region, Family, and Individual in the Chinese Examination System,' p. 560.

27. Always assuming, once again, that the chance that one family member would gain office is *independent* of the chance of any other member. (This is what allows

simple multiplication of the chances for each of the three ancestors to find the overall chance for all three.) This assumption, like Kracke's own assumption that three ancestors' failure to hold office perfectly predicts failure by all other relatives, would seem on its face an unlikely one. Just how unlikely, however, seems to depend on which list is in question. In the 1148 list, while overall 66.7 per cent of fathers, 71.3 per cent of grandfathers, and 77.7 per cent of great-grandfathers had held office, leading one to expect that (if the three were independent of each other) the total proportion of candidates with no official ancestry recorded should be $(0.667)(0.713)(0.777)$, or only 36.9 per cent, the actual figure is 56.2 per cent; the difference must be the result of an association of the chances for office for one of the three with the chances for the others.

In other words, the ancestral offices in the 1148 list are to a significant degree clustered in the descent lines of particular candidates: if a man has had one officeholding ancestor, it is disproportionately likely that he has had others.

In the 1256 list, on the other hand, there is virtually no such clustering. Here 76.3 per cent of fathers, 86.9 per cent of grandfathers and 84.3 per cent of great-grandfathers had held no office; assuming again that the three chances are independent of one another, the proportion of candidates with no recorded official ancestry should in this year be $(0.763)(0.869)(0.843)$, or 55.9 per cent; the actual figure is 57.8 per cent, only very slightly higher. In fact the mean chance of the three ancestors, 0.825, differs only slightly from the five-in-six chance assumed in the discussion above (which of course was derived simply by taking the approximate cube root of 57 per cent).

This suggests that in 1256 the lack of office by one lineal ancestor bore little or no relation to the chances of office for another: ancestral offices were, far more nearly than in 1148, scattered randomly among the ancestors of successful candidates.

If one assumes that, where the chance for one lineal ancestor helps predict the chance for another, the chances for three lineal ancestors will in turn help predict the chances of other, nonlineal relatives, then the 1148 figures allow us to surmise that the percentage of all relatives who held office was almost surely significantly lower for those without than for those with office among the three recorded ancestors (but do not allow us to conclude how many had *no* official relatives); for 1256 it is possible, judging from the figures, that the proportion of all relatives with office was as high (or nearly so) for those without official ancestry recorded as for those with.

The two lists, then, seem to represent quite different situations. The difference may reflect a major shift between Northern and Southern Sung that will be discussed in Chapter 3: see especially pp. 115–23 below. The 1148 list follows the fall of Northern Sung by only twenty-one years, less than the age of the average candidate; most, if not all, of the fathers, grandfathers, and great-grandfathers of the 1148 candidates must have lived their lives and pursued their careers largely within Northern Sung. In the 1256 list, issued 130 years after the fall of the north, virtually all of the ancestors must be Southern Sung men. The clustering of officeholding ancestors in particular descent lines in 1148, then, surely reflects the success of certain Northern Sung families in pursuing a strategy focused on gaining office for as many members as possible in every generation. The more random scattering of ancestral offices in 1256 must similarly reflect a Southern Sung strategy directed less exclusively toward officeholding. And if, as was certainly true in Fu-chou (see p. 65), a striking number of new elite families emerged or rose in the early decades of Southern Sung, the 1148 list may catch many sons of these families at the precise moment of their rise. The 1148 list, in other words, may by its location in time capture considerably more real movement of relatively 'new blood' into the bureaucracy than the 1256 list, despite the near identity of the overall percentages derived from them. The two lists in fact seem to represent quite different situations despite the similarity of the overall percentages derived from them: this is a further indication of the diagnostic weakness of Kracke's 'mobility' figures.

28. Sudō, 'Sōdai kanryōsei,' pp. 48–77; Kracke, 'Family vs. Merit', p. 116. The family of Tung Te-yüan, for example, would be counted by Kracke as having only a 'minor' tradition of office, since of his three ancestors only his great-grandfather had held office (*Shao-hsing shih-pa nien t'ung-nien hsiao-lu* 12a). Actually, Tung Te-yüan's patrilineal kinsmen had produced eighteen *chin-shih* by the time he passed: the earliest was in 1014, 134 years before Te-yüan's degree. (See Appendix I, no. 59; also see *WWC* 32/20b–21b.)

29. The four are: Chao Pang of Nan-feng County, *Shao-hsing etc.* 57b; Ch'en Ju of Lin-ch'uan County, ibid. 12a; Huang Wen-ch'ang of Nan-feng County, ibid. 32b; and Tung Te-yüan of Yün-kai canton in Yung-feng County, Chi-chou (annexed to Fu-chou's Lo-an County in the following year), ibid. 12a.

30. The fourteen are: Chang Kuei-lung of Lo-an County, *Pao-yu ssu-nien teng-k'o lu* 26b; Chang Chün-chung of Lo-an County, ibid. 81a; Chang Sheng-tzu of I-huang County, ibid. 41b; Chang Yu-hsin of Lin-ch'uan County, ibid. 20b; Chao Pi-ch'üan of Lin-ch'uan County, ibid. 68a (recorded there only as imperial family member; for Lin-ch'uan residence see *TCLC* 36/8a); Chao Pi-kun of Chin-ch'i County, ibid. 16a; Chao Yü-hsi of Lin-ch'uan County, ibid. 28b (again, recorded there only as imperial family member; for Lin-ch'uan residence see *TCLC* 36/8a); Ch'en Chen-yen of Ch'ung-jen County, ibid. 33a; Ch'en Yüan-fa of Lin-ch'uan County, ibid. 90b; Chu Yu-chi of Chin-ch'i County, ibid. 96b; Ho Shih of Lo-an County, ibid. 14b; Liao Tzu-shih of Lo-an County, ibid. 12b; Teng Fei-ying of Chin-ch'i County, ibid. 63b; Tseng Hui-ti of Lo-an County, ibid. 11a.

31. Chao Pi-ch'üan, Pi-kun, and Yü-hsi; see note 30 above. Kracke's policy is apparently to count imperial lineage members as mobile or not mobile in just the same way as other candidates, on the basis of the presence or absence of office among the three recorded ancestors; Sudō's policy, to exclude imperial lineage members from his calculations, seems altogether more reasonable, since it is at least odd to call a descendant of an emperor who gets a degree upwardly mobile, especially as from mid-Southern Sung on imperial relatives appear in vast numbers on the *chin-shih* lists of all regions of South China. In the present study I specify whether imperial lineage members are being excluded or included with respect to all statistics.

32. These are Huang Wen-ch'ang and Tung Te-yüan in 1148 (see n. 29 above) and Chang Kuei-lung, Chang Sheng-tzu, Ch'en Yüan-fa, Chu Yu-chi, and Teng Fei-ying in 1256 (see n. 30 above).

33. See n. 30 above.

34. *TCLA* 7/11b; *KHLA* 5/12a.

35. *TCLA* 7/20a; *KHLA* 5/2b.

36. *TCLA* 7/10b; *KHLA* 5/9b.

37. *TCLA* 7/11a; *KHLA* 7/19b.

38. See n. 29 above.

39. See n. 30 above.

40. *KHFC* 42/20a; *TCCJ* 7c/10b; *KHCJ* 1/57b–58a. For full information on this family see Appendix I, no. 4.

41. Ch'en Yüan-chin, *Yü-shu lei kao* 6/4a–6b. Ch'en Chen-yen must then have been, strictly speaking, Yüan-chin's second cousin once removed rather than his nephew as in the gazetteers; but such an extended use of the term *chih* may not be unusual.

42. See n. 29 above.

43. *KHTH* 1/22a, 4/5a; *TCIH* 11/4b.
44. See n. 30 above.
45. *TCLA* 7/11b; *KHLA* 5/4b.
46. *TCLA* 7/10a; *KHLA* 5/5b.
47. *TCLA* 7/10b; *KHLA* 5/9b.
48. See n. 30 above.
49. *TCLA* 7/11b; *KHLA* 5/12a.
50. *TCLA* 7/10a; *KHLA* 5/2b.
51. *TCLA* 7/10a; *KHLA* 5/3a.
52. *TCLA* 7/10a; *KHLA* 5/3a. For full information on these families see Appendix I, nos. 52 and 53.
53. Tseng Feng, *Yüan-tu chi* 19/10a–13a.
54. Tseng Feng, 19/10a–13a.
55. *TCLA* 7/4b; *KHLA* 5/17a.
56. See n. 30 above.
57. *WWC* 78/6a–b.
58. *KHFC* 61/9b; *KHLA* 7/8b–9a.
59. See n. 30 above.
60. Huang Chen, 97/10b–12b.
61. *TCLC* 36/6b.
62. *TCLC* 36/6b.
63. *TCLC* 36/6b.
64. *TCLC* 36/8a.
65. *KHFC* 56/7b; *SYHA* 77/14b–15a; *SYHAPI* 77/20a.
66. Liu K'o-chuang, 162/11a–15b.
67. For the sources on this family see Appendix I, no. 31.
68. Huang Chen, 97/10b–12b.
69. *TCIH* 25/3b, 4a, 5a; *KHIH* 5/6a, 7a, 9b, 14a; and see Appendix I, no. 58.
70. *KHCC* 4/3a–b; *TCCC* 17a/2a–b; and cf. Appendix I, no. 42.
71. See Appendix I, no. 18 for the sources on the Ho family.
72. Thus one may calculate for greater Fu-chou at least two different sets of 'mobility rates,' meaning rates of entry of 'new men' onto the *chin-shih* lists. If one counts all men for whom no official background is *known* as instances of mobility, one gets rates that, while varying considerably by county, are quite high indeed. However in this case one is judging as mobile 201 *chin-shih* on whom no biographical information survives but their names and the dates of their degrees. If one excludes these completely unknown cases and considers only men for whom some further information, however slight, is available (433 men, excluding members of the imperial family), quite a different set of rates emerges. This situation is tabulated below:

County	Rate A			Rate B		
Lin-ch'uan	197/289	=	68.2%	61/153	=	39.9%
I-huang	36/ 95	=	37.9%	21/ 80	=	26.2%
Nan-feng	44/ 89	=	49.5%	16/ 61	=	26.2%
Ch'ung-jen	33/ 74	=	44.6%	20/ 61	=	32.8%
Chin-ch'i	18/ 44	=	41.0%	12/ 38	=	31.6%
Lo-an	15/ 43	=	34.9%	12/ 40	=	30.0%
TOTAL	343/634	=	54.1%	142/433	=	32.8%

Here Rate A is the proportion of all *chin-shih* for whom no previous family office is known; Rate B is the proportion of *chin-shih* on whom some biographical information survives for whom no previous family office is known. Thus it will be seen that over two-thirds of the *chin-shih* of whom anything more than a name and date is known can be shown to have had previous family members in office. If one includes in this group a further 112 *chin-shih* who were members of the imperial lineage, the proportion of men not new to the bureaucracy rises to 74 per cent. The remaining 26 per cent cannot by any means all be assumed to be new: for most the available biographical information deals only with their own life and official career and sheds no light on their ancestry; thus for the *chin-shih* of whom anything is known the several Rates B above must be considered maxima.

This leaves the question how to view the men of whom no record but their *chin-shih* listings survives. A common approach in mobility studies of China has been to assume that where information is unavailable or sketchy, ancestry must have been 'obscure' (meaning 'not prominent' rather than, tautologically, 'unclear'). To follow this assumption seems to me the height of methodological carelessness. To be plausible it must imply one of two other assumptions: either that the information now available reflects, at least in its proportions, the records left by Sung men when they lived and died; or else that the survival of such records, once created, has been significantly determined by the ancestry (not the prominence in his own lifetime) of each man. For the former assumption there is little reasonable basis: the ultimate source of most of the biographical information on a man available to us now will have been his record of conduct or funerary inscription (for these provided the basis for other biographical records, such as those in official or private histories, and were even a chief source for the compilation of genealogies), and these two sorts of record appear to have been a required part of the ritual of living and dying for all members of the educated or wealthy stratum, extending far beyond *chin-shih* or officials and their families. There seems no reason whatever to suppose that a man who attained the status of *chin-shih* would have been less likely to have had such records composed for him by a family member, local man, or fellow-official of some literary repute simply because his ancestors had not held office.

Given this, the issue must shift to the survival of the records once composed: one might argue that a *chin-shih* whose ancestors had also held office was more likely than other *chin-shih* to have his record of conduct and funerary inscription written by men of particular fame (an argument which would be difficult to support on the basis of the records that have survived), and that the collected works of such authors, containing the records and inscriptions they composed, have been more likely to survive than those of less famous men. This argument too would encounter considerable difficulties. In the sources one can find mention of, in all, 101 sets of collected works (excluding purely poetic collections) produced by Fu-chou men in Sung. The authors of all of these were men of considerable literary prominence at least within their prefecture and frequently nationally: it is to this that we owe the fact that their works are mentioned at all in contemporary sources. Of the lot, only nineteen collected works have survived to the present day, and several of these only as fragments. Nor have the works of the most famous authors most consistently survived. Thus we have the works of Wang An-shih and one of his brothers, An-li, but not those of two other brothers, An-jen and An-kuo, or those of his father, I, and son, P'ang. The writings of Tseng Kung have survived in large part, but from his brother Tseng Chao, equally famous in his own day, we have only four chapters of an original fifty, and the works of his other brother, Tseng Pu, whose assistant-ministership was the highest office among the three, are entirely lost. The two hundred chapters of the works of Yüeh Shih, first *chin-shih* from Fu-chou in Sung, one of eight in his own family, the author of the *T'ai-p'ing huan-yü chi*, have not survived (Yüeh Shih was generally regarded by later generations of

Fu-chou men as the most outstanding author in nonpoetic genres that the prefecture had produced); and only 2 of 250 chapters remain of the works of the
Northern Sung chief minister and master lyric poet, Yen Shu. On the other hand,
we possess the complete works of both Hsieh I and his brother Hsieh K'o, well
known in their own time as members of the circle of poets associated with Huang
T'ing-chien but by no means the most famous poets produced by Fu-chou;
neither ever reached office, and while both were comfortably ensconced in Fu-
chou elite society, neither was unusually prominent except as a poet.

In short, what is available to us now is only a fraction of the records produced
by some of the most famous and powerful men of Sung, and neither fame nor
family seems decisively to have influenced survival: the factors that have led to
the destruction at different times of most of what was originally available have
been so various that it is impossible to argue that any consistent principle of
selection — social or otherwise — has been at work. I would argue then that the
lack of any information on 201 Sung Fu-chou *chin-shih* is adequately explained
by the loss of this enormous quantity of sources, leaving no need for appeal to
any presumed trait of the men themselves; and therefore that the maximum rates
of movement obtained for men on whom biographical information *has* survived
may quite plausibly be representative of these other men as well.

73.   The number of men treated is of course restricted by limitations in the sources:
these reduce both the background information on known first *chin-shih* and the
chances of being able to show to begin with that a man was the first from his
family. Further, the thirty-four differ widely in the amount and kinds of information available. Most importantly, lists of prefectural graduates exist only for
three counties (Ch'ung-jen, I-huang, and Lo-an), while only for I-huang do the
lists specify which prefectural graduates eventually received facilitated degrees
(*t'e-tsou-ming*). For men from other counties any knowledge of a previous family
history of success in the prefectural exams, or of facilitated degrees, is dependent
on chance mentions in funerary inscriptions and other biographical sources, which
by no means tend to stress such information.

74.   One of the exceptions is Sun Yu-ch'ing, of whom we know only that his grandfather had been a clerk and administered the prefectural jail. Clerical positions in
local governments were in Sung universally regarded as inevitably highly lucrative,
though illicitly so; the opportunities must have been especially attractive in a post
that involved one in legal processes. Thus at least as regards wealth Sun may be
no exception after all; as noted above (p. 59), Yu-ch'ing may have been
preceded in the prefectural exams by his father. Still, the impression one receives
from Sung sources is that the holders of clerical positions were excluded from
honorable status within local society, and although one knows nothing of the
possible social position or connections of Sun's other relatives, his case is interesting as a *possible* instance of intergenerational movement from clerical status
into 'legitimate' office. The other exception, Chi Fu, came from a very wealthy
family of whose history little is recorded. See nos. 6 and 23 in the list appended
to this chapter.

75.   It is true that one sometimes finds, in a funerary inscription or biography, descriptions of the hardship which poverty caused for some future degreeholder or
high official as he struggled to gain a knowledge of the classics. In many of these
cases, however, the poverty in childhood proves to have been the result of a
father's early death and represents a decline from an earlier period of wealth or
official and scholarly prominence. Such men could often rely on aid from inlaws
or associates dating from before the father's death; here established social ties
obviated the immediate need for wealth. But wealth must have been much more
important as a foundation for families working their way 'up' for the first time,

who could not rely on old ties to help them but rather had to think of establishing them for the future.

76. Lu Chiu-yüan, 28/7a–11a. In an earlier version of this study I read this passage as evidence, in itself, of a process of local recommendation of men for admission to the prefectural exam: '[. . .] people would ask him *whose name should be recommended.*' However, it is clear, first, that *chien*, which I had translated as 'recommended,' may be an abbreviation of *hsiang-chien*, a common expression for a man's 'sendup' by the prefecture on passing the prefectural exam; and second, that *tang*, which I had translated as 'should,' is in fact often used when a diviner's or fortuneteller's prediction is being referred to: such-and-such a thing 'is to' happen. Since Huang Shih is precisely a specialist in the 'Arts of the Five Phases,' it seems almost certain that it is his prediction of the future, not simply his opinion of the proper course of action, that is being asked for here. The Lus (or 'people') are asking, then, not whom they *should* recommend *for* the exam, but who *will* be 'recommended' *in* it, that is, pass it.

77. Wen T'ien-hsiang, *Wen-shan hsien-sheng ch'üan-chi* 9/319.

78. This is *SHY*, *hsüan-chü* 16/8b–9a.

79. On this point I agree with Chaffee, p. 228.

80. Wen T'ien-hsiang, 9/319.

81. See Araki, pp. 56–7, citing a 1007 edict from *SS*, ch. 155, *hsüan-chü* 1, and a 1007 edict from *SHY*, *hsüan-chü* 3, *k'o-chü t'iao-chih*.

82. *SHY*, *hsüan-chü* 16/8b–9a. See also Chaffee, p. 228.

83. This does not appear to have been a legal requirement, and in the case of another prefecture, Brian McKnight has shown that 5 per cent of Hang-chou prefects in Northern Sung were Hang-chou natives (McKnight 'Administrators of Hang-chou under the Northern Sung,' p. 190). In Fu-chou, however, something like a geographic rule of avoidance seems to have existed already in Sung: no Fu-chou prefect listed in the gazetteers or elsewhere can be identified as a Fu-chou man; nor can any of the county administrators or vice-administrators be identified as men of that county. Conversely, of the hundreds of Fu-chou men for whom at least one official position is known, none is recorded to have held prefectural office in Fu-chou or county office in his own county (a few cases are known in which a Fu-chou man held a county post in a Fu-chou county not his own).

84. This will have been true even though the formal requirements for candidacy, for which the guarantor's assurances were required, were not particularly restrictive. That they were not seems clear from Chaffee, pp. 226–241.

85. Quoted in Conrad Schirokauer, 'Neo-Confucians under Attack: the Condemnation of Wei-hsüeh,' p. 180.

86. Lu Chiu-yüan, 36/10b.

87. On this point compare Jerry Dennerline's discussion of the role of the Restoration Society in the examinations in the late Ming. The signalling of academic/political alignments by the style of a candidate's essay was clearly, for the Restoration Society, a quite deliberate tactic. (Jerry Dennerline, *The Chia-ting Loyalists: Confucian Leadership and Social Change in Seventeenth-Century China*, pp. 33–4.)

88. The uncertainty hinges on the impossibility of demonstrating beyond question that the Ch'ung-jen men surnamed Chan, ten of whom passed the prefectural exam before the splitting off of Lo-an from Ch'ung-jen *and none thereafter*, are the same family as the Ya-pei Chans of Lo-an, who lived on territory formerly part of Ch'ung-jen, contributed their market place as the site for the county seat at Lo-an's creation, and produced prefectural graduates down to the end of Sung. The evidence is convincing but does not constitute a proof. See Appendix I, no. 1.

89. *TCIH* ch. 25, *KHIH* ch. 5, passim.

90. For instance, the Chengs of Lo-an (Appendix I, no. 9); the Fus of Chin-ch'i (Appendix I, no. 74); the Hous of I-huang (Appendix I, no. 19); the Tengs of Chin-ch'i (Appendix I, no. 47); and the Ts'aos of I-huang (Appendix I, no. 50). Jao Yen-nien (see Appendix I, no. 31) was offered office in return for his relief grain sales in 1210, but declined; and the prefect Huang Chen promised office to a number of men contributing to famine relief in 1271. (Huang Chen, 75/15a–16b.)

91. The I-huang facilitated degrees are listed in *TCIH* ch. 25, *KHIH* ch. 5; the 1148 *chin-shih* exam produced 457 facilitated degrees as compared to 330 regular *chin-shih*; in the first year in which facilitated degrees were granted, 970, there were 106 compared to 8 regular *chin-shih* (Kracke, 'Family vs. Merit', p. 110; Araki, p. 290; Ma Tuan-lin, 32/305.)

92. The chance of success in the special exam seems to have varied with time. Li Hsin-ch'uan tells us that the practice had been to accept one out of every two candidates, but that in 1178 this was lowered to one in three out of concern at the inflated numbers of officeholders. However:

> '[. . .] after this, there were constantly celebratory proclamations of grace [*ch'ing-pei*: possibly proclamations issued in honor of the emperor's birthday?] in which all those who had ever not achieved selection were passed and given office [. . .] Subsequently this became well-established precedent; reductions were no longer possible.' (Li Hsin-ch'uan, *Chien-yen i-lai ch'ao-yeh tsa-chi* 15/4b–5a).

As Li was writing before 1216, the practical effects of the reduction to one in three cannot have lasted long before the custom of universal qualification by grace established itself. It would seem then that in later Southern Sung it was virtually impossible for those technically qualified for the exam not to achieve (eventually) a facilitated degree; earlier the chance had been one in two.

93. In Southern Sung Fu-chou this privilege of *kuan-hu* status, however, actually extended to households that had produced one prefectural graduate. See *Ming-kung shu-p'an ch'ing-ming chi*, p. 163. On the question of tax payments and an agent's responsibility, see *Ch'ing-yüan t'iao-fa shih-lei*, p. 428. I am indebted to Joseph McDermott for these references. (See McDermott, p. 144.)

94. Officials, of course, were subject to administrative disciplinary action, which could sometimes be fairly harsh.

95. The essay is addressed to 'the Professor, Wang Po-keng.' Presumably this is a courtesy-name, since the two other people mentioned who are not themselves participants in the sacrifice are called by their courtesy-names. The courtesy-name given for Wang Ko in other contexts, however, is not Po-keng but Hsin-min. Yet for a variety of reasons one may be quite sure that Po-keng is Wang Ko and not some other Wang entirely. In the first place, the essay refers to 'the death-announcement of Shu-yeh.' Shu-yeh is the courtesy-name of Wang Ko's younger brother, Wang Hsin, the appropriate person to send out a death-announcement for Wang Ko. Second, Wang Ko died, as we know from a mention in Hsieh K'o's sacrificial essay for Hsieh I, in the fall of 1110; the sacrificial essay for Wang Po-keng is dated in the spring of 1111. Finally, there is the evidence of the structure of names. It was common for the given names or courtesy-names (or both) of brothers to be formed on some single pattern. Wang Ko and Wang Hsin, for instance, share the uppermost strokes in the characters of their given names. (In 'Hsin' these are the grass radical; in 'Ko' they technically are not, but their form is almost the same.) Now Po-keng contains two elements: the first, 'Po-', is commonly used to indicate the first of a series of brothers. The second, 'keng', means to change, to alter, to replace: this seems clearly related

to the 'Ko' in Wang Ko, which also can mean to change, to replace or substitute. Compare Wang Hsin's courtesy-name, Shu-yeh: here the first element, 'Shu-', forms part of the same series for brothers' names as 'Po-', but is used for a brother who stands third or later in line; it can also have the more general sense of 'younger brother.' The second element, 'yeh', means wilderness, fields, countryside, rustic. Wang Hsin's given name, 'hsin,' means a kind of wild grass that grows in marshes. The connection with 'yeh,' wilderness, would seem clear on its face; it appears even stronger when one notes that the two appear together in a line from the Mencius (here Hsin is part of the name of a state, Yu-Hsin: *Mencius* V.A.7: 'Yi Yin plowed in the wilds [or fields] of Yu-Hsin.') and turn up in later literature as a compound: 'Hsin-yeh', the wilds (or fields) of (Yu-)Hsin. (See Morohashi, IX: 31056-19.) Thus Wang Hsin's courtesy-name stands in the same relation to his given name as the courtesy-name Po-keng does to the given name of Wang Ko; the two courtesy-names are formed on a common pattern and contain just the elements ('Po-' and 'Shu-') that one might expect for an elder and younger brother. There can be no doubt, I think, that Wang Po-keng is Wang Ko.

96. Hsieh I, 10/14a–b.
97. Hsieh I, 10/12b.
98. Hsieh I, 7/2a–2a.
99. Lü Pen-chung, *Tung-lai Lü Tz'u-wei shih-yu tsa-chih*, 2.
100. Hsieh K'o, end matter.
101. Hsieh K'o, 10/2a–2a.
102. Hsieh I, 9/18b–20b.
103. Hsieh I, 8/10a–12a.
104. His mother's father's name was Chiang Chü-ch'ing; a Chiang Chü-yüan (with the same 'Chü-' in his name) was a *chin-shih* in 1049, two years before the mother was born. See also Hsieh I, 9/20a.
105. The word *ti*, which I translate as 'younger brother' in the sacrificial essay, can be applied more generally to any younger male relative of ego's generation.
106. Hsieh I, 10/1a–3b.
107. Hsieh I, 8/13b–15a; *TCLC* 36/2a.
108. Hsieh I, 8/12a–13b and 9/2b–4a.
109. Hsieh I, 10/5a–12a.
110. It is possible that they were of the same family as Huang Shu's mother's brother Wu Ti-chi, or as the woman surnamed Wu who was Ch'en Yen-kuo's mother. See Hsieh I, 9/8b–12a.
111. See *SS* 376/7b.
112. For Lu Chiu-yüan's students and scholarly friends, see especially *SYHA* ch. 57 and 58; *SYHAPI* ch. 57 and 58. The extensive correspondence by Lu preserved in his collected works illustrates the same principle. See Lu Chiu-yüan, ch. 1–17.
113. Essentially the same point has recently been made by Patricia Ebrey in her study and translation of Yuan Ts'ai's household manual (*Family and Property in Sung China: Yuan Ts'ai's Precepts For Social Life*, pp. 3–11, especially pp. 3–5). Ebrey uses the term *shih-ta-fu* rather than simply *shih*; the two, as she notes (p. 5 n. 3), were equivalent.
114. *TCLA* 7/11a, 20b, 8/17b; *KHLA* 5/4a, 9b, 6/20b.
115. *TCLA* 8/36a; *KHLA* 7/8b. Also see Tseng Feng, 19/10a–13a, and *SHY, fang-yü* 6, p. 27.
116. Tseng Feng, 20a–21a; *TCLA* 1/27b–28a. For Tung Te-hsiu (to whom Tseng Feng refers by his courtesy name, Chung-hsiu) see *TCLA* 8/13a, *KHLA* 6/21a, and *SYHA* 77/14a.
117. Tseng Feng, 19/10a–13a.
118. *TCLA* 7/10a, 17a, 17b; *KHLA* 5/2b, 6a, 6b.

119. *TCLA* 7/17a; *KHLA* 5/5b.
120. *TCLA* 6/17a; *KHLA* 5/6a.
121. *TCLA* 7/16b; *KHLA* 5/6b.
122. *TCLA* 7/12a, 22b; *KHLA* 5/5a, 11b.
123. *TCLA* 7/12a, 24b; *KHLA* 5/5a, 14a.
124. *TCCJ* 7c/3b, 8b, 8b/5a; *KHCJ* 1/52b, 53a.
125. For Wang Tsao, see his funerary inscription in Sun Ti, *Hung-ch'ing chü-shih chi* 34/12a; Wang was appointed prefect of Fu-chou in 1133, see *KHFC* 39/7b; while there he requested in a memorial to the throne the abolition of Fu-chou's navy yard as a burden on the local people: see Wang Tsao, *Fu-ch'i chi* 1/9b–13a. For Han Chü, see *SS* 445/7a–b, which mentions that he was in Fu-chou at his death in 1135; according to *TCLC* 47b/2a, he came to Fu-chou to live near the end of his life because of his long friendship with Wang Tsao, then prefect, and Tseng Yü, son of Tseng Pu and member of the Nan-feng Tseng lineage (see Appendix I, no. 54). For Sun Ti there is no adequate single biographical source; a list of those available is in *CPT* pp. 1913–14, but considerable additional information on his life can be gleaned from his own collected writings. Sun passed through Fu-chou in 1131 or 1132 on his way to Kuang-hsi circuit, to which he had been banished for crimes supposed to have been committed while administrator of the capital prefecture, Lin-an Fu. As a rash of bandit activity in nearby prefectures of Chiang-hsi made travel perilous at this time, Sun stayed on for some time in Fu-chou and became well acquainted with a number of local men. See Sun Ti, 36/16a, 37/4b, 15b.
126. Ho I appears in the inscription as 'Wu I of Moon Lake,' but this is a mistake: 'Moon Lake' is the appellation of *Ho* I (see e.g., *CPT* p. 1259) and there is no other record of a Wu of this name from Ch'ung-jen. The error probably results from a simple transfer of the Wu surname down from the two names (Wu Tseng and Wu Chien) listed directly above it in the inscription.
127. *TCCJ* 7b/2b, 7c/5a, 8a/2a; *KHCJ* 1/48b; *KHFC* 47/23a–b.
128. *TCCJ* 7c/5a, 8b/3a–4a; *KHCJ* 1/48a, 4/22b–23b; Hung Mai, *chih-i* 2/4a–b.
129. *TCCJ* 7b/3a; *KHCJ* 1/49b; *KHFC* 47/36b; Hung Mai, *san-jen* 1/1b–2a.
130. All of this information on Ch'en Yüan-chin's family comes from Ch'en K'ai's funerary inscription in Ch'en Yüan-chin, 6/4a–6b.
131. Chi Fu appears in *KHFC* 47/12a–b and elsewhere as Chi Chi-fu but in his funerary inscription, which I follow here, as Chi Fu (n. 132 below).
132. Hsieh I, 10/5a–12a.
133. *KHNF* 5/2b.
134. Tseng Kung, *Yüan-feng lei-kao* 46/8b–9a. For the Tsengs as a family see Appendix I, no. 54.
135. *TCCJ* 7b/4a, 7c/9a; *KHCJ* 1/53a–b, 4/40a–41a.
136. *TCCJ* 7c/5a; *KHCJ* 1/48b; for their relationship see *TCCJ* 7b/4a and *KHCJ* 1/53a–b.
137. *WWC* 24/5b–7b.
138. *TCCJ* 8b/5b–6a; *KHCJ* 4/40a–41a.
139. *TCLC* 36/4b.
140. Chu Hsi, *Chu Wen-kung wen-chi* 91/27b–29a.
141. *TCIH* 25/7a, 25a; *KHIH* 5/19b, 22b.
142. *TCIH* 25/21b; *KHIH* 5/16a.
143. *TCIH* 25/22b; *KHIH* 5/16a.
144. Sun Ti, 37/4b; *TCIH* 45g/90a–92a.
145. *TCIH* 25/3b, 11a; *KHIH* 5/4b, 6/62; *KHFC* 47/12a.
146. *TCIH* 25/5b, 18b; *KHIH* 5/13a; *KHFC* 42/11b, 12a, 18b.
147. *TCIH* 25/19b; *KHIH* 5/10b.
148. *TCLA* 7/11b, 23a; *KHLA* 5/4b, 12b.

149. *WWC* 32/17a–18b.
150. *TCLA* 8/12b; *KHLA* 6/6a; *KHFC* 69a/5a; *SYHA* 63/21b. On Huang Kan, see his funerary inscription in the appendix to his collected works: Huang Kan, *Mien-chai chi*; on his prefectship in Fu-chou see the numerous documents concerning the prefecture scattered through his works, and the very brief notice in *KHFC* 39/11a.
151. *TCLA* 8/12b; *KHLA* 6/6a; *KHFC* 69a/5a; *SYHA* 63/21b. On the Lin-ju Academy, also called the Ju-shui Academy and founded in 1249, see *YLTT* 2265/8b–10a.
152. *KHNF* 5/3a; *MKNF* 9/7b.
153. Lu Chiu-yüan, 28/4a–6a.
154. *TCCJ* 7c/9a; *KHCJ* 1/53a–b, 55a–b.
155. *KHFC* 69a/3b; *TCCJ* 8d/8b; *KHCJ* 4/26b–27a.
156. *SYHA* 77/11a; *SYHAPI* 77/16a.
157. Hung Mai, *san-jen* 1/46b–5a.
158. *TCCC* 17a/2a; *KHCC* 4/3a.
159. Lu Chiu-yüan, 28/7b–11a.
160. *TCCJ* 7b/3b, 8b; *KHCJ* 1/52a–b; *KHFC* 47/48a–b.
161. Wei Liao-weng, *Ho-shan hsien-sheng ta-ch'üan chi* 79/4a–6a.
162. Wei Liao-weng, 79/4a–6a.
163. Wei Liao-weng, 79/4a–6a and 6a–8a. On Wu Hsieh see *TCCJ* 7b/3a; *KHCJ* 1/49b, 4/38b; *KHFC* 59/4a; *SYHAPI* 45/16b. On Wu Hang see *TCCJ* 8e/1b; *KHCJ* 4/22a–b; *KHFC* 59/4a; *SYHAPI* 45/17a. On Wu Tseng see *TCCJ* 7c/5a, 8b/3a–4a; *KHCJ* 1/48a, 4/22b–23b; *KHFC* 46/16b; Lou Yüeh, *Kung-k'uei chi* 52/11b–13b; Hung Mai, *chih-i* 2/4a–b.
164. *WWC* 57/8a–b.
165. E.g., Li Ting in 1153 (*TCCJ* 7c/5a, *KHCJ* 1/48b); Li Sung in 1162 (*TCCJ* 7c/6a; *KHCJ* 1/49b); Li Ch'ung in 1162 and 1171 (*TCCJ* 7c/6a; *KHCJ* 1/49b–50a); Li Po-yin in 1177 (*TCCJ* 7c/6a; *KHCJ* 1/50a); Li Chin-ch'ing in 1180 (*TCCJ* 7c/6b; *KHCJ* 1/50a); Li Wen-cho in 1198 (*KHCJ* 1/5b).
166. Lu Chiu-yüan, 28/1a–2a.
167. Lu Chiu-yüan, 28/6a–7b, 27/8a–10a.
168. Lu Chiu-yüan, 28/6a–7b, 27/8a–10a.
169. *WWC* 61/15a–16b; Yü Chi, 43/2b–4b.
170. *TCCC* 17a/3a–b; *KHCC* 4/3a, 5/8a–b.
171. *TCCC* 17b/6b; *KHCC* 4/40a; Wei Su, *T'ai-p'u yün-lin chi, hsü-chi* 1/12b–13a.
172. Sung Lien, *Sung hsüeh-shih chi* 12/449–50.
173. *WWC* 22/8a–b.
174. *TCCJ* 7b/3a; *KHCJ* 4/24b–26b.
175. *KHFC* 47/24a; *TCCJ* 8a/2a–6a; Yüan Hsieh, 12/1a–35a.
176. Ch'en Tsao, *Chiang-hu ch'ang-weng chi* 35/13a–16a. See Chapter 2, n. 89 for a detailed account of the evidence on the Lo family.
177. *TCCC* 7a/2a; *KHCC* 4/3a, 5/8a–b; *KHFC* 47/33b–34a; *SYHAPI, pieh-fu* 2/91a–b.
178. Lu Chiu-yüan, 27/1a–8a.
179. Lu Chiu-yüan, 27/1a–8a and 28/3a–4a, 12a–16b.
180. Chou Pi-ta, 20/16b–17b.
181. *KHFC* 42/22b.
182. Ch'eng Chü-fu, *Hsüeh-lou chi* 22/8a–9b; *KHFC* 42/22a; *SYHAPI* 58/48a.
183. *KHFC* 42/22a.
184. *KHFC* 42/22b.
185. Ch'eng Chü-fu, 22/8a–9b.
186. *KHFC* 42/11a.
187. Yü Chi, 43/1a–2b.
188. *TCCC* 17a/2b, 18/10a; *TCLC* 36/8b.
189. See especially *TCCC* 22a/1a–5a, 33f/7b–9b; *KHCC* 5/5b–7a; Chou Pi-ta, 20/16b–17b; *WWC* 32/20b–21b.

190. Lu Chiu-yüan, 27/1a–8a. Lu Yün's preface is preserved in the thirteenth edition of the Teng genealogy, compiled in 1946, which I examined at the canton seat of Huang-t'ung canton, Chin-ch'i County (near the old Teng residence) in June of 1985.
191. *KHFC* 42/12a.
192. *KHFC* 57/2b; Lu Chiu-yüan, 16/8b–10b; *SYHA* 77/2a.
193. The I-huang gazetteers appear to have omitted all *chin-shih* information for this year, but see *WWC* 32/15a–16b.
194. *TCIH* 25/10b; *KHIH* 5/4a.
195. *WWC* 32/15a–16b.
196. *TCLA* 7/11b, 22b; *KHLA* 5/4a, 12a.
197. Tseng Feng, 19/10a–13a; *TCLA* 7/4b; *KHLA* 5/17a.
198. *TCCJ* 7c/7a–b; *KHCJ* 1/50b–51a.
199. Ch'en Tsao, 35/13a–16a.
200. *TCIH* 25/4b; *KHIH* 5/11a–b.
201. Ibid., and *KHFC* 42/9b.
202. *TCIH* 25/9b, 11a; *KHIH* 5/3a, 4a; Lu Hsin-yüan, *Sung shih i* 36/5a; *SYHAPI* 98/7a.
203. *TCIH* 25/11a, 12a; *KHIH* 5/4b, 5b.
204. *TCIH* 25/3b, 12a; *KHIH* 5/5b, 6a.
205. *TCIH* 31/2a–b.
206. Sun Ti, 35/15a; *TCIH* 45g/93a–95a.
207. *TCIH* 25/4a, 12a; *KHIH* 5/5b, 8b.
208. *TCIH* 25/9b; *KHIH* 5/3a.
209. *TCLH* 37/1b.
210. Ko Sheng-chung, 12/4b–7b.
211. *TCCC* 7a/3b; *KHCC* 5/21a–b; *KHTH* 3/10a; *TCTH* 11/8a; *WWC* 81/8a–9a.
212. Sung Lien, 22/804b–806a; Li Ts'un, *Ssu-an chi* 23/18a–21b; *KHFC* 57/10a.
213. Sung Lien, 22/804–806; *SYHAPI* 77/25b.
214. *WWC* 79/8b–10a.
215. *TCLC* 36/5b.
216. *WWC* 61/15a–16b; Yü Chi, 43/2a; Lu Chiu-yüan, 27/8a.
217. Lu Chiu-yüan, ch. 36 (*nien-p'u*), under these years.
218. *TCIH* 25/5b, 22a, 19/7b–8a; *KHIH* 5/16a–b; *KHFC* 47/37b–38a; *WWC* 32/13b–15a.
219. *WWC* 32/13b–15a; *TCIH* 25/9a, 18a, 22a; *KHIH* 5/12b, 16b.

Chapter 2

1. The sources that underlie the reconstruction of each family are listed fully in Appendix I.
2. The table begins in 976, rather than 960 (the first year of the dynasty in the usual reckoning), because the Southern T'ang kingdom was not incorporated into the Sung empire until 975; it ends in 1276 rather than 1278 or 1279 because the Yüan conquest of Fu-chou was in fact complete by 1275–6.
3. Thus five families who immigrated to Fu-chou during Sung after first achieving office elsewhere are omitted. In general the basis for a family's inclusion in this table or in Appendix I has been that it could be reconstructed over a period exceeding one generation, and that information other than a simple association of names was available – at minimum a place of residence, perhaps offices or local activities of members. Thus occasional cases in which the gazetteer exam lists indicate one graduate or degreeholder to have been the son or grandson of another, where no other information is available on either man, are excluded from Table I. Such cases, however, have of course been used in constructing the

apparent mobility rates tabulated in note 72 to Chapter 1. There are several families in Table II, however, whose recorded membership in the local elite begins so late in Southern Sung that one cannot be certain that more than one generation is involved: these are the Ch'üeh family of Lo-an County (Appendix I, no. 15), the Huang family of T'ung-fu in Lo-an County (Appendix I, no. 29), the T'an family of I-huang County (Appendix I, no. 46), and the Wang family of Lo-an County (Appendix I, no. 62). These cases are included on the one hand in order not to exclude evidence that new elite families continued to emerge throughout Sung, and on the other hand because all are associated with a definite place of residence and can be shown on gazetteer evidence to continue as elite families into the Yüan dynasty.

4. Similarly the Ch'ung-jen County gazetteers, which do list prefectural graduates, generally give kinship, residence, or other biographical information only for the most prominent men, in particular those who reached high office.

5. I refer here to claims, not of descent from T'ang aristocrats (for these see p. 67, but of connections to Sung families still flourishing in nearby counties. Examples are the claim of the Lo-shan Tsengs of Lo-an County to be a branch of the Sung-ch'i Tseng lineage in neighbouring Yung-feng County, Chi-chou (*WWC* 32/5a–6b); the claim of the Wei family of Chin-ch'i to have diverged from a many-branched Wei lineage in Lin-ch'uan (Wei Su, 6/1a–2a and 10/21b–23a); and the claim of the Tseng family of Chin-ch'i County to descent from one of the Tsengs of Nan-feng County (Ch'eng Chü-fu, 17/2b–4a; Yü Chi, 17/2b–4a; Yü Chi, 40/4b–6a; Liu Hsün, *Shui-yün-ts'un kao* 3/4a–6a; Wei Su, 5/10b–11b).

An exception to the general minimizing tendency of Table II has been my decision that, where a prefectural graduate or officeholder is recorded within twenty-five years of the end of Sung, the family may be assumed to have continued to the end. In fact most of these families with a brief gap in documentation at the end of Sung reappear in the sources as elite families in Yüan, soon after Sung's fall. Ten families have their last recorded prefectural graduate or official more than ten years before the end of Sung. If one counted all these families as leaving the local elite at the last date recorded, it would reduce the overall average period of elite membership by only about three years; in any case to proceed this way would be unrealistic, since one can presume that nearly all the men in question would have lived for some time after achieving a degree or reaching office.

6. I have dealt with the Sung–Yüan transition in Fu-chou in an unpublished paper, 'From Sung to Yüan: Continuities in the Local Elite of Fu-chou, Chiang-hsi,' presented at the 33rd Annual Meeting of the Association for Asian Studies, Toronto, March 14, 1981, and in 'Marriage, Descent Groups, and the Localist Strategy in Sung and Yüan Fu-chou.'

7. These six are as follows:

(a) The Ch'en family of Tung-ch'uan in Lo-an County (Appendix I, no. 7). According to Wu Ch'eng's preface to their genealogy, re-edited in Yüan, the family had not declined from its Sung prominence fifty years after the Yüan conquest (*WWC* 32/11b–12a). In fact the editor of the genealogy, named Ch'en Wen-hsiu, was the father of Wu Ch'eng's wife; the marriage took place under Yüan. (See the funerary inscription of Ch'en's wife, surnamed Lai, in *WWC* 67/14b.) As Wu Ch'eng was one of the two most prominent men of Fu-chou during Yüan (the other was Yü Chi), this marriage itself attests to the Ch'en family's local elite status in Yüan. Another member of the family, Ch'en Shih-kuei, in cooperation with his brother rebuilt the Lo-an County school in 1312. (See his funerary inscriptions in *WWC* 82/1a–3a and in Ho Chung, 4/9a–10b.)

(b)   The Cheng family of Lo-an County (see Appendix I, no. 9). The most
prominent Sung member of this family, Cheng Sung, during the early years
of Yüan was Wu Ch'eng's protector and host for eight years: Wu returned to
his own home in 1283. Cheng, in the first years after the fall of Sung, had
supplied his private militia to the supporters of a Sung restoration, but was
ultimately granted an amnesty by the Yüan state and lived on until 1307.
(See *WWC* 74/3a–5a, and Wu Ch'eng's own record of conduct in *WWC* end
matter.)

(c)   The Ch'üeh family of Lo-an County (see Appendix I, no. 15). Several
members of this family are mentioned as Yüan officeholders in the Lo-an
gazetteers. (See especially *KHLA* 5/23–25b.)

(d)   The Huang family of T'ung-fu in Lo-an County (see Appendix I, no. 29).
This family produced two *chin-shih* after the revival of the examinations in
Yüan: one in 1318 and one in 1330. (See *KHLA* 5/20b–21a; *TCLA* 7/12b–
13a.)

(e)   The Wang family of Lo-an County (see Appendix I, no. 62). This family
produced a *chin-shih* in the examination of 1351 and prefectural graduates
in 1308, 1344, 1353, and 1356. (See *KHLA* 5/21–22b; *TCLA* 7/26a–
27b.)

(f)   The Wu family of Hsien-k'ou in Ch'ung-jen County (see Appendix I, no. 69).
This is the family of Wu Ch'eng, who after refusing Yüan offices several
times finally accepted an academic post in 1306. His sons too held office
under Yüan, and his grandson Wu Li reached the *chin-shih* in 1351. (See Wu
Ch'eng's record of conduct in *WWC*, end matter, and in Yü Chi, 44/2b–4a;
also *TCCJ* 7c/72 and *KHCJ* 4/31a–32a.)

8.   See pp. 71–73.
9.   The first is Chao Chi-chih in 1135. See *TCLC* 36/4b.
10.   It is important to note the difference between these figures and those tabulated
in n. 72 to Chapter 1. Here the question is one of membership in a long-lived elite
family; there the issue was whether a man's relatives had achieved office before
his *chin-shih*. Thus in the present case the group of 409 includes a number of
chin-shih who are known to have been their family's first officeholder, and many
more who may have been. On the other hand, the 'non-mobile' group in n. 72
included some men whose family cannot be reconstructed over a long enough
period to justify inclusion in Table II, but who are known to have had at least
one relative in office before their *chin-shih*. There the object was to establish
maximum rates of movement of 'new' men into office; here it is simply to show
that this group of relatively stable families represent too high a proportion of the
officeholding and degreeholding population to be dismissed as atypical.
11.   Of course there is a fair number of families whose claims of origin, if any, simply
have not survived. But the absence in the available records of *any* claim to early
T'ang or pre-T'ang local roots is a very striking bit of – admittedly negative –
evidence.
12.   The medieval Chinese aristocracy has been the subject of an enormous secondary
literature in Asian languages, though it is only more recently that it has attracted
considerable attention from Western researchers. An excellent brief introduction
to work on various aspects of the subject is provided by the footnotes and bibliographic postscript of D.C. Twitchett's article on the composition of the T'ang
elite (Twitchett, 'The Composition of the T'ang Ruling Class'), itself a major
contribution to the discussion. Two other important works by Western scholars
should be cited: David Johnson's overall study of the medieval clans (Johnson,
Medieval Chinese Oligarchy), with a very important examination of the lists of
choronyms and their associated surnames discovered at Tunhuang or reconstructed

from the *T'ai-p'ing huan-yü chi*, and Patricia Ebrey's painstaking reconstruction and case study, from Han through T'ang, of a single clan, the Ts'uis of Po-ling (Ebrey, *Aristocratic Families*). The Tunhuang lists are also discussed in Twitchett's article above. Ebrey's work is one of two book-length studies of a single clan for the medieval period: the other is Moriya Mitsuo's pathbreaking monograph on the Wangs of T'ai-yüan (Moriya, *Rikuchō monbatsu no ichi kenkyū*). Shorter studies exist by Johnson on the Chao Chün Lis (Johnson, 'The Last Years of a Great Clan'), by Takeda Ryūji on the Yangs of Hung-nung (Takeda, 'Monbatsu to shite no Kōnō Yōshi ni tsuite no ichi kōsatsu'), by Yano Chikara on the P'ei, Wei, Chang, and Cheng clans (Yano, 'Shōshi kenkyū kō;' (Teishi kenkyū;' 'Ishi kenkyū;'), and by Mao Han-kuang on the Lang-yeh Wangs (Mao, 'Wo-kuo chung-ku ta shih-tsu chih ko-an yen-chiu – Lang-yeh Wang shih').

13. The view of most of T'ang political history as a process of the rise of a new *chin-shih*-bureaucrat class of relatively lowly origins at the expense of the old aristocratic families of the period of disunion was present already in the work of Naitō Torajirō (Naitō, 'Gaikekuteki Tō-Sō jidai kan') but emerged in its earliest fully articulated form in the work of the great Chinese scholar Ch'en Yin-k'o (Ch'en, *T'ang-tai cheng-chih chih shu-lun*). Ch'en's arguments strongly influenced E.G. Pulleyblank's study of the An Lu-shan rebellion and its social and political contexts (Pulleyblank, *The Background of the Rebellion of An Lu-shan*). Ch'en's views have been attacked or modified from all possible directions: some have placed the beginnings of the breakdown of the aristocratic polity before T'ang (Ochi Shigeaki, 'Gi-Shin Nanbokuchō no saikakyū kanryōsō ni tsuite') or even seen the old aristocracy as having largely dissolved before T'ang began (Nunome, 'Tōsho no kizoku'); but the view that aristocratic elements maintained much of their power even through the factional struggles of middle and late T'ang has established itself more successfully (e.g. Tonami Mamoru, 'Chūsei kizokusei no hōkai to hekisho sei'). Both David Johnson's examination of T'ang chief ministers and Sun Kuo-tung's comparison of the backgrounds of prominent men of early T'ang, late T'ang, and Northern Sung have demonstrated fairly clearly that the medieval great clans continued to produce very substantial proportions, even the majority, of high officials right to the end of T'ang (Johnson, *Medieval Chinese Oligarchy*, pp. 131–52; Sun, 'T'ang–Sung chih she-hui men-ti chih hsiao-jung.'

14. Johnson, *Medieval Chinese Oligarchy*, p. 165, no. 49.

15. Johnson, *Medieval Chinese Oligarchy*, pp. 92–3, 105–203. Ebrey, *Aristocratic Families*, pp. 81–2, deals with the dispersal of much of the Ts'ui clan from its home base during Sui and early T'ang. There will no doubt also have been some clans or members of clans for whom the choronym still corresponded to their place of residence.

16. This view too goes back to Naitō Torajirō. Both Ebrey and Johnson support it: Ebrey, *Aristocratic Families*, pp. 112–15; Johnson, *Medieval Chinese Oligarchy*, 141–52.

17. For Robert Hartwell claims of T'ang and pre-T'ang great clan descent, whether true or not, are an integral part of the social identity of the 'professional elite' of Northern Sung. See Hartwell, 'Demographic, Political, and Social Transformations of China, 750–1550,' pp. 411–12. See also Chapter 3, pp. 119–21 and note 76.

David Johnson's detailed study of the history of the Chao Chün Lis ('The Last Years of a Great Clan') deals brilliantly with the clan's origins and with the transformation of its character under T'ang. As to early Sung, I find Johnson's general conclusion – that the social meaning of great clan descent had entirely changed – quite well founded. In specifics, however, I think Johnson goes too far in suggesting that mentions of great clan choronyms in Sung funerary inscriptions often were not even intended as serious claims of descent. More generally, I am uncomfortable with the view – not Johnson's alone – that because claims are general and vague, or because they cannot be confirmed by step-by-step tracings of ancestry, they must therefore be false. It is clear from the remarks of Sung authors that written genealogies were lost or destroyed in great numbers during the social upheavals of late T'ang and Five Dynasties; this has been amply documented by Johnson and others. Under these conditions it seems to me perfectly plausible that men whose ancestors had in fact been great clan members would have found themselves, in Sung, aware of their own prestigious descent (which would have become part of the family's oral tradition) but unable – for lack of genealogical records by then destroyed – to trace precisely the steps of that descent beyond two or three generations. In such a situation false claims, being harder to detect, would probably have been made more often; but this does not alter the likelihood that many claims were true. That descendants of the T'ang great clans should have vanished almost without trace from the social and political elite of China in the course of the T'ang–Sung transition seems to me most improbable, and possibly without historical parallel elsewhere.

As to the claims of the Fu-chou families dealt with here, for only two is there much evidence beyond the claim itself. These two, however, make an interesting contrast. The Tseng family of Nan-feng County originally claimed descent from the Tsengs of the state of Lu – thus ultimately from Confucius' disciple Tseng Tzu. The claim appears in the earliest surviving funerary inscription of a member of the Nan-feng family, that of Tseng Chih-yao, written by Ou-yang Hsiu at the request of Chih-yao's grandson Tseng Kung in 1046, some thirty-four years after Chih-yao's death (Ou-yang Hsiu, 21/1a–4a). By lucky happenstance both the letter in which Tseng Kung requested the inscription (Tseng Kung, 15/5a–8b) and Ou-yang Hsiu's reply to the request (Ou-yang Hsiu, 47/10b–11b) have survived. In his letter Ou-yang called attention to some points in the Tsengs' claimed line of descent in the period from Chou to Han which seemed to him to conflict with what was recorded in independent historical sources. While he had reproduced the Tsengs' claims in his inscription, here he indicated his doubts to Tseng Kung. Tseng Kung in a reply thanked Ou-yang elaborately for his inscription, but regarding the doubts as to the descent claim he noted: 'I have ventured not to receive your instruction, but will consider it more carefully.' (Tseng Kung, 16/3b–5b). In another tomb inscription for Tseng Chih-yao, written by Wang An-shih at Tseng Kung's request in 1057 (eleven years after Ou-yang Hsiu's inscription), the same descent claims appeared again (Wang An-shih, 92/1a). However, in 1084 Tseng Kung's brother Tseng Chao compiled a new genealogy for the Tsengs. This work, long since lost, is mentioned in Tseng Chao's own record of conduct (Yang Shih, *Kuei-shan chi* 29/2a–20b), and Chao's preface to it is quoted, in part, in a Yüan dynasty preface to a later version of the genealogy. According to Tseng Chao at this time:

> The line of the old generations of our family was composed by Wen Yen-po and Kao Shih-lien and contains things that one dare not believe. Through the disorder of late T'ang and Five Dynasties there are further matters that cannot be determined. I have personally searched among the remnants of old collected works and have even gone to the region's stone records and bronze inscriptions and the like, and have obtained names for six generations; there are still things that cannot completely be known (Yü Chi, 40/4b–6a).

The Kao Shih-lien referred to here was one of the compilers of the T'ang genealogical work called *Chen-kuan shih-tsu chih*, done in 638; thus it would appear that the Nan-feng Tsengs' genealogical records for the earliest stages of their ancestry were derived (or were believed or claimed to be derived) from a section of that work devoted to a Tseng descent line. Tseng Chao, however, would seem to have taken Ou-yang Hsiu's doubts to heart; his preface represents a withdrawal of the family's confidence in its claims to ancient ancestry. The new genealogy evidently limited its scope to a mere six generations before (or possibly including) Tseng Chao's own. Thus in this case we have a claim to which not even the family at issue was willing to maintain a firm commitment.

A rather different case is the claim of the Lu family of Chin-ch'i County to descent from a great Six Dynasties and T'ang clan, the Lus of Wu Chün (i.e. of Su-chou). This claim, made in a number of funerary inscriptions (e.g. Lu Chiu-yüan, 27/1a), was supported by the Southern Sung poet Lu Yu, of the same surname but from a family in Yüeh-chou. In a preface to the collected works of Lu Huan-chih of the Chin-ch'i family, Lu Yu noted that this family had not lost its genealogy even in the disorder of Five Dynasties and so could still trace its exact line of descent from the T'ang clan; he implied that the achievement was unusual (Lu Yu, *Wei-nan wen-chi* 15/5b). This descent claim, based on a surviving genealogy that at least one contemporary judged as genuine, seems to be of a different order from that of the Tsengs.

18. The more recent places of origin named by families that claim great clan descent are, however, included. In identifying great clan choronyms mentioned in Sung Fu-chou sources I have used the several clan lists reproduced by David Johnson (Johnson, *Medieval Chinese Oligarchy*, pp. 217–31). These appear also in Ikeda On, 'Tōdai no gunbō hyō;' Ikeda was in fact the one who first reconstructed one of the lists, from the *T'ai-p'ing huan-yü chi*.

19. The ten are: (1) a Ch'eng family of Ch'ung-jen County, claiming descent from the Ch'engs of Kuang-p'ing (*WWC* 73/6a–7a; cf. Johnson, p. 224); (2) a Chiang family of Lin-ch'uan County, claiming descent from the Chiangs of Chi-yang (Hsieh I, 9/18a and 20b; cf. Johnson, pp. 217 and 225); (3) the Li family of Ch'ung-jen County, claiming descent from a Ch'eng-chi Li family which may be the same as the Lis of Lung-hsi (Wei Liao-weng, 79/4a–6a; cf. Johnson, pp. 222–31; and see Appendix I, no. 36); (4) the Lo family of Ch'ung-jen, claiming descent from the Los of Yü-chang (Yüan Hsieh, 12/1a–35a; cf. Johnson, pp. 218, 227, and 231; and see Appendix I, no. 41); (5) the Lu family of Chin-ch'i County, claiming descent from the Lus of Wu Chün (see note 17 above; cf. Johnson, pp. 218, 226, and 230; and see Appendix I, no. 42); (6) the Ts'ai family of Lin-ch'uan, claiming descent from the Ts'ais of Chi-yang (Su Sung: *Su Wei-kung wen-chi* 57/9b–14a; cf. Johnson, pp. 217, 225, 228; and see Appendix I, no. 49); (7) the Tseng family of Nan-feng County, claiming descent from the Tsengs of Lu-kuo (see note 18 above; cf. Johnson, pp. 217–18, 225, and 229; and see Appendix I, no. 54); (8) the Tseng family of Lo-an County, similarly claiming descent from the Lu-kuo Tsengs (Tseng Feng, 17/1a; cf. Johnson, loc. cit.; and see Appendix I, no. 52); (9) the Wang family of Lin-ch'uan, claiming descent from the Wangs of T'ai-yüan (Wang An-shih, 96/2a; cf. Johnson, pp. 223 and 229; and see Appendix I, no. 61); (10) the Wu family of Hsin-t'ien in Chin-ch'i County, claiming descent from the Wus of P'u-yang (Li Ts'un, ch. 24; cf. Johnson, pp. 217, 225, and 228; and see Appendix I, no. 66). Of these only the Ch'engs and the Chiangs do not appear in Table I.

20. These last three are: (a) the ancestor of Li Shih-hua of Ch'ung-jen (1266–1351), who is reported to have come to Fu-chou as an official during the K'ai-yüan period (713–41) of T'ang (Sung Lien, 50/1–2); (b) the eighteenth-generation ancestor of a late Sung prefectural graduate named Yüeh Yüan: eighteen generations' distance would place this man as well (very approximately) in mid-T'ang

(*WWC* 55/10b–11a); (c) the ancestor of the Wu family of Ch'ing-yün canton in Ch'ung-jen, whose genealogy was shown to Wu Ch'eng in early or middle Yüan by a man identified as of the nineteenth generation; again nineteen generations' distance would place the founding ancestor roughly in middle T'ang (*WWC* 32/8b–9a).

The other four families are: (1) the Chu family of Chin-ch'i, whose ancestor Chu Man is said simply to have arrived in T'ang (Sung Lien, 49/77a ff.; and see Appendix I, no. 12); (2) the Chu family of Lo-an, whose first ancestor served as *ssu-ma* of the prefecture at the end of T'ang (*WWC* 75/8a–9b; and see Appendix I, no. 13); (3) the Li family of Ch'ung-jen, whose ancestors' arrival in Fu-chou would appear to have fallen at the end of T'ang, judging by the number of generations recounted in the funerary inscription of Li Yen-hua (Wei Liao-weng, 79/4a–6a; and see Appendix I, no. 36); (4) the Tseng family of Nan-feng County, whose ancestor Tseng Hung-li is reported to have arrived late in T'ang (*MKNF* 3/8b–9b and 14/2a–b; *TCChCh* 8/2b–3a; and see Appendix I, no. 54).

21. The seventeen are: (1) An Ai family of Lin-ch'uan County (Ch'eng Chü-fu, 22/16a–17a); (2) a Chang family of Lin-ch'uan (Huang Chen, 97/10b–12b); (3) the Hsieh family of Lin-ch'uan County, of which Hsieh I, born in 1069, was a fifth-generation member (Hsieh I, 9/18b–20b; and see Appendix I, no. 21); (4) the Jao family of Lin-ch'uan (Lü Nan-kung, *Kuan-yüan chi* 19/5b; and see Appendix I, no. 32); (5) the Ko family of Chin-ch'i County (Lu Chiu-yüan, 7a–11a; and see Appendix I, no. 34); (6) the Liu family of Nan-feng County (Liu Hsün, 8/1a–2b; and see Appendix I, no. 40); (7) the Liu family of Chin-ch'i County (Wei Su, *hsü-chi* 1/12b–13a; and see Appendix I, no. 39); (8) a Ch'eng family of Ch'ung-jen (*WWC* 73/6a–7a); (9) the Lu family of Chin-ch'i (see note 18 above; and see Appendix I, no. 42) (10) an Ou-yang family of Ch'ung-jen County (Ou-yang Ch'e, *Ou-yang hsiu-chuan chi* 7/6a–8a); (11) the Teng family of Chin-ch'i (Wei Su, 3/14b–16b; and see Appendix I, no. 47); (12) the Ts'ai family of Lin-ch'uan County (Su Sung, 57/9b–14a; and see Appendix I, no. 49); (13) the Tseng family of Lo-an (Tseng Feng, 17/1a, and see Appendix I, no. 52); (14) the Ts'ao family of I-huang (*WWC* 32/15a–16b; and see Appendix I, no. 50); (15) the Yen family of Lin-ch'uan (Ou-yang Hsiu, *Ou-yang Wen-chung kung chi*, 7a–12a; and see Appendix I, no. 73); (16) the Yü family of Chin-ch'i (Li Ts'un, 24/16a–17a; and see Appendix I, no. 81); (17) a Yüan family of Lin-ch'uan (Yü Chi, 43/12b–13b). Of these, only the Ais, Changs, Ch'engs, Yüs, and Yüans do not appear in Table I.

22. These seven are: (1) a Chang family of Chin-ch'i (Wei Su, 6/15b–16a); (2) the Ch'en family of Tung-ch'uan in Lo-an (Ho Chung, 4/9a–10b; and see Appendix I, no. 7); (3) the Lo family of Ch'ung-jen (Yüan Hsieh, 12/1a–35a, and see Appendix I, no. 41); (4) the Wu family of Hsin-t'ien in Chin-ch'i (Li Ts'un, 23/4a–7a; and see Appendix I, no. 66); (5) the Wu family of Lin-ch'uan (Yü Chi, 43/2a; and see Appendix I, no. 71); (6) a Yü family of Ch'ung-jen (*WWC* 32/10a–11a); (7) the Yü family of Lin-ch'uan (Ch'eng Chü-fu, 18/5a–6b; and see Appendix I, no. 82). Of these, only the Changs and the Yüs of Ch'ung-jen do not appear in Table 1.

It is important to note that some of the attributions of date of arrival in this and the previous two footnotes are approximate, calculated by counting back the numbers of generations (assuming roughly a thirty-year average) or the round numbers of years that are recorded in the sources. In the case of the present group of 'early Sung' arrivals this approximation is especially broad: for some of these we are told only, for instance, that 'when Nan-T'ang submitted to Sung, then they moved' to Fu-chou, or that 'with the rise of Sung, they moved.' Some of these may have arrived after the beginning of the eleventh century and so belong with the group in n. 23 below; some of those determined by counting generations may have arrived earlier, before Sung absorbed Southern T'ang. A few such cases, however, would not much affect the evidence for the shift in migration patterns discussed on pp. 67–9.

23. Eleven of these sixteen, who arrive with a previous history of office, are discussed on pp. 71–3 and in notes 34 and 35 below. The other five are: (1) the Chan family of Lo-an, whose founder arrived as registrar of Ch'ung-jen County in 1034 (*TCLA* 1/27a; *WWC* 32/2b–3a. and see Appendix I, no. 1); (2) the Huang family of Pa-t'ang in Lo-an, arriving in 1014 (*WWC* 32/17a–18b; and see Appendix I, no. 28); (3) a Chou family of Ch'ung-jen, arriving around 1127 (*WWC* 40/1a–b); (4) the Li family of Lin-ch'uan, arriving in the later eleventh century (*YLTT* 10422/3a–6a; and see Appendix I, no. 37); (5) the Teng family of Lin-ch'uan, arriving in the second half of the twelfth century (*KHFC* 57/2b; Lu Chiu-yüan, 16/8b–10a; and see Appendix I, no. 47).

24. Aoyama Sadao's studies of Northern Sung families from various regions of the empire have shown that their ancestors very commonly are said to have changed residence once or several times during the Five Dynasties. See the last eight works by Aoyama in the List of Works Cited.

25. The late T'ang, Five Dynasties, and early Sung immigrants have been grouped together largely because of the approximateness of the dates of arrival (see above, n. 22): they form a group of cases falling roughly in the tenth century, with some in the late ninth and perhaps a few in the early eleventh. By combining them one can be fairly sure that all the migrants who arrived during the rule of the Wu and Southern T'ang kingdoms have been included. The regional autonomy maintained formally by the two kingdoms was probably already a fact at the end of T'ang and may have continued to some degree into the early decades of Sung. Note that no map has been made for immigrants arriving earlier in T'ang, as the number known is simply too small (see n. 20 above) for any pattern to emerge.

26. The only exception to this rule, the ancestor of the Ai family of Lin-ch'uan (n. 21 above), came from Mu-chou, which in Sung was in Liang-che circuit but lay just to the east of the Chiang-nan-tung circuit border.

27. Again, Mu-chou, home of the Ai ancestor, lay outside Wu and Southern T'ang (in the kingdom of Wu-Yüeh) but directly bordered them. Otherwise one may note that Shao-wu Chün, origin of the ancestor of the Yü family of Chin-ch'i (n. 21), was part of the territory of Southern T'ang but not that of Wu. It would appear that most of the recorded migration in the Five Dynasties period actually took place during Southern T'ang (937–75), since many of the sources in dating an ancestor's arrival specifically mention Southern T'ang, while none mentions Wu.

28. This is, however, a point on which further research, to establish similar maps for other prefectures in the Chiang-nan region, could shed a good deal of light; it could certainly be done with little difficulty on the basis of the same sort of evidence as is used here. There are good grounds for certain speculations as to the results; for example, it is almost inconceivable that one would not find significant numbers of migrants to the region from North China in the tenth century. My own guess would be that such migrants came chiefly to Chin-ling (or earlier to Yang-chou, the Wu capital) and certain other prefectures whose political and economic importance in the region predates Sung; that these prefectures acted in effect as collection points, with migrants branching out in turn (perhaps often through official posting) to more peripheral prefectures such as Fu-chou; and that the effect of the Wu and Southern T'ang statehood and boundaries, combined with the political and military situation in other regions, was to direct migration from the major prefectures inward, to prefectures which in earlier periods of unification might have been relatively unattractive to would-be emigrants. If all this proves to be true, then the predominance of short-distance

moves I have found for Fu-chou in the tenth century may reflect only that the individual steps of a sequence of migrations were fairly short. This still contrasts with the later period, when single-step long-distance moves seem to have been common.

29. These four are: (1) Liu Hsi-t'i, ancestor of the Liu family of Nan-feng, who held office (along with his father and grandfather) under Southern T'ang (see his funerary inscription in Liu Hsün, 8/1a–2b; and see Appendix I, no. 40); (2) the ninth-generation ancestor of Ch'eng Yüan of Ch'ung-jen, who served as sheriff of the district and settled there (see the funerary inscription of Ch'eng Yüan's wife, a woman surnamed Lo,[b] in *WWC* 73/6a–7a); (3) Ou-yang Chün, who served Southern T'ang and around 970 retired to his home in Lu-ling County, Chi-chou, then moved to Ch'ung-jen (see the funerary inscription of his descendant Ou-yang Ch'e in Ou-yang Ch'e, 7/6a–8a); (4) Ts'ai I, ancestor of the Ts'ai family of Lin-ch'uan, who moved from Chin-ling to Lin-ch'uan; his father had held office under Southern T'ang (see the funerary inscription of their descendant Ts'ai Ch'eng-hsi in Su Sung, 57/9b–14a; and cf. Appendix I, no. 49). Of these, only Ch'eng Yüan's ancestor definitely was posted to office in Fu-chou and then settled there.

30. The five are: (1) the ancestor of the Chu family of Lo-an, made *ssu-ma* of Fu-chou at the end of T'ang (see the funerary inscription of his descendant Chu Kuei-fa, in *WWC* 75/8a–9b; and cf. Appendix I, no. 13); (2) Li Te-ling, who held office in Fu-chou between 713 and 741 and settled in Ch-ung-jen (see the funerary inscription of his descendant Li Shih-hua in Sung Lien, 23/847–48); (3) Tseng Hung-li, ancestor of the Tsengs of Nan-feng, who became administrator of Nan-feng between 874 and 879 and ultimately settled there (*MKNF* 3/8b–9b and 14/2a–b; *TCChCh* 8/2b–3a; Huang Chin, *Chin-hua Huang hsien-sheng wen-chi* 32/13a–14b; and see Appendix I, no. 54); (4) the ancestor of the Wu family of Ch'ing-yün canton in Ch'ung-jen, who in mid-T'ang came to Fu-chou as registrar of Ch'ung-jen, married the daughter of a man of the county, and settled there (see the preface to the family's genealogy in *WWC* 32/8b–9a and the funerary inscription of descendant Wu Te-fu in *WWC* 86/1a–2a; and cf. Appendix I, no. 68); (5) Chu Man, ancestor of the Chu family of Chin-ch'i, who held office during T'ang and moved to Chin-ch'i (see the funerary inscription of his descendant Chu Ssu-jung in Sung Lien, 19/706–708; and cf. Appendix I, no. 12). The first four all clearly held office in Fu-chou.

31. This is the Yüeh family of I-huang County. Yüeh Shih, the first Sung *chin-shih* from Fu-chou, had held office under Southern T'ang (*SS* 306/10b; Tseng Kung, *Lung-p'ing chi* 14/1a–b), and the founding ancestor had migrated some time in mid-T'ang (see n. 20 above).

32. This is the ancestor of the Ts'ao family of I-huang: see n. 21 above.

33. Here again the claims of some families to great clan ancestry, which of course imply a long background of official service, are not included in the discussion. Three of these families (the Ch'engs, the Ts'ais, and the Tsengs: see above, nn. 29 and 30) are nevertheless included among the eleven with pre-Sung official ancestry, since they make specific claims to ancestors who held office while living at some residence more recent than the putative great-clan home.

34. Five of these are discussed in note 35 below. (Note that the Chan family of Lo-an – see above, n. 23 – is not included among the eleven families. This is because nothing is known of the family before its arrival in Fu-chou, and because the Ch'ung-jen office claimed for its founder cannot be independently confirmed. The Chans, who do later become quite a successful local family, seem in any case set off from the other families mentioned here by their arrival in the *early* eleventh century; note that the other ten appear to arrive no earlier than late Northern

Sung, near the end of the eleventh century.) The other six are: (1) Huang Sheng, an 1103 *chin-shih*, holder of several prefectships between then and 1138, and descendant of a series of officials, who is claimed as an ancestor by a late Sung or early Yüan woman of Chin-ch'i County. Huang Sheng's own funerary inscription confirms that, though originally of P'u-ch'eng County in Chien-chou, and resident since his grandfather's time in Lo-p'ing County, Jao-chou, he was buried in Chin-ch'i. See Wei Su, 9/2a–3a, and Wang Ying-ch'en, *Wen-ting chi* 20/249–50. (2). Huang Jen-chieh, who came to Fu-chou as the sheriff of Lin-ch'uan County and took up residence there; his sons Huang I-kang, I-ming, and I-yung all became disciples of Chu Hsi. See *KHFC* 59/9b–10a; *SYHA* 69/36a; *SYHAPI* 63/20b and 69/143a; and the funerary inscription of a woman surnamed Kuo in Huang Kan 38/35a–37a, where I-yung is identified as from Hsin-ch'eng County in Lin-an Fu. (3) Kuan Chien of Lung-ch'üan County in Ch'u-chou, who came to Fu-chou in the middle 1100s as administrative aide to the Intendancy for Ever-Normal Granaries, which had its seat there, and made his residence in Lin-ch'uan. By 1186 he had reached the post of Judical Intendant of Kuang-tung circuit, serving concurrently as acting prefect of Kuang-chou and Military Intendant of the same circuit; his son Kuan Chan in 1212 held the same posts for Kuang-hsi circuit. Nothing is known of later members of the family, and no *chin-shih* of this surname is recorded in the Fu-chou gazetteers. See *KHFC* 47/34a–35a; Wu T'ing-hsieh, *Nan-Sung chih-fu nien-piao* 61a. (4) Liu Ch'ing-yin of Lin-chiang Chün, prefect of Ch'üan-chou and descendent of several central officials, who moved to Chin-ch'i in the early or middle twelfth century. His son and grandson also held office. See the funerary inscription of his Yüan descendant Liu Yu-ting in Wei Su, 5/24a–25b, and the preface to some ancestral writings done for Yu-ting's sons by Wu Ch'eng in *WWC* 45/5b–7a. (5) Shih Ying-chi, prefect of an unidentified prefecture and a member of an important family of Mei-shan County, Mei-chou, that had held office for at least two generations before him. He came to live in Ch'ung-jen County near the end of Sung. See the funerary inscription of his son Shih Shih-mei in *WWC* 72/4a–6b. (6) Yü Tien, great-grandson of Hsiao-tsung's assistant minister, Yü Yün-wen, and member of a Szechwan family that had produced many officials in the four generations before him. Near the end of Sung he settled in Ch'ung-jen. The family left no Sung record of its presence in the Fu-chou local elite (there was scarcely time), but became one of the most important families of the prefecture in Yüan, when Tien's grandson Yü Chi reached a post of considerable prestige, if not power, in the new dynasty's central government. See Yü Chi's funerary inscription in Ou-yang Hsüan, *Kuei-chai wen-chi* 9/23a.

35. I discuss each of these five families in detail below.

(1) Ch'ao: Late in Northern Sung, a man named Ch'ao Kung-mai was made vice-administrator of Chien-ch'ang Chün, Fu-chou's southeastern neighbor, and took up residence in Fu-chou. (See the funerary inscription of Kung-mai's son Ch'ao Tzu-yü in Chou Pi-ta, 75/1a–3a.) Kung-mai was a member of an enormously successful officeholding family, originally of Ch'ing-feng County, Shan-chou, and more recently based in Chü-yeh County, Chi-chou, just to the east of the Northern Sung capital at K'ai-feng Fu; among his ancestors were assistant ministers and other high officials. (See the funerary inscriptions and biographies of various relatives in Tseng Kung, *Yüan-feng lei-kao* 46/11a–b; Wang An-shih, 95/9b–11a; *SS* 444/2a–b; for further information see *CPT* pp. 1946–58, which lists forty-six men of the Ch'ao surname, almost all from this family.) At least two of Ch'ao Kung-mai's sons remained in Fu-chou; Ch'ao Tzu-yü (see above) and Ch'ao Tzu-shei, whose son Ch'ao Pai-t'an passed the prefectural exam in 1174 and achieved the *chin-shih*

the next year. (See *KHIH* 5/17a, 6/16a; *TCIH* 25/22b, 29/8a–b; *KHFC* 47/19b–20a; *SYHA* 77/16a.) For confirmation that Pai-t'an was Kung-mai's grandson, thus that Tzu-shei was Kung-mai's son, see the preface to Kung-mai's collected works in Lu Yu, 14/10b–12a, which says that the writings were brought together by Kung-mai's grandson Pai-t'an.) No later members of the family are known in Fu-chou.

(2) Meng: Probably at roughly the same time as Ch'ao Kung-mai's move, an officeholder from a Meng family of K'ai-feng Fu also migrated south and settled in Lin-ch'uan County. The family had a long history of official success in Sung, having moved to K'ai-feng when its ancestor Meng Jih-hsin passed the *ming-ching* examination in 988. (See the funerary inscription of Meng Tse in Han Yüan-chi, *Nan-chien chia-i kao* 21/11a–14a.) The precise time of the family's move to Fu-chou is unclear: a Yüan preface to their genealogy identifies a *'t'e-chin-kung'* as the first to move south, in the third generation after Meng Jih-hsin, and a *'chung-t'ai-kung'* as the first to live in Lin-ch'uan, in the fourth generation. The first of these is clearly Meng Tse's grandfather, who is identified in Tse's inscription as *'t'e-chin'* (a high official title) and falls in the right generation counting down from Jih-hsin. The second, then, is either Meng Tse's father or someone else of his generation. As Tse himself lived from 1118 to 1181, it is likely that a move in his father's generation would have taken place near the end of Northern or the beginning of Southern Sung. Since this is a northern family it is probable that the move was occasioned by the fall of North China to the Chin in 1126–7. After the move the family continued producing high officials for at least three generations, well into the thirteenth century, with one *chin-shih* in 1175. Meng Tse himself reached no higher than administrative aide to the Military Intendancy of Ching-hu-nan circuit, and his three sons are not known to have held any but minor local posts. However, the 1175 *chin-shih*, a man named Meng Huan, reached Intendant of Ever-Normal Granaries of Kuang-tung circuit and then Supervisory Official of the Fiscal Intendancy of the same circuit: see *KHFC* 47/42a–b; *SYHA* 77/12b. A man named Meng Chih of the same family rose to be prefect of Yüeh-chou, and his son Meng Tien, in the middle thirteenth century, was Supervisory Official of the Fiscal Intendancy of Chiang-tung circuit and acting prefect of T'ai-p'ing-chou: see *KHFC* 47/41a–42a. If one examines Meng Tse's funerary inscription, one finds that his father's name is Chien, written with the metal radical; his own name, Tse, is written with the water radical; his sons' names are K'ai, Chi, and Ch'i, all written with the wood radical; and his grandson's is Yen, written with the fire radical. This is clearly a sequential arrangement of generational radicals associated with the cycle of the Five Phases: metal, water, wood, fire and – not directly attested here – earth. Meng Chih – wood radical – and his son Meng Tien – fire radical – fit perfectly into the sequence implied by Tse's inscription, and so can be identified as respectively of Tse's sons' and grandsons' generations. Meng Huan – water radical – must be of Tse's own generation. Thus although the exact relationships of all these men cannot be reconstructed, their generational and temporal succession is clear. A preface to the family's Yüan dynasty genealogy records that it continued sending members into office right down to the end of Sung: see *WWC* 57/5b–6a.

(3) Huang: Members of a third important Northern Sung family came to Fu-chou in Southern Sung: this was the lineage of the poet Huang T'ing-chien, two branches of which produced migrants to Fu-chou. A first cousin once removed of Huang T'ing-chien named Huang Piao (one generation lower than

T'ing-chien), moved to Lin-ch'uan County during (probably) the 1150s or 1160s (*KHFC* 47/43a). His sons Huang Jung and Huang Lo both used hereditary privilege to enter office and had fairly successful official careers. (For Jung, see *KHFC*, 46/1b; for Lo, see his funerary inscription in *YLTT* 7651/7b–13b, which mentions his burial in Lin-ch'uan Hsien, as well as *KHFC* 46/1b, and Lu Hsin-yüan, *Sung shih i* 22/2a.) Lo's two sons again obtained office through hereditary privilege, while Jung's two sons, Huang Fu and Huang Yung, passed the *chin-shih* exam from Fu-chou together in 1208 (*KHFC* 42/14b). A marker was established in Fu-chou's prefectural city to commemorate the two brothers' achievement (*YLTT* 10950/1b). No later descendants in Fu-chou are known.

A more distant relative of Huang T'ing-chien named Huang Tz'u-shan, the son of a *chin-shih* and himself a high official, settled in Lin-ch'uan in or around the 1130s. His son Huang Mu-chih, born in 1131, entered office by hereditary privilege and reached the posts of prefect of Chün-chou and Military Intendant for the forces under that jurisdiction. Mu-chih's two sons, Huang Luan and Huang Shao-tsung, passed the *chin-shih* exam from Fu-chou in 1184 and 1187 respectively. (See Mu-chih's funerary inscription in Chou Pi-ta, 78/11a–15a, and *KHFC* 42/13a–b.) Mu-chih's grandnephew Huang Ssu-yung also has a surviving funerary inscription (Huang Kan, 38/11a–13a): his adoptive father Huang Feng-chi, a grandson of Huang Tz'u-shan and the son of Mu-chih's brother, passed the prefectural exam in the late twelfth century. Ssu-yung's two sons both married daughters of prominent families, one the granddaughter of Chu Hsi, the other the daughter of the 1187 Fu-chou *chin-shih* Wang K'o-chin (for whom see *TCLC* 37b/1b, 43/6a–b; *KHFC* 59/8a; *SYHAPI* 43/25b). These marriages must have taken place before around 1210, when the inscription was written. Thus this line's elite status can be carried down to the first decades of the thirteenth century. No later descendants in Fu-chou are known.

For Huang Tz'u-shan's relationship to Huang T'ing-chien the only direct evidence is the biography of Tz'u-shan by the Yüan Fu-chou man Wei Su, which is reproduced in whole or in part by a variety of later sources (Wei Su, *hsü-chi* 8/10b; Lu Hsin-yüan, *Sung shih i* 27/18). No surviving Sung source specifies such a relationship, and the two lines were of different districts of Hung-chou (Tz'u-shan from Feng-ch'eng County, T'ing-chien from Fen-ning County), but neither fact makes the relationship impossible. Both lines claim an origin in Chin-hua County in Wu-chou, *not* a T'ang choronym. (See Huang Ssu-yung's funerary inscription in Huang Kan, 38/11a–13a, and that of T'ing-chien's relative Huang Lo in *YLTT* 7651/7b–13b.)

(4) Lin: In 1109 a man named Lin Kung-hsüan, from the 'other' Fu-chou, in Fu-chien circuit, passed the *chin-shih* examination. He eventually rose to the post of Military Intendant of the armies under the jurisdiction of Ch'iung-chou in Kuang-nan-hsi circuit, and on leaving that office sojourned in Fu-chou while awaiting a new appointment, then settled there. (See Liang K'o-chia, (*Ch'un-hsi*) *San-shan chih* 27/15a for the *chin-shih* listing for Lin Kung-hsüan; for his office and his move to Fu-chou see his grandson's biography in *KHFC* (47/39a–b.) Kung-hsüan's grandsons Lin Wen-chung and Lin Meng-ying (the latter a student of Lu Chiu-yüan: see *SYHA* 77/10b, and a letter from Lu to Meng-ying in Lu Chiu-yüan, op. cit., 9/10b–12b) both passed the *chin-shih* exam from Fu-chou in 1175 (*KHFC* 42/12a, 47/38b–39a and 39a–b). Wen-chung's son Lin Tzu-cheng passed in 1202 (*KHFC*, 42/14a), and Meng-ying's nephew Lin Yen-shan in 1220 (*KHFC*, 42/15b). No later record of the family exists.

(5) Lou: In the late twelfth or early thirteenth century, a man named Lou Shih became the last known immigrant founder of an important Sung Fu-chou family when he moved from his native place, Chia-hsing County in Hsiu-chou, to Lin-ch'uan. (See the funerary inscription of his great-grandson Wen-fu in Ch'eng Chü-fu, 18/11b–12b). Shih's cousin Lou Chi had been an assistant minister around 1210, but Shih himself was not an official, and the family had nothing like the long and manifold history in office of the Ch'aos, Huangs, or Mengs. (For the relationship between Shih and Chi see Ch'eng Chü-fu, 18/11b–12b. For Chi himself see his funerary inscription in 97/1a–13b.) Shih's son Lou Pi-chung held a low academic post in Chung-chou; his son Lou Chien was also a minor officeholder and passed the prefectural exam in 1240. Chien's three sons were all prefectural graduates, and one, Lou Nan-liang, passed the *chin-shih* exam in 1268. Later family members held office in Yüan. (See Ch'eng Chü-fu, 18/11b–12b; Yü Chi, 43/13b–15b; *WWC* 30/1a–2a; *SYHAPI* 84/12b and 26a; *KHFC* 66/1b.)

36. A further example of an immigrant officeholding family is the imperial lineage. From a perusal of the various provincial gazetteers' *chin-shih* lists, where imperial lineage members are recognizable by their surname (Chao) and the generational elements prescribed for the given names of all male members, it is clear that relatives (usually distant) of the Sung emperors flowed in vast numbers into virtually all prefectures south of the Yangtse in the years following the fall of the north in 1127. Fu-chou is no exception: the first imperial Chao obtained his *chin-shih* in 1135 (this is Chao Chi-chih: *TCLC* 36/4b), to be joined by several more in the next few decades: the numbers increase to a flood in the thirteenth century. In all, 112 members of the imperial lineage attained *chin-shih* from Fu-chou in Southern Sung, over a fifth of the total for the prefecture. In view of these numbers it is startling how little evidence there is of the Chaos' presence in the local scheme of things during the same period. Sung marriages between members of Fu-chou local elite families and Chaos are virtually unrecorded; nor is there much record of Chao participation in the kinds of activities typical of other Fu-chou elite members: construction of bridges, temples, or schools; local defense; famine relief. Nor do they appear prominently among the members of local philosophical schools: of the very large number of Fu-chou men recorded to have studied with Lu Chiu-yüan or his brother Lu Chiu-ling, only one is a Chao. (This is Chao Tuan-i, *chin-shih* in 1214: *KHFC* 42/16a, 47/27a–b; *SYHAPI* 58/37a. Lu Chiu-yüan's collected works include several letters to men surnamed Chao, but none of these appears to be from Fu-chou.) For a smaller family it would be dangerous to argue from such purely negative evidence; but as it is clear that hundreds or more probably thousands of Chaos must (at least formally) have maintained residence in Fu-chou in order to account for over a hundred *chin-shih*, the absence of evidence in this case surely cannot reflect mere lacunae in the sources. If, as I argue below, immigrant officeholding families were not easily integrated into the local elite during Sung, then the Chaos are surely the paradigm case. That despite this they were highly successful in the competition for degrees right down to the end of Sung does not significantly weaken the argument I make elsewhere, since imperial lineage members were by law specially privileged in the examination process. See Chaffee, pp. 190–2.

37. Huang Chen's efforts at famine relief in Fu-chou are documented in great detail in his collected works, *Huang-shih jih-ch'ao*, ch. 75 (containing his memorials to the court and to circuit officials) and ch. 78 (containing his public notices issued to the people of Fu-chou). The use of non-native residents as his agents in the countryside is recorded in two notices issued in the fourth month of 1271. Only the second of these is included in the *Ssu-k'u ch'üan-shu chen-pen* edition

of Huang's works (which is the edition I cite elsewhere), in ch. 78, pp. 15b–16b; but both are found, following one another, in the Tzu-ch'i Feng-shih Keng-yü Lou edition at the Jinbun Kagaku Kenkyūjo in Kyoto, in ch. 78, pp. 7b–8a. Huang's term in the first notice is *yü-kuei shih-ta-fu*, 'sojourning men of rank and gentlemen'; this is ambiguous, as *shih-ta-fu*, 'gentlemen,' may or may not here be modified by *yü*, 'sojourning.' In the second notice, however, the question is resolved when Huang uses only the terms *chi-yü*, 'sojourners; men living in a place other than their original home,' and *yü-kuei*, 'sojourning men of rank.'

38. Thus in the early 1200s the administrator of Lin-ch'uan County, Huang Kan, in judging the suit brought by a Lo-an County man identified only as Prefect Tseng (Tseng *chih-fu*) against one Huang Kuo-ts'ai, remarks on Tseng's characterizing himself as a 'recently arrived sojourning resident' and rejects the claim on the grounds that Tseng is living where his parents had lived already; he scolds Tseng for making the claim 'and so denigrating, in order to rise above, the lineage and neighborhood of his father and elder brothers' (Huang Kan, 32/8b–9a). Why Tseng should want to make such a claim becomes clear in view of Huang Kan's earlier remark about the suit: 'When this county received the Intendancy's order to supervise the investigation, I saw that [Tseng's suit] was unreasonable, but through its having to do with a sojourning resident family I did not want to speak sternly of its impropriety' (Huang Kan, 32/8a–b). Evidently Tseng knew that by calling himself a non-native he could earn special consideration from officials judging his suit. This could not have been based on inside knowledge that Huang Kan was particularly susceptible to the claim, since the plaints Huang quotes from had been made originally to officials in Lo-an, and the case had only later been sent down extraordinarily to Huang by the financial intendancy for his special investigation.

39. For example, the private militia of the Teng family of Chin-ch'i County; the similar force maintained by the Fu family of the same district; and the fort and defense force founded by Hou Ting of I-huang County in the 1230s (see Chapter 5, pp. 139–47 and 148).

40. See the examples listed in n. 46 to Chapter 5.

41. See Huang Chen's comments on the problem of the troops in rural forts, discussed in Chapter 5, pp. 137–38.

42. See the funerary inscription of Meng Tse (Han Yüan-chi, 21/11a–14a) regarding his construction of dwellings for his entire lineage, numbering over a thousand people, and the neighborhood's admiration of the harmony maintained within so large a group.

43. As the Ch'aos were a northern family, many of them may have come south with the fall of the north in 1127, but Ch'ao Tzu-yü's funerary inscription (Chou Pi-ta, 75/1a–3a) recounts the circumstances of his father Kung-mai's move to Fu-chou in a way that suggests that only he made the move; and it is known, for example, that Kung-mai's father's cousin, Ch'ao Ch'ien-chih, moved not to Fu-chou but to Hsin-chou after the north fell (*CPT*, p. 1957). As for the Huangs, the first cousin of Huang Lo and Huang Jung, a man named Huang Sun (whose name shared his cousin's generational indicator), was according to his funerary inscription buried in the family's original home district, Fen-ning County; Fu-chou is mentioned only as the place Huang Sun visited to mourn his cousin's death (Yeh Shih, *Shui-hsin chi* 17/11a–13b). Similarly the funerary inscription of the son of Huang Mu-chih's first cousin Huang Ch'ü-hua, a man named Huang Ch'ou-jo, makes no mention of Fu-chou, identifies Ch'ou-jo's place of residence as Feng-ch'eng County in Hung-chou, and records his burial at 'the old family home' (*ku-li*) (Liu K'o-chuang, 142/4b). Thus neither Huang Piao nor Huang Tz'u-shan would appear to have been accompanied by their brothers in their move to Fu-chou.

44. *WWC* 32/17a–18b; and see Appendix I, no. 28.
45. See the funerary inscription of Ko Keng in Lu Chiu-yüan, 28/7a–11a; and cf. Appendix I, no. 34.
46. See the record of conduct of Lu Chiu-ling in Lu Chiu-yüan, 27/1a–8a, and cf. Appendix I, no. 42.
47. Ch'en Yüan-chin, 6/4a–6b; and see Appendix I, no. 4.
48. Hsieh I, 10/5a–12a. See also Chapter 1, pp. 54–5.
49. Ho Hsi-chih, *Chi-lei chi* 5b–7b; and see Appendix I, no. 9.
50. See T'u's funerary inscription in Sun Ti, *Nan-lan-ling Sun shang-shu ta-ch'üan chi* 52/5b–8b, and in *TCIH* 45g/93a–95a; and cf. Appendix I, no. 58.
51. See his funerary inscription in Ch'en Yüan-chin, 6/9a–11b.
52. The occasional opposite claim of 'poverty' is, I think, to be taken with more than a grain of salt, or at best as describing a relative condition. Lu Chiu-yüan, for example, uses the term to describe his own family, despite the abundant other evidence of their considerable material resources (leadership of the county militia; management of a community granary apart from their own lineage granary; maintenance of a family school that took in students from other families; owner-ship of a drug business that employed large numbers of family members and other workers: see Appendix I, no. 42, as well as the reference cited below). As I have noted in the previous chapter, Lu's claim of poverty seems mainly to refer to the lack of extensive *landed* holdings. Even here the notion seems to be a relative one, since Lu notes that (in the absence of the drug business) the family's stores of grain from their own holdings would 'only' suffice to feed for several months a household that appears to have numbered in the hundreds (Lu Chiu-yüan, 28/3a–4a). A similar case is the claim of poverty made (by others) for Chu Shih of Nan-feng County: if true it seems to have been irrelevant, since Chu's mother came from the enormously powerful, wealthy, and officially successful Tseng family of the same county. (See Chapter 1, p. 55; also *KHNF* 5/2b; Tseng Kung, *Yüan-feng lei-kao*, 46/8b–9a; Hung Mai, *I-chien chih*, *TSCC* edition, 20/154.) In any case Chu Shih's personal wealth is apparently no indication of the wealth of his family, since he had given up his claim to his grandfather's property in favor of his younger brother, keeping only the ancestral house for himself (*SYHAPI* 4/139a).

    In some cases – and Chu Shih's may be one – what is referred to as poverty may simply be an unostentatious style of life adopted as a deliberate choice. The funerary inscription of a later Southern Sung woman tells us that 'her husband's lineage was quite rich, and only her husband's household preserve a scholarly simplicity' (*shou-ju-su*). (*WWC* 78/8a–9a) See also Chapter 1, n. 75.

53. Occasionally, isolated figures do exist for a single household. Thus, the estate of Yüeh I of I-huang County, whose division was decided in 1271 by the prefect Huang Chen when Yüeh died without heir, yielded over 40 000 strings of cash to his relations and 21 000 *shih* of stored rice, along with 2200 *liang* of silver and 32 *liang* of gold, to the government (Huang Chen, 78/3a–40b). The cash and rice could have supplied the entire summer and autumn tax and Harmonious Purchase quotas for all of Chin-ch'i County (population: about 140 000) for one year at about the same time (*TCCC* 9/1a–b; *KHCC* 2/1a–2a). Judging from Huang's comments on the case, it does not appear that he considered Yüeh particularly wealthy.

54. One example is the Lu family, mentioned below. As for the others: the funerary inscription of Ko Chi-tsu of Chin-ch'i tells us that he contributed to increasing his family's wealth by engaging in trade; but this was after the Yüan conquest, when conditions had perhaps changed (*WWC* 80/12a–13a). The gazetteer biography of Tseng Shu-ch'ing of Nan-feng mentions his planning to transport

Chiang-hsi porcelain he had purchased to the north for sale there; the plans fell
through when natural disasters in the north led Tseng to believe there would be
little market for the goods (*MKNF* 23/2a; see also *SS* 459/10a). The funerary
inscription of a woman surnamed Lo (1236–1301) reports that her husband's
family, surnamed Ch'eng, had founded a drug business, probably as an adjunct
to her husband's career as a travelling physician for high officials and great families
(*WWC* 73/6a–7a). Finally, in Huang Chen's disposition of the estate of Yüeh I
(see the preceding note), one of the claimants, a man named Yüeh Wen-huan, is
said to have opened a dyer's shop (Huang Chen, 78/36a–40b).

55. See the references cited in n. 52.
56. *TCLA* 7/11a, 20b, 8/17b, 36a; *KHLA* 5/4a, 9b, 6/20b, 7/8b; and see Appendix I,
no. 1.
57. For a case of control of a market town by a single lineage in late Ch'ing, see
Freedman, *Chinese Lineage and Society: Fukien and Kwangtung*, pp. 82ff.; other
cases are briefly mentioned on p. 91.
58. A number of other elite families, however, lived in places that prove to have been
market towns under the Ming: here I follow the lists of place names given in the
Ming Chia-ching period gazetteer of Fu-chou, dated 1554. In Chin-ch'i County,
for instance, there is Ch'ing-t'ien Hsü in the thirty-sixth *tu* (*CCFC* 4/44b), which
appears in Sung sources (simply as Ch'ing-t'ien) as the home of the Lu family,
who we know were involved in trade (Lu Chiu-yüan, 36/1a; Lo Ta-ching, *Ho-lin
yü-lu* 5/9–10); also Huang-fang Shih in the eighteenth *tu* (*CCFC* 4/40b), identified in a Chin-ch'i gazetteer as the home of a Huang family (*TCCC* 17a/1a–b;
and see Chapter 6, n. 101). In I-huang County there is a T'an-fang Shih in the
fourth *tu* of Tai-hsien canton (*CCFC* 4/35b), identified in I-huang gazetteers as
the home of the T'an family (*TCIH* 25/30b, 33b; *KHIH* 5/25a, 28b; and see
Appendix I, no. 46, for contemporary testimony that confirms the identification);
a Hou-fang Shih in the eighteenth *tu* of Ch'ung-hsien canton (*CCFC* 4/33b),
identified by the gazetteers as the home of the Hou family (see Appendix I,
no. 19); and Ts'ao-fang Shih in the first *tu* of Hsien-kuei canton (*CCFC* 4/34a),
named in an early Yüan genealogy preface as the home of the Ts'ao family (*WWC*
32/15a–16b; and see Appendix I, no. 50). Each of these Ming towns is associated
with only one reconstructed Sung elite family. As the population of the prefecture seems not to have increased dramatically between Sung and Ming (*CCFC*
7/1a–2b), there is no reason to assume an expansion in the number of market
towns in the meantime; most of the Ming market towns may have been market
towns in Sung as well. If so, some or all of these families may have functioned
in these towns as the Chans did in theirs.
59. The thirteen are: Chao Pi-kun, *chin-shih* 1256, an imperial lineage member (*Pao-
yu ssu-nien teng-k'o lu* 162); Chou Kuo-hua, *chin-shih* 1220, and Chou Mai, *chin-
shih* 1138, both members of the Ma-shan Chou family (*TCCC* 17a/2a–b; *KHCC*
4/2b, 3b; *KHFC* 42/9b, 16a; and see Appendix I, no. 10); Chu Ying-lung, *chin-
shih* 1250, Chu Yu-chi, *chin-shih* 1256, and Chu Yüan-ch'ing, *chin-shih* 1211,
all members of the Ming-yang Chu family (*TCCC* 17a/2b, 3a; *KHCC* 4/3b; *KHFC*
42/15a, 19b, 20a; *Pao-yu ssu-nien teng-k'o lu* 96b; and see Appendix I, no. 12);
Huang Yen, *chin-shih* 1187, the grandson of Huang Yen-yüan, who had been
chin-shih in 1112 (*KHFC* 42/13a, 61/1b; *TCCC* 17a/2b, 22a/1a; *KHCC* 4/1a,
3b); Hung Chih-chang, *chin-shih* 1132, younger cousin of Hung Chih-jou, who had
been *chin-shih* in 1118 (*TCCC* 17a/1b, 2a; *KHCC* 4/2a–b; *KHFC* 42/8a, 9a);
Tseng Hung-tzu, *chin-shih* 1250, Tseng Yü, *chin-shih* 1220, and Tseng Yüan-tzu,
chin-shih 1271, all descendants of Tseng Ching, a member of the Tseng family of
Nan-feng, who had moved to Chin-ch'i (*TCCC* 17a/2b, 3a; *KHCC* 4/3b; *KHFC*
42/16a, 49/29b; Ch'eng Chü-fu, 17/2b–4a; and see Appendix I, no. 51); Tseng

Tzu-liang, *chin-shih* 1268, descendant of another migrant offshoot of the same family (*TCCC* 17a/3a, 24/2a; *KHCC* 4/4a, 5/18a–b, *KHFC* 59/11b; Huang Chin, 32/13a–14b); and Wu Su, *chin-shih* 1128, a member of the Northern Sung Wu family discussed in Chapter 3, n. 59 (*TCCC* 17a/1b; *KHCC* 4/2b; *KHFC* 42/9a; and see Appendix I, no. 65).

60. These are Ho Kuo-jui, *chin-shih* 1160 (*TCCC* 17a/2a; *KHFC* 42/11a), whose place of residence, identified as Ho-yüan, cannot be located in the Chin-ch'i gazetteer place-name lists or on available topographic maps; and three others for whom no place of residence is recorded: Feng Hsing-tzu, *chin-shih* 1265, whom the gazetteers identify as a man of Lin-ch'uan but who is called a Chin-ch'i man in the funerary inscription of his daughter's daughter (Wei Su, 4/9b–11b); Kuei Yu-lung, *chin-shih* 1160 (*TCCC* 17a/2a; *KHCC* 4/3a; *KHFC* 42/11a); and Yang Yü-lung, *chin-shih* 1187 (*TCCC* 17a/2b; *KHFC* 42/13a).

61. The Ko family is represented by Ko Feng-shih, *chin-shih* 1169 (*TCCC* 17a/2a; *KHCC* 4/3a; *KHFC* 42/11b; and see Appendix I, no. 34); the Liu family by Liu Yao-fu, *chin-shih* 1172 (*TCCC* 17a/2b, 17b/16b; *KHFC* 42/12a, 47/38a–b; *WWC* 22/8a–b; Wei Su, *hsü-chi* 1/12b–13a; cf. Appendix I, no. 39); the Lu family by Lu Chiu-ling, *chin-shih* 1169, Lu Chiu-yüan, *chin-shih* 1172, Lu Chün, *chin-shih* 1211, and Lu Yün, *chin-shih* 1142 (*TCCC* 17a/2a–b; *KHCC* 4/3a, 3b, 5/8a–b; and see Appendix I, no. 42); the Teng family by Teng Fei-ying, *chin-shih* 1256, Teng Kang, *chin-shih* 1220, and Teng Yüan-kuan, *chin-shih* 1265 (*TCCC* 17a/2b, 3a, 18/10a; *KHFC* 42/20a, 21b; *TCLC* 36/8b; *Pao-yu ssu-nien teng-k'o lu* 63b; and see Appendix I, no. 47); the Wei family by Wei Kuo-ts'ai, *chin-shih* 1235, and Wei Yen-chen, *chin-shih* 1262 (*KHCC* 4/4a; *TCCC* 17a/3a; *TCLC* 36/8a; and see Appendix I, no. 63); and the Wu family by Wu K'o-sun, *chin-shih* 1274, and Wu Ming-yang, *chin-shih* 1271 (*TCCC* 17a/3b; *KHCC* 4/4a, 5/21a–b; *KHFC* 61/6b–7b; *TCTH* 13c/10b–11a; *KHTH* 3/10a, 4/7a–8a; Ch'eng Chü-fu, 16/12–13b; and see Appendix I, no. 66).

62. On Map 6 this can be seen clearly for the Lu, Wu, and Ko families, but is not obvious for the Teng and Wei families, as the map, and the 200 000 : 1 topographic maps on which it is based, show the river systems only in part. However, a map in the very detailed 50 000 : 1 topographic series available at Osaka University shows clearly that Huang-t'ung Shih and the Yün-lin mountains are served by streams that flow (ultimately) north into the Hsin River system. The map in question is listed as no. 23 of the series of Chien-ch'ang in Nunome Chōfu, *Chūgoku hondo chizu mokuroku*, p. 149.

63. See n. 61 above.

64. This is the Chu family of Ming-yang: cf. n. 59 above.

65. The basic sources are: Teng P'ang's biographies in *TCCC* 22a/1a–5a and *KHCC* 5/5b–7a, the latter quoting at length a preface written by Hsieh Fang-te for a contemporary account of the Teng family; the letter from Hsieh Fang-te to Teng Yüan-kuan preserved in *TCCC* 33f/7b–9b; Chou Pi-ta's note on discussions of the Chin-ch'i militia in the capital in 1175 (in Chou Pi-ta, 20/16b–17b); and Lu Chiu-ling's funerary inscription, recording at some length the family's 1175 debate over their current role in the militia, with an account of their involvement in 1127 (Lu Chiu-yüan, 27/1a–8a).

66. Chou Pi-ta, 20/16b–17b, and Lu Chiu-yüan, 27/1a–8a.

67. *TCCC* 22a/1a–5a, and *KHCC* 5/5b–7a.

68. Lu Chiu-yüan, 28/7a–11a.

69. *TCTH* 13b/1a.

70. This inscription is for Wu Ch'en-tzu. See Yü Chi, 18/21a–22b.

71. *TCCC* 22a/1a–5a.

72. Chou Pi-ta, 20/16b–17b.

73. *TCTH* 13b/1a.
74. Lu Chiu-yüan, 28/7a–11a.
75. Lu Chiu-yüan, 27/1a–8a. The remark appears in Lu Yün's preface to the Tengs' genealogy, which I examined at the canton seat of Huang-t'ung canton, Chin-ch'i County, in June 1985.
76. Sung Lien, 22/804–6; *SYHAPI* 77/25b.
77. See *KHFC* 47/23a–b, which closely reproduces *SS* 401/3b–4b.
78. See his record of conduct in Yüan Hsieh, 12/1a–35a.
79. Lu Hsin-yüan, *Sung shih i* 29/10a; *KHFC* 47/48a–b; *TCCJ* 7c/8b; *KHCJ* 1/52a–b; *WWC* 75/15b; *SYHAPI* 45/15b.
80. Ch'en Yüan-chin, front matter; *TCCJ* 7c/8b, 8b/5a; *KHCJ* 1/52b, 53a.
81. See Huang Chen's notice to the taxed households of Lo-an County, urging them to offer grain for sale to relieve famine:

> The single county of Lo-an is not like the other counties: it is secluded among countless mountains, not accessible to boat traffic. The wealthy families who store up grain [here] have not been subject to Harmonious Purchase, but only to the autumn tax. (Huang Chen, 78/6b–19b).

Further on Huang makes it clear that Lo-an was inaccessible only from the other districts of Fu-chou: discussing absentee estates owned in Lo-an by a Lo family of neighboring Yung-feng County, Chi-chou, he notes:

> While this county is not accessible to boat traffic, there is one small stream, the Niu-t'ien, which flows straight across to Yung-feng in Chi-chou. In a single-oared small boat one can slip past the border.

Thus water transport of a modest kind was possible out of Lo-an into Chi-chou (cf. Map II), but not into the other districts of Fu-chou by way of the Ch'ung-jen River.

82. Wei Liao-weng, 79/4a–6a.
83. Wei Liao-weng, 79/4a–6a; *TCCJ* 7c/3b; *KHCJ* 1/46b.
84. *WWC* 57/8a–b.
85. *TCCJ* 7c/4b; *KHCJ* 1/47b–48a.
86. Ch'en Yüan-chin, 6/4a–6b.
87. Yüan Hsieh, 12/1a–35a.
88. 'Ch'i chia shih hsiu ju-yeh erh men-hu wei chen.'
89. First of all, a man named Lo Min-te is recorded as contributing his lands for the reconstruction of a temple located within a mile of Lo Tien's lineage residence (*KHCJ*, ch. 3). As Lo Tien's funerary inscription tells us that his agnates (*tsu*) were quite numerous, and as they seem to have been ramified over an area surrounding a residence at Kao-ch'i – Lo Tien's father had moved from the main residence there to 'Wu-hsing Springs of Kao-ch'i' – it is very probable that a man of the surname contributing to a temple so close by was a kinsman. The same Lo Min-te also began the reconstruction of another temple, in the west quarter of the county seat, which was continued in elaborate style after his death by his two sons and was completed in 1152. The inscriptional record for this temple notes that one of the sons had held office some time before in Ching-hu-nan circuit (*KHCJ*, 3/8a–9a). Lo Tien himself was also apparently associated with the county seat's west quarter (he may have maintained a separate residence there), since a special commemorative gate was later established there in his honor (*CCFC* 4/23a–24a). Another man of the surname, Lo Yen, rebuilt a third temple, also in the west quarter of the county seat, some time after 1127 (*KHCJ* 3/11a; *TCCJ* 7c/16b); this man passed the prefectural examination in 1153 (*KHCJ* 1/48b; *TCCJ* 7c/5a). Further, the funerary inscription of the wife of a Ch'ung-jen

man named Miu Chao lists two of Lo Tien's brothers, and a third man of the Lo surname, among the husbands of her granddaughters; among her *daughters'* husbands are two other men surnamed Lo, both identified as officeholders (Ch'en Tsao, 35/13a–16a). As Lo Tien's mother is also known to have been surnamed Miu (Yüan Hsieh, 12/1a–35a; Hung Mai, *chih-ting* 4/5a), and as this woman's inscription was written on behalf of an unidentified man, serving in the capital, who called himself her grandson through the maternal line – almost certainly Lo Tien himself – these other two Los are surely earlier officeholding members of Lo Tien's family. One of them, Lo Wei, has a name that appears to share a generational indicator with the name of Lo Yen above. Finally, Miu Chao's wife was herself the daughter of a family that had earlier produced a number of degreeholders and prefectural graduates. In sum, it seems clear that the Lo family had emerged into the local elite and the ranks of officeholders by shortly after the fall of Northern Sung.

90. See Appendix I, no. 67.
91. *TCCJ* 7b/1b, 7c/1b; *KHCJ* 1/43b–44a; *KHFC* 42/4a.
92. This is Wu Yu-lin. There are two reasons for thinking him a member of the same family: his residence in the county seat, and his disinterment and reburial with honors by the county administration during Shao-hsing (1131–62), precisely the period when the Wu family was attaining its greatest local reputation academically. See *TCCJ* 7b/1 b; *KHCJ* 1/43b, 4/36a–b; *KHFC* 47/28a; Liu Chih, *Chung-su chi* 14/23a–24a.
93. *TCCJ* 7b/2b; *KHCJ* 1/47a–b; *KHFC* 42/9b.
94. *TCCJ* 1g/3a, 8e/1b; *KHCJ* 4/22a–b; *KHFC* 59/4a; *SYHAPI* 45/17a; Lou Yüeh, 52/11b–13b.
95. *TCCJ* 7b/3a; *KHCJ* 4/38b; *KHFC* 49/4b; *SYHAPI* 45/167a.
96. *TCCJ* 7c/5a, 8b/3a–4a; *KHCJ* 1/48a, 4/22b–23b; *KHFC* 59/5a; Lou Yüeh, 52/11b–13b; Hung Mai, *chih-i* 2/4a–b.
97. *TCCJ* 7b/3a; *KHCJ* 1/49b; *KHFC* 47/36b; *SYHAPI* 44/79a; Hung Mai, *san-jen* 1/1b–2a.
98. Wei Liao-weng, 79/4a–5a.
99. Ch'en Yüan-chin, 6/4a–6b.
100. Hung Mai reports that in the year before Lo Tien's *chin-shih* he took lodging with the family of a Wu Te-hsiu of his county seat, as the family's teacher. Hung Mai's anecdote is the only mention of Wu Te-hsiu's name in the Fu-chou sources. However, as Hung refers to Lo Tien only by his courtesy name (Lo Ch'un-po), it seems likely that Te-hsiu is similarly Wu's courtesy name. Now the courtesy names of Wu Hang (see above) and his brothers Wu Hsieh, Wu Kuang, and Wu T'ao are, respectively, Te-yüan, Te-shen, Te-ch'iang, and Te-shao. Here the shared element Te- is obviously a generation marker; its occurrence again in the name of Lo Tien's host Wu Te-hsiu makes it very probable that he was a brother or cousin of the other four. The evidence for Lo Tien's association with their family, then, seems reasonably strong.
101. The Miu family with which Lo Tien's own was intermarried (see n. 89 above) seems to have had marriage relations with Li Liu's as well: Li Liu's wife came from a Miu family described as a 'leading lineage' of Ch'ung-jen County (see the funerary inscription of Miu Mu in *WWC* 72/7a–8b); and according to the funerary inscription of Miu Chao's wife (n. 89), Miu Chao's father's second wife had been surnamed Li, and one of his granddaughters married a officeholder also of the Li surname.
102. See Hung Mai, *chih-i* 2/6a–b, and Huang Chen, 78/24a–b; and cf. Appendix I, no. 11.
103. Hung Mai, *chih-i*, 2/6a–b; *TCCJ* 7c/4b; *KHCJ* 1/48a.

104. Hung Mai, *chih-i* 2/6a–b; *TCLA* 7/18a; *KHLA* 5/6b.
105. Hung Mai, *chih-i* 2/6a–b; *TCLA* 7/18b; *KHLA* 5/7b.
106. Wei Liao-weng, 79/4a–6a.
107. Ch'en Tsao, 35/13a–16b; *TCCJ* 7c/7a, 7b; *KHCJ* 1/50b, 51a; and cf. Appendix I, no. 43.
108. None of the place-names mentioned in Miu funerary inscriptions can be found in the gazetteers or on modern maps. However, two men of the same surname are listed in the gazetteers in Ming, as *chin-shih* in 1479 and 1585, and identified as men of the forty-third *tu* (*KHCJ* ch. 1; *TCCJ* ch. 7b). This is in precisely the same area as the residences of the families with whom the Sung Mius are connected; thus I tentatively accept this as the home of the Miu family. (For the location of the forty-third *tu*, see *TCCJ* 1b/4a and 28b.)
109. The men in question are Cheng Ying-yu (*TCLA* 7/22b; *KHLA* 5/12a) and Huang Te-i (*TCLA* 7/22b; *KHLA* 5/12b). For their families see Appendix I, nos. 9 and 29.
110. See the funerary inscription of Cheng Sung in *WWC* 74/3a–5a, and the postface to the inscription of his adoptive mother (surnamed Huang) reproduced in Ho Hsi-chih, 5b–6b.
111. *TCLA* 1/27a, 8/36a, and ch. 7, passim.; *KHLA* 7/8b and ch. 5, passim.; and cf. Appendix I, no. 1.
112. *TCCJ* 7c/4a; *KHCJ* 1/47a; *WWC* 74/10b–13b; and see Appendix I, no. 18.
113. They did, however, intermarry in Southern Sung. Chan Ch'ung-p'u, mentioned in *WWC* 74/10b–13b as an in-law of Ho Yao, is a member of this Chan family: see *TCLA* 7/24a; *KHLA* 6/6a–b.

Chapter 3

1. As to the date of this letter, it is known that Wang Ling died in 1059 (see his funerary inscription in Wang An-shih, 97/1a–2a) and that his wife married him when she was (by Chinese reckoning) twenty-four, which will have been in 1058 (see her funerary inscription in Wang Ling, *Kuang-ling chi, fu-lu* 13b). The letter thus cannot have been written after 1058. In the letter Wang An-shih mentions that Wang Ling is presently in Chiang-yin. This county in Liang-che circuit was during the middle of the eleventh century an independent prefecture, but had earlier been and would later be subordinate to Ch'ang-chou, with which it shared a border. Wang An-shih refers to having had contact with Wang Ling at this time, which places him in or close to Chiang-yin. It is known that Wang An-shih was appointed prefect of Ch'ang-chou in 1057 and left that office the next year. In view of Ch'ang-chou's proximity to Chiang-yin, the letter must have been written during Wang An-shih's tenure there.
2. Wang An-shih, 74/12a–13a.
3. In both letters Wang addresses Wu Fen as *erh-chiu*, 'second maternal uncle'; Wang's mother was the daughter of Wu Min, Wu Fen's father: see her funerary inscription in Tseng Kung, *Yüan-feng lei-kao* 45/4b–6a.
4. The reference to 'poverty' here should again be taken in a relative sense. Wang Ling was the descendant of three generations of low-ranking officials (Wang An-shih, 97/1a–2a), and Wang An-shih himself goes on to imply that his income from teaching was not inconsiderable. The issue was whether he was wealthy enough to suit Wu Fen.
5. Wei T'ai, *Tung-hsien pi-lu* 14/106. The original passage has 'Western Capital' where I have 'Southern Capital'; the events in question, however, must have taken place during Yen's earlier tenure in the late 1020s as Guardian (*liu-shou*) of the Southern Capital, as is clear from Yen's own funerary inscription (Ou-yang Hsiu, *Wen-chung kung chi* 22/7a–12a) and from the account of his interaction

with Fan Chung-yen during his tenure in the Southern Capital in Johanna Fischer, 'Fan Chung-yen (989–1052): das Lebensbild eines chinesischen Staatsmannes,' pp. 56–7.

6. Huang Kan, 38/11a–13a.

7. Note that the inscription goes on to praise Yu for going *against* custom by choosing for his sons wives from 'poor' families. Here the context makes it likelier than ever that 'poor' should actually be read 'poorer,' since the contrast is with men who choose wives not simply from rich families but from families richer than their own. (The inscription has earlier called Yu's own family 'a rich lineage.') The inscription is important otherwise as the only clear reference in Fu-chou sources to the question of the relative position of wife-givers and wife-takers. This issue has been a focus of some controversy among anthropologists studying China. An examination of the question for Ch'i-nan village in Taiwan by Emily Ahern (Ahern, 'Affines and the Rituals of Kinship') is especially important for carefully distinguishing the various possible aspects of 'relative position' and limiting its firm conclusions to the ritual aspect, in which Ahern shows quite beyond doubt that in Ch'i-nan wife-givers are regarded and treated as superior. She notes also that Ch'i-nan residents generally hold that a wife-giving family ought also to be *economically* superior to its wife-taking partner – that economics ideally should jibe with ritual. Now Wu Ch'eng's remarks in Yu Te-hung's funerary inscription – if reliable – suggest that in Sung Fu-chou as well it was thought the norm for the wife-givers to be richer than the wife-takers. Here, however, the stress on the gains to be had from a dowry suggests that Fu-chou wife-takers were not liable to the heavy obligations of gifts to the bride's family which in Ch'i-nan symbolize their ritual indebtedness – or at least that any such gifts did not have to compensate (even nearly) for the dowry. A fuller study of these questions might be possible for Sung. A first step has been taken by Patricia Ebrey in 'Women in the Kinship System of the Southern Sung Upper Class.'

8. Ho Hsi-chih, 5b–6b.

9. One case is also known of a man's being chosen as a son-in-law as a direct reward for his aid to the woman's family. Cheng Sung of Lo-an County intervened around 1271 on behalf of a wealthy household in a dispute with the prefect over the family's obligation to sell its stored grain as part of the prefect's famine relief program. Through his intervention the situation was resolved in a way satisfactory to the wealthy family, who 'were grateful and formed marriage ties with him,' giving him their daughter as his wife. (*WWC* 74/3a–5a; and see Chapter 6, p. 160). Here it would appear that the wife-giving family was regarded as transferring, in the person of their daughter, something of net value to the wife-taker, something appropriate as a reward for aid. This again seems to jibe with the Ch'i-nan situation as described by Ahern.

10. The context is a legal judgment in which Huang is rebuking a complainant for denigrating the family of his father's second wife. See Huang Kan, 32/5a–10b.

11. These are nos. 13, 14, 21, 24, 34, and 37 (see legend to Map 7). Note that no. 21, in Ch'u-chou, while not in the Che River valley, directly borders prefectures that are, and that no. 24, in Hu-chou, similarly borders Hang-chou, sited near the mouth of the Che; thus both cases perhaps belong with the Che River concentration.

12. This is the woman surnamed Hou, of Nan-feng County, whose husband was Hsieh Pi of Hsi Hsien in Hui-chou, no. 1 on Map 7.

13. The short-term records of the Ts'ais, Tsengs, Wangs, Yens, and Yüehs in the *chin-shih* examination were to be equalled only by a very few other Fu-chou families in Sung. This is all the more impressive when one considers that the five had their success precisely in the period when the total numbers of *chin-shih* granted in Fu-chou (and in the empire as a whole) were lowest.

14. The Ts'ai family first appears in the Fu-chou sources with the *chin-shih* degree of
Ts'ai Wei-shan in 988 (*KHFC* 42/2b). The family was to produce twelve more
chin-shih, five of them by 1057 (*KHFC* 42/2b, 3b; *TCLC* 36/2a; Su Sung, 57/9b–
14a). The offices held by most of these men are not recorded and may well not
have been very high; but the 1015 *chin-shih* Ts'ai Tsung-yen reached the prefectship of Nan-chien-chou in Fu-chien circuit, and his grandson Ts'ai Ch'eng-hsi, a
1057 *chin-shih*, in 1074 had an imperial audience and was made an attaché in the
Censorate, later rising successively to be Corrector for the Chi-hsien Library and
Superintendent of Public Matters of the Towns and Districts of K'ai-feng Fu,
then K'ai-feng Prefectural Judge, and then K'ai-feng Prefectural Staff Supervisor
and concurrently Superintendent of the Books of the Finance Commission; finally
in 1084 he was sent out to be Assistant Fiscal Intendant of Huai-nan circuit and
died in that post, aged forty-nine (Su Sung, 57/9b–14a). While his highest salary-
rank was only of the seventh grade, the functional posts he held were offices of
considerable responsibility, auguring well for his future prospects had he not died;
in particular, posts in the local administration of the capital city and prefecture
were in Northern Sung often entrées to career paths leading to the highest offices
in the state. On this point see Kinugawa Tsuyoshi's study of the backgrounds and
careers of the first forty chief ministers of Northern Sung (Kinugawa, 'Sōdai
saishō kō.') Cf. Appendix I, no. 49.

The Tseng family's first officeholder was Tseng Chih-yao, a *chin-shih* in 983
(*KHNF* 5/1b; *KHFC* 42/1b). In all some thirty *chin-shih* were to come from this
family, fifteen by 1065 (*KHNF* ch. 5, passim.). Chih-yao served as Fiscal Intendant first of Liang-che circuit, later of Ching-hsi circuit (Wang An-shih, 92/1a–
4b; Ou-yang Hsiu, *Ou-yang Wen-chung kung chi* 21/1a–4a). The career of his
son Tseng I-chan, a 1024 *chin-shih*, was cut short by accusations of impropriety
(Ch'en Shih-tao, *Hou-shan chi* 16/10b–11b; Wang An-shih, 93/1a–3b); but in
the next generation three of I-chan's sons – Tseng Kung, Tseng Chao, and Tseng
Pu – also received the *chin-shih* and after 1068 reached positions of influence
in the capital during the first dominance of the New Laws party (Tseng Kung,
Yüan-feng lei-kao, end matter; Yang Shih, 29/2a–20b; Tu Ta-kuei, *Ming-ch'en
pei-chuan wan-yen chi, hsia*, 20/1a). Tseng Chao continued to hold central office
during the succeeding anti-reform administration (Yang Shih, 29/2a–20b), and
Tseng Pu, in the provinces in this period, eventually reached the post of chief
councillor under Hui-tsung (Tu Ta-Kuei, 20/1a). Later both brothers fell afoul
of the dictator Ts'ai Ching, were demoted to insignificant local posts, and died
in Jun-chou. Cf. Appendix I, no. 54.

The first known prominent member of the Wang family was Wang Kuan-chih,
who received the *chin-shih* in 1000 (*KHFC* 42/1b); eight other members of the
family were to earn the degree by 1067 (*KHFC* ch. 42, passim.). Kuan-chih held
a number of prefectships and was for a time Judicial Intendant of Huai-nan
circuit, Wang An-shih, 98/2b); his nephew Wang I ended as vice-administrator
of Chiang-ning Fu (Tseng Kung, *Yüan-feng lei-kao*, 44/6b–8b). I's son Wang
An-shih rose to serve as chief councillor under Shen-tsung and to institute the
series of large-scale reforms ever since associated with his name. Cf. Appendix I,
no. 61.

The Wu family of Chin-ch'i County first reached office in Sung when Wu Min
passed the *chin-shih* examination in 992 (*TCCC* 17a/1a; *KHCC* 4/1a); the family
was to produce three other *chin-shih* in Northern Sung, as well as a number of
officials who reached their posts through hereditary privilege. The offices held
by this family seem not to have been as high as those of the others discussed here;
Min is known to have reached a salary-rank of the seventh grade, but his functional office is not recorded (Wang An-shih, 98/10a–b). As will be seen, however,
the family intermarried early with both the Wangs and the Tsengs.

Note that I do not here count Wu Piao-wei, *chin-shih* 985, and his grandson
Wu Hsiao-tsung, *chin-shih* 1070, as members of this Wu family, despite gazetteer
testimony that they are related to Wu Min (e.g., *TCCC* 26/1b; *KHCC* 4/40a),
because the funerary inscriptions written for Hsiao-tsung's brother Hsing-tsung
and for Wu Min's sons Wu Fan and Wu Fen by Wang An-shih, who was related
by marriage to all of them, provide no support for the relationship (Wang An-shih,
94/12a–13a and 98/10a–b). If the gazetteers are correct, however, two more
chin-shih must be counted among the members of the family. Cf. Appendix I,
no. 65.

Fu-chou's first Sung *chin-shih* was Yüeh Shih of I-huang County, who passed
in 980 (*KHIH* 5/1a; *TCIH* 25/ab; *TCCJ* 7b/1a; *KHCJ* 1/43a). His sons and grandsons achieved six more degrees by 1034. Shih held a post in the Institute of
History in the capital, as well as two prefectships (*SS* 306/10b; *TCCJ* 8d/1a–3a).
His son Yüeh Huang-mu served as Fiscal Intendant of Kuang-hsi and Shen-hsi
circuits, then in several posts in the capital, including Prefect of K'ai-feng Fu
and Administrator of the Bureau of Administrative Personnel, reaching a salary-
rank of the fourth grade (*SS*, loc. cit.; *KHFC* 47/26a–27a; *TCCJ* 8b/1b–2b).
Cf. Appendix I, no. 72.

The Yen family's first Sung officeholder was Yen Shu, granted the *chin-shih*
in 1005 at the age of fourteen through a special examination for candidates too
young for the regular competition (*KHFC* 42/2b). By 1079 his family had produced four more *chin-shih* (*KHFC* ch. 42, passim.). Yen Shu himself reached the
post of chief councillor in the 1040s, the first Fu-chou man to rise so high.
(Ou-yang Hsiu, *Ou-yang Wen-chung kung-chi*, 22/7b–12b). Cf. Appendix I,
no. 73.

15. There is not space here to give a separate account of each of these families. Those
for whose history there are important sources not already cited in the legend for
Map 7 are indicated below:

No. 5   (Wang of Chiang-tu County): Tseng Kung, *Yüan-feng lei-kao* 44/1a–2a.
No. 6   (Kuan of Ch'ien-t'ang County): Tseng Kung, 45/7a–8a, 15b–16b.
No. 7   (Chiang of K'ai-hua County): Ch'eng Chü, *Pei shan chi* 19/7b–10a.
Nos. 8 and 9 (Ch'iang of Ch'ien-t'ang County): Tseng Hsieh, *Yün-chuang chi*
        5/5a–28b.
Nos. 11 and 19 (Chu of T'ien-ch'ang County): Tseng Kung, 46/2a–b; see also
        CPT pp. 579, 621.
No. 12   (Ch'ao of K'ai-feng Fu): Tseng Kung, 46/7a–b.
No. 14   (Su of Mei-shan County): Tseng Kung, 43/7a–8b; see also *CPT*, pp.
        4304–5; 4312–24; 4331–33.
No. 15   (Wu of Shao-wu Chün): Yang Shih, 30/12b–15a.
Nos. 16 and 17 (Chou of Hai-ling County): Wang An-shih, 96/7b–8b.
No. 18   (Shen of Yang-tzu County): Wang An-shih, 90/13a–14a.
No. 20   (Wu of P'u-ch'eng County): Ou-yang Hsiu, *Ou-yang Wen-chung kung
        chi* 32/5b–10b.
No. 22   (Chang of Sha County): *SS* 299/3a.
No. 25   (Wang of Kuang-ling County): Wang An-shih, 97/1a–2a.
No. 27   (Kuo of T'ai-yüan Fu): Liu Chih, 11/18a–23a.
No. 33   (Fu of Lo-yang County): Su Shih, *Su Tung-p'o chi* 37/1a–9b.
No. 34   (Yang of Ho-fei County): *SS* 295/14b–15a.
No. 35   (Li of Chien-an County): *SS* 300/12a–13a.
No. 36   (Chang of Ho-nan Fu): *SS* 306/8b–10a.
No. 37   (Fan of Ch'ing-chou): Chao Ting-ch'en, *Chu-yin chi-shih chi* 18/7b–
        10a.

16. Tseng Kung, 46/1b–2b.
17. Wang An-shih, 96/7b–8b.
18. See for instance *SS* 306/10b for the Yüehs and *MKNF* 14/2a–b for the Tsengs.
19. Lou Yüeh, 97/13b–22a.
20. The funerary inscription of Wu Ting-weng, Wu Chien's descendant, recounts the family's early history in this way:

> Their ancestors lived in Chin-ling; when Southern T'ang submitted to Sung, they came to live at Lin-ch'uan's East Gate, bought fields in Chin-ch'i [County], and built a house east of the [Lin-ch'uan] city to live in. In the prefecture there were many of the Wu surname; [this family] were distinguished by calling them the 'East Gate Wus.' For generations they were a cultivated family [*ju-chia*], but hid their virtue and did not achieve fame. (Yü Chi, 43/2a.)

The rather unusual reference to the place where the family acquired their lands probably indicates that they did not, at least at first, own fields in their own district.

21. There are five exceptions: nos. 2, 3, 23, 28, and 30. In each of these cases the surname of one partner is that of a family which is already known to have had other marriage connections with the second partner's family; I have added these uncertain cases here to show the possibility that the connection was repeated.
22. In I-huang County, for example, we find that the 1256 *chin-shih* Chang Sheng-tzu was the son of a woman surnamed Ts'ao, and the husband of a woman surnamed Hsü (*Pao-yu ssu-nien teng-k'o lu* 41b). Both are surnames of highly successful I-huang families. Chang Sheng-tzu was a man of 'I-nan,' the southern part of the county seat; the Ts'ao family's residence lay just outside the seat, to the west; the two Hsü families were located close together to the northeast, again not far from the seat. (For these families see Appendix I, nos. 2, 24, 25, and 50.) Similarly, a Hsü family of I-huang, producing degreeholders at least from 1145 to the end of Sung, was resident in the county seat (cf. Appendix I, no. 26). Women of this surname, otherwise unidentified, appear as wives of Wu K'un-sun and Li Lung of I-huang (*WWC* 83/4a–5a and 76/4b–6b respectively); both men were also residents of the county seat (see Appendix I, no. 70 for the Wus; *TCIH* 25/33a and *WWC* 30/20b for Li Lung). In Nan-feng County, a Huang family that had produced *chin-shih* in Northern Sung, and continued to do so for at least the first half of Southern Sung, had its residence not far to the northwest of the county seat. A man of this family, Huang Wen-sheng, married a woman surnamed Tseng, and his daughter married a man named Tseng Lin-tsung (Lu Chiu-yüan, 28/4a–6a). The most prominent family of the county was the Tseng family (above, n. 14), which at least in Northern Sung had maintained a residence in the county seat (see Appendix I, no. 54). Such examples could be multiplied considerably.
23. Hsieh K'o, 10/3a–4b, 4b–5b; Hsieh I, 9/15b–17a and 10/3b–5a.
24. See Chapter 1, pp. 49–52, as well as the various funerary inscriptions for local men in the works of Hsieh I and Hsieh K'o. The picture is not absolutely clear, however. Consider Hsieh K'o's marriage to the daughter of a *chin-shih* from Chin-ch'i County: is this comparable to the inter-district marriages in Map 8? To answer the question one would need to know *where* in Lin-ch'uan County Hsieh K'o lived, and where in Chin-ch'i his wife's family lived. It is not impossible that within the prefecture the Northern Sung pattern extended even to some families without any officeholders. Outside the prefecture, however, the pattern seems clear.
25. See, for the Lus, marriages no. 16 and no. 20 on Map 9, no. 3 on Map 10; for the Hos, nos. 11, 12, 13 on Map 9; for the Lis, nos. 5, 11, 17, 18, 31 on Map 9,

nos. 6 and 7 on Map 10; for the Los, see Chapter 2, note 89; for the Tungs, see nos. 10, 11, 12, and 13 on Map 10.

26. For the full sources on the Tungs see Appendix I, no. 59; here the major references are the funerary inscriptions of Tung Ch'ang-i and Tung I in Chou Pi-ta, 72/7a– 9a and 75/11b–12a respectively, and that of Tung Kuan in Wang T'ing-kuei, *Lu-ch'i wen-chi* 44/3a–5b.

27. In 1198 Tung Ch'ang-i's remains were removed from their original burial place in the prefectural city in Lu-ling, where they had rested for eighteen years, to the Tungs' ancestral burial grounds in what was now Lo-an County. His funerary inscription explains the transfer as undertaken 'to fulfill the wish for intimacy;' the move suggests a reorientation by his descendants toward the family's ancestral home and hence away from its old prefecture.

28. The real proportion is in all probability considerably higher, since a number of the funerary inscriptions cited include the names and offices of other marriage partners who, while not identifiable from other sources, either have surnames not recorded among Fu-chou elite members, or else hold offices of a level that would make them likely to appear in other Fu-chou sources if in fact they were Fu-chou people.

29. This case may actually belong with the Tungs, *et al.*, above. While Yen Ta-cheng was a descendant of Yen Shu (see above. n. 14) of Lin-ch'uan and was buried in that county, it would seem that his ancestors may have been living elsewhere in the interim. In an account of his career in his funerary inscription we find:

> Later he was able to go to live as a sojourner [*yü-chü*] in Lin-ch'uan, making the veranda of a Buddhist temple his dwelling, and acquiring barely several tens of mou of fields; he sold off half of them in order to travel to Ch'ang-sha [where he was appointed to a new office]. (Ts'ao Yen-yüeh, *Ch'ang-ku chi* 20/19a–23b)

Earlier, in reference to his having held a subordinate post in the military governor-generalship of Ch'eng-tu Fu circuit, we learn:

> The Szechwan staff positions were known for being lucrative; those who held them all became wealthy. [Ta-cheng] took very sparingly, and used it to support those of his lineage who were in the western prefectures.

Both the reference to his 'living as a sojourner' with no house of his own in Lin-ch'uan, and the remark on his support of relatives 'in the western prefectures' (presumably Szechwan or the Ching-hu circuits?) suggests that Yen's family was no longer strongly rooted in Fu-chou and that his burial there may have been in the nature of a return.

30. On this question the pioneer among Western scholars is Hartwell, who established the shift in marriage patterns through research on Sung fiscal officials and developed an explanation that anticipates a good part of what will be argued further on. The elite retrenchment from a preoccupation with high office to a concern with local interests which Hartwell deduced chiefly from marriage and migration patterns is confirmed by the other sorts of changes that will be shown in the present chapter. (Robert Hartwell, 'Demographic, Political, and Social Transformations of China,' pp. 405–22.) See pp. 119–21.

The transformation of marriage patterns emerges also (and quite independently) from the work of the Japanese scholar Ihara Hiroshi, work which deserves wider notice in the West. Ihara first examined Sung elite marriage in articles on two lower-Yangtse prefectures, Ming-chou and Wu-chou ('Sōdai Meishū ni okeru kanko no kon-in kankei' and 'Sōdai Ushū ni okeru kanko no kon-in kankei'), then approached the issue in more general terms in an article on 'the meaning of marriage' for Sung officials ('Sōdai kanryō no kon-in no imi ni tsuite'). Here he proposed, on the basis of several examples, that Southern Sung marriage was more constricted geographically, more locally rooted, than Northern Sung marriage, and that the more farflung Northern Sung marriage pattern must in some way be connected to a tendency for official families to emigrate from their homes. The shift in Southern Sung, he argues, may be explained, first, by the movement of the capital to Hang-chou, which made the economic and political centers of the state coincide; and second, by the growing numbers of *chin-shih* who were unable to hold functional offices owing to the expansion of the official pool. *Chin-shih* without office, Ihara suggests, could not rely on office and official connections alone to support their families' position, and so fell back on local social networks instead. Third, the general geographic constriction of Southern Sung may, Ihara thinks, play some role. I find the connection of the shift of capitals to marriage patterns, as suggested by Ihara, rather obscure, since marriage patterns seem to have contracted both for those who lived near the new capital and for those who lived far away. As to the second point, a good many Fu-chou men who *did* reach functional posts, and rather high ones, in Southern Sung, still maintained the more local marriage pattern: it is hard then to explain it by an increase in the number of officeless *chin-shih*. But in tying the marriage question to migration, and in noting in passing the potential value of wide-ranging marriage for factional conflict, Ihara has made suggestions that are very valuable indeed. Compare my own discussion on pp. 115–23 and Hartwell, pp. 405–22.

31. Liu Pin, *P'eng-ch'eng chi* 39/517.
32. The P'o-yang basin was in fact virtually shut out of the Council of State during much of later Southern Sung. This important fact of Southern Sung central politics was, I believe, first pointed out by Sudō Yoshiyuki in a survey of Sung chief and assistant ministers that formed part of his major study of Sung land-holding and its relation to the official system (Sudō Yoshiyuki, 'Sōdai kanryōsei to daitochishoyū,' pp. 9–33). Even Sudō's study, however, did not reveal the full extent of the phenomenon, because Sudō used circuits or groups of circuits, rather than physiographic regions, as his units. Thus in the period of the P'o-yang basin's exclusion an occasional councillor came from Chiang-tung circuit (which Sudō combined with Chiang-hsi in his analysis), but always from the sections of that circuit that lay *outside* the P'o-yang basin.
33. For Lu Chiu-yüan's students and associates outside Fu-chou I rely on *SYHA* and *SYHAPI*.
34. See Tseng Kung's letter to a Chiang-hsi circuit intendant concerning his application to be considered as a Lin-ch'uan resident in order to gain admission to the county school: Tseng Kung, 15/14a–15a. The grandmother was there because several of her daughters had married Lin-ch'uan men.
35. See the references cited for no. 12 in the legend for Map 9.
36. On Merit Cloisters see Kenneth Ch'en, *Buddhism in China*, pp. 272–3; and for a comprehensive treatment see Chikusa Masaaki, 'Sōdai funji kō.'
37. *TCCJ* 2d/1b–3a and 8d/2b–3a.
38. *TCIH* 13/6a reports that the Yün-feng (Buddhist) Temple at Huo-yüan (for which a later reconstruction by a descendant of Yüeh Shih is recorded in *WWC* 49/13a) was rebuilt in the 880s by a man named Yüeh Tien.
39. *TCCJ* 10b/1a.
40. Here I exclude the Tung family discussed above: in the first place they may have taken up their residence in the Chi-chou prefectural city in Northern Sung and simply continued it after the transfer of their ancestral home to Fu-chou; in the second place they may have been following a pattern typical of Chi-chou but not Fu-chou families in Southern Sung. On the whole the circumstances surrounding their position are so atypical as to justify considering them an isolated case.

41. See the funerary inscription of Li Ch'ou in *WWC* 75/15b–17a.
42. The Nan-fu Pavilion, just south of the county seat (*KHCJ* ch. 3) and a shrine called the Mei-feng Tz'u just north of the family's original residence (*WWC* 46/1a–3a).
43. See Li Ch'ou's funerary inscription, *WWC* 75/15b–17a.
44. He contributed new chambers and arhat figures to the P'u-an Temple in the county seat in 1205 (*KHCJ* 3/11a; *TCCJ* 2d/16b), and had earlier dug out a Moon Lake as part of an estate in the southern suburbs (*TCCJ* 1g/1b).
45. See Hung Mai's record in *TCCJ* 7/6a–8a.
46. Occasionally there is a seeming exception: Li Liu of Ch'ung-jen played a major role in organizing and financing the rebuilding of the Wen-ch'ang Bridge in Fu-chou city in 1225–6. But this was a project initiated by local officials, who persuaded Li to take part: it was not a spontaneous act by Li or his family.
47. 'Poems on thinking of Ying,' as becomes clear further on in Hung's note, was in fact the title of a series of poems written by Ou-yang Hsiu; Ou-yang wrote two prefaces for these poems. 'Ying' is Ying-chou in Ching-hsi-pei circuit, where Ou-yang had held office and to which he always hoped to return someday to live. It was his reading of Ou-yang's prefaces that prompted Hung Mai to record his thoughts, along with excerpts from Ou-yang.
48. Hung Mai, *Jung-chai sui-pi wu chi*, v. II, 16/153–54.
49. Chao I, *Kai-yü ts'ung-kao* 18/4a–b. I owe this reference to Ihara Hiroshi and Chikusa Masaaki, cited below.
50. Cf. the work of Ihara Hiroshi cited in note 30 above, and his 'Nan-Sō Shisen ni okeru . . .' The issue is the subject also of an important article by Chikusa Masaaki, who treats at some length the case of Su Shih's acquisition of lands far from his ancestral home, Mei-shan County in Mei-chou: see Chikusa Masaaki, 'HokuSō shidaifu no baiten.'
51. Su Sung, 57/9b–14a.
52. Yü Hsi-lu, *Chen-chiang chih*, chapter on examinations.
53. *TCLC* 36/3a and 4a.
54. Thus even the most reliable Nan-feng County gazetteer lists both Tseng Yen (below, n. 56) and his cousin Tseng Huan as *chin-shih* from Nan-feng (*KHNF* 5/5a), despite convincing evidence that their families were quite firmly settled in Liang-che circuit well before their time.
55. *TCLC* 36/3b and 5a.
56. Tseng Chao and his brother Tseng Pu had settled in Jun-chou, in Liang-che circuit, late in their lives (Yang Shih, 29/176; Tu Ta-Kuei, 10/1a; *Ching-k'ou ch'i-chiu chuan* 2/4b–6b; Yü Hsi-lu, 196/a). While Chao on his death was taken back to Nan-feng County for burial (Yang Shih, 29/17b), Pu was buried in Jun-chou (Wang Tsao, 28/1a–b), and Chao's widow too stayed on and was buried there (Tseng Hsieh, 5/28b–31a), as was her son Tseng Hsün, Hsieh's father, who died while on his way back to Liang-che to mourn for his mother – evidence of her residence there at the time of death (Wang Tsao, 28/1a–b). Tseng Hsieh moved again to live in Te-ch'ing County, Hu-chou (also in Liang-che circuit), where Tseng Yen was raised; Yen himself was buried in Ch'ien-t'ang County, the family home of his mother, grandmother, and great-grandmother (Lou Yüeh, 97/13b–22a). The last direct evidences of the presence of sons or grandsons of Tseng Chao and Tseng Pu in Nan-feng County date from before 1127. These are a construction record by Tseng Wu – Tseng Chao's grandson, who died in 1127 – written in his youth on the occasion of his first visit to a temple that his uncle Tseng Pu had built in the 1090s; and another inscription, dated 1098, recording construction in Nan-feng by Tseng Chi, a son of either Chao, Pu, or their brother Tseng Kung. See *MKNF*, 3/8b–9b and 27b–29a respectively.

57. Wang Kuan-chih (above, n. 14), the family's first *chin-shih*, was first buried at Ho-chou in Huai-nan-hsi circuit; on his widow's death his remains were moved to be buried with hers in Yang-tzu County of neighboring Chen-chou (Wang An-shih, 96/2a–4a). Also buried in Chen-chou was his son Wang Shih-hsi (Wang An-shih, 93/7a–b); the two generations of burial there probably indicate that Chen-chou had become a long-term base for his branch of the family.

58. Wang Kuan-chih's brother Wang Yung-chih was buried in Lin-ch'uan County (Wang An-shih, 83/3b). His son Wang I (Wang An-shih's father) reached the post of vice-administrator of Chiang-ning Fu, died, and was buried there (Tseng Kung, 44/6b–8b). From this time on Chiang-ning, directly across the Yangtse from Chen-chou (where the other branch lived: see n. 57), appears to have become the second home of this branch of the family (Chang Hsüan, *Chin-ling hsin-chih* 13b/46a). While Wang An-shih is known to have lived and studied in Lin-ch'uan County in his youth (see Wang-An-shih, 83/3b and 10b–11a, as well as *YLTT* 10950/1b), on his retirement he came back 'home' to Chiang-ning Fu and was given the honorific title of Supervisor of that prefecture. When his brother Wang An-shang was made Judicial Intendant of Chiang-tung circuit, the office of the intendancy was moved to Chiang-ning for his convenience – a reflection chiefly of the family's power but also of its firm association with this residence (Chang Hsüan, 13b/46a). Two other brothers, Wang An-kuo and Wang An-jen, were both buried in Chiang-ning (Wang An-shih, 96/1b–2b and 91/8a–9a). Fu-chou commentators at the end of Sung and in Yüan seem to have been in agreement that the Wangs had moved *en masse* to Chiang-ning Fu and that few or no descendants remained in Fu-chou. In Yüan the Fu-chou man Wei Su wanted to acquire a genealogy of the Wang family but could not locate a recent one in Fu-chou or in Chiang-ning Fu and so entrusted the making of a new one to a descendant of the family who was living neither in Fu-chou nor in Chiang-ning but in Chu-chi County, Yüeh-chou: none of this man's relatives had had occasion to visit Fu-chou for seven generations (Wei Su, 10/2a–b). Wei's older contemporary Yü Chi, in prefacing a genealogy of the Tseng family, commented on the fortunes of other great families of Northern Sung Fu-chou: '[. . .] the descendants of the Wangs moved to live in Chin-ling [i.e., Chiang-ning Fu]; their descendants [today] are extremely few' (Yü Chi, 4/4a–6a). But cf. also n. 63 below.

59. The information on the Wus is less complete than one might wish. Wu Fen, the son of Wu Min (above, n. 14), is known to have moved to T'ang-chou and to have been buried there; one of his daughters was widowed early and moved back to T'ang-chou and her natal family; on her death she was buried near her father's tomb (Wang An-shih, 98/10a–b; Wang Ling, *fu-lu* 13b–14b). As for the rest of the family, it is known that Fen's brother Wu Fan was buried in Chin-ch'i County (Wang An-shih, 98/8a–b); but Fan's grandson Wu Ch'üeh was buried in Ch'ang-chou in Liang-che circuit, where he had earlier held office. The choice of his burial place was not a matter of happenstance, as he died in Ch'u-chou, where his son was then holding office, and was deliberately taken back to Ch'ang-chou for burial; it is thus virtually certain that he or his son had established a residence there (Sun Ti, 58/14b–18a). Wu Ch'üeh's son Wu Su is the last of the family to be recorded on the Fu-chou exam lists (in 1128) or in other local sources (*KHFC* 42/9a; *KHCC* 4/2b; *TCCC* 17a/1b); it is likely that the later silence reflects the departure from Fu-chou of this second branch of the family.

60. According to the funerary inscription of a granddaughter of Yüeh Shih (above, note 14):

> [. . .] with the abolition of the Li family's kingdom, Shih submitted to serve this dynasty. His sons and grandsons included many famous men. They then moved their family to become men of Ho-nan. (Wang An-shih, 99/9b–10b.)

Essentially the same account is given in the inscription of the wife of one of Yüeh Shih's grandsons (Yin Chu, *Ho-nan hsien-sheng wen-chi* 15/6b–7b). The move to Loyang must have taken place in the early eleventh century. In late Northern Sung the charitable estate that the family had established in I-huang was confiscated by the government because the family was not present, the tenants had run off, and the land had fallen out of cultivation (*TCIH* 14/23a–b; *KHIH* 3/1b–2b, 18a–b). The Yüeh family did not, however, disappear from Fu-chou forever: descendants of Yüeh Shih are found in the exam lists in Southern Sung (see Appendix I, no. 72). The earliest surviving gazetteer of Fu-chou reports that members of the family returned to the ancestral home in I-huang from the north on the fall of Northern Sung in 1127 (*CCFC* 11/3b).

61. Yen Shu (above, n. 14) was buried in Hsü-chou (Ou-yang Hsiu, 22/7b–12b), as were the wives of two of his sons, hence probably the sons themselves. This suggests a move away from Fu-chou similar to those above; but Yen Shu's grand-nephew Yen Fang, born in Shu's own household, is known to have built a hall for contemplation and study in Lin-ch'uan, the family's county of origin, and to have been buried there (Hsieh I, 7/6a–7b and 9/4a–8b). All other members of the family for whom information survives were also buried in Lin-ch'uan, down into Southern Sung, and one of them, Yen Ta-cheng, is known to have lived there for at least part of his life (Hsieh I, 9/11a–12a; Huang Kan, 38/35a–37a; Ts'ao Yen-yüeh, 20/19a–23b). Thus despite unclear connections to Hsü-chou for two generations in Northern Sung, connections to Fu-chou seem to have been maintained throughout the dynasty. The family was honored by local officials near the end of Sung (*YLTT* 10950/1b); in the last years of the dynasty, the Fu-chou prefect Huang Chen prefaced writings of Shu and other family members shown him by their descendants (Huang Chen, 91/23a–24b); and in Yüan, Yü Chi wrote a genealogy preface for a descendant of Yen Shu who was then abbot of a Buddhist temple in Lin-ch'uan (Yü Chi, 32/8a–9a). See also Appendix I, no. 73. There is, however, evidence that the family presence in Fu-chou had been tenuous in certain periods: see n. 29 above.

62. See Map 7, nos. 16–19, 23, 24.

63. Hung Mai, for example, writing of events that took place in the 1130s, refers to one Wang Ch'un, the grandson of Wang An-shih's brother An-kuo, as 'Wang Ch'un of Lin-ch'uan' (Hung Mai, *chih-keng* 10/3a–b). A great-grandson of another brother, An-li, appears in the same work as 'Wang Huan of Lin-ch'uan'. (Hung Mai, *chih-ching* 3/6a–b.)

64. See Map 7, no. 20.

65. See Map 7, no. 25.

66. See Map 7, nos. 5, 6, 8, 10, 11.

67. See Map 7, nos. 12, 13, 14.

68. See Map 7, nos. 32 and 34.

69. Or *heads*: 'family' here does not necessarily correspond to 'household', and in the absence of formal lineage organization a 'family' need not have had any single head.

70. See Kinugawa, 'Sōdai saishō kō.'

71. See Umehara, 'Sōsho no kirokukan to sono shūhen.'

72. Umehara, p. 159 and n. 65, cites Ou-hang Hsiu's testimony on this point.

73. I owe this point to Robert Hartwell. It is implicit as well in Ou-yang Hsiu's complaint cited above.

74. Kinugawa, 'Sōdai saishō kō,' and Umehara, 'Sōsho no kirokukan to sono shūhen'.

75. See nn. 34 and 35 in Chapter 2.

76. Hartwell, 'Demographic, Political, and Social Transformations,' pp. 405–22. This analysis had been developed by Hartwell in a series of unpublished papers

beginning in 1976 and rests on more than a decade of research, of unparalleled breadth, into Sung economic policy, factional struggle, bureaucratic organization, elite behavior, and demography. My own discussion, particularly in what immediately follows, does not parallel Hartwell's in every respect; but his analysis has provided from early on an organizing principle for the patterns I have seen emerging in my Fu-chou research. The dependence of my argument, in this chapter in particular, on his work is obvious.

77. The shift may not have coincided precisely with the Northern Sung/Southern Sung boundary, and certainly need not have been sudden. I am prepared to believe that the 'Southern Sung strategy' was beginning to emerge in the last decades of Northern Sung, even while other families continued to pursue the older strategy. That even during a period of overlap the two strategies were associated with 'groups' distinguishable in other ways, however, I would tend to doubt. On the prefectural examination in the capital in Northern and Southern Sung, see Chaffee, pp. 192–3.

78. See de Bary, 'A Reappraisal of Neo-Confucianism,' pp. 100–6; Michael Freeman, 'Lo-yang and the Opposition to Wang An-shih: the Rise of Confucian Conservatism,' pp. 128–30.

79. See the funerary inscription of Tseng's son Hsün in Wang Tsao, 27/17b–18b.

80. This idea was suggested to me, I believe, by Karen Alvarez in conversations in Kyoto in 1977.

81. See Schirokauer, 'Neo-Confucians under Attack.'

82. My thoughts on this question grow partly out of conversation with James Polachek in Princeton in the fall of 1984. On the academy movement in Southern Sung see Chaffee, pp. 158–165; Terada Gō, *Sōdai kyōiku kaisetsu*, pp. 262–23; Linda Walton-Vargö, 'Education, Social Change, and Neo-Confucianism.' On academies or literary societies and politics in later dynasties see John Meskill, *Academies in Ming China*; Charles Hucker, 'The Tung-lin Movement of the late Ming Period;' William Atwell, 'From Education to Politics: The Fu She;' Jerry Dennerline, *The Chia-ting Loyalists*, pp. 23–68; James Polachek, 'Literati Groups and Literati Politics in Early Nineteenth-Century China,' pp. 157–206.

Chapter 4

1. Lu Chiu-yüan, 7/9a–11a.
2. Lu Chiu-yüan, 7/11a–12b.
3. Lu Chiu-yüan, 5/11a–13a; 8/1a–2b; 8/3a–4b; 9/4a–5a.
4. Lu Chiu-yüan, 1/12b–13a; 8/4b–8a; 9/6b–7a; 9/10a–b.
5. Lu Chiu-yüan, 8/11a–15b.
6. Lu Chiu-yüan, passim. in citations above; and 10/2b–4a.
7. Lu Chiu-yüan, 11/7b–8a.
8. Tseng Chao, *Ch'ü-fu chi* 4/4a–6a. See also Chapter 3, p. 107.
9. *KHFC* 59/4b.
10. Chou-Pi-ta, 20/16b–17b. See also Chapter 5, p. 142.
11. Huang Chen, 42/41a. See Chapter 5, n. 26.
12. *TCLA* 8/17a.
13. Liu Hsün, 14/2a–5a.
14. *WWC* 74/17b.
15. *WWC* 74/3a–5a; and see Chapter 6, pp. 159–60.
16. Huang Chen, 78/33a–b.
17. *WWC* 76/1a.
18. On Ch'ing dynasty school-temples and the sacrificial tablets worshipped there (which also included, as in Sung, those to Confucius and his disciples), see Stephen Feuchtwang, 'School-Temple and City God.' Also see Lawrence G. Thompson, *The Chinese Way in Religion*, pp. 146–8.

19. I have found no reference to them as *shen*, the term used for the gods of popular religion and the state cult.

20. My discussion of the general character of the shrines is partly speculative: for Sung they remain almost unstudied. Terada Gō touches on them in his *Sōdai kyōiku kaisetsu*, pp. 272–7. I have benefited greatly from conversations with my student Ellen Neskar, who is in the process of undertaking research on the shrines, their spread in Sung, and their connections to the Neo-Confucian movement. Note that the shrines discussed here are precisely and only those devoted to *local* worthies, to men connected in some way, during their own lives, to Fu-chou. On similar shrines devoted to men with no necessary connection to the prefecture, see the discussion in Chapter 7, pp. 194–96.

21. Yen was the dedicatee of the Yen Lu-kung Altar in the prefectural city. *TCLC* 15/24a–30a; Tseng Kung, *Yüan-feng lei-kao*, Ch. 18.

22. Sacrifices to Su took place at the Su Chung-yung Kung Altar in Ch'ung-jen's county seat. *TCCJ* 2b/19a–20a.

23. *TCLC* 15/20a–b.

24. *TCLC* 15/30a.

25. The nineteen, their shrines, and the relevant dates are as follows:

> The Shrine of Former Worthies in the prefectural city, next to the prefectural school, built around 1180, sacrificed to Yen Shu, Wang An-shih, Tseng Kung and his brother Tseng Chao, Wang Ko, Hsieh I, Hsieh K'o, Ou-yang Ch'e, Wu Hang, and Li Hao. To these were added, around 1210, Tseng Chi-li and Lo Tien. In 1229 the shrine was rebuilt in a different part of the school compound. *TCLC* 16/10aff.

> The Shrine of the Two Masters Lu was built in 1193 at the county school in Chin-ch'i County to sacrifice to the brothers Lu Chiu-yüan and Lu Chiu-ling. Later this became the Shrine of the Three Masters Lu when sacrifices were rendered to a third brother, Lu Chiu-shao. Still later Lu Chiu-yüan's leading local disciple, Fu Tzu-yün, also began receiving sacrifices here. *KHFC* 33b/17b–22b.

> Another Shrine of the Three Lus was built around 1215 near the prefectural school. *TCLC* 16/6b–10a.

> The Ch'in-shan Shrine, established in 1242 in the Chin-ch'i county seat, also sacrificed to the three Lus. *TCCC* 7/4b.

> The Shrine of the Four Worthies, built around 1202, offered sacrifices to Wu Hang, his younger brother Wu Hsieh, and their lineage-mates Wu I and Wu Tseng. *TCCJ* 2b/3b.

> The Shrine of the Two Worthies was built in 1223 in the county seat of Ch'ung-jen County to sacrifice to Wu Hang and Ou-yang Ch'e. *TCCJ* 2b/3a.

> The Shrine of Master Huang Mien-chai was built around 1241 in the prefectural city to sacrifice to the former Fu-chou prefect Huang Kan. *TCLC* 16/17a.

26. *TCLC* 14/17a.

27. De Bary, 'A Reappraisal of Neo-Confucianism.'

28. De Bary, *The Liberal Tradition in China*, especially pp. 32–4; Hymes, 'On Academies, Community Institutions, and Lu Chiu-yüan,' unpublished paper presented at the Conference on Neo-Confucian Education, Princeton, August 30–September 4, 1984.

29. On academies see Chapter 3, n. 82. In Fu-chou, seventeen private institutions bearing the name *shu-yüan* (academy) are known from gazetteers or collected

works to have been established in Sung. Fourteen of these were founded in Southern Sung.

30. On the community granary and other Sung granaries see Sogabe Shizuo, 'Sōdai no sansō oyobi sono ta,' in his *Sōdai saikeishi no kenkyū*, pp. 465–94. I have benefited also from reading unpublished work on Sung community granaries by Richard von Glahn. The final form of Chu Hsi's plan is found in Chu Hsi, 99/5a–22a; for an earlier version see 77/25a–27b. For an account of the relation of Chu's scheme to that of Wei Shan-chih, see 79/18b–20a. The relationship is also touched on by Wang Po in a comprehensive discussion of community granaries and alternative schemes: Wang Po, *Lu-chai chi* 7/123–7.

31. On the community compact, see Wada Sei, *Shina chihō jichi*, pp. 51–2, 119–45, 224–30; de Bary, *The Liberal Tradition in China*, pp. 32–4; and Monika Übelhör, 'The Community Covenant (*Hsiang-yueh*) of Sung and its Educational Significance,' unpublished paper presented at the Conference on Neo-Confucian Education, Princeton, August 30–September 4, 1984.

32. De Bary, *The Liberal Tradition in China*, p. 33. For Chu's categorization of the *I-li* see Ueyama Shumpei, 'Shushi no "Karei" to "Girei keiten tsū kai",' pp. 238–41.

33. Note, however, that one of the institutions treated here, the community compact, had originated as the plan of a *Northern* Sung man, Lü Ta-chün. Lü was an associate of the anti-reform party during Wang An-shih's regime. As Monika Übelhör has pointed out, his application of the plan in his home county of Lan-t'ien followed by only a few years Wang's promulgation of the *pao-chia* law. It does not seem unreasonable to speculate that the plan was at its origin a conscious alternative to *pao-chia*. There is reason to believe that many of the elements of the line of thought that Chu Hsi was to inherit from the Ch'eng brothers (and others) were first worked out during the period of exile in Lo-yang of the opponents of Wang An-shih: see Michael Freeman, 'Lo-yang and the Opposition to Wang An-shih.' This may apply as well to the stress on local spheres of action that we find crystallized in Chu Hsi's institutional program.

Chapter 5

1. Huang Chen, 75/19a–20a. The three forts in Lo-an mentioned here appear also in the 'Troops and Defense' (*ping-fang*) section of the Sung Ching-ting period (1260–4) Fu-chou gazetteer that survives partially in what remains of the *Yung-lo ta-tien*; here their dates of establishment, numbers of troops, and troops' salaries are supplied as well (*YLTT* 10950/10a–12b; the forts are listed on 11b–12a). The three are listed again among 'seven forts of Fu-chou' in a section of the *Sung shih*'s military monograph devoted to forts established in Southern Sung (*SS* 192/14b), though here Tseng-t'ien is miswritten as Hui-t'ien.

2. There were in fact nine such forts, seven of which are known to have been created in Southern Sung (for the other two no dates are available). Much remains unclear about the official military system in Fu-chou during Sung. The fragmentary late Sung gazetteer and all later gazetteers give information only on Southern Sung (though they do not make this clear), but earlier information can be pieced together from scattered references in the military monograph of the *Sung shih*. The first Northern Sung emperors had established and maintained a distinction between the 'imperial armies' (*chin-chün*), forces in theory directly subordinate to the emperor, composed of the most able and best-trained troops in the empire, used in combat, and in principle alternating tours of duty in the provinces with periods of service in the capital; and the 'borough armies' (*hsiang-chün*), forces originating as the remnants of the Five Dynasties period local forces after the transfer of the best troops to the *chin-chün*, stationed permanently in each

prefecture, and used only for labor duties. (See *SS* 187/1a–9a and 189/1a–4b respectively, both of which make clear the tendency for the distinction to be muddied with time.) It would appear that in around 1041 a command of imperial army troops with the name *Hsüan-i* was created and stationed at Fu-chou; this was one of an enormous number of such new commands, all called *Hsüan-i*, created for most of the prefectures of China at the same time (*SS* 187/14a). In the period before 1070 – perhaps from the beginning of Sung – Fu-chou was also the site of three commands of borough army troops, named *Chien-chung ch'i-she*, *Pao-chieh*, and *Lao-ch'eng* (*SS*, 189/5a, 5b, and 6a respectively). In 1070 a major consolidation, rationalization, and reduction of troop units was instituted for both the imperial and borough armies (*SS*, 187/5a–b and 189/3a–4a). The chief effect of this in Fu-chou was a change of names: the *Hsüan-i* command was changed to *Chiao-yüeh chung-chieh* (*SS*, 188/4b), while the *Chien-chung ch'i-she* command was changed to *Hsiao-yung*. The *Pao-chieh* and *Lao-ch'eng* commands kept their old names (*SS*, 189/9b). After the fall of Northern Sung, according to the *Sung Shih*, there were two commands of imperial army troops in Fu-chou: one called *Chung-chieh* – undoubtedly a simple shortening of *Chiao-yüeh chung-chieh* above – and one called *Wu-hsiung* (*SS* 189/11a; see also *YLTT* 10950/10b). As Southern Sung borough army units, the *Sung Shih* lists only the *Hsiao-yung* and *Lao-ch'eng* commands above (*SS* 189/11b). As the gazetteer fragment tells us that this *Lao-ch'eng* unit was also sometimes called *Pao-chieh*, it is probable that it was the product of the combining of the Northern Sung *Lao-ch'eng* and *Pao-chieh* commands (*YLTT* 10950/11a). The same source lists a third Southern Sung borough army command, called *Chuang-ch'eng*; again there is no indication of its origin, though there had been a command of this name in nearby Hung-chou during Northern Sung (*SS* 189/6b and 9b). It would appear that by middle or late Southern Sung the imperial and borough army units in Fu-chou – all of which had been stationed in or near the prefectural city – had largely disappeared, since the gazetteer fragment refers to them as from 'the old registers,' and since all but one of the old barracks in Fu-chou had been abandoned (*YLTT* 10950/ 11a). In their place were the nine forts. The Ch'eng-nan Fort just south of the prefectural seat and the Lu-ch'i Fort sited on Fu-chou's border with Chien-ch'ang Chün (and subordinate jointly to both prefectures) may have existed already in Northern Sung, as no date of creation is recorded for either (*YLTT* 10950/11b–12a). Of the others the earliest created were the County Fort and Tseng-t'ien Fort in Lo-an County discussed by Huang Chen: both were built in 1149 at the county's creation (ibid.). The county itself was founded in order to strengthen government control of an area plagued by bandits (*TCCJ* 9f/33b–35a), and the two forts were no doubt intended to be a major instrument of such control. A third was established in 1155 at Pei-shan, where the northwest corner of Lo-an bordered Hsin-kan County of Lin-chiang Chün and Feng-ch'eng County of Hung-chou; it was named Pei-shan Fort and was subordinated simultaneously to all three prefectures, which paid its troops' salaries in rotation (*YLTT*, 10950/11b–12a). The next active period in fort building came in 1230 after Fu-chou and surrounding prefectures were overrun by bandits from T'ing-chou (in Fu-chien) and elsewhere. (On this banditry see the very brief mention in *SS* 41/5a; see also Liu Hsün, 13/2b–7b; *TCLC* 31/2b–3a; *TCLA* 5/3a–4a; *TCCC* 14/1a; *TCCJ* 5b/1b–2a; *MKNF* 8/5a–6b; *CCFC* ch. 10; and the biography of Teng P'ang in *TCCC* 22/1a–5a.) When the bandits had finally been 'pacified' the Fu-chou prefect Huang Ping established two new military units called the Ch'i-ma and Ch'i-pu armies (literally 'banner cavalry' and 'banner infantry'), totalling roughly three hundred men, and stationed them at newly built forts at the prefectural city. At the same time he established two other new forts: one, the Chao-hsi Fort mentioned by Huang Chen, was sited in the extreme south of Lo-an, the other, Hu-p'ing Fort, on the southern border of I-huang County (*YLTT*, 10950/11a–12a). This, then, made the full complement of nine forts. What must be noted is that all but two of the nine appear clearly to have been established as a remedy for the government's inability to control banditry in the countryside. Yet as Huang Chen's memorial shows, the remedy failed, as the fort troops themselves proved uncontrollable.

3. *YLTT* 10950/11a.

4. Most of the contemporary references to Fu-chou bowmen deal with their use to pursue and arrest single individuals charged with crimes or wanted in connection with lawsuits. The one evidence of their use against larger threats in the countryside is an anecdote retold by Hung Mai in his *I-chien chih*: here we find that in 1159 a bandit named Hsieh Chün-chiu of I-huang County gathered a force of a hundred men and broke open graves and plundered in the countryside, finally killing a local man of official rank. Two patrols of bowmen were sent out to deal with Hsieh's gang: the first fled on its first meeting with the bandits, while the second fought them and in the end was decimated. This group of bandits was hardly a large one in comparison to others in Fu-chou before and after, but the sheriff's bowmen proved quite ineffectual against it. It should be noted that Hung Mai and his informant do not tell this tale to show the weakness of county bowmen: the facts of their performance are incidental to the point of the story, which is the touching loyalty of two dogs kept by the bowmen's captain. See Hung Mai, *chih-ching* 7/2b–3a. None of the numerous other accounts of Fu-chou banditry mentions any participation by county bowmen in fighting.

5. The Hung Mai story cited above mentioned local *pao-wu* units as of 1159, but their role in the events was to assemble after the fighting was over and notify the county of what had occurred. Huang Kan, who had administered Lin-ch'uan County in the first years of the thirteenth century, from a later post addressed a memorial to the court in which he recounted the details of an official *pao-wu* organization he had found already in existence ('not yet completely abolished') when he served in Lin-ch'uan: the function of the organization was 'to investigate perversity and villainy in order to protect the rural communities' (Huang Kan, 24/11b–13a). But again, no source on anti-bandit defense mentions official *pao-wu* units as combatants. On *pao-wu* in Southern Sung, see especially Sudō Yoshiyuki's comprehensive article on the subject (*Sudō, Tō-Sō shakai keizaishi kenkyū*, pp. 681–734); see also McKnight, *Village and Bureaucracy*, pp. 33, 39, 40–3, 49, 91–3, 180. It is important to bear in mind that the term *pao-wu* (originating simply as a compound of two names of hierarchical units within a military or police organization: *pao* and *wu*) could be applied in Sung to any privately run militia as well as the officially-organized units discussed here. Sudō discusses both sorts of *pao-wu* under a single rubric, but the difference is crucial.

6. As I have commented in n. 2, the establishment of forts in Southern Sung is itself evidence of this concern; the 1230 débâcle showed the inadequacy of the forts established in early Southern Sung, and the new forts created in 1230 must rather quickly have gained independence of official authority if Huang Chen's testimony forty years later is accurate.

7. For summary accounts of a large number of these local militia forces, none of them in Fu-chou, see the article headed 'Militia and Patrolling Societies after Chien-yen' in the *Sung shih* monograph on the military (*SS* 192/13b–14b). The proper role of such troops in the national defense was the object of rather heated controversies at court: see Teraji Jun, 'Nan-Sō seiritsuki ni okeru mingen bushō soshiki to Ken-en nenkan no seiji katei.'

8. *SS* 24/6a. See also Kyō Heinan, 'Nan-Sō no chūgijunshasei ni tsuite.'
9. *TCCC* 22/1a–5a; *KHCC* 5/5b–7a.
10. *YLTT* 10950/12a.
11. Chou Pi-ta, 20/16b–17b.
12. See *TCCC*, 22/1a–5a; *KHCC* 5/5b–7a.
13. Chou Pi-ta, 20/16b–17b.
14. Lu Chiu-yüan, 27/1a–8a.
15. Lu Chiu-yüan, 28/7a–11a.
16. *TCTH* 13b/1a; Yü Chi, 18/21a–23b.
17. The gazetteer biography of one Lan Hsi-ch'uan reports that when a bandit named P'an K'uei led his followers from Kuei-ch'i into Chin-ch'i, Lan commanded one of three units of militia troops that met and defeated him. The others were the Teng and Fu societies. Whether the claim of coequality with the Tengs and Fus can be accepted is doubtful. (Why did contemporaries not refer to the Three Societies of the Tengs, Fus, and Lans?) It seems much more likely that Lan, like Ko Keng, was commander of a subordinate unit under one or the other (most probably the Tengs: see below). The source base for this account is relatively weak: the biography appears in the 1870 but not in the 1682 edition of the Chin-ch'i gazetteer. The 1870 edition cites an earlier edition of 1823 as its source. I have not been able to consult this edition. It may be that it cites some earlier source other than previous editions of the gazetteer or even that the 1682 edition has simply omitted a biography that still earlier editions had included; but in the absence of definite information, the possibility that the account in the 1870 edition is without foundation cannot be dismissed.

The biography of Teng P'ang in the T'ung-chih period gazetteer of Chin-ch'i (*TCCC* 22/1a–5a) gives the names of a number of men who received rewards for their role in the militia after its defeat of bandits in 1230; aside from known lineal descendants of Teng P'ang, Fu An-ch'ien, and Ko Keng, as well as three other Tengs and one other Fu, the list includes a Principal General (*cheng-chiang*) named Huang Yüan-lung, a Staff Officer (*ts'an-mou*) named Shang-kuan Ts'ung-lung, and a Secretary (*shu-chi*) named Li Fang, all of whom received appointments as students at the prefectural school; and Divisional Generals (*pu-chiang*) named Li Hsiung-fei, Li Pi-sheng, Shang-kuan Ch'ien, P'eng Shou-hsün, Hu Nan, and T'u An-kuo. Judging by surnames alone one might guess that one family surnamed Li and one surnamed Shang-kuan each supplied more than one member of this group; but again, nothing is known of these or of any other families represented here, and none of these surnames is that of a reconstructed Chin-ch'i County local elite family.
18. See *TCCC* 5/2b; *KHCC* 5/7b; *KHFC* 61/5b; and for the Tengs, see Wei Su, 3/14b–6b.
19. Most of the information given here and below on the campaigns of the militia comes from Teng P'ang's biographies (*TCCC* 22/1a–5a and *KHCC* 5b/7a).
20. On these tea bandits, aside from sources already cited, see also *SS* 34/11a–b; *SHY chih-kuan* 62, *chih-kuan* 72, and *ping* 13; Li Hsin-ch'uan, *Chien-yen i-lai ch'ao-yeh tsa-chi* 14/12b–13a. None of these sources makes clear the nature of these bandits or of their grievances. An anecdote in the *Ho-lin yü-lu* of the Southern Sung man Lo Ta-ching informs us that the bandit leaders were in fact tea merchants (Lo Ta-ching, 6/24–25) but again gives no idea of the reason for their uprising. All these references come from Saeki Tomi's invaluable compilation of source material on Sung tea (Saeki, *Sōdai chahō kenkyū shiryō*, pp. 823–30). Saeki has also dealt briefly with the tea bandits in an article, suggesting that their banditry grew out of the private military units that tea merchants in the Ching-hu region are known to have maintained for the protection of their goods and themselves (Saeki, *Chūgokushi kenkyū*, pp. 409–20).

21. Chou Pi-ta, 20/16b–17b.
22. '*Shih chu ku fu*': for this phrase see for instance *Tso Chuan*, Duke Yin, 6th year; this seems to be the source of its use with this meaning.
23. Chou Pi-ta, 20/16b–17b.
24. Lu Chiu-yüan, 27/1a–8a.
25. This is an awkward attempt to translate *hao-hsia wu-tuan-che*.
26. Aside from Chou Pi-ta's record of Liu Yao-fu's account on the one hand and Lu Chiu-yüan's record of conduct for Lu Chiu-ling on the other, a third source appears to record Chiu-ling's involvement in the militia. Chiu-ling's own collected works have not survived; but the late Southern Sung scholar Huang Chen included in his daily notes on ancient and modern books a number of Sung collected works, Lu Chiu-ling's among them. Huang's very brief summaries of scattered items in the collection include one of a letter from Lu to an unidentified administrator of Chin-ch'i County, discussing the organization of defense against bandits. Lu urged consideration of a number of issues, which Huang lists: 'What men should be used, what troops are capable in battle, how they are to be distributed among the posts and forts, how they are to be provisioned, who is to be put in command. [. . .]' (Huang Chen, 42/41a). While the letter is undated, there can be little doubt that it originates from the 1175 defense preparations.
27. See, for example, *SYHA* 77/19a; *SYHAPI* 77/29a; and the two letters from Lu to Liu in Lu Chiu-yüan, 4/9a–12b.
28. Aside from the sources already cited, there are Wu Ch'eng's preface to Liu's collected works (*WWC* 22/8a–b) and two Yüan prefaces to his lineage's genealogy (Wei Su, *hsü-chi* 1/12b–13a; Sung Lien, 12/449–450).
29. *SYHA*, 77/19a; *SYHAPI*, 77/29a.
30. A grandson of Lu Chiu-yüan's elder brother Chiu-ssu, named Lu Chün, is recorded to have been recruited by the Chiang-hsi military intendant Li Yü onto his staff to help in the planning of defense against bandits in Chi-an County in neighboring Chi-chou (*SYHAPI* 58/36b; *KHFC* 47/45b). Li Yü took up the post of military intendant on being made prefect of Hung-chou in 1211 (Wu T'ing-hsieh, p. 20), and an uprising by aboriginal bandits had apparently begun in Chi-chou in 1210 (*TCCC* 22/3a), so a 1211 date for Lu Chün's participation seems secure. The Teng Society is recorded to have played an important part in the suppression of the 1210 outbreak (ibid.); thus the Tengs may once again have found themselves in principle subordinate to a Lu. However, Lu Chün's new role as a staff member at the military intendancy in Hung-chou was quite different from (and at a far greater distance from the action than) the direct local participation of his forebears.
31. There is disagreement in the sources as to which Teng led the forces at Han-p'o Fort: the gazetteer biography of Fu T'i identifies him as Teng K'o-chi (*KHFC* 46/31a), but according to Teng P'ang's biography K'o-chi was the commander-in-chief and 'aided the prefectural city,' while his son Teng Ch'ih-chih commanded the troops at Han-p'o Fort (*TCCC* 22/3a–b). There is reason to think that the Fu family had shifted their residence from the south of the district to the northeastern area occupied already by the Tengs and Lus; if so this may have contributed to their loss of independence. See Appendix I, no. 74.
32. *SHY, ping* 2, 50–58.
33. Lu, according to Chou Pi-ta, was made *tu-she*. Technically in the official regulations this was the title, not of an officer, but of his unit itself: the highest unit, comprising five 'societies' (*she*). The commander of such a unit was to be known as *tu-she-cheng*, 'supersociety director.' The correspondence, however, is close

enough: Chou Pi-ta may have been using a kind of shorthand. Lu O did indeed direct a unit that spanned more than one 'society' (in this case, two): the Two Societies of the Tengs and Fus. Chou Pi-ta, 20/16b–17b.

34. For the titles of other Chin-ch'i militia officers, see *TCCC* 22/1a–5a; *KHCC* 5/ 5b–7a. A few are listed in note 17 above.

35. *YLTT* 10950/11b–12a.

36. *TCCC* 22a/1a–5a.

37. Chou Pi-ta, 20/16b–17b.

38. On the sacking of these prefectures and further incursions into Hsing-kuo Chün, Hung-chou, and Fu-chou, see *SS* 45/1a.

39. *SS* 425/11a. This appears to be the only mention of the Chin-ch'i militia in the *Sung shih*. According to the biography, Hsieh had been chosen by Wu Ch'ien for a place on his staff when Wu took up the post of Pacification Commissioner for Chiang-tung and Chiang-hsi Circuits, and had received an order to organize militia defense. The events are undated here, but judging by the context cannot be less than two years after Hsieh's *chin-shih* in 1256 (*SS* 45/1a). However, neither Wu Ch'ien's own biography (*SS* 418/1a–3b) nor the *Sung-shih* annals for the years 1257 through 1262, when Wu died (*SS* 44/5a–45/8a), mention this office among the many that Wu held in these years. The office itself is mentioned only as being received by Chao K'uei in 1259, with the note: '[. . .] the official armies and militia troops of Jao-chou, Hsin-chou, Yüan-chou, Lin-chiang Chün, Fu-chou, and Lung-hsing Fu [all prefectures in the P'o-yang Lake region] were to be under his command' (*SS* 44/10b). Now, in Hsieh Fang-te's funerary inscription we find: 'In 1259 Chao K'uei was Pacification Commissioner of Chiang-tung and Chiang-hsi and chose Hsieh as his subordinate [. . .] He was ordered to recruit troops for aid for the Yangtse, spent 100,000 strings in paper currency, and obtained several thousand militiamen of Hsin-chou and Fu-chou' (Hsieh Fang-te, *T'ieh-shan chi* 16/7b–10b). These are clearly the same events as those described in the *Sung Shih* biography; it would seem then that the latter has misidentified Hsieh's superior. In Teng P'ang's biography one finds, for 1261:

> Hsieh Fang-te of Hsin-chou was deputed by the Pacification Commissioner [. . .] Chao K'uei, to pay out money and grain to recruit militia troops for defense. He thereupon persuaded the Two Societies of the Tengs and the Fus and various great families to unite their efforts. [. . .] (*TCCC* 22a/4b–5a)

This account is surely derived from the same sources as that in Hsieh's *Sung shih* biography. As for the date (1261), it is probably the year in which the Tengs responded to the recruitment efforts rather than actually the year in which Hsieh was ordered to begin recruiting them. See also n. 41 below.

40. *TCCC* 33f/7b–9b.

41. Near the beginning of the letter we find the phrase: 'From *keng-hsü* until today, for ten years [. . .]' (*tzu keng-hsü chih chin shih nien*). A *keng-hsü* year had occurred in 1250, so ten years afterward would be 1260. It would seem that Chao K'uei came to his office in 1259 and ordered Hsieh Fang-te to organize militia defense in that year or in 1260; that Hsieh communicated with the Tengs during 1260; and perhaps (see n. 39 above) that matters were settled in 1261.

42. For Teng Yüan-kuan see *TCCC* 17a/3a; *KHFC* 42/21b; *TCCC* 22a/5a.

43. *TCCC* 33f/7b–9b.

44. *TCCC* 22a/5a.

45. The bestowal of office on ancestors of Ts'ao Shih-hsiu (*chin-shih* in 1106) for anti-bandit activity has been mentioned in Chapter 1, n. 90; and the funerary inscription of Jao Huai-ying of Lin-ch'uan County, who died sometime before 1068, similarly records his successful campaign against local bandits (Lü Nan-kung,

19/5b–8a). The *Sung shih* further records the existence of an officially organized seven-thousand-man anti-bandit militia in Fu-chou as of 1079 (*SS* 191/10a). Whether any of the participants in this organization came from the families that were the mainstays of the later militia cannot be shown.

46. For purposes of reference I provide a list here:

    (a) *1127 to 1135*

        (1) Hsü Tso-lin of I-huang County, a prefectural graduate in 1115 and member of an old officeholding family (see Appendix I, no. 23), first around 1127 used his influence to persuade local youths not to rise in support of bandits passing through, and then in 1133 organized a force of a hundred or so, and successfully warded off the incursions into I-huang of the bandit Yang Shih-hsiung. See Sun Ti, *Nan-lan-ling Sun shang-shu ta-ch'üan chi* 33/10b–11a; *TCIH* 25/15a, 36/1a–b; *KHIH* 5/9a, 36b–37a; *KHFC* 66/2a.

        (2) Kuo Jen-shih of Ch'ung-jen County, not an officeholder or of identifiable family, around 1127 organized a local society to defend his county against southward penetrations by Chin troops. See *KHFC* 61/9a.

    (b) *1230*

        (1) Chao Pu-tz'u of Ch'ung-jen County, not an officeholder but a member of the imperial lineage, in 1230 formed a troop of about three hundred men and defended his locality against bandits. See *KHCJ* 4/73b.

        (2) Cheng Feng-hsiang and Cheng Hsin, two brothers from a rich family in Lo-an County, in 1230 used their family's wealth to organize a militia and protect their neighborhood. Not an officeholder before this, Feng-hsiang received a low office for his defense role. See Ho Hsi-chih, 5b–6b; *WWC* 74/3a–5a.

        (3) Hou Ting of I-huang County, member of an old officeholding family (see Appendix I, no. 19), after the bandit destruction of the 1230s, built Lung-chi Fort near his residence and manned it with militiamen. Not (apparently) an officeholder before this, by the time the events were recorded he had been appointed county sheriff of Hsin-feng County in neighboring Kan-chou; it seems likely that he had received office as a reward for his undertaking. See Pao Hui, *Pi-chou kao-lüeh* 4/9b–11b; *TCIH* 7/5a.

        (4) Huang Ch'ung of Ch'ung-jen County, not an officeholder, led militia troops (*pao-wu*) in defending the area for several *li* around his residence. See Ch'en Yüan-chin, 6/14b–17a.

        (5) Huang Tsai of Nan-feng County, whose father Huang Ta-shou had been a prominent poet as well as a student of Chu Hsi, after 1230 received office for his role in defense against bandits, and through recommendations eventually reached prefect of Feng-chou in Kuang-nan-tung circuit. See Li O, *Sung-shih chi-shih* 71/12a; Lu Hsin-yüan, *Sung-shih chi-shih hsiao-chuan pu-cheng* 4/11a; *MKNF* 9/1b, 26/6b. Also see Appendix I, no. 30.

        (6) Tung Chü-i of Lin-ch'uan County was a *chin-shih* in 1181, with an elder brother who had passed in 1178 and two sons who passed in 1220 and 1232; after his retirement, in 1230, he spent his own money and grain to assemble popular troops and defend the prefecture. See *KHFC* 42/12b, 47/42b; *TCLC* 36/5a–b, 6b, 7b.

    (c) *End of Sung*

        (1) Ch'en Yü of Lin-ch'uan County, descendant of an 1148 *chin-shih* but himself a failed examination candidate, was prominent in the defense of

his locality against bandits at the Sung-Yüan transition. See *WWC* 87/ 9b—11b. See also Appendix I, no. 6.

(2) Cheng Sung of Lo-an County, son of Cheng Feng-hsiang above, and recipient of an office in 1275 as reward for his restoration of the old course of the Ju River, received fields with rents totalling 800,000 *shih* from the government as support for popular troops he was to train; after the fall of Sung he used these troops in support of those working for a restoration. See *WWC* 74/3a—5a. Also see Appendix I, no. 9.

(3) Tseng Yu-lung of Nan-feng County, descendant of the 1132 and 1163 *chin-shih* Tseng Fa and Tseng Tsun, thus a member of the prominent Nan-feng Tseng family (see Chapter 3, n. 14 and Appendix I, no. 54) and himself a prefectural graduate in 1264, at the change of dynasties was relied upon by 'the authorities' to lead local militia troops (*pao-wu*) in protecting his locality against disorder. As he was to hold office under Yüan as professor in the Nan-feng school, it seems likely that 'the authorities' in this case were the Mongols, and that he played his militia role immediately after the Yüan conquest. See *MKNF* 10/6b, 26/7b; Liu Hsün, 8/4a—6a.

(d) For Northern Sung see n. 45 above.

47. See *TCCC* 22a/1a—5a.
48. See n. 46 above.
49. See n. 46 above.
50. See n. 46 above.
51. See n. 46 above.
52. Lu Chiu-yüan, 27/1a—8a.
53. Service in the *official* military forces, however, in at least one case (and probably many more) spanned several generations. The Hsia family of Lo-an County served as officers of Tseng-t'ien Fort in Lo-an from its founding until the end of Sung. See *WWC* 75/6b—8a and 74/8b—10b; and cf. Appendix I, no. 76.
54. See n. 46 above.
55. These are in *TCLC* 31/2b—3a; *TCLA* 5/3b—4a; *TCCC* 14/1a; *TCCJ* 5b/1b—2a; *MKNF* 8/5a—6b. A detailed account of banditry and social disorder in Nan-feng County from 1229 down into Yüan is given by Liu Hsün in his collected works (Liu Hsün, 13/2b—7b) and reproduced in *KHNF* 14/77a—80b. Teng P'ang's gazetteer biographies also give details on bandits and other invaders faced by the Tengs (*TCCC* 22a/1a—5a and *KHCC* 5/5b—7a).
56. Sun Ti, *Nan-lan-ling* . . . 33/10b—11; *TCIH* 36/1a—b; *TCCC* 22a/1a; *KHFC* 32/3a.
57. *KHFC* 32/28a—31b; *TCCJ* 2c/6b—7b, 2d/34a, 9g/2b—3b; *WWC* 49/2b—4a.
58. *TCIH* 12/1b, 13/2b, 8a, 45/13b—15a; *KHFC* 32/37a; see also Chen Te-hsiu, *Chen Wen-chung kung chi* 36/22a—23a on the 1230 bandits' deliberately sparing the household of Ts'ao Yao-tzu, and Pao Hui, 4/9b—11b on the seriousness of the destruction in I-huang that year.
59. *KHLA* 7/8b; *KHFC* 61/9b; *TCLA* 2/25b—27a; and Chen Te-hsiu, 25/24b—26b.
60. *WWC* 32/17a—18b.
61. *MKNF* 8/5a—6b; Liu Hsün, 13/2b—7b.
62. It should be noted that Chin-ch'i's county administrative office was itself burned in 1276, and that the Lu family was burned out of its residence at about the same time (*TCCC* 8/1a, Ch'eng Chü-fu, 14/6a—7a). It would appear, however, that by this time the Chin-ch'i militia, or at least the Teng family, had retired from the field: Teng P'ang's biography tells us that Teng Cho, then the commander of the militia, in 1273 led his men to guard the prefectural city, but fell ill and was borne back to his home, where he died. The biography records no date of militia action later than 1273 until after the Yüan gained control of Fu-chou. Teng

Hsi-yen, heir to the leadership role, was then appointed by Yüan as Inspector (*hsün-chien*) of the district (*TCCC* 22a/5a; Wei Su 3/14b–16b; *WWC* 79/10a– 11b). The Tengs served Yüan quite effectively, aiding in the control of 'bandits' and the re-establishment of local order, until around 1295, when the Teng Society was officially abolished and Teng Hsi-yen was given office as sheriff of Li-shui County in Chien-ning Fu, the first of several local posts he was to hold under the new dynasty (Wei Su, 3/14b–16b; *WWC*, 79/10a–11b). It is most improbable that the Tengs would have been employed in the service of Yüan in this way had they been much involved in resistance to the conquest of Fu-chou in the decisive years of 1275 and 1276. Thus it seems likely that the destruction in Chin-ch'i in 1276 occurred while the leaders of the Chin-ch'i militia sat things out.

63. G. William Skinner, 'Mobility Strategies in Late Imperial China: A Regional Systems Analysis,' p. 355.

Chapter 6

1. See Appendix I, no. 12.
2. Hsieh I, 8/18a–20a.
3. *MKNF* 23/2b–3a.
4. Ch'en Tsao, 35/13a–16a.
5. Ch'en Yüan-chin, 6/9a–11b.
6. *YLTT* 10950/5a–b.
7. *YLTT* 10950/5a–b. On Sung granaries in general the best summary account is an article by Sogabe Shizuo, 'Sōdai no sansō oyobi sono ta'. This covers the Ever-Normal Granaries, Charitable Granaries, and community granaries in detail and a variety of others more briefly.
8. Of course under conditions of free movement of grain one would expect that if a Normal-Sale or Ever-Normal Granary functioned to reduce grain prices in the city, this would affect prices in the countryside as well. However, the total stock of rice of the Normal-Sale Granary at its founding in 1252 was fourteen thousand *shih*, to be sold over the next several years with only a three thousand *shih* re-plenishment in 1254 (*YLTT*, 10950/5a–6). Several individual private sellers of rice are known each to have disposed of similar or far greater quantities in the single famine year of 1271 (Huang Chen, 75/15a–16b), and the prefecture's Harmonious Purchase program in the same year reduced by seventy-five thousand *shih* the supply of rice available to local private purchasers (Huang Chen, 75/12b–14a); in such a context the sale of not more than a few thousand *shih* each year in the prefectural city cannot have made much of an impact on the rice market of the prefecture as a whole.
9. For instance Lu Chiu-yüan, in a letter written in around 1188 to the professor of the prefectural school, notes that 'Chin-ch'i County has never had any *t'i-chü* money or grain,' i.e., any money or grain from the Intendancy of Ever-Normal Granaries in the prefectural city. See Lu Chiu-yüan, 8/6a–8a.
10. Lu Chiu-yüan, 36/40b ff.
11. Lu Chiu-yüan, 1/12b–13a.
12. The account of the Lus' community granary given here is assembled from refer-ences in several of Lu Chiu-yüan's letters: these are a letter to Chou Ju-ch'ien (Lu Chiu-yüan 1/12b–13a); two letters to a Professor Ch'en, probably Ch'en Wan who served as professor of the Fu-chou prefectural school from 1188 to 1192 (Lu, 8/4b–8a); a letter to an Intendant Huang, probably Huang Wei-chih who was Chiang-hsi Intendant of Ever-Normal Granaries from 1189 to 1191 (Lu, 9/10a–b); and a letter to a Prefect Yang, probably Yang Ch'ien who became prefect of Fu-chou in 1190 (Lu, 9/6b–10a). The recipients of these letters, where not identified

by full name in Lu's collected works, have been identified with the aid of the lists of men holding office in Fu-chou in *KHFC* 35/6a–16a.

13. Lu Chiu-yüan, 8/4b–8a.
14. Chu Hsi, 80/22a–23b.
15. Chu Hsi, 80/22a–23b.
16. *SYHA* 77/12a; *SYHAPI* 77/17a.
17. See Appendix I, no. 50.
18. *TCIH* 45b/28a–29a; Chen Te-hsiu, 36/22a–23a.
19. For this Jao family see Appendix I, no. 33.
20. See Appendix I, no. 31.
21. Huang Chen in two places refers to a County Sheriff Jao who is refusing during the famine to make loans from the community granary he administers (Huang Chen, 75/9b–10b and 78/21a–22b); the first of these references gives the man's full name: Jao Li. Now Jao Li is identified elsewhere as the son of Jao Ying-tzu of Ch'ung-jen County, a *chin-shih* in 1232, who was in turn the grandson of Jao Yen-nien (Liu K'o-chuang, 62/11a–15b). Jao Yen-nien had attained lasting fame for his large-scale sales of grain at low prices during a famine in around 1210 (*KHCJ* 4/26b–27a; *KHFC* 69a/3b; *SYHA* 77/11a; *SYHAPI* 77/16a; Huang Chen, 78/5b–6b and 97/10b–12b). Community granaries seem frequently to have been founded on the heels of involvement in relief grain sales in a famine; and Jao Yen-nien is known to have studied with Lu Chiu-yüan and to have been acquainted with Chen Te-hsiu (*KHCJ*, 4/26b–27a; *KHFC* 69a/3b), who was involved in the foundation of various kinds of relief granaries while in office (see Chen Te-hsiu, 24/13b–16a, 40/12a–14a). It thus seems very likely that the community granary administered by Jao Li in the 1270s had been founded by his great-grandfather Yen-nien, probably around the time of the famine in 1210.
22. *TCCC* 22a/4a–b.
23. Pao Hui, 4/9b–11b.
24. Huang Chen, 87/36b–396.
25. Huang Chen, 75/9b–10b.
26. Huang Chen, 87/36b–39a.
27. Lu Chiu-yüan, 8/4b–8a.
28. Lu Chiu-yüan, 9/10a–b.
29. Similarly, according to an inscriptional record by Chen Te-hsiu, when in the first decades of the thirteenth century a man surnamed Shih was prefect of Chien-chou and wanted to establish relief institutions in the countryside, he first considered reviving the community granary program that Chu Hsi had instituted in the same prefecture some fifty years before, but decided that the potential problems of collection were too great. Instead he oversaw the establishment of some ninety rural *Kuang-hui* (literally 'Broad Benefit') granaries, modeled on the Ever-Normal Granaries of Northern Sung and so in essence the same as the Normal-Purchase Granaries of Fu-chou. In the case recorded here the system was that 'the purchase price will follow the level of the time, and when selling it will be somewhat reduced' (that is, reduced from the market price at the time of sale, not reduced from the earlier purchase price). See Chen Te-hsiu, 24/13b–16a.
30. *TCIH* 45b/28a–29a.
31. See Appendix I, no. 31 and no. 4.
32. Huang Chen, 78/33a–b.
33. Huang Chen, 75/9b–10b.
34. This question, however, is complicated. In Chu's own first version of the plan, he had departed from Wei Shan-chih's original by charging interest (twenty percent) without any provision for an eventual suspension. He was persuaded to abandon permanent interest by Wei himself, who argued against what he saw – precisely – as

Chu's imitation of the Green Sprouts farm loan program of Wang An-shih. See Chu Hsi, 79/18b–20a.

35. Chu Hsi established his first community granary in Ch'ung-an County with rice left over from famine relief that he had administered the year before (Chu Hsi, 77/25a–27b); Lu Chiu-shao undertook the administration of his community granary in 1188, the year after his brother Chiu-kao had been deputed as the local supervisor of relief grain sales during a drought (Lu Chiu-yüan, 28/12a–16b); other examples could be supplied for Fu-chou and elsewhere.

36. Lu Chiu-yüan, 28/7b–11a.

37. Lu Chiu-yüan, 28/12a–16b.

38. I list these here (apart from those mentioned in the text):

(1) Chang Yu-hsin of Lin-ch'uan County, *chin-shih* in 1256: aided Huang Chen in encouraging grain sales in 1271. See Huang Chen, 97/10b–12b.

(2) Chao Jo-liu of Ch'ung-jen County, a member of the imperial lineage: fl. c. 1230, but no date is given for his sales of grain. See *KHCJ* 4/74a.

(3) A man surnamed Chu of Lin-ch'uan County, not an officeholder and of unknown family background: lived 1102–85, but no date is given for his grain sales. See Ch'en Tsao, 35/9b–11a.

(4) Huang Ch'ung of Ch'ung-jen County, not an officeholder and of unknown family background: lived 1171–1242, but no date is given for his involvement in relief sales. See Ch'en Yüan-chin, 6/14b–17a.

(5) Huang Yü-sun of Lo-an County, a student at the county school: in 1271 sold 13,000 *shih*. See Huang Chen, 75/15a–16a.

(6) Jao Yen-nien of Ch'ung-jen County, not an officeholder but a member of the prominent Ch'ung-jen Jao family (see Appendix I, no. 31): recommended for office (but would not go) for his sales of relief rice in around 1210. See *KHFC* 69a/3b; *TCCJ* 8d/8b; *KHCJ* 4/26b–27a; Huang Chen, 97/10b–12b.

(7) A woman surnamed Kuo, wife of Yen Sun of Lin-ch'uan County, who was a member of the prominent Yen family of Lin-ch'uan (see Chapter 3, n. 14 and Appendix I, no. 73): lived c. 1135–1213, but no dates are given for her sales of rice. See Huang Kan, 38/35a–37a.

(8) T'an Huai of I-huang County, member of the household of an officeholder, perhaps a member of the prominent I-huang T'an family (see Appendix I, no. 46): in 1271 sold 34,617 *shih*. See Huang Chen, 75/15a–16a.

(9) T'an Ai of I-huang County, member of the household of a man with the title of Postal Inspector, perhaps a member of the prominent I-huang T'an family (see Appendix I, no. 46): in 1271 sold 31,217 *shih*. See Huang Chen, 75/15a–16a.

(10) Tseng Chieh of Nan-feng County, not an officeholder but a member of the prominent Nan-feng Tseng family (see Appendix I, no. 54): lived in late Northern Sung, but no dates are given for his sales of grain. See *MKNF* 23/2b–3a, 26/5a, 7b.

(11) Wang K'uang of Lin-ch'uan County, not an officeholder and of unknown family background: lived 1027–78, but no dates are given for his grain sales. See Lü Nan-kung, 20/5b–7a.

(12) A man surnamed Wei of Chin-ch'i County, an administrative officer in the financial intendancy, perhaps a member of the prominent Chin-ch'i Wei family (see Appendix I, no. 63): in 1271 sold 8,400 *shih*. See Huang Chen, 75/15a–16b.

(13) Wu Shih-shun of Lin-ch'uan County, not an officeholder and of unknown family background: lived 1047–1114, but no dates are given for his sales of grain. See Hsieh K'o, 10/2a–3a.

(14) Yen Shih-k'o of Lin-ch'uan County, an officeholder and probably a member of the prominent Yen family of Lin-ch'uan (see Chapter 3, n. 14 and Appendix I, no. 73): in 1271 sold 11,980 *shih* of rice in various forms. See Huang Chen, 75/15a–16a.

(15) Yu Te-hung of Lo-an County, not an officeholder but a member of a 'rich lineage': played an active role in the relief grain sales in 1271. See *WWC* 74/17a–18b.

39. Officials were frequently reluctant to use methods that required extensive record-keeping or registration for fear that the program would be manipulated by prefectural or county clerks to their own ends (or for fear that local families' charges of such clerical manipulation would paralyze the program). On this see: a memorial from around 1205 by the Fu-chou prefect Huang Kan on relief grain sales (Huang Kan, 29/6b–8b); Huang Chen's assurances to local wealthy families in 1271 that clerks and paperwork would play no part in his relief program (Huang Chen, 78/7a–10a); and the discussions of various methods in Tung Wei's early thirteenth-century handbook on famine relief, which will be dealt with further below (Tung Wei, *Chiu-huang huo-min shu*, ch. 2, passim). The first two of these sources make equally clear their authors' conviction that the ultimate source of famine relief must precisely be the wealthy families in the countryside.

40. Huang Kan, 38/11a–13a.

41. Huang Chen, 78/7a–16b.

42. An exception is Hsü Ying-ch'ang, a *chin-shih* in 1242 who served as administrator of Tao-chou (*TCLA* 7/11a; *KHLA* 5/4a; *KHFC* 42/18b); he is referred to in this list as Hsü Tao-chou, that is by an abbreviation of his title, Tao-chou Prefect.

43. Huang Chen, 78/16b–19b. The order is Huang's own. I omit here Hsü Ying-ch'ang above, a man referred to as *Chia-t'ou* Yen, whose title marks him as a *pao-chia* officer, and two men surnamed Lo, referred to as members of a great lineage of Hu-hsi in neighboring Yung-feng County, Chi-chou, who own extensive absentee estates in Lo-an County. Men of this surname and with the residence identification 'Hu-hsi' appear on the examination lists of the Yung-feng gazetteer from 1189 on, with twelve *chin-shih* beginning in 1190 (*TCYF* 15/15a–18a, 16/13a–20a).

44. See Appendix I.

45. The drawing of conclusions from identity of surnames here requires some comment. It might be objected that certain surnames may simply have been common in the county or the prefecture and so likely to recur in any list of local men, regardless of family. The evidence, however, suggests otherwise. Where the sources provide the names of local bandits, for instance, these virtually never share surnames with reconstructed elite families living in the same county. Similarly, between the reconstructed families of any pair of counties the average overlap of surnames is only 20 per cent. In the present case, on the other hand, 61 per cent of the surnames of reconstructed Lo-an County elite families appear in Huang Chen's list of rice hoarders, and 80 per cent of those in Huang's list appear among the reconstructed elite families. Here the extent of the coincidence seems striking enough to justify my inference.

46. Huang Chen, 78/24a–b.

47. See for instance the county map of Lo-an in *TCLA*, front matter. This map makes it clear that Lung-i is in the same (thirty-first) *tu* as a place called Shan-t'ang, which (unlike Lung-i itself) can be found on existing topographic maps of Fu-chou in more or less the spot that the rather vague gazetteer map would lead one to expect. (The topographic map in question is no. 65 in the 50,000: 1 series for the Chien-ch'ang region listed on p. 149 of Nunome, *Chūgoku hondo chizu mokuroku*) This in turn determines more precisely the location of Lung-i itself.

48. Huang Chen, 78/24a–b.
49. Huang Chen, 78/25b–27a.
50. Huang Chen, 78/27a–28a.
51. *WWC* 74/3a–5a.
52. *WWC* 74/3a–5a.
53. Sometimes, but not necessarily always. It would appear that Huang was successful in forcing the community granary of the Jao family of Ch'ung-jen County to make loans of its rice. In a public notice Huang remarked: 'This prefecture, because County Sheriff Jao was rich but inhumane, not responding to repeated exhortations, has already sent out a unit of troops to pressure him.' (Huang Chen, 78/22b.) Elsewhere in Huang's collected works a memorial to the court explains that the refusal of the community granary owner and manager, Jao Li, formerly Sheriff of Ku-ch'eng County, to make the expected loans of rice, has compelled him to take action to force the issue: he requests the court's attention and approval (Huang Chen, 75/9b–10b). Through an exceptional piece of historiographic luck the events as seen from the court have been preserved in the *Sung shih*:

> In the sixth month [. . .] of 1271, Fu-chou's Huang Chen reported that in the prefecture's relief of famine and exhortation of sharing, the former Ku-ch'eng Sheriff Jao Li, having accumulated 200,000 *shih* of rice, stingily refused to open his granary, and that although he [Huang] had already overseen the lending, one ought [also] to punish his violation of the prohibition of export. It was decreed that Jao Li be demoted two grades. (*SS* 46/9b)

Thus punitive measures were taken against Jao Li, and the forced lending of the granary's rice was apparently accomplished. The contrast with the case of the K'angs is striking, all the more so as Jao Li was an officeholder while the K'angs, it seems, were not. Perhaps a local official could sometimes exert *more* leverage over an officeholder than over a commoner, by threatening to ask the court to demote or remove him. This will have depended, of course, on the quality of the connections that each had with decisionmakers at court.

54. Huang Chen, 78/16b–19b.
55. Huang, 75/15a–16b. Note the surnames of the men: two officeholding T'ans of I-huang, a Huang of Lo-an, a Yen of Lin-ch'uan, and a Wei of Chin-ch'i (see n. 38 above). Once again these are all surnames of reconstructed local elite families living in the same counties at this period.
56. Huang Chen, 78/19b–21b. Nothing is known of this Nan-t'ang Jao family before this time. However, in the gazetteer of Tung-hsiang County (a Fu-chou county created in Ming out of territory taken from Lin-ch'uan, Chin-ch'i and two counties of other prefectures) there is a biography of a Yüan man, claimed retrospectively as a native of this district, named Jao Tsung-lu: his place of residence is listed as Nan-t'ang (*KHTH* 4/27a). The place-name section of the same gazetteer lists Nan-t'ang as in Yen-shou canton. This is one of the cantons transferred from Lin-ch'uan at Tung-hsiang County's creation (*KHTH* 1/16a; *TCLC* 2/6b–7a); and indeed Huang Chen, in 1271, places the Jao residence in the seventy-seventh *tu* in Yen-shou canton. Jao Tsung-lu also appears in contemporary sources: Wu Ch'eng composed a funerary inscription of Jao's wife (*WWC* 80/10b–12a) as well as an inscriptional record for a tower built by Jao in around 1320, in which Wu calls him a man 'of Lin-ch'uan's eastern cantons' (*tung-hsiang*)(*WWC* 42/17a–19a). It appears from a number of other references in Sung and Yüan sources that the phrase 'the eastern cantons' was already in colloquial use as a name for the area of the district that later was cut off to create Tung-hsiang, and indeed that this was the origin of the name Tung-hsiang. All of these sources thus seem to

confirm each other: evidently the Nan-t'ang Jao family was still locally prominent about fifty years after its confrontation with Huang Chen.

57. Huang Chen, 78/19b–21b.
58. This assumption was made explicit in Chu Hsi's plan for famine relief in Nan-k'ang Chün (Chu Hsi, *pieh-chi* 9/8a–9a), and is implied in two sources on Fu-chou. Lu Chiu-yüan, in his letter to Professor Ch'en (see n. 10 above), explains why the Lu community granary's location makes it particularly useful:

> In all the district this is the only place without rich people or great families. What one calls the farming people [here] are either tenants on *k'o-chuang* [literally 'guest estates,' here probably simply meaning estates let out to tenants] or else renters of government land [. . .] What I call '*k'o-chuang*' too are frequently those of absentee official households, *who in normal times cannot provide relief to these farmers.* (Lu Chiu-yüan, 8/4b–8a; emphasis mine)

Here the clear implication is that if the owner households were not absentees the responsibility for relief of their tenants would be theirs. Similarly in the funerary inscription of Huang Ssu-yung we are told that because of his sales of grain at lowered prices, 'those who worked for his family did not move away in famine years' (Huang Kan, 38/11a–13a).

59. Joanna F. Handlin, 'The Philanthropy of Ch'en Lung-cheng (1585–1645),' unpublished paper presented at the annual meeting of the Association for Asian Studies, Washington, 1984.
60. For Fu-chou, the famine-relief documents of Huang Chen, already extensively cited, provide many examples. Huang Kan, in a memorial during the famine in his term, similarly describes the steps he is taking to *compel* relief sales by hoarding families (Huang Kan, 29/6b–8b).
61. Huang Chen, 78/10a–12b.
62. Huang Chen, 78/16b–19b.
63. Huang Chen, 78/33a–b.
64. *SYHA* 57/3a.
65. This story is told by Chen Te-hsiu about the Ts'ao family of I-huang County and the bandits of 1230 (Chen Te-hsiu, 36/22a–23a).
66. Yüan Ts'ai, 3/4b.
67. The family earned particular fame for maintaining its property (hence its status as a single household) undivided for ten generations; in 1242 an imperial edict ordered the official marking of their residence in commemoration of their familial virtue and harmonious coresidence (Lu Chiu-yüan, 36/4a–b). The memorial by the Chin-ch'i County administrator requesting the honor for the Lus had mentioned the family's clear division of labor among the brothers of Lu Chiu-yüan (one managing household finances, one running the family drug business, one teaching in the family school, etc.): this seems to have been a feature of their household organization that was particularly admired. The same point is noted by the late Southern Sung man Lo Ta-ching in an appreciative discussion of the Lu family (Lo Ta-ching, 5/9–10).
68. Pao Hui's 1248 inscriptional record of the edict marking the Lu household devotes considerable attention to Lu Chiu-shao's family rules, and at the end tells us that though the Lus have not been without financial worries, 'their prop has been (Chiu-shao's) instruction in pure-heartedness and simple and frugal manage-ment to assure sufficiency of food' (*TCCC* 33d/20a–22a).
69. *SYHA* 57/2b–3a.
70. *SYHA* 57/3a.
71. *SYHA* 5/3a.

72. On these issues see Patricia Ebrey's discussion of the views of Yuan Ts'ai and others (Lu Chiu-shao included) in *Family and Property in Sung China*, pp. 37–51 and 75–80; see also Ebrey, 'Conceptions of the Family in the Sung Dynasty,' especially pp. 224–9.
73. See for instance the bibliographic notice on the work by Uematsu Tadashi in Hervouet, *Sung Bibliography*, pp. 183–4.
74. On Tung Wei, see his funerary inscription in Ch'eng Pi, *Ming-shui chi* 10/1aff., and *SYHAPI* 25/106b. My attention was first drawn to Tung's book by the very useful article on the subject by Yoshida Toru: see his '*Kyūkō Katsumin Sho* to Sōdai no kyūkō seisaku.'
75. Tung Wei, 2/33–34.
76. Tung Wei, 2/32–33. Tung also mentions the existence, as of 1181, of a decree enjoining local officials against this practice.
77. Tung Wei, 2/34.
78. I follow Burton Watson, trans., *Records of the Historian: Chapters from the Shih chi of Ssu-ma Ch'ien*, p. 334.
79. *Mencius* VI.A.2. I follow D.C. Lau, trans., *Mencius*, p. 160.
80. See Huang Chen, 78/5b–6b, 16b–19b; Huang Kan, 29/6b–8b. For Huang Kan's case there is also an inscriptional record of the shrine built to him in the prefectural city in 1241, some thirty years after his term in Fu-chou: the record mentions that during a period of bad harvests, profit-seekers 'had struggled to sneak rice downstream' (i.e., down the Ju River to the P'o-yang Lake). See *TCLC* 16/17a–19a.
81. Huang Chen, 78/5b–6b.
82. Huang Kan, 25/9b–10a.
83. Lu Chiu-yüan, 16/1b–2a.
84. See Introduction, note 54.
85. *YLTT* 2754/10a–15a. Several points should be noted about these lists: first, while for the vast majority of dams listed nothing but a name is given (no information as to location), a comparison of these lists to those of Ch'ing dynasty dams in Ch'ing gazetteers reveals duplication ranging from 80 or 90 per cent in certain counties down to 50 or 60 per cent in others. Since in the Ch'ing lists the locations of the dams are given (by canton and, within canton, by *tu*), it is possible on the basis of the massive or total duplication of names between Sung and Ch'ing to demonstrate quite conclusively that the Sung lists group the dams by canton within each county. Even more striking, for several counties the canton groupings are arranged according to the numbering of the *tu* in each canton. Thus *YLTT* 2754/10b–12a lists Sung dams in Lin-ch'uan County. Working from the rightmost to the leftmost column on these pages, column 4 lists dams identified in the Ch'ing gazetteer as in Lin-ju canton (*tu* nos. 1 to 4); column 5 lists dams identified in the Ch'ing gazetteer as in Ch'ang-ning canton (*tu* nos. 5 to 8) and Ling-t'ai canton (*tu* nos. 9 to 13); column 6 lists dams identified in the Ch'ing gazetteer as in Chou-hsien canton (*tu* nos. 14 to 17), and so on up through the *tu* numbering scale to columns 26 and 27 (the second and third columns on p. 12a), which list dams identified in the Ch'ing gazetteer as in Hsin-feng canton (*tu* nos. 101 to 109; no *tu* has a higher number). See *TCLC* 6/6b–19b. Thus virtually all the Sung dams can be located rather precisely (down to the *tu*) on the basis of the correspondence to the Ch'ing gazetteer lists. I first observed this duplication of dam names between Sung and Ch'ing lists in this list of Lin-ch'uan County dams and in the lists for Chung-jen County and I-huang County in *YLTT* 2754/12b–13a and 13a–b respectively. The remaining lists were more puzzling until it became clear that some transposition of counties had occurred. Thus the list given under 'Lin-ch'uan: old gazetteer,' ending with the annotation 'the above

are all in Fu-chou Fu, Lin-ch'uan county' (*YLTT* 2754/12a–b), actually lists dams in Yen-fu canton and Pai-ma Yung-ho canton of *Chin-ch'i* County (cf. *TCCC* 3/15b–20b). Likewise what follows the list for I-huang County, up through the 114th dam, in the middle of the third column of p. 14a, though presented as the first part of the list for Chin-ch'i County, is actually a complete list for *Lo-an* County (cf. *TCLA* 1/15b–17a). (Note that Sudō, *Tō-Sō shakai keizaishi kenkyū*, p. 746, mistakes the 'Lin-ch'uan: old gazetteer' list for a complete list of dams in Lin-ch'uan County.) What follows this, up to the annotation 'the above are all in Chin-ch'i County,' is in fact a list for the remaining cantons of Chin-ch'i. These lists are thus enormously valuable but have required some decipherment and re-arrangement to make them usable.

86. The relative numbers for the counties seem to belie an annotation that precedes the lists: 'In Lin-ch'uan and Ch'ung-jen there is much flat land, so dams and storage ponds are plentiful; in Chin-ch'i, I-huang, and Lo-an, there are many mountains and valleys, so streams and springs are plentiful.' The statement does make sense, however, if one supposes that the names 'Ch'ung-jen' and 'Chin-ch'i' have here exchanged places. In view of the general condition of the lists as outlined above, this is far from implausible, and it accords better with the appearance of the counties' terrain on modern topographic maps.

87. *TCLC* 21/4b–5a gives population figures for 1260–4 broken down into rural and urban households (within the overall division into *chu-hu* and *k'o-hu*).

88. *SHY*, *shih-huo* 61, pp. 68–9, *shui-li t'ien*. This point as to the relative size of Chiang-hsi irrigation works has been made previously on the basis of the same evidence in Satake Yasuhiko, 'Sōdai Kanshū no sobyō.'

89. *YLTT* 2754/10b.

90. Ch'en Tsao, 35/3a–16a.

91. Ch'en Tsao, 35/13a–16a.

92. *KHCJ* 4/74b–75a.

93. The only reconstructible Wang family of Lin-ch'uan County is that of Wang An-shih, which by this time had moved away from Fu-chou (see Chapter 3, nn. 57, 58). A number of Lin-ch'uan men surnamed Wang passed the *chin-shih* exam during Southern Sung, but there is no way of knowing whether Wang Chi-weng was related to any (or all) of these.

94. *KHFC* 66/1a; and see the record for a later reconstruction of the dam in *TCLC* 5/5a–7a.

95. *WWC* 74/3a–5a.

96. Here and below, Sung dams have been located by matching them to the lists in the Ch'ing gazetteers: see n. 85 above. For the Lu Family Dam the references are *YLTT* 2754/12a, column 4, and *TCCC* 3/16b, column 10.

97. For the Lus' residence here, see for instance Lu Chiu-yüan's *nien-p'u* (Lu Chiu-yüan, 36/1a) or Lo Ta-ching, 5/9–10.

98. *YLTT*, 54/12a, column 8; *TCCC* 3/18b, column 11.

99. *TCCC*, 3/19a, column 5. For the Kos' residence here, see *TCCC* 17a/2a, 22a/5b–6a; *KHCC* 4/3a.

100. *YLTT* 2754/14b, column 1; *TCCC* 3/9b, column 9.

101. In the collected works of the Lin-ch'uan man Hsieh I there appear two funerary inscriptions, one for a Huang Shih-liang (1032–1109), and one for his brother (identifiable as such because his son Shu is mentioned as Shih-liang's nephew), whose given name is not recorded. Huang Shih-liang's inscription tells us that his family had been wealthy locals for about two hundred years, that his son passed the prefectural exam, and that Shih-liang was buried at a place called Chü-lin in Kuei-te canton, Chin-ch'i County (Hsieh I, 9/2b–4a).

102. *YLTT* 2754/13b, column 1; *TKIH* 6/1b–10b, under Ch'ung-hsien canton, *tu* 11, second dam listed.

103. See *TCIH* ch. 25 and *KHIH* ch. 5, passim, and cf. Appendix I, no. 45. For the location of Huang-pei in the eleventh *tu* of Ch'ung-hsien canton see *TCIH*, front matter: maps.

104. *YLTT* 2754/13a, column 8; *TKIH*, 6/1b–10b, under Ch'ung-hsien canton, *tu* 14, first dam listed, here called 'Little Yüeh Dam.'

105. Cf. Appendix I, no. 72. For the location of Huo-yüan in the fourteenth *tu* of Ch'ung-hsien canton, see *TCIH* 2/8a.

106. *SHY*, *shih-huo* 61, pp. 68–9, *shui-li t'ien*.

107. See the record for Ch'ung-jen County administrator Fan Ying-ling's reregistration of land in that county in 1221, about seventy-five years after the last previous registration (*KHFC* 23/16a–17a), and the similar record of Chin-ch'i County administrator Chang Li's reregistration in about 1226, roughly eighty years after the last previous one (*TCCC* 33c/20b–22a). No such registration is known for any other Fu-chou county after the national registration (*ching-chieh*) program of the 1140s; as inscriptional records of official projects tend to be the best preserved of all sources, the absence of records here is probably significant.

108. Huang Chen, 88/20a–21b.

109. See for instance Huang Chen, 78/7a, columns 3 and 4, where Huang promises the wealthy households that he will 'not assign quotas (of relief grain to be sold), not force down prices, not establish official markets (for relief grain), and never retain paperwork in the offices and so give you future worries about clerks using registers to cause trouble;' and 78/8b, column 5: 'Since the authorities are not, through official paperwork, encouraging the craftiness of clerks, those who [must] mediate between public and private, between high and low, are the gentlemen of good will in the rural communities.'

110. Huang Chun, 88/20a–21b.

111. For the location of South Lake see *YLTT* 2265/8b–10a. Chia-lo Dam appears in the Sung lists for I-huang County as Hsia-lo Yung-feng Dam in Hsien-kuei canton (*YLTT* 2754/13a, column 5): on the interchanging of the characters *chia* and *hsia*, see Morohashi, v. 1, p. 853, no. 835, heading III, subheading 6. The Hsia-lo Yung-feng Dam appears as Yung-feng Dam in *TKIH* 6/1b–10b, under Hsien-kuei canton, *tu* 3. The third *tu* of Hsien-kuei canton can in turn be located on gazetteer maps just outside the county seat, to the east (*TCIH* front matter: maps). As for Ch'ung-jen County's Yung-feng Dam, it is recorded in the Sung list as in Ch'ang-an canton (*YLTT* 2754/12b, column 3) and in the Ch'ing gazetteer under Ch'ang-an canton's fourth *tu* (*KHCJ* 3b/1a–56b); this location is confirmed on Ch'ing gazetteer maps (*TCCJ* front matter: pictures and maps, p. 5a). The Wan-chin Dam does not appear in the Sung list, which was compiled some seven to ten years before Huang Chen's record; but the Ch'ing gazetteer records it under the fourth *tu* – the same location as the Yung-feng Dam (*KHCJ*, 3b/1a–56b); and the same gazetteer map shows Wan-chin Dam lying slightly farther west (thus farther from the county seat) than Yung-feng Dam (*TCCJ*, front matter). Now on a modern topographic map the Wan-chin Dam is shown sited about a mile west-southwest of the county seat (this is map no. 54 in the 50,000:1 series for the Chien-ch'ang region listed on p. 149 of Hunome, *Chūgoku hondo chizu mokuroku*). Yung-feng Dam is not shown but must be still nearer the city in the same general area.

112. See Chao Yü-chou's inscriptional record for the second project in *TCLC* 5/5a–7a.

113. See Ho I's inscriptional record in *TCCJ* 9f/22a–24b.

114. See for instance Li Yüan-pi, *Tso-i tzu-chen*, Ch. 2.

115. This reflects the nature of the sources. Records of bridgebuilding come, with hardly any exceptions, not from collected works or biographies but from the sections of local gazetteers dealing with construction. The extant Ch'ing gazetteers,

in dealing with Sung bridges, draw indirectly but almost exclusively on their Sung forerunners; these began to be compiled only in Southern Sung. Where gazetteers are not the only surviving source of information, or where Ch'ing gazetteers – as is quite common – draw on other kinds of earlier sources, one does not find the same shortage of Northern Sung data. In this respect bridges are an unusual case.

116. This was first built as a pontoon bridge around 1165 by the Fu-chou prefect; in 1175, having been washed away in the interim, it was restored by the Lin-ch'uan County administrator with funds supplied by circuit intendants. A few years later it was washed away again; not until around 1202 was it restored, this time as a stone bridge, by the prefect Wang Fang. In 1225 half its length was damaged by fire, and a new prefect organized repair work with the aid of a number of important local men. See the inscriptional record by Li Liu in *TCLC* 7/3a–5a.

117. Originally a pontoon bridge, this was rebuilt in stone by the 1076 *chin-shih* Chu Yen (for the Nan-feng Chu family, see Chapter 1, p. 55 and Appendix I, no. 14) in 1095. Between 1131 and 1208 it was destroyed three times and rebuilt by county administrators. Destroyed once more, it was replaced with a pontoon bridge in about 1225. In 1229 bandits burned this, and the county administrator restored it; but it was destroyed again in 1235. In 1241 the new county administrator Huang Tuan-liang rebuilt it once more, found a man from among the local elite to take on the post of supervisor of the bridge, and established an estate with a yearly rent of sixty-six *shih* of rice to support maintenance expenses. See *MKNF* 2/18a–19a, with Huang Tuan-liang's own inscriptional record; also see the 1247 'Record of the Chu Family's Hidden Virtue' by the Chien-ch'ang Chün vice-administrator Chiang An-chih in *KHNF* 13/11a–12a.

118. This was built in stone by county officials in cooperation with local men between 1248 and about 1263, but was soon destroyed by fire. In 1270 the county vice-administrator Chao Jo-shu got the local man Ch'en Ch'un-chung (son of Ch'en Yüan-chin, see Chapter 2, p. 77f.; for the Ch'en family see also Appendix I, no. 4) to organize local men in rebuilding the bridge, at an expense of 11,000 strings of cash.

119. This bridge had been built (always of wood) and destroyed several times between the founding of the county and 1235, when a new prefect, Huang Wei, undertook the construction of a new bridge in stone, apparently with some financial help from local men of wealth. See the inscriptional record in *TCLA* 1/19b–21a. In 1266 the bridge, since destroyed, was rebuilt by the county administrator T'ang Chiu-ling, again apparently with some local aid. See the inscriptional record by Ho Shih in *KHLA* 9/19a–21a.

120. For these, see *TCIH* 6/1b–6a; *TCLA* 1/24b–25b; *TCCJ* 1f/18a–22b; *MKNF* 2/18a–19a, 26b–27a, 31a–b, 35a–b; *KHTH* 1/11a.

121. See the inscriptional record by the County administrator Chou Meng-jo in *TCIH* 45b/21a. Though not himself an officeholder, T'u was almost certainly a member of the very prominent officeholding I-huang family of the same surname: cf. Appendix I, no. 58.

122. *TCLC* 7/3a–5a.

123. See notes 117 through 119 above.

124. See note 117 above.

125. On the reasons for this see note 115 above.

Chapter 7

1. Thus apart from the domestic ancestral cult. On this and on worship of ancestors beyond the household level, as for instance the worship of common ancestors by lineage-like associations of households, the Fu-chou sources offer very little

information. On the emergence of lineage-like descent groups in Southern Sung Fu-chou cf. Hymes, 'Marriage, Descent Groups, and the Localist Strategy in Sung and Yüan Fu-chou.'

2. *SYHA* 57/2b.
3. The Fu-chou sources are rather uninformative as to the particular forms of Buddhism practised in the prefecture. Where specific doctrines are mentioned they are usually of Pure Land origin. This is not very enlightening, since Pure Land teachings pervaded a wide variety of independent sects and movements in the Sung. Some temples have the word *ch'an*, 'meditation,' in their names. But this cannot be taken as showing doctrinal affiliation with Ch'an (Zen) Buddhism, since the term *ch'an* was in Sung used for one of three common forms of temple categorized as to function, not denomination. (See Takeo Giken, *Sōdai Bukkyōshi no kenkyū*, pp. 64–9.) Thus an inscriptional record for an I-huang County temple called the I-ch'üan Ch'an Hall specifically mentions that its head and founder was a teacher of Pure Land (*TCIH* 45b/3b–4a).
4. Sun Ti, *Nan-lan-ling Sun shang-shu ta-ch'üan chi* 31/5a–7a.
5. *TCCC* 7/6b–10b; *TCCJ* 2d/1a–53a; *TCIH* 13/1a–12b; *TCLA* 2/39a–43a; *TCLC* 18/2a–35b. Material in collected works is too abundant and too scattered to list here.
6. For example, the 1876 prefectural gazetteer reproduces a map of the prefectural city from the Ching-ting period (1260–4) of Sung. Nine Buddhist temples appear on the map; of these only three are familiar from gazetteer lists and surviving inscriptional records (*KHFC*, front matter: maps, pp. 2b–3a). Similarly, Chou Pi-ta's *Journal of a Return to Lu-ling* (*Kuei Lu-ling jih-chi*), which records Chou's passage through Chin-ch'i and Nan-feng Counties, makes specific mention of five Buddhist temples. None is named on gazetteer lists or in surviving construction records. (Chou Pi-ta, 165/15b–21a.)
7. For Wang An-shih's donation of lands to the Ch'eng-pei Temple in Chin-ch'i County, see *CCFC* 4/40a and *KHCC* 13/10b. See also Wang An-shih, 83/3b. On the family see Appendix I, no. 61, and Chapter 3, n. 14.
8. On Tseng Chih-yao's construction of a Hall of Buddhas in early Sung for a temple that was later the burial site of Tseng Kung and ultimately became a Merit Cloister for the family, see Liu Hsün, 3/4a–6a. On the family see Appendix I, no. 54, and Chapter 3, n. 14.
9. T'u Chi and his sons and nephews built the I-ch'üan Temple in I-huang County between 1092 and 1104 (*TCIH* 45b/3b–4a). On the family see Appendix I, no. 58.
10. On Yüeh Shih's construction of Buddhist temples in Ch'ung-jen County see *TCCJ* 2d/1b, 30b, 31a, 34b–35a. On the family see Appendix I, no. 72, and Chapter 3, n. 14.
11. On temple construction evidently by Lo Tien's kinsmen, see Chapter 2, n. 89. On the family see Appendix I, no. 41.
12. Chou K'un recorded the renovation of the Yung-hsing Temple at Liu-yüan in Chin-ch'i because his grandfather had earlier made donations to it (*TCCC* 33d/8b–10a). For the family see Appendix I, no. 10.
13. Sun Ti, *Nan-lan-ling Sun shang-shu ta-ch'üan chi* 31/5a–7a.
14. *TCCC* 9/1a–b; *KHCC* 2/1a–2a.
15. Tseng Feng, 19/10a–13a.
16. Ch'en Tsao, 35/13a–16a.
17. Tseng Kung, *Yüan-feng lei-kao* 17/7a–8a.
18. Liu Hsün, 3/4a–6a.
19. Hsieh I, 8/18a–20a.
20. Wang An-shih, 73/10a–11a.

21. *TCIH* 45b/39a–40a. So-called Writing-Brush Pagodas (*wen-pi t'a*), built in the shape of brushes and intended to improve 'wind and water' conditions for academic pursuits in their area, were common in later times. (The collocation appears in Morohashi Tetsuji, *Dai kanwa jiten,* vol. V, p. 5231, nos. 13450–791.) I know of no Sung case besides this one. The Pagoda in this instance was not, evidently, built in the shape of a brush; this may have been a later refinement introduced after the practise and name had become widespread.

22. Hung Mai, *chih-ching* 2/1a.

23. Hung Mai, *ting* 3/1a–b.

24. Hsieh I, 7/12b–14b.

25. *TCIH* 45b/35b–36a.

26. For Taoist temples we have, apart from the gazetteer lists and inscriptional records in collected works on which one depends for Buddhist temples, extensive lists and other records in a 'mountain monograph' for Hua-kai Mountain, a local Taoist cult center. This is the *Hua-kai shan Fou-ch'iu Wang Kuo san chen-chün shih-shih*, *Tao tsang* 556–557.

27. The conclusion that such local cult centers grew more important in Southern Sung, indeed became the chief focus of Taoist belief in the region, is drawn from research in progress and rests on a large body of material that cannot be adequately cited here.

28. See for instance *WWC* 46/1a–3a.

29. *Hua-kai shan Fou-ch'iu Wang Kuo san chen-chün shih-shih* 5/6b.

30. *Hua-kai shan* [...] *shih-shih* 5/10b–11b.

31. *Hua-kai shan* [...] *shih-shih* 5/12b–13a.

32. Chou Pi-ta, 165/15b–21a.

33. See Map 15, nos. 13–16 and 19.

34. Wu I in 1186 rebuilt the Hsing-lo (Taoist) Temple (*TCCJ* 2d/42b), and a Wu family had donated land for the Chao-ch'ing (Taoist) Temple, whose location right next to the county seat strongly suggests that this is the same Wu family (*WWC* 47/8b–10b).

35. Some time after 1140 a Wu family built a Hall of Buddhas for the Fu-shou Temple in the northern part of the county seat, requested and were granted a new name for it: the Kuan-yin Temple (*TCCJ* 2d/1a). Again the location suggests that this is the same Wu family. See Appendix I, no. 67.

36. *TCLC* 7/3a–5a.

37. These are the South Bridge in Ch'ung-jen County, built around 1115 by monks of the Hsin-hsing Temple (*TCCJ* 1f/20a), and a pontoon bridge in the south of I-huang County, built around 1170 under the direction of the head monk of the K'u-chu Temple (*TCIH* 13/7b).

38. *YLTT* 10959/6a–b.

39. Huang Chen, 78/28a–29a.

40. The Wu-lin Temple in Lin-ch'uan County performed sacrifices for members of the Jao family of T'ang-fang in the same county at the end of Southern Sung (*WWC* 46/10a–11b). The prominent officeholder Tsou Chi of I-huang County was sacrificed to for two hundred years after his death by the Ch'ih-sung Temple near his place of burial (*WWC* 47/12b–14b). On the death of the mother of Yü Tou-hsiang of Chin-ch'i County, near the end of Southern Sung, Yü built a sacrifical hall for her and donated newly bought lands to the nearby Tung-lin Temple to guarantee the hall's permanent support and care (*WWC* 74/5b–7a). Lo Yü of Ch'ung-jen County, a son of the assisting councillor Lo Tien, in the early thirteenth century built a tomb for his parents and entrusted its management to a relative who was a Buddhist monk (Liu Tsai, *Man-t'ang chi* 23 (19b–20a). Finally there is the case of the Tseng family's Merit Cloister, which cared for the tomb of Tseng Kung.

41. In Yüan a Taoist temple is reported to have been built by the widow of Tsou Ming-shan of I-huang County for the performance of sacrifices to Ming-shan and his parents (*WWC* 47/12b–14b). It is not impossible that there may have been such cases in Sung as well; still the significantly greater importance of Buddhism in this and other functions seems clear.

42. Lü Pen-chung, *Tung-lai Lü Tzu-wei shih-yu tsa-chih*, p. 1; Hsieh I, 7/1a. For Wang Ko see also *TCLC* 36/3a; *KHFC* 5/1a–b; *Chiang-hsi shih-she tsung-p'ai t'u-lu*, pp. 25–6.

43. *SYHA* 23/7b; *SYHAPI* 23/13a; Lu Hsin-yuan, *Sung-shih chi-shih pu-i* 28/22a; *Chiang-hsi shih-she tsung-p'ai t'u-lu*, pp. 19–20.

44. *SYHA* 77/19a; *SYHAPI* 77/29a; see also *WWC* 22/8a–b.

45. Sung Lien, 12/449–50; Wei Su, *hsu-chi* 1/12b–13a.

46. See n. 40 above.

47. *WWC* 47/14b–16a.

48. Yü Chi, 32/8a–9a.

49. *WWC* 47/7b–8b.

50. See Appendix I, nos. 38, 52, 1, 7, and 59.

51. *KHLA* 5/11a, 14a; *TCLA* 7/11a, 21b.

52. See Chapter 6, n. 39.

53. *WWC* 47/7b–8b.

54. For the T'ans see Appendix I, no. 46. As for the Tus: an I-huang County man named Tu Tzu-yeh, who had passed the prefectural examination in 1056 and received a facilitated degree in 1073, was the teacher of Wang An-shih. His kinsman Tu Ch'ien passed the prefectural exam in 1075 and 1087, and his grandson Tu Yü-te achieved the *chin-shih* degree in 1135. See *TCIH* 25/9b, 11a, 12a, 17a, 31/2b–3a; *KHIH* 5/3a, 4a–b, 5b, 11a–b; Lu Hsin-yüan, *Sung shih i*, 36/5a; *SYHAPI* 98/7a.

55. Again I am deducing identity of families from coincidence of surnames; here, however, the correspondence is perfect and the conclusion (given the move of the temple from one district to another) almost inescapable.

56. For an example of a *wu* dealing with a demon that has kidnapped a village woman, see Hung Mai, *ting* 20/4a–5a. For a *wu* who serves a god (*shen*) and uses his power to capture demons (*kuei-mo*), see Hung Mai, *i* 15/1a–b.

57. Chieh Ch'i-ssu (1272–1344) discusses this in a farewell composition for a doctor from a prefecture neighboring Fu-chou. See his *Chieh Wen-an kung ch'üan chi* 8/15a–16b. For *wu* as healers in Fu-chou see for instance Hung Mai, *ting* 20/2b–3a and *pu* 2/1b–2a.

58. Tseng Chao, 4/4a–6a.

59. This is Tseng Wu's record for the Ch'i-shan *ching-she*, in *MKNF* 3/8b–9b.

60. None of them, unfortunately, in Fu-chou. The lists, though voluminous, are far from complete.

61. It is recorded that around 1120 a man of the Chin dynasty enshrined and honored as a god in Lo-an County was enfeoffed as Marquis of Excellent Fame and Reliable Aid (*TCLC* 15/18b). The dedicatees of the Four Immortals' Shrine on Pa Mountain in Ch'ung-jen County were first enfeoffed in 1231, and 'promoted' in 1234 (Huang Chen, 88/33b–35b). The *Hua-kai shan* [. . .] *shih-shih* records the enfeoffment and promotion of the Three Immortals in ch. 1.

62. Hung Mai, *chih-i* 2/5b–6a and 4a–b respectively.

63. Hung Mai, *chih-i* 2/4a–b.

64. Hung Mai, *ping* 9/6b–7a and *san-jen* 1/4b–5a respectively.

65. Hung Mai, *ping* 12/4a–b.

66. *TCLC* 15/18b.

67. Huang Chen, 88/33b–35b.

68. Huang Chen, 78/47b–50a.
69. Huang Chen, 78/46b–47a and 79/21b–22b.
70. Huang Chen, 75/29a–30b. A White Lotus Temple is recorded to have existed in Chin-ch'i County more than sixty years earlier. See Huang Kan, 32/17a–19b.
71. *SHY*: *li* 20/9b.
72. *SHY*: *li* 20/9b–10b.
73. *YLTT* 10950/7a. 'The state' is my translation of *she-chi* in this context. The term has as its primary meaning the gods of the earth and grain or the altars that sacrifice to these, but is frequently used to symbolize the state itself, which was responsible for the gods and their altars.
74. Huang Kan, 32/17a–19b.
75. *YLTT* 10950/9a; *TCCC* 7/1a; *TCCJ* 2b/1b; *TCIH* 11/19a.
76. *YLTT* 10950/7a–b. From the late Sung gazetteer map of the prefectural city preserved in a Ch'ing gazetteer it is evident that there were actually two City God temples in the city, one managed by the prefectural administration and one by that of Lin-ch'uan County. See *KHFC*, front matter: maps, pp. 2b–3a.
77. Thus most are called *hsing-miao*, literally 'travelled shrines.' Among these shrines of non-Fu-chou origin were:

    (1) The Tung-yüeh hsing-miao, devoted to some seventy-four gods and goddesses associated with the national altars at Mt T'ai in Shantung. *YLTT* 10950/7b.
    (2) The Yang-shan fu-hui hsing-miao, devoted to a deity associated with Yang Mountain in nearby I-ch'un County, Yüan-chou. *YLTT* 10950/7b; and cf *SHY*: *li* 20/84–85 and Morohashi, vol. I, no. 400-40.
    (3) The Wu-hsien ling-shun hsing-miao, devoted to a god associated with Wu-yüan County, Hui-chou. *YLTT* 10950/8a.
    (4) The Tz'u-shan lieh hsing-miao, devoted to a Han man of Wu-ling, Chang Ping, known after his apotheosis as the Great Emperor of Tz'u-shan. *YLTT* 10950/8a; and cf. Morohashi, vol. VIII, no. 24676-39.
    (5) The Shu san-wang hsing-miao, devoted to three men of Szechwan first deified in their own region. *YLTT* 10950/8a.
    (6) The Tzu-ming-shan fu-hui hsing-miao, devoted apparently to a number of deities, at least one of which must have been associated with an unidentified mountain called Tzu-ming. *YLTT* 10950/8a.

78. *YLTT* 10950/7b.
79. She was worshipped at the Tzu-ming-shan shrine, no. 6 in n. 77 above.
80. See Stephen Feuchtwang, 'School-Temple and City God,' pp. 583–4.
81. Tseng Feng, 19/10a–13a.
82. *TCLC* 7/3a–5a.
83. The Kuang-chiao Temple in the Ch'ung-jen County countryside was restored in that year by the county administrator Su Chien. See *TCCJ* 2d/43b.
84. See Huang Chen's record for the Shrine of the Four Immortals of Pa Mountain (there called Hsiang Mountain) in Huang Chen, 88/33b–35b; and Wu Ch'eng's record for the Shrine of Mei Peak in *WWC* 46/1a–3a.
85. Hung Mai, *chih-ching* 9/6a–b.
86. This is surely the implication of *Hua-kai shan* [. . .] *shih-shih* 5/11b–12b.
87. *SHY*: *li* 5/18.
88. See *TCLC* 18/9a–13b. The inscriptional records transcribed there are for later reconstructions of the temple or of the associated branch shrine for the deities of Mt T'ai. The note in *TCLC* 18/9a has the T'ien-ch'ing Temple built in 1004, which would be a temporal anomaly; but the retrospective account in the 1108 inscription by Wu K'o in *TCLC* 18/9aff. places the temple's founding after Chen-tsung's performance of the *feng* and *shan* sacrifices, which occurred in

1008 and was directly followed by the decree ordering the creation of T'ien-ch'ing temples. It is possible that the branch shrine for the Mt T'ai deities was founded as early as 1004, though this too seems denied by Wu K'o's record. The note giving the date as 1004 may simply be an error. Note that Wu K'o also presents the temple's founding as a spontaneous act of local people; but this is clearly belied by the existence of a decree ordering the same act uniformly throughout the empire.

89. Suzanne Cahill, 'Taoism at the Sung Court: The Heavenly Text Affair of 1008,' pp. 40–1.
90. *TCLC* 18/12b–13b. This 1215 inscription for the repair of the hall recalls the 1012 decree and the Fu-chou founding that followed. For the decree itself see also *SHY: li* 5/18.
91. Michel Strickmann, 'The Longest Taoist Scripture.'
92. Strickmann, pp. 336–9.
93. Strickmann, p. 346.
94. *TCIH* 13/2b places the founding in the Hsüan-ho region period; as the innovations of Lin Ling-su, especially those directed against Buddhist establishments, began to be rescinded in 1120, the Fu-chou founding surely cannot have occurred later than 1119. See Strickmann, p. 347.
95. On the Jao-chou case see Strickmann, p. 346, n. 44, which cites Hung Mai, *ping* 11/1a–b.
96. Chu Hsi, *Chu Tzu ta-ch'üan wen-chi* 79/2b–4a.
97. On this point see also Chaffee, p. 162.
98. Pi Yüan, *Hsü tzu-chih t'ung-chien* 167:4562. See James T.C. Liu, 'How Did a Neo-Confucian School Become the State Orthodoxy?,' esp. p. 502. Pi Yüan does not mention local sacrifices, and I have found no evidence that these were specifically required by the 1234 decree. But Chu Hsi makes clear in his Wu-yüan shrine inscription that the presence of the Ch'engs and Chou in the national sacrificial statutes would have been, for him, justification enough for a local shrine. Thus the national order presumably had some influence. Still, the founding of local shrines and the performance of local sacrifices should not be seen as an automatic result of the instituting of sacrifices at the capital. This seems clear from Huang Chen's account of conditions as he found them on his arrival in Fu-chou: see below.
99. Huang Chen, 94/13b–14a.
100. Huang Chen, 94/13b–14a.
101. Lu Chiu-yüan, 26/4a–5b.

Chapter 8

1. This is the conclusion of Umehara Kaoru in his important study of the Sung household-grade system, 'Sōdai no kotōsei o megutte.'
2. For the basic study of these '*fang-t'ien chün-shui*' programs, which had been preceded by similar but abortive efforts in 1000 and 1043, see Sudō Yoshiyuki, *Chūgoku tochi seido*, pp. 431–509.
3. *TCIH* 14/23a–b; *KHIH* 3/1b–2b and 3/18a. These place the increase during the 1072 program; but from other sources it seems clear that this was applied only in North China. Probably the K'ang-hsi gazetteer editors (or the editors of some earlier gazetteer that was their source), having before them a source which referred to a *fang-t'ien* program, assumed that this was the first, Wang An-shih's own, and so added its date (1072) when they copied out the source. The increase must actually have taken place around 1112 during the second program, which covered the whole empire.
4. Wang Te-i, 'Li Ch'un-nien yü Nan-Sung t'u-ti ching-chieh'; Sogabe Shizuo, 'Nan-Sō no tochi keikai hō.'

5. On the wide variety of local service arrangements in Southern Sung, see Brian McKnight, *Village and Bureaucracy*, pp. 73–94.

6. For example, the county administrator of Chin-ch'i Hsien who decided to begin taxing income from porcelain manufacture. See the letter of protest in Lu Chiu-yüan, 10/4a–5a.

7. Thus Huang Kan, while administrator of Lin-ch'uan County, issued a proclamation exhorting the locals against their love of litigation. An excerpt:

> The people of Lin-ch'uan are refined and capable in writing; they are firm, and do not bend. Thus with its illustrious succession of famous men in previous generations, Lin-ch'uan has been most prosperous. But the abuse of its customs makes of its firmness a delight in contention and of its literary cultivation a skill in lawsuits. Of unbridled customs none is more severe than this. The holder of this post, untalented, has through some error received a county [office]; during the two months of his stay [so far] he has read through several thousand pages of plaints. Struggles over trifles continue for months and years. (Huang Kan, 34/15a–16b)

A similar account of Ch'ung-jen County appears in the works of the Buddhist monk Hui-hung:

> Ch'ung-jen is a subordinate county of Fu-chou. Its scenery is clear and splendid; its people's customs are vigorous and fine. However, its territory adjoins Nan-k'ang and Lu-ling, and [their customs] have, perhaps, lapped over into it. As a consequence suits are numerous and it has the reputation of a troublesome county [*chü-i*]. (Hui-hung, 23/23a–24a.)

Fu-chou's reputation was typical of its region, as Hui-hung's testimony suggests. On litigiousness in Sung Chiang-hsi, see Miyazaki, 'Sō-Gen jidai no hō to saiben kikō', especially pp. 246–52.

8. On Harmonious Purchase in Southern Sung Fu-chou, see Huang Kan, 27/1a–2a; and Huang Chen, Ch. 75 and passim.

9. See Shiba Yoshinobu, 'Sōdai shiteki seido no enkaku.'

10. Shiba, 'Sōdai shiteki seido no enkaku.'

11. See n. 8 above.

12. Huang Kan, 27/1a–2a, refers to the court's 'disbursing gold and coin and sending envoys to make Harmonious Purchase;' Huang Chen mentions 'purchase capital' supplied by the center in a memorial, 75/16b–18a, and in two public proclamations, 78/36a–40b and 40b–41b.

13. Huang Chen, 78/40b–41b.

14. Lu Chiu-yüan, 8/1a–2b.

15. Huang Kan, 29/6b–8b.

16. Huang Chen, 75/25b–26b.

17. Huang Chen, 78/36a–40b, 40b–41b.

18. There were other taxes, of course; but there were other lands, other crops, and other enterprises as well.

19. Huang Kan, 32/1a–5a.

20. Huang Kan, 32/5a–10b. Even here it is only the offense of 'oppressing his neighborhood to advance himself' that is at issue. As to the deaths, Huang comments: 'May the wrong of Huang Ssu's and Li Wu's being brought guiltless to their deaths be somewhat redressed in the afterlife.'

21. Huang Kan, 32/10b–13b.

22. Lu Chiu-yüan, 8/8a–10b.

23. Lu Chiu-yüan, 9/8a–b.

Conclusion

1. I have explored this issue in more detail in Hymes, 'Marriage, Descent Groups, and the Localist Strategy.'
2. Or of Lu Chiu-shao. Ebrey has identified in the work of Yüan Ts'ai an approach to social life she calls the *'chia* orientation.' (Ebrey, 'Conceptions of the Family in the Sung Dynasty,' pp. 224–9; see also her *Family and Property in Sung China*, especially pp. 75–171.) I have elsewhere argued that a partly similar orientation toward the *chia* may explain certain omissions and peculiarities in the form of Neo-Confucianism propagated by Lu Chiu-yüan. See Hymes, 'On Academies, Community Institutions, and Lu Chiu-yüan.'
3. John Dardess, *Confucianism and Autocracy: Professional Elites in the Founding of the Ming Dynasty*, especially pp. 13–84.
4. Hymes, 'Marriage, Descent Groups, and the Localist Strategy.'
5. Beattie, *Land and Lineage in China*, passim.; Dennerline, *The Chia-ting Loyalists*, p. 104, pp. 119–20. Note that Dennerline mentions elite marriages crossing county lines as examples of relatively 'distant' marriages; there is no suggestion of frequent marriage outside the region.
6. The phrase was suggested to me by David Johnson.

GLOSSARY

The list that follows includes all Chinese personal names, place names, and miscellaneous words and phrases appearing in the body of this study, except for titles and authors of works cited. Personal names appearing only in Appendix I are not listed.

Ai (surname) 艾
An-jen (County) 安仁
An-shou Hall 安壽堂
An-yüan Temple 安元寺
Ao-ch'i (River) 鰲溪
Cha-p'u 渣浦
Chai-pien 砦卞
chai-ping 寨兵
Chan (surname) 詹
Chan Ch'ung-p'u 詹崇樸
Chan-hsü 詹墟
Chan Ta-t'ung 詹大通
Chan Yüan-chi 詹元吉
ch'an 禪
Ch'an-tsu Temple 禪祖寺
Chang[a] (surname) 張
Chang[b] (surname) 章
Chang Chieh-fu 章節夫
Chang Chün-chung 張濬中
Chang Kuei-lung 張桂龍
Chang K'uei 張奎
Chang Mu 張穆
Chang O 張鍔
Chang Ping 張秉
Chang Shen 章森
Chang Sheng-tzu 張聲子
Chang Ta 張達
Chang Tzu-hsien 章子先
Chang Wen-huan 章文渙
Chang Wen-kang 張文剛
Chang Yu-hsin 章又新
Chang Yung 張詠
Chang Yüan-ting 張元定

Ch'ang-an (canton) 長安
Ch'ang-chou 常州
Ch'ang-ning (canton) 長寧
Ch'ang-sha 長沙
Chao (surname) 趙
Chao Chi-chih 趙勣之
Chao-ch'ing Temple 昭清觀
Chao Ch'un-chung 趙純中
Chao Chün 趙郡
Chao-hsi Fort 招攜寨
Chao-hsien (canton) 招仙
Chao-hsien Temple 招仙觀
Chao I 趙翼
Chao Jo-liu 趙若流
Chao Jo-shu 趙若澍
Chao Ju-ch'ien 趙汝謙
Chao Ju-yü 趙汝愚
Chao K'uei 趙葵
Chao Pang 趙邦
Chao Pi-ch'üan 趙必烇
Chao Pi-kun 趙必棍
Chao Pu-tz'u 趙不玭
Chao Tuan-i 趙端頤
Chao Yü-hsi 趙與誏
Ch'ao (surname) 晁
Ch'ao Ch'ien-chih 晁謙之
Ch'ao Kung-mai 晁公邁
Ch'ao Pai-t'an 晁百談
Ch'ao Tzu-shei 晁子誰
Ch'ao Tzu-yü 晁子與
Che (River) 浙
Che-hsi 浙西
Che-tsung 哲宗

ch'e 車
ch'e-t'ien pei 車田陂
ch'e-t'ou pei 車頭陂
Chen-chou 眞州
Chen-kuan shih-tsu chih 貞觀氏族志
Chen Te-hsiu 眞德秀
Chen-tsung 眞宗
Ch'en (surname) 陳
Ch'en Chen-yen 陳震炎
Ch'en Chien-su 陳見素
Ch'en Chih-ch'i 陳之奇
Ch'en Ch'un-chung 陳純中
Ch'en Chün-ch'ing 陳俊卿
Ch'en Ju 陳孺
Ch'en K'ai 陳凱
Ch'en K'ang-ch'eng 陳康成
Ch'en Lung-cheng 陳龍正
Ch'en Meng-chien 陳夢薦
Ch'en Ming-shih 陳命世
Ch'en P'eng-fei 陳鵬飛
Ch'en Shih-kuei 陳仕貴
Ch'en Ting-te 陳定德
Ch'en Tsung-li 陳宗禮
Ch'en Tzu-sheng 陳子升
Ch'en Wan 陳綰
Ch'en Wen-hsiu 陳文秀
Ch'en Yen-kuo 陳彥國
Ch'en Yü 陳瑜
Ch'en Yüan-chin 陳元晉
Ch'en Yüan-fa 陳元發
Cheng (surname) 鄭
cheng-chiang 正將
Cheng-chüeh Temple 正覺寺
Cheng Feng-hsiang 鄭鳳翔
Cheng-ho 正和
Cheng Hsin 鄭莘
Cheng Kuo-hua 鄭國華
Cheng Sung 鄭松
Cheng Ying-yu 鄭應酉
Ch'eng (surname) 程
Ch'eng-chi 成紀
Ch'eng I 程頤
Ch'eng-nan Fort 城南寨
Ch'eng-pei Temple 城陂院
Ch'eng-tu Fu 成都府
Ch'eng-tu-fu 成都府
Ch'eng-tu shih-tsu p'u 成都世族譜
Ch'eng Yüan 程遠

Chi (surname) 季
Chi-an 吉安
Chi Ch'ing-ch'ing 季清慶
Chi-chou 吉州
Chi Fu 季復
Chi-shui (County) 吉水
Chi Tuan-ch'ing 季端慶
chi-wen 祭文
Chi-yang 濟陽
chi-yü 寄寓
Ch'i-chen Temple 祈眞寺
Ch'i chia shih hsiu ju-yeh erh men-hu
    wei-chen 其家世修儒業而門戶
    未振
ch'i-ma 旗馬
ch'i-pu 旗步
chia 家
chia-chuang 家狀
Chia-hsing (County) 嘉興
chia-li 家禮
Chia-lo Dam 假樂陂
chia-pao chuang 家保狀
chia-shou 甲首
chia-t'ou 甲頭
chia-wu 甲戊
Chiang (surname) 江
Chiang An-chih 江安止
Chiang-chou 江州
Chiang Chü-ch'ing 江巨卿
Chiang Chü-yüan 江巨源
Chiang-hsi 江西
Chiang-nan-hsi 江南西
Chiang-nan-tung 江南東
Chiang-ning Fu 江寧府
Chiang Pao 江襃
chiang-t'ien chung ch'e pei 漿田中
    車陂
Chiang Tower 江樓
Chiang-tu (County) 江都
Chiang-tung 江東
Chiang Yeh 江野
Chiang-yin 江陰
Ch'iang (surname) 強
Ch'iang Hsing-fu 強行父
Chiao-yüeh chung-chieh 教閱忠節
Chieh Ch'i-ssu 揭俟斯
chien 薦
chien (industrial prefecture) 監

Chien-an (County) 建安
Chien-ch'ang Chün 建昌軍
Chien-chou 建州
Chien-chung ch'i-she 揀中騎射
chien-chü 薦舉
Chien-ning (County) 建寧
Chien-shan Pavilion 見山亭
Chien-yang (County) 建陽
Ch'ien-chia ch'e hsiao-kang pei 牽家
　　車小港陂
Ch'ien-chin 千金
Ch'ien-chou 虔州
Ch'ien-shan (County) 鉛山
Ch'ien-t'ang (County) 錢塘
Ch'ien-ying (canton) 遷鶯
chih 姪
Chih-lo Garden 直樂園
chih-ta 直達
Ch'ih-chou 池州
Ch'ih-sung Temple 赤松
Chin (dynasty) 金
Chin-ch'i (County) 金溪
Chin-chiang (County) 晉江
chin-chün 禁軍
Chin-hsien (County) 進賢
Chin-hua (County) 金華
Chin-ling 金陵
chin-shih 進士
Ch'in Kuei 秦檜
ching 經
ching-chieh 經界
Ching-hsi-nan 京西南
Ching-hsi-pei 京西北
Ching-hu 荊湖
Ching-hu-pei 荊湖北
Ching-hu-nan 荊湖南
Ching-k'ou 京口
Ching-men Chün 荊門軍
Ching-te Chen 景德鎮
Ching-ting 景定
ch'ing 頃
Ch'ing (dynasty) 清
Ch'ing-chiang (River) 清江
Ch'ing-chou 青州
Ch'ing-feng (County) 清豐
Ch'ing-ho 清河
ch'ing-pei 慶霈
Ch'ing-t'ien Hsü 青田墟

Ch'ing-yün (canton) 青雲
chiu-chü 僦居
Chiu-huang huo-min shu 救荒活民書
Ch'iu (surname) 邱
Ch'iung-chou 瓊州
Chou 州
Chou (surname) 周
Chou Ch'i-wu 周棲梧
Chou Hsiao-jo 周孝若
Chou Hsin-fu 周信甫
Chou Kuang 周光
Chou Kuei-fang 周桂芳
Chou Kuo-hua 周國華
Chou Mai 周邁
Chou Pi-ta 周必大
Chou Shan-fu 周山父
Chou T'an 周譚
Chou Tun-i 周敦頤
Chou-t'ung Dam 周通陂
Chou Wu-chung 周武仲
Chou Yen-hsien 周彥先
Chu (surname) 朱
Chu-chi (County) 諸暨
Chu-ch'i 珠溪
Chu Ching 朱京
Chu Hsi 朱熹
Chu Hsia 朱夏
chu-hu 主戶
Chu Kuei-fa 朱桂發
Chu Liang 朱亮
Chu Man 朱滿
Chu Ming-chih 朱明之
chu pei 苧陂
chu-p'u chih fen 主僕之分
Chu Shih 朱軾
Chu Shih-heng 朱世衡
Chu Ssu-jung 朱嗣榮
Chu Te-yu 朱德由
chu-tien chih fen 主佃之分
Chu Yeh 朱埜
Chu Yen 朱彥
Chu Ying-lung 朱應龍
Chu Yu-chi 朱酉吉
Chu-yüan 朱源
Chu Yüan-ch'ing 朱元慶
Ch'u 楚
Ch'u-chou 處州
ch'üan-nung wen 勸農文

Chuang-ch'eng 莊城
Ch'un-hsi 淳熙
Chung-chieh 忠節
Chung-hsiu 仲修
Chung-i (canton) 忠義
Chung-i hsün-she 忠義巡社
Chung-shan Temple 鐘山寺
Chung-t'ai kung 中太公
Ch'ung-an (County) 崇安
Ch'ung-chüeh Temple 崇覺寺
Ch'ung-hsien (canton) 崇仙
Ch'ung-hsing Yüan 崇興院
Ch'ung-jen (County) 崇仁
Ch'ung-Jen (River) 崇仁
Ch'ung-ning 崇寧
chü 舉
chü-i 劇邑
chü-jen 舉人
Chü-jen 居仁
chü-tzu 舉子
Chü-yeh (County) 鉅野
Ch'ü-chou 衢州
Ch'üan-chou 泉州
Ch'üeh (surname) 闕
chün[a] 軍
chün[b] 郡
Chün (Mountain) 軍
erh-chiu 二舅
Fan Chung-yen 范仲奄
Fan Shih-chi 范世基
Fan Ying-ling 范應鈴
Fang (surname) 方
Fang Pi-chung 方必中
fang-t'ien chün-shui 方田均稅
Fen-ning (County) 分寧
Feng-ch'eng (County) 豐城
Feng-ch'in 奉親
Feng-chou 封州
Feng Hsing-tzu 馮興子
Feng Te-i 馮得一
Feng Wen-tsai 馮文載
fo-ching 佛經
fu 府
Fu (surname) 傅
Fu (River) 撫
Fu An-ch'ien 傅安潛
Fu-chai 復齋
fu-cheng 副正

Fu-chien 福建
Fu-ch'ing Temple 福慶寺
Fu-chou 撫州
Fu-chou (Fu-chien) 福州
Fu Pi 富弼
fu-ping 府兵
Fu-sheng Temple 福勝院
Fu T'i 傅梯
Fu Yang-feng 傅陽鳳
Hai-ling (County) 海陵
Han (dynasty) 漢
Han Chü 韓駒
Han-kuang (County) 浛光
Han-p'o Ridge 韓婆嶺
Hang-chou 杭州
hao 豪
hao-hsia wu-tuan-che 豪俠武斷者
Ho (surname) 何
Ho Chan 何湛
Ho-chou 和州
Ho Chung 何中
Ho-fei (County) 合肥
Ho Hsi-chih 何希之
Ho Hung-chung 何宏中
Ho I 何異
Ho Ku 何穀
Ho Kuo-jui 何國瑞
Ho Lin 何霖
Ho Meng-lung 何孟龍
Ho Meng-niu 何孟牛
Ho-nan Fu 河南府
Ho Shih 何時
Ho Ssu 何思
Ho T'ien-sheng 何天盛
Ho Yao 何堯
Ho-yüan 何源
Hou (surname) 侯
Hou-fang Shih 侯坊市
Hou Shu-hsien 侯叔獻
Hou Ting 侯錠
Hou-t'u-huang ti-chih miao 后土皇地
　　祇廟
Hsi (County) 歙
Hsi-fang 西坊
Hsia (surname) 夏
Hsia Chieh 夏楷
Hsia Hsiung 夏雄
Hsia-lo Yung-feng Dam 下樂永豐陂

Hsia-shih 峽石
Hsia Yu-lan 夏友蘭
Hsia-yüan 峽源
hsiang (borough) 廂
hsiang (canton, community) 鄉
hsiang-chien 鄉薦
Hsiang-chou 襄州
hsiang-chü li-hsüan 鄉舉里選
hsiang-chün 廂軍
hsiang-li 鄉禮
Hsiang (Mountain) 相
hsiang-ping 鄉兵
hsiang-she 鄉社
hsiang-ting 鄉丁
Hsiang-yang (County) 襄陽
hsiang-yüeh 鄉約
hsiao-mai 小麥
Hsiao-pei 小陂
Hsiao-tsung 孝宗
Hsiao-yung 効勇
Hsieh (surname) 謝
Hsieh Chiu-ch'eng 謝九成
Hsieh Chün-chiu 謝軍九
Hsieh Fang-te 謝枋得
Hsieh I 謝逸
Hsieh K'o 謝薖
Hsieh Kung-tan 謝公旦
Hsieh Ling-yün 謝靈雲
Hsieh Mai 謝邁
Hsieh Min-hsing 謝敏行
Hsieh O 謝諤
Hsieh Pi 謝泌
Hsieh Shu 謝樞
Hsieh Ta-jen 謝大任
Hsieh Yüan 謝源
Hsieh Yüan-li 謝元禮
hsien 縣
hsien (Immortal) 仙
hsien i shih chu ku fu 縣亦視諸故府
Hsien-k'ou 咸口
Hsien-kuei (canton) 仙桂
Hsien-p'ing (County) 咸平
hsien-tz'u 仙祠
Hsien-yu (County) 仙遊
Hsin (River) 信
Hsin-ch'eng (County) 新城
Hsin-chien (County) 新建
Hsin-chou 信州

Hsin-feng (canton) 新豐
Hsin-hsing Temple 新興寺
Hsin-kan (County) 新淦
Hsin-min 新民
Hsin-t'ien 新田
Hsin-yeh 莘野
hsing 姓
Hsing-hua chün 興化軍
Hsing-kuo Chün 興國軍
Hsing-lo Temple 興樂觀
hsing-miao 行廟
Hsiu-chen Temple 修眞觀
Hsiu-chou 秀州
Hsiu-ning (County) 休寧
Hsiung (surname) 熊
Hsiung Hsiang 熊相
Hsiung P'u 熊溥
Hsü[a] (surname) 胥
Hsü[b] (surname) 許
Hsü[c] (surname) 徐
Hsü-chou 許州
Hsü Chung-fu 許中復
Hsü Fu 徐復
Hsü Meng-ling 許夢齡
Hsü Shih-wei 許世緯
Hsü Shih-ying 徐世英
Hsü Ta-nien 許大年
Hsü T'ang 許堂
Hsü Te-hsin 許德新
Hsü Tso-lin 胥作霖
Hsü Tzu-an 許子安
Hsü Tzu-shih 徐子石
Hsü Ying-ch'ang 許應昌
Hsüan-ho 宣和
Hsüan-i 宣毅
hsün-chien 巡檢
hsün-hsia 巡轄
hsün-hsia ma-p'u 巡轄馬鋪
hu-chang 戶長
Hu-chou 湖州
Hu-hsi 湖西
Hu Nan 胡南
Hu-p'ing Fort 湖坪寨
Hua-kai (Mountain) 華蓋
Huai (River) 淮
Hua-yen Temple 華嚴寺
Huai-jen 懷仁
Huai-nan 淮南

Huai-nan-hsi 淮南西
Huai-nan-tung 淮南東
Huai-tung 淮東
Huan-ch'i Academy 環溪書院
Huang (River) 黄
Huang (surname) 黄
Huang Chen 黄震
Huang Chieh 黄介
Huang Chien 黄監
Huang Ch'ing-ch'en 黄慶臣
Huang-chou Bridge 黄洲橋
Huang Ch'ou-jo 黄疇若
Huang Ch'ung 黄鍾
Huang Ch'ung-i 黄崇義
Huang Ch'ü-hua 黄去華
Huang-fang Shih 黄坊市
Huang Feng-chi 黄逢吉
Huang Fu 黄符
Huang Hsi 黄希
Huang I-kang 黄義剛
Huang I-ming 黄義明
Huang I-yung 黄義勇
Huang Jen-chieh 黄仁傑
Huang Jung 黄榮
Huang Kan 黄榦
Huang Kuo-ts'ai 黄國材
Huang Lo 黄犖
Huang Luan 黄欒
Huang Lü-chung 黄履中
Huang Mien-chai 黄勉齋
Huang Mu-chih 黄牧之
Huang-pei 黄陂
Huang Piao 黄霦
Huang Ping 黄炳
Huang Ping-yen 黄丙炎
Huang P'u 黄溥
Huang Shao-tsung 黄紹宗
Huang Sheng 黄陞
Huang Shih 黄實
Huang Shih-liang 黄士艮
Huang Shu 黄洙
Huang Ssu-yung 黄思永
Huang Sun 黄畚
Huang Ta-shou 黄大受
Huang Te-i 黄德一
Huang Te-li 黄得禮
Huang-t'ien Chen 黄田鎮
Huang T'ing-chien 黄庭堅
Huang Tsai 黄載
Huang Tuan-liang 黄端亮
Huang-t'ung Shih 黄通市
Huang Tz'u-shan 黄次山
Huang Wei 黄維
Huang Wei-chih 黄維之
Huang Wen-ch'ang 黄文昌
Huang Wen-sheng 黄文晟
Huang Yen 黄炎
Huang Yen-yüan 黄彥遠
Huang Yung 黄墉
Huang Yü-sun 黄與孫
Huang Yüan-lung 黄元龍
Huang Yüeh 黄鉞
Hui-an (canton) 惠安
Hui-chou 徽州
Hui-hung 惠洪
Hui-t'ien 會田
Hui-tsung 徽宗
Hung Chih-chang 洪知彰
Hung Chih-jou 洪知柔
Hung-chou 洪州
Hung Mai 洪邁
Huo-yüan (Yüeh residence) 霍源
Huo-yüan (Yü residence) 火源
I (River) 宜
i-chia 抑價
I-chien chih 夷堅志
I-ch'un (County) 宜春縣
I-ch'üan Ch'an Hall 義泉禪院
I-huang (County) 宜黄
I-huang (River) 宜黄
I-li ching-chuan t'ung chieh 儀禮通解
I-nan 邑南
i-shih 義士
i-ts'ang 義倉
I-tung 邑東
Jao (surname) 饒
Jao Chieh 饒節
Jao-chou 饒州
Jao Huai-ying 饒懷英
Jao Li 饒立
Jao Meng-k'uei 饒夢夔
Jao Shih-heng 饒時亨
Jao Tsung-lu 饒宗魯
Jao Tzu-yung 饒子庸
Jao Tz'u-wei 饒次魏
Jao Yen-nien 饒延年

Jao Ying-lung 饒應龍
Jao Ying-tzu 饒應子
Jen-tsung 仁宗
jen-wu 人物
Jih-chi 日記
ju 儒
Ju (River) 汝
ju-chia 儒家
Ju-pi 如壁
Ju-shui Academy 汝水書院
Jui-chou 瑞州
Jui Hui 芮煇
Jun-chou 潤州
Jung-chai sui-pi 容齋隨筆
Jung-ch'in 榮親
K'ai-feng Fu 開封府
K'ai-hua (County) 開化
K'ai-yüan 開元
Kan (River) 贛
Kan (surname) 甘
Kan-chou 贛州
kan-jen 幹人
Kang-tung 港東
K'ang (surname) 康
K'ang-chou 康州
Kao-an 高安
Kao-ch'i 高坘
Kao Shih-lien 高士廉
Kao-tsung 高宗
keng-hsü 庚戌
keng-pei ch'e pei 埂背車陂
Ko (surname) 葛
Ko Chi-tsu 葛繼祖
Ko Feng-shih 葛逢時
Ko Keng 葛賡
ko-pu 葛布
Ko Ts'ai-mei 葛才美
k'o-chuang 客莊
k'o-hu 客戶
k'o-mi 客米
k'ou 口
Ku-ch'eng (County) 穀城
ku-li 故里
Ku-t'ang 古塘
K'u-chu Temple 苦竹院
kuan 觀
Kuan (surname) 管
Kuan Chan 管湛

Kuan Chiang-chün 關將軍
Kuan Chien 管鑑
kuan-chih 館職
Kuan Ching-hui 關景暉
kuan-hu 官戶
Kuan-ti 關帝
Kuan-yin 觀音
Kuan-yin Temple 觀音寺
Kuang-ch'ang (County) 廣昌
Kuang-chiao Temple 廣教寺
Kuang-chou 廣州
Kuang-hsi 廣西
Kuang-hui 廣惠
Kuang-nan-hsi 廣南西
Kuang-nan-tung 廣南東
Kuang-p'ing 廣平
Kuang-tse 光澤
Kuang-tung 廣東
kuei 鬼
kuei-mo 鬼魔
Kuei (surname) 桂
Kuei-ch'i (County) 貴溪
Kuei-lin 桂林
Kuei Lu-ling jih-chi 歸廬陵日記
Kuei Yu-lung 桂友龍
K'uei-chou 夔州
kung 功
Kung (surname) 龔
Kung Huan 龔煥
Kung Meng-k'uei 龔孟夔
kung-te yüan 功德院
Kuo (surname) 郭
Kuo Jen-shih 郭仁實
Kuo Shen-hsi 郭申錫
Lai (surname) 賴
Lan (surname) 藍
Lan Hsi-ch'uan 藍習傳
Lang-chou 閬州
Lao-ch'eng 牢城
Lei-chou 雷州
li 禮
li (township) 里
Li (surname) 李
Li Chieh-fu 李介夫
Li Ch'ih 李持
Li Chin-ch'ing 李進卿
Li Ch'ou 李疇
Li Ch'un 李椿

Li Chü-ch'uan 李巨川
Li Chün 李峻
Li Fang 李芳
Li Hao 李浩
Li Hsiu 李修
Li Hsiu-yung 李修永
Li Hsiung-fei 李雄飛
Li Hu 李琥
Li I 李沂
Li-i Bridge 立義橋
Li Liu 李劉
Li Lung 李龍
Li Pi-sheng 李必勝
Li Po-yin 李伯尹
li-pu shang-shu 吏部尚書
Li Shih-hua 李士華
Li-shui (County) 溧水
Li Sung 李松
Li Te-ling 李德靈
Li Te-yüan 李德遠
Li Ting 李鼎
Li Wen-cho 李文灼
Li Yen-hua 李彥華
Li Yü 李玨
Li-yüan 禮源
liang 兩
Liang (surname) 梁
Liang-che 兩浙
Liang Ch'eng-chang 梁成章
Liao Chüeh-chen 廖覺眞
Liao Shih 廖實
Liao Tzu-shih 廖子實
Lin (surname) 林
Lin (River) 臨
Lin-an Fu 臨安府
Lin-chiang Chün 臨江軍
Lin-ch'uan Chün 臨川郡
Lin-ch'uan (County) 臨川
Lin-ju (canton) 臨汝
Lin-ju (County) 臨汝
Lin-ju Academy 臨汝書院
Lin Kung-hsüan 林公選
Lin Ling-su 林靈素
Lin Meng-ying 林夢英
Lin Pao 林保
Lin Tsu-hsia 林祖洽
Lin Tzu-cheng 林子正
Lin Wen-chung 林文仲

Lin Yen-shan 林彥掞
Ling-kan chün-shan miao 靈感軍山廟
Ling-ku 靈谷
Ling-t'ai (canton) 靈台
Liu (surname) 劉
Liu Chang 劉璋
Liu Ch'ing-yin 劉慶因
Liu-fang 流坊
Liu Hsi-t'i 劉希逖
Liu Hsieh 劉爕
Liu Hsün 劉壎
Liu Kuo-chen 劉國珍
liu-shou 留守
Liu Sung (dynasty) 劉宋
Liu Tao-cheng 劉道正
Liu T'ien-ch'i 劉天麒
Liu Yao-fu 劉堯夫
Liu Yu-ting 劉有定
Liu Yüan-kang 留元岡
Lo[a] (surname) 羅
Lo[b] (surname) 駱
Lo-an (canton) 樂安
Lo-an (County) 樂安
Lo Ch'un-po 羅春伯
Lo Min-te 羅敏德
Lo Pang-yen 羅邦彥
Lo Pi-yüan 羅必元
Lo Pin 羅彬
Lo-p'ing (County) 樂平
Lo-shan 羅山
Lo Tien 羅點
Lo Wei 羅衛
Lo-yang (County) 洛陽
Lo Yen 羅衍
Lo Yü 羅愚
Lou (surname) 婁
Lou Chi 婁機
Lou Chien 婁建
Lou Nan-liang 婁南艮
Lou Pi-chung 婁必中
Lou Shih 婁郂
Lou Wen-fu 婁文輔
lu (circuit) 路
Lu (state) 魯
Lu (surname) 陸
Lu-ch'i 盧溪
Lu Ch'ih-chih 陸持之
Lu Chiu-hsü 陸九敍

Lu Chiu-kao 陸九皋
Lu Chiu-ling 陸九齡
Lu Chiu-shao 陸九韶
Lu Chiu-ssu 陸九思
Lu Chiu-yüan 陸九淵
Lu-chou 廬州
Lu Chün 陸濬
Lu Ho 陸賀
Lu Huan-chih 陸煥之
Lu-kang Academy 鹿岡書院
Lu-kung 魯公
Lu-kuo 魯國
Lu-ling (County) 廬陵
Lu O 陸謂
Lu Yu 陸游
Lu Yün 陸筠
lu-shih ts'an-chün 錄事參軍
Lung-chi Fort 龍磧塞
Lung-chou 隆州
Lung-ch'üan (County) 龍泉
Lung-hsi 隴西
Lung-hsing Fu 隆興府
Lung-i 龍義
Lung-yen Temple 龍巖寺
Lü (surname) 呂
Lü Hao-wen 呂好問
Lü Hsi-che 呂希哲
Lü Pen-chung 呂本中
Lü Ta-chün 呂大鈞
Lü Tsu-ch'ien 呂祖謙
Ma-ku (Mountain) 麻姑
Ma-shan 麻山
Ma-tsu 馬祖
mai 麥
Mao-sheng 茂生
Mei-chou 眉州
Mei-feng Tz'u 梅峯祠
Mei Peak 梅峯
Mei-shan (County) 眉山
Meng (surname) 孟
Meng Chi 孟楫
Meng Ch'i 孟杞
Meng Chien 孟鑑
Meng Chih 孟植
Meng Huan 孟渙
Meng Jih-hsin 孟日新
Meng K'ai 孟楷
Meng Tien 孟點

Meng Tse 孟澤
Meng Yen 孟炎
Miao-tuan 妙端
Miao-yen 妙嚴
Ming (dynasty) 明
Ming-chou 明州
Ming-kung shu-p'an ch'ing-ming chi
    明公書判清明集
Ming-yang 名揚
Miu (surname) 繆
Miu Chao 繆昭
Miu Mu 繆穆
Mo Jo 莫若
Mo Lei-hsien 莫雷顯
Mu-chou 睦州
Nan-an Chün 南安軍
Nan-ch'ang 南昌
Nan-ch'eng (County) 南城
Nan-chien-chou 南劍州
Nan-feng (County) 南豐
Nan-fu Pavilion 南阜亭
Nan Hsüan 南軒
Nan-k'ang Chün 南康軍
Nan-t'ang 南塘
Nan-ts'un 南村
Nan-yüan 南源
Neng-kai-chai man-lu 能改齋漫錄
Ning-tsung 寧宗
Niu-t'ien (River) 牛田
o-ti 遏糴
Ou-yang (surname) 歐陽
Ou-yang Ch'e 歐陽澈
Ou-yang Chün 歐陽俊
Ou-yang Hsiu 歐陽修
Pa (Mountain) 巴
Pa-t'ang 巴塘
Pai-hu kiln 白滸窰
Pai-ma 白馬
Pai-ma Yung-ho (canton) 白馬永和
Pai-yün Temple 白雲寺
Pan-ch'iao 板橋
P'an K'uei 潘逵
pang-kuo li 邦國禮
P'ang (surname) 龐
pao 保
pao-cheng 保正
pao-chia 保甲
Pao-chieh 保節

Pao Hui 包恢
Pao-t'ang (River) 寶塘
Pao-t'ang Dike 寶塘堤
pao-wu 保伍
Pao Yang 包揚
Pao-ying Temple 寶應寺
Pei-shan 杯山
P'eng (surname) 彭
P'eng-li 彭蠡
P'eng Shou-hsün 彭壽勳
Pi-yung 辟雝
Piao-hu 表湖
ping-fang 兵防
p'ing-tiao ts'ang 平糶倉
p'o-chia 破家
Po-ling 博陵
Po Pei 博陂
P'o-yang (County) 鄱陽
P'o-yang (Lake) 鄱陽
pu 布
pu-chiang 部將
pu chih so-pien 不知所辨
p'u 僕
P'u-an Temple 普安寺
P'u-ch'eng (County) 浦城
P'u-t'ien 莆田
P'u-yang 濮陽
Sha (County) 沙
Shan-chou 潭州
Shan-t'ang 山碭
shan-yüan lu-ti 山園陸地
Shang-ch'eng Temple 上成寺
Shang-fang Temple 上方觀
Shang-kuan Ch'ien 上官謙
Shang-kuan Ts'ung-lung 上官從龍
Shao-hsing 紹興
Shao-wu Chün 邵武郡
she 社
she-chi 社稷
she-tu-t'ung 社都統
she-ts'ang 社倉
shen 神
Shen (surname) 沈
Shen Chi-ch'ang 沈季長
Shen-hsi 陝西
Shen-hsiao Temple 神霄觀
shen-miao 神廟
Shen-tsung 神宗

shen-tz'u 神祠
sheng 升
sheng-yüan 省元
shih 士
shih (family) 氏
shih (rice measure) 石
Shih (surname) 師
shih-chia 世家
Shih-men 石門
Shih-pei 石陂
Shih Shih-mei 師世美
shih-ta-fu 士大夫
shih-te 實得
Shih Ying-chi 師應極
shou ju-su 守儒素
Shu Dam 述陂
shu-chi 書記
Shu san-wang hsing-miao 蜀三王行廟
Shu-yeh 叔野
shu-yüan 書院
shuang-kang k'ou ch'e pei 雙港口車陂
shui 說
shui-ch'e pei 水車陂
shuo 說
ssu-li ts'an-chün 司理參軍
ssu-ma 司馬
Ssu-ma Ch'ien 司馬遷
ssu-tien 祀典
Su (surname) 蘇
Su Chien 蘇緘
Su-chou 蘇州
Su (Mountain) 疏
Su Shih 蘇軾
Sui (dynasty) 隋
Sun (surname) 孫
Sun Hsün 孫洵
Sun Ti 孫覿
Sun Yen 孫彥
Sun Yu-ch'ing 孫有慶
Sun Yu-pin 孫幼賓
Sung (dynasty) 宋
Sung shih 宋史
Sung-ch'i 松溪
Sung-Yüan hsüeh-an 宋元學案
Ta-hua-tsang Temple 大華藏寺
Ta-kuan 大觀
Ta-ming Fu 大名府
ta ssu-t'u 大司徒

Tai (surname) 戴
T'ai-chou 泰州
T'ai-ho 太和
T'ai-p'ing-chou 太平州
T'ai-p'ing huan-yü chi 太平寰宇記
T'ai-tsung 太宗
T'ai-yüan 太原
Tan-t'u (County) 丹徒
T'an (surname) 譚
T'an Ai 譚鍠
T'an-fang Shih 譚坊市
T'an Huai 譚槐
tang 當
T'ang (dynasty) 唐
T'ang Chiu-ling 唐九齡
T'ang-chou 唐州
T'ang-fang 唐坊
Tao-chou 道州
tao-hsüeh 道學
tao-min 道民
tao-shih 道士
Tao-teng 道燈
Te-ch'iang 德強
t'e-chin kung 特進公
Te-ch'ing (County) 德清
Te-shao 德紹
Te-shen 德深
Te-yüan 德遠
t'e-tsou ming 特奏名
Teng (surname) 鄧
Teng Ch'i 鄧啓
Teng Ch'ih-chih 鄧持之
Teng Cho 鄧卓
Teng Chou 鄧輈
Teng Fei-ying 鄧非英
Teng-Fu erh she 鄧傅二社
Teng Hsi-yen 鄧希顏
Teng Hu 鄧虎
Teng Kang 鄧剛
Teng K'o-chi 鄧克濟
Teng P'ang 鄧雱
Teng Wen-tzu 鄧文字
Teng Yüan-kuan 鄧元觀
Teng Yüeh-li 鄧約禮
ti 弟
ti-k'o 地客
ti-kung-lang 廸功郎
t'i-chü 提舉

tien-hu 佃戶
t'ien 田
T'ien-ch'ang (County) 天長
T'ien-ch'ing Temple 天慶觀
T'ien-ning Temple 天寧寺
T'ien-shou (canton) 天授
T'ien-wang Temple 天王寺
ting 丁
T'ing-chou 汀州
tou 斗
Ts'ai (surname) 蔡
Ts'ai Ch'eng-hsi 蔡承禧
Ts'ai Ching 蔡京
Ts'ai Chü-hou 蔡居厚
Ts'ai I 蔡倚
Ts'ai Pien 蔡卞
Ts'ai Tse-chi 蔡擇吉
Ts'ai Tsung-yen 蔡宗晏
Ts'ai Wei-shan 蔡爲善
Ts'ai-yüan Temple 菜園院
ts'an-mou 參謀
Ts'ao (surname) 曹
Ts'ao-fang Shih 曹坊市
Ta'ao Kun 曹壤
Ts'ao Shih-hsiu 曹時修
Ts'ao Yao-tzu 曹堯咨
Ts'ao Yen-yüeh 曹彥約
Tseng (surname) 曾
Tseng Chao 曾肇
Tseng Chi 曾績
Tseng Chi-li 曾季貍
Tseng Chia 曾斝
Tseng Chieh 曾偕
Tseng chih-fu 曾知府
Tseng Chih-yao 曾致堯
Tseng Ching 曾經
Tseng Fa 曾發
Tseng Feng 曾丰
Tseng Hsieh (Lo-an) 曾澥
Tseng Hsieh (Nan-feng) 曾協
Tseng Hsin 曾莘
Tseng Hsün 曾繏
Tseng Huan 曾煥
Tseng Hui 曾滙
Tseng Hui-ti 曾惠廸
Tseng Hung-li 曾洪立
Tseng Hung-tzu 曾鴻子
Tseng I-chan 曾易占

Tseng I-ts'ung 曾易從

Tseng I-yüan 曾一元

Tseng Kua 曾适

Tseng Kung 曾鞏

Tseng Lin-tsung 曾林宗

Tseng Pu 曾布

Tseng Shu-ch'ing 曾叔卿

Tseng-t'ien 曾田

Tseng-t'ien Fort 曾田寨

Tseng Tsun 曾樽

Tseng Tsung 曾縱

Tseng Tzu 曾子

Tseng Tzu-liang 曾子艮

Tseng Wu 曾悟

Tseng Yeh 曾燁

Tseng Yen 曾炎

Tseng Ying-lung 曾應龍

Tseng Yu-lung 曾友龍

Tseng Yung 曾泳

Tseng Yü 曾鈺

Tseng Yüan-tzu 曾淵子

Tsou (surname) 鄒

Tsou Chi 鄒極

Tsou Chih-ming 鄒智明

Tsou Fan 鄒璠

Tsou Ming-shan 鄒明善

Tsou T'ao 鄒陶

Tsou Tsung-kao 鄒宗皋

Tsou Tz'u-ch'en 鄒次陳

Tsou Yü 鄒餘

tsu 族

tsu-shih 族師

Ts'ui (surname) 崔

Tsung-an 宗安

Tsung-hsin 宗信

tu 都

Tu (surname) 杜

Tu-ch'ang (County) 都昌

Tu Ch'ien 杜潛

tu-pao 都保

tu-pao-cheng 都保正

tu-pao-fu-cheng 都保副正

tu-she 都社

tu-she-cheng 都社正

tu-ts'ang 都倉

Tu-tsung 度宗

Tu Tzu-yeh 杜子野

Tu Yü-te 杜育德

T'u (surname) 涂

T'u An-kuo 涂安國

T'u Cheng-sheng 涂正勝

T'u Chi 涂濟

T'u Chung-sheng 涂中勝

T'u Hsiang-chung 涂祥仲

T'u Hui 涂恢

T'u Ssu-yu 涂四友

T'u Ta-hsiang 涂大向

T'u Ta-k'uei 涂大馗

T'u Ta-lin 涂大琳

Tung (surname) 董

Tung Ch'ang-i 董昌裔

Tung-ch'uan 東川

Tung Chü-i 董居誼

Tung-hsiang (County) 東鄉

Tung Hung-tao 董鴻道

Tung I 董億

Tung Ko 董革

Tung Kuan 董觀

Tung-lin Temple 東林寺

Tung-shan Temple 東山寺

Tung Te-hsiu 董德修

Tung Te-yüan 董德元

Tung T'ien-ching 董天經

Tung T'ien-yin 董天隱

Tung-t'ing (Lake) 洞庭

Tung Wei 董煟

t'ung-ch'e 簡車

Tung-yüeh hsing-miao 東嶽行廟

T'ung-fu 同富

t'ung-i che 同役者

T'ung-kang 桐岡

t'ung-ling 統領

tzu keng-hsü chih chin shih nien 自庚
戌至今十年

Tzu-ming-shan fu-hui hsing-miao 自鳴
山孚惠行廟

tz'u 祠

Tz'u-shan lieh hsing-miao 祠山烈
行廟

wa-yao pei 瓦窰陂

Wan-chin Dam 萬金陂

Wan K'ai 萬開

Wang (surname) 王

Wang An-jen 王安仁

Wang An-kuo 王安國

Wang An-li 王安禮

Wang An-shang 王安上
Wang An-shih 王安石
Wang Ch'en 王忱
Wang Chi 王幾
Wang Chi-weng 王積翁
Wang Chien 王檢
Wang Ch'un 王椿
Wang Fu 王阜
Wang-hsien 望仙
Wang Huan 王煥
Wang I 王益
Wang Ko 汪革
Wang K'o-chin 王克勤
Wang Kuan-chih 王貫之
Wang K'uang 王曠
Wang Ling 王令
Wang P'ang 王雱
Wang Po-keng 汪伯更
Wang Shih-hsi 王師錫
Wang Tsai 王宰
Wang Tsao 汪藻
wang-tsu 望族
Wang Wen-ch'ing 王文慶
Wang Wu-chiu 王無咎
Wang Yung-chih 王用之
Wei (surname) 危
Wei (surname of Tseng Pu's wife) 魏
Wei Ch'en 危琛
Wei Ho 危和
Wei Kuo-ts'ai 危國材
Wei Shan-chih 魏掞之
Wei Su 危素
Wei T'ai 魏泰
Wei Yen-chen 危炎震
Wen-ch'ang Bridge 文昌橋
Wen-lin Academy 文林書院
Wen-ming Bridge 文明橋
wen-pi t'a 文筆塔
Wen T'ien-hsiang 文天祥
Wen Yen-po 溫彥博
wu 巫
Wu (kingdom) 吳
Wu[a] (surname) 吳
Wu[b] (surname) 鄔
Wu An-ch'ih 吳安持
Wu Ch'e 吳澈
Wu Ch'en-tzu 吳辰子
Wu Ch'eng 吳澄
Wu-ch'eng (County) 烏程

wu-chiang shuang-kang k'ou ch'e pei
　　烏江雙港口車陂
Wu Chien 吳漸
Wu Ch'ien 吳潛
Wu Ch'ih 吳墀
Wu-chou 婺州
Wu Chü-hou 吳居厚
Wu Ch'üeh 吳慤
Wu Chün 吳郡
Wu Fan 吳蕃
Wu Fen 吳賁
wu-fu 五服
Wu Hang 吳沆
Wu Hao 吳號
Wu Hsiao-tsung 吳孝宗
Wu Hsieh 吳澥
Wu-hsien ling-shun hsing-miao 五顯
　　靈順行廟
Wu-hsing 五星
Wu Hsing-tsung 吳興宗
Wu-hsiung 武雄
Wu Hsün 吳恂
Wu Hung 吳洪
Wu I 吳鎰
Wu Jung 吳榮
Wu Kan 吳感
Wu K'o 吳可
Wu K'o-ch'eng 鄔克成
Wu K'o-sun 吳可孫
Wu Kuang 吳洸
Wu K'un-sun 吳困孫
Wu Li 吳里
Wu-lin Temple 武林寺
Wu Lung-ch'i 鄔龍啓
Wu Meng 吳蒙
Wu Meng-hsi 吳夢儶
Wu Min 吳敏
Wu Ming-yang 吳名揚
Wu-ning (County) 武寧
Wu Pang-chi 吳邦基
Wu Piao-wei 吳表微
Wu Ping-jo 吳炳若
Wu Shih-liang 武師亮
Wu Shih-shun 吳仕舜
Wu Ssu 吳思
Wu Su 吳槊
Wu-t'ang 吳塘
Wu T'ao 吳濤
Wu Te-fu 吳德夫

Wu Te-hsiu 吳德秀
Wu Te-p'u 吳德溥
Wu Ti-chi 吳廸吉
Wu T'ien-kuei 吳天桂
Wu Ting-weng 吳定翁
Wu Tseng 吳曾
Wu Wan 吳萬
Wu Wen-sheng 吳文盛
Wu Yu-lin 吳有鄰
Wu Yü 吳玨
Wu-yüan (County) 婺源
Wu-Yüeh 吳越
Ya-pei 崦背
Yang (surname) 楊
Yang Ch'a 楊察
yang-chia ch'e pei 楊家車陂
Yang Ch'ien 楊遷
Yang-chou 揚州
Yang-shan 仰山
Yang-shan fu-hui hsing-miao 仰山孚
　　惠行廟
Yang Shih-hsiung 楊世雄
Yang-tzu (County) 揚子
Yang Yü-lung 楊遇龍
yao-ch'ien pei 窯前陂
Yeh Chu 葉耒
Yeh T'ao 葉濤
Yen (surname) 晏
Yen Chao-su 晏昭素
Yen Chen-ch'ing 彥眞卿
Yen-ch'eng Shih 嚴城市
Yen Ch'eng-yü 晏成裕
Yen chia-t'ou 鄢甲頭
Yen Fang 晏防
Yen-fu (canton) 延福
Yen Fu-hsin 晏復新
Yen Hsiu-mu 晏修睦
Yen Shih-k'o 晏時可
Yen-shou (canton) 延壽
Yen Shu 晏殊
Yen Sun 晏巽
Yen Ta-cheng 晏大正
yin 隱
Yin (County) 鄞
Ying-chou (Ching-hsi-pei) 穎州
Ying-chou (Kuang-tung) 英州
Ying-hsiu (canton) 穎秀
Ying-tse Shrine 英澤廟
Yu (surname) 游

yu-ming wu-shih 有名無實
Yu Te-hung 游德洪
Yung-feng Dam 永豐陂
Yung-feng (County) 永豐
Yung-hsing Temple 永興觀
yung-wu 用物
Yü (River) 盱
Yü[a] (surname) 余
Yü[b] (surname) 俞
Yü[c] (surname) 虞
Yü-chang 豫章
Yü Chi 虞集
yü-chü 與舉
Yü-kan 餘干
yü-kuei 寓貴
yü-kuei shih-ta-fu 寓貴士大夫
Yü Pang-kuang 余邦光
Yü-shu Academy 魚墅書院
Yü Tien 虞玨
Yü Tou-hsiang 余斗祥
yü-yung 雩禜
Yü Yün-wen 虞允文
yüan 園
Yüan (dynasty) 元
Yüan (surname) 袁
Yüan-chou 袁州
Yüan Hung-tao 袁宏道
Yüan Li-ch'u 袁立初
Yüan Shih-ch'eng 袁世成
Yüan Ts'ai 袁采
Yüeh (surname) 樂
Yüeh-chou (Liang-che) 越州
Yüeh-chou (Ching-hu-pei) 岳州
Yüeh Dam 樂陂
Yüeh Fei 岳飛
Yüeh Hsü-kuo 樂許國
Yüeh Huang-mu 樂黃目
Yüeh Huang-shang 樂黃裳
Yüeh I 樂誼
Yüeh Shih 樂史
Yüeh Ta-chang 樂大章
Yüeh Tien 樂琠
Yüeh Wen-huan 樂文煥
Yüeh Yüan 樂淵
Yün Chuang 雲莊
Yün-feng Temple 雲峯寺
Yün-kai (canton) 雲蓋
Yün-lin (Mountain) 雲林

LIST OF WORKS CITED

Ahern, Emily. 'Affines and the Rituals of Kinship.' In *Religion and Ritual in Chinese Society*. Ed. Arthur P. Wolf. Stanford: Stanford University Press, 1974, pp. 279–307.

Aoyama Sadao 青山定雄. 'Zui-Tō-Sō sandai ni okeru kosu no chiikiteki kōsatsu 隋唐宋三代における戸数の地域的考察.' *Rekishigaku kenkyū* 歴史学研究 (o.s.) VI, nos. 4 and 5 (1936).

——. 'Godai-Sō ni okeru kōsei shinkō kanryō 五代宋における江西新興官僚.' In *Wada hakushi kanreki kinen tōyōshi ronsō* 和田博士還暦記念東洋 史論叢. Tokyo: Kodansha, 1951, pp. 19–37.

——. 'Sōdai ni okeru shisen kanryō no keifu ni tsuite 宋代における四川官僚 の系譜について.' In *Wada hakushi koki kinen tōyōshi ronsō* 和田博士 古稀記念東洋史論叢. Tokyo: Kodansha, 1960, pp. 37–48.

——. 'The Newly-Risen Bureaucrats in Fukien at the Five Dynasty–Sung Period, with Special Reference to their Genealogies.' *Memoirs of the Research Department of the Tōyō Bunko*, 21 (1962), pp. 1–48.

——. 'Sōdai ni okeru kahoku kanryō no keifu ni tsuite 宋代における華北官 僚の系譜について (I).' *Seishin joshi daigaku ronsō* 聖心女子大学論叢, 21 (1963), pp. 21–41.

——. 'Sōdai ni okeru kahoku kanryō no keifu ni tsuite 宋代における華北官 僚の系譜について (II).' *Seishin joshi daigaku ronsō* 聖心女子大学論叢, 25 (1965), pp. 19–49.

——. 'Sōdai ni okeru kahoku kanryō no keifu ni tsuite 宋代における華北官 僚の系譜について (III).' *Chūō daigaku bungakubu kiyō* (*shigakuka*) 中央大学文学部紀要（史学科）, 12 (1967), pp. 67–110.

——. 'Sōdai ni okeru kōsei shusshin no kōkan no konin kankei 宋代におけ る江西出身の高官の婚姻関系.' *Seishin joshi daigaku ronsō* 聖心女子 大学論叢, 29 (1967), pp. 17–33.

——. 'Sōdai ni okeru kanan kanryō no keifu ni tsuite – toku ni yōsukō ryūiki o chūshin to shite 宋代における華南官僚の系譜について—特に揚子江 流域を中心として." *Chūō daigaku bungakubu kiyō* 中央大学文学部 紀要, 72 (1974), pp. 51–76.

Araki Toshikazu 荒木敏一. *Sōdai kakyo seido kenkyū* 宋代科舉制度研究. Kyoto: Tōyōshi-Kenkyū-Kai, 1969.

Beattie, Hilary. *Land and Lineage in China: A Study of T'ung-ch'eng, Anhwei, in the Ming and Ch'ing Dynasties*. Cambridge: Cambridge University Press, 1979.

Bielenstein, Hans. 'The Census of China during the Period AD 2–742.' *Bulletin of the Museum of Far Eastern Antiquities*, 19 (1947), pp. 125–63.

Cahill, Suzanne E. 'Taoism at the Sung Court: The Heavenly Text Affair of 1008.' *Bulletin of Sung and Yüan Studies* 16 (1980), pp. 23–44.

Cha Lung-a 札隆阿 et al. *I-huang Hsien chih* 宜黃縣志. Tao-kuang edition, 1824.

Chaffee, John. 'Education and Examinations in Sung Society (960–1279).' Diss. University of Chicago 1979.

Chang, Chung-li. *The Chinese Gentry: Studies in their Role in Nineteenth-Century Chinese Society*. Seattle: University of Washington Press, 1955.

Chang Hsing-yen 張興言 et al. *I-huang Hsien chih* 宜黃縣志. T'ung-chih edition, 1871.

Chang Hsüan 張鉉. *Chin-ling hsin chih* 金陵新志. Chih-cheng edition, 1344.

Chang Kao 張淏. *K'uai-chi hsü-chih* 會稽續志. Ch'ing printing of Sung Pao-ch'ing edition, 1808.

Chang Lei 張耒. *Chang Yu-shih wen-chi* 張右史文集. SPTK edition.

Chang Shih 張栻. *Chang Nan-hsüan hsien-sheng wen-chi* 張南軒先生文集. TSCC edition.

Ch'ang Pi-te 昌彼得 et al. *Sung-jen chuan-chi tzu-liao so-yin* 宋人傳記資料索引. Taipei: Ting-wen shu-chü, 1973.

Chao I 趙翼. *Kai-yü ts'ung-k'ao* 陔餘叢考. Tu-shu cha-chi ts'ung-k'an, first collection.

Chao Ting-ch'en 趙定臣. *Chu-yin chi-shih chi* 竹隱畸士集. SKCSCP, first collection.

Chen Te-hsiu 眞德秀. *Chen Wen-chung kung chi* 眞文忠公集. SPTK, first compilation.

Ch'en Chen-sun 陳振孫. *Chih-chai shu-lu chieh-t'i* 直齋書錄解題. SKCSCP, pieh-chi.

Ch'en Ch'ien 陳潛 et al. *Ch'ung-jen Hsien chih* 崇仁縣志. K'ang-hsi edition, 1673.

Ch'en, Jerome. 'Sung Bronzes: an Economic Analysis.' *Bulletin of the School of Oriental and African Studies*, 28, no. 3 (1965), pp. 613–26.

Ch'en, Kenneth. *Buddhism in China: A Historical Survey*. Princeton: Princeton University Press, 1964.

Ch'en Po-ch'üan 陳柏泉. 'Chiang-hsi Lin-ch'uan Nan-feng yao-chih tiao-ch'a 江西臨川南豐窯址調查.' *K'ao-ku* 考古, no. 12 (1963), pp. 686–9.

——. 'Ch'ung-jen Hsien T'ai-ho Ssu t'a ch'uan-ming 崇仁縣太和寺塔磚銘.' *Wen-wu* 文物, no. 4 (1963), pp. 52–3.

Ch'en Shih-tao 陳師道. *Hou-shan chi* 後山集. SPPY edition.

Ch'en Tsao 陳造. *Chiang-hu ch'ang-weng chi* 江湖長翁集. SKCSCP, fifth collection.

Ch'en Yin-k'o 陳寅恪. *T'ang-tai cheng-chih shih shu-lun* 唐代政治史述論. Taipei: Lo-t'ien ch'u-pan she, 1970.

Ch'en Yüan-chin 陳元晉. *Yü-shu lei-kao* 漁墅類稿. SKCSCP, first collection.

Cheng Yüeh 鄭鈇 et al. *Nan-feng Hsien chih* 南豐縣志. K'ang-hsi edition, 1683.

Ch'eng Chü 程俱. *Pei-shan chi* 北山集. SKCSCP, third collection.

Ch'eng Chü-fu 程鉅夫. *Hsüeh-lou chi* 雪樓集. Taipei: Kuo-li Chung-yang T'u-shu-kuan, photographic reprint of Yüan edition.

Ch'eng Fang 程芳 et al. *Chin-ch'i Hsien chih* 金溪縣志. T'ung-chih edition, 1870.

Ch'eng Pi 程珌, *Ming-shui chi* 洺水集. Ming Ch'ung-chen edition.

Ch'eng Ying-lin 程應麟 and P'eng Kua-fan 彭适凡. 'Chiang-hsi Fu-chou fa-hsien Yüan-tai ho-tsang-mu 江西撫州發現元代合葬墓.' *K'ao-ku* 考古, no. 7 (1964), pp. 370–2.

Chiang-hsi shih-she tsung-p'ai t'u-lu 江西詩社宗派圖錄. TSCC edition.

Chieh Ch'i-ssu 揭傒斯. *Chieh Wen-an kung ch'üan-chi* 揭文安公全集. SPTK, first collection.

Chikusa Masaaki 竺沙雅章. 'Hoku Sō shidaifu no shikyo to baiten – omo ni Tōha sekicho o shiryō to shite 北宋士大夫の徙居と買田— 主に東坡尺牘を資料として.' *Shirin* 史林, 54, no. 2 (1971), pp. 28–53.

——. 'Sōdai sessai no tōmin ni tsuite 宋代浙西の道民について.' *Tōyōshi kenkyū* 東洋史研究, 36, no. 3 (1977), pp. 74–100.

——. 'Sōdai funji kō 宋代墳寺考.' *Tōyō gakuhō* 東洋学報, 61, nos. 1–2 1979), pp. 35–67.

Ching-k'ou ch'i-chiu chuan 京口耆舊傳. SKCSCP, *pieh-chi*.

Ch'ing-yüan t'iao-fa shih-lei 慶元條法事類. Tokyo: Koten Kenkyūkai, 1968.

Chou Pi-ta 周必大. *Wen-chung chi* 文忠集. SKCSCP, second collection.

Chu Chuan-yu. 'A History of Chinese Journalism in the Sung Dynasty.' *Synopses of Monographical Studies in Chinese History and Social Sciences*, 5 (1969), pp. 67–88.

Chu Hsi 朱熹. *Chu Wen-kung wen-chi* 朱文公文集. SPTK, first compilation.

Chu K'uei-chang 朱奎章 et al., *Lo-an Hsien chih* 樂安縣志. T'ung-chih edition, 1871.

Chu Mu 祝穆. *Fang-yü sheng-lan* 方輿勝覽. Sung edition at National Central Library, Taipei.

Chu Shih-chia 朱士嘉. *Chung-kuo ti-fang-chih tsung-lu* 中國地方志總錄. Shanghai: Shang-wu yin-shu kuan, 1935.

Ch'ü, T'ung-tsu. *Local Government in China under the Ch'ing*. Stanford: Stanford University Press, 1962.

Ch'üan Han-sheng 全漢昇. 'Nan-Sung t'ao-mi ti sheng-ch'an yü yün-hsiao 南宋稻米的生產與運銷.' *Kuo-li chung-yang yen-chiu-yüan li-shih yü-yen yen-chiu-so chi-k'an* 國立中央研究院歷史語言研究所集刊, 10 (1948), pp. 404–32.

——. 全漢昇. 'Sung-mo ti t'ung-huo p'eng-ch'ang chi ch'i tui-yü wu-chia ti ying-hsiang 宋末的通貨膨脹及其對於物價的影響.' *Kuo-li chung-yang yen-chiu-yuan li-shih yü-yen yen-chiu-so chi-k'an* 國立中央研究院歷史語言研究所集刊, 10 (1948), pp. 193–222.

Clark, Hugh R. 'Consolidation on the South China Frontier: The Development of Ch'üan-chou, 699–1126.' Diss. University of Pennsylvania, 1981.

Dardess, John. *Conquerors and Confucians: Aspects of Political Change in Late Yüan China*. New York: Columbia University Press, 1973.

Davis, Richard. 'The Shih Lineage at the Southern Sung Court.' Diss. Princeton University, 1980.

de Bary, Wm. Theodore. 'A Reappraisal of Neo-Confucianism.' In *Studies in Chinese Thought*. Ed. Arthur F. Wright. Chicago: University of Chicago Press, 1953, pp. 81–111.

——. *The Liberal Tradition in China.* New York: Columbia University Press, 1983.

Dennerline, Jerry. *The Chia-ting Loyalists: Confucian Leadership and Social Change in Seventeenth-Century China.* New Haven: Yale University Press, 1981.

Eberhard, Wolfram. *Das Toba-Reich Nordchinas.* Leiden: E.J. Brill, 1949.

——. *Social Mobility in Traditional China.* Leiden: E.J. Brill, 1962.

——. *A History of China.* 3rd edition. Berkeley: University of California Press, 1969.

——. *Conquerors and Rulers: Social Forces in Medieval China.* Leiden: E.J. Brill, 1970.

Ebrey, Patricia B. *The Aristocratic Families of Early Imperial China: A Case Study of the Po-ling Ts'ui Family.* Cambridge: Cambridge University Press, 1978.

——. 'Women in the Kinship System of the Southern Song Upper Class.' In *Women in China*, edited by Richard Guisso and Stanley Johannesen. New York: Philo Press, 1981, pp. 113–128.

——. 'Conceptions of the Family in the Sung Dynasty.' *Journal of Asian Studies* 43 (1984): 219–45.

——. *Family and Property in Sung China: Yuan Ts'ai's Precepts for Social Life.* Princeton: Princeton University Press, 1984.

Elvin, Mark. *The Pattern of the Chinese Past.* Stanford: Stanford University Press, 1973.

Fairbank, John K., ed. *The Cambridge History of China.* Volume 10: *Late Ch'ing, 1800–1911.* Part I. Cambridge: Cambridge University Press, 1978.

——, Edwin O. Reischauer, and Albert M. Craig. *East Asia: Tradition and Transformation.* Boston: Houghton Mifflin Co., 1973.

Fang Chan 方湛 et al. *Lo-an Hsien chih* 樂安縣志. K'ang-hsi edition, 1683.

Fang Hao 方豪. 'Sung-tai jen-k'ou k'ao-shih 宋代人口考實.' In *Sung-shih yen-chiu chi* 宋史研究集, fifth collection. Taipei: Chung-hua ts'ung-shu pien-shen wei-yüan-hui, 1969, pp. 257–300.

Fang Hsüan-ling 房玄齡. *Chin shu* 晉書. SPPY edition.

Fei Hsiao-t'ung. *Earthbound China.* Chicago: University of Chicago Press, 1945.

——. 'Peasantry and Gentry in China.' *American Journal of Sociology*, 52, no. 1 (1946), pp. 1–17.

Feuchtwang, Stephen. 'School-temple and City God.' In *The City in Late Imperial China.* Ed. G. William Skinner. Stanford: Stanford University Press, 1977, pp. 581–608.

Fischer, Johanna. 'Fan Chung-yen (989–1052): das Lebensbild eines chinesischen Staatsmannes.' *Oriens Extremus* 2, no. 1 (1955), pp. 39–85.

Freedman, Maurice. Review of *The Chinese Gentry*, by Chang Chung-li. *Pacific Affairs*, 29, no. 1, pp. 78–80.

——. *Lineage Organization in Southeastern China.* London: Athlone Press, 1958.

——. *Chinese Lineage and Society: Fukien and Kwangtung.* London: Athlone Press, 1966.

Freeman, Michael. 'Lo-yang and the Opposition to Wang An-shih: The Rise of Confucian Conservatism, 1068–1086.' Diss. Yale University 1973.

Golas, Peter J. 'Rural China in the Sung.' *Journal of Asian Studies*, 39, no. 2 (1980), pp. 291–325.

Goodrich, L.C. 'The Development of Printing in China and its Effects on the Renaissance under the Sung Dynasty.' *Journal of the Hong Kong Branch of the Royal Asiatic Society*, 3 (1963), pp. 36–43.

——, and Feng Chia-sheng. 'The Early Development of Firearms in China.' *Isis* 36, no. 2 (1946), pp. 114–29.

Haeger, John. *Crisis and Prosperity in Sung China*. Tucson: University of Arizona Press, 1975.

Han Wei 韓維. *Nan-yang Chi* 南陽集. SKCSCP, second collection.

Han Yüan-chi 韓元吉. *Nan-chien chia-i kao* 南澗甲乙稿. SKCSCP, pieh-chi.

Hartwell, Robert. 'Markets, Technology, and the Structure of Enterprise in the Development of the Eleventh-Century Chinese Iron and Steel Industry.' *Journal of Economic History* 26 (1966), pp. 29–58.

——. 'A Cycle of Economic Change in Imperial China: Coal and Iron in Northeast China, 750–1350.' *Journal of the Economic and Social History of the Orient* 10, no. 1 (1967), pp. 102–59.

——. 'The Evolution of the Early Northern Sung Monetary System.' *Journal of the American Oriental Society* 87, no. 3 (1967), pp. 280–9.

——. 'Demographic, Political, and Social Transformations of China, 750–1550.' *Harvard Journal of Asiatic Studies* 42 (1982), pp. 365–442.

Hasebe Gakuji 長谷部樂爾. *Sekai tōshi zenshū* 世界陶磁全集. Vol. 12: *Sō* 宋. Tokyo: Shogakukan, 1977.

Hervouet, Yves. *A Sung Bibliography*. Hong Kong: Chinese University Press, 1978.

Hino Kaisaburō 日野開三郎. 'Sōdai no kiko o ronjite koko mondai ni oyobu 宋代の詭戸を論じて戸口問題におよぶ.' *Shigaku zasshi* 史学雑誌, 47, no. 1 (1936), pp. 83–105.

Ho Chung 何中. *Chih-fei-t'ang kao* 知非堂稿. Ch'ing printed edition at Jinbun Kagaku Kenkyujo, Kyoto.

Ho Hsi-chih 何希之. *Chi-lei chi* 雞肋集. Ch'ing printed edition at Seikadō, Tokyo.

Ho, Ping-ti. 'Early-ripening Rice in Chinese History.' *Economic History Review*, second series, 9, no. 2 (1956), pp. 200–18.

——. *Studies on the Population of China*, 1368–1953. Cambridge: Harvard University Press, 1959.

——. 'Aspects of Social Mobility in China, 1368–1911.' *Comparative Studies in Society and History*, 1, no. 4 (1959).

——. *The Ladder of Success in Imperial China: Aspects of Social Mobility, 1368–1911*. New York: Columbia University Press, 1962.

——. 'An Estimate of the Total Population of Sung-Chin China.' In *Études Song in Memoriam Étienne Balazs Série I: Histoire et Institutions*. Fasc. 1, 1970, pp. 3–53.

Hsieh Fang-te 謝枋得. *T'ieh-shan chi* 疊山集. SPTK, second compilation.

Hsieh I 謝逸. *Ch'i-t'ang chi* 溪堂集. SKCSCP, *pieh-chi*.

Hsieh K'o 謝薖. *Hsieh Yu-p'an wen-chi* 謝幼槃文集. Shanghai Han-fen-lou photographic reprint of Sung edition.

Hsü Ta-ching 許大經 et al. *Fu-chou Fu chih* 撫州府志. Chia-ching edition, 1554.

Hsü Ying-jung 許應鑅 et al., *Fu-chou Fu chih* 撫州府志. Kuang-hsü edition, 1876.

Hua-kai shan Fou-ch'iu Wang Kuo san chen-chün shih-shih 華蓋山浮邱王郭三眞君實事. *Tao Tsang* 道藏 556–57.

Huang Chen 黃震. *Huang-shih jih-ch'ao* 黃氏日鈔. SKCSCP, second collection.

Huang Chin 黃溍. *Chin-hua Huang hsien-sheng wen-chi* 金華黃先生文集. SPTK, first compilation.

Huang Kan 黃幹. *Mien-chai chi* 勉齋集. SKCSCP, second collection.

Huang Tsung-hsi 黃宗羲. *Sung-Yüan hsüeh-an* 宋元學案. SPPY edition.

Huang Yen-p'ing 黃彥平. *San-yü chi* 三餘集. SKCSCP, fifth collection.

Hui-hung 惠洪. *Shih-men wen-tzu ch'an* 石門文字禪. SPTK, first compilation.

Hung Mai 洪邁. *I-chien chih* 夷堅志. Kyoto: Chūbun Shuppansha, 1975. (Except where other edition is noted.)

——. *Jung-chai sui-pi wu-chi* 容齋隨筆五集. Kuo-hsüeh chi-pen ts'ung-shu edition.

Hymes, Robert P. 'Marriage, Descent Groups, and the Localist Strategy in Sung and Yuan Fu-chou.' In *Kinship Organization in Late Imperial China, 1000–1940*. Edited by Patricia B. Ebrey and James L. Watson. Forthcoming from University of California Press.

Ihara Hiroshi 伊原弘. 'Sōdai Meishū ni okeru kanko no kon-in kankei 宋代明州における官戸の婚姻関系.' *Chūō daigaku daigakuin ronkyū* 中央大学大学院研究年報, 1 (1972).

——. 'Sōdai Ushū ni okeru kanko no kon-in kankei 宋代婺州における官戸の婚姻関系.' *Chūō daigaku daigakuin kenkyū nenpō* 中央大学大学院論究, 6, no. 1 (1974), pp. 33–42.

——. 'Nan-Sō Shisen ni okeru Goshi no seiryoku – Go Gi no ran zenshi 南宋四川における呉氏の勢力—呉曦の亂前史.' In *Aoyama hakushi koki kinen Sōdaishi ronsō* 青山博士古稀紀念宋代史論叢. Tokyo: Seishin Shobō, 1974, pp. 1–33.

——. 'Sōdai kanryō no kon-in no imi ni tsuite 宋代官僚の婚姻の意味について.' *Rekishi to chiri* 歴史と地理, 254 (1976), pp. 12–19.

——. 'Nan-Sō Shisen ni okeru teikyo shijin – Seidofuro-Shishūro o chūshin to shite 南宋四川における定居士人—成都府路・梓州路を中心として.' *Tōhōgaku* 東方学, 54 (1977).

Ikeda On 池田温. 'Tōdai no gumbō hyō 唐代の郡望表.' *Tōyō gakuhō* 東洋学報, 42, no. 4, pp. 412–30.

Johnson, David. *The Medieval Chinese Oligarchy*. Boulder: Westview Press, 1977.

——. 'The Last Years of a Great Clan: The Li Family of Chao Chün in Late T'ang and Early Sung.' *Harvard Journal of Asiatic Studies*, 37, no. 1 (1977), pp. 5–102.

Katō Shigeshi 加藤繁. *Tō-Sō jidai ni okeru kingin no kenkyū* 唐宋時代における金銀の研究. Tokyo, 1924.

——. 'On the *Hang* or Association of Merchants in China, with Special Reference to the Institution in the T'ang and Sung Periods.' *Memoirs of the Research Department of the Tōyō Bunko* 9 (1936): 45–83.

——. 加藤繁. *Shina keizaishi kōshō* 支那經濟史考證. Tokyo: Tōyō Bunko, 1953.

Kinugawa Tsuyoshi 衣川強. 'Sōdai saishō kō – Hoku-Sō zenki no baai 宋代宰相考—北宋前期の場合.' *Tōyōshi kenkyū* 東洋史研究, 24, no. 4 (1966), pp. 39–76.

———. 'Sōdai no meizoku – Kanan Ryōshi no baai 宋代の名族— 河南呂氏の場合.' *Kōbe shōka daigaku jinbun ronshū* 神戸商科大学人文論集, 9, nos. 1 and 2 (1973), pp. 134–66.

Ko Sheng-chung 葛勝仲. *Tan-yang chi* 丹陽集. Ch'ang-chou hsien-che i-shu edition.

Kracke, E.A. 'Family Versus Merit in Chinese Civil Service Examinations under the Empire.' *Harvard Journal of Asiatic Studies*, 10 (1947), pp. 105–23.

———. *Civil Service in Early Sung China, 960–1067.* Cambridge: Harvard University Press, 1953.

———. 'Region, Family, and Individual in the Chinese Examination System.' In *Chinese Thought and Institutions.* Ed. John K. Fairbank. Chicago: University of Chicago Press, 1957, pp. 251–68.

Kuan Wei-lan 官蔚藍. *Chung-hua min-kuo hsing-cheng ch'ü-hua chi t'u-ti jen-k'ou tsung-chi piao* 中華民國行政區劃土地人口總計表. Taipei: Pei-k'ai ch'u-pan-she, 1955.

Kuhn, Philip A. *Rebellion and its Enemies in Late Imperial China.* Cambridge: Harvard University Press, 1970.

K'ung Wu-chung 孔武仲. *Tsung-po chi* 宗伯集. Yü-chang ts'ung-shu edition.

Kyō Heinan 喬炳南. 'Nan-Sō no chūgijunshasei ni tsuite 南宋の忠義軍社制について.' 帝塚山大学論集 *Tezukayama daigaku ronshū*, 8 (1976), pp. 18–33.

Lau, D.C., trans. *Mencius.* Harmondsworth: Penguin Books, 1970.

Lee, Thomas H.C. 'A Report on the Recently Excavated Sung Ship at Quanzhou and a Consideration of its True Capacity.' *Sung Studies Newsletter*, nos. 11 and 12 (1976), pp. 4–9.

Li Chi-fu 李吉甫. *Yüan-ho chün-hsien t'u-chih* 元和郡縣圖志. TSCC edition.

Li Hsin-ch'uan 李心傳. *Chien-yen i-lai ch'ao-yeh tsa-chi* 建炎以來朝野雜記. Sung-shih tzu-liao ts'ui-pien, first collection.

———. *Chien-yen i-lai hsi-nien yao-lu* 建炎以來繫年要錄. Sung-shih tzu-liao ts'ui-pien, first collection.

Li Hsing-yüan 李興元 et al. *Chi-an Fu chih* 吉安府志. Shun-chih edition, 1660.

Li Kou 李覯. *Chih-chiang Li hsien-sheng wen-chi* 直講李先生文集. SPTK, first compilation.

Li Kuang-jun 黎廣潤 et al. *Nan-feng Hsien chih* 南豐縣志. Republican edition, 1923.

Li O 李鶚. *Sung-shih chi-shih* 宋詩紀事. Taipei: Ting-wen shu-chü, 1970.

Li Shih-fen 李士棻 et al. *Tung-hsiang Hsien chih* 東鄉縣志. T'ung-chih edition, 1869.

Li Ts'un 李存. *Ssu-an chi* 俟巷集. SKCSCP, second collection.

Li Yüan-pi 李元弼. *Tso-i tzu-chen* 作邑自箴. SPTK edition.

Liang Ch'i 梁奇 et al. *Tung-hsiang Hsien chih* 東鄉縣志. K'ang-hsi edition, 1665.

Liang K'o-chia 梁克家. *San-shan chih* 三山志. Ming Ch'ung-chen printing of Sung Ch'un-hsi edition.

Lin, Shuen-fu. *The Transformation of the Chinese Lyrical Tradition: Chiang K'uei and Southern Sung Tz'u Poetry*. Princeton: Princeton University Press,1978.

Liu Ch'en-weng 劉辰翁. *Hsü-ch'i chi* 須溪集. SKCSCP, fourth collection.

Liu Chih 劉摯. *Chung-su chi* 忠肅集, SKCSCP, pieh-chi.

Liu Hsü 劉昫 et al. *Chiu T'ang shu* 舊唐書. SPPY edition.

Liu Hsün 劉壎. *Shui-yün-ts'un kao* 水雲村稿. SKCSCP edition.

——. *Yin-chu t'ung-i* 隱居通議. Tu-shu-chai ts'ung-shu edition.

Liu, James T.C. 'How Did a Neo-Confucian School Become the State Orthodoxy?' *Philosophy East and West*, 23 (1973), pp. 483–505.

——. 'Lüeh-lun Sung-tai wu-kuan-ch'ün tsai t'ung-chih chieh-chi chung ti ti-wei 略論宋代武官群在統治階級中的地位.' In *Aoyama hakushi koki kinen Sōdaishi ronsō* 青山博士古稀紀念宋代史論叢. Tokyo: Seishin Shobō, 1974, pp. 477–91.

Liu K'o-chuang 劉克莊. *Hou-ts'un hsien-sheng ta-ch'üan chi* 後村先生大全集. SPTK, first compilation.

Liu Pin 劉攽. *P'eng-ch'eng chi* 彭城集. TSCC edition.

Liu Tsai 劉宰. *Man-t'ang chi* 漫塘集. Chia-ts'ung-t'ang ts'ung-shu edition.

Lo Jung-pang, 'Maritime Commerce and its Relation to the Sung Navy.' *Journal of the Economic and Social History of the Orient* 12 (1969), pp. 57–101.

Lo Ta-ching 羅大經. *Ho-lin yü-lu* 鶴林玉露. Taipei: K'ai-ming shu-tien, 1967.

Lo, Winston W. 'Circuits and Circuit Intendants in the Territorial Administration of Sung China." *Monumenta Serica* 31, (1974–75), pp. 39–107.

Lo Yüan 洛原. 'Sung Tseng Kung mu-chih 宋曾鞏墓志.' *Wen-wu* 文物, no. 3 (1973), pp. 29–32.

Lou Yüeh 樓鑰. *Kung-k'uei chi* 攻媿集. SPTK, first compilation.

Lu Chiu-yüan 陸九淵. *Hsiang-shan hsien-sheng ch'üan-chi* 象山先生全集. SPTK, first compilation.

Lu Hsin-yüan 陸心源. *Sung-shih chi-shih pu-i* 宋詩紀事補遺. Taipei: Ting-wen shu-chü, 1970.

——. *Sung-shih chi-shih hsiao-chuan pu-cheng* 宋詩紀事小傳補正. Taipei: Ting-wen shu-chü, 1970.

——. *Sung shih i* 宋史翼. Sung-shih Tzu-liao ts'ui-pien, first compilation.

Lu Mei 陸湄. *Yung-feng Hsien chih* 永豐縣志. K'ang-hsi edition, 1684.

Lu Yu 陸游. *Wei-nan wen-chi* 渭南文集. SPTK, first compilation.

Lü Nan-kung 呂南公. *Kuan-yüan chi* 灌園集. SKCSCP, first collection.

Lü Pen-chung 呂本中. *Tung-lai Lü Tzu-wei shih-yu tsa-chih* 東萊呂紫微師友雜志. TSCC edition.

Ma Tuan-lin 馬端臨. *Wen-hsien t'ung-k'ao* 文獻通考. Taipei: Hsin-hsing shu-chü, 1962.

Mao Han-kuang 毛漢光. 'Wo-kuo chung-ku ta-shih-tsu chih ko-an yen-chiu – Lang-yeh Wang shih 我國中古大士族之個案研究 — 瑯琊王氏.' *Chung-yang yen-chiu-yüan li-shih yü-yen yen-chiu-so chi-k'an* 中央研究院歷史語言研究所集刊, 37, no. 2, pp. 577–610.

Marsh, Robert. *The Mandarins: Circulation of Elites in China*. New York: Free Press, 1961.

McDermott, Joseph. 'Land Tenure and Rural Control in the Liangche Region during the Southern Sung.' Diss. Cambridge University, 1979.

McKnight, Brian. 'Administrators of Hangchow under the Northern Sung: A Case Study.' *Harvard Journal of Asiatic Studies*, 30 (1970), pp. 185–211.

——. *Village and Bureaucracy in Southern Sung China*. Chicago: University of Chicago Press, 1971.

Medley, Margaret. *The Chinese Potter: A Practical History of Chinese Ceramics*. New York: Charles Scribner's Sons, 1976.

Meskill, John. *An Introduction to Chinese Civilization*. New York: Columbia University Press, 1973.

Mihelich, Mira Ann. 'Polders and the Politics of Land Reclamation During the Northern Sung Dynasty 960–1126.' Diss. Cornell University 1979.

Ming-kung shu-p'an ch'ing-ming chi 明公書判淸明集. Tokyo: Koten Ken-kyūkai, 1964.

Miyazaki Ichisada 宮崎市定. 'Tokushi sakki 讀史箚記.' *Shirin* 史林, 21, no. 1, pp. 124–58.

——. 'Sō-Gen jidai no hōsei to saiban kikō – *Gentenshō* seiritsu no jidaiteki. shakaiteki haikei 宋元時代の法制と裁判機構——元典章成立の時代的社會的背景.' In his *Ajiashi kenkyū* アジア史研究. Kyoto: Tōyōshi-Kenkyū-Kai, vol. IV, pp. 170–305.

Morita Kenji 森田憲司. '*Seido shizokufu* shōkō 成都氏族譜小考.' *Tōyōshi kenkyū* 東洋史研究, 36, no. 3 (1977), pp. 101–27.

Moriya Mitsuo 守屋美都雄. *Rikuchō monbatsu no ichi kenkyū* 六朝門閥の一研究. Tokyo, 1961.

Naitō Torajirō 內藤虎次郎. 'Gaikakuteki Tō-Sō jidai kan 概括的唐宋時代觀.' *Rekishi to chiri* 歷史と地理, 9, no. 5 (1922), pp. 1–12.

Nan-feng T'an-shih hsü-hsiu tsu-p'u 南豐譚氏續修族譜. 1920 edition, in gene-alogies collection of Columbia University East Asian Library.

Needham, Joseph. 'The Chinese Contribution to the Development of the Mariner's Compass.' In *Clerks and Craftsmen in China and the West*. Cambridge: Cambridge University Press, 1970, pp. 239–49.

Nunome Chōfu 布目潮渢. 'Tōsho no kizoku 唐初の貴族.' *Tōyōshi kenkyū* 東洋史研究, 10, no. 3 (1950), pp. 164–74.

——. *Chūgoku hondo chizu mokuroku: Tōkyō daigaku sōgō kenkyū shiryōkan josō shiryō* 中國本土地圖目錄：東京大學總合研究資料館所藏資料. Osaka: Osaka Daigaku Ajiashi Kenkyūkai, 1976.

Ochi Shigeaki 越智重明. 'Gi-Shin Nanbokuchō no saikakyū kanryōsō ni tsuite 魏晉南北朝の最下級官僚層について.' *Shigaku zasshi* 史学雑誌. 74, no. 7 (1965), pp. 1–37.

Otagi Hajime 愛宕元. 'Godai Sōsho no shinkō kanryō – Rinshi no Mashi o chūshin to shite 五代宋初の新興官僚——臨淄の麻氏を中心として.' *Shirin* 史林, 57, no. 4 (1974), pp. 57–105.

Ou-yang Ch'e 歐陽澈. *Ou-yang hsiu-chuan chi* 歐陽修撰集. SKCSCP, fourth collection.

Ou-yang Hsiu 歐陽修. *Ou-yang Wen-chung kung chi* 歐陽文忠公集. SPTK, first compilation.

——. et al. *Hsin T'ang shu* 新唐書. SPPY edition.

Ou-yang Hsüan 歐陽玄. *Kuei-chai wen-chi* 圭齋文集. SPTK, first compilation.

Ou-yang Shou-tao 歐陽守道. *Sun-chai wen-chi* 巽齋文集. SKCSCP, second collection.

Overmeyer, Daniel. *Folk Buddhist Religion: Dissenting Sects in Traditional China*. Cambridge: Harvard University Press, 1976.

Pao Hui 包恢. *Pi-chou kao-lüeh* 敝帚藁略. SKCSCP, third collection.

Pao-yu ssu-nien teng-k'o lu 寶祐四年登科錄. In *Sung-Yüan k'o-chü san-lu pen*. Ed. Hsü Nai-ch'ang. 1923.

Pi Yüan 畢沅, *Tzu chih t'ung chien* 續資治通鑑.

Pulleyblank, E.G. *The Background of the Rebellion of An Lu-shan*. London: Oxford University Press, 1955.

Saeki Tomi 佐伯富. *Sōdai chahō kenkyū shiryō* 宋代茶法研究資料. Kyoto: Tōhō Bunka Kenkyūjo, 1941.

———. *Chūgokushi kenkyū* 中國史研究. Vol. I. Kyoto: Tōyōshi-Kenkyū-Kai, 1969.

Satake Yasuhiko 佐竹靖彦. 'Sōdai Kanshū no sobyō 宋代贛州事情素描.' In *Aoyama hakushi koki kinen Sōdaishi ronsō* 青山博士古稀紀念宋代史論叢. Tokyo: Seishin Shobō, 1974, pp. 99–122.

Schirokauer, Conrad. 'Neo-Confucians Under Attack: The Condemnation of *Wei-hsüeh*.' *In Crisis and Prosperity in Sung China*. Ed. John Haeger. Tucson: University of Arizona Press, 1975, pp. 163–98.

Schoppa, R. Keith. 'The Composition and Functions of the Local Elite in Szechwan, 1851–1874.' *Ch'ing-shih Wen-t'i*, 2, no. 10 (1973), pp. 2–23.

Shao-hsing shih-pa nien t'ung-nien hsiao lu 紹興十八年同年小錄. In *Sung-Yüan k'o-chü san-lu pen* 宋天科舉三錄本. Ed. Hsü Nai-ch'ang 徐乃昌. 1923.

Shao Tzu-i 邵子彝 et al. *Chien-ch'ang Fu chih* 建昌府志. T'ung-chih edition, 1872.

Shen Yüeh 沈約. *Sung shu* 宋書. SPPY edition.

Sheng Ch'üan 盛銓 et al. *Ch'ung-jen Hsien chih* 崇仁縣志. T'ung-chih edition, 1873.

Shiba Yoshinobu 斯波義信. *Sōdai shōgyōshi kenkyū* 宋代商業史研究. Tokyo: Kazama Shobō, 1968.

———. *Commerce and Society in Sung China*. Translated by Mark Elvin. Ann Arbor: Center for Chinese Studies, 1970.

———. 'Sōdai shiteki seido no enkaku 宋代市糴制度の沿革.' In *Aoyama hakushi koki kinen Sōdaishi ronsō* 青山博士古稀紀念宋代史論叢. Tokyo: Seishin Shobō, 1974, pp. 123–59.

Shuang Kuei 雙貴 et al. *Yung-feng Hsien chih* 永豐縣志. T'ung-chih edition, 1872.

Skinner, G. William. 'Marketing and Social Structure in Rural China.' *Journal of Asian Studies*, 24, no. 1 (1964), pp. 1–43.

———. 'Mobility Strategies in Late Imperial China: A Regional Systems Analysis.' In *Regional Analysis*. Ed. Carol A. Smith. New York: Academic Press, 1976, Vol. 1, pp. 327–64.

———. *The City in Late Imperial China*. Stanford: Stanford University Press, 1977.

Sogabe Shizuo 曾我部靜雄. *Sōdai zaisei shi* 宋代財政史. Tokyo: Daian, 1941.

———. 'Sōdai no koko tōkei ni tsuite no shin kenkyū 宋代の戶口統計について の新研究.' *Tōa keizai kenkyū* 東亞經濟研究, 26, no. 3 (1942), pp. 26–40.

———. 'Zoku Sōdai no koko tōkei ni tsuite no shin kenkyū 續宋代の戶口統計 についての新研究.' *Tōa keizai kenkyū* 東亞經濟研究, 27, no. 3 (1943), pp. 14–27.

———. 'Zokuzoku Sōdai no koko tōkei ni tsuite no shin kenkyū 續續宋代の戶

口統計についての新研究.' *Tōa keizai kenkyū* 東亞經濟研究, 27, no. 4 (1943), pp. 47–51.

——. 'Nan-Sō no tochi keikai hō 南宋の土地経界法.' In his *Sōdai seikeishi no kenkyū* 宋代政経史の研究. Tokyo: Yoshikawa Hiroshi Bunkan, 1974, pp. 405–42.

——. 'Sōdai no sansō oyobi sono ta 宋代の三倉及びその代.' In *Sōdai seikeishi no kenkyū* 宋代政経史の研究 (Tokyo, 1974), pp. 465–94.

Spence, Jonathan. *Ts'ao Yin and the K'ang-hsi Emperor*. New Haven: Yale University Press, 1966.

Strickmann, Michel. 'The Longest Taoist Scripture.' *History of Religions* 17 (1978): 331–54.

Stuermer, John. 'Polder Construction and the Pattern of Landownership in the T'ai-hu Basin During the Southern Sung Dynasty.' Diss. University of Pennsylvania, 1980.

Su Pai 蘇白. 'Nan-Sung ti tiao-pan yin-shua 南宋的雕版印刷.' *Wen-wu* 文物, no. 1 (1962), pp. 15–28.

Su Shih 蘇軾. *Su Tung-p'o chi* 蘇東坡集. SPPY edition.

Su Sung 蘇頌. *Su Wei-kung wen-chi* 蘇魏公集. SKCSCP, fourth collection.

Sudō Yoshiyuki 周藤吉之. 'Sōdai kanryōsei to daitochishoyū 宋代官僚制と大土地所有.' *Shakai kōseishi taikei* 社會構成史體系 8 (1950).

——. *Chūgoku tochi seidoshi Renkyū* 中國土地制度史研究. Tokyo: Tōkyō Daigaku Shuppansha, 1954.

——. *Sōdai keizaishi kenkyū* 宋代經濟史研究. Tokyo: Tokyo University Press, 1962.

——. *Tō-Sō shakai keizaishi kenkyū* 唐宋社會經濟史研究. Tokyo: Tokyo University Press, 1965.

Sun Kuo-tung 孫國棟. 'T'ang-Sung chih she-hui men-ti chih hsiao-jung 唐宋之社會門第之消融.' *Hsin-ya hsüeh-pao* 新亞學報, 4, no. 1 (1959), pp. 212–305.

Sun Ti 孫覿. *Nan-lan-ling Sun shang-shu ta-ch'üan chi* 南蘭陵孫尚書大全集. Sung edition from rare books collection of National Library, Peiping.

Sung hui-yao chi-pen 宋會要輯本. Taipei: Shih-chieh shu-chü, 1963.

Sung Lien 宋濂. *Sung hsüeh-shih chi* 宋學士集. TSCC edition.

—— et al. *Yüan shih* 元史. SPPY edition.

Sung Shee 宋晞. *Sung-shih yen-chiu lun-ts'ung* 宋史研究論叢. Taipei: Chung-kuo wen-hua yen-chiu-so, 1961.

Takahashi Yoshirō 高橋芳郎. 'Sōdai tenko no mibun mondai 宋代佃戶の身分問題.' *Tōyōshi kenkyū* 東洋史研究, 37, no. 3 (1978), pp. 64–91.

Takao Giken 高雄義堅. *Sōdai Bukkyōshi no kenkyū* 宋代仏教史の研究. Kyoto: Hyakkaen, 1975.

Takeda Ryūji 竹田龍兒, 'Monbatsu to shite no Kōnō Yōshi ni tsuite no ichi kōsatsu 門閥としての弘農楊氏についての一考察.' *Shigaku* 史學, 31 (1958), pp. 613–43.

Tanigawa Michio 谷川道雄. 'Bukōchō matsunen yori Gensōchō shonen ni itaru seisō ni tsuite 武后朝末年より玄宗朝初年にいたる政争について.' *Tōyōshi kenkyū* 東洋史研究, 14, no. 4 (1956), pp. 295–318.

Teng Ming-shih 鄧名世. *Ku-chin hsing-shih shu pien-cheng* 古今姓氏書辨證. TSCC edition.

Terada Gō 寺田剛. *Sōdai kyōikushi kaisetsu* 宋代教育史概説. Tokyo: Hakubunsha, 1965.

Teraji Jun 寺地遵. 'Nan-Sō seiritsuki ni okeru mingen bushō soshiki to Ken-en nenkan no seiji katei 南宋成立期における民間武装組織と建炎年間の政治過程.' *Shigaku kenkyū* 史学研究, 137 (1977), pp. 26–48.

Thompson, Lawrence G. *The Chinese Way in Religion*. Encino: Dickenson Publishing Company, 1973.

T'o T'o 脱脱 et al. *Sung shih* 宋史. SPPY edition.

Tonami Mamoru 礪波護. 'Chūsei kizokusei no hōkai to hekishosei 中世貴族制の崩壊と辟召制.' *Tōyōshi kenkyū* 東洋史研究, 21, no. 3 (1962), pp. 1–26.

Ts'ao Yen-yüeh 曹彦約. *Ch'ang-ku chi* 昌谷集. SKCSCP, first collection.

Tseng Chao 曾肇. *Ch'ü-fu chi* 曲阜集. Ch'ien-yen tsung-chi chün-shu edition.

Tseng Feng 曾丰. *Yüan-tu chi* 緣督集. SKCSCP, second collection.

Tseng Hsieh 曾協. *Yün-chuang chi* 雲莊集. SKCSCP, pieh-chi.

Tseng Kung 曾鞏. *Lung-p'ing chi* 隆平集. SKCSCP, second collection.

——. *Yüan-feng lei-kao* 元豐類稿. SPTK, first compilation.

Tsou Hao 鄒浩. *Tao-hsiang hsien-sheng wen-chi* 道鄉先生文集. Ch'ing printed edition, 1870.

Tu Ta-kuei 杜大珪. *Ming-ch'en pei-chuan wan-yen chi* 名臣碑傳琬琰集.

Tu Yu 杜佑. *T'ung tien* 通典. Kuo-hsüeh chi-pen ts'ung-shu edition.

Tung Wei 董煟. *Chiu-huang huo-min shu* 救荒活民書. TSCC edition.

T'ung Fan-yen 童範儼 et al. *Lin-ch'uan Hsien chih* 臨川縣志. T'ung-chih edition, 1870.

Twitchett, D.C. *Financial Administration Under the T'ang Dynasty*. Second edition. Cambridge: Cambridge University Press, 1970.

——. 'Merchant, Trade, and Government in Late T'ang.' *Asia Major* 14, no. 1 (1968), pp. 63–93.

——. 'The Composition of the T'ang Ruling Class: New Evidence from Tunhuang.' In *Perspectives on the T'ang*. Ed. Arthur Wright and D.C. Twitchett. New Haven: Yale University Press, 1973, pp. 47–85.

Ueyama Shumpei 上山春平. 'Shushi no "Karei" to "Girei keiten tsū kai" 朱子の"家禮"と"儀禮經傳通解". *Tōhō gakuhō* 東方学報, 54 (1982), pp. 173–256.

Umehara Kaoru 梅原郁. 'Sōdai no kotōsei o megutte 宋代の戸等制をめぐって.' *Tōhō gakuhō* 東方学報, 41 (1970), pp. 375–414.

——. 'Sōsho no kirokukan to sono shūhen 宋初の寄禄官とその周辺.' *Tōhō gakuhō* 東方学報, 48 (1975), pp. 135–182.

Wada Sei 和田清. *Shina chihō jichi* 支那地方自治. Tokyo: Kyūkōshoin, 1975.

Wakeman, Frederic. *Strangers at the Gate: Social Disorder in South China, 1839–1861*. Berkeley: University of California Press, 1966.

——. *The Fall of Imperial China*. New York: Free Press, 1975.

—— and Carolyn Grant, eds. *Conflict and Control in Late Imperial China*. Barkeley: University of California Press, 1975.

Walton-Vargö, Linda. 'Education, Social Change, and Neo-Confucianism in Sung-Yuan China: Academies and the Local Elite in Ming Prefecture (Ningpo).' Diss. University of Pennsylvania 1978.

Wan Ssu-t'ung 萬斯同. *Sung-chi chung-i lu* 宋季忠義錄. Ssu-ming ts'ung-shu edition.

Wang An-shih 王安石. *Lin-ch'uan chi* 臨川集. SPTK, first compilation.

Wang Ch'eng 王稱. *Tung-tu shih-lüeh* 東都事略. Sung-shih tzu-liao ts'ui-pien, first collection.

Wang Chih 王質. *Hsüeh-shan chi* 雪山集. TSCC edition.

Wang Hsiang-chih 王象之. *Yü-ti chi-sheng* 輿地紀勝. Taipei: Wen-hai ch'u-pan-she, 1962.

Wang Ling 王令. *Kuang-ling chi* 廣陵集. Wu Ssu-lan manuscript edition.

Wang Po 王柏. *Lu-chai chi* 魯齋集. TSCC edition.

Wang Te-i 王德毅. 'Li Ch'un-nien yü Nan-Sung t'u-ti ching-chieh 李椿年與南宋土地經界.' In *Sung-shih yen-chiu chi* 宋史研究集, no. 7. Taipei: Chung-hua ts'ung-shu pien-shen wei-yüan-hui, 1973, pp. 441–80.

Wang T'ing-kuei 王庭珪. *Lu-ch'i wen-chi* 盧溪文集. SKCSCP, third collection.

Wang Tsao 汪藻. *Fu-ch'i chi* 浮溪集. SPTK, first compilation.

Wang Ts'un 王存. *Yüan-feng chiu-yü chih* 元豐九域志. Taipei: Wen-hai ch'u-pan-she, 1962.

Wang Tzu-ts'ai 王梓材 and Feng Yün-hao 馮雲濠. *Sung-Yüan hsüeh-an pu-i* 宋元學案補貴. Ssu-ming ts'ung-shu edition.

Wang Ying-ch'en 汪應辰. *Wen-ting chi* 文定集. TSCC edition.

Wang Yu-nien 王有年 et al. *Chin-ch'i Hsien chih* 金溪縣志. K'ang-hsi edition, 1682.

Watson, Burton, trans. *Records of the Historian: Chapters from the Shih Chi of Ssu-ma Ch'ien*. New York: Columbia University Press, 1969.

Wei Liao-weng 魏了翁. *Ho-shan hsien-sheng ta-ch'üan chi* 鶴山先生大全集. SPTK, first compilation.

Wei Su 危素. *T'ai-p'u yün-lin chi* 太樸雲林集; *pu-i* 補遺; *hsü-pu* 續補; *wen-chi* 文集; *hsü-chi* 續集. Republican edition at Jinbun Kagaku Kenkyūjo, Kyoto.

Wei T'ai 魏泰. *Tung-hsüan pi-lu* 東軒筆錄. TSCC edition.

Wen T'ien-hsiang 文天祥. *Wen-shan hsien-sheng ch'üan chi* 文山先生全集. Kuo-hsüeh chi-pen ts'ung-shu edition.

Wittfogel, K.A. 'Public Office in the Liao Dynasty and the Chinese Exam System.' *Harvard Journal of Asiatic Studies*, 10 (1947), pp. 13–40.

Wou, Odoric. 'The Political Kin Unit and the Family Origin of Ch'ing Local Officials." In *Perspectives on a Changing China: Essays in Honor of Professor C. Martin Wilbur on the Occasion of his Retirement*. Ed. Joshua A. Fogel and William T. Rowe. Boulder: Westview Press, 1979, pp. 69–87.

Wu Ch'eng 吳澄. *Wen-chung kung chi* 文忠公集. SKCSCP, second collection.

Wu T'ing-hsieh 吳廷燮. *Nan-Sung chih-fu nien-piao* 南宋制撫年表. In *Erh-shih-wu shih pu-pien*. Shanghai: K'ai-ming shu-tien, 1935.

Wu Tseng 吳曾. *Neng-kai-chai man-lu* 能改齋漫錄. TSCC edition.

Yanagida Setsuko 柳田節子. 'Sōdai tochi shoyūsei ni mirareru futatsu no katachi 宋代土地所有制にみられる二つの型.' *Tōyō bunka kenkyūjo kiyō* 東洋文化研究所紀要, 29 (1963), pp. 95–130.

Yang Shih 楊時. *Kuei-shan chi* 龜山集. SKCSCP, fourth collection.

Yang Wan-li 楊萬里. *Ch'eng-chai chi* 誠齋集. SPTK, first compilation.

Yano Chikara 矢野主稅. 'Shōshi kenkyū kō 張氏研究考.' *Shakai kagaku ronsō* 社會科學論叢, 5 (1955), pp. 1–39.

——. 'Teishi kenkyū 鄭氏研究.' *Shakai kagaku ronsō* 社會科學論叢, 8 (1958),

pp. 21–36; 9 (1959), pp. 1–8; 10 (1960), pp. 1–10.

——. 'Ishi kenkyū 韋氏研究.' *Shakai kagaku ronsō* 社會科學論叢, 11 (1961), pp. 49–64; 12 (1962), pp. 26–42.

——. 'Haishi kenkyū 裴氏研究.' *Shakai kagaku ronsō* 社會科學論叢, 14 (1964), pp. 17–48.

Yeh Shih 葉適. *Shui-hsin hsien-sheng wen-chi* 水心先生文集. SPTK, first compilation.

Yen Chen-ch'ing 顏眞卿. *Wen-chung chi* 文忠集. TSCC edition.

Yin Chu 尹洙. *Ho-nan hsien-sheng wen-chi* 河南先生文集. SPTK, first compilation.

Yoshida Toru 吉田寅. '*Kyūkō katsumin sho* to Sōdai no kyūkō seisaku "救荒活民書"と宋代の救荒政策.' In *Aoyama hakushi koki kinen Sōdaishi ronsō* 青山博士古稀紀念宋代史論叢. Tokyo: Seishin Shobō, 1974, pp. 447–75.

Yu Chih-chang 尤犀章 et al. *I-huang Hsien chih* 宜黃縣志. K'ang-hsi edition, 1666.

Yung-lo ta-tien 永樂大典. Peking: China Bookstore, 1960.

Yü Chi 虞集. *Tao-yüan hsüeh-ku lu* 道園學古錄. SPTK, first compilation.

Yü Hsi-lu 俞希魯. *Chen-chiang chih* 鎮江志. Hua-wen shu-chü reprint of Yüan Chih-shun edition.

Yüan Fu 袁甫. *Meng-chai chi* 蒙齋集. SKCSCP, pieh-chi.

Yüan Hsieh 袁燮, *Chieh-chai chi* 絜齋集. SKCSCP, pieh-chi.

Yüan Ts'ai 袁采. *Yüan-shih shih-fan* 袁氏世範. TSCC edition.

Yüeh Shih 樂史. *T'ai-p'ing huan-yü chi* 太平寰宇記. Taipei: Wen-hai ch'u-pan-she, 1962.

Zurndorfer, Harriet. 'The *Hsin-an ta-tsu-chih* and the Development of Chinese Gentry Society 800–1600.' *T'oung Pao* 68 (1981), pp. 154–215.

INDEX

Absentee landowning, *see* landowning, absentee
Academic assignments (*kuan-chih*), 115
Academic connections, 9, 102, 103, 117, 122–3, 281 n.112
Academies, local, 8, 9, 32, 56, 60, 104, 122–3, 128, 132–4, 195, 271 n.13, 314 nn.28, 29
Academy, Imperial, 57, 58
Adoption, 58
Affines, 9–10, 37, 40, 42, 115–16, 261 n.25
Agents (*kan-jen*), 48, 280 n.93
Agriculture (*see also* rice, wheat, tea, tenancy, dams, water control, waterwheels), 11, 21, 56, 74, 119, 133, 253–8
Ahern, Emily, 304 n.7
Alvarez, Karen, 313 n.80
Ancestors, worship of, 58, 163, 164, 179, 332 n.1, 334 n.40
Ao-ch'i Bridge, 174
Ao-ch'i River, 174, 262 n.33
Aoyama Sadao, 291 n.24
Aristocracy, of Six Dynasties and T'ang, 3, 4, 5, 66, 216, 217, 286 n.12, 287 nn.13–18
Armies, 21, 138, 315 n.2

Banditry, 18, 23, 24, 39, 56, 58, 60, 75, 83, 126, 127, 138, 142, 143, 147, 148, 149, 150, 154, 163, 201, 282 n.125, 315 n.2, 318 nn.17, 20, 319 n.30, 320 n.45, 321 n.46, 322 n.55, 328 n.65, 332 n.117
Barley, 22, 255
Beattie, Hilary, 216, 273 n.24
Boroughs (*hsiang*), 265 n.50
Bowmen, 138, 207, 317 n.4
Bridges, 8, 9, 52, 104, 111, 174–5, 182–3, 190, 265 n.51, 310 n.46, 331 n.115, 332 nn.116–19, 334 n.37
Bronze, 22, 75, 259

Buddhism (*see also* temples, monks), 107, 109, 111, 119, 149, 151, 174, 175, 177, 178–84, 193, 333 n.3

Cahill, Suzanne, 192
Chaffee, John, 132–3, 268 nn. 91, 93, 269 n.97
Chan Ch'ung-p'u, 303 n.113
Chan family, 47, 53, 74, 184, 279 n.88, 291 n.23, 292 n.34, 303 n.113
Chan Yüan-chi, 53
Chang Chieh-fu, 39
Chang Chin-ch'eng, 32
Chang, Chung-li, 271 n.22
Chang Chün-chung, 38, 40
Chang family, 38, 54
Chang Li, 331 n.107
Chang O, 54
Chang Sheng-tzu, 307 n.22
Chang Shih-kao, 99
Chang Tzu-hsien, 39
Chang Wei-shan, 83
Chang Wen-huan, 39, 40
Chang Yu-hsin, 39, 40, 325 n.38
Ch'ang-chou, 113
Chao Chi-chih, 286 n.9, 296 n.36
Chao family, *see* imperial lineage
Chao I, 112
Chao Jo-liu, 325 n.38
Chao Jo-shu, 332 n.118
Chao Ju-ch'ien, 153
Chao Ju-yü, 46
Chao K'uei, 320 n.39
Chao Pang, 38
Chao Pu-tz'u, 148, 321 n.46
Chao-hsi Fort, 137
Ch'ao Ch'ien-chih, 297 n.43
Ch'ao family, 71, 95, 293 n.35, 297 n.43
Ch'ao Kung-mai, 293 n.35, 297 n.43
Ch'ao Pai-t'an, 293 n.35
Ch'ao Tzu-shei, 293 n.35
Ch'ao Tzu-yü, 293 n.35, 297 n.43
Charitable estates, *see* estates
Charity, 9, 129, 151–2, 154–5, 157–8, 162–7, 179